Managing Organizational Change

A Multiple Perspectives Approach

Fourth Edition

Ian Palmer

Richard Dunford

David A. Buchanan

MANAGING ORGANIZATIONAL CHANGE: A MULTIPLE PERSPECTIVES APPROACH, FOURTH EDITION

Published by McGraw Hill LLC, 1325 Avenue of the Americas, New York, NY 10121. Copyright © 2022 by McGraw Hill LLC. All rights reserved. Printed in the United States of America. Previous editions © 2017, 2009, and 2006. No part of this publication may be reproduced or distributed in any form or by any means, or stored in a database or retrieval system, without the prior written consent of McGraw Hill LLC, including, but not limited to, in any network or other electronic storage or transmission, or broadcast for distance learning.

Some ancillaries, including electronic and print components, may not be available to customers outside the United States.

This book is printed on acid-free paper.

1 2 3 4 5 6 7 8 9 LCR 24 23 22 21

ISBN 978-1-260-04371-6 (bound edition)
MHID 1-260-04371-1 (bound edition)
ISBN 978-1-264-07161-6 (loose-leaf edition)
MHID 1-264-07161-2 (loose-leaf edition)

Executive Portfolio Manager: *Michael Ablassmeir*
Product Developer: *Laura Hurst Spell*
Marketing Manager: *Lisa Granger*
Content Project Managers: *Melissa M. Leick, Bruce Gin*
Buyer: *Laura Fuller*
Designer: *Matt Diamond*
Content Licensing Specialist: *Gina Oberbroeckling*
Cover Image: *HT-Pix/Getty Images*
Compositor: *Aptara®, Inc.*

All credits appearing on page or at the end of the book are considered to be an extension of the copyright page.

Library of Congress Cataloging-in-Publication Data

Names: Palmer, Ian, 1957- author. | Dunford, Richard, author. | Buchanan, David A., author.
Title: Managing organizational change : a multiple perspectives approach / Ian Palmer, Richard Dunford, David A. Buchanan.
Description: Fourth edition. | New York, NY : McGraw-Hill Education, [2022] | Includes index.
Identifiers: LCCN 2020031288 (print) | LCCN 2020031289 (ebook) | ISBN 9781260043716 (hardcover) | ISBN 9781264071616 (spiral bound) | ISBN 9781264071531 (ebook) | ISBN 9781264071579 (ebook other)
Subjects: LCSH: Organizational change. | Organizational change—Management.
Classification: LCC HD58.8 .P347 2022 (print) | LCC HD58.8 (ebook) | DDC 658.4/06—dc23
LC record available at https://lccn.loc.gov/2020031288
LC ebook record available at https://lccn.loc.gov/2020031289

The Internet addresses listed in the text were accurate at the time of publication. The inclusion of a website does not indicate an endorsement by the authors or McGraw Hill LLC, and McGraw Hill LLC does not guarantee the accuracy of the information presented at these sites.

mheducation.com/highered

DEDICATIONS

From Ian   To Dianne, Matthew, and Michelle

From Richard   To Jill, Nick, and Ally

From David   To Lesley with love—and thanks

Acknowledgments

A number of people have contributed to this edition, and we owe them all a debt of gratitude, including Francis Adeola, University of New Orleans; Terrence R. Bishop, Northern Illinois University; Frederick Brockmeier, Northern Kentucky University; Lesley Buchanan; and James Cornwell, U.S. Military Academy. We must also thank the many change managers—too many to name—with whom we have explored the issues addressed in this book, for their time, their insights, and their willingness to share their experiences with us.

Brief contents

Preface x

PART 1 Groundwork: Understanding and Diagnosing Change 1

    1 Managing Change: Stories and Paradoxes 3

    2 Images of Change Management 29

    3 Why Change? Contemporary Pressures and Drivers 63

    4 What to Change? A Diagnostic Approach 103

PART 2 Implementation: The Substance and Process of Change 139

    5 What Changes? 141

    6 Purpose and Vision 175

    7 Change Communication Strategies 211

    8 Resistance to Change 249

    9 Organization Development and Sense-Making Approaches 281

    10 Change Management Perspectives 319

PART 3 Running Threads: Sustainability and the Effective Change Manager 353

    11 Sustaining Change versus Initiative Decay 355

    12 The Effective Change Manager: What Does It Take? 387

Name Index 425

Subject Index 433

Contents

Preface x

Part 1
Groundwork: Understanding and Diagnosing Change 1

1 Managing Change: Stories and
   Paradoxes 3

   Learning Objectives 3
   Stories about Change: What Can
   We Learn? 4
   The Starbucks Story 5
   The Sears Story 7
   The Detroit Story 10
   Tension and Paradox: The State
   of the Art 11
   Assessing Depth of Change 16
   What's Coming Up: A Roadmap 18
   Change Diagnostic: The Starbucks
   Story 20
   Change Diagnostic: The Sears Story 21
   Change Diagnostic: The Detroit Story 23
   Exercise 1.1 Writing Your Own Story
   of Change 24
   Additional Reading 25
   Roundup 25
   References 26

2 Images of Change Management 29

   Learning Objectives 29
   What's in a Name: Change Agents, Managers,
   or Leaders? 30
   Images, Mental Models, Frames,
   Perspectives 31
   The Six-Images Framework 32
   Six Images of Change Management 36

Using the Six-Images Framework 45
Self-Assessment: What Is Your Image of
Managing Change? 49
Self-Assessment: Scoring 51
Exercise 2.1: Assessing Change Managers'
Images 52
Exercise 2.2: Turnaround at Beth
Israel 53
Additional Reading 56
Roundup 57
References 58

3 Why Change? Contemporary Pressures
   and Drivers 63

   Learning Objectives 63
   Internal Organization Change
   Drivers 64
   Environmental Pressures for Change 66
   Why Do Organizations Not Change after
   Crises? 88
   Exercise 3.1: COVID-19 Consequences 90
   Exercise 3.2: Top Team Role Play 91
   Exercise 3.3: Case Analysis—The Netflix
   Story 92
   Exercise 3.4: The Reputation Trap—Can You
   Escape? 94
   Additional Reading 96
   Roundup 96
   References 98

4 What to Change? A Diagnostic
   Approach 103

   Learning Objectives 103
   Organizational Strategy and
   Change 112

Diagnosing Readiness for Change   121

Agile Organization   125

Exercise 4.1: Scenario Planning   130

Exercise 4.2: Readiness for Change
Analysis   131

Additional Reading   133

Roundup   134

References   135

Part 2
Implementation: The Substance and Process of Change   139

5   What Changes?   141

Learning Objectives   141

What Changes?   142

Organizational Culture   153

Digital Transformation and the Social
Matrix   159

Exercise 5.1: The Mattel Toy Story   166

Exercise 5.2: Organizational Culture
Assessment   168

Exercise 5.3: How Will Digital Transformation
Affect Your Organization?   168

Additional Reading   168

Roundup   169

References   172

6   Purpose and Vision   175

Learning Objectives   175

Missions and Visions: Fundamental
or Fads?   176

Mission: Why Are We Here?   178

Vision: Where Are We Going?   183

Why Visions Fail   192

Linking Vision to Change:
Three Debates   194

Exercise 6.1: Interviewing Change
Recipients   201

Exercise 6.2: Analyze Your Own
Organization's Mission and Vision   202

Exercise 6.3: The Role of Vision at Mentor
Graphics   202

Additional Reading   203

Roundup   204

References   206

7   Change Communication
Strategies   211

Learning Objectives   211

The Change Communication Process   212

Gender, Power, and Emotion   217

Language Matters: The Power of
Conversation   222

Change Communication Strategies   228

Contingency Approaches to Change
Communication   231

Communication Channels and the Impact of
Social Media   235

Exercise 7.1: Listen to Who's Talking   239

Exercise 7.2: How Defensive
Are You?   240

Exercise 7.3: Social Media at the
Museum   241

Additional Reading   242

Roundup   243

References   245

8   Resistance to Change   249

Learning Objectives   249

WIIFM, WAMI, and the Dimensions of
Resistance   250

Benefits   251

Causes   254

Symptoms   261

Managers as Resisters   263

Managing Resistance   265

Exercise 8.1: Diagnosing and Acting   272

Exercise 8.2: Jack's Dilemma   272

Exercise 8.3: Moneyball   273

Additional Reading   274

Roundup   274

References   277

9   Organization Development and Sense-Making Approaches   281

Learning Objectives   281

Alternative Approaches to Managing Change   282

Organization Development (OD)   282

Appreciative Inquiry (AI)   293

Positive Organizational Scholarship (POS)   295

Dialogic Organization Development   297

Sense-Making   300

Exercise 9.1: Reports from the Front Line   307

Exercise 9.2: Designing a Large-Scale Change Intervention   307

Exercise 9.3: Making Sense of Sense-Making   307

Exercise 9.4: Interpreting the Interpreter: Change at Target   308

Exercise 9.5: Change at DuPont   309

Additional Reading   311

Roundup   311

References   313

10   Change Management Perspectives   319

Learning Objectives   319

Options for Managing Change   320

Why Change Fails   321

Change by Checklist   323

Stage Models   327

The Process Perspective   333

Contingency Approaches   336

Exercise 10.1: Develop Your Own Change Model   343

Exercise 10.2: Getting Boeing Back in the Air   343

Exercise 10.3: Did Heinz Choke on the 3G Recipe?   346

Additional Reading   348

Roundup   348

References   351

**Part 3
Running Threads: Sustainability and the Effective Change Manager   353**

11   Sustaining Change versus Initiative Decay   355

Learning Objectives   355

Initiative Decay and Improvement Evaporation   356

Praiseworthy and Blameworthy Failures   359

Actions to Sustain Change   361

Words of Warning   369

Exercise 11.1: A Balanced Set of Measures   374

Exercise 11.2: Treating Initiative Decay   374

Exercise 11.3: The Challenger and Columbia Shuttle Disasters   375

Additional Reading   380

Roundup   381

References   383

12   The Effective Change Manager: What Does It Take?   387

Learning Objectives   387

Change Managers: Who Are They?   388

Change Managers: What Kind of Role Is This?   399

Change Management Competencies   401

Political Skill and the Change Manager   404

Developing Change Management
Expertise   411

Exercise 12.1: Networking—How Good
Are You?   414

Exercise 12.2: How Resilient Are You?   415

Exercise 12.3: How Political Is Your
Organization?   417

Additional Reading   418

Roundup   419

References   421

Name Index   425

Subject Index   433

Preface

The previous edition of this book was published in 2016. Since then, the organizational world has continued to change dramatically. The aftermath of the global financial crisis is still with us; there are fresh and severe geopolitical tensions; environmental concerns are increasingly urgent; the focus on corporate social responsibility has intensified; organizations are under pressure to demonstrate their environmental, social, and governance (ESG) credentials; technological developments continue to surprise; and cybersecurity is a constant concern. Organizations have to consider how to manage demographic trends including an ageing, multigenerational, and multicultural workforce. Consumer preferences and expectations change radically and rapidly. Stir into this mix the impact of social media, where positive and critical views of organizations and their products and services—along with personal and corporate reputations—can be shared instantly and globally.

What Do CEOs Think?

The business magazine *Fortune* carries out an annual survey of U.S. chief executives, asking them about trends and challenges. The 2019 survey (Murray, 2019) found that the main challenges facing these CEOs were:

- cybersecurity
- technological change
- increased regulation
- shortages of skilled labor
- competition from China
- shareholder activism

They were positive about the economy and business opportunities, particularly in America, and 65 percent said that they expected to be employing more people in two years' time and planned to continue investing in artificial intelligence (AI); 60 percent said that they had already used AI to improve efficiency and cut costs; and 22 percent had used AI to create new products and services. However, around half were expecting a recession within two years.

How do CEOs feel about wider social issues and criticisms of large organizations in particular? Over 70 percent said they thought that capitalism was not in crisis but that "some tweaking" to better serve society would be appropriate. Over 40 percent felt that their business strategy should include finding ways to address major social problems. They also felt that companies such as Amazon, Facebook, and Google had grown so large and influential that they needed additional regulation.

Murray, A. 2019. 2019 CEO survey: The results are in. *Fortune* 179(6):3.

From a management perspective, the drivers or catalysts for change are now more numerous and unpredictable. The pace of change has not slackened: more pressures, more opportunities, more changes, faster changes. Failure to respond to those pressures and opportunities, and in some cases failure to respond quickly enough, can have significant individual and corporate consequences. The "agile organization" has become fashionable—and is perhaps strategically indispensable. Many companies are experimenting with new ways of organizing—co-working spaces, no hierarchy, social enterprises, virtual teams, and platform organizations. The personal and organizational stakes appear to have increased.

The management of organizational change thus continues to be a topic of strategic importance for most sectors, public and private. Current conditions have continued to increase the importance of this area of management responsibility. This new edition, therefore, is timely with regard to updating previous content, while introducing new and emerging trends, developments, themes, debates, and practices.

In light of this assessment, we continue to believe that the multiple perspectives approach is particularly valuable, recognizing the various ways in which change can be progressed and highlighting the need for tailored and creative approaches to fit different contexts. Our images of how organizational change should be implemented affect the approaches that we take to understanding and managing change. Adopting different images and perspectives helps to open up new and more innovative ways of approaching the change management process. We hope that this approach will guide and inspire others in pursuing their own responsibilities for managing organizational change.

This text is aimed at two main readers. The first is an experienced practicing manager enrolled in an MBA or a similar master's degree program or taking part in a management development course that includes a module on organizational change. The second is a senior undergraduate, who may have less practical experience, but who will probably have encountered organizational change directly through temporary work assignments or internships or indirectly through family and friends. Our senior undergraduate is also likely to be planning a management career, or to be heading for a professional role that will inevitably involve management—and change management—responsibilities. Given the needs and interests of both our readers, we have sought to present an appropriate blend of research and theory, on the one hand, and practical management application, on the other.

Instructors who have used our previous editions will find familiar features in this update. The chapter structure and sequence of the book remain much the same, with minor adjustments to accommodate new material. The overall argument is underpinned by the observation that the management of organizational change is in part a rational or technical task and is also a creative activity, with the need to design novel strategies and processes that are consistent with the needs of unique local conditions. We hope that readers will find the writing style and presentation clear and engaging. We have maintained the breadth of coverage of the different traditions and perspectives that contribute to the theory and practice of managing change, with international examples where appropriate.

What's New in This Edition?

The new content for this edition includes the following:

Real-world examples. We draw on the experience of change in the following organizations, including a U.S. city and baseball team and one nation-state. Examples range from full-length cases to short vignettes: Airbnb, Alibaba, Best Buy, Beth Israel Deaconess Medical Center, BlackRock, Boeing, BP, British Army, Carnival Cruise Line, Chobani, Continental Airlines, Detroit, DuPont, Estée Lauder, FedEx, Etsy, Facebook, Ford, General Motors Poland, Goldman Sachs, Google, HP, IBM, Instagram, Intuit, Johnson & Johnson, Kaiser Permanente, Kraft Heinz, Lego, Levi Strauss, McDonald's, Mattel, Mentor Graphics, a Siemens Business, Microsoft, NASA, Netflix, Nike, Oakland Athletics, Progressive Insurance, Sandvik AB, Sears, Semco, Spotify, Starbucks, Swiss Re, Thai Union, Twitter, Uber, Unilever, U.S. Postal Service, Vanuatu, YouTube, and Zumba Fitness.

Leadership language. The power of meaningful stories is well known. But the role of language in articulating vision and mission statements is less well understood. However, research on organization mission statements has found that concrete imagery works, and abstractions do not, with regard to encouraging support for change. In addition, support for change is more likely to be forthcoming when vision statements emphasize continuity as well as change (chapters 1 and 6).

Change managers and change leaders. We argue that the distinction between leaders and managers is blurred and that these are different labels for the same role. However, research offers counterintuitive advice with regard to the complementary roles of middle managers and senior executives. Middle managers may be better able to initiate change, because they have a better understanding of frontline operations. Senior leaders may be better able to execute change, because they have more power and better access to resources (chapters 2 and 8).

The world out there. Conditions in the external environment of the organization continue to become more turbulent, volatile, and unpredictable. The nature of globalization is also changing, creating more pressures and opportunities, as well as more change drivers and catalysts (chapter 3).

COVID-19 consequences. The World Health Organization declared a global pandemic in March 2020, following an outbreak of a zoonotic coronavirus, COVID-19, for which there was no treatment or cure at the time of writing. To stop the virus from spreading, countries closed borders and introduced social distancing. These steps had a major impact on social life, working patterns, and most businesses, driving major organizational changes. Exercise 3.1 asks readers to consider the nature of these changes and the long-term consequences (chapter 3).

Technology as a change driver. Robots, cobots, machine learning, artificial intelligence, automation. Emerging technologies are reshaping the world of work, probably creating more benefits and opportunities than downsides. Many organizations are undergoing digital transformations. Professional roles are no longer immune to automation. The change implications are significant, requiring careful management (chapter 3).

Initiative overload. Too much change is a problem for many organizations. This leads to a dilution of effort and misallocation of resources. Why does this happen? What can be done to manage multiple change initiatives more effectively? (chapter 4).

Agile organization. Adaptability is a strategic priority in a turbulent, unpredictable world. "Agile" has its roots in the concepts of "mechanistic and organic" systems, "segmentalist and integrative" cultures, and "built to change" organizations. The core concept is based on the classic concept of autonomous, self-managing teams, but the approach needs "agile managers" in new roles, able to balance flexibility with stability (chapter 4).

Social media. Social media platforms have become increasingly important as a general management tool, contributing to change management by improving communications, employee voice, and involvement and by building momentum for change. Many organizations have yet to exploit fully these opportunities, and there is a need to balance the opportunities with the risks (chapters 5 and 7).

The purpose-driven organization. Purpose, or organizational mission, is now recognized as a driver of competitive advantage, and thus of change. But the concept is not always taken seriously by organizations, which often produce vague, abstract statements of purpose. We consider the evidence that supports clarifying the organization's mission or purpose and consider the language in which purpose is best articulated (chapter 6).

Pragmatic resistance to change. Everyday resistance to change can benefit the organization by preventing or reshaping poorly designed change initiatives (chapter 8).

Has resistance to change been exaggerated? New research shows that employees often welcome the opportunities that new technologies have to offer. This positive approach contrasts with the beliefs and expectations of many managers (chapter 8).

Counterproductive work behavior (CWB). Evidence suggests that some types of damaging CWB can be triggered by change initiatives. Why does this happen? What can be done about it? (chapter 8).

Evidence-based implementation. A systematic review of the research suggests that there are 10 steps to successful change. Most organizations seem to ignore the evidence, and this may contribute to the reportedly high failure rate of major change initiatives (chapter 10).

Change resourcing. Contrary to accepted wisdom, research now suggests that, at least in some circumstances, underfunding a change initiative can be advantageous. How can this be? (chapter 10).

Transformational change. What is the nature of transformations? Why do as many as three-quarters fail? Many of the causes of failure are predictable. What can organizations do to improve the odds of success? (chapter 10).

Issue-selling. Why multimodal approaches are more successful for pitching change initiative ideas to senior management: how to choose the right combination of words, body language, and visual imagery (chapter 12).

Collective change agency. Responsibility for change management rarely rests with one individual, or even with a small group. Now, different models of change delivery units are emerging. Which approach best fits your organization? (chapter 12).

The politics of change. Management political games can disrupt or stop change initiatives. Political skill is critical for the change manager. The constructive aspects of "playing politics" are now widely recognized, challenging the negative stereotype of politics as harmful "dirty tricks" (chapter 12).

Chief transformation officer (CTO). A new kind of change agent, a "high-level orchestrator" of change. What is the nature of this role, and what capabilities are required? (chapter 12).

Pedagogy

The pedagogical features in the text include:

- learning outcomes identified at the beginning of each chapter
- a mix of short and longer "high-impact" case studies of organizational change
- case studies of "new economy" as well as "old economy" organizations
- organizational diagnostic and self-assessment exercises for personal and classroom use
- movie recommendations, identifying films and clips that illustrate theoretical and practical dimensions of organizational change management
- YouTube clip recommendations, following up case and research accounts with commentary from the managers and researchers concerned
- a "roundup" section at the end of each chapter, with reflections for the practicing change manager, summarizing the key learning points linked to the learning outcomes
- suggestions for further reading at the end of each chapter.

Instructors will also find useful the experiential learning exercises in the edited collection by Schwartz et al. (2019).*

Since our book was first published, we have continued our conversations with managers who have been using it as part of their teaching, consulting, and other change activities. In many of these conversations, it was reassuring to hear how our multiple perspectives framework strikes the right chord with them, opening up new, innovative, and different

---

*Schwarz, G. M., Buono, A. F., and Adams, S. M. (eds.) 2019. *Preparing for high impact organizational change: Experiential learning and practice.* Cheltenham UK: Edward Elgar Publishing.

ways of seeing, thinking, conceptualizing, and practicing organizational change. We hope that this new and updated fourth edition will continue to inspire our various change journeys, and we look forward to more conversations along the way.

Additional Resources

Instructors. If you are looking for teaching materials in this subject area, such as case studies, discussion guides, organizational diagnostics, self-assessments, company websites, audio-visual materials (feature films, YouTube clips) to use in lectures and tutorials, then go to: connect.mheducation.com.

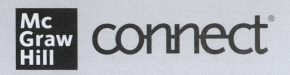

Instructors: Student Success Starts with You

Tools to enhance your unique voice

Want to build your own course? No problem. Prefer to use our turnkey, prebuilt course? Easy. Want to make changes throughout the semester? Sure. And you'll save time with Connect's auto-grading too.

65%

Less Time Grading

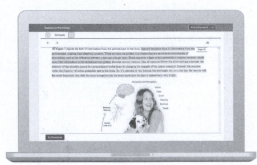

Laptop: McGraw Hill; Woman/dog: George Doyle/Getty Images

Study made personal

Incorporate adaptive study resources like SmartBook® 2.0 into your course and help your students be better prepared in less time. Learn more about the powerful personalized learning experience available in SmartBook 2.0 at **www.mheducation.com/highered/connect/smartbook**

Affordable solutions, added value

Make technology work for you with LMS integration for single sign-on access, mobile access to the digital textbook, and reports to quickly show you how each of your students is doing. And with our Inclusive Access program you can provide all these tools at a discount to your students. Ask your McGraw Hill representative for more information.

Padlock: Jobalou/Getty Images

Solutions for your challenges

A product isn't a solution. Real solutions are affordable, reliable, and come with training and ongoing support when you need it and how you want it. Visit **www.supportateverystep.com** for videos and resources both you and your students can use throughout the semester.

Checkmark: Jobalou/Getty Images

Students: Get Learning That Fits You

Effective tools for efficient studying

Connect is designed to make you more productive with simple, flexible, intuitive tools that maximize your study time and meet your individual learning needs. Get learning that works for you with Connect.

Study anytime, anywhere

Download the free ReadAnywhere app and access your online eBook or SmartBook 2.0 assignments when it's convenient, even if you're offline. And since the app automatically syncs with your eBook and SmartBook 2.0 assignments in Connect, all of your work is available every time you open it. Find out more at **www.mheducation.com/readanywhere**

> *"I really liked this app—it made it easy to study when you don't have your textbook in front of you."*
>
> - Jordan Cunningham,
>   Eastern Washington University

Everything you need in one place

Your Connect course has everything you need—whether reading on your digital eBook or completing assignments for class, Connect makes it easy to get your work done.

Calendar: owattaphotos/Getty Images

Learning for everyone

McGraw Hill works directly with Accessibility Services Departments and faculty to meet the learning needs of all students. Please contact your Accessibility Services Office and ask them to email accessibility@mheducation.com, or visit **www.mheducation.com/about/accessibility** for more information.

Top: Jenner Images/Getty Images, Left: Hero Images/Getty Images, Right: Hero Images/Getty Images

PART 1

Groundwork: Understanding and Diagnosing Change

CHAPTER 1 Managing Change: Stories and Paradoxes

CHAPTER 2 Images of Change Management

CHAPTER 3 Why Change? Contemporary Pressures and Drivers

CHAPTER 4 What to Change? A Diagnostic Approach

The central theme of the four chapters in Part 1 is *groundwork*. How are we to approach an understanding of organizational change? With what approaches, perspectives, or images of change management should we be working? What drivers and pressures produce organizational change? What diagnostic tools can we use to decide what aspects of the organization and its operations will need to change or will benefit from change?

Chapter 1

Managing Change: Stories and Paradoxes

Learning Objectives

By the end of this chapter you should be able to:

LO 1.1 Understand how stories of change can contribute to our knowledge of theory and practice.

LO 1.2 Explain why managing organizational change is both a creative process and a rational process.

LO 1.3 Identify the main tensions and paradoxes in managing organizational change.

LO 1.4 Evaluate the strengths and limitations of our current understanding of this field.

"The human mind is a story processor, not a logic processor."

Jonathan Haidt, social psychologist

3

LO 1.1 LO 1.2 Stories about Change: What Can We Learn?

Changing organizations is as exhilarating as it is messy, as satisfying as it is frustrating, as creative as it is rational. This book recognizes these tensions and how they affect those who are involved in managing change. Rather than pretend that these tensions do not exist or that they are unimportant, we confront them head-on, considering how they can be addressed and managed, recognizing the constraints that they can impose. We also want to demonstrate how the images that we have about the way in which change should be managed, and our image of the role of change agents, affect how we approach change and the outcomes that we think are possible.

To begin this exploration, we present three stories of recent changes. The first concerns how Roz Brewer restored the "buzz" at Starbucks. The second concerns the organizational model introduced at Sears Holdings in an unsuccessful attempt to restore falling sales and profits. The third describes how Mike Duggan, mayor of Detroit, transformed the city's fortunes. These stories each address different problems: a coffeehouse chain, a retailer, and a city. But they illustrate common issues concerning the management of change. Each account opens with a set of assessment questions. We ask that you think through the answers for yourself. What can we learn about change management from stories like these? You will find our answers to these questions at the end of the chapter.

Our aim is to demonstrate that stories about change can be a valuable source of practical lessons, as well as help to contribute to our general understanding of change. This narrative perspective has a number of advantages. Stories are a familiar and popular medium. They give us rich information set in context. They enable us to put ourselves at the center of the action. They encourage us to consider how we could transfer the issues that we are reading about into our own experience.

These stories are, of course, each distinctive, one-off. How can they contribute to knowledge and practice in general, in other sectors and organizations? Stories are one of our main ways of knowing, communicating, and making sense of the world (Dawson and Andriopoulos, 2017; Gabriel, 2019). Our stories have actors: change leaders, other managers, staff, customers, etc. They make decisions that lead to actions that trigger responses: acceptance, resistance, departure. There is a plot: a serious problem that could be solved by organizational change. There are consequences: To what extent did the change solve the problem, and were other problems created along the way? The sequence of events unfolds in a typical manner: . . . and then . . . and then. This tells us *why* the outcomes were reached. These narratives do not simply describe what happened with a change initiative. They also provide us with *explanations*. These are *process narratives*. Process narratives have advantages over more traditional (quantitative, statistical) research methods (Mohr, 1982; Langley et al., 2013):

- They tell us about the context, give us a sense of the whole, a broader frame of reference.
- Complexity can be expressed within a coherent sequence of events.
- The nature and significance of the causal factors acting on events are exposed.
- The narrative patterns transcend individual cases.

This approach is based on what is called *narrative knowing* (Langley and Tsoukas, 2010; Vaara et al., 2016)—understanding events through the stories that are told about them. Because stories can reveal the mechanisms, or logics, behind a sequence of events, they are *process theories*. (We will explore process perspectives on change in chapter 10.) What combinations of factors drive, slow down, accelerate, or block the change process? The three stories that follow explain the relative success of the changes in Starbucks, Sears, and Detroit. We will ask you to consider the extent to which those explanations, each based on a single unique case narrative, can be applied to managing organizational change in general, in other settings.

LO 1.1   The Starbucks Story

Issues to Consider as You Read This Story

1. To what extent can management expertise in general, and change management expertise in particular, translate from one company and sector to another?
2. What elements of Roz Brewer's approach to change management would be appropriate for you to use in your organization?
3. Do you think that senior executives should be closely involved with the frontline day-to-day operations of the business as Brewer was?

The Context

Founded in 1971, based in Seattle, with over 30,000 locations, 330,000 employees, and annual revenues of around $25 billion, Starbucks is the largest seller of coffee in the world.

The Problem

Roz Brewer joined Starbucks' business in America as chief operating officer in 2017, the first woman and first African-American to hold such a senior position in the company. In her new role, she had a number of problems to deal with. The company's iconic founder and executive chairman, Howard Schultz, had decided to leave the company after three decades. After five years of exceptional growth, sales had stalled. In 2018, the company was accused of racial bias after a manager called police to deal with two Black men who had been waiting for a friend in an outlet in Philadelphia; they had not bought drinks and refused to leave when asked. Some customers called for a Starbucks' boycott after a social media video of the arrest went viral. When Brewer analyzed Starbucks' business operations in detail in her first three months, she found that the company was "melting down behind the coffee bar." Paradoxically, this was the result of the success of the mobile order and pay system; customers placed their orders through an app before coming to the store. But the stores were not ready for the sudden increase in orders. Crowds of customers jostled each other as they waited for their drinks, and stressed baristas struggled to keep up with the flow. She also found that 40 percent of employees' time was spent on tasks away from the customers, such as counting milk jugs three times a day and unnecessarily restocking the floor with cups. And like many other organizations, there were too many development and change initiatives being run by corporate headquarters.

The Solution

Brewer was not an obvious choice for the role at Starbucks. Her previous position was as a senior executive at Walmart. Investors were skeptical that her experience with a big-box retailer could translate to a "high touch" coffee shop business. And she preferred green tea to coffee. However, one of Brewer's colleagues at Walmart said, "Roz is a tough cookie. She's into the details. She's not a fluffy person. She gets things done." Another colleague said, "She's an operator. She's not just a person with a point of view and vision. She can execute" (Kowitt, 2019, pp. 86 and 88).

Schultz had managed the company by instinct and intuition. Brewer, who trained as a chemist, focused on the numbers and sought to bring some discipline and order to the stores. Brewer and her team simplified, eliminated, or automated tasks to allow store staff to spend more time with customers. Dedicated baristas were appointed to handle the mobile orders in stores where those were popular. Cleaning was carried out when the stores were closed. Two-thirds of the corporate projects were stopped. Only those relating to three priorities—beverage innovation, store experience, and the digital business—were allowed to continue. Brewer earned a reputation for making tough decisions. For example, she asked her team to assess the benefits and disadvantages of Mercato—Starbucks' fresh food business that was introduced, with much publicity, to 1,500 stores in 2017. The assessment showed that Mercato did not fit the company's priorities, so she killed it. She also cut specialist stand-alone, time-limited offers, like the Unicorn Frappucino. These were popular with only a small number of customers, and they complicated the baristas' work. She had the development team work instead on simpler products that could be made with existing ingredients. Following analysis of the timing of customer visits to stores and focusing on converting occasional midday customers to "rewards" members (who account for 40 percent of sales), Brewer was able to grow the afternoon business, which was traditionally a slack period.

Following what became known as "the Philadelphia incident," Brewer flew to Philadelphia to apologize in person to the two men, and she organized racial bias training for 175,000 employees. Brewer also spent a lot of her time visiting the stores, talking to employees, and assessing their pride in the business. Do employees who recognize her look her in the eye? Brewer says, "If they look down at their feet, they're not proud about the store. Ninety-nine percent of the time I'm right about that" (Kowitt, 2019, p. 91). Brewer sees Starbucks' stores as more than coffee shops; they are also public spaces, like libraries, serving the needs of employees and communities. In some shops, if they think that safety will be increased, managers have been allowed to install needle boxes in restrooms, for the disposal of drug users' syringes. "Brewer wants baristas to make the perfect flat white or pour-over. But she also wants them trained in how to deal with the hardest social situations they could possibly encounter so that everyone feels like they belong in Starbucks" (Kowitt, 2019, p. 92).

The Outcome

Starbucks' sales growth recovered, proving Brewer's critics wrong. By 2018, there were 15 million rewards members, who spend three times as much as nonmembers. Afternoon customers started to generate 50 percent of beverage sales, and in 2019 Starbucks saw its best sales growth in three years. Starbucks' stock price rose 70 percent between 2017 and 2019.

Case Sources

Kowitt, B. 2019. How Starbucks got its buzz back. *Fortune*, 180(4):84–92.

> On *YouTube,* find 'Starbucks COO Roz Brewer on big changes at Starbucks' (2019; 6 minutes).

LO 1.1 The Sears Story

Issues to Consider as You Read This Story

1. How would you describe Eddie Lampert's leadership style?
2. How would you assess his approach to implementing major organizational change—in this case restructuring the whole company with a new organizational model?
3. On balance, how would you assess his new organizational model?
4. What lessons about managing organizational change can we take from this experience and apply to other organizations, in this or other sectors?

The Setting

A household name in America, Sears was once the world's largest retailer. In October 2018, the company filed for Chapter 11 bankruptcy, and its remaining assets were sold to a hedge fund, ESL Investments, owned by Eddie Lampert. What happened?

Sears Holdings Corporation was a specialty retailer, formed in 2005 by the merger of Kmart and Sears Roebuck. The merger was the idea of Eddie Lampert, a billionaire hedge fund manager who owned 55 percent of the new company and who became chairman. Based in Illinois, the company operated in the United States and Canada, with 274,000 employees, 4,000 retail stores, and annual revenues (2013) of $40 billion. Sears and Kmart stores sold home merchandise, clothing, and automotive products and services. The merged company was successful at first, due to aggressive cost cutting.

The Problem

By 2007, two years after the merger, profits were down by 45 percent.

The Chairman's Solution

Lampert decided to restructure the company. Sears was organized like a classic retailer. Department heads ran their own product lines, but they all worked for the same merchandising and marketing leaders, with the same financial goals. The new model ran Sears like a hedge fund portfolio with autonomous businesses competing for resources. This "internal market" would promote efficiency and improve corporate performance. At first, the new structure had around 30 business units, including product divisions, support functions, and brands, along with units focusing on e-commerce and real estate. By 2009, there were over 40 divisions. Each division had its own president, chief marketing officer, board of directors, profit and loss statement, and strategy that had to be agreed on by Lampert's executive committee. With all those positions to fill at the head of each unit, executives competed for the roles, each eager to run his or her own multibillion-dollar business. The new model was called SOAR: Sears Holdings Organization, Actions, and Responsibilities.

When the reorganization was announced in January 2008, the company's share price rose 12 percent. Most retail companies prefer integrated structures, in which different divisions can be compelled to make sacrifices, such as discounting goods, to attract more shoppers. Lampert's colleagues argued that his new approach would create rival factions. Lampert disagreed. He believed that decentralized structures, although they might appear "messy," were more effective and they produced better information. This would give him access to better data, enabling him to assess more effectively the individual components of the company and its assets. Lampert also argued that SOAR made it easier to divest businesses and open new ones, such as the online "Shop Your Way" division.

Sears was an early adopter of online shopping. Lampert (who allegedly did all his own shopping online, but had no previous experience in retailing) wanted to grow this side of the business, and investment in the stores was cut back. He had innovative ideas: smart-phone apps, netbooks in stores, and a multiplayer game for employees. He set up a company social network called Pebble, which he joined under the pseudonym Eli Wexler, so that he could engage with employees. However, he criticized other people's posts and argued with store associates. When staff worked out that Wexler was Lampert, unit managers began tracking how often their employees were "Pebbling." One group organized Pebble conversations about random topics just so they would appear to be active users.

The Chairman

At the time of the merger, investors were confident that Lampert could turn the two companies around. One analyst described him as "lightning fast, razor-sharp smart, very direct." Many of those who worked for him described him as brilliant (although he could overestimate his abilities). The son of a lawyer, it was rumored that he read corporate reports and finance textbooks in high school, before going to Yale University. He hated focus groups and was sensitive to jargon such as "vendor." His brands chief once used the word *consumer* in a presentation. Lampert interrupted, with a lecture on why he should have used the word *customer* instead. He often argued with experienced retailers, but he had good relationships with managers who had finance and technology backgrounds.

From 2008, Sears' business unit heads had an annual personal videoconference with the chairman. They went to a conference room at the headquarters in Illinois, with some of Lampert's senior aides, and waited while an assistant turned on the screen on the wall opposite the U-shaped table and Lampert appeared. Lampert ran these meetings from his homes in Greenwich, Connecticut; Aspen Colorado; and subsequently Florida, earning him the nickname, "The Wizard of Oz." He only visited headquarters in person twice a year because he hated flying. While the unit head worked through the PowerPoint presentation, Lampert didn't look up, but dealt with his emails or studied a spreadsheet until he heard something that he didn't like—which would then lead to lengthy questioning.

In 2012, he bought a family home in Miami Beach for $38 million and moved his hedge fund to Florida. Some industry analysts felt that Sears' problems were exacerbated by Lampert's penny-pinching cost savings, which stifled investment in its stores. Instead of store improvements, Sears bought back stock and increased its online presence. In 2013, Lampert became chairman and chief executive, the company having gone through four other chief executives since the merger.

The Outcomes

Instead of improving performance, the new model encouraged the divisions to turn against each other. Lampert evaluated the divisions and calculated executives' bonuses, using a measure called "business operating profit" (BOP). The result was that individual business units focused exclusively on their own profitability, rather than on the welfare of the company. For example, the clothing division cut labor to save money, knowing that floor salespeople in other units would have to pick up the slack. Nobody wanted to sacrifice business operating profits to increase shopping traffic. The business was ravaged by infighting as the divisions—behaving in the words of one executive like "warring tribes"—battled for resources. Executives brought laptops with screen protectors to meetings so that their colleagues couldn't see what they were doing. There was no collaboration and no cooperation. The Sears and Kmart brands suffered. Employees gave the new organizational model a new name: SORE.

The reorganization also meant that Sears had to hire and promote dozens of expensive chief financial officers and chief marketing officers. Many unit heads underpaid middle managers to compensate. As each division had its own board of directors, some presidents sat on five or six boards, which each met monthly. Top executives were constantly in meetings.

The company had not been profitable since 2010 and posted a net loss of $170 million for the first quarter in 2011. In November that year, Sears discovered that rivals planned to open on Thanksgiving at midnight, and Sears' executives knew that they should also open early. However, it wasn't possible to get all the business unit heads to agree, and the stores opened as usual, the following morning. One vice president drove to the mall that evening and watched families flocking into rival stores. When Sears opened the next day, cars were already leaving the parking lot. That December, Sears announced the closure of over 100 stores. In February 2012, Sears announced the closure of its nine "The Great Indoors" stores.

From 2005 to 2013, Sears' sales fell from $49.1 billion to £39.9 billion, the stock value fell by 64 percent, and cash holdings hit a 10-year low. In May 2013, at the annual shareholders' meeting, Lampert pointed to the growth in online sales and described a new app called "Member Assist" that customers could use to send messages to store associates. The aim was "to bring online capabilities into the stores." Three weeks later, Sears reported a first-quarter loss of $279 million, and the share price fell sharply. The online business contributed 3 percent of total sales. Online sales were growing, however, through the "Shop Your Way" website. Lampert argued that this was the future of Sears, and he wanted to develop "Shop Your Way" into a hybrid of Amazon and Facebook. The company's stock market valuation fell from $30 billion in 2007 to $69 million in October 2018, while carrying $5 billion in debt. Revenues in 2018 were $16.7 billion, down from $50.7 billion in 2007. Sears had around 3,500 stores in America in 2007, and young shoppers rarely visited the 866 stores that remained in August 2018. Sears filed for Chapter 11 bankruptcy in 2018, and Lampert resigned as chief executive, but stayed on as chairman.

Case Sources

Kimes, M. 2013. At Sears, Eddie Lampert's warring divisions model adds to the troubles. *Bloomberg Businessweek*, July 11. http://www.businessweek.com/articles/2013-07-11/at-sears-eddie-lamperts-warring-divisions-model-adds-to-the-troubles.

Forbes (n.d.), #2057 Edward Lampert, http://www.forbes.com/profile/edward-lampert.

Sears Holdings, http://www.searsholdings.com.

Sears holdings, *Wikipedia*, http://en.wikipedia.org/wiki/Sears_Holdings.

Shop Your Way, http://www.shopyourway.com.

The Economist. 2018. The collapse of an American retail giant. October 20. https://www.economist.com/business/2018/10/20/the-collapse-of-an-american-retail-giant.

On *YouTube,* find 'The fall of a retail icon: why Americans stopped shopping at Sears' (2018, 6 minutes).

LO 1.1 The Detroit Story

Issues to Consider as You Read This Story

1. Mike Duggan transformed Detroit without a "management textbook" plan for change. Why do you think he was successful?
2. What aspects of Duggan's change management style would be appropriate for you to use in your organization?
3. To what extent can we generalize from managing change in a Midwestern American city to managing change in commercial organizations?

The Context

Detroit, Michigan, has a population of over 4 million people. It was once the fourth largest city in America. In the early twentieth century, Henry Ford and other motorcar manufacturers made Detroit famous as the automotive capital of the world; Detroit is also known as the Motor City and Motown. But decades of decline, starting in the 1970s, made Detroit famous as America's worst urban disaster story, as an iconic city in America's Midwestern rust belt.

The Problem

Oil crises in the 1970s meant that customers wanted smaller, fuel-efficient vehicles, not the "gas guzzlers" that Detroit made. In the late twentieth century, with falling employment in the motor industry and other businesses leaving, Detroit's population fell. As skilled workers found employment elsewhere, the proportion of poor people in the city's population increased. These factors led to a smaller tax base, lower property prices, abandoned homes, and higher crime rates. The city administration was corrupt, and several officials (including the mayor) were imprisoned. In 2011, half of Detroit's property owners failed to pay their taxes.

By 2013, Detroit was bankrupt, and $18.5 billion in debt. When the current mayor, Mike Duggan, was elected in 2013, 40 percent of the city's streetlights and 25 percent of the fire hydrants were not working and 40,000 properties were vacant. The city had stark racial, economic, and social divisions. In the run-up to his election, Duggan organized house parties with small groups of residents across Detroit. In total, 8,000 people turned up to these meetings, and Duggan described this experience as powerful:

> You go to a house party at Mack and Beals, where the people had an abandoned house on each side of their property, and their streetlights were out, they have one perspective on the city of Detroit. And then you go to Indian Village and they have a different perspective. And East English Village has a different perspective. But the aspirations of the people

of the city are really the same. They want their neighborhoods back. They want the police to show up. They want the abandoned buildings dealt with. And they want to be able to stay in their neighborhood and not leave. They did teach me about the different issues in those neighborhoods. They were enormously educational. Anyone can come up to me from any neighborhood in this city, and I'm able to have a conversation about their problems and what we're going to do about them.

The Solution

Duggan's past experience involved turning around the Detroit Medical Center, which had lost $500 million over the six years, before he was appointed chief executive in 2004. The Center generated over $57 million net income in 2012. Duggan's priority as mayor of Detroit was once again to reverse the decline. He describes his strategy as "focusing on the boring."

> Get the boring stuff right—streetlights, fire hydrants, ambulance response times—and the rest falls into place. If each individual person says, OK my job is to get the grass cut in the parks; my job is to get the tractors repaired 20 percent faster to get the grass cut in the parks, turnaround occurs. People get into public service because something in their heart wants them to help people, and over time the bureaucracy beats that idealism out of them. We are trying to bring idealism back.

Duggan continued to hold weekly meetings with residents, in their homes, where he asked them what he could fix next.

The Outcomes

Bankruptcy brought some debt relief. Wealthy Detroit families invested in redevelopment, which brought sports teams and businesses back to the city. Entrepreneurial start-ups came to Detroit for its low costs and light traffic and because "rust belt" became trendy. Now the streetlights work, the fire hydrants have been repaired, and the city's population is growing again. In 2018, Duggan bid to host the new U.S. headquarters for Amazon (subsequently awarded to northern Virginia). "Mike Duggan is an unremarkable guy who has done unremarkable things to achieve extraordinary results."

Case Sources

Hagen, N. 2018. Halting Detroit's decline. *Financial Times*, January 8, p. 24. https://www. crainsdetroit.com/awards/mike-duggan-making-improbable-inevitable.

On *YouTube,* find 'The revitalization of Detroit — Talks at GS', (2016, 15 minutes).

LO 1.3 LO 1.4 Tension and Paradox: The State of the Art

tension   when two or more ideas are in opposition to each other
paradox   when two or more apparently correct ideas contradict each other

From a management perspective, organizational change is seen as problematic. How do we persuade people to accept new technologies that will make their skills, knowledge, and working practices obsolete? How quickly can people who find themselves with new roles, and new relationships, learn to operate effectively after a major reorganization? How about this new system for capturing and processing customer information? We prefer the old system because it works just fine. Change can be difficult. Change that is not well managed, however, can generate frustration and anger.

Most estimates put the failure rate of planned changes at around 60 to 70 percent (Bucy et al., 2017; Stouten et al., 2018; Keller and Schaninger, 2019). There is, therefore, no shortage of advice. However, that advice is both extensive and fragmented. The literature—research and other commentary—can be difficult to access, and to absorb, for several reasons:

many perspectives	There are contributions from different academic disciplines and theoretical perspectives—there are several *literatures*.
rich history	Work dating from the 1940s is still interesting and useful; recent research has not necessarily made previous commentary irrelevant.
range of concepts	The concepts that are used vary in scale, from schools of thought or perspectives on change, through methodologies, to single tools.
blurred boundaries	Depending on the definitions of change and change management in use, the boundaries of the topic vary between commentators.
varied settings	As with our stories, evidence and examples come from a range of organizational types and contexts, using different methodologies.

LO 1.2

Many perspectives is the most significant of these properties. That is usually seen as a problem—"the experts can't agree." We disagree and prefer instead to emphasize the advantages in adopting a multiple-perspectives approach to the management of organizational change. First, a perspective that works in one context may not work well in a different setting: We will explore contingency frameworks in chapter 10. Second, this is a way of opening up debate: "Should we define our problem in these terms, or in some other way?" Third, multiple perspectives encourage the search for creative solutions: "Can we combine ideas from two or more approaches and adapt them to fit our context?" We will meet all these characteristics again in later chapters.

The practicing manager, less interested in theoretical perspectives, wants to know "what works?" It is difficult to give a clear answer to that question, too, for the following reasons:

many variables	Even with simple changes, the impact is multidimensional, and measuring "effectiveness" has to capture all the factors to produce a complete picture.
slippery causality	It is difficult to establish cause and effect clearly across complex processes that unfold over time, usually at the same time as lots of other changes.
many stakeholders	Different stakeholders have different views of the nature of the problem, the appropriate solution, and the desirable outcomes. Whose measures should we use?

What works well in one setting may not work well in another. The broad outlines of a good change strategy are widely known and accepted. However, what matters is the detail, concerning how an intervention is designed for a particular organization. For example, most practical guidelines begin by suggesting that change will be more readily accepted if there is a "sense of urgency" that underpins the business case for change. That sense of urgency can be seen in the issues facing Starbucks, in the falling profitability at Sears, and in the many problems in Detroit. Note, however, that there are many different ways in which a sense of urgency can be established and communicated. Some methods emphasize the (negative) "burning platform" that heightens anxiety and encourages escape. Other approaches encourage a (positive) "burning ambition" to confront and solve the problem.

What works depends on the context. It is rarely possible to just do what someone else has done. Change is in part a rational process; we know what kinds of issues need to be taken into account. Change is also a creative process; it is always necessary to design—to create—an approach that is consistent with local circumstances. However, creatively adapted, such accounts of how other organizations have handled change can be helpful in addressing similar problems in other settings.

LO 1.3   The field of change management is also rich in tensions and paradoxes. We will explore six of these briefly, in the form of key questions. These issues will also appear in later chapters. You will probably encounter further tensions in your reading across the subject and in practice. How these tensions and paradoxes are managed has implications for the process and outcomes of change.

Transformational Change, or Sweat the Small Stuff?

Where to start—with sweeping radical changes, or a gradual process of incremental initiatives? We will explore a simple model for "locating" the scale of change in the next section. However, faced with geopolitical, economic, demographic, sociocultural, and technological developments, most organizations seem to think in terms of deep transformational change. The Sears story reflects this view, implementing whole-organizational changes to deal with survival threats. In contrast, Roz Brewer at Starbucks began by focusing on operational details—"behind the coffee bar"—and Mike Duggan turned Detroit around by focusing on "the boring stuff." A focus on transformation may mean that minor changes are seen as less valuable and important and are overlooked in favor of "high impact" initiatives. This could be a mistake. Moore and Buchanan (2013), for example, demonstrate how an initiative designed to fix small problems quickly in a hospital generated major improvements for almost no cost. In this case, "sweating the small stuff" was an enabling strategy, getting people involved (the small problems were identified by staff), establishing a reputation for getting things done, and creating the platform for further developments. Shallower changes can facilitate and complement the deeper initiatives, and evidence suggests that these should not be underestimated.

Systematic Tools, or Messy Political Process?

If one looks below the surface of cases of managed change, one can always discern the ever-present effect of the "other side" of organizational life. The ambiguities, uncertainties, ambivalences, tensions, politics and intrigues are always involved, and are influential and addressed in some manner—however half-cocked, fudged, guessed at, messed up or little understood.

(Badham, 2013, p. 24)

Most practical guidelines on change implementation (chapters 9 and 10) suggest a systematic sequence of steps, with support from diagnostic tools and assessments (chapters 4 and 5). We have already suggested that change is a creative process as well as a rational one. It is also a political process. Organizations are political systems, and because there are often "winners and losers," change is a political process. The systematic tools-based approach, the creativity, and the politics work hand in hand. We will explore the political skills that change managers require later (chapter 12). It is important to recognize that, despite what the textbook or the change management consultant says, those systematic tools are only part of the answer to, "how to do it, and how to get it right."

Organizational Capabilities, or Personal Skills?

Starbucks' founder Howard Schultz grew the company on a combination of instinct and intuition. Roz Brewer brought a different style, based on the evidence, data, and the numbers. Either of these approaches works well in the right context, particularly with regard to whether or not the organization will welcome change. We thus need to pay attention to organizational readiness and capabilities, as well as individual personalities and skills, to understand the change drivers and barriers (chapter 5). The skills of change agents are, of course, also important. However, skilled change agents struggle in rules-based organizations, and agile organizations still need capable change agents. We will explore the capabilities of effective change managers in chapter 12.

Rapid Change, or the Acceleration Trap?

The pace of change—social, political, economic, technological—appears to have accelerated. Can organizations keep up? There is now a considerable amount of advice on how to speed up change, to accelerate the pace. Rapid change, however, can cause problems. Can people keep up? Change too fast, and you run the danger of destabilizing the organization and creating staff burnout (Buchanan and Macaulay, 2019). There is also, therefore, advice on how to manage "painless change," and how to avoid "the acceleration trap" (see chapter 8).

Change Has Never Been So Fast

That this is an age of change is an expression heard frequently today. Never before in the history of mankind have so many and so frequent changes occurred. These changes that we see taking place all about us are in that great cultural accumulation which is man's social heritage. It has already been shown that these cultural changes were in earlier times rather infrequent, but that in modern times they have been occurring faster and faster until today mankind is almost bewildered in his effort to keep adjusted to these ever-increasing social changes. This rapidity of social change may be due to the increase in inventions which in turn is made possible by the accumulative nature of material culture [i.e., technology]. (Ogburn, 1922, pp. 199–200).

Change Leader, or Distributed Leadership?

There is a personality at the heart of each of our stories: Roz Brewer, Eddie Lampert, Mike Duggan. It seems that the fate of change is in the hands of the leader. This is rarely the case. It is widely assumed that change needs a champion, a senior figure, who sets the direction, inspires others, and drives the project. A lot of work has gone into identifying the competencies of this "ideas champion," the effective change leader. This parallels work on the capabilities of effective leaders in general (although the evidence says that leadership success is highly contingent). However, in most organizations, change is not a solo performance but a team effort. There is usually a "guiding coalition" of more or less senior managers, who guarantee permission for change, oversee progress, and unblock problems. Different models of change delivery units have evolved (chapter 12). Research has shown how change is often driven by large numbers of organizational members, through "distributed leadership" or "leadership constellations," or "leadership in the plural." As you read the case history "The Vanuatu Plastics Ban," note the number of individuals, groups, agencies, government ministers, and government departments contributing to this change. Vanuatu is a nation state, not a company, but this distributed approach to implementing change is typical.

The Vanuatu Plastics Ban

Vanuatu in the South Pacific is made up of 80 islands stretching over 1,000 kilometers, with a population of 300,000 people. Three and a half hours flight time from Sydney on the east coast of Australia, Vanuatu's coral reefs and World War II wrecks are popular with scuba divers.

Ocean plastic is a global problem, harming marine life and polluting the food chain. It is estimated that by 2050, there will be more plastic by volume in the world's oceans than fish. Most of this marine pollution comes from East Asian and Pacific countries. The United Nations has "declared war" on marine litter, noting that a garbage truck of plastic is dumped into the ocean every minute. Vanuatu makes a tiny contribution to global plastic waste. However, the waste damages the islands' ecosystems and biodiversity. Vanuatu hosted cleanup days to develop awareness of the problems that plastics created. But after these cleanups, the plastic waste would gradually return.

Solution: First Phase

The war on plastic in Vanuatu started with a campaign organized by Christelle Thieffry and Georges Cumbo. Having seen the plastic rubbish on the beaches around the capital Port Vila, they launched their Facebook page in March 2017, calling for a ban on plastic bags. Their Facebook campaign attracted a lot of support, so they launched a petition in May 2017, gaining 2,000 signatures. Their efforts attracted the attention of politicians. In July 2017, the Prime Minister, Charlot Salwai, announced the government's intention to eradicate plastic bags within a year.

In 2018, Vanuatu banned single-use plastics, including bags and polystyrene containers, with fines

of $175 to $900 for violations (World Bank, 2019). When the ban was introduced, it was resisted. But people became accustomed to the idea, and shops became more comfortable about not giving shoppers plastic bags. Ellen Jimmy, a stallholder in Port Vila's market, said that her business had not been harmed by the ban, and customers rarely complained (Visser, 2019).

Solution: Second Phase

Donna Kalfatak became Director of Vanuatu's Department of Environmental Protection and Conservation in 2019. To implement the second phase of the plastics ban, she worked with Vanuatu's waste management team, the Ministry of Climate Change, and the Ministry of Foreign Affairs. The Centre for Environment, Fisheries, and Aquaculture Science conducted a waste audit and concluded that the ban should be extended to disposable diapers, drinking straws, grocery packaging, Styrofoam food containers, and plastic cutlery. Christina Shaw and her colleagues at Dive Against Debris gathered further data. The Minister of Foreign Affairs and External Trade, Ralph Regenvanu, announced the expanded list of banned items, endorsed by the Council of Ministers, in December 2019.

The Outcomes

The ban had an immediate effect, with locals noting the absence of trash on the capital's streets and urban areas. The ban was helped by the islands' handicrafts tradition of making biodegradable bags woven from pandanus fronds. Sales of these bags grew, benefitting those who made them (Bulvanua

(Continued)

Arts and Crafts Cooperative members). But bottle caps and chip packets still wash up on the beaches, and plastic bags and water bottles have not disappeared. To evade the ban on bags, some shops packaged fruits and vegetables in plastic netting. These will eventually be banned, too.

Foreign Minister Ralph Regenvanu thinks that Vanuatu's success may be explained by the fact that it is a small country. Only one company that makes plastic products and the government have helped them to adapt to the new regulations. Regenvanu says, "It's because we're so small that we can do it. We're like a little laboratory for being able to do things like this. One of the advantages here is that it is so small that you can do things that you may think impossible in other places" (Visser, 2019).

Case Sources

Visser, N. 2019. Vanuatu has one of the world's strictest plastic bans. It's about to get tougher. *Huffington Post*, February 24. https://www.huffingtonpost.com.au/entry/vanuatu-plastic-ban-law-ocean-pollution_n_5c6ee757e4b0f40774cd355d.

World Bank. 2019. Meet the innovator battling plastic waste in Vanuatu: Donna Kalfatak. June 4. https://www.worldbank.org/en/news/feature/2019/06/04/meet-the-innovators-battling-plastic-waste-in-vanuatu-donna-kalfatak.

Find on *YouTube,* 'Local Impact Story Big Blue Vanuatu' (2018, 1.38 minutes)

Learning Lessons, or Implementing Lessons?

Change following crises, accidents, misconduct, failures, and other extreme events often does not happen. There is always an investigation, which produces recommendations for preventing such an event from happening again (or at least reducing the probability). The evidence shows that those recommendations are often ignored. One might assume that, in such circumstances, change would be welcome, rapid, and straightforward. The distinction between passive learning (identifying lessons) and active learning (implementing changes) is important here. The latter does not automatically follow. Why is that not the case? In exploring "why organizations change' in chapter 3, we will also consider why organizations do not change, when perhaps they should.

The perceptive reader will have noticed that the answer to each of these six paradoxes, these six questions, is in every case "both." We need big change and small change. Change is at the same time a systematic process and a political one. We need both organizational and individual capabilities. The pace of change must, if possible, vary with circumstances. It almost always takes "a cast of characters" that includes champions and supporters to drive change. There is no point in learning lessons if we do not then implement them. As noted earlier, the way in which these tensions are confronted and managed both drives and constrains the change process and influences the outcomes.

LO 1.4 Assessing Depth of Change

We have noted the tension between transformational change and the small stuff. Depth is one metaphor that can be used to categorize change. Figure 1.1 presents a framework for that assessment.

At the bottom of Figure 1.1 sits the "small stuff" that may not even be regarded as "change." In the middle of the scale, we have "sustaining innovation" that involves

FIGURE 1.1
Assessing Depth of Change

Off the scale	Disruptive innovation Frame-breaking, mold-breaking Redraw dramatically organization and sector boundaries
Deeper	Paradigm shift, strategic change New ways of thinking and solving problems, whole system change New ways of doing business
Deep change	Change the mission, vision, values, the organization's philosophy, in order to symbolize a radical shift in thinking and behavior
	Change the organization's definition of success Create new goals, objectives, targets
Sustaining innovation	Improve business planning to symbolize a shift in thinking Tighten up on documentation, reporting, controls
	Reallocate resources Grow some departments, cut others, create new units
Shallow change	Fine-tuning: cut costs, improve efficiencies Constantly "nibble away" making minor improvements
Not on the scale	"Sweat the small stuff"—quickly solve the minor annoying problems that nobody has bothered to fix; "grease the wheels"

improving on current practices. At the top of the scale is "disruptive innovation," which involves radically new business models and working methods (Christensen et al., 2015). Clearly, in considering change in an organization, the proposed solution should be consistent with the diagnosis of the problem. Using shallow changes to address strategic challenges may not be appropriate. Attempting to solve minor difficulties with disruptive innovation could consume disproportionate amounts of time and resources.

Shallow changes are often easier to implement than frame-breaking changes. Transformational "off the scale" changes are more challenging because they are costly and time consuming and affect larger numbers of people in more significant ways, potentially generating greater resistance. However, in most organizations, several changes at different depths are likely to be under way at the same time (see the box "Turnaround at Etsy"). Many large organizations have thus established corporate project or program management offices (PMOs), or delivery units, to support and coordinate their multiple initiatives (Ward and Daniel, 2013; Wylie and Sturdy, 2018).

One of the tensions in this framework concerns the ambitions of the individual manager. When one is interviewed for the next promotion, stories about the impact of the deep transformations for which one has been responsible are typically more impressive than stories about minor stuff. If an initiative looks like "change for the sake of change," find out who will be adding it to their resumé.

Turnaround at Etsy

When an organization is in trouble, should management focus on changing the high-level strategy or on fixing "the small stuff"? Here is an example of a company that did both, while cutting the number of change initiatives that were running.

Founded in 2005 and based in New York, Etsy is an e-commerce company linking customers with suppliers of handmade and vintage items such as jewelry, bags, clothing, toys, art, craft supplies, and furniture, with 60 million items for sale at any given time. But in this sector, Etsy is a small company, with less than 900 staff, competing with large e-commerce companies (such as Amazon Handmade), which offer fast, consistent, and reliable online shopping.

When Josh Silverman became chief executive in 2015, Etsy was making a loss. Sales were slowing. A major investor wanted the company to be sold if business did not improve. Etsy had 800 active business development initiatives. Silverman cut half of these, and most of the rest were fast-tracked to completion in weeks rather than months or years. Technical resources were moved to a cloud platform to give the technical team more time to focus on Etsy's issues. In his first few weeks in the job, Silverman made a quarter of the employees redundant—a decision he described as "tough love." Etsy has 40 million active buyers, but 60 percent make a purchase only once a year, with the average shopper spending $100 annually. With its ethos of "keeping commerce human," Etsy has a loyal base of customers and suppliers. To grow, Etsy has to reach beyond this core group.

Silverman also focused on the "nuts and bolts" of the online business. An autocorrect feature was added to the website's search box. Customers were reassured about the safety of using credit cards for online payments. Silverman made sellers use the company's own payments system, allowing Etsy to charge transaction fees and standardize the checkout procedure. Tools to support the sellers were introduced, including a dashboard to track orders and streamline payments. The search algorithm was redesigned: While it used to prioritize low-value items that sold more often, it now finds higher-priced items of better quality, encouraging shoppers to consider buying a desk, for example, when searching for a desk lamp. The new algorithm also prioritizes sellers who offer free shipping.

What Silverman has not changed, however, is Etsy's youthful, idealistic organizational culture. The headquarters in Brooklyn has a bicycle garage, local food in the cafeteria, and a plan to offset its shipping-related carbon dioxide emissions. Sales revenue rose by 65 percent over two years, to $604 million in 2018. The company has been profitable for two years, and its stock value was five times higher in 2019 than when Silverman took over (based on Wahba, 2019).

LO 1.4   What's Coming Up: A Roadmap

This text is divided into three parts. Part 1, including this chapter, sets out the *groundwork* and is concerned with understanding and diagnosing change and with different images of change management. Part 2 focuses on *implementation*, exploring the substance of change, the role of vision, managing resistance, developing communication strategies, and several approaches to the implementation process. Part 3 examines two *running threads*, which relate to all the previous chapters. The first concerns managing the sustainability of change, which we argue has to be considered from the beginning, and not managed as an afterthought. The second running thread is an assessment of what it takes to be an effective change manager—which is, of course, the theme of the book as a whole. Figure 1.2 sets out a roadmap, an overview of the content.

FIGURE 1.2
To Be an Effective Change Manager, This Is What You Need . . .

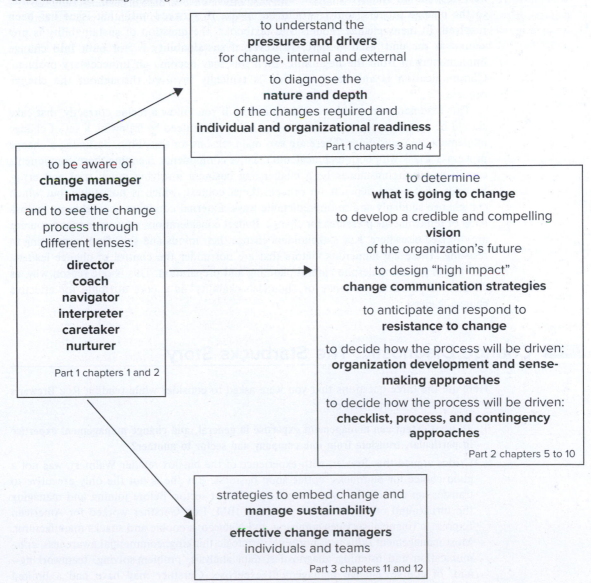

to understand the
pressures and drivers
for change, internal and external

to diagnose the
nature and depth
of the changes required and
individual and organizational readiness

Part 1 chapters 3 and 4

to be aware of
**change manager
images**,
and to see the change
process through
different lenses:

**director
coach
navigator
interpreter
caretaker
nurturer**

Part 1 chapters 1 and 2

to determine
what is going to change

to develop a credible and compelling
vision
of the organization's future

to design "high impact"
change communication strategies

to anticipate and respond to
resistance to change

to decide how the process will be driven:
**organization development and sense-
making approaches**

to decide how the process will be driven:
**checklist, process, and contingency
approaches**

Part 2 chapters 5 to 10

strategies to embed change and
manage sustainability

effective change managers
individuals and teams

Part 3 chapters 11 and 12

One of the main assumptions underpinning this roadmap is that our images of the roles of change leaders affect how we approach the other issues on the map. Remember, for example, how the different change leadership styles adopted by Roz Brewer at Starbucks, Eddy Lampert at Sears, and Mike Duggan in Detroit colored their approaches to designing and implementing the changes that they wanted to implement. This explains why "images," chapter 2, is at the center of the figure. However, by necessity, a book such as this follows a linear sequence for presentational reasons. This is not necessarily the sequence in which change leaders will need to consider these issues or in which instructors will wish to introduce and explore these themes. What will work best depends on context. In some cases, the question of "vision" may be fundamental to the change process, and it would be unwise to proceed until that issue has been resolved. In many change models and textbooks, the question of sustainability is presented at the end, as it is here. However, if sustainability is not built into change implementation from the beginning, then this may become an unnecessary problem. Communication is another issue that is typically involved throughout the change process.

This roadmap comes with an added caution. If you follow a recipe correctly, that cake should be perfect; enjoy. However, success is not guaranteed by following a set of change implementation guidelines. There are two main reasons for this. First, designing a change process is a task with both technical and creative components; blending these components can in many circumstances be a challenging business involving much trial and error. Second, what works depends on organizational context, which is not stable, but which can change suddenly and in unpredictable ways. External conditions can change, intensifying or removing the pressures for change. Budget considerations may mean that resources are diverted elsewhere. Key stakeholders change their minds and shift from supporting to resisting. There are numerous factors that are not under the control of change leaders, and things go wrong despite careful planning and preparation. This is one reason why, as chapter 12 explains, resilience or "bouncebackability" is a core attribute for effective change leaders.

LO 1.1   Change Diagnostic: The Starbucks Story

Here are the three questions that you were asked to consider while reading Roz Brewer's story, followed by our answers.

1. **To what extent can management expertise in general, and change management expertise in particular, translate from one company and sector to another?**

   Critics argued that Brewer, with experience of the big-box retailer Walmart, was not a good choice for Starbucks' coffee shop business. But she is not the only executive to transfer her capabilities to a completely different sector. Before joining and managing the turnaround of the computer company IBM, Lou Gerstner worked for American Express, a financial services company, and Nabisco, a cookie and snacks manufacturer. Most management skills are "portable": strategic thinking, commercial awareness, communication and listening, diagnostics, data analysis, problem-solving, teamworking—and, of course, change management expertise. Gerstner may have had a limited understanding of how computers work or how they were made, but he had people around him who did and on whose expertise he could draw. It was probably easier for Brewer to develop an operational understanding of Starbucks' business.

2. **What elements of Brewer's approach to change management would be appropriate for you to use in your organization?**

The main elements of Brewer's approach were:

- Focus on the evidence, not on intuition.
- Understand in detail how the company meets the needs of its customers.
- Be prepared to make tough, controversial decisions.
- When the company makes a mistake, apologize openly and take remedial action.
- Develop rapport and empathy with employees.
- See the organization as a part of the community, not just as a bunch of sales outlets.

3. **Do you think that senior executives should be closely involved with the frontline day-to-day operations of the business as Brewer was?**

This is a difficult judgment call. If you want to make improvements, it helps if you have a good understanding of the details of the operations that you want to change. Often, top management is accused of being too remote from the day-to-day, of not understanding frontline operations, and of making poor (or even unworkable) decisions as a result. Frontline staff members often complain that they never see top management or that any visits management does make are too short to be worthwhile. Understanding the operational details of the business can thus enhance management credibility and establish goodwill with employees on the frontline. However, acquiring that understanding takes time for someone not familiar with the business. Brewer spent three months doing little else. Shouldn't top management focus on more important strategic issues? There is also a danger that frontline and middle managers will feel threatened by a senior executive appearing to do their jobs. If you want to know what is going wrong, why not ask them, rather than doing it for yourself? It is helpful to pause and consider the benefits and disadvantages, before dropping into the operational details, as Brewer did. Should you draw on the expertise of the current team instead of doing this yourself?

LO 1.1 Change Diagnostic: The Sears Story

Is this the Sears story or the Eddie Lampert story? One commentator said that, as well as the other issues facing retailers, Sears had a unique problem—Lampert himself. Here are the four questions that you were asked to consider while reading the Sears story, followed by our answers.

1. **How would you describe Eddie Lampert's leadership style?**

Lampert could be described as a transformational leader. He was highly intelligent and decisive. He was innovative, concerning both the company structure and its service delivery. He had a clear and interesting vision for the online future of the business. Check out Shop Your Way for yourself.

However, he also appears to have been an autocratic leader. There is little evidence to suggest that he either sought or considered the views of others, including his senior colleagues, before making business-critical decisions. He was something of a recluse, preferring to meet with his division heads infrequently and through a video link (and he rarely allowed media interviews). His "engagement" with staff through the company's social network was more confrontational than consultative.

2. **How would you assess his approach to implementing major organizational change—in this case restructuring the whole company with a new organizational model?**

   If rapid action is necessary to rescue an organization that is experiencing extreme difficulties, then an autocratic approach may be appropriate. It takes time to pause, to ask everyone else what they think should be done, to process that feedback, to develop a more widely informed decision, to check that with those involved, and then to implement the approach. By that time, the company could be bust. Lampert's "crisis management" style may thus have been appropriate immediately after the merger. Although profitability was declining, it is debatable whether that approach was appropriate in 2008.

   A more prudent approach in this case would probably have been to listen to the views of colleagues, at all levels of the company, and to take those into account, before imposing that reorganization. There could have been many other ways in which to achieve the required end results, including improved divisional and corporate performance, and data transparency. Whatever restructuring was implemented, it was probably going to be more successful if those who were affected understood the decision, had contributed significantly to it, and had agreed with it. "Behavioral flexibility" is one of the core capabilities of managers and leaders at all levels in an organization. This means adapting one's overall approach and personal style to fit the circumstances. Lampert did not do that.

3. **On balance, how would you assess his new organizational model?**

   From 2005 to 2013, the company's sales, profits, and share value fell. Although not mentioned in the case account, many experienced executives left the company, frustrated by the impact of the restructuring. Divisional collaboration was stifled, and it appears that the competition stimulated by the new organizational model was not healthy competition. The model, therefore, appears to have been damaging to the company's performance and to its reputation. The new model, however, made it easier for Lampert to set up the online business as a division run independently of the other units. The balance of benefits and costs, however, appears to be weighted on the costs side.

4. **What lessons about managing organizational change can we take from this experience and apply to other organizations, in this or other sectors?**

   Change leaders need to adapt their style to fit the context. An autocratic style can rapidly resolve a crisis. In other circumstances, "decisive action" may leave others feeling that they have been excluded, and they may decide to undermine decisions that they feel were ill-advised (especially where the approach was considered to be idiosyncratic), as well as imposed on them.

LO 1.1 Change Diagnostic: The Detroit Story

Here are the three questions that you were asked to consider while reading Mike Duggan's story, followed by our answers.

1. **Mike Duggan transformed Detroit without a "management textbook" plan for change. Why do you think he was successful?**

   First, Duggan did not have a detailed plan to "sell" to Detroit's residents and employees. He had a single, clear aim—to reverse the city's decline. The operational details came from the residents themselves, and most, if not all, of the employees were also Detroit residents. Instead of telling the residents what he wanted to do, he asked them what they wanted him to do. As he was doing what the residents were asking him to do, there was no resistance to the changes that he made. Second, the changes that he introduced were immediately visible and beneficial: The streetlights and the fire hydrants worked again, and the city's population started to grow. Third, he won support for these changes from more affluent residents, creating a "virtuous circle," which enticed entrepreneurs to the city, which became fashionable. This could be described as a textbook case of participative change management, although there was no formally documented change strategy.

2. **What aspects of Duggan's change management style would be appropriate for you to use in your organization?**

   Duggan's change management style had four components. First, he had previous successful turnaround experience and sincerely believed that he could do a similarly good job for Detroit. Second, he was willing to listen and to learn from those on the ground before launching into a major change program. Third, he paid attention to the operational details of the city's infrastructure, in the belief that minor improvements would be cumulative and transformational. Fourth, he trusted the public-service idealism of the city's employees. Self-belief, willingness to listen, attention to detail, trust in others—are those attributes useful for you in your change management role?

3. **To what extent can we generalize from managing change in a Midwestern American city to managing change in commercial organizations?**

   Can we take general advice from a sample of one? The answer to this question, traditionally, is "no." But this is misleading. Of course, we can. We are always looking at single instances and asking ourselves, "Would that work for me or for my organization?" The technical term for this is *naturalistic generalization*; we naturally consider whether or not the behaviors and methods and techniques that we see, in single examples, would apply to us in some way. We can ask whether Duggan's approach to Detroit's residents would apply to a chief executive's approach to employees. We can consider how Duggan's focus on the "small, boring stuff" could contribute to a change program in a commercial organization or public-sector agency. Duggan's belief in the idealism of his employees applies in other parts of the public sector (healthcare, for example), and also in some commercial organizations.

EXERCISE 1.1

Writing Your Own Story of Change

LO 1.1

Think of a change that you have experienced, in either your work or personal life. We would like to ask you to write a story about that experience. Here is a definition of a story to help you:

> A story expresses how and why life changes. It begins with a situation in which life is relatively in balance: You come to work day after day, week after week, and everything's fine. You expect it will go on that way. But then there's an event—in screenwriting, we call it the "inciting incident"—that throws life out of balance. You get a new job, or the boss dies of a heart attack, or a big customer threatens to leave. The story goes on to describe how, in an effort to restore balance, the protagonist's subjective expectations crash into an uncooperative objective reality. A good storyteller describes what it's like to deal with these opposing forces, calling on the protagonist to dig deeper, work with scarce resources, make difficult decisions, take action despite risks, and ultimately discover the truth. (McKee, 2003, p. 52)

Plan A

Write down your experience of change in about one page, and then answer these questions:

- What made this experience a "story"?
- What lessons for managing change can you take from your story?
- Compare these with the lessons from the Starbucks, Sears, and Detroit stories. Which are the same?
- From your experience, what new lessons have you added, particularly for future changes in which you might be involved?
- In small groups, share your lessons with colleagues. Which lessons are similar, and what are the differences among you?
- What three main conclusions can you take from these stories about managing change?

Plan B

In small groups of around four to six people, ask each group member to tell their story of change, taking only three or four minutes each. Record key elements of each story on flipchart paper. When everyone has told their story, answer the following questions:

- What are the common themes and issues across these stories?
- What are the differences between these stories?
- Of the change lessons from Starbucks, Sears, and Detroit, which are revealed in the groups' stories and which are absent? What are the implications of this?
- Are there any further lessons embedded in these stories that could apply to future changes in which group members may be involved?
- What three main conclusions can you take from these stories about managing change?

Additional Reading

Barsoux, J. L., and Narasimhan, A. 2017. What everyone gets wrong about change management. *Harvard Business Review* 95(6):78–85. Notes that three-quarters of change efforts are unsuccessful. The answer, they argue, is to align three factors: the catalyst for transformation, the organization's "quest" or strategy, and leadership capabilities. In other words, successful change depends on a combination of organizational and individual characteristics.

Christensen, C. M., and Carlile, P. R. 2009. Course research: Using the case method to build and teach management theory. *Academy of Management Learning and Education* 8(2):240–51. Explains how to use stories and case studies in management teaching, to develop, test, and improve theory.

Colvile, R. 2016. *The great acceleration: How the world is getting faster, faster.* London: Bloomsbury. Argues that almost everything we do—walking, travelling, communicating, processing information, buying things, you name it—is getting faster. He also claims that this is beneficial, because we are wealthier and better informed than we were. But organizations that are not able to keep up with the pace of change will suffer, and many of us now feel overwhelmed by too much information.

Gabriel, Y. 2019. Case studies as narratives: Reflections prompted by the case of Victor, the wild child of Aveyron. *Journal of Management Inquiry* 28(4):403–408. Argues from an unusual basis, that stories and case studies can give us considerable insights and are thus valuable vehicles for developing and sharing management knowledge.

Hughes, M. 2011. Do 70 per cent of all organizational change initiatives really fail? *Journal of Change Management* 11(4):451–64. Challenges the evidence behind the argument that so many change initiatives fail, suggesting that this has been exaggerated.

Roundup

Successful change is not guaranteed, despite the care and attention given to implementation planning. If there is one firm prediction that we can make about change, it is that it will go wrong, however meticulously designed. Why? By definition, we are always doing it for the first time—in this organization, facing these problems, with these resources, given the past history—and so on. One cannot confidently predict what will happen. The change leader is always building the plane as it flies. This is not an argument against planning; it is an argument for recognizing when things are going wrong, learning from that, and adapting accordingly. So this text does not set out to tell change leaders what to do. Such perspectives perpetuate the problem by creating the illusion that the outcomes can be kept under control if carefully planned steps are followed. Most people's experience of organizations suggest that they are complex and untidy—and political—arenas. Acknowledging these characteristics is the first step to taking a more realistic view of what change leaders can expect to achieve. As discussed in chapter 2, it is more appropriate to think in terms of *shaping* the change process rather than *controlling* it. We hope that reflective change leaders will accept that choices must be made for change to proceed and that these are informed choices, not adopted on the grounds that there is one best way to approach the process.

Here is a short summary of the key points that we would like you to take from this chapter, in relation to each of the learning objectives:

LO 1.1   * *Understand how stories of change can contribute to our knowledge of theory and practice.* Stories can be read as process narratives, which explain what happened in a given context. These explanations are therefore theories of change, pointing to the combination of factors interacting over time, leading to more or less successful change. Although those theories cannot be copied simply to other organizations and contexts, they are still a rich source of general lessons, and aspects of one organization's approach can be adapted to fit other organizational contexts, if appropriate.

LO 1.2   * *Explain why managing organizational change is both a creative and a rational process.* As with management practice in many other areas, what is going to work well when it comes to implementing change depends on the organizational context. Although general guidelines help to identify the factors to take into consideration, the details have to be determined by local, informed management and staff judgment. That is a creative process.

LO 1.3   * *Identify the main tensions and paradoxes in managing organizational change.* Should we focus on transformational changes, or do we need to sweat the small stuff as well? Should change be a rational, systematic process, or do we need to recognize the political dimension? What is more important, organizational capabilities or individual skills in implementing change? Should we accelerate the changes or adopt a more measured pace? Do we rely on one change champion or recognize the distributed contributions of many change agents? Once we have learned the lessons from a crisis or other extreme event, how do we ensure that these are put into practice?

LO 1.4   * *Evaluate the strengths and limitations of our current understanding of this field.* There is a significant amount of commentary, but little consensus. Most of the advice says much the same thing, but the failure rate of change is still high. The commentary is highly fragmented and includes multiple perspectives and conceptualizations. Evidence comes from a range of different settings and approaches, and contributions from the last century are still relevant today. Establishing cause and effect with regard to change and outcomes is made difficult by the many variables and the many stakeholders typically involved.

References   Badham, R. 2013. *Short change: An introduction to managing change.* Sumy, Ukraine: Business Perspectives.

Barsoux, J. L., and Narasimhan, A. 2017. What everyone gets wrong about change management. *Harvard Business Review* 95(6):78–85.

Buchanan, D., and Macaulay, S. 2019. The seven deadly myths of change. *Training Journal* (November):29–31.

Bucy, M., Fagan, T., Maraite, B., and Piaia, C. 2017. *Keeping transformations on target*. New York and London: McKinsey & Company.

Christensen, C. M., and Carlile, P. R. 2009. Course research: Using the case method to build and teach management theory. *Academy of Management Learning and Education* 8(2):240–51.

Christensen, C. M., Raynor, M., and McDonald, R. 2015. Disruptive innovation. *Harvard Business Review*, 93(12):44–53.

Dawson, P., and Andriopoulos, C. 2017. *Managing change, creativity and innovation*, 3rd ed. London: Sage Publications.

Denis, J. L., Lamothe, L., and Langley, A. 2001. The dynamics of collective leadership and strategic change in pluralistic organizations. *Academy of Management Journal* 44(4):809–37.

Gabriel, Y. 2019. Case studies as narratives: Reflections prompted by the case of Victor, the wild child of Aveyron. *Journal of Management Inquiry* 28(4):403–8.

Hagen, N. 2018. Halting Detroit's decline. *Financial Times* (January 8):24.

Hughes, M. 2011. Do 70 per cent of all organizational change initiatives really fail? *Journal of Change Management* 11(4):451–64.

Keller, S., and Schaninger, B. 2019. *A better way to lead large-scale change*. New York: McKinsey & Company.

Kimes, M. 2013. At Sears, Eddie Lampert's warring divisions model adds to the troubles. *Bloomberg Businessweek*, July 11. http://www.businessweek.com/articles/2013-07-11/at-sears-eddie-lamperts-warring-divisions-model-adds-to-the-troubles.

Kowitt, B. 2019. How Starbucks got its buzz back. *Fortune* 180(4):84–92.

Langley, A., and Tsoukas, H. 2010. Introducing perspectives on process organization studies. In *Process, sensemaking, and organizing*, ed. T. Hernes and S. Maitlis (1–26). Oxford: Oxford University Press.

Langley, A., Smallman, C., Tsoukas, H., and Van de Ven, A. H. 2013. Process studies of change in organization and management: Unveiling temporality, activity, and flow. *Academy of Management Journal* 56(1):1–13.

McKee, R. 2003. Storytelling that moves people. *Harvard Business Review* 81(6):51–55.

Mohr, L. B. 1982. *Explaining organizational behavior: The limits and possibilities of theory and research*. San Francisco: Jossey-Bass Publishers.

Moore, C., and Buchanan, D. A. 2013. Sweat the small stuff: A case study of small scale change processes and consequences in acute care. *Health Services Management Research* 26(1):9–17.

Ogburn, W. F. 1922. *Social change: With respect to culture and original nature*. New York: B.W. Huebsch.

Stouten, J., Rousseau, D. M., and De Cremer, D. 2018. Successful organizational change: Integrating the management practice and scholarly literatures. *Academy of Management Annals* 12(2):752–88.

Vaara, E., Sonenshein, S., and Boje, D. M. 2016. Narratives as sources of stability and change in organizations. *Academy of Management Annals* 10(1):495–560.

Visser, N. 2019. Vanuatu has one of the world's strictest plastic bans. It's about to get tougher. *Huffington Post*, February 24. https://www.huffingtonpost.com.au/entry/vanuatu-plastic-ban-law-ocean-pollution_n_5c6ee757e4b0f40774cd355d.

Wahba, P. 2019. Crafting a comeback at Etsy. *Fortune* 180(2):33–35.

Ward, J., and Daniel, E. 2013. The role of project management offices (PMOs) in IS project success and management satisfaction. *Journal of Enterprise Information Management* 26(3):316–36.

Wylie, N., and Sturdy, A. 2018. Structuring collective change agency internally: transformers, enforcers, specialists and independents. *Employee Relations* 40(2):313–28.

Source of the chapter opening quote: Wylie Communications, Quotes on the power of storytelling. https://www.wyliecomm.com/writing-tips/creative-communications/storytelling/quotes-on-the-power-of-storytelling.

Chapter opening silhouette credit: CharlotteRaboff/Shutterstock

Chapter 2

Images of Change Management

Learning Objectives

By the end of this chapter you should be able to:

LO 2.1   Evaluate the use that different authors make of the terms *change agent*, *change manager*, and *change leader*.

LO 2.2   Understand the importance of organizational images and mental models.

LO 2.3   Compare and contrast six different images of managing change and change managers.

LO 2.4   Explain the theoretical underpinning of different change management images.

LO 2.5   Apply these six images of managing change to your personal preferences and approach and to different organizational contexts.

"We all have mental models: the lens through which we see the world that drive our responses to everything we experience. Being aware of your mental models is key to being objective."

Elizabeth Thornton, author

LO 2.1 What's in a Name: Change Agents, Managers, or Leaders?

This chapter focuses on those who drive and implement change. We first consider how those individuals are described, and then explore different ways in which their roles can be understood. This is not just a theoretical discussion. An understanding of organizational change roles has profound practical implications for the way in which those roles are conducted. And if you are in a change management role, now or in the future, the way in which you understand your position will affect how you fulfill those responsibilities and whether you are more or less successful. We will thus explore different mental models or images of the change management role.

The use of terms in this field has become confused, and we first need to address this problem. Do the terms *change agent*, *change manager*, and *change leader* refer to different roles in relation to organizational change? Or are these labels interchangeable?

For most of the twentieth century, the term *change agent* typically referred to an external expert management consultant who was paid to work out what was going wrong in an organization and to implement change to put things right. This model is still in use. Many external change agents use the "process consultation" approach popularized by Schein (1999). Here, the role of the "expert" is to help members of the organization to understand and solve their own problems.

Today, a change agent is just as likely to be a member of the organization as an external consultant. The term is now often used more loosely, to refer to anyone who has a role in change implementation, regardless of that person's job title or seniority. Given the scale and scope of changes that many organizations face, a significant number of internal change agents may be a valuable—perhaps necessary—resource. Internal change agents usually have a better understanding than outsiders of the problems that need to be solved and the changes that would lead to improvements. In short, when you see the term *change agent*, it is important to check the meaning that is intended, unless it is obvious from the context.

Conventional wisdom says that managers and leaders play different roles (Zaleznik, 1997; Kotter, 1990). For John Kotter (2012), change management involves the basic tools and structures with which small-scale changes are controlled. Change leadership, in contrast, marshals the driving forces and visions that produce large-scale transformations. His point is that we need more change leaders. In a series of studies, Kniffin et al. (2019) found that the traditional distinction between managers and leaders is deeply embedded in popular thinking and that leadership is evaluated more positively than management. Management is associated with terms such as supervises, fires, bosses, oversees, and budgets. Leadership is associated with terms such as inspires, encourages, motivates, guides, and teaches. Leadership has become more fashionable. Graduate business schools in the 1970s used management-related terms in their mission statements; today almost all use leader-related terms.

One explanation for this emphasis on leadership lies with the language used by the media and influential commentators. Leaders are routinely praised. Managers are regularly dismissed as bureaucratic paper pushers. Another explanation lies with today's turbulent social and economic conditions that favor the change-oriented roles associated with leadership. Kniffin et al. (2019, p. 5) argue that:

> These findings speak to what has been referred to as an infatuation with or romance of leadership in our society, where leadership is often loved for personal, historical, and ideological reasons rather than any direct connection to the facts of a situation. Beyond seeming to confirm this love of leadership, our findings highlight that this preference may come at the high cost of failing to appreciate the value of management in many situations.

In other words, "people learn to love prototypical leadership characteristics via repeated exposure to exhortations that they should" (p. 17).

The argument that management and leadership are distinct has two main flaws. The first concerns the assumption that large-scale transformations are more meaningful and potent and are therefore more valuable than small-scale change. They are not, as the discussion of "depth of change" (Figure 1.1) in chapter 1 suggested. The second flaw concerns the belief that distinct definitions of management and leadership concepts will survive contact with practice. They do not. It may be possible to define clear categories in theory, but in practice these roles overlap and are indistinguishable. The general distinction between management and leadership is challenged by Mintzberg (2009, pp. 8–9) who argues, "I don't understand what this distinction means in the everyday life of organizations. Sure, we can separate leading and managing conceptually. But can we separate them in practice? Or, more to the point, should we even try?" He asks, how would you like to be managed by someone who doesn't lead, or isn't led by someone who doesn't manage? "We should be seeing managers *as* leaders, and leadership as management practiced well."

In short, management versus leadership is not a distinction worth arguing over and may be more simply resolved by a combination of personal and contextual preference. In this book, we will use the terms *change management* (or *manager*) and *change leadership* (or *leader*) synonymously.

LO 2.2 Images, Mental Models, Frames, Perspectives

More important than the terminology, the internal mental *images* that we have of our organizations influence our expectations and our interpretations of what is happening, and of what we think needs to change and how (Morgan, 2006; Hatch and Cunliffe, 2012; Bolman and Deal, 2017). We typically hold these images, metaphors, frames of reference, or perspectives without being conscious of how they color our thinking, perceptions, and actions. These images or mental models help us to make sense of the world around us, by focusing our attention in particular directions. The key point is that while an image or mental model is a way of seeing things, a standpoint drawing our attention to particular issues and features, it is also a way of *not* seeing things, shifting our attention away from other factors, which may or may not be significant.

For example, if we have a mental image of organizations as machines, then we will be more aware of potential component "breakdowns" and see our role in terms of maintenance and repair. In contrast, if we think of organizations as political arenas, we are more likely to be aware of the hidden agendas behind decisions and try to identify the winners and losers. We are also likely to see our role, not as maintaining parts of a smooth-running machine, but as building coalitions, gathering support for our causes, and stimulating conflict to generate innovation. Shifting the lens again, we may see our organizations as small societies or "microcultures." With this image, we are more likely to focus on "the way things get done around here" and on how to encourage the values that are best aligned to the type of work that we do. A microculture image highlights the importance of providing vision and meaning so that staff identity becomes more closely associated with the work of the organization. Each frame thus orients us toward a different set of issues.

There are no "right" and "wrong" images here. These are just different lenses through which the world in general, and organizations in particular can be seen and understood. The images or lenses that we each use reflect our backgrounds, education, life experiences, and personal preferences. There are some problems for which a "machine" image may be more appropriate, and other problems where a "microculture" image is relevant. Some problems may best be understood if they are approached using two or three images or lenses at a time.

Those who are responsible for driving and implementing change also have their own images of organizations—and more importantly, *images of their role as change manager*. Those images clearly influence the ways in which change managers approach the change process, the issues that they believe are important, and the change management style that they will adopt. Like the child with a hammer who treats every problem as if it were a nail, the change manager is handicapped in drawing on only one particular image of that role. It is therefore important, first, to understand one's personal preferences—perhaps biases—in this regard. It is also important, second, to be able to switch from one image of the role to another, according to circumstances. This ability to work with *multiple perspectives, images, or frames concerning the change management role* is, we will argue, central to the personal effectiveness of the change manager and also to the effectiveness of the change process.

We will outline six different "ideal type" images of managing change, describing the assumptions that underpin each image and the theoretical views that support them. We will then explore how change managers can draw from and use these multiple perspectives and images of managing change.

LO 2.3 The Six-Images Framework

How are our images or mental models of organizational change formed? To answer this question, Palmer and Dunford (2002) argue that two dimensions of change are particularly important. The first dimension concerns *choice of change management approach*. The second concerns *expectations concerning the outcomes* of the change process. Of the many dimensions of the change management process, these two are particularly important because they concern the *how*, or the way in which change will be implemented, and the *results*, or what the change hopes to achieve.

With regard to the first of these dimensions, change management can be seen as either a *controlling* or a *shaping* activity. These images represent extreme points on a continuum and reflect the traditional distinction between autocratic/directive and participative/engaging management styles (e.g., Katz et al., 1950; Tannenbaum and Schmidt, 1958). Second, there are three broad images of the expected change outcomes, which can be seen as either *intended*, *partially intended*, or *unintended*. Outcomes do not always depend entirely on the decisions and actions of those who are implementing the change. Change outcomes can be affected by events and developments outside the organization, beyond the direct

TABLE 2.1
Images of
Change
Management

	Images of Managing	
Images of Expected Change Outcomes	**Controlling (Roles and Activities)**	**Shaping (Enhancing Capabilities)**
Intended	director	coach
Partially intended	navigator	interpreter
Unintended	caretaker	nurturer

control of change managers, whose intentions may be swamped by those external factors. How change managers understand those outcomes thus influences their image of the change management role. Combining these models of managing change and of expectations of change outcomes leads to the six images summarized in table 2.1: *director, coach, navigator, interpreter, caretaker, nurturer.*

Management as Controlling

The image of management as a controlling function has deep historical roots, based on the work of Henri Fayol (1916; 1949) and his contemporaries (Gulick and Urwick, 1937) who described what managers do, captured by the clumsy acronym POSDCoRB. This stands for Planning, Organizing, Supervising, Directing, Coordinating, Reporting, and Budgeting—activities that the change manager, as well as the general manager, may be expected to carry out (Kniffin et al., 2019). This reflects a "top-down," hierarchical view of managing, associated with the image of organization as a machine. The manager's job is to drive the machine in a particular direction. Staff members are given defined roles. Resources (inputs) are allocated to departments to produce efficiently the required products and/or services (outputs). Mintzberg (2009) also describes management roles in terms of deciding, focusing, scheduling, communicating, controlling, leading, networking, building coalitions, and getting things done. This is the "hard" dimension of management. But Keller and Shaninger (2019, p. 3) are not alone in emphasizing the importance of focusing on both the "hard and soft" elements of change management, concerning performance and organizational health:

> Performance is what an enterprise does to deliver improved financial and operational results for its stakeholders. Health describes how effectively people work together to pursue a common goal. To deliver successful change at scale, leaders should emphasize performance- and health-related efforts equally.

Management as Shaping

This image of management as a shaping function, enhancing both individual and organizational capabilities, also has deep roots, based on the "human relations" school of management from the 1930s (Roethlisberger and Dickson, 1939; Mayo, 1945) and on the organization development movement (Bennis, 1969; Cheung-Judge and Holbeche, 2015). This image is associated with a participative management style that encourages involvement in decision making in general, and in deciding the content and process of change in particular. Employee involvement in change is based on two assumptions. First, those who are closest to the action will have a better understanding of how things can be improved. Second, staff members are more likely to be committed to making changes work if they have contributed to the design of those changes. Managing people is thus concerned with shaping (and not directly controlling) behavior in ways that benefit the organization.

The contemporary concern with "employee engagement" is another manifestation of this image. The polling organization Gallup (2017) studied employee engagement in 155 countries. They found that 85 percent of employees worldwide are not engaged or are actively disengaged in their jobs and describe this as an "engagement deficit." Levels of engagement vary from country to country, but no region exceeded 40 percent of employees engaged. The figure for Eastern Europe was 15 percent; Western Europe, 10 percent; France, Italy and Spain, below 10 percent; United Kingdom, 11 percent; Australia and New Zealand, 14 percent; Norway, 17 percent; and the United States and Canada, 30 percent. Gallup (2017) argues that these figures reflect a waste of potential. Employers with the most engaged workforces—those in the top 25 percent, with around 70 percent of employees saying they were engaged—were 17 percent more productive and 21 percent more profitable than those in the bottom 25 percent. Gallup (2017, p. 7) also concludes that addressing the engagement deficit would contribute to the implementation of beneficial organizational change:

> The resulting sense of empowerment benefits both the employee and the organization. Employees who strongly agree that their opinions count at work are more likely to feel personally invested in their job. Gallup's global data suggest that without such opportunities, workers are more likely to doubt their ability to get ahead by working hard—a devastating blow to their motivation and productivity. Higher levels of autonomy also promote the development and implementation of new ideas as employees feel empowered to pursue entrepreneurial goals that benefit the organization.

There is no argument concerning which of these images—controlling or shaping—is "correct" and which is "wrong." It is possible to marshal argument and evidence in support of both frames. We have to ask, however, which would be more appropriate or effective in given circumstances.

Table 2.1 also identifies three dominant images of change outcomes, based on the extent to which it is expected that change outcomes can be wholly planned and achieved, or not. Change outcomes can be achieved as intended or partially achieved, or unintended outcomes can be achieved. This is a continuum, from wholly intended to wholly unintended, rather than three discrete categories.

Intended Change Outcomes

The dominant assumption of this image is that intended change outcomes can be achieved, as planned. This assumption underpins much of the commentary on organizational change and has dominated the practical advice offered to change managers for over half a century (Burnes, 2017).

The consulting company McKinsey, for example, advises a carefully planned approach to improving the chances of success of planned transformations (their research suggests that 30 percent fail to deliver their intended benefits). They describe the process as going through six stage gates: idea, identified, validated, planned, executed, and realized (Bucy et al., 2017).

These six stages represent a "change pipeline." At each stage of the pipeline, however, value can be lost, which means that the end result falls short of the original intent. This happens, in part, because smaller initiatives, which can account for a significant component of a program's overall value, often attract less management attention. To reduce the "impact leakage" through the pipeline, Bucy et al. (2017) offer three pieces of advice. First, be relentless: Assume that most initiatives will not achieve all that is expected, and do not lose sight of the minor changes that can contribute to the end result. Second, focus resources: Do not ask individual change managers to lead more than three initiatives at any one time, recruit more initiative owners, and limit the number of milestones and metrics. Third, plan and adapt: Plan the milestones, reduce delays, and initiate weekly actions for initiative owners.

In this image, therefore, the intended outcomes of a change program are achieved by following the right steps, planning, allocating resources appropriately, and focusing on all the components of an initiative that contribute to the final results. Managing change is a technical matter that involves following the correct sequence of actions. When things go wrong, it is because steps in the process or particular issues have been overlooked.

Partially Intended Change Outcomes

In this image, it is assumed that some, but not all, planned change outcomes are achievable. Power, competing interests, organizational politics, embedded processes, and different skill levels affect a manager's ability to produce intended outcomes. As Mintzberg and Waters (1985) note, the link between initial intent and final outcome is not necessarily a direct one. This is due to the fact that both intended and unintended consequences may emerge from the actions of change managers; intended outcomes may be adapted along the way, or externally imposed forces may modify what was originally intended. Change goals can be altered or ignored by "everyday resistance" to initiatives that are seen as undesirable or unworkable by those who are affected (McCabe et al., 2019). For these reasons, change initiatives do not always deliver all the outcomes that were planned.

Unintended Change Outcomes

Less attention has been paid to this image in commentary on change management, but this is a common theme in mainstream organization theory. This image recognizes that managers often have great difficulty in achieving the change outcomes that were intended. This difficulty stems from the variety of internal and external forces that can push change in unplanned directions. Internal forces can include interdepartmental politics, long-established working practices that are difficult to dislodge, and deep-seated perceptions and values that are inconsistent with desired changes. External forces can include confrontational industrial relations, legislative requirements (tax demands, regulatory procedures), or industry-wide sectoral trends (trade wars, stock market volatility). These forces typically override the influence of individual change managers, whose intentions can be easily swamped. On occasion, of course, intentions and outcomes may coincide, but this is often the result of chance rather than the outcome of planned, intentional change management actions.

How to Achieve Unintended Change Outcomes

Hope (2010) describes how middle managers "redefined" senior management plans for change in the claims handling division of a Nordic insurance company. The claims handling process was time consuming and costly, and it was difficult for customers. Middle management, however, did not agree with the changes that senior management proposed and were concerned that, as they would be responsible for the implementation, they would be blamed if anything went wrong. A back office management team, who called themselves "The Gang of Four," decided to implement their own proposals instead. The tactics they used to influence the change outcomes included:

- disobeying management decisions about project representation
- handpicking loyal and skilled people to fill project roles

- taking control over the subproject staffing
- controlling information gathering by deciding what questions were to be asked
- producing a memo supporting their own position and aims
- holding back information, and distributing information selectively
- questioning the expertise of the external consultants
- taking advantage of the new division head and his lack of local experience
- rejecting unfavorable decisions, and insisting on a "replay" to reach different outcomes

Middle management was thus able to implement its own more effective proposals.

LO 2.3 LO 2.4 Six Images of Change Management

Table 2.1 identifies six different images of change management, each dependent in turn on contrasting images of the role of the change manager, on the one hand, and of expectations concerning change outcomes, on the other. We can now outline each of these images and their theoretical underpinnings.

1. Change Manager as Director (*Controlling Intended Outcomes*)

The *director* image views management as controlling, and change outcomes as being achievable as planned. The change manager's role here, as the title indicates, is to steer the organization toward the desired outcomes. This assumes that change involves a strategic management choice upon which the well-being and survival of the organization depends. Let us assume that an organization is "out of alignment" with its external environment, say with regard to the information demands of a changing regulatory system and the more effective responses of competitors. The change management response could involve a new corporate information technology (IT) system to apply data analytics to more efficiently capture "big data" (George et al., 2014). The director image assumes that this can be mandated, that the new system can be implemented following that command, and that it will work well, leading to a high-performing organization that is more closely aligned to its external environment.

What theoretical support does this image have? As chapter 10 will explain, there are a number of "*n*-step" models, guidelines, or "recipes" for change implementation that are based on the image of the change manager as director. The change manager is advised to follow the steps indicated (the number of steps varies from model to model), more or less in the correct sequence and regardless of the nature of the change, to ensure successful outcomes. These models are united by the optimistic view that the intended outcomes of change can be achieved, as long as change managers follow the model, as discussed earlier. Kotter (2007; 2012b) developed one of the best known *n*-step models. He advocates working systematically through the eight steps in his approach, more or less in sequence, and not missing or rushing any of them. Even Kotter acknowledges that change is usually a messy, iterative process. Nevertheless, he remains confident that, if followed correctly, his "recipe" will increase the probability of a successful outcome.

As chapter 10 also explains, *contingency theories* argue that there is no "one best model" for change managers to follow. These perspectives argue that the most appropriate approach is contingent; that is, it depends on the context and on the circumstances (Stace and Dunphy, 2001; Balogun et al., 2016). Contingency theorists thus part company with *n*-step "best practice" guides, suggesting that a range of factors such as the scale and urgency of the change, and the receptivity of those who will be affected, need to be considered when framing an implementation strategy. In other words, the "best way" will depend on a combination of factors—but as long as the change manager takes those factors into account and follows the contingent model, then the intended outcomes should be delivered.

2. Change Manager as Navigator (*Controlling Some Intended Outcomes*)

In the *navigator* image, control is still at the heart of change management action, although external factors mean that, although change managers may achieve some intended change outcomes, they may have little control over other results. Outcomes are at least partly emergent rather than completely planned and result from a variety of influences, competing interests, and processes. For example, a change manager may wish to restructure the business using "agile" autonomous teams to streamline new product design and development (Brosseau et al., 2019). Although a change manager may be able to set up agile teams (an intentional outcome), getting them to work effectively may be challenging if there is a history of distrust, information hoarding, and boundary protection by the business units. In this situation, functional managers may appoint to the agile teams people who they know will keep the interests of their department uppermost and block any decisions that might decrease their organizational power—an unintended outcome of setting up the teams in the first place.

Exploring why change initiatives stall, Eric Beaudan (2006, p. 6) notes that "No amount of advance thinking, planning and communication guarantees success. That's because change is by nature unpredictable and unwieldy. The military have a great way to put this: 'no plan survives contact with the enemy'." He also argues that "leaders need to recognize that the initial change platform they create is only valid for a short time. They need to conserve their energy to confront the problematic issues that will stem from passive resistance and from the unpredictable side effects that change itself creates" (Beaudan, 2006, p. 6). Change may be only partially controllable, with change managers navigating the process toward a set of outcomes, not all of which may have been intended.

What theoretical support does this image have? Processual theories (see chapter 10) argue that organizational changes unfold over time in a messy and iterative manner and thus rely on the image of change manager as navigator (Langley et al., 2013; Dawson and Andriopoulos, 2017). In this perspective, the outcomes of change are shaped by a combination of factors, including:

- the past, present, and future *context* in which the organization functions, including external and internal factors
- the *substance* of the change, which could be new technology, process redesign, a new payment system, or changes to organizational structure and culture
- the implementation *process*—tasks, decisions, timing *political behavior*, inside and outside the organization
- *interactions* between these factors.

The role of the change manager is not to direct, but to identify options, accumulate resources, monitor progress, and navigate a way through this uncertainty, ambiguity, and complexity.

Change managers must accept that there will be unanticipated disruptions and that options and resources need to be reviewed. Change navigators are also advised to encourage staff involvement. For senior management, rather than directing and controlling the process, the priority is to ensure receptivity to change (Rafferty et al., 2013) and that those involved have the skills and motivation to contribute. However, given the untidy, nonlinear nature of change, navigators—consistent with the metaphor—have room to maneuver; the course of change may need to be plotted and replotted in response to new information and developments. There is no guarantee that the final destination will be as initially intended. In some instances, change may be ongoing, with no clear end point.

3. Change Manager as Caretaker (*Controlling Unintended Outcomes*)

In the caretaker image, the (ideal) management role is still one of control, although the ability to exercise that control is severely constrained by a range of internal and external forces that propel change relatively independent of management intentions. For example, despite the change manager's desire to encourage entrepreneurial and innovative behavior, this may become a failing exercise as the organization grows; becomes more bureaucratic; and enacts strategic planning cycles, rules, regulations, and centralized practices. In this situation, the issues linked to inexorable growth are outside the control of an individual change manager. In this rather pessimistic image, at best managers are caretakers, shepherding their organizations along to the best of their ability.

Theoretical support for the caretaker image can be drawn from three organizational theories: life-cycle, population ecology, and institutional theory.

Life-cycle theory views organizations passing through well-defined stages from birth to growth, maturity, and then decline or death. These stages are part of a natural, developmental cycle. There is an underlying logic or trajectory, and the stages are sequential (Van de Ven and Poole, 1995; Van de Ven and Sun, 2011). There is little that managers can do to prevent this natural development; at best they are caretakers of the organization as it passes through the various stages. Harrison and Shirom (1999) identify the caretaker activities associated with the main stages in the organizational life cycle, and these are summarized in table 2.2. Change managers thus have a limited role, smoothing the various transitions rather than controlling whether or not they occur.

TABLE 2.2

Life-Cycle Stages and Caretaker Activities

Developmental Stage	Caretaker Activities
Entrepreneurial Stage Founder initiates an idea	• Make sure that resources are available • Establish market niche • Design processes to aid innovation and creativity • Ensure founder generates commitment to vision
Collectivity Stage Coordination through informal means as group identity develops	• Coordinate communication and decision making • Build cohesion and morale with goals and culture • Develop skills through appropriate reward systems
Formalization Stage Formalization of operations emphasizing rules and procedures, efficiency, and stability	• Facilitate shift to professional management • Monitor internal operations and external environment • Focus procedures on efficiency and quality • Strike balance between autonomy, coordination, and control
Elaboration Stage Change and renewal as structure becomes more complex and environment changes	• Adapt current products, and develop new ones • Ensure structure facilitates divisional coordination • Plan for turnaround, cutbacks, and renewal

Source: Adapted from Harrison and Shirom (1999), pp. 307–14.

Population ecology theory focuses on how the environment selects organizations for survival or extinction, drawing on biology and neo-Darwinism (White et al., 1997). Whole populations of organizations can thus change as a result of ongoing cycles of *variation*, *selection*, and *retention*:

• Organizational *variation* occurs as the result of random chance.
• Organizational *selection* occurs when an environment selects those that best fit the conditions.
• Organizational *retention* involves forces (e.g., inertia and persistence) that sustain organizational forms, thus counteracting variation and selection.

Some population ecology theorists suggest that there are limited actions that change managers can take to influence these forces, such as:

• interacting with other organizations to lessen the impact of environmental factors
• repositioning the organization in a new market or other environment

In general, however, this perspective implies that managers have little influence over change where whole populations of organizations are affected by external forces. For example, managers of many financial institutions struggled to deal with the widespread global crisis triggered by the collapse of Lehman Brothers, an investment bank, in September 2008. That event affected adversely the global population of finance organizations (and the governments that had to recapitalize them).

Institutional theory argues that change managers take broadly similar decisions and actions across whole populations of organizations. The central concern of this perspective is not to explain change, but to understand "the startling homogeneity of organizational forms and practices" (DiMaggio and Powell, 1983, p. 148; Oertel et al., 2016). These similarities can be explained by the pressures associated with the interconnectedness of organizations that operate in the same sector or environment. DiMaggio and Powell (1983) distinguish three pressures, which in practice interact:

- *coercive*, including social and cultural expectations, and government-mandated changes
- *mimetic*, as organizations imitate or model themselves on the structures and practices of other organizations in their field, often those which they consider to be more successful
- *normative*, through the professionalization of work such that managers in different organizations adopt similar values and working methods that are similar to each other

Not all organizations succumb to these pressures; there are what DiMaggio and Powell call "deviant peers." However, the assumption is that these external forces are inexorable and individual managers have only limited ability to implement change outcomes that are not consistent with these forces. At best, change managers are caretakers with little influence over the long-term direction of change.

4. Change Manager as Coach (*Shaping Intended Outcomes*)

In the *coach* image, the assumption is that change managers (or change consultants) can intentionally shape the organization's capabilities in particular ways. Like a sports coach, the change manager shapes the organization's or team's capabilities to ensure that, in a competitive situation, it will be more likely to succeed. Rather than dictating the state of each play as the director might do, the coach relies on establishing the right values, skills, and "drills" so that the organization's members can achieve the desired outcomes.

What theoretical support does this image have? Organization development (OD) theory reinforces the "shaping" image of the change manager as coach, by stressing the importance of values such as humanism, democracy, and individual development (see chapter 9). OD "interventions" are designed to develop skills, reduce interpersonal and inter-divisional conflict, and structure activities in ways that help the organization's members to better understand, define, and solve their own problems (Ibarra and Scoular, 2019). As the OD movement evolved, the emphasis shifted from team-based and other small-scale interventions to organization-wide programs, designed to "get the whole system in the room" (Burnes and Cook, 2012; Cheung-Judge and Holbeche, 2015). As a movement underpinned by values, OD advocates can be evangelical about helping organization members to develop their own problem-solving skills to achieve intended outcomes, claiming that the approach works and that it produces results with less resistance, greater speed, and higher commitment.

5. Change Manager as Interpreter (*Shaping Some Intended Outcomes*)

The change manager as *interpreter* has the task of creating meaning for others, helping them to make sense of events and developments, which, in themselves, constitute a changed organization. It is up to change managers to represent to others just what these changes mean. However, there are often competing interpretations of the same issues, especially where there are different groups who do not necessarily share common interests and perceptions (Buchanan and Dawson, 2007). This suggests that only some meanings—and therefore some change intentions—are likely to be realized.

What theoretical support does this image have? Architect of the influential processual perspective on organizational change, Pettigrew (1985, p. 442) sees the "management of meaning" as central. He argues, "The management of meaning refers to a process of symbol construction and value use designed to create legitimacy for one's own ideas, actions, and demands, and to delegitimize the demands of one's opponents." The change manager seeking to introduce significant, strategic change may thus be faced with the prospect of trying to create a story that will dislodge a well-established ideology, culture, and system of meaning. Change managers, of course, do not have a monopoly on story-telling skills; sometimes the stories of others are better, and they "win."

The interpreter image is central to Weick's (1995; 2000) sensemaking theory of organizational change. Sensemaking, Weick explains, is what we do when we face a problem—a surprise or a crisis, for example—and have to work out how we are going to respond. For sensemaking to work in these situations, however, four factors have to be present. First, it has to be possible to take some action to address the problem; almost any action will do, as long as experiment and exploration are allowed. Second, that action must be directed toward a purpose or goal. Third, the context must allow people to be attentive to what is happening and to update their understanding accordingly. Fourth, people need to be allowed to share their views openly, in a climate of mutual trust and respect. Weick calls these four components of sensemaking *animation*, *direction*, *attention*, and *respectful interaction*.

Weick (2000, p. 225) also observes that emergent, continuous, cumulative change is the norm in most organizations. The textbook focus on planned, transformational, revolutionary, disruptive change is partial and misleading. Emergent change involves the development of new ways of working that were not previously planned:

> The recurring story is one of autonomous initiatives that bubble up internally; continuous emergent change; steady learning from both failure and success; strategy implementation that is replaced by strategy making; the appearance of innovations that are unplanned, unforeseen, and unexpected; and small actions that have surprisingly large consequences.

Emergent changes are thus driven by continuous sensemaking, often by frontline staff, and not by senior management. Indeed, top-team intervention may inhibit change. Weick (2000, p. 234) argues that, while the four sensemaking activities of animation, direction, attention, and respectful interaction are necessary for learning, adaptation, and change, "they are also the four activities most likely to be curbed severely in a hierarchical command-and-control system." For successful change, Weick concludes, management must become interpreters, recognizing that "organizational change is emergent change laid down by choices made on the front line. *The job of management is to author interpretations and labels that capture the patterns in those adaptive choices. . . . management doesn't create change. It certifies change*" (Weick, 2000, p. 238; emphasis added).

The interpreter image of change management may be particularly significant during an economic downturn and recession, when commitment and loyalty to employers are likely to deteriorate. In this context, there may be problems getting staff to support major change programs, triggering passive resistance and turnover. To build that support, management needs to try and change the mindset and associated behaviors by offering a positive interpretation of events (Basford and Schaninger, 2016).

Interpreters at Work: Four Conditions for Changing Mindsets

Emily Lawson and Colin Price (2003) argue that the success of change relies on persuading individuals to change their "mindsets"—to think differently about their jobs and the way in which they work. They identify three levels of organizational change. First, desired outcomes (increase revenue) can often be achieved without changing working practices (selling noncore assets, for example). Second, employees can be asked to change working practices in line with current thinking (finding ways to reduce waste, for example). The third level involves fundamental changes in organizational culture, in collective thinking and behavior—from reactive to proactive, hierarchical to collegial, inward looking to externally focused. There are four conditions for changing mindsets at level three:

Employees will alter their mindsets only if they see the point of the change and agree with it—at least enough to give it a try. The surrounding structures (reward and recognition systems, for example) must be in tune with the new behaviour. Employees must have the skills to do what it requires. Finally, they must see people they respect modelling it actively. Each of these conditions is realized independently; together they add up to a way of changing the behaviour of people in organizations by changing attitudes about what can and should happen at work. (Lawson and Price, 2003, p. 32)

In a contested climate, managers as interpreters "need to be able to provide legitimate arguments and reasons for why their actions fit within the situation and should be viewed as legitimate" (Barge and Oliver, 2003, p. 138). Downsizing, for example, is one situation where competing interpretations are inevitable. Change managers may portray this action as a way of strengthening the organization in the face of environmental pressures, thus protecting the jobs of those who remain. Others, however, may tell different stories, of management incompetence and of underhand ways of "outplacing" politically troublesome individuals or even whole departments, under the cover of "efficiency." Good stories can be more inspiring and motivational than a detailed business case. Balogun et al. (2016) regard stories as devices to make the content of new strategies easier to understand, enhancing individuals' ability to translate change into meaningful actions for themselves. Vaara et al. (2016) explore how senior management narratives concerning strategy and vision contribute to organizational stability and change by making sense of circumstances and events. In other words, when it comes to interpreting the meaning of change for others, the effective interpreter tells better stories than the competition.

6. Change Manager as Nurturer (*Shaping Unintended Outcomes*)

The image of change manager as *nurturer* assumes that small changes can have a major impact on the organizations and that managers may be unable to control fully the outcomes of these changes. However, they can nurture the organization and its staff, developing qualities that enable positive self-organizing. Future directions and outcomes can be nurtured or shaped, but the ability to produce specific intended outcomes is limited by wider, and sometimes chaotic, forces and influences. Checinski et al. (2019) claim that the failure rate of public-sector transformations, at 80 percent, is higher than in the private sector. In determining the outcomes of change, they emphasize the decisive impact of people practices, one of which is nurturing the capabilities that are required to succeed with major transformation programs and that are often lacking in the public sector.

TABLE 2.3
Chaos Theory and Change Management

Change Management Actions	Core Elements
Managing transitions	Destabilize people Get them involved in decision making and problem-solving
Building resilience	Develop ability to absorb change
Destabilizing the system	Create a state of tension; act as devil's advocate Seek disconfirmation of organizational beliefs Nurture creativity to cope with a chaotic environment
Managing order and disorder, the present and the future	Balance the needs for order and change
Creating and maintaining a learning organization	Make continuous learning available to everyone

Source: Adapted from Tetenbaum (1998).

Perspectives supporting the nurturer image include chaos theory and Confucian/Taoist theory.

Chaos theory argues that organizational change is nonlinear, is fundamental rather than incremental, and does not necessarily entail growth (table 2.3). Chaos theorists, drawing also on complexity theory, explore how organizations "continuously regenerate themselves through adaptive learning and interactive structural change. These efforts periodically result in the spontaneous emergence of a whole new dynamic order, through a process called self-organization" (Lichtenstein, 2000, p. 131). The phenomenon of self-organization is driven by the chaotic nature of organizations, which in turn is a consequence of having to grapple simultaneously with both change and stability. In this context, the change manager has to nurture the capacity for self-organization, with limited ability to influence the direction and nature of the spontaneous new orders that may emerge. This may sound abstract and puzzling, but this describes the emergent strategy—and nurturing capabilities—that the successful Brazilian entrepreneur Ricardo Semler (2000; 2019) adopted in his iconic manufacturing company Semco (Kuiken, 2010). This explains how Semco successfully diversified into electronics (see the box "Semco: A Chaotic Business?").

Confucian/Taoist theory—or rather philosophy—adopts assumptions with regard to organizational change that are fundamentally different from Western views (Marshak, 1993). Change is regarded as:

- cyclical, involving constant ebb and flow
- processual, involving harmonious movement from one state to another
- journey-oriented, involving cyclical change with no end state
- based on maintaining equilibrium, or achieving natural harmony
- observed and followed by those who are involved, who seek harmony with their universe
- normal rather than exceptional

Semco: A Chaotic Business?

Semco is a well-known South American manufacturing business. The company has a flat hierarchy and emphasizes staff empowerment to engage in decisions about virtually all company issues, from strategy to setting their own salaries. This is "a big company that has no rules" (Kruse, 2016). Ricardo Semler, the Brazilian majority owner of Semco, discussed how the company moved away from manufacturing, making industrial pumps and white goods, and into e-business and other services that now account for 75 percent of its business. Many of the company practices and philosophies illustrate principles of chaos theory. Semler says that the company "went digital without a strategy." Revenues went from $4 million to $160 million over 20 years. He attributes this success to what some might term a chaotic management style, whereby, in his words:

[R]ather than dictate Semco's identity from on high, I've let our employees shape it through their individual efforts, interests, and initiatives.

That rather unusual management philosophy has drawn a good deal of attention over the years. The way we work—letting our employees choose what they do, where and when they do it, and even how they get paid—has seemed a little too radical for mainstream companies.

[S]ome of the principles that underlie the way we work will become increasingly common and even necessary in the new economy. In particular, I believe we have an organization that is able to transform itself continuously and organically—without formulating complicated mission statements and strategies, announcing a bunch of top-down directives, or bringing in an army of change-management consultants. (Semler, 2001, pp. 51–52)

Taoist Approach to Change Leadership

Richard Pascale and Jerry Sternin (2005) discuss the role of change leaders in circumstances where there are no "off the shelf" remedies or coping strategies for dealing with the organization's problems. The role of the leader, they argue, is to be a facilitator rather than a "path breaker." This means identifying and encouraging the "positive deviants" in the organization, who are already doing things differently—and better. The key "is to engage the members of the community you want to change in the process of discovery, making them the evangelists of their own conversion experience" (p. 74). To illustrate what is involved, they quote the well-known Taoist poem written by Lao-tzu:

Ivy Close Images/Alamy Stock Photo

Learn from the people
Plan with the people
Begin with what they have
Build on what they know
Of the best leaders
When the task is accomplished
The people all remark
We have done it ourselves

Organizational change outcomes from this standpoint are not intended so much as produced through the nurturing of a harmonious Yin-Yang philosophy in which each new order contains its own negation. Embedded in this philosophy, therefore, is an image of the change manager as nurturer.

LO 2.5 Using the Six-Images Framework

Each of these images of managing change represents a Weberian "ideal type." They are "ideal" in the sense that a "pure" version of the concept may not exist, but they give us a set of benchmarks, or templates, against which practice can be compared. (Note: "Ideal" does not in this case mean "desirable.") These images are not separate categories. They form a continuum from controlling so shaping management roles and from planned to unintended outcomes. The boundaries of these six images are blurred, and their elements may overlap in practice.

These six images are enduring, each having, as we have seen, differing theoretical underpinnings. Nevertheless, the *caretaker* and *nurturer* images are less frequently discussed in relation to change management—although they are more widely accepted in other domains of organizational theory, particularly where there is less focus on practice. In contrast, the *director, navigator, coach,* and *interpreter* images involve more active, intentional, and directional views of the ability of change managers to deliver organizational change, whether through control or shaping actions. In this sense, they are more positive images than caretaking and nurturing, which reflect a more reactive view of managerial effectiveness—in terms of both why changes occur and the extent to which these changes are driven by management intentions. Managers do not like to feel that they are insignificant players in their organizational worlds. Rather, the assumption that they are able to produce positive and intentional change is an important component of the Western change management lexicon.

The need to be seen to be producing positive intentional change was demonstrated to us in the following example. A well-known change consultant based in Washington, DC, told us how he intended to use the six-image framework in a major international organization to help the staff understand the impact of the culture of the organization and its many competing discourses of change. The company agreed to use the framework and requested copyright permission. However, some senior executives argued against using it, "because it might legitimate managers not assuming responsibility for initiating and managing change; it might give them an out." This was for two reasons. First, there was the possibility of seeing change have unintended outcomes. Second, there was the possibility that change managers would have minimal impact where the organization was dominated by enforced change from the outside. The six-image framework was not used.

This example is instructive, for the following reasons. Some commentators distinguish between topics that are "sacred" and those that are "profane." Some topics are not to be questioned, and to do so is not legitimate. The experience of our Washington consultant indicates that the idea that change can be controlled to produce intentional outcomes is sacred. It is profane to suggest otherwise—that managers may be overwhelmed by forces beyond their control. The view that we would like to promote in this text is that it is time to end this divide. It is necessary to recognize that, in the long run, such a distinction is unhelpful. This stance hinders change managers by discouraging a reflective, self-critical view of their actions and of what is achievable in any given context.

So, how should the six-images framework be used in practice? There are three interrelated issues where reflection on the part of the change manager is valuable: surfacing assumptions about change, assessing dominant images of change, and using multiple images and perspectives of change.

Surfacing Assumptions About Change

The six-image framework guides us in reflecting on the images and assumptions we hold about managing change. As we noted at the start of this chapter, we all have mental models that help us simplify and make sense of the complex organizational worlds in which we operate. At the same time as they simplify and illuminate, they turn our attention toward some things and away from others. Being aware of the mental models with which we work helps us to think more carefully about their relevance and the extent to which the assumptions they entail are really ones that are going to be of assistance to us in approaching organizational change.

Being aware of these images enables change managers to assess the assumptions that are being made by others with whom they are working or from whom they are taking advice. Resulting from this assessment may be actions to reorient the images that others have of the particular change in which they are involved by providing new images through which the change can be seen.

For example, a change manager working with a navigator image may get others, who may view change through a director image, to acknowledge that unanticipated outcomes may occur as change unfolds. The navigator may persuade others to accept that one possibility of engaging in a change is that their current view of what is desired at the end may shift as the process unfolds and new possibilities emerge. In this sense, awareness of differing change management images can lead to an educational process within a change team. It requires encouragement of conversations around images and assumptions about the anticipated change, testing these with the group, and ensuring that all members of the team share common change image(s). This ensures that individual change managers are not talking past one another and making assumptions that are not shared by others.

Assessing Dominant Images of Change

The six-images framework encourages change managers to reflect on whether they are dominated by one particular image and on the limitations of that perspective. For example, the director image turns our attention to the outcomes we want to achieve and the steps needed to get there. At the same time, however, it turns our attention away from whether the outcomes are really achievable (or desirable) and whether unintentional outcomes also might occur should we pursue a particular change course.

The framework also directs attention to whether the organization in which the change is to occur is dominated by a particular view of what is achievable and how change should unfold. Some organizations are dominated by a particular view of how things should get done—almost to the point where the view is part of the "genetic coding" of the organization and is therefore seen as natural and not open for negotiation. In this case, change managers whose images are not consistent with the dominant organizational image may experience frustration and stress as they work with a change that may be seen as less legitimate or irrelevant.

Using Multiple Images and Perspectives of Change

It is possible that a change manager's "image-in-use" may depend on that manager's personal preferences, or it may be an unconscious decision based simply on the use of a familiar approach. One of the advantages of exposure to the range of images is to reduce the likelihood of a change manager using a single image because of a lack of understanding of the range of options. The six-images framework directs attention to the range of available options and to how their use may vary between contexts. A conscious choice of image-in-use can be based on at least the following four sets of considerations.

Image-in-Use Depends on the Type of Change

Change managers may assess some types of change as being more amenable to one image or approach rather than another. An interpreter might be seen as possible for one but not another type of change. Change managers are thus advised to adjust their image of change and the perception of what is possible depending on the situation. Anderson and Anderson (2001), for example, adopt a coaching image, arguing that developmental and transitional change can be managed from this perspective, but not transformational change. They draw on a navigator image in relation to transformational change, arguing that there are too many intangibles that can inhibit the achievement of predetermined outcomes; what is required is a mindset that accepts that organizations can be led into the unknown without the end point being predictable in advance.

Image-in-Use Depends on the Context of the Change

As chapter 10 explains, management approach should ideally be consistent with the context. In some settings, organizational members may be unhappy with the status quo and ready for change. The appropriate image-in-use in this context could be coach or interpreter, involving people to identify desired change outcomes and how those should be achieved. Where change faces hostility and resistance and intended outcomes are thus in jeopardy, a caretaker or navigator image may be more appropriate. However, if change is necessary for the organization's survival, then a director image may necessary.

Image-in-Use Depends on the Phase of Change

Change processes pass through different phases (see chapter 10). Change managers may thus choose to use different images at different stages of the process or depending on perceptions of the phase that change has reached. For example, in initiating an externally imposed or encouraged change (such as the Malcolm Baldrige Quality Awards), to continue as an accredited supplier, change managers may feel that the caretaker image is appropriate as change was not generated internally. However, as change progresses, an interpreter image may become relevant, conveying to staff new meanings associated with the implementation, such as enhanced professionalism and the possibility of diversifying into new areas.

Do You Want Kale with That?

The Context

The American fast-food company McDonald's is based in Chicago, Illinois, and is one of the world's largest employers, with a global chain of 37,000 outlets. Despite the company's success, McDonald's faces criticism for its unhealthy menu (burgers and fries); industrial-style food production methods; and low-skill, boring, low-wage jobs ("McJobs").

The Problem

When Steve Easterbrook became global chief executive in 2015, customer tastes were changing and sales had fallen for the first time in a decade. Millennials, in particular, wanted tastier and fresher food. The company had been slower than its competitors to recognize and respond to these trends. Easterbrook said, "People's palates are getting broader and they're far more interested in where the food comes from, what's in it and how it gets there." Customers were going to rival chains, and McDonald's had to "sharpen up" fast.

The Solution

Easterbrook's turnaround strategy was radical. He replaced almost all the global leadership team, many of whom were accustomed to working at a slower pace and had a lower risk appetite. He also cut several layers of middle management, reducing overheads. This also streamlined the bureaucracy,

allowing the company to introduce new products and services more quickly. The menu across the whole chain was revised, with healthier food, gourmet burgers, artisan buns, and locally sourced fresh beef rather than frozen. Customers placed their orders at touchscreen kiosks, food was cooked fresh, and orders were delivered to tables. A home delivery service was also introduced.

The Outcomes

Easterbrook's radical approach appears to have been successful. Profits have grown, returns to shareholders have increased, and McDonald's market value doubled, to $140 billion, between 2015 and 2018. The chain now sells vegan burgers in Scandinavia and kale salad in California. These options are not yet available in the United Kingdom (Duke, 2018).

What image, or images, of change management does Steve Easterbrook's approach illustrate? To what extent is his approach appropriate in this organizational context? What image, or images, of managing change would you have used in this context?

Case Sources

Duke, S. 2018. The wizard from Watford shaking up McDonald's. *The Sunday Times Business Section* (January 7):6.

On *YouTube,* find 'Steve Easterbrook McDonald's CEO on Turnaround Plan, Customer Growth' (2017, 12 minutes).

Image-in-Use Depends on Simultaneous Involvement in Multiple Changes

At any given time, in any one organization, there are often many changes unfolding, in different business units or across the organization as a whole. Some of those changes could be externally driven, and a caretaker image may apply. Where externally generated change is not negotiable—a change in legislation, for example, demanding compliance—then a director image may be necessary. Other initiatives, however, may be internally generated, and a director image may again be appropriate to achieving desired outcomes in a controlled way. This implies that skilled and reflective change managers are able to adapt, to move between images depending on how conditions are developing. It may also be appropriate to manage simultaneously with multiple images where these are related to different but concurrent initiatives.

SELF-ASSESSMENT

What Is Your Image of Managing Change?

LO 2.5

What is your image of how to manage change? Based on the six-image framework, this assessment sets out a series of beliefs, some of which are contradictory. The aim is to profile your beliefs and to encourage reflection concerning your approach to change. This is an assessment, and not a test; there are no right or wrong answers. It should take only 10 to 15 minutes to complete and score.

Rate each statement (tick the appropriate box) with regard to how closely it reflects your views, using this scale:

1	2	3	4	5
Strongly Disagree	Disagree	Neither Agree nor Disagree	Agree	Strongly Agree

		1	2	3	4	5
1	Communications should emphasize the inevitability of change and how best to cope with or survive it.	❑	❑	❑	❑	❑
2	Managers don't have to do anything about resistance to change because in the long run it won't have any impact.	❑	❑	❑	❑	❑
3	Managers' ability to control change is limited because other forces propel change regardless of managers' actions.	❑	❑	❑	❑	❑
4	The aim of communication about change is to send clear, unambiguous messages so that organization members understand what is going to happen and what is required of them.	❑	❑	❑	❑	❑
5	Articulating a vision is essential to successful change; top management should do this early in the process.	❑	❑	❑	❑	❑
6	Communication about change needs to foster supportive conditions and to convey the need for members to be ready to engage in change as it unfolds, often in unpredictable ways.	❑	❑	❑	❑	❑
7	Although managers can exert some control over how change unfolds, external factors also affect the process.	❑	❑	❑	❑	❑
8	A search for the deepest values of the organization is required to find a vision that resonates with the organization's members; a CEO cannot provide a vision.	❑	❑	❑	❑	❑
9	Organizational change is unpredictable, and resistance may or may not affect the outcomes, but managers should respond to resistance anyway, as this could address the arguments.	❑	❑	❑	❑	❑
10	An appropriate vision for change will most likely emerge through consultation with the organization's members.	❑	❑	❑	❑	❑
11	Probably the best way for managers to implement change is to shape staff abilities to succeed in the new circumstances.	❑	❑	❑	❑	❑

(Continued)

12	Communicating about change involves attending to the varied interests of stakeholders and persuading them of the benefits of change or, if necessary, modifying changes to produce the best outcome in a given situation.	❏	❏	❏	❏	❏
13	It is generally possible for managers to have significant control over how change happens in their organization.	❏	❏	❏	❏	❏
14	Managers should help resisters develop the capacity to cope with particular organizational changes.	❏	❏	❏	❏	❏
15	Communication about change should ensure that organization members are "on the same page" about the values linked to the change and the actions appropriate to those values.	❏	❏	❏	❏	❏
16	A vision for organizational change emerges from the clash of chaotic and unpredictable change forces; a vision cannot be articulated early in a change process.	❏	❏	❏	❏	❏
17	Although managers cannot directly control how change happens in an organization, they can nurture staff capabilities, and thus encourage positive self-organizing.	❏	❏	❏	❏	❏
18	Managers should redirect change to go around resistance, when that occurs, rather than try to overcome it.	❏	❏	❏	❏	❏
19	To implement change successfully, managers must interpret the change for organization members and help them to make sense of what is going on.	❏	❏	❏	❏	❏
20	Visions for organizational change are likely to have a limited impact unless they are consistent with events unfolding outside the organization; change comes less from a vision and more from the influence of external forces.	❏	❏	❏	❏	❏
21	Communication about change is best done with a persuasive account, to ensure that as many people as possible, inside and outside the organization, share a common understanding.	❏	❏	❏	❏	❏
22	Managers should deal with resistance to change by helping the organization members understand the changes and what these imply for their own roles.	❏	❏	❏	❏	❏
23	Leaders cannot impose a vision for change as competing stakeholders have different views; effective change management involves navigating these tensions.	❏	❏	❏	❏	❏
24	Managers can and should overcome resistance to change.	❏	❏	❏	❏	❏

Source: This assessment was designed by, and is reproduced here with the permission of Jean Bartunek, Professor of Management and Organization, Boston College, MA.

SELF-ASSESSMENT

Scoring

Transfer your ratings to this table. Add the ratings for each image, and calculate your average.

	Director			Coach	
4	_____	10		_____	
5	_____	11		_____	
13	_____	14		_____	
24	_____	15		_____	
Total:	_____	Total:		_____	
÷ 4 = average:	_____	÷ 4 = average:		_____	

	Navigator			Interpreter	
7	_____	8		_____	
12	_____	19		_____	
18	_____	21		_____	
23	_____	22		_____	
Total:	_____	Total:		_____	
÷ 4 = average:	_____	÷ 4 = average:		_____	

	Caretaker			Nurturer	
1	_____	6		_____	
2	_____	9		_____	
3	_____	16		_____	
20	_____	17		_____	
Total:	_____	Total:		_____	
÷ 4 = average:	_____	÷ 4 = average:		_____	

You will have an average score of between 1 and 5 for each image. Consider the following questions, and where possible compare your answers with colleagues:

1. What are your two highest scores? These are your "dominant" images. Check your understanding of those images with the descriptions in table 2.4.

2. Do any of these images of change management involve actions that you would be uncomfortable taking? Why?

3. If you have one or two dominant images, how do you feel about being advised to use the other, low-scoring images, if conditions indicate that would be more appropriate?

4. If your six scores are similar, does this mean that you are able to act differently in different change settings?

TABLE 2.4
Six Images of Change Management

Image	Sound Bite	Approach to Change	When to Use
Director	"This is what is going to happen."	Management choice, command, and control	When urgent change is required for survival, and change manager has better knowledge of solutions
Navigator	"I will tell you what I would like to happen."	Plan with care, but expect the unexpected	When the organization's history, culture, context, and politics will affect change plans
Caretaker	"Let us explore what might be possible."	Accept the force of external context factors, and adapt as necessary	When environmental forces are overwhelming, affecting the entire sector
Coach	"How can we develop our capability to deal with change?"	Shape systemic capabilities—values, skills, drills—to respond effectively to change	When the organization's members need to resolve interpersonal conflicts and build an understanding to solve their own problems
Interpreter	"We need to think differently about this."	Manage meaning through interpretations that explain and convey understanding to others	When different stakeholders have competing views of the same issues and they do not share common interests
Nurturer	"This is everybody's problem. How will we fix it?"	Develop resilience, encourage involvement, continuous learning, and self-organizing	When faced with competing and changing external pressures, requiring constant regeneration and adaptive learning

We will refer to these images of change management throughout the book. We would therefore like you to reflect on the following additional questions:

1. Is it likely that most people will have one dominant image of change management?
2. Are change leaders more likely to be successful if they remain faithful to their dominant style(s)?
3. Are change leaders who have the capacity to apply a range of different images more likely to be successful?
4. In your judgment, do most managers have the behavioral flexibility to move between different styles, or do they tend to apply just one or a limited range of approaches?

EXERCISE 2.1

Assessing Change Managers' Images

LO 2.2

Your task, individually or in a small group, is to find and interview two people who have managed organizational change or who have been directly involved in change implementation. Design a "topic guide" for your interviews. This should cover, for example: the organizational context; your interviewees' roles in relation to change; the nature of the changes in which they were involved; why those changes were significant; how the changes were implemented covering key decisions, actions, turning points, and crises; how your interviewees would describe their personal management styles; the outcomes of those changes—successful, or not. If possible, choose to interview managers from different organizations and sectors, to provide contrast. Once you have collected this interview evidence, consider the following questions:

- Which images of change did those two managers illustrate?
- How did those images affect their change management decisions and actions?
- Where they drew on more than one image, to what extent were those related to
- type of change?
  - context of change?
  - phase of change?
  - their involvement in more than one change at the same time?
- What other factors did you identify?
- What conclusions can you draw from your analysis about the effects of images and mental models on the way that your interviewees approached their change management roles?

EXERCISE 2.2

Turnaround at Beth Israel

Issues to Consider as You Read This Story

1. Identify five factors that explain the success of this corporate turnaround.
2. Describe Paul Levy's role and contributions to this turnaround.
3. What insights does this story have to offer concerning the role of the change leader?
4. What lessons about managing organizational change can be taken from this experience and applied to other organizations, in healthcare and in other sectors? Or, are the lessons unique to Beth Israel Deaconess Medical Center?

LO 2.5

The Setting

Since a merger with Lahey Health in 2019, Beth Israel Deaconess Medical Center (BIDMC) has been part of Beth Israel Lahey Health, an integrated healthcare system based in Boston, Massachusetts. In 2019, BIDMC had 700 beds and 1,250 doctors, most of whom also held faculty positions at Harvard Medical School. BIDMC also provides clinical education in nursing, social work, radiologic technology, ultrasound, and occupational therapy. BIDMC cared for victims of the Boston Marathon bombing in 2013 (including one of the bombers) and is the official hospital of the Boston Red Sox major league baseball team. It is also a leading research institution, receiving $230 million in research funds in 2019. However, the survival of BIDMC was once in question.

This is the story of a corporate turnaround, rescuing the organization from financial disaster and restoring its reputation, competitiveness, and profitability. Beth Israel Deaconess Medical Center was originally created in 1996 by the merger of two hospitals. The business case was based on the view that the larger organization would be better able to compete with, for example, Massachusetts General Hospital and Brigham Women's Hospital. The two merged hospitals had different cultures. Beth Israel had a casual management style that encouraged professional autonomy and creativity. Deaconess Hospital was known for its rules-based top-down management. Staff members were loyal to their own organization. After the merger, the Beth Israel culture dominated, and many Deaconess staff, especially nurses, left to join the competition.

(Continued)

The Problems

By 2002, BIDMC was losing $100 million a year and faced a "financial meltdown." There were problems with the quality and safety of care, with low staff morale and poor relationships between clinical staff and management. The media attention was damaging BIDMC's reputation.

The Solutions

External management consultants recommended drastic measures to turn around the hospital's finances, and Paul Levy was appointed chief executive officer of BIDMC in 2002. Levy had no healthcare background and little knowledge of hospitals. He felt that gave him an advantage, as he was a "straight talker" and could act as an "honest broker." But staff members were skeptical at first.

Levy's turnaround strategy was based on two themes: transparency and commitment to quality. His first action was to share with all staff the full scale of the financial difficulties to create "a burning platform" from which escape would only be possible by making radical changes. His second approach was to signal absolute commitment to the continuous improvement of quality to build trust and establish a sense of common purpose. Levy described his management style:

> Perhaps I had an overly developed sense of confidence, but my management approach is that people want to do well and want to do good and I create an appropriate environment. I trust people. When people make mistakes, it isn't incompetence, it's insufficient training or the wrong environment. What I've learned is that my management style can work.

Phase 1

With the hospital "bleeding money," urgent action was necessary. Levy accepted some of the management consultants' recommendations, and several hundred jobs were lost in an attempt to restore financial balance. He refused to reduce nursing levels, but the financial crisis was resolved.

Phase 2

Medical staff members were tired of poor relationships with management. In 2003, Levy hired Michael Epstein, a doctor, as chief operating officer. Epstein met with each clinical department to win their support for the hospital's nonclinical objectives and to break down silo working. Kathleen Murray, who had joined BIDMC in 2002, was director of performance assessment and regulatory compliance. The hospital had no annual operating plans, and she set out to correct this, starting with two departments that had volunteered to take part in phase 1: orthopedics and pancreatic surgery. Other departments soon joined in. Operating plans had four areas to address: quality and safety, patient satisfaction, finance, and staff and referrer satisfaction. One aim was to make staff proud of the outcomes and create a sense of achievement. Although the performance of doctors would now be closely monitored, the introduction of operating plans was seen as a major turning point.

Phase 3

To help address the view that medical errors were inevitable, Levy appointed Mark Zeidel as chief of medicine. Zeidel introduced an initiative that cut "central line infection" rates, reducing costs as well as harm to patients, and providing the motivation for more improvements. The board of directors was not at first convinced that performance data should be published, but Levy was persuasive. He put the information on his public blog, which he started in 2006, and it soon became popular with staff, the public, and the media, with over 10,000 visitors a day. Levy explained:

> The transparency website is the engine of our work. People like to see how they compare with others, they like to see improvements. Transparency is also important for clinical leaders and our external audience of patients and insurers. We receive encouraging feedback from patients. We've also managed to avoid a major controversy with the media despite our openness. Transparency's major societal and strategic imperative is to provide creative tension within hospitals so that they hold themselves accountable. This accountability is what will drive doctors, nurses and administrators to seek constant improvements in the quality and safety of patient care.

Other performance data were published for the hospital and for individual departments. This included measures to assess whether care was evidence-based, effective, safe, patient-centered, timely, efficient, and equitable. Progress in meeting priorities for quality and safety could be tracked on the hospital's website, and the data were used by staff to drive quality improvements. The board also set tough goals to eliminate preventable harm and increase patient satisfaction. Every year, staff members were invited to summarize their improvement work in poster sessions, featuring the work of 95 process improvement teams from across the hospital.

Levy hired staff with expertise in LEAN methods. Previously an option, training in quality and safety became mandatory for trainee doctors, who had to take part in improvement projects. The culture was collaborative, and nurses had the respect of doctors. Patients often chose BIDMC for the quality of nursing care. The departmental quality improvement directors met twice a month to share experience. Department meetings routinely discussed adverse events. A patient care committee fulfilled a statutory requirement for board oversight of quality and safety. The office of decision support collected data on complication rates, infection rates, department-specific quality measures, and financial goals. A senior nurse said: "We felt a sense of ownership with issues of quality. We have dashboards up in the units to see how we are doing. Staff know what the annual operating goals are, as they are actively involved in setting them and integrating them into their work."

The Outcomes

By 2010, BIDMC was one of the leading academic health centers in the United States, with state-of-the-art clinical care, research, and teaching. BIDMC now competes effectively with other healthcare organizations, and with revenues of $3.53 billion in 2018, attracts over $200 million a year in research funding.

Postscript

Paul Levy resigned in January 2011. He explained his decision in a letter to the board of directors, making this available to staff and the public on his blog. The letter included the following remarks:

> I have been coming to a conclusion over the last several months, perhaps prompted by reaching my 60th birthday, which is often a time for checking in and deciding on

(Continued)

the next stage of life. I realized that my own place here at BID had run its course. While I remain strongly committed to the fight for patient quality and safety, worker-led process improvement, and transparency, our organization needs a fresh perspective to reach new heights in these arenas. Likewise, for me personally, while it has been nine great years working with outstanding people, that is longer than I have spent in any one job, and I need some new challenges.

Case Sources

Abbasi, K. 2010. *Improvement in practice: Beth Israel Deaconess case study*. London: The Health Foundation.

BIDMC, About BIDMC, https://www.bidmc.org/about-bidmc.

Levy, P. 2011, Transitions. *Not Running a Hospital*, January 7. http://runningahospital.blogspot.co.uk/2011/01/transitions.html.

The Health Foundation. 2012. Beth Israel Deaconess case study: summary, October 8. https://www.youtube.com/watch?v53mF3u0nIWVQ.

On *YouTube,* find 'Beth Israel Deaconess case study: summary' (2012, 5 minutes).

Additional Reading

Battilana, J., and Casciaro, T. 2013. The network secrets of great change agents. *Harvard Business Review* 91(7/8):62–68. Research concluding that it is the networks of change agents that can make them more successful, especially where the nature of their networks ("bridging" or "cohesive") matches the type of change that they are pursuing.

Chatman, J. 2014. Culture change at Genentech: Accelerating strategic and financial accomplishments, *California Management Review* 56(2):113–29. A study of successful change in a pharmaceuticals company. The senior vice president, Jennifer Cook, said: "My leadership philosophy is that individuals are people first and employees second. Our best employees make a choice to come to work every day and we have to earn the right to have them want to come back. The way I look at it is that I'm bringing a framework and infrastructure as a way to harness the group's thinking, but it's their thinking" (p. 113).

Ibarra, H., and Scoular, A. 2019. The leader as coach. *Harvard Business Review* 97(6):110–19. Argues that to deal with disruptive change, leaders have to become coaches to those they supervise, asking questions rather than giving answers, supporting and not judging, facilitating rather than directing. Coaching must also become an organizational capability.

Pascale, R. T., and Sternin, J. 2005. Your company's secret change agents, *Harvard Business Review* 83(5):72–81. Argues that the leader's role is not to direct change but to identify and encourage the organization's "positive deviants" who are creating new solutions and ways of working on their own initiative. Thus supports the *nurturer* image of the change manager, shaping conditions that again will lead to unpredicted outcomes.

Roundup

Reflections for the Practicing Change Manager

- To what extent are you more comfortable with one or another of the six images described in this chapter in terms of your own (current or anticipated) approach to managing change?

- Why is this the case?

- What are the strengths and limitations of the images that you have identified as most relevant to you?

- What skills do you think are associated with each image to use it well?

- Are there areas of personal skill development that are needed for you to feel more comfortable in using other change management images?

- Have you worked in an organization that was dominated by particular images or approaches to change?

- What barriers would you face in trying to bring consideration of alternative images in these organizations? What strategies could you use to assist you in overcoming these barriers?

- As a small group exercise: Compare your responses to the above questions. Where do you differ from colleagues? Why do those differences arise?

Here is a short summary of the key points that we would like you to take from this chapter, in relation to each of the learning outcomes:

LO 2.1   * *Evaluate the use that different authors make of the terms change agent, change manager, and change leader.*

Some commentators argue that the distinction between change managers and change leaders is clear and significant. We have argued, in contrast, that in practice these two roles are closely intertwined. This is a semantic squabble that is not worth arguing about. The term *change agent* traditionally refers to an external consultant or adviser, and although that role is still common, the term today is used more loosely, to refer to internal as well as external change agents.

LO 2.2   * *Understand the importance of organizational images and mental models.*

The images or mental models that we all have provide us with ways of understanding the world around us. Although these images are useful, we have to appreciate that "ways of seeing" are also "ways of not seeing." Focusing on specific attributes of a situation, of necessity means overlooking other attributes—which may sometimes be important. Change managers approach their task with an image of the organization, an image of the change process, and an image of their role in change. These mental models—our "images-in-use"—have profound implications for change management practice.

LO 2.3   * *Compare and contrast six different images of managing change and change managers.*

We explored six images of the change manager: director, navigator, caretaker, coach, interpreter, and nurturer. Each is based on different assumptions about the role of management (controlling versus shaping) and about the change outcomes being sought (intended, partly intended, unintended).

LO 2.4   * *Explain the theoretical underpinning of different change management images.*
Each image finds support in organizational theory and change management theory, which was explored briefly. Nevertheless, it is important to recognize that these images, which have strikingly different implications for practice, are based on research evidence and theory.

LO 2.5   * *Apply these six images of managing change to your personal preferences and approach and to different organizational contexts.*
We identified three uses of the six-image framework: surfacing assumptions, assessing dominant images, and using multiple perspectives and images. There are no right or wrong images of change management. It is valuable to be able to interpret problems and solutions in general, and change processes in particular, from different standpoints. This "multiple perspectives" approach can help to generate fresh thinking and creative solutions.

This framework has other uses, explored in later chapters. One concerns the assessment of change as successful or not. That judgment is often related to one image rather than another. We often ask: Was it managed well? What went right? What went wrong? Did we achieve what we wanted? However, judging success is open to interpretation. As Pettigrew et al. (2001, p. 701) argue, "Judgements about success are also likely to be conditional on who is doing the assessment and when the judgments are made." The six-image framework highlights the need to raise conversations early about judging the success of change and to ensure a broadly common view of that judgment across the organization.

References

Abbasi, K. 2010. *Improvement in practice: Beth Israel Deaconess case study*. London: The Health Foundation.

Anderson, L. A., and Anderson D. 2001. Awake at the wheel: Moving beyond change management to conscious change leadership. *OD Practitioner* 33(3):4–10.

Balogun, J., Hope Hailey, V., and Gustafsson, S. 2016. *Exploring strategic change*. 4th ed. Harlow, Essex: Pearson.

Barge, J. K., and Oliver, C. 2003. Working with appreciation in managerial practice. *Academy of Management Review* 28(1):124–42.

Basford, T., and Schaninger, B. 2016. Winning hearts and minds in the 21st century. *McKinsey Quarterly* 2:122–26.

Battilana, J., and Casciaro, T. 2013. The network secrets of great change agents. *Harvard Business Review* 91(7/8):62–68.

Beaudan, E. 2006. Making change last: How to get beyond change fatigue. *Ivey Business Journal* (January/February):1–7.

Bennis, W. G. 1969. *Organization development: Its nature, origins, and prospects*. Reading, MA: Addison Wesley.

Bolman, L., and Deal, T. 2017. *Re-framing organizations: Artistry, choice, and leadership.* 6th ed. San Francisco, CA: Jossey Bass.

Brosseau, D., Ebrahim, S., Handscomb, C., and Thaker, S. 2019. *The Journey to an agile organization.* New York and London: McKinsey & Company.

Buchanan, D. A., and Dawson, P. 2007. Discourse and audience: Organizational change as multi-story process. *Journal of Management Studies* 44(5):669–86.

Bucy, M., Fagan, T., Maraite, B., and Piaia, C. 2017. *Keeping transformations on target.* New York and London: McKinsey & Company.

Burnes, B. 2017. *Managing Change: A strategic approach to organizational dynamics.* 7th ed. Harlow, Essex: Pearson.

Burnes, B., and Cook, B. 2012. The past, present and future of organization development: Taking the long view. *Human Relations* 65(11):1395–429.

Chatman, J. 2014. Culture change at Genentech: Accelerating strategic and financial accomplishments. *California Management Review* 56(2):113–29.

Checinski, M., Dillon, R., Hieronimus, S., and Klier, J. 2019. *Putting people at the heart of public-sector transformations.* London and New York: McKinsey & Company.

Cheung-Judge, M.-Y., and Holbeche, L. 2015. *Organization development: A practitioner's guide for OD and HR.* 2nd ed. London: Kogan Page.

Dawson, P., and Andriopoulos, C. 2017. *Managing change, creativity and innovation.* 3rd ed. London: Sage Publications.

Di Maggio, P. J., and Powell, W. W. 1983. The iron cage revisited: Institutional isomorphism and collective rationality in organizational fields. *American Sociological Review* 48(2):147–60.

Duke, S. 2018. The wizard from Watford shaking up McDonald's. *The Sunday Times Business Section* (January 7):6.

Elizabeth Thornton Quotes. (n.d.). BrainyQuote.com. Retrieved November 13, 2019, from https://www.brainyquote.com/quotes/elizabeth_thornton_735226.

Fayol, H. 1916. Administration industrielle et générale. *Bulletin de la Societe de l'Industrie Minérale* 10:5–164.

Fayol, H. 1949. *General and industrial management.* Translated by C. Storrs. London: Sir Isaac Pitman & Sons.

Gallup. 2017. *State of the global workplace: Executive summary.* Washington DC: Gallup.

George, G., Haas, M., and Pentland, A. S. 2014. Big data and management. *Academy of Management Journal* 57(2):321–26.

Gulick, L., and Urwick, L. 1937. *Papers on the science of administration.* New York: Institute of Public Administration.

Harrison, M. I., and Shirom, A. 1999. *Organizational diagnosis and assessment*. Thousand Oaks, CA: Sage Publications.

Hatch, M. J., and Cunliffe, A. L. 2012. *Organization theory: Modern, symbolic and postmodern perspectives*. 3rd ed. Oxford: Oxford University Press.

Hope, O. 2010. The politics of middle management sensemaking and sensegiving. *Journal of Change Management* 10(2):195–215.

Ibarra, H., and Scoular, A. 2019. The leader as coach. *Harvard Business Review* 97(6):110–19.

Katz, D., Maccoby, N., and Morse, N. C. (1950). *Productivity, supervision, and morale in an office situation*. Ann Arbor, MI: University of Michigan Institute for Social Research.

Keller, S., and Schaninger, B. 2019. *A better way to lead large-scale change*. New York: McKinsey & Company.

Kniffin, K. M., Detert, J. R., and Leroy, H., L. 2019. On leading and managing: Synonyms or separate (and unequal)? *Academy of Management Discoveries* (published online early).

Kotter, J. P. 1990. *A force for change: How leadership differs from management*. New York: Free Press.

Kotter, J. P. 2007 (first published 1995). Leading change: why transformation efforts fail. *Harvard Business Review* 85(1):96–103.

Kotter, J. P. 2012a. *Leading Change*. 2nd ed. Boston, MA: Harvard University Press.

Kotter, J. P. 2012b. Accelerate! *Harvard Business Review* 90(11):44–52.

Kruse, K. 2016. The big company that has no rules. *Fortune*, August 29. https://www.forbes.com/sites/kevinkruse/2016/08/29/the-big-company-that-has-no-rules.

Kuiken, B. 2010. Where is Semco now? *Organization 5.0*, http://www.organization-5point0.com/literature/articles/where-is-semco-now-visit-2010.

Langley, A., Smallman, C., Tsoukas, H., and Van de Ven, A. H. 2013. Process studies of change in organization and management: Unveiling temporality, activity, and flow. *Academy of Management Journal* 56(1):1–13.

Lawson, E., and Price, C. 2003. The psychology of change management. *The McKinsey Quarterly* Special Edition: The value in organization: 31–41.

Lichtenstein, B. B. 2000. Self-organized transitions: A pattern amidst the chaos of transformative change. *Academy of Management Executive* 14(4):128–41.

McCabe, D., Ciuk, S., and Gilbert, M. 2019. There is a crack in everything: An ethnographic study of pragmatic resistance in a manufacturing organization. *Human Relations* (published online first), pp. 1–28.

McCreary, L. 2010. Kaiser Permanente's innovation on the front lines. *Harvard Business Review* 88(9):92–97.

Marshak, R. J. 1993. Lewin meets Confucius: A re-view of the OD model of change. *Journal of Applied Behavioral Science* 29(4):393–415.

Mayo, E. 1945. *The social problems of an industrial civilization*. Cambridge, MA: Harvard University Press.

Mintzberg, H. 2009. *Managing*. Harlow, Essex: Financial Times Prentice Hall.

Mintzberg, H., and Waters, J. A. 1985. Of strategies deliberate and emergent. *Strategic Management Journal* 6(3):257–72.

Morgan, G. 2006. *Images of organization*. 3rd ed. London: Sage Publications.

Oertel, S., Thommes, K., and Walgenbach, P. 2016. Organizational failure in the aftermath of radical institutional change. *Organization Studies* 37(8):1067–87.

Palmer, I., and Dunford, R. 2002. Who says change can be managed?: Positions, perspectives and problematics. *Strategic Change* 11(5):243–51.

Pascale, R. T., and Sternin, J. 2005. Your company's secret change agents. *Harvard Business Review* 83(5):72–81.

Pettigrew, A. M. 1985. *The awakening giant: Continuity and change in ICI*. Oxford: Basil Blackwell.

Pettigrew, A. M., Woodman, R. W., and Cameron, K. S. 2001. Studying organizational change and development: Challenges for future research. *Academy of Management Journal* 44(4):697–713.

Rafferty, A. E., Jimmieson, N. L., and Armenakis, A. A. 2013. Change readiness: a multilevel review. *Journal of Management* 39(1):110–35.

Roethlisberger, F. J., and Dickson, W. J. 1939. *Management and the worker*. Cambridge, MA: Harvard University Press.

Schein, E. 1999. *Process consultation revisited: Building the helping relationship*. Reading, MA: Addison-Wesley.

Semler, R. 2000. How we went digital without a strategy. *Harvard Business Review* 78(4):51–58.

Semler, R. 2001. *Maverick!: The success story behind the world's most unusual workplace*. London: Random House Business.

Semler, R. 2019. *Radical*. Valencia: Maximo Potencial.

Stace, D. A., and Dunphy, D. 2001. *Beyond the boundaries: Leading and re-creating the successful enterprise*. 2nd ed. Sydney: McGraw Hill.

Tannenbaum, R., and Schmidt, W. H. 1958. How to choose a leadership pattern. *Harvard Business Review* 36(2):95–101.

Tetenbaum, T. J. 1998. Shifting paradigms: From Newton to chaos. *Organizational Dynamics* (Spring):21–32.

Vaara, E., Sonenshein, S., and Boje, D. M. 2016. Narratives as sources of stability and change in organizations. *Academy of Management Annals* 10(1):495–560.

Van de Ven, A. H., and Poole, M. S. 1995. Explaining development and change in organizations. *Academy of Management Review* 20(3):510–40.

Van de Ven, A. H., and Sun, K. 2011. Breakdowns in implementing models of organizational change. *Academy of Management Perspectives* 25(3):58–74.

Weick, K. E. 1995. *Sensemaking in Organizations*. Thousand Oaks, CA/London: Sage Publications.

Weick, K. E. 2000. Emergent change as a universal in organizations. In *Breaking the code of change*, ed. M. Beer and N. Nohria (223–41). Boston, MA: Harvard Business School Press.

White, M. C., Marin, D. B., Brazeal, D. V., and Friedman, W. H. 1997. The evolution of organizations: Suggestions from complexity theory about the interplay between natural selection and adaptation. *Human Relations* 50(11):1383–401.

Zaleznik, A. 1997. Real work. *Harvard Business Review,* 75(6):53–63.

Source of the chapter opening quote: Elizabeth Thornton Quotes. (n.d.). BrainyQuote. com. Retrieved November 13, 2019, from BrainyQuote.com Web site: https://www. brainyquote.com/quotes/elizabeth_thornton_735226

Chapter opening silhouette credit: FunKey Factory/Shutterstock

Chapter 3

Why Change? Contemporary Pressures and Drivers

Learning Objectives

By the end of this chapter you should be able to:

LO 3.1 Identify internal organizational factors that trigger change.

LO 3.2 Understand the environmental pressures that can trigger organizational change.

LO 3.3 Explain why organizations often fail to change following crises.

LO 3.4 Relate differing images of managing change to pressures for change.

"Change? Change? Why do we need change? Things are quite bad enough as they are."

Robert Gascoyne-Cecil, 3rd Marquess of Salisbury, and UK Prime Minister to Queen Victoria, 1885–1892

LO 3.1 Internal Organization Change Drivers

Why change? Organizations face many pressures for change. However, the evidence suggests that a high proportion of planned change programs fail to meet their objectives. To understand why managers embark on apparently risky change ventures, we explore in this chapter the internal and environmental pressures for change. We then explore why "remedial" change often does not happen where it would be expected, following accidents, disasters, and other crises.

The external, environmental pressures—some would argue imperatives—for change are now overwhelming, and we will focus mainly on those in this chapter. The internal change drivers can, of course, also be important in some circumstances (Figure 3.1). These include:

- low performance and morale; high stress and staff turnover
- inadequate skills and knowledge base; need for training and reskilling
- relocation of head office and facilities
- reallocation of responsibilities to address new priorities, problems
- new product and service delivery innovations

FIGURE 3.1
Internal Organizational Change Drivers

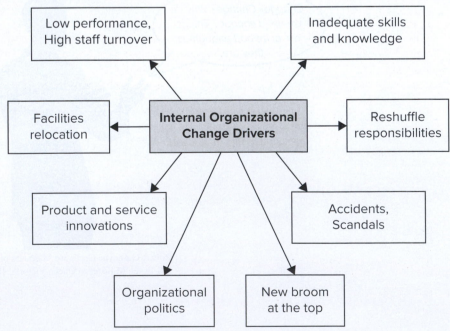

- accidents, scandals, failures, and governance issues leading to damaged reputation
- new senior managers, who want to "make their mark"
- internal organizational politics

The last four of these are particularly important—product and service innovations, accidents and scandals, new management, and organizational politics. Netflix, for example, changed its DVD-by-mail business into a subscription video on demand (SVOD) service, offering customers new products and new ways of delivering them (Lev-Ram, 2019a). Having cheated vehicle emissions tests, Volkswagen in 2015 was forced to consider changes to management and organizational culture to restore its reputation (Ewing, 2018). The safety reputation of Boeing (see Exercise 10.2 in chapter 10) was damaged in 2019 by the loss of 346 lives when two 737 Max aircraft crashed, allegedly due to faulty anti-stall software (Stacey, 2019). Roz Brewer, appointed chief operating officer at Starbucks in 2017, made her mark by restoring the company's sales growth, based on her personal observation of customer service and the introduction of new working practices (Kowitt, 2019). (See the box "Pressure on Airbnb to Change.")

Pressure on Airbnb to Change

In October 2019, the website *Vice* published a story about a company that was using fake identities to fool guests into booking attractive sounding but substandard accommodations. The *Vice* story argued that it was Airbnb's "lax oversight" that enabled this to occur and that Airbnb did little to help the victims either logistically or financially.

In the same month, in an affluent San Francisco suburb, in a house booked through Airbnb, over 100 people were attending a "mansion party" promoted through social media when gunfire erupted, killing five people and wounding four others. The house owners openly expressed their frustration with Airbnb, given that the owners' explicit instructions included a guest limit and banning of parties.

Although expressions of concerns about fraud and safety were not new for Airbnb, the timing of these incidents was unfortunate as they occurred shortly after the company had announced its intention to go public in 2020. *Fortune* magazine journalist Aric Jenkins (2020, p. 68) said, "With trust plummeting among investors and customers, Airbnb's leaders scrambled." What changes could Airbnb make that would restore confidence in the company?

Kanter (2003) notes that "new broom" top executives have a number of advantages because they

- are more likely to be able to create energy for change.
- are not constrained by past practice.
- can confront the organization's "sacred cows," and other long-running problems.

Board-level power struggles are rarely reported in detail, but these can often lead to changes in organizational structure and strategy, depending on the disagreements that triggered the struggles in the first place (Buchanan and Badham, 2020). Organizational politics is played at all levels of an organization and, contrary to the popular stereotype of dirty tricks and back-stabbing, politics can often generate positive organizational benefits (see Using Politics to Engineer Change).

Using Politics to Engineer Change   *Chief executive, UK hospital*

There are occasions where I can see that something is going to happen, and I've encouraged it to happen. For example, over the last couple of years, there's been a difficult relationship with the commissioner [the body which purchases healthcare from providers such as hospitals]. It's been a confrontational relationship that has not benefitted patients. What I have done this year is set up a contractual situation that is going to crash. And it's that crash that will stop that behaviour forever. It could be a crash for the hospital, or it could be a crash for the commissioner, but it doesn't matter. I've made it go nuclear this year, deliberately, because the incremental changes have gone unnoticed. A deficit of several million pounds is either going to land suddenly on our side of the books, or suddenly on the commissioning side of the books. I've contrived to make that happen so that it won't go unnoticed, to expose something that needs to be tackled. This is an accounting manoeuvre—the health system isn't actually going to lose any money. I could gradually let it rot over the years, until somebody realizes that this had gone on for too long and we need action to change it. But we are a successful organization, and we are able to take a risk on things like this, draw attention to it, and that's what those organizations need.

This is not a complete list of internal drivers for change. Managers and staff regularly identify ideas for improvement, many of which (the "small stuff") can be implemented simply and quickly, without the need for a formal change or project management process. The job description of most managers includes, implicitly or explicitly, a duty to find ways to improve performance. But as the following section explains, the more powerful drivers of organizational change today are external, arising from trends and developments in the wider environment. Organizations—including management—may be able to ignore staff ideas about how to change and improve things. Environmental trends, developments, and pressures that are overlooked can threaten the organization's survival.

LO 3.2 Environmental Pressures for Change

That's Disruption

Disruption isn't just one of the most overused words in management writing; it's also one of the most imprecisely used. When we say industry disruption is accelerating, we mean that in many sectors, critical foundations of industry structure—the economic fundamentals, the power balance between buyers and sellers, the role of assets, the types of competitors, even the borders of industries—are rapidly shifting. While that degree of change can be uncomfortable or even destructive, it can also contain the seeds of opportunity. For example, Airbnb is the world's largest provider of accommodation—but owns no property. Alibaba is the world's largest retailer—but owns no warehouses—That's disruption. (Greenberg et al., 2017, pp. 41 and 45)

The external environment for most organizations has altered dramatically since our previous edition in 2016. Social, financial, economic, technological, political, and geopolitical conditions have become much more turbulent and unpredictable. Some of these issues may appear to be remote, but they can affect radically the conditions under which businesses, small and large, have to operate: currency exchange rates, interest rates and the cost of debt, changing tariff and nontariff barriers to trade, regulations concerning carbon emissions, tax incentives and disincentives, consumer perceptions and preferences, and legislation affecting competition and consumer protection. An extreme example of external environmental pressure is the COVID-19 pandemic (2019–2020), which has driven major organizational changes across most sectors of the economy. Exercise 3.1 asks readers to assess the nature and long-term consequences of these changes in particular.

Organizations have to respond to these trends. Failure to respond to the opportunities and risks in appropriate ways can have negative consequences (see Transformation at Best Buy).

Transformation at Best Buy

Organizations often have to respond to several environmental pressures at the same time—economic, technological, organizational, and demographic. Best Buy is a good example.

Founded in 1966 as an audio specialist store, Best Buy is now an American multinational consumer electronics retailer based in Richfield, Minnesota. Faced with declining revenues in the 2010s, chief executive Hubert Joly and chief financial officer Corie Barry reinvented the company. Their transformation strategy involved adding new services to attract more customers and partnering with other companies (including Amazon) to set up "shop-in-shops" (where other brand owners rent space in a Best Buy store). They introduced price matching, sped up delivery for online purchases, and reduced the floorspace devoted to selling physical music, as streaming became popular.

As a result, Best Buy's shares quadrupled in value and its market capitalization reached $20 million in 2019. The company plans to diversify further, into wearable technology and digital healthcare. These are growth areas, with an ageing population that is tech-savvy. Best Buy is now the largest consumer electronics retailer in America and was rated "The Most Sustainable Company in the United States" by *Barron's* (a financial magazine) in 2019. The company ranks 72 in the 2018 *Fortune* 500 list of the largest U.S. companies by revenue. Taking over from Joly (who became executive chairman) in 2019, Corie Barry became the 30th female chief executive of a *Fortune* 500 company (Wahba, 2019).

Managers face a paradox. On the one hand, they are advised to change rapidly or perish (Greenberg et al., 2017). On the other, they are advised to avoid the risks of implementing too many changes at the same time (Hollister and Watkins, 2018). As noted earlier, the evidence suggests that around 70 percent of planned organizational changes fail. As failures appear to be widespread and widely acknowledged, what encourages managers to embark on such risky ventures? One answer is based on an economic perspective and is aligned to "management as control" images and assumptions:

> In competitive economies, firm survival depends on satisfying shareholders. Failure to do this will lead investors either to move their capital to other companies, or to use their influence to replace senior management. Managers thus introduce change to improve organizational performance in terms of profitability and higher company share prices.

An alternative view, aligned with "management as shaping" images and assumptions, is the organizational learning perspective.

Organizations and human systems are complex and evolving and cannot be reduced to a single objective of maximizing shareholder value. Change is also related to the need to increase an organization's adaptive capacity—because ways of increasing shareholder value, and the knowledge underpinning that goal, are likely to change over time. Change is based on the desire to build capacity to respond to, and to shape, external pressures and demands.

Change is not simply a matter of reacting to events. Organizations and individuals can anticipate trends and opportunities and be proactive as well. It has been argued that, given the need to navigate high levels of turbulence and adapt quickly to changing conditions, organizations need to focus on "next practice" as well as "best practice" (Mohrman and Lawler, 2012). As table 3.1 suggests, the ways in which managers experience triggers of change, and those to which they attend, will be influenced by their images of managing change.

LO 3.4

TABLE 3.1
Images of Change and Understanding the Pressures

Image	Understanding the Pressures for Change
Director	Change is a result of strategic pressure, entering new markets, or correcting an internal problem to improve efficiencies. These pressures are controllable, and the management task is to direct the organizational response.
Navigator	Change results from strategic threats and opportunities and from the need to deal with internal problems. However, the best response may not be obvious, given the many and often conflicting priorities that management faces and the range of influences and competing interests that need to be considered.
Caretaker	There are many pressures for change, and managers cannot control this agenda. External pressures arise from new regulations or market conditions, for example. Internal pressures can be triggered by growth or operational innovations. These pressures can be overwhelming and difficult to resist. The role of management, as caretakers, is to look after the organization as it is buffeted by these pressures, having limited choice in the actions that need to be taken in response.
Coach	The pressures for change are constant. They arise from the need to coordinate teamwork, values, and mindsets and to generate the collaboration that leads to improved organizational outcomes. Change pressures are therefore continuous and developmental and help to shape the organization's capabilities to respond to further change and to further improve performance.
Interpreter	Given the many internal and external pressures for change, staff members need management to provide meaning, to help understand "what is going on." Those who will be affected need to understand the significance of their roles, what needs to happen and why, and where the organization is heading. Managers must help to make sense of changes. This is a sensemaking role, providing clarity and contributing to individual identity and to organizational commitment.
Nurturer	Organizations change as a result of a variety of forces, some weak, some strong. The weaker pressures, however, can have a disproportionate impact on the organization. These pressures may not all be rational but may instead be chaotic and difficult to coordinate. The management role, therefore, is to nurture or to develop the organization's adaptive capacity to respond to those challenges.

Environmental pressures take many forms and include both opportunities and threats. Figure 3.2 identifies six current environmental pressures that are leading to the most profound organizational changes: shifts in the nature of globalization, corporate response to divisive issues, climate change, changing expectations of work, demographic trends, and technological innovation. Most, if not all, of these pressures are active at the same time, and all may be considered a priority.

FIGURE 3.2
Environmental Pressures for Organizational Change

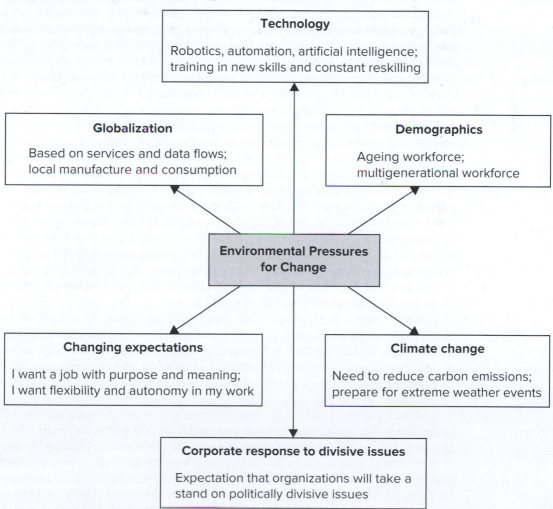

Technology

Robotics, automation, artificial intelligence; training in new skills and constant reskilling

Globalization

Based on services and data flows; local manufacture and consumption

Demographics

Ageing workforce; multigenerational workforce

Environmental Pressures for Change

Changing expectations

I want a job with purpose and meaning; I want flexibility and autonomy in my work

Climate change

Need to reduce carbon emissions; prepare for extreme weather events

Corporate response to divisive issues

Expectation that organizations will take a stand on politically divisive issues

Globalization with a Digital Profile

Although domestic pressures may seem dominant, organizations are not immune from developments in the wider global environment. London and Lund (2019; Lund et al., 2019) observe that, since the mid-2000s, the nature of globalization has changed. Trade in physical goods is "flattening" while cross-border data flows are "soaring." Globalization is developing a new digital profile, creating both new opportunities and fresh risks. Organizational resilience and flexibility—or agility—is critical in this fluid context. Traditional sources of competitive advantage do not apply as patterns of globalization are reshaped, as technology developments redefine whole sectors, and as changing social pressures and consumer demands challenge business models.

Anti-globalization sentiment has grown, particularly as some employees have seen their jobs moved to other countries. Some governments have responded with protectionist measures to limit free trade, resulting in trade wars, higher tariffs for imported goods, and renegotiated trade agreements. Although globalization has generated benefits, for countries, organizations, and employees, those benefits have been unevenly distributed; many have gained, but many feel that they have been "left behind" and have either suffered or experienced few gains. Governments have done little to support workers and communities suffering from global industry shifts. The next phase of globalization will have to be more inclusive if the benefits are to be achieved without disruption. Employing organizations will be expected to contribute to this inclusive approach.

Global trends have implications for corporate strategy. Traditional globalization may have gone into reverse, but trade in services has continued to rise: information technology (IT) services, helpdesks, telecoms, call centers, transport, business services, education, tourism, healthcare, music and video streaming, Internet search, and email. Cross-border services appear to be growing 60 percent faster than trade in goods, and services typically generate more economic value than traditional trade statistics reveal (Lund et al., 2019, p. vi). The services component of manufactured goods has also become more important. For example, around 30 percent of the value of an automobile comes from the services that go into it, including research and development, design, accounting and legal services, engineering, distribution, logistics, marketing, and sales. The United States has a large surplus in traded services, the total value of which is difficult to measure accurately but which may now be greater than that of traded goods.

This new pattern of globalization has workforce implications. As research and development, innovation, and intangible assets become more important and knowledge-intensive, a more highly skilled workforce is required. As manufacturing becomes more automated, companies will need higher levels of technical, engineering, and maintenance skills. It has long been apparent that highly skilled staff members are required to operate and maintain sophisticated technologies.

Another trend that London and Lund (2019) identify is that the trade intensity of manufactured goods is falling. In other words, more goods are now sold in the countries in which they were made, and the volume of output that is traded across borders is falling. For example, most of what is made in China is sold in China. Intraregional trade is now growing faster than long-haul trade. This is the result of a trend toward regionalization, as exemplified by the European Union and the Asia-Pacific region. With information sharing on social media, consumer tastes change rapidly, thus shortening product life cycles. The need to reduce time to market for new products is encouraging closer collaboration with suppliers, who for preference should be located nearby and not on the other side of the planet. This encourages the location of production close to markets rather than in remote locations from which goods could take a month to reach their market. Domestic supply chains are also less concerned with tariffs. These developments all contribute to falling cross-border trade.

Corporate Response to Divisive Issues

Society's expectations of business have changed, and customers want to know more about what the organizations they deal with are doing. Generation Z (see the "Demographic Trends" section), in particular, believe that companies have a duty to address social and environmental issues and are more likely to be loyal to businesses that match their values. Organizations are thus now expected to take a stand on social and politically divisive issues such as climate change, the environment, pollution, child labor, sexual harassment, racial discrimination, and, particularly in America, gun control. Whatever an organization decides will attract some customers and alienate others. Nike's stock fell sharply in 2018 when it used the football quarterback Colin Kaepernick in its advertising. Kaepernick became known for kneeling during the U.S. national anthem to protest against police brutality and racism against African-Americans. Praised for his actions by many, he was seen as "unpatriotic" by others and faced calls to be fired from his team. Nike's stock fell, but revenue quickly recovered (Derousseau, 2019).

In a survey of 14,000 consumers in 14 countries, 60 percent said that they decide whether to buy or to boycott products because of a company's views on social or political issues (Bond, 2017). In February 2018, the shooting at Marjory Stoneman Douglas High School in Parkland, Florida, which killed 17 students and injured 17 others, highlighted the gun control debate in America. A former school pupil opened fire with a legally acquired AR-15 semi-automatic rifle. Following this incident, many companies cut their ties with the National Rifle Association (NRA), cancelling special discount deals for NRA members, to show their disagreement with the NRA's pro-gun values (Edgecliffe-Johnson, 2018). BlackRock, an investment management company, announced that it was excluding gun makers and retailers from its socially responsible investment funds. BlackRock's chief executive, Larry Fink, said that the company must "make a positive contribution to society" (Masters, 2018).

Another organization affected by the Parkland incident is Dick's Sporting Goods. Dick's is America's largest sporting goods retailer, based in Pennsylvania, selling sports equipment, clothing, footwear—and guns. The Parkland shooter had bought a shotgun from Dick's, but not the weapon that he used at the school. Dick's is one of the four largest sellers of firearms in the United States. Founded in 1948, it now has over 700 stores and 30,000 employees and is a *Fortune* 500 company. After Parkland, Dick's chief executive, Ed Stack, decided to stop selling AR-15s and similar assault-style automatic rifles, stopped the sale of guns altogether in 125 stores, stopped selling guns to anyone under the age of 21, and ordered a review of the company's entire hunting business. The immediate result was a drop in sales that cost Dick's $300 million.

Sales started to make a comeback in 2019. But the incident prompted Stack to change the company's strategy to offset the continuing loss in sales, by targeting serious athletes as well as the more casual shoppers Dick's tended to attract. He put baseball batting cages and indoor golf driving ranges into the stores to help customers choose their equipment. Stack said that being a large seller of firearms, "made us part of the problem. We sold that kid in Parkland a shotgun. He should never have been able to buy a shotgun from us." Will Dick's post-gun strategy be a success? (Wabha, 2019).

Stating an opinion on a controversial issue of public interest may therefore not be enough on its own. To demonstrate support for a stance, more or less significant and visible organizational changes may be required, to both operations and strategy, as in Dick's case. Building a reputation in a particular area may, however, incur costs and lower the organization's performance, at least in the short term.

Climate Change

Each year, the World Economic Forum asks participants—political and business leaders from around the globe—for their views on the threats that they think will arise over the next 10 years. In 2019, the top five future threats were seen as:

- extreme weather events
- climate change
- natural disasters
- cyber attacks
- data fraud

The top three future threats concern the environment. In America, those threats are already present. In 2018, there were 14 weather disasters, with economic losses of more than $1 billion in each case, including Hurricanes Florence and Michael and the California wildfires (which struck the state again in 2019). Those losses amount to more than double the annual average of losses between 1980 and 2018. Incidents such as these affect business in many ways, for example, by damaging or destroying lives, facilities, and infrastructure and by disrupting communications, supply chains, and distribution channels. Making appropriate organizational changes to anticipate and manage these as well as other risks is likely to become increasingly important over the next decade—and perhaps beyond.

Greener Cruising

New regulatory requirements can trigger major organizational changes. Cruise liners, container ships, and oil tankers are among the world's biggest polluters. They burn "bunker fuel," which is highly sulfurous and emits more toxic gas and harmful particles than motor vehicle fuel. The maritime industry is vital to world trade and to a significant volume of tourism, but it is responsible for 2.5 percent of global greenhouse gas emissions. From 2020, the United Nations' International Maritime Organization wants to reduce this environmental impact by requiring all international vessels to stop using fuel with 3.5 percent sulfur content and to use 0.5 percent sulfur fuel instead. Cleaner fuel, however, is 30 to 60 percent more expensive, costing the industry an extra $30 billion a year. The UN is also considering speed limits for shipping to reduce carbon emissions further.

How are shipping companies responding to these environmental and regulatory challenges? New technology is part of the solution. Carnival Cruise Line (a subsidiary of Carnival Corporation), founded in 1972 and based in Florida, is the world's largest international cruise ship line. Carnival operates 26 ships, with 35,000 employees, carrying 5 million passengers a year. The company is introducing a new air lubrication system that creates a layer of bubbles between the ship and the water, reducing drag, increasing fuel efficiency, and saving up to $1 million a year per ship. Other approaches that Carnival is adopting include scrubbers to cut pollution, sleeker ship designs to reduce drag further, and cleaner alternative fuels such as liquid natural gas.

The maritime industry has a poor environmental record. Carnival was fined $40 million in 2016 for discharging plastic and food waste into the ocean and dumping "grey" wastewater from showers and kitchens. In front of a U.S. district judge in June 2019, Carnival chief executive Arnold Donald said, "The company pleads guilty. We acknowledge the shortcomings. I am here today to formulate a plan to fix them." The plan included audits to spot violations, improved staff training, better waste management systems, and more effective pollution incident reporting. Reinforcing Carnival's commitment to reducing the company's environmental impact, vice president for marine technology, Mike Kaczmarek simply says, "Our ships have to be in compliance" (Alsever, 2019, p. 38). The organizational changes that are required to ensure compliance, however, are not so simple.

The damage from climate change could cost the insurance industry billions of dollars. Global losses from human-made and natural catastrophes ("nat-cats") and disasters are rising, reaching their highest ever level in 2017 due to hurricanes, thunderstorms, wildfires, and flooding; total global economic losses that year were $337 billion, and over 11,000 lives were lost (Bevere et al., 2018). Most insurance payouts in 2018 were related to nat-cats in North America. Hurricane Dorian, which hit the Bahamas in August 2019, was expected to cost insurers between $1.5 billion and $3 billion (Ball, 2019).

The insurance sector is in the front line of addressing the impact of climate change on society and on business. How is the sector responding? Swiss Re, based in Zurich, is the world's largest reinsurance company (selling policies to other insurance companies that want to protect themselves from large claims). As extreme weather events have become more unpredictable and damaging, assessing the risks for insurance purposes has become more difficult. In a world that is getting warmer, there are two main categories of business risk. The first is *transition risk*, concerning the possibility of sunk investments losing value as regulations concerning carbon emissions become more strict. This could apply, for example, to coal mines, oil fields, and conventional car plants, which could become "stranded assets." The second category is *physical risk*; higher temperatures are leading to more intense storms, rising sea levels, and wildfires, all of which can destroy valuable assets.

Swiss Re is dealing with these issues in two ways. The first, and more problematic, concerns the development of more sophisticated approaches to disaster-modelling and risk assessment. The traditional method of extrapolating from the past is less helpful as weather events become more extreme, and what used to be "normal" no longer applies. One confident prediction is that climate change will produce a future very different from the past. The second approach is to stop insuring businesses that mine or burn coal, much to the annoyance of companies in those sectors, and to shift assets to low-carbon areas. Other insurance and reinsurance companies have taken similar steps: Allianz, Munich Re, AXA, SCOR, Chubb.

Climate campaigners are of course delighted by these responses. The aim at Swiss Re is to have a carbon-neutral investment portfolio and insurance book by 2050. Poland still generates 80 percent of its electricity from coal. A Polish anti-coal activist, Kuba Gogolewski, is quoted as saying, "When you look at where climate change can be tackled, it's actually reinsurance—and reinsurance in the most-developed countries—where we have the most leverage" (Ball, 2019, p. 130). Reinsurance may thus be instrumental in persuading other sectors and organizations to "go green," if the alternative is to go without insurance.

BlackRock and Climate Change

BlackRock is the world's largest asset management firm, with $7 trillion in investments. As a result, chief executive Laurence Fink's annual letter to the CEOs of the world's largest companies gets a lot of attention. In his 2020 letter, he said:

The evidence on climate risk is compelling investors to reassess core assumptions about modern finance.

Even if only a fraction of the science is right today, this is a much more structural, long-term crisis.

BlackRock would begin to remove itself from investments that "present a high sustainability-related risk.

Commenting on Fink's letter, *New York Times* journalist Andrew Sorkin said, "BlackRock's decision may

(Continued)

give CEOs license to change their own companies' strategy and focus more on sustainability. Such a shift could also provide cover for banks and other financial institutions that finance carbon-emitting businesses to change their own policies" (Sorkin, 2020).

Find on *YouTube,* 'BlackRock CEO Fink sees climate change becoming an investment risk' (2020, 3:28 minutes).

Changing Expectations of Work

The relationships between society in general and employees, on the one hand, and employing organizations on the other, is also changing. Society expects organizations to operate ethically and to consider the environment; corporate social responsibility has become a given. Employees are increasingly looking for meaningful work that serves a wider social purpose and expect their voices to be heard, particularly with regard to how work is performed (through autonomous teams, for example). Jack (2019) notes that MBA candidates now expect to combine profit with a higher purpose, with social impact, to make a difference. Business schools are combining traditional subjects with classes focusing on environmental, social, and governance (ESG) concerns; impact investing; and sustainable finance. Flexible modes of work, including remote working, that allow better work–life balance are also becoming increasingly popular, as are freelancing and labor-sharing platforms (Fuller et al., 2019). Skills shortages encourage the employment of older workers.

Makeover at Estée Lauder

The Context

Founded in 1946 and based in New York, Estée Lauder is a multinational cosmetics company, making skin care, makeup, perfume, and hair care products. It includes several well-known brands including Aramis, Aveda, Bobbi Brown, Clinique, DKNY, Jo Malone, Smashbox, and Tommy Hilfiger.

The Problem

When Estée Lauder's president and chief executive, Fabrizio Freda, joined the company in 2008, the brand was dated and the company's market value was shrinking. The company had a traditionally older customer base, and sales revenue was falling. How should the company respond to these demographic trends?

The Solution

One of Freda's first challenges was to persuade younger customers to buy Estée Lauder products. Millennials were a key target customer group, because they buy more cosmetic products than their parents, but they are not loyal to particular brands. Freda made a number of changes:

- The company continued its strategy of brand acquisitions—including Smashbox, Becca, and Too Faced—to broaden customer appeal and reduce the traditional dependence on skin care.

- Online sales were introduced to complement the traditional focus on department stores.

- Selling to Asia and Latin America reduced the company's dependence on the U.S. market.

- Freda set up a five-person in-house team called The Compass, to forecast beauty industry trends 10 years ahead. This group's forecasts have been accurate, including predicting the growth in demand for new "instant results" skin care products.

- He hired more millennials, who now make up 67 percent of the workforce.

- He set up a "reverse mentoring" scheme, pairing senior leaders with younger colleagues. Freda's own mentor taught him how to use Facebook, and "She shows me what's new on Instagram or YouTube or the new retail model that she would shop in. Most importantly, I learn what's cool."

The Outcomes

Freda exploited the crisis to weaken resistance to the changes that he felt were necessary. By 2018, the company's market value had risen eight-fold, from $6.6 billion to $53 billion, and the share price had tripled since 2007—outperforming the share price of their French rival L'Oréal by 165 percent. These changes were made during and after the global financial crisis of 2008. Freda commented, "You should never let a big crisis pass without taking advantage of doing all the changes, because during a normal period it's less clear to the people why they have to change, and there is more resistance" (based on Daneshkhu, 2018).

Find on *YouTube,* '6 core values at Estée Lauder companies via Fabrizio Freda' (2017, 16 minutes)

Organizations that do not respond to these expectations may have problems recruiting staff and may experience higher staff turnover. Meeting these expectations, however, is not necessarily damaging for the organization. Increasing flexibility and autonomy can increase work motivation and performance. In other words, "problems" with employee expectations may encourage management to implement changes to work design and employment conditions that they should consider making anyway.

Demographic Trends

From a change management perspective, demographic trends pose interesting new challenges for management in the twenty-first century. Life expectancy is rising, and the population is ageing. This is a global phenomenon, affecting most countries, apart from sub-Saharan Africa. At the same time, birth rates are falling. With fewer young people looking for work, organizations will need to find ways to encourage older workers to stay in what is becoming an age-diverse workforce. Other demographic trends include global migration, triggered in part by wars and famine, and improved communications and transport. Migration not only creates social and political tensions but also contributes to a richer ethnic, cultural, and religious mix in a given workforce. Migrants can of course help to address the labor and skill shortages created by an ageing population. There is now a premium on the ability to manage this diversity of generational and cultural values, needs, and preferences.

Population statistics paint a consistent picture:

- Around half of all the human beings who have ever been over 65 are alive today, and by 2035, over 1.1 billion people—13 percent of the world's population—will be over 65.
- For most of human history, those over 65 have not exceeded 3 or 4 percent of the population. In developed economies, those over 65 now make up about 15 percent of the population. This will reach 25 percent on average by 2050, and 40 percent in Korea and Singapore.
- In the United States, the old-age dependency ratio—the proportion of those aged 65 and over as a percentage of the labor force—was 24 percent in 2019. In the United Kingdom, it was 29 percent. In Japan, it was 50 percent and is forecast to rise to 79 percent by 2050 (Chand and Tung, 2014).

An ageing population has social and organizational consequences. The generation born after the Second World War have been celebrating their 60th birthdays and considering retirement, since around 2006. But not everybody retires at 60 or 65; many of those who do then "unretire," and go back to full- or part-time work. Organizations will have to learn how to manage them. Will older workers adapt to new technologies and take orders from youngsters? These are new problems, and there is little experience on which to draw. If you are going to live to be 100, as more of us are doing, then you have one-third of your life left if you retire at 65 (Gratton and Scott, 2016; 2017). Changes to human resource policies and working practices will be required to deal with these trends.

What management issues does an ageing workforce create? Let's start with the negative stereotype. Older workers are seen as expensive, poor performers, less motivated, lacking technology skills, with a limited ability to learn, and resistant to change. Age discrimination is thus widespread, discouraging organizations from recruiting and developing older workers. Another problem is that younger managers find it difficult to manage older, more experienced colleagues (Kunze and Menges, 2017).

Research shows that the negative stereotype is false and that the business case for employing older workers—the unretired—is strong. In comparison with younger colleagues, older workers tend to be better, or at least equally good, in the following areas (Marvell and Cox, 2016, pp. 8–9):

- practical skills and knowledge, experience, insights, judgment
- eagerness to share their expertise with and to mentor others
- communication skills
- problem-solving ability, handling difficult situations
- engagement, commitment, reliability, lower turnover
- understanding the needs of older customers or clients
- contributing to age-diverse teams, combining perspectives, encouraging innovation

Unretirement Is Popular

As life expectancy increases, more people are deciding to "unretire"—to carry on working after the traditional retirement age of 65. According to the U.S. Census Bureau and Bureau of Labor Statistics, the number of retirement-age Americans still in the labor force doubled between 1985 and 2019 (Wasik, 2019). Around 20 percent of Americans who are 65 or older—10.6 million people—are either working or are looking for work; 78 percent in that age group and looking for work report being in good health—up from 69 percent in 1985. A survey of 2,500 UK employees found that 52 percent were planning to carry on working after they had retired from their primary employment (Brown, 2019). In addition, 45 percent planned to work past the age of 70, and 10 percent planned to work into their 80s. Motives for unretirement vary. Many find work fulfilling and rewarding, and others may need the extra income. Most simply want to avoid a "cliff-edge" retirement.

Catering to the needs of older workers can benefit organizations facing skill shortages as fewer young people join the workforce. Older workers are not interested in pursuing a career, so they are not looking for "fast-track" positions. Organizations need to consider changing their human resource management policies relating to older workers by introducing more part-time positions, flexible working, bridge jobs, and phased retirement.

From their research with employees and managers, Zheltoukhova and Baczor (2016, p. 13) found that older workers (55+), due to their accumulated experience and skills, were seen as the most talented and employable of all underrepresented groups in the workforce:

> Older workers were seen to have a more positive attitude to work, but lower potential to develop, compared with young people. They were also rated the highest on their ability to hit the ground running, levels of relevant experience and skills, and being highly networked and connected.

With regard to resistance to change, a study of 3,000 workers in 93 companies in Germany found that older employees were *less* resistant than their younger colleagues (Kunze et al., 2013). This may be because older workers have better strategies for coping with and adapting to changing environments.

Older employees may have motives for working that are different from those of younger generations. It has been suggested that the unretired return to work for many reasons: money, stimulation, intellectual challenge, meaning, to continue adding value, and social contact. But most of us want these outcomes. One motive that does distinguish older workers is the desire for flexible working, to allow them to care for elderly parents and grandchildren, and in some cases to manage their own health.

There are several low-cost approaches to attracting and retaining the skills and knowledge of older workers (Chartered Institute for Personanel and Development, 2016):

- Conduct workforce planning and age-diversity monitoring.
- Build an age-diverse culture that values all age groups, with inclusive recruitment.
- Support employee health and well-being; some older workers have long-term health conditions.
- Help employees to balance work and caring responsibilities.
- Allow more flexibility in working time.
- Provide training and development based on potential, not on age.
- Tailor the retirement process to individual needs, e.g., phased retirement.
- Tailor job roles to suit individual needs and expectations.
- Train line managers to deal with the needs of an age-diverse workforce.

Increasing life expectancy also contributes to a multigenerational workforce. Table 3.2 shows the makeup of this workforce, from Veterans to Generation Z (included for completeness, Alphas are too young to work). It is possible to find all five working generations in the same organization. The point is that each generation seems to have its own approach to work. In this discussion, we will overlook Veterans, because their numbers are now low.

Any differences between the generations are likely to have been shaped by social context—the defining events and conditions to which we are exposed and which shape our attitudes, core beliefs, and work values. When Baby Boomers were born, for example, there were no televisions or mobile phones. In contrast, Gen Z have never known a world without touch-sensitive screens and the Internet. Traditionally, management policies and practices have been applied consistently to all employees. With an age-diverse workforce,

TABLE 3.2
The Six Generations*

Veterans, born 1925 to 1942; also known as the silent generation, matures, traditionalists

Baby Boomers, 1946 to 1964; also just called Boomers

Generation X, 1965 to 1979, also known as post Boomers, baby busters

Generation Y, 1980 to 1994; also known as millennials, nexters, echo Boomers

Generation Z, 1995 to 2010/2015; also known as Gen C—connected, communicating, clicking

Generation Alpha, 2010 to present; the first generation to all be born in this century, surrounded by technology

*Note: These dates are approximate; there is disagreement over the precise years separating the different generations.

that consistency may no longer be appropriate. The evidence is mixed, but there may be differences in approach to work across the generations:

- *Baby Boomers.* They are now retiring, but many are still active members of the workforce. They are said to value high-quality colleagues, intellectual stimulation, autonomy, flexibility, new experiences and challenges, giving something back, and recognition (Hewlett et al., 2009).

- *Generation X.* Now in their 40s and 50s, they will not begin to retire until around 2030. They play a major role in the workforce and have had a significant impact on today's social and technological climate. They are seen as ambitious, strategic, autonomous, persuasive, people-oriented, socially confident, and drivers for change (Hudson Consulting, 2014, p. 11).

- *Generation Y.* Also known as millennials, by 2025 they will comprise 75 percent of the global workforce. A study by Deloitte, a management consultancy, found that their main reasons for choosing to work for an organization included work–life balance, flexibility (which is more important than pay), sense of meaning and purpose, professional development, and impact on society and the environment. They are also independent and resist micromanagement, comfortable with technology and social networks, open-minded, multiculturally aware, and ethical (Groom, 2016). However, they can have a strong sense of entitlement, poor interpersonal and decision-making skills, and a weak work ethic, and can appear overconfident (Chartered Management Institute, 2014).

- *Generation Z.* Now making up over 40 percent of the population of America and Europe, Gen Z was born between 1995 and 2010/15 (Francis and Hoefel, 2018). As they are computerized, connected, communicating, content-centric, community-oriented, and always clicking, they have also been called Gen C. This is the first generation to have grown up with the Internet, social media, and mobile computing, for whom 24/7 mobile and Internet connectivity are taken for granted and for whom freedom of expression is the norm. These technologies encourage flexible forms of working and less hierarchical organizations and blur the boundaries between work and personal life. As personal relationships rely on social networks, blogs, and messaging platforms, this creates fast-moving business and political pressures as information and ideas spread quickly.

Technology and teamwork are particularly important to Gen Z, who bring their own devices (smartphones, tablets) to work rather than use clumsy corporate resources. This means more work can be done by virtual project groups, with fewer face-to-face meetings and less frequent travel (Calnan, 2017). Organizations will have to change working conditions and practices to accommodate those preferences and to exploit the opportunities.

In the context of managing organizational change, the contributions of vision (chapter 6) and communications (chapter 7) are central to engaging commitment and motivation. Human resource management policies will need to emphasize teamwork, collaboration, flexible working, flexible retirement, project work, short-term assignments, support for external causes, and eco-friendly work environments. Another valuable practice may involve intergenerational mentoring; Boomers welcome the chance to mentor Gen Ys, who can share their better understanding of social networking. There is also evidence to suggest that age-diverse teams have higher levels of satisfaction and performance (see the box "McDonald's Happy Teams").

McDonald's Happy Teams

Having many generations in the same workforce may be beneficial. Research by the fast-food chain McDonald's UK found that employees in age-diverse teams had higher job satisfaction and performed better. McDonald's surveyed 32,000 staff members and found that multigenerational teams were 10 percent happier than those working in their peer group. A survey of 1,000 customers found that over 80 percent liked to see a mix of ages in a restaurant team, because it improved the atmosphere. Older workers deliver better service and mentor younger staff. Levels of customer service were 20 percent higher in restaurants with staff aged 60 and over.

Claire Hall, McDonald's UK chief people officer, said, "Teams that bring a mix of people of different ages and at different life stages are fundamental to creating a happy and motivated workplace and to delivering a great customer experience." The age range of staff at McDonald's in the United Kingdom is an incredible 75 years—from 16 to 91.

Case Sources

Based on Clarke (2016).

https://workplaceinsight.net/bridging-the-generation-gap-is-the-key-to-a-happier-workforce/.

Technology

Changing Jobs

The world of work faces an epochal transition. By 2030, according to a recent McKinsey Global Institute report, as many as 375 million workers—or roughly 14 per cent of the global workforce—may need to switch occupational categories as digitization, automation, and advances in artificial intelligence (AI) disrupt the world of work. The kinds of skills companies require will shift, with profound implications for the career paths individuals will need to pursue. (Illanes et al., 2018, p. 1)

The Harvard Business School Project on Managing the Future of Work identified several forces driving organizational change (Fuller et al., 2019). The most significant of these is new technology:

- Robotics and automated systems that replace human labor
- Artificially intelligent systems that augment human capabilities
- Rapid technology-based shifts in customer preferences that create new business models and ways of working (Airbnb, Netflix, Spotify, Taskrabbit, Uber)
- Monetizing free web services and underused assets such as personal consumption data

This study also found that employees are more open to change, retraining, and new opportunities—and are more adaptive and optimistic—than management believe they are (Fuller et al., 2019, p. 122).

Technology will drive organizational change for the foreseeable future, affecting corporate strategy, the organization of work, working practices, and the design of jobs and tasks. Technology has also encouraged the creation of new models of employment based on remote working and virtual teaming, freelancing through online labor exchange platforms, and temporary "gigging" where employers and employees find each other online. There are few sectors, and few organizations, that will not be affected by robotics, automation, artificial intelligence, and other related technology developments. The pace of innovation is such that there is probably more change and disruption to come.

Even technology giants such as Facebook are under pressure to change. As Lev-Ram (2019b, p. 48) notes, "On the way to building an empire worth half a trillion dollars, [Mark Zuckerberg] and his company have connected friends old and new, but they have also inadvertently found themselves in the middle of controversies from hate speech to data breaches." As a result, Facebook may have to change aspects of how it does business, including how it manages content, to balance free expression and safety and to improve data privacy. According to Zuckerberg, Facebook "is moving from a reactive model of how we're handling this stuff to one where we are building systems to get out ahead." Lev-Ram (2019b, p. 48) comments, "Facebook may be changing, but it aims to preserve what it's got until it figures out a way to replace the business too much change would jeopardise."

Although new technologies will create new opportunities and benefits for organizations, employees, and consumers, there are at least four concerns. The first is that new technologies will create mass unemployment. Those in routine office jobs and manufacturing were traditionally under threat, but artificial intelligence has now moved into the domain of knowledge workers: accountants, doctors, lawyers, and managers. The second is that changes to the nature of work will create a two-tier workforce, divided between a skilled and well-paid elite, on the one hand, and unskilled, poorly paid employees who perform boring, routine, manual or "screen sitting" tasks that are either difficult or uneconomical to automate. The third concerns the risk of exploitation facing self-employed gigging workers. The fourth concerns a potential increase in cybercrime as computerization becomes more pervasive.

These are social problems, but they affect individual organizations. Unemployment and inequality can generate resistance to change and conflict. The perceived exploitation of employees can damage an organization's reputation and make recruitment harder. All organizations are exposed to "insider" attacks carried out by disgruntled employees. The concerns about new technology thus have to be addressed at an organizational level as well as at a national level.

It is difficult to overestimate the scale of the changes to the nature of work that technology will generate. Work can be classified as routine (repetitive) or nonroutine (varied, requiring flexibility). The latter are more difficult to codify because of the many exceptions. Work can also be classified in terms of whether manual (physical) or cognitive (intellectual) capabilities are more important. Traditionally, routine physical work has been more readily automated. However, Frey and Osborne (2017) note that many nonroutine manual and cognitive tasks can now be computerized, including equipment maintenance, quality screening vegetables, hospital surgery, driving a car in city traffic, deciphering poor handwriting, financial trading, fraud detection, and medical diagnostics.

Robots were traditionally used for routine manufacturing. We now have humanoid robots that walk on two legs, mobile robots that shuttle pallets around warehouses, and autonomous vehicles. The common feature of these developments is mobility, thanks to advances in hardware (sensors and materials), software, and large data sets or "big data." Moving around and working alongside humans, cobots—collaborative robots—handle jobs that used to need human dexterity and eyesight. Cobots can do things that humans find physically difficult or unpleasant. They are light and easy to move between tasks and do not require specialist programming skills. They can be used by smaller organizations, which could not afford expensive traditional robots. Given their capabilities, cobots can help organizations to retain older workers. Research by MIT and BMW found that robot–human teams were 85 percent more productive than either working alone (Hollinger, 2016). This does not mean that robot applications are without problems (see the box "Robots Not Welcome Here").

Robots Not Welcome Here

Robots may not always deliver the benefits they promise. Fletcher (2018) describes the experience of an animal charity in San Francisco that had security problems with break-ins, vandalism, and local drug users who made staff and visitors feel unsafe. They employed a 1.5-meter-tall Knightscope security robot. The robot patrolled nearby car parks and alleyways, taking video recordings and saying "hello" to passersby. However, it was accused of harassing homeless people. Calls for retribution appeared on social media, and the charity suffered more vandalism. The Knightscope was regularly tipped over, covered by a tarpaulin, and smeared with barbecue sauce (and worse). Other robots have been tripped up by angry office workers, and a robot in another city in America accidentally knocked over a toddler.

Robots with artificial intelligence routinely provide care for children and the elderly; they work in hospitals, perform surgery, deliver customer care, and play a range of analytical roles in offices. But Fletcher sees the spread of workplace robots as a major challenge:

> How far are we willing to—or should we at all—let robots into the workplace? What kinds of roles are acceptable and which are not? Most importantly, who sets the rules for how they behave, and how they decide on priorities when interacting with people?

Will knowledge workers be replaced by machines, like manual workers before them? Not necessarily. Artificial intelligence (AI) can be used to automate jobs and replace people. But intelligence augmentation (IA) systems do not replace individual expertise and enable us to work faster and more effectively. This means that knowledge workers have more time to deal with interesting, complex, and challenging tasks, making them more productive. For example, automated decision support for air traffic controllers increases their accuracy and performance. A study of an automated dispensing system in a hospital found that this reduced the amount of time pharmacists spent in the dispensary and allowed them to spend more time with patients on wards (Hislop et al., 2017). IA systems are also used to aid medical diagnosis and by law firms to search documents for litigation and due diligence purposes.

Two main developments are reshaping AI today. The first is machine learning, which involves "training" algorithms how to operate using existing data. Machine learning programs use pattern recognition to create generalized rules that make sense of future inputs. Advanced machine learning systems, given enough data, can teach themselves and improve their own performance. The second development is deep learning, which uses layers of pattern recognition based on complex neural networks that are designed to simulate our brain functions. A study at King's College London found that deep learning methods more than doubled the accuracy of brain age assessments when using data from MRI scans (Dellot and Wallace-Stephens, 2017, p. 20).

Why should organizations invest in artificial intelligence? A survey of 250 executives identified the business benefits, shown in table 3.3 (Davenport and Ronanki, 2018, p. 112).

TABLE 3.3
Business Benefits of Artificial Intelligence

Benefits	% of Executives Citing as AI Benefit
Enhance features, functions, and performance of products	51
Optimize internal business operations	36
Free up workers to be more creative by automating tasks	36
Make better decisions	35
Create new products	32
Optimize external processes like marketing and sales	30
Pursue new markets	25
Capture and apply scarce knowledge where needed	25
Reduce head count through automation	22

The main objective was to make existing products better. Only 22 percent mentioned reducing head count, but 36 percent mentioned freeing up workers to be more creative. The same survey found a number of challenges facing companies seeking to develop AI:

- problems integrating AI with existing processes and systems
- expensive technologies and expertise
- lack of management understanding of AI and how it works
- lack of people with appropriate expertise
- technology that has been "oversold"

AI Everywhere

Johnson & Johnson, a consumer-goods firm, and Accenture, a consultancy, use AI to sort through job applications and pick the best candidates. AI helps Caesars, a casino and hotel group, guess customers' likely spending and offer personalized promotions to draw them in. Bloomberg, a media and financial information firm, uses AI to scan companies' earnings releases and automatically generate news articles. Vodafone, a mobile operator, can predict problems with its network and with users' devices before they arise. Companies in every industry use AI to monitor cybersecurity threats and other risks, such as disgruntled employees. (Bass, 2018, p. 3)

Will robots, automation, and smart machines generate mass unemployment? Frey and Osborne (2017) made headlines by predicting that around 47 percent of employment in the United States would be at risk over the coming decade. This estimate was based on an analysis of the "automation potential" of over 700 occupations. Those with low scores were mainly in healthcare, education, and creative roles, such as recreational therapists, dieticians, choreographers, surgeons, school teachers, and set designers. Occupations with a middling score included dental assistants, embalmers, shoe and leather workers, commercial pilots, teacher assistants, advertising sales agents, and computer programmers. Occupations with a high automation potential included insurance underwriters, watch repairers, cargo and freight agents, umpires and referees, legal secretaries, real estate brokers, and telemarketers.

An approach based on automation potential overlooks three sets of complicating factors. The first is that the net effect on employment depends on opposing processes—replacement effects and compensatory mechanisms. New technologies create unemployment by substituting equipment for people, such as self-service checkouts in supermarkets. However, compensatory mechanisms also come into play—processes that lead to the creation of new products, services, and jobs or that delay or reduce replacement effects. In the past, those who have been replaced by technology have (sooner or later) found work in other sectors, supplying the new products and services generated by new technologies. It was predicted in the 1980s that automation would lead to redundancies, and we would have to worry about how to use our new leisure time. The economist John Maynard Keynes made a similar prediction in the 1930s. These predictions have never come true.

Computerizing Lego

Lego, the profitable (and privately owned) Danish toy manufacturer, famous for its colored bricks, is not immune from computerization. The company's traditional business model is simple, transforming plastic that costs $1 a kilo into Lego box sets that sell for $75 a kilo. However, children increasingly play games on iPads and smartphones, and Lego's sales growth slowed after 2010. How can an organization like Lego compete in the evolving digital world?

Lego's first experiment with the online game *Lego Universe* was not successful. They then developed a partnership with a Swedish company, Mojang, which designed *Minecraft*, a popular computer game based on virtual landscapes resembling Lego building blocks. Lego sold sets based on the game. Lego partnered with TT Games to develop video games based on Lego set themes such as *Star Wars* and *Legends of Chima*. The Lego Movie (Warner Bros, 2014) generated $500 million on release. In partnership with Google, *The Lego Movie* was accompanied by a video game, new construction sets (the Sea Cow pirate ship, and the hero Emmet Brickowski), and a website (www.buildwithchrome.com). The movie sequel appeared in 2017. Another innovation was *Lego Fusion*. Items built with Lego bricks are captured using a smartphone or tablet, which imports them into a 3D digital online world where users can play using their own designs. Lego was one of the most-watched brands on YouTube. The bricks and physical play are important, but Lego's chief executive, Jørgen Vig Knudstorp, said, "I see digital as an extra experience layer" (Milne, 2014). With record sales and earnings, Lego became the world's most popular and most profitable toymaker in 2015; it is estimated that, on average, every person on earth owns 102 Lego bricks (Milne, 2015).

There are many compensatory mechanisms. New products and services need new infrastructure (factories, offices, distribution chains), which create jobs in those areas. The reduced costs from technological innovation lead to lower prices, which increase demand for other goods and services—creating more jobs. New technologies are not always implemented rapidly; it takes time to solve technical and organizational problems, and scrapping existing facilities can be costly. The benefits of new technologies may not at first be clear, and organizations often experiment with and introduce new systems gradually, to hedge the risks. Investment in new technologies is based on the expectation that the organization's market will expand, in which case the existing workforce may be retained, if not increased. Finally, new technologies do not always live up to their promise and may not be able to do everything that the "old" technology could do. This explains why many homes still have traditional landlines, and there is still a demand for vinyl records, compact discs, printed books, and radios. Autonomous vehicles could replace truck drivers. But it will take time to replace the fleet of conventional trucks, and the self-driving kind will still have to be loaded, programmed with their destinations, unloaded, cleaned, maintained, and serviced. They will also have to be manufactured, advertised, and distributed to dealerships and customers in the first place.

A second complicating factor is that automation does not always take over whole jobs; it performs individual tasks. Most jobs are made up from bundles of different tasks. It may not be possible to automate an entire job, but some tasks could be done (and done better) by machine. However, few will complain if automation does the work that is dangerous, boring, or strenuous, leaving more time for the more interesting, challenging, value-creating activities.

There is a third set of complicating factors. Many jobs (or tasks) may not be automated even though that would be possible. The nature of the task is critical. Most customers want to talk to a human being when they ask a call center for help, and how many of us will fly in an automated aircraft with no pilot? The cost of labor is important: It may be cheaper to pay people to clean your home than to buy a robot. Power relations can also stop or delay change: Trade unions and powerful professional groups can resist the implementation of new technologies that adversely affect their members.

Automation Anxiety and a Workless Future?

Our findings suggest that, while a significant proportion of jobs could be fully displaced by new machines (15 per cent of private sector jobs over the next 10 years, according to our YouGov poll), grim predictions of mass automation and widespread economic strife do not stand up to scrutiny. Machines are still incapable of performing many tasks, and very few can comprehensively automate whole jobs. Occupations are more likely to evolve than be eliminated, and new ones will emerge in the long run. Low-skilled workers will probably face the greatest disruption, but sectors vary significantly in their automation potential and we are likely to see a continued growth in human-centric roles in health care, social care and education. (Dellot and Wallace-Stephens, 2017, p. 42)

The impact of new technology thus depends on the interplay between replacement effects and compensatory mechanisms, on the extent to which tasks can be automated, and on other factors that can discourage or delay computerization. Compensation effects have ensured in the past that computerization has created more jobs than have been replaced. But with so many clever new technologies, is the balance between replacement and compensation changing? Technology may be developing so rapidly that those who are displaced may not be able to "reskill" themselves fast enough. New technology has created many new business models. Banks, taxi drivers, camera makers, music and book publishers, and universities—among others—have seen their traditional business models undermined by faster-moving and cheaper competitors whose products and services are more appealing to Internet-savvy consumers.

Where Have the People Gone?

Nike uses advanced automation to make Flyknit Racer trainers. These are made with a special knitting machine and use less labor and fewer materials than most running shoes; automation can halve labor costs and cut material costs by a fifth. Nike plans to use more automation and is experimenting with laser cutting and automated gluing in its factory in Mexico. Nike employs almost half a million people making footwear in 15 countries and takes pride in being an ethical and sustainable business.

What impact will automation have on the workforce? Growing sales will allow Nike to automate further while keeping its current employees. The main motive for automating production is not cost cutting, but the need to adapt the company's products to meet changing consumer tastes. Shoe manufacturing is complex, involving around 200 pieces (across 10 sizes), which traditionally were cut and glued manually. Lead times for new products could run to several months. With automation, Nike can get a new trainer to market in three or four weeks. If the company continues to grow, jobs will be created and not lost (Bissell-Linsk, 2017). For similar reasons, Mercedes-Benz replaced robots with humans on some production lines, because the machines were not agile enough to keep up with demand for customized products (Hollinger, 2016).

Lund et al. (2019) conclude that although we are seeing major workforce transformations, job displacement and job creation will go hand in hand, with growth in demand for labor in some areas:

> The future of work is not just about how many jobs could be lost and gained. Technology is altering the day-to-day mix of activities associated with more and more jobs over time. The occupational mix of the economy is changing, and the demand for skills is changing along with it. Employers will need to manage large-scale workforce transformations that could involve redefining business processes and workforce needs, retraining and moving some people into new roles, and creating programs for continuous learning. This could be an opportunity to upgrade jobs and make them more rewarding. The choices that employers make will ripple through the communities in which they operate. (Lund et al., 2019, p. 1)

Lund et al. (2019, p. 9) also argue that the main effects of automation will be to augment human capabilities: "As machines perform some tasks, the time that is freed up can be reallocated into different, and often higher-value, activities. More workers will need to work side by side with machines and use them to become more productive."

These trends will not lead to widespread deskilling. As technology becomes more sophisticated, the need for formal education and technical knowledge and skills will increase. Fuller et al. (2019) predict a shortage of workers with the skills required to work effectively in rapidly evolving jobs. Frey and Osborne (2017) identify three bottlenecks that will prevent or at least delay further computerization: the problems that computer systems have with complex perceptual and manipulation tasks, social intelligence tasks, and creative intelligence tasks. Frey et al. (2016, pp. 51–52) identify 10 skills that will continue to be important and in demand despite the increasing computerization of work:

1. sensemaking—understanding the deeper meaning of what is being expressed
2. social intelligence—understanding others and the effect you have on them
3. novel and adapting thinking—taking creative approaches to new situations
4. cross-cultural competency—understanding different cultural norms and expectations
5. computational thinking—especially the ability to apply machine learning methods creatively
6. new media literacy—understanding how to use mobile, multimedia, online information
7. transdisciplinarity—understanding concepts across several different disciplines
8. design mindset—able to develop tasks and processes to achieve desired outcomes
9. cognitive load management—ability to decide which information is important
10. virtual collaboration—the ability to work effectively as a member of a virtual team.

The work of chief executives and other senior managers requires a high degree of social intelligence as they deal with senior colleagues and other officials to discuss future plans and strategies, coordinate activities, resolve problems, and negotiate and approve contracts and agreements. Consequently, most (but not all) management, business, and finance occupations where social intelligence is necessary face a low risk of being affected by computerization, as with many jobs in education, healthcare, the arts, and media. Engineering and science occupations where creative intelligence is required are also low risk. Lawyers are low risk, but paralegals and legal assistants are high risk. In general, high skill–high wage occupations are least susceptible to computerization.

In summary, robotics, automation, and AI are likely to create a mix of bad news and good news, but the good news will probably outweigh the bad (Lawrence et al., 2017; Wisskirchen et al., 2017).

The bad news is:

- AI and robotics will transform many jobs and destroy others in the short term.
- Employees in jobs that require low to medium skill and qualifications will be most affected.
- Those who are displaced may lack sufficient training and may not readily find other work.
- Income inequality between those in "lovely" and "lousy" jobs could lead to social conflict.

The good news is:

- New technologies will create new organizational opportunities and new jobs.
- Sudden mass redundancies are unlikely.
- Time saved with the use of intelligent IT systems will reduce production costs.
- New technologies will take over dangerous, monotonous tasks.
- AI and robotics free up time for employees to do more interesting and valuable work.
- Older employees and those with disabilities can be better integrated.
- New job models will encourage the creation of personalized working conditions.
- Employees will supervise rather than participate in production.
- AI and robotics will contribute to a growth in prosperity.

The change management implications are therefore:

- Recognize that employees may be more open to change than you think.
- New technology can support demands for more flexible, autonomous working.
- Employee engagement in the change process will maximize benefits and counter resistance.
- Training is vital to meet demand for experienced, skilled personnel with technical knowledge.
- Reskilling, upskilling, and continuous learning are a human resources policy imperative.
- Avoid creating a two-tier workforce that could generate resentment and resistance to change.

Lund et al. (2019, p. 14) conclude:

To take full advantage of what automation technologies can do for innovation and productivity, employers will need to rethink business processes and workflows—all of which may require large-scale workforce transformations. Several factors will shape their decisions: the state of their current digital initiatives, the share of current work that machines can handle, whether technology complements existing labor or substitutes for it, the diversity of current roles, the education level of the current workforce, turnover rates, and the customer experience. Large-scale workforce transformation requires vision and adept leadership from the entire management team—and it has implications for the company's overall strategy, operations, talent needs, capital investment, geographic footprint, diversity goals, and external reputation. As the demand for labor shifts across the country, these changes will affect the geography of consumer purchasing power.

Start-ups Also Have to Change—or Pivot

Change is often associated with large, well-established organizations. However, organizations don't have to be large or established for change management to become an issue. Ries (2019) argues that capacity for a specific kind of change—"the pivot"—is a key competence for many start-ups.

A start-up's strategy typically includes "a business model, a product road map, a point of view about partners and competitors, and ideas about who the customer will be" (p. 22). The strategy includes propositions and expectations that may or may not prove to be well-founded. Therefore, a leader has to address the question: "Are we making sufficient progress to believe that our original strategic hypothesis is correct, or do we need to make a major change" (p. 149). In other words, do we stick with the original plan, or "pivot"? A pivot is "a structured course correction designed to test a new fundamental hypothesis about the product, strategy, and engine of growth" (p. 149).

Instagram began as Burbn, an app with a range of functions including identity check, posting of plans, and photo posting and sharing, with comment and like features. However, the founders came to believe that the future lay in simplicity. They decided to focus on just the most popular feature, photo posting, and rebranded the app as Instagram. Twitter began as Odeo, a platform for discovering and subscribing to podcasts. However, when Apple announced that iTunes would include a podcasting platform, Odeo pivoted to become "a microblogging platform where contacts could share and read one another's status updates in real-time" and was rebranded as Twitter (*CB Insights*, 2018).

YouTube began as a dating site that gave people the capacity to upload videos of themselves talking about what they were looking for in a partner. However, following an underwhelming response, its founders pivoted to being a platform onto which people could upload videos of any kind.

Ries (2019, pp. 149–150) concludes, "There is no bigger destroyer of creative potential than the misguided decision to persevere, [and those who] cannot bring themselves to pivot, on the basis of feedback from the marketplace, can get stuck in the land of the living dead, neither growing enough nor dying, consuming resources and commitment from employees and other stakeholders but not moving ahead."

LO 3.3 Why Do Organizations Not Change after Crises?

Why would organizations not implement change following accidents, crises, and disasters, to prevent further similar events? This is a situation in which it might be assumed that change would be welcome, automatic, and straightforward. Expectations and receptiveness should be high, resistance low. The evidence shows, however, that these assumptions are often incorrect. One iconic example is the losses of the NASA space shuttles *Challenger* (1986) and *Columbia* (2003), the causes of which displayed striking similarities (Vaughn, 1996; Columbia Accident Investigation Board, 2003; Mahler and Casamayou, 2009). The NASA shuttle losses were complex incidents, and they have been subjected to exhaustive analysis, but two conclusions are significant. First, although the immediate causes of these disasters were technical (O-ring failure; foam insulation failure), the main contributory causes were organizational: budget pressures, launch program expectations, management style, and subcontractor relationships. Second, there were failures in organizational learning (see Exercise 11.3 in chapter 11). Mahler and Casamayou (2009) offer an interesting analysis of what NASA learned from the *Challenger* disaster, what was not learned from that event, and what was learned but subsequently forgotten—leading ultimately to the *Columbia* disaster.

One of the main reasons for failures to change after extreme events thus concerns organizational learning difficulties. Toft and Reynolds (2005) distinguish between passive learning (identifying lessons) and active learning (implementing changes). Many organizations, it appears, focus on passive learning, but overlook active learning or find that difficult to achieve.

In explaining why organizations do not change following crises, Edmondson (2011, p. 49) notes the effort that goes into after-action reviews, postmortems, and investigations; "time after time I saw that these painstaking efforts led to no real change." The problem, Edmondson argues, is that most managers think that failures are bad (some are) and that learning from these events is straightforward; ask people what went wrong, and tell them to avoid similar mistakes in the future. Both of those views, she argues, are incorrect. Failure is not always bad, and learning from failures is complex; it is almost always necessary to look further than "procedures weren't followed." That involves what she calls "first-order reasoning," or looking at immediate causal factors such as the failed O-ring. She argues that it is also necessary to understand the second- and third-order reasons. That is challenging because complex failures typically involve combinations of many events across different parts of an organization over time. Edmondson (2011, p. 54) advocates the use of multidisciplinary team-based analysis to explore those kinds of issues and offers the following example:

> A team of leading physicists, engineers, aviation experts, naval leaders, and even astronauts devoted months to an analysis of the Columbia disaster. They conclusively established not only the first-order cause—a piece of foam had hit the shuttle's leading edge during launch—but also second-order causes: a rigid hierarchy and schedule-obsessed culture at NASA made it especially difficult for engineers to speak up about anything but the most rock-solid concerns.

Edmondson also argues that organizational failures lie on a continuum, from praiseworthy (innovative experiments that just didn't work) to blameworthy (deliberate sabotage). However, speaking of this continuum (which we will consider again in chapter 11), she notes:

> When I ask executives to consider how many of the failures in their organizations are truly blameworthy, their answers are usually in single digits—perhaps 2% to 5%. But when I ask how many are treated as blameworthy, they say (after a pause or a laugh) 70% to 90%. The unfortunate consequence is that many failures go unreported and their lessons are lost. (Edmondson, 2011, p. 50)

For effective post-incident change, Edmondson (2018) argues, the organization needs a "psychologically safe environment" in which failures can be discussed openly:

1. There must be a shared understanding of the kinds of failures that can occur in a particular context and why openness is important for learning.
2. Those who report failures—the "messengers"—should be praised, rather than shot.

3. Known problems must be acknowledged, and mistakes admitted openly and honestly.

4. To defuse resistance and defensiveness, management must invite participation, seeking ideas and creating opportunities for staff to analyze failures and explore remedies.

5. There must be clarity concerning actions that are blameworthy, so boundaries are clear and people are accountable.

Buchanan (2011; Buchanan and Moore, 2016) argues that explanations for failures in post-incident change also lie in the altered nature of the organizational context. Most commentary focuses on change with *progressive*, developmental agendas: restructuring, quality, process redesign, innovation, new technology, and working practices—aimed at cost reduction, quality, time to market, "agility," customer service, growth, market share, and profitability. Changes following extreme events, in contrast, have *defensive* agendas, which aim to prevent things from happening. Implementing a defensive agenda may be less appealing for the change manager, as the indicator of the success of that agenda is the nonoccurrence of the next event. That may be less exciting than the development of something new (products, systems, business models), which, in career terms, is also likely to be more rewarding. It may be helpful, therefore, in a post-incident context, to design a change agenda that marries progressive and developmental components with defensive, preventive elements.

EXERCISE 3.1

COVID-19 Consequences

LO 3.2

The global pandemic that began in December 2019 was caused by a flu-like zoonotic coronavirus that jumped from animals to humans and appeared to have originated in Wuhan, China. At the time of writing, COVID-19 had a fatality rate around 10 times higher than that of the normal flu and there was no cure or vaccine. As infection rates and deaths climbed, healthcare systems were overwhelmed with patients and a lack of beds, personal protective equipment for hospital staff, and equipment such as ventilators to treat respiratory problems. Doctors and nurses also caught the disease, further reducing hospital capacity.

The main strategy for slowing the spread of the virus was *lockdown*. Countries closed their borders, airlines grounded planes, and cruise ships were not allowed to dock. These measures were stricter in some countries than in others. Typically, the public was told to stay indoors, to go out only for shopping and exercise, and to keep 6 feet "social distance" from others. Shops, offices, construction sites, public houses, and restaurants closed. Factories making food and medical supplies stayed open. Although there were few shortages, shoppers were panic-buying and stockpiling, and queues outside supermarkets became the new norm. The only exceptions to the "stay indoors" rule were key workers, in healthcare, emergency services, and food production and distribution. Those who could not work from home were out of a job and had to depend on employer support (if available) or state aid. Work for many freelancers in the "gig economy" dried up.

What were the implications for organizational change? More people started working from home, if their jobs allowed. Restrictions on travel made videoconferencing popular. Shoppers made more online purchases. Some businesses repurposed their premises: For example, some local bars and restaurants (which were shut) sold groceries and snacks (open for food distribution), and some manufacturers switched to making medical equipment. This raised several questions. Would employees who had become accustomed to working from home want to go back to the office? Would shoppers who had become accustomed to online purchasing and home delivery want to go back to brick-and-mortar stores? Would companies that created new business models go back to their previous ways of working or develop their new approaches?

Your Task

1. Choose an organization whose operations were affected by this pandemic—not necessarily your current employer—or choose an affected sector in which you have an interest.

2. Identify the changes that this organization or sector implemented because of the COVID-19 pandemic, in working practices, customer relationships, and core business models. Which changes were mandatory, and which did it implement on its own initiative?

3. Assess which of these changes were temporary, for the duration of the pandemic, and which would be long lasting.

4. Why is the human resource management function critical in this context?

EXERCISE 3.2

Top Team Role Play

LO 3.4

1. In groups of 3, choose an organizational change with which you are familiar, perhaps in your current employment or in an organization about which you have recently been reading. If neither of those options works, then for the purposes of this exercise, invent an organization and a change initiative.

2. Now revisit table 3.1, "Images of Change and Understanding the Pressures." Each person in your group must choose one of those images of managing change and will play that role.

3. Your group is now in a senior management board meeting. You are discussing an agenda item at the request of the chairperson of your board, who wants to know why the organization is going through the change that you have identified.

4. Debate how you will respond to the chairperson's request, with members of your group (board) playing their role based on the change management image that they have selected.

5. When you have decided how you are going to respond to the chair's request, consider the following questions:

   - Did one of your images better explain the rationale for change than the others, and why?

   - On reflection, what criteria did you use for making this judgment with regard to the comparative advantage of a particular image?

   - Is there an image with which you personally have a particular affinity or preference? Why? What would it take for you to change that preference?

EXERCISE 3.3

Case Analysis— The Netflix Story

LO 3.1

LO 3.2

Organizations change in response to a mix of internal and external factors. As you read this account of change at Netflix, the video streaming service, identify the change drivers affecting this business.

1. What environmental factors are driving change at Netflix?

2. What are the internal drivers of change at Netflix?

3. Netflix faces strong competition from other organizations in its sector. What is your assessment of Netflix's approach to beating the competition?

4. To what extent is the organization culture at Netflix key to its competitive advantage? Given the nature of the competition, what changes to Netflix's culture would be advisable?

The Context

What kind of company is Netflix? The company's cofounder and chief executive, Reed Hastings, wanted to create a unique organizational culture, particularly with regard to employee empowerment:

> I pride myself on making fewer and fewer decisions. Sometimes I can go a whole quarter without making a decision. We're like the anti-Apple. They compartmentalize. We do the opposite. Everyone gets all the information. We encourage employees to figure out how to improve the culture, not how to preserve it. (Schleier, 2019)

Employees at Netflix are paid higher than the industry standard. There is no dress code and no vacation limits. But there is full accountability, transparency, and what Hastings calls radical honesty:

> We want people to speak the truth. We said to disagree silently is disloyal. It's not okay to let a discussion go through without saying your piece.

Netflix is a subscription video on demand (SVOD) company, founded in 1997 by Reed Hastings and Marc Randolph as a DVD-by-mail service, based in California. When content licensing rights became expensive, Netflix had to develop a new business model. This also meant creating its own programs—movies and television series—and delivering them by online streaming. Subscribers enjoyed watching shows that Netflix streamed, such as *Mad Men*, but that show was made by AMC, so it didn't generate brand loyalty. That changed when Netflix invested $100 million in two seasons of *House of Cards,* which was an instant success; people talked about it and associated it with Netflix.

Netflix has 150 million subscribers in 190 countries, with revenues in 2019 of $20.169 billion. The content department employs 400 people worldwide. This success is based on cloud computing that enables seamless video streaming, and data-driven personalization that predicts what viewers want to watch. But Netflix is not a technology company. It is in the entertainment business.

The Problem

Netflix made video streaming entertainment possible and popular. Today, however, Netflix faces competition from other SVOD providers: Amazon Prime (with 100 million subscribers), CBS All Access, Apple TV+, Disney Plus, HBO Max, NBCUniversal, BritBox, Hotstar, Salto, WarnerMedia. Some of those companies—Disney, WarnerMedia, and

NBCUniversal, for example—own the content on which Netflix has relied in the past, such as the television series *Friends* and *The Office*. To keep subscribers happy, Netflix has to replace shows like these with content of similar quality (such as *Seinfeld*, which it licensed from Sony Pictures Television until 2021). Price competition is another issue. A monthly subscription to Apple TV+ is $4.99 and Disney Plus charges $6.99, which includes access to content from Marvel, Lucasfilm, and Pixar. Netflix subscribers in the United States pay between $8.99 and $15.99.

In mid-2019, Netflix revealed that it had lost U.S. subscribers for the first time in eight years, and growth had slowed in other markets. The company's stock fell 10 percent in one day. The problem? Weak content. Not enough hits like *Stranger Things*, a science fiction story first shown in 2016. Netflix has to be as good at producing programs with global appeal as it is at delivering those programs to subscribers. Ted Sarandos, chief content officer, says, "Our challenge every day is making a show you can't live without" (Lev-Ram, 2019a, p. 78).

The Solution

Netflix has made big changes by investing in new content, spending $12 billion in 2018 to produce 700 new programs. The content budget for 2019 was $15 billion. Much of the new content is aimed at subscribers outside the United States, where most growth is coming from. There are Netflix production hubs in London, Madrid, and Toronto, and content teams in other markets including Mexico. To finance this investment, Netflix has accumulated $12.6 billion in debt. Successful programs such as *Stranger Things* have been promoted in partnership with, for example, Burger King, Coca Cola, and Nike, who have all released "Stranger-themed" products. Over 40 million households streamed at least part of the third season of *Stranger Things* in the four days after it was released. Earlier in the year, only 17 million people watched the first episode of the final season of HBO's *Game of Thrones*.

Netflix has created a team of experienced content developers, who represent a range of ethnicities, races, and sexual orientations. Their job is to produce programs, in different categories, that will appeal to different audience segments, in different markets. Many of the senior members of this team are women. The leading actors in one of Netflix's popular shows, *Glow*, are all women, as are the show's creators. Illustrating the problems of choosing content, Netflix cancelled *OA,* a supernatural drama about a missing blind woman who comes back to her family in Michigan with her vision inexplicably restored. The series was costly to make and attracted a small audience. Loyal fans, however, were angry that the show had been cancelled; they erected billboards, organized a flash mob in Times Square, started a petition to save the series, and protested outside Netflix offices in New York and Hollywood. The show was cancelled anyway, demonstrating that Netflix was prepared to behave more like a traditional broadcast network or Hollywood studio. However, low-budget programs that attract a loyal niche of viewers can sometimes be viable. Expensive shows that do not attract large audiences are likely to be cut.

With competition for talent as well as subscribers, Netflix has to provide a creative environment in which film and program directors and writers want to work. The company has a reputation among artists and viewers for its willingness to develop specialist content. Writers, directors, and actors like the freedom and pace at Netflix, the flat organizational structure, and the fact that there are no senior executives constantly telling them what to do.

(Continued)

The Outcomes

It is not yet clear how well Netflix's strategy is working. Competing services have substantial catalogs of valuable content, and they have the resources to produce more. Asked if he was concerned about the competition, Marc Randolph said:

> I think actually for Netflix, it's nice. It gives them some discipline in terms of saying how are we going to compete and maintain our edge, maintain our prevalence in the streaming world. But I'm not worried. You know, Netflix always behaves like a startup, which means it's always willing to do what it has to do to make sure it meets customer needs in the future and not relying on what it did in the past.
>
> I mean, the only thing Netflix does is streaming and movies. They are very disciplined, very focused. Whereas you look at Disney, which of course, has a studio, but they also have theme parks and they have cruise ships. You look at Apple, which, of course, has the retail stores and its hardware. The time that I think I'll be worried about Netflix is when they come out with the Netflix theme park or the Netflix cell phone. (Brown, 2019)

In other words, according to Randolph, the "secret weapon" for Netflix is *focus*. If you are a Netflix subscriber, you will be able to judge the success of the company's strategy for yourself.

Case Sources

Brown, B. 2019. Netflix co-founder Marc Randolph says company's "secret weapon" sets itself apart from Disney, other streaming services, *Fox News Channel*, November 9. https://www.foxnews.com/tech/netflix-co-founder-marc-randolph-says-companys-secret-weapon-sets-itself-apart-from-disney-other-streaming-services.

Lev-Ram, M. 2019a. Once upon a time at Netflix. *Fortune* 180(4):74–82.

Schleier, C. 2019. Netflix's Reed Hastings revolutionized the way people watch movies, TV shows, *Investor's Business Daily*, January 17. https://www.investors.com/news/management/leaders-and-success/netflixs-reed-hastings-revolutionized-the-way-people-watch-movies-tv-shows.

TED Talk. 2018. Reed Hastings: How Netflix changed entertainment—and where it's heading. April. https://www.ted.com/talks/reed_hastings_how_netflix_changed_entertainment_and_where_it_s_headed?language=en (20 minutes).

EXERCISE 3.4

The Reputation Trap—Can You Escape?

LO 3.2

What happens if a company cannot change how it is viewed by consumers? As you read this case, consider the following questions:

1. What does this case reveal about the challenges faced by successful businesses? Is it possible to be too successful?

2. How does a successful organization determine whether an environmental change is a brief fad or fashion to be ignored, or a development that requires a fundamental rethink of the way in which it does business?

3. What change issues does this case raise with regard to the significance of reputation?

4. What actions would you recommend be taken by Big Food and the fast-food companies that have been caught in the reputation trap?

Try this simple test. Say the following out loud: Artificial colors and flavors. Pesticides. Preservatives. High-fructose corn syrup. Growth hormones. Antibiotics. Gluten. Genetically modified organisms. If any one of these terms raised a hair on the back of your neck, left a sour taste in your mouth, or made your lips purse with disdain, you are part of Big Food's multibillion-dollar problem. In fact, you may even belong to a growing consumer class that has some of the world's biggest and best-known companies scrambling to change their businesses. (Kowitt, 2015, p. 61)

Fortune magazine prides itself on being able to feel and report "the pulse" of U.S. business. In 2014 and 2015, two articles by Beth Kowitt, "Fallen Arches" and "The War on Big Food," explored the impact that consumer preference for healthy foods was having on Big Food organizations such as General Mills and Kraft Heinz, and also on some fast-food outlets like McDonald's and Subway. A growing number of consumers are suspicious of processed foods. Ironically, although processing (e.g., salting and curing) has traditionally been associated with reducing the risk of illness from the food we eat, food processing is now seen as the antithesis of healthy eating.

The annual sales of processed food are declining, but these are the core products of multi-billion dollar Big Food companies. Since 2009, the top 25 food and beverage companies in the United States have lost market share equivalent to $18 billion. Some fast-food companies are also facing a similar shift in consumer preferences. For example, in 2014, in their U.S. operations, McDonald's reported four consecutive quarters of falling sales and an overall 30 percent drop in profit, while Subway's sales dropped 3 percent, or $400 million.

Big Food has reacted by increasingly marketing their products as "natural," reviewing their product recipes and acquiring many small health and natural food companies. However, this has not resolved their reputational problem. According to Gary Hirshberg, founder and chairman of Stonyfield Farm, "there's enormous doubt and scepticism about whether large companies can deliver naturality and authenticity" (Kowitt, 2014, p. 64). According to Don Thompson, CEO of McDonald's, "people today are questioning the integrity and quality of the food at a much higher level" (Kowitt, 2014, p. 116). However, some fast-food brands, such as Chipotle Mexican Grill (annual growth rate 20 percent) and Firehouse Subs, are thriving in this environment, but not McDonald's or Subway. McDonald's seems to be suffering from its past success, which built its reputation as the quintessential fast-food brand. Today, however, it is operating in an environment where a growing number of customers are choosing "fresh and healthy" rather than "fast and convenient" (Kowitt, 2015, p. 109). The challenge for McDonald's is to convince customers that it can be both.

However, "fresh" brings its own challenges. In 2015 and 2016, hundreds of customers became sick after eating at Chipotle. Despite quickly making changes to its food safety practices, the reputational effect was substantial, and customers stayed away in droves. It was not until mid-2019 that Chipotle's share price returned to its 2015 pre-crisis level (Yaffe-Bellany, 2019).

Subway might seem to be a strange brand to have suffered from the "move to health" given that its growth has in the past been due to its positioning as a healthy alternative to "traditional" fast food. As one indicator of Subway's success, it is "the world's most ubiquitous restaurant chain" with over 41,000 locations in 100 countries, half of these in the United States. However, according to Darren Tristan, executive vice-president of the industry research firm Technomic, Subway's problem is that "fresh" no longer means what Subway offers. For example, people want meat that has been freshly cut, not a precut

(Continued)

slice peeled off wax paper. Subway has also been criticized for using the food additive azodicarbonide (E927, a flour bleaching and dough conditioning agent) in its bread.

Despite the attention, Subway is still the most popular restaurant chain in America and is still criticized for the high calorie count and salt content in its sandwiches. The sector faces other market changes, such as customers ordering by app, and food delivery aggregators selling meals from a range of outlets direct to customers (Stack, 2018).

Case Sources

Harwell, D. 2015. The rise and fall of Subway, the world's biggest food chain, *The Washington Post*, May 30. http://www.washingtonpost.com/business/economy/the-rise-and-fall-of-subway-the-worlds-biggest-food-chain/2015/05/29/0ca0a84a-fa7a-11e4-a13c-193b1241d51a_story.html (accessed June 20, 2015).

Kowitt, B. 2014. Fallen arches: can McDonald's get its mojo back? *Fortune* (December 1):106–16.

Kowitt, B. 2015. The war on big food, *Fortune* (May 21):61–70.

Stack. 2018. Is Subway actually healthy? December 20. http://www.stack.com/a/is-subway-actually-healthy.

Additional Reading

Bevan, S., Brinkley, I., Bajorek, Z., and Cooper, C. 2018. *21st century workforces and workplaces*. London: Bloomsbury. An informed review of the contemporary trends affecting organizations and the nature of work, assessing the evidence rather than the hype.

McAffee, A., and Brynjolfsson, E. 2017. *Machine, platform, crowd: Harnessing the digital revolution*. London and New York: W.W. Norton & Co. Explores how artificial intelligence will transform business and the nature of work, also emphasizing the role of platforms (Uber, Airbnb), and the "crowd"—informal, decentralized, self-organizing participants.

Stillman, D., and Stillman, J. 2017. *Gen Z @ Work: How the next generation is transforming the workplace*. New York: HarperBusiness. Argues that Gen Z are different from Millennials. Technologically sophisticated, independent, pragmatic, competitive, suffering from FOMO (fear of missing out on anything), accustomed to a sharing economy with no hierarchies.

Wilson, J., and Daugherty, P. R. 2018. Collaborative intelligence: Humans and AI are joining forces. *Harvard Business Review* 96(4):114–23. Explores examples of the performance gains achieved when humans and smart machines collaborate; artificial intelligence will have the most significant impact when it augments human workers instead of replacing them.

Roundup

Reflections for the Practicing Change Manager

- To what extent can you identify the external environmental pressures for change in your organization?

- To what extent can you influence whether and how to change?

- Do you relate better to one or more of the change management images outlined in table 3.1, with regard to the organizational changes in which you are involved? Why is this the case?

- Which of the possible reasons for avoiding change that have been discussed in this chapter have you experienced? On reflection, how might you have contributed to overcoming those avoidance tactics? And how would you judge your likely success in that attempt?

- How easy is it to raise issues in your organization about the rationale for specific changes? Is there a dominant rationale? And if so, why?

- What personal criteria might you adopt to ensure that you are initiating change "for the right reasons"? Set out some key questions that might help to guide you in the future, to ensure that your rationale for change is clear to you and those who will be affected.

Here is a short summary of the key points that we would like you to take from this chapter, in relation to each of the learning outcomes:

LO 3.1 * *Identify internal organizational factors that trigger change.*
We explored eight internal triggers of organizational change: low performance, inadequate skills and knowledge, facilities relocation, a reshuffling of responsibilities, product and service innovations, accidents and scandals, new top management, and organizational politics. These are only some of the main internal factors triggering change, and the last four of these are particularly significant.

LO 3.2 * *Understand the environmental pressures that can trigger organizational change.*
We explored four external pressures that are driving radical organizational change. *Globalization*, which has developed a digital profile, switching from trade in goods to trade in services, and which has encouraged companies to locate production closer to customers, using local suppliers. *Climate change*, which is encouraging businesses to switch to low-carbon methods and to plan for the risks of extreme weather events and other climate catastrophes. *Changing expectations of work,* with employees asking for greater autonomy, more flexibility, and work that has a sense of purpose. *Demographic trends*, with an ageing and multigenerational workforce, and the need to find ways to encourage older workers to remain in employment. *Technology*, which is starting to automate professional knowledge work as well as routing manual tasks but which will probably create more jobs than are replaced and will require higher degrees of knowledge, skill, and continuous learning. These pressures for change are interrelated, and all are active at the same time. These pressures are constantly shifting with local, national, and international trends and developments.

LO 3.3 * *Explain why organizations often fail to change following crises.*
Although it might be expected that change following accidents, failures, and other crises would be straightforward, this is not always the case. The causes of these incidents are usually complex and systemic, requiring systemic solutions that can be difficult and costly to implement. Many organizations are good at passive learning—identifying lessons—but not so good at active learning—implementing those changes. Not all failures are blameworthy; some are praiseworthy. Most failures, however, are treated as blameworthy, and this is a further barrier to active learning as it maintains a psychologically unsafe environment. The post-incident change agenda is often a defensive one, designed to stop such incidents from happening again. This is less appealing to change managers

who can experience more challenge and career rewards from implementing progressive change. It may be helpful to combine defensive agendas with progressive agendas to progress the former.

LO 3.4   * *Relate differing images of managing change to pressures for change.*

Chapter 2 discussed three uses of the six-images framework: surfacing assumptions, assessing dominant images, and using multiple perspectives. We argued that there are no "right" and "wrong" images of change management and that it is valuable to be able to interpret problems and solutions in general, and change processes in particular, from different standpoints. This "multiple perspectives" approach can help to generate fresh thinking and creative solutions. In this chapter, we have seen how external and internal pressures or drivers do not necessarily lead to change; those pressures are filtered through the perceptions of the need for change, and those perceptions are in turn colored by the images that managers have of the change process. One manager's reaction to a particular external or internal pressure, therefore, may be different from that of others. The issues discussed in this chapter suggest that more successful change managers are likely to be those who have a clear, personal understanding about the pressures on them to change their organizations, a well-developed rationale for what they are attempting to achieve, and a clear view of the likely effects of their actions.

References

Alsever, J. 2019. Big ships tack to a greener future. *Fortune* 180(5):37–38.

Ball, J. 2019. Racing a rising tide. *Fortune* 180(5):126–34.

Bass, A. S. 2018. GrAIt expectations. *The economist special report AI in business*, March 31.

Bevere, L., Schwartz, M., Sharan, R., and Zimmerli, P. (2018). *Sigma: Natural catastrophes and man-made disasters in 2017.* Zurich, Switzerland: Swiss Re Institute.

Bissell-Linsk, J. 2017. Robotics in the running. *Financial Times* (October 23):23.

Bond, S. 2017. Shoppers buy or boycott brands based on values. *Financial Times* (June 19):18.

Brown, J. 2019. Half of UK adults plan to work past retirement, finds survey. *People Management*, November 1. https://www.peoplemanagement.co.uk/news/articles/half-uk-adults-plan-work-past-retirement-finds-survey.

Buchanan, D. A. 2011. Good practice, not rocket science: Understanding failures to change after extreme events. *Journal of Change Management* 11(3):273–88.

Buchanan, D. A., and Badham, R. 2020. *Power, politics, and organizational change.* 3rd ed. London: Sage Publications.

Buchanan, D. A., and Moore, C. 2016. Never say never again: Post-incident change and the investigation trap. *Journal of Change Management* 16(3):159–183.

Calnan, M. 2017. Generation Z more motivated by teamwork than the average worker. *People Management*, August 17. https://www.peoplemanagement.co.uk/news/articles/generation-z-motivated-teamwork (accessed October 23, 2019).

CB Insights 2018. From Instagram to Slack: 9 successful startup pivots. November 1. https://www.cbinsights.com.research/startup-pivot-success-stories.

Chand, M., and Tung, R. L. 2014. The ageing of the world's population and its effects on global business. *Academy of Management Perspectives* 28(4):409–29.

Chartered Institute for Personnel and Development 2016. *Creating longer, more fulfilling working lives: Employer practice in five European countries.* London: Chartered Institute for Personnel and Development.

Clarke, R. 2016. Employees are happier in age-diverse teams, says study. *HR Review*, September 7. http://www.hrreview.co.uk/hr-news/employees-happier-age-diverse-teams-says-study/101053.

Columbia Accident Investigation Board. 2003. *Columbia Accident Investigation Board Report, Volumes I to VI.* Washington, DC: National Aeronautics and Space Administration and the Government Printing Office.

Daneshkhu, S. 2018. Estée Lauder chief Fabrizio Freda on winning over millennials. *Financial Times* (March 12):24.

Davenport, T. H., and Ronanki, R. 2018. Artificial intelligence for the real world. *Harvard Business Review* 96(1):108–16.

Dellot, B., and Wallace-Stephens, F. 2017. *The age of automation: Artificial intelligence, robotics and the future of low-skilled work.* London: RSA Action and Research Centre.

Derousseau, R. 2019. The pros and cons of politics. *Fortune* 179(3):47–48.

Edgecliffe-Johnson, A. 2018. US companies cut corporate ties with National Rifle Association. *Financial Times* (February 26):4.

Edmondson, A. 2011. Strategies for learning from failure. *Harvard Business Review* 89(4):48–55.

Edmondson, A. 2018. *The fearless organization: Creating psychological safety in the workplace for learning, innovation, and growth.* Hoboken, NJ: John Wiley & Sons.

Ewing, J. 2018. *Faster, higher, further: The inside story of the Volkswagen scandal.* London: Corgi.

Fletcher, S. 2018. What makes a good robot co-worker? *People Management*, January 15.

https://www.peoplemanagement.co.uk/voices/comment/good-robot-worker.

Francis, T., and Hoefel, F. 2018. *"True Gen": Generation Z and its implications for companies.* Sau Paulo: McKinsey & Co.

Frey, C. B., and Osborne, M. A. 2017. The future of employment: How susceptible are jobs to computerization? *Technological Forecasting & Social Change* 114(C):254–80.

Frey, C. B., Osborne, M. A., and Homes, C. 2016. *Technology at work v2.0: The future is not what it used to be.* London and Oxford: Citigroup/University of Oxford, Oxford Martin School.

Fuller, J. B., Wallenstein, J. K., Raman, M., and de Chalendar, A. 2019. Your workforce is more adaptable than you think. *Harvard Business Review* 97(3):118-26.

Gratton, L., and Scott, A. 2016. *The 100-year life: Living and working in an age of longevity*. London: Bloomsbury.

Gratton, L., and Scott, A. 2017. The corporate implications of longer lives. *MIT Sloan Management Review* 58(3):63-70.

Greenberg, E., Hirt, M., and Smit, S. 2017. The global forces inspiring a new narrative of progress. *McKinsey Quarterly* (2):33-52.

Groom, B. 2016. Inside the mind of a millennial, *Work* (Spring):29-35.

Harwell, D. 2015. The rise and fall of Subway, the world's biggest food chain. *The Washington Post* (May 30):5.

Hewlett, S. A., Sherbin, L., and Sumberg, K. 2009. How Gen Y and Boomers will reshape your agenda. *Harvard Business Review* 87(7/8):71-76.

Hislop, D., Coombs, C., Taneva, S., and Barnard, S. 2017. *Impact of artificial intelligence, robotics and automation technologies on work*. London: Chartered Institute for Personnel and Development.

Hollinger, P. 2016. Meet the cobots: Humans and robots learn how to work together on the factory floor. *Financial Times* (May 5):17.

Hollister, R., and Watkins, M. D. 2018. Too many projects. *Harvard Business Review* 96(5):64-71.

Hudson Consulting. 2014. *The great generational shift: Why the differences between generations will reshape your workplace*. New York and London.

Illanes, P., Lund, S., Mourshed, M., Rutherford, S. and Tyreman, M. 2018. *Retraining and reskilling workers in the age of automation*. New York: McKinsey & Company.

Jack, A. 2019. Business students want to succeed—and do good. *Financial Times* (October 21):19.

Jenkins, A. 2020. Coping with a bad trip at Airbnb. *Fortune* 181(1):66-75.

Kanter, R. M. 2003. Leadership and the psychology of turnarounds. *Harvard Business Review* 81(6):58-67.

Kowitt, B. 2014. Fallen arches: Can McDonald's get its mojo back? *Fortune* (December 1):106-16.

Kowitt, B. 2015. The war on big food. *Fortune* (May 21):61-70.

Kowitt, B. 2019. How Starbucks got its buzz back. *Fortune* 180(4): 84-92.

Kunze, F., and Menges, J. I. 2017. Younger supervisors, older subordinates: An organizational-level study of age differences, emotions, and performance. *Journal of Organizational Behavior* 38(4):461-86.

Kunze, F., Boehm, S., and Bruch, H. 2013. Age, resistance to change, and job performance. *Journal of Managerial Psychology* 28(7/8):741–60.

Lawrence, M., Roberts, C., and King, L. 2017. *Managing automation: Employment, inequality and ethics in the digital age*. London: Institute for Public Policy Research.

Leaf, C. 2019. What scares the world. *Fortune* 179(3):124.

Lev-Ram. M. 2019a. Once upon a time at Netflix. *Fortune* 180(4):74–82.

Lev-Ram. M. 2019b. About face. *Fortune* 179(4):46–53.

London, S., and Lund, S. 2019. *Globalization's next chapter*. Washington, DC: McKinsey & Company.

Lund, S., Manyika, J., Woetzel, J., Bughin, J., Krishnan, M., Seong, J., and Muir, M. 2019. *Globalization in transition: The future of trade and value chains*. Washington, DC: McKinsey Global Institute.

Mahler, J. G., and Casamayou, M. H. 2009. *Organizational learning at NASA: The Challenger and Columbia accidents*. Washington, DC: Georgetown University Press.

Marvell, R., and Cox, A. 2016. *Fulfilling work: What do older workers value about work and why?* London: Institute of Employment Studies and Centre for Ageing Better.

Masters, B. 2018. BackRock's gun-free funds show ethical investing is a good bet. *Financial Times* (April 11):11.

Milne, R. 2014. Lego: King of the castle. *Financial Times* (July 10):13.

Milne, R. 2015. Lego shores up title of most profitable toymaker. *Financial Times* (February 26):18.

Mohrman, S. A., and Lawler, E. E. 2012. Generating knowledge that drives change. *Academy of Management Perspectives* 26(1):41–51.

Ries, E. 2019. *The Lean Startup*. New York: Penguin Random House.

Schleier, C. 2019. Netflix's Reed Hastings revolutionized the way people watch movies, TV shows, *Investor's Business Daily*, January 17. https://www.investors.com/news/management/leaders-and-success/netflixs-reed-hastings-revolutionized-the-way-people-watch-movies-tv-shows.

Sorkin, A. R. 2020. BlackRock C.E.O. Larry Fink: Climate crisis will reshape finance. February 24. https://www.nytimes.com/2020/01/14/business/dealbook/larry-fink.

Stacey, K. 2019. Senators castigate Boeing over anti-stall system. *Financial Times* (October 30):12 (US edition).

Toft, B., and Reynolds, S. 2005. *Learning from disasters: A management approach*, 3rd ed. Houndmills, Basingstoke: Palgrave Macmillan.

Vaughan, D. 1996. *The Challenger launch decision: Risky technology, culture, and deviance at NASA*. Chicago: University of Chicago Press.

Wahba, P. 2019. Can Best Buy keep winning? *Fortune* 179(5):5.

Wasik, J. 2019. Why working past retirement age may make sense. *Forbes*, June 3. https://www.forbes.com/sites/johnwasik/2019/06/03/why-working-past-retirement-age-may-make-sense.

Wisskirchen, G., Biacabe, B. T., Bormann, U., Muntz, A., Niehaus, G., Soler, G. J., and von Brauchitsch, B. 2017. *Artificial intelligence and robotics and their impact on the workplace.* London: International Bar Association Global Employment Institute.

Yaffe-Bellany, D. 2019. Chipotle, with food-safety issues behind it, recovers strongly. *New York Times*, July 23. https://www.nytimes.com/2019/07/23/business/chipotle-stock-earnings.html.

Zheltoukhova, K., and Baczor, L. 2016. *Attitudes to employability and talent.* London: Chartered Institute for Personnel and Development.

Chapter opening silhouette credit: CharlotteRaboff/Shutterstock

Chapter 4

What to Change? A Diagnostic Approach

Learning Objectives

By the end of this chapter, you should be able to:

LO 4.1   Understand the use of diagnostic models in planning organizational change.

LO 4.2   Use strategic analysis tools to assess the need for organizational change.

LO 4.3   Diagnose organizational receptiveness to and individual readiness for change, and use those assessments as the basis for action to increase receptiveness and readiness.

LO 4.4   Diagnose the degree of "agility" that an organization requires to operate effectively in an often uncertain and unpredictable business context.

"Well, in our country," said Alice, still panting a little, *"you'd generally get to somewhere else—if you run very fast for a long time, as we've been doing."*

"A slow sort of country!" said the Queen. *"Now, here, you see, it takes all the running you can do, to keep in the same place. If you want to get somewhere else, you must run at least twice as fast as that!"*

LO 4.1   Organizational Models

The theme of this chapter is *diagnosis*. With regard to organizational change, what is the problem? Can we improve our understanding of the context and nature of the problem? And can this diagnostic approach help us to solve the problem, or problems, that we find? In short—what has to change? This chapter introduces a number of diagnostic frameworks and tools. Some diagnostic models consider the operation of the organization as a whole, such as the 7-S model. Others, such as "scenario planning," start with strategy. Some are designed to explore specific aspects of the change process, such as organizational and individual readiness for change. The "agile" approach suggests that organizations can be designed in ways that make "change management" tools redundant.

The way in which these diagnostic models, frameworks, and tools are deployed depends on the image of change management (chapter 2) in use.

Director	You can use these diagnostics to strengthen your knowledge base and confidence with regard to what needs to change, identifying key relationships and focusing on where change is needed and the results that you want.
Navigator	You will also find these diagnostics useful to "map" the organization's environment and help you to assess appropriate responses.
Caretaker	You will be less impressed by the capability of these diagnostics to support change, but those which focus on the external environment (PESTLE and scenario planning) help to identify trends and developments to which the organization should respond.
Coach	You will probably be more interested in diagnostics, which focus on goals and on the capabilities required to achieve them.
Interpreter	You will find particularly useful the diagnostics, which emphasize images, framing, and cognitive maps.
Nurturer	With your interest in emergent strategy, you may not be convinced of the value of this diagnostic approach.

Who does the diagnosing? Some perspectives see this as a senior management role, perhaps also involving external consultants and advisers. Those consultants may use their diagnostic expertise to help clients to manage the change process, rather than to decide the content of the changes. However, other perspectives emphasize the need to involve at the diagnostic stage those who will be affected by change; involvement can strengthen commitment to the change process, and thus increase the probability of success. Some organization development (OD) consultants explicitly reject the role of "diagnostician," arguing that their role is to help the organization's members to do this for themselves.

One problem that you will meet in this chapter concerns the number of diagnostics that we discuss; see the summary in table 4.1. You are not going to be able to remember all these. So, why present them? We have included these models for two reasons. The first is to give a comprehensive account of the field. Even if several of these models are of little use to you today, you may need to turn to them in the future. The second and related reason is that these models are part of the change manager's toolbox. Different

TABLE 4.1
Change Diagnostics and Their Uses—A Summary

Diagnostic	Use When You Want to . . . .
Six-box model	Simplify the complexity, focus on key problems
	Be reminded of the systemic implications of actions in one area
7-S model	Recognize interconnectedness
	Pay attention to the "soft" factors as well as structure and strategy
Star model	Recognize interconnectedness and "knock on" effects
	Align your strategy, structure, people, processes, and rewards
Four-frame model	See the organization through different lenses at the same time
	Generate a deeper understanding to develop creative solutions
Gap analysis	Develop a change agenda that addresses future conditions
	Generate understanding and consensus around the agenda
PESTLE framework	Understand the impact of multiple environmental pressures
	Exploit future opportunities and deal with risks and threats
Scenario planning	Encourage creative thinking and acceptance of uncertainty
	Prioritize, plan, and implement future-oriented changes
Elements of strategy	Identify changes necessary to pursue a given strategy
	Develop an integrated package of self-reinforcing changes
Strategic inventory	Clarify and validate strategic assumptions
	Decide what changes are necessary to drive strategy
Cultural web	Map and understand the components of the organizational culture
	Challenge that which is taken for granted, and identify barriers to change
Receptive context	Determine how receptive the organization is to change
	Decide action to increase receptiveness if necessary
Absorptive capacity	Assess the organization's ability to assimilate and apply new ideas
	Increase absorptive capacity with appropriate actions
Force-field analysis	Assess the driving and restraining forces for a given change
	Manage the balance of forces to encourage the change
Readiness for change analysis	Assess organizational and individual readiness for a given change
	Identify the "groundwork" needed before the change goes ahead
Individual readiness	Assess individual readiness for a given change
	Take appropriate steps to increase individual readiness
Stakeholder mapping	Identify how those affected could influence the change process
	Manage stakeholders, given their power and their interest
Agile organization model	Ensure that change is quick and smooth
	Create an organization design that maximizes flexibility and adaptability

The Spotify Model Suits Spotify, but Is It Right for You?

The digital music, podcast, and video streaming service Spotify has attracted a lot of interest in how it operates internally, including its team structure and cultural values. The level of interest has been such that these practices have been called the "Spotify Model"—a simple, agile, flat organizational structure based on autonomous teams or "squads," with few bureaucratic rules.

However, the director of engineering at Spotify, Marcin Floryan, cautions that what people call The Spotify Model is a simplified description of what Spotify does. For a start, the company is continually evolving. Although "the model" can give people a sense of how things are done at Spotify, it should not be seen as something that can be copied in another organization, much less as a guarantee of success (Linders, 2016).

Similarly, argues consultant Jurrian Kamer (2018), "When people copy The Spotify Model, it often happens through a top-down directive, without taking a close look at what kind of culture and leadership is needed to make it work." What is needed, argues Kamer, is diagnosis and not the copying of some pre-existing model. A diagnostic approach involves:

1. Ask yourself if there is a clear picture of what issues you are trying to solve with a new organizational model.

2. Involve not just your leadership team but also a wide variety of people in the organization to gather ideas and co-create a picture of the desired future state. A good question to ask is, "What is holding us back from doing the best work of our lives?"

3. Appreciate what is going really well, and decide what you definitely want to keep.

4. Take inspiration from a wide variety of work practices and companies. Look at different models of self-organization that fit different scale and risk contexts.

5. Figure out which of your main capabilities you need to upgrade and where in the organization they are based.

Find on *YouTube*, "Spotify Engineering Culture" (parts 1 and 2; by Henrik Kniberg) (2017; 2019, 13:13 minutes).

---

tools help address different problems. Where one tool or approach is unsatisfactory, another may be valuable. Sometimes, using two or more tools at the same time produces better results than only using one. So, if you are studying this chapter as a student, skim these models to get an overview and stop on three or four that are especially interesting. If you are reading this chapter as a practitioner, focus on the diagnostics that you think are relevant to the change projects in which you are currently involved.

Our treatment of change diagnostic models is based on the following assumptions:

- Managers and staff have their own views of "how things work." "Diagnosis" with regard to organizational change is going to happen whether or not explicit diagnostic tools are used.

- Implicit causal models have the power to influence how we think about organizational issues and problems and what we believe are the appropriate courses of action.

- The option of not using a diagnostic model, therefore, is not available. We use either an implicit model or an explicit one.

- Implicit models based on experience can provide valuable insights. However, implicit models have limitations. First, they may be based on the limited experience of a small number of people. Second, because they are implicit, it is difficult for others to understand the assumptions underlying decisions based on those models.

Explicit models are helpful in at least five ways (Burke, 2013). They:

1. *Simplify complexity.* They help to address the complexity of complex, multivariate situations, reducing the complexity with a manageable number of categories.
2. *Highlight priorities.* They help to prioritize the issues that need most attention.
3. *Identify interdependencies.* They identify key organizational interdependencies (e.g., strategy and structure).
4. *Provide a common language.* They provide a common language with which different stakeholder groups can discuss organizational properties.
5. *Offer a process guide.* They can offer guidance with respect to the appropriate sequence of actions in a change process.

Each of the models discussed here has a different focus on aspects of organizational functioning. No one model, or small collection of models, can be described as "best." It is always important to choose, or to adapt, a model that fits the organization's problem, by triggering discussion and analysis among those involved, leading ultimately to action. With regard to problem-solving, the debate that a model prompts can be more important than the model itself. Our aim is to show the variety of available models and to give you a basis from which to choose those that fit your interests and purposes.

The Six-Box Organizational Model

Marvin Weisbord (1976, p. 431) developed one of the first organizational diagnostics, which he described as "my efforts to combine bits of data, theories, research, and hunches into a working tool that anyone can use." In the context of our discussion of implicit and explicit models, it is interesting to note that Weisbord subtitled his article, "Six Places to Look for Trouble with or without a Theory." It is not surprising that his model is based on sets of factors or "boxes":

1. *Purposes.* What business are we in?
2. *Structure.* How do we divide up the work?
3. *Rewards.* Do all tasks have incentives?
4. *Helpful mechanisms.* Do we have adequate coordinating technologies?
5. *Relationships.* How do we manage conflict among people?
6. *Leadership.* Does someone keep the other five boxes in balance?

Weisbord (1976, p. 431) uses a radar screen analogy: "Just as air controllers use radar to chart the course of an aircraft—height, speed, distance apart and weather—those seeking to improve an organization must observe relationships among the boxes and not focus on any particular blip."

As a change diagnostic, therefore, this model has two main applications. First, in providing a small set of categories that simplify (perhaps oversimplify) the complexity of an organization, this facilitates the process of deciding which factors or sets of factors are generating problems, and which therefore require attention. Second, it reminds the change manager to consider the wider systemic implications of actions that address only one or two of those categories or boxes.

The 7-S Framework

Robert Waterman et al. (1980) developed the 7-S framework while they were working as management consultants with McKinsey & Company. They argue that organizational effectiveness is influenced by many factors and that successful change depends on the relationships among them. In an approach similar to that of Weisbord (1976), they identify seven sets of factors (see Figure 4.1).

- *Structure* in this framework refers to the formal organization design.
- *Strategy* concerns how the organization plans to anticipate or respond to changes in its external environment to strengthen its competitive position.
- *Systems* are the formal and informal procedures that determine how things get done, such as budgeting, cost accounting, IT, and training systems. Waterman et al. (1980, p. 21) note that one way to change an organization without disruptive reorganization is to change the systems.
- *Style* refers to patterns of management actions, how managers spend their time, what they pay attention to, the signals they send about priorities, and their attitude to change.
- *Staff* can refer to appraisal, training, and development processes, and also to attitude, motivation, morale—but more importantly in this framework, this refers to how managers are developed.
- *Skills* concern what an organization does best, expressed in the dominant attributes and capabilities that distinguish it from its competitors.
- *Superordinate goals* refer to the organization's guiding concepts, values, aspirations, and future direction. These are sometimes captured by the term "vision," discussed in chapter 6. In later versions of the 7-S framework, these goals are also referred to as "shared values."

FIGURE 4.1
The 7-S Framework

Source: Based on Waterman et al. (1980, 18).

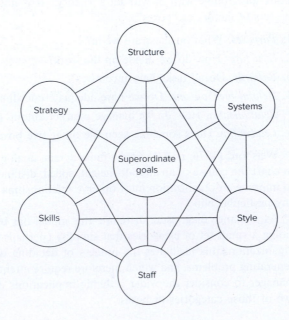

As a change diagnostic, this framework emphasizes the interconnectedness of the seven sets of factors and also argues that the "soft" issues (style, staff, skills, shared values) are just as important as structure and strategy. Waterman et al. (1980, p. 17) explain:

> Our assertion is that productive organization change is not simply a matter of structure, although structure is important. It is not so simple as the interaction between strategy and structure, although strategy is critical too. Our claim is that effective organizational change is really the relationship between structure, strategy, systems, style, skills, staff, and something we call superordinate goals. (The alliteration is intentional: it serves as an aid to memory.)

The framework thus identifies the areas on which to focus, the questions to ask, and the relationships and alignments to consider when planning organizational change. A full 7-S analysis, exploring each of the elements of the framework in depth, can be rich and valuable but is time consuming.

Applying 7-S to Intuit

In 2000, Steve Bennett, vice president of GE Capital, became chief executive of Intuit, a financial software and services company with three products, Quicken, TurboTax, and QuickBooks, which, respectively, had 73, 81, and 84 percent of their markets. However, given this market dominance, many analysts felt that Intuit was less profitable than it should be. The company also had a reputation for slow decision making, allowing competitors to steal a number of market opportunities. Bennett wanted to change all that. In his first few weeks, he visited most of Intuit's locations, addressed most of its 5,000 employees, and spoke personally to each of the top 200 executives. He concluded that staff members were passionate about the firm's products but that not much attention was being paid to internal processes (based on Higgins, 2005).

In terms of the 7-S framework, this is what he did:

Strategy. To expand Intuit's portfolio, he expanded the product range by acquisition.

Structure. He created a flatter structure and decentralized decision making, giving business units greater control and responsibility for the product process from development to delivery.

Systems. The rewards system was more closely aligned to achieving strategic objectives.

Style. He emphasized the need for a performance-oriented focus, and he provided a vision for change, putting effort into "selling" that vision.

Staff. He built on the commitment of staff to Intuit's products by emphasizing the critical role of quality and efficiency in maintaining and building the company's reputation.

Skills. To enhance staff capabilities in the areas of quality and efficiency, resources were allocated to training and development, and some select managers were hired from GE in specific skill areas.

Superordinate goals. Bennett's approach was "vision-driven," with his paper, "Steve's Dream for Intuit" outlining strategic objectives and how they would be achieved; to "sell" this vision, he communicated constantly with staff.

As a result of Bennett's changes, operating profits increased in 2002 and 2003 by 40 to 50 percent. By 2014, Intuit had global revenues of over $5 billion, with 8,000 employees in the United States, Canada, United Kingdom, India, and other countries (www.intuit.com).

FIGURE 4.2
The Star Model

Based on Galbraith
et al. (2002).

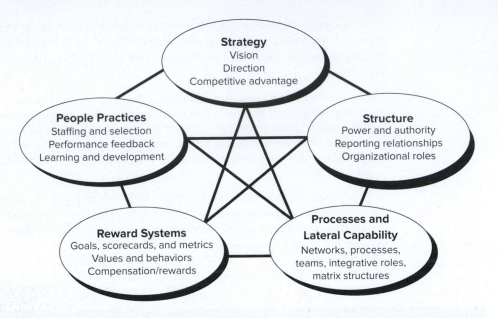

The Star Model

The star model of organizational design, developed by Galbraith et al. (2002), argues that for an organization to be effective, its strategy, structure, processes, rewards, and people practices have to be in alignment (see Figure 4.2). This model thus overlaps with the McKinsey 7-S framework.

Strategy in this model plays a dominant role, because if the strategy is not clear, then there is no basis for making other design decisions.

Structure is defined as the formal authority relationships and grouping of activities, as shown on an organization chart.

Processes and lateral capability concern the formal and informal systems that coordinate the organization's activities.

Reward systems relate to how performance is measured and compensated in ways that align individual actions to organizational objectives.

People practices concern the organization's human resource policies and practices; selection, training and development, performance management.

As a change diagnostic, this model emphasizes how these five elements are interconnected. Changes in one area are almost certain to affect others and not always in predictable ways. Despite the significance of strategy, organizational performance will suffer if one or more of the five sets of factors are out of alignment with the others. For example, although changing the structure may be relatively straightforward and visible, this can have little or no impact on performance without complementary changes elsewhere in the organization. Galbraith et al. (2002) explain the implications of misalignment of each of the five "points of the star," as summarized in table 4.2.

TABLE 4.2
The Implications of Misalignment

Design Component	Leads to...	Implications for Practice
Strategy If strategy is missing, unclear, or not agreed	*confusion*	No common purpose People pulling in different directions No criteria for decision making
Structure If structure is not aligned to strategy	*friction*	Inability to mobilize resources Ineffective execution Lost competitive advantage
Processes If coordinating mechanisms are left to chance	*gridlock*	Lack of collaboration across boundaries Long decision and innovation cycle times No sharing of information and best practice
Rewards If metrics and rewards do not support the goals	*internal competition*	Diffused energy, wrong results Low standards Frustration and staff turnover
People If staff are not enabled and empowered	*low performance*	Effort without results Low job satisfaction

Based on Galbraith et al. (2002).

The Four-Frame Model

Lee Bolman and Terry Deal (2017) explain four different frames or lenses, each providing a different perspective on how an organization functions. Their aim is to promote the value of "multiframe thinking," which means seeing the same situation in different ways. Problems arise, they argue, when we become locked into our one favored way of seeing the world—and our organization—and then fail to see other critical aspects or issues. We met frames before, in chapter 2, in our discussion of mental models; same thing. The *structural* frame in this model concerns the organization of groups and teams. The *human resource* frame concerns how the organization is tailored to satisfy human needs and build effective interpersonal relationships and teamwork. The *political* frame concerns how power and conflict are dealt with and how coalitions are formed. The *symbolic* frame relates to how the organization builds a culture that gives purpose and meaning to work and builds team cohesion. The four-frame model is illustrated in Figure 4.3 (Bolman and Deal, 2017, p. 20).

Each frame is associated with a metaphor. The structural frame sees the organization as a machine, and the problem concerns efficient design. The human resource frame treats the organization as a family, and the task is to meet the needs of both the organization and its members. The political frame sees organizations as sites of collaboration and conflict, as the interests of internal and external stakeholders sometimes overlap and sometimes differ. For the symbolic frame, the essence of the organization lies with its culture—symbols, beliefs, values, norms, rituals, and meanings.

As a change diagnostic, the four-frame model invites the change manager to see the organization through several different lenses at the same time. This can deepen an understanding of problems and helps to generate creative solutions by highlighting previously unseen, or unconsidered, possibilities.

FIGURE 4.3
The Four-Frame Model

	Frame			
	Structural	**Human Resource**	**Political**	**Symbolic**
Organizational Metaphor	Factory or machine	Family	Jungle	Theatre, carnival, temple
Central Concepts	Roles, goals, policies, technology, environment	Needs, skills, relationships	Power, conflict, competition, politics	Culture, meaning, metaphor, ritual, ceremony, stories, heroes
Image of Leadership	Social architecture	Empowerment	Advocacy and political savvy	Inspiration
Basic Leadership Challenge	Attune structure to task, technology, environment	Align organizational and human needs	Develop agenda and power base	Create faith, beauty, meaning

Metaphorical Diagnostics

In many situations, diagnosis of the need for and substance of change can be enhanced by capturing the perspectives of a wide range of the staff who are involved—at all levels. However, getting people to talk about the "as is" situation and what needs to change can sometimes be awkward. A useful technique for overcoming this potential blockage builds on the concept of "frames," asking people to describe their organization (or part of the organization) and how it works using a metaphor (an image or a simile): "My organization is like a well-oiled machine." "My division is a shark-infested pond."

In our experience, when asked, most people quickly generate such an image: "My organization is like a dinosaur—large, slow-moving, unresponsive to change, and headed for extinction." These images differ from one individual to another and become the basis of discussion, as their originators provide further detail about what they intended to convey with their metaphor.

LO 4.2   Organizational Strategy and Change

In this section, we shift the focus from organizational models, to strategic analysis tools. Strategy is a major driver of change, but it is not the only factor. Here, we explain six tools that are in common use for exploring and shaping an organization's strategy. These are gap analysis, the PESTLE framework, scenario planning, elements of strategy, the strategic inventory, and the cultural web.

Gap Analysis

Gap analysis is a simple, flexible, and widely used tool for reviewing the current "as is" state of an organization and what has to change. This involves asking three questions:

1. Where are we now?
2. Where do we want to get to?
3. What do we need to do to get there?

These are general questions that almost always elicit a response—from staff at all levels in an organization—and they are therefore a good basis for discussion. A key issue concerns the degree of consensus in the responses of those who are asked. If everyone agrees, then action may be rapid. However, if rapid action is not necessary in the circumstances, it can be useful deliberately to orchestrate a challenge to the consensus. That challenge could reinforce the consensus view, or it could prompt a reconsideration of "taken for granted" assumptions. A low degree of consensus prompts further attention to the organization's goals, on the grounds that commitment to action should have a reasonably broad base of agreement, at least concerning the first two questions. Agreement on the third question may be desirable, but it is not necessary as long as there is commitment to support the formal decision on the course of action to be taken.

Gap analysis is flexible with regard to focus and timescale. The first question can relate to the organization as a whole or to one or more divisions. If appropriate, it can address a range of other specific issues: where are we now—with regard to staff engagement, updating our information systems, developing new product lines, streamlining our procurement processes, and so on. The second question may ask about where we want to get to in six months, or two years, or five years, and so on. The simplicity and flexibility of this tool make it both easy to use and powerful.

As a change diagnostic, this can be a helpful way of establishing a change agenda (what do we need to do to get there?) that has been explored in depth and that is understood by those involved. Through open discussion, the resultant agenda can gain a high degree of consensus, but the disagreements that have been aired will also be known and understood. One problem with gap analysis is that it often suggests a felt need for deep, transformational change (see Figure 1.1, page 17), which immediately generates an overwhelming and potentially resource-intensive agenda.

PESTLE Framework

PESTLE is an environmental scanning tool, which provides a structured method for organizing and understanding complex trends and developments across the Political, Economic, Social, Technological, Legal, and Ecological factors that can affect an organization. Figure 4.4 shows a typical PESTLE analysis. This is an illustration and is not comprehensive. The tidy categories in the figure can overlap in practice; legislative changes may be politically motivated, and ecological concerns reflect changing social values and preferences. The point of the analysis, however, is to identify the environmental factors that may affect the organization now and in the future.

Environmental complexity makes prediction hazardous. We can predict demographic trends with some accuracy, with respect to mortality and gender and age profiles. We can

FIGURE 4.4

PESTLE Analysis for a Retail Organization

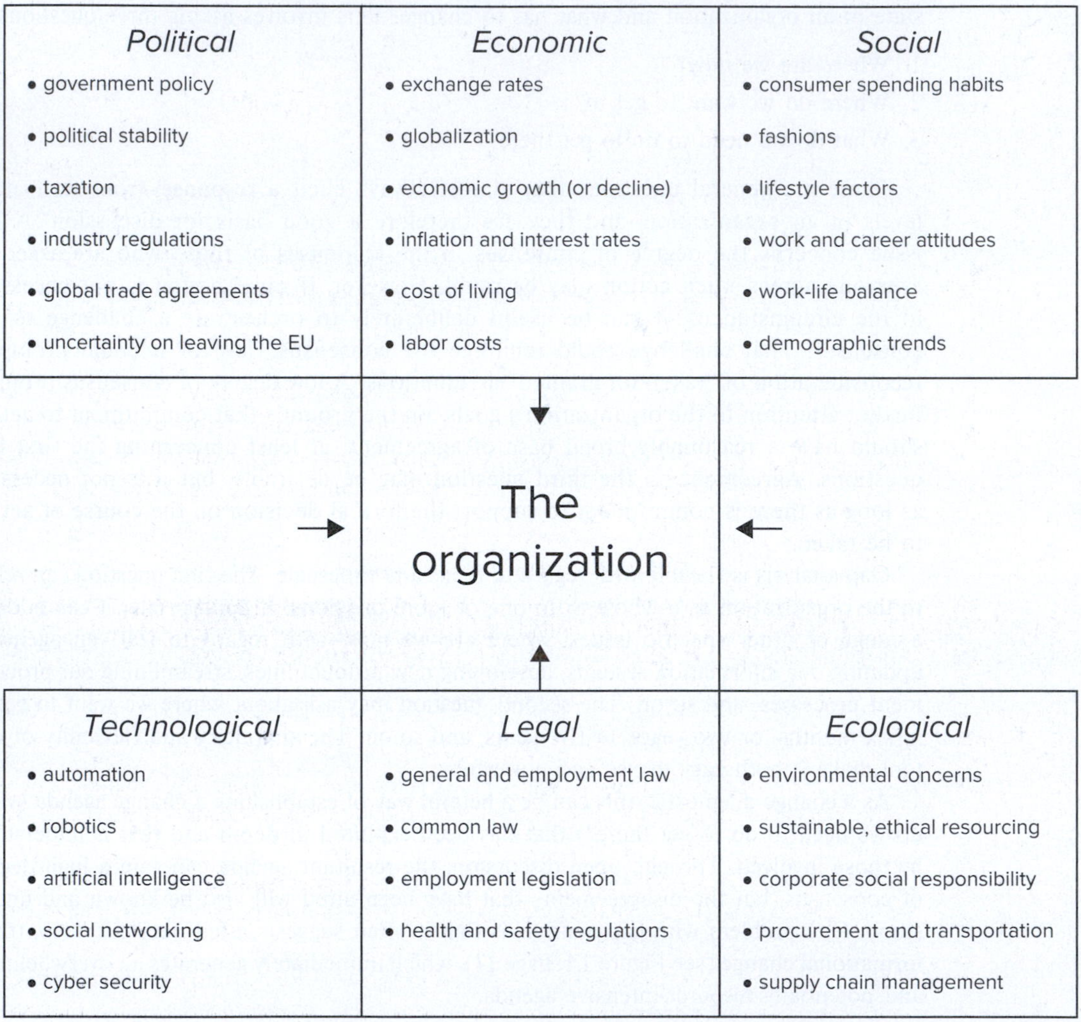

Political	*Economic*	*Social*
• government policy	• exchange rates	• consumer spending habits
• political stability	• globalization	• fashions
• taxation	• economic growth (or decline)	• lifestyle factors
• industry regulations	• inflation and interest rates	• work and career attitudes
• global trade agreements	• cost of living	• work-life balance
• uncertainty on leaving the EU	• labor costs	• demographic trends

| | The organization | |

Technological	*Legal*	*Ecological*
• automation	• general and employment law	• environmental concerns
• robotics	• common law	• sustainable, ethical resourcing
• artificial intelligence	• employment legislation	• corporate social responsibility
• social networking	• health and safety regulations	• procurement and transportation
• cyber security		• supply chain management

Source: Based on Morrison and Weeks (2017, 4).

normally predict economic trends with some confidence in the short to medium term—say two to three years. Trends in social values and lifestyles, politics, technological innovation, or the impact of new technology cannot be predicted with much confidence—although that does not stop journalists and others from making the attempt. Predicting geopolitical events, such as terrorist attacks and wars, is even more difficult. PESTLE analysis thus relies heavily on informed guesswork and judgement.

As a change diagnostic, the environmental audit that PESTLE produces can be used to guide strategic decision making and contingency planning, exploit opportunities, and address potential threats and risks (Morrison and Weeks, 2017). The resultant agenda may involve immediate change initiatives and can also include longer-term change planning.

Scenario Planning

Scenario planning involves the imaginative development of one or more likely pictures of the characteristics of the possible futures for an organization sometimes, but not necessarily, considering "best case/worst case" possibilities. The organization can then plan an appropriate response to those futures (Verity, 2003). Recent concerns with regard to geopolitical risks have made scenario planning more popular (see the box "Work in 2022: Colorful Scenarios"). The results of a PESTLE analysis can, of course, contribute to scenario development. The Royal Dutch Shell company was responsible for developing scenario planning in the 1970s, and this tool is thus also known as the "Shell method."

Scenario planning combines environmental scanning with creative thinking to identify the most probable future scenario as a basis for planning and action. In the field of corporate strategy, scenario planning is used to explore best-case/worst-case possibilities and to encourage creative out-of-the-box thinking. (You can see an example of this in "Work in 2022: Colorful Scenarios.")

Work in 2022 *Colorful Scenarios*

The consultancy company PricewaterhouseCoopers used scenario planning to explore the future of work (Houghton and Spence, 2016). They developed three possible scenarios for 2022:

Orange world   *Small is beautiful.* Networks of small, specialized enterprises replace big companies. People work on short-term contracts exploring job opportunities online through portals developed by craft guilds.

Green world   *Companies care.* Demographic change, climate, and sustainability are key business drivers. Employment law, employee relations, and corporate responsibility are vital in this heavily regulated environment.

Blue world   *Corporate is king.* Large corporations are like mini-states providing staff with housing, health, education, and other welfare benefits. Human capital metrics are sophisticated, and people management is as powerful as finance.

If none of these models turns out to be correct, will this have been a waste of time? No, because those who are used to thinking in innovative, lateral ways about the future are likely to be able to respond more quickly to what does actually happen.

As a change diagnostic, scenario planning encourages creative "blue skies" decision making to identify the most probable futures for the organization. This analysis then forms the basis for prioritizing, planning, and acting to implement appropriate changes. Exercise 4.2 invites you to carry out a scenario planning exercise for an organization with which you are familiar.

TABLE 4.3
Elements of
Strategy

1. **Corporate mission: What is our core business?**
   • In what product categories, market segments, or regions/countries will we compete? What technologies are core to our business?

2. **Tactics: How will we achieve our mission?**
   • Will we depend on internal growth, partnerships, licensing, franchising, or mergers and acquisitions?

3. **USPs*: How will we stand out from the competition?**
   • Will we stand out because of our brand, reputation, cost, product quality, styling, or customization?

4. **Pace: How quickly will we move?**
   • Will we expand slowly or rapidly? In what sequence will we undertake our actions?

5. **Competitive logic: Are we a low-cost or premium quality provider?**
   • Will we compete on price and volume through cost reduction based on economies of scale and scope, or high price (lower volume) based on quality product/service and/or unique features?

* USPs = Unique selling points

Elements of Strategy

Strategy is often considered to be at the heart of change because it addresses the basic issues with which an organization has to deal: What are we seeking to achieve, and how? Strategy and change intersect because strategies can change ("change of strategy") and change may be necessary to realize a set strategy ("change for strategy"). Donald Hambrick and James Fredrickson (2001) developed a framework that characterizes organization strategy in terms of five mutually reinforcing elements, which they called "arenas," "vehicles," "differentiators," "staging," and "economic logic." They argue that misalignment of these elements of strategy suggests the need for change. Table 4.3 summarizes their framework, using current terminology.

From this perspective, only when all five strategic elements have been determined is it possible to assess the structures and systems that will be appropriate to pursuing the strategy. However, before moving to this stage, it is important to test the quality of the proposed strategy. One approach concerns the key evaluation criteria summarized in Table 4.4 (based on Hambrick and Fredrickson, 2001).

As a change diagnostic, therefore, this analysis identifies the organizational changes that are necessary to pursue a desired strategy. If for any reason (cost, time, expertise) those changes are difficult or impossible to implement, then the strategy may have to be reconsidered. This approach can also help to generate an integrated package of change initiatives that are mutually self-reinforcing and that are aligned with organization strategy. Although integration and alignment may sound like straightforward advice, this can often be difficult to achieve in practice. For example, problems arise when changes that are optimal for one division of an organization undermine activities and changes in other divisions (see point 5 in Table 4.4 about spreading resources too thinly).

TABLE 4.4

Testing the Quality of Your Strategy

Key Evaluation Criteria

1. **Is your strategy consistent with wider business trends and developments?**
   - Is your proposed core business consistent with evidence on business trends, does your strategy recognize what it takes to succeed in this environment, and will your business model produce a reasonable profit margin?

2. **Are your organization's key capabilities consistent with those required to be competitive in this business?**
   - With your particular mix of resources, does this strategy give you a good head start on your competitors?
   - Can you pursue this strategy in a way that keeps you ahead of the competition?

3. **Are your USPs sustainable?**
   - Are there solid grounds for being confident that competitors won't simply copy you, or are you planning further innovation to create other new market opportunities?

4. **Is your strategy internally consistent?**
   - Do the five elements of strategy—mission, tactics, USPs, pace, and competitive logic—consistently reinforce each other?

5. **Are your resources adequate to fulfill the strategy's ambitions?**
   - Do you have the finances, time, management capability, and other resources to achieve the strategy, or are these resources going to be spread too thinly?
   - If your existing resources are insufficient, do you have a feasible plan to acquire needed resources?

6. **Can you actually implement this strategy?**
   - Do key stakeholders support your strategy? If significant change is needed for the strategy to be implemented, is the organization as a whole ready for major change, and do you have a capable strategic change leadership team?

The Strategic Inventory

Strategy is about the future, committing resources to activities based on "assumptions, premises and beliefs about an organization's environment (society and its structure, the market, the customer, and the competition), its mission, and the core competencies needed to accomplish that mission" (Picken and Dess, 1998, p. 35). These assumptions, premises, and beliefs, often formed over time through experience, become a "mental grid" through which new information is sifted and interpreted. To the extent that this grid comprises assumptions and beliefs that accurately reflect the environment, the quality of strategic decision making is enhanced. However, when assumptions fail to reflect key elements of the business environment, they can lead to the adoption of inappropriate strategies, a phenomenon known as "strategic drift."

As a change diagnostic, identifying and validating management's strategic assumptions can be useful in assessing whether or not strategy is consistent with key elements of the business environment. This assessment can then identify whether an organization's

Assumptions and Strategy *Strategic Drift and the Beech Starship*

In the early 1980s, Raytheon Co. acquired Beech, a light-aircraft company that had fallen on hard times. The managers appointed by Raytheon proposed to reinvigorate Beech by producing an advanced turboprop aircraft based on the latest carbon-fiber technology. It was expected that this technology would enable Beech to compete at the lower end of the business jet market, with a product that was 60 percent the price of competitors, as well as being more fuel efficient. An 85 percent scale model "Starship" was built, and on the basis of good reviews, Beech announced that it would invest in a new factory to make the plane, which would be ready for sale in two years (Picken and Dess, 1998).

This initiative was based on several assumptions:

1. Beech could complete the design of the new aircraft and get Federal Aviation Administration (FAA) certification within two years.

2. The new carbon-fiber technology would not be a significant problem, even though it was not covered by the existing regulations.

3. Sufficient aircraft would be built to justify the expenditure on a new factory.

However, the FAA had never certified an all-composite aircraft and insisted on compliance with the standards for metal aircraft. This led to a redesign, which increased the weight, which required a bigger engine, which needed more fuel, which meant more weight, which meant further redesign, and so on. Eventually, the Starship made it to market, but it was four years late, carried only 6 passengers rather than 10, and cruised at 335 knots instead of 400. The price advantage over jets had also disappeared. The expected demand failed to materialize, and the production line was closed.

strategy should be a focal point for change. To establish the degree of consensus on dominant strategic assumptions, Joseph Picken and Gregory Dess (1998) developed a "strategic inventory" (see table 4.5).

Picken and Dess (1998) suggest that, where there is consensus on strategic assumptions, the organization should seek an independent validation to check for biases. Where significant divergence exists, attention should focus on which (and whose) assumptions are currently embedded in strategy and which (and whose) can be independently validated. The strategic inventory involves a more sophisticated analysis than that provided by the widely used SWOT approach to understanding an organization's Strengths, Weaknesses, Opportunities, and Threats. The danger with SWOT analysis is that it becomes a listing not of strengths but "perceived strengths," not weaknesses but "perceived weaknesses," and so on. It may simply capture existing beliefs, the current dominant logic, which may need to be challenged to improve organizational performance.

The Cultural Web

Organizational culture is often seen as a response to performance problems and is a component of many change diagnostics (Johnson et al., 2017). This perspective describes organizational culture in terms of a "cultural web" that has seven elements (see Figure 4.5):

1. *The paradigm.* The set of assumptions commonly held throughout the organization with respect to basic elements of the business such as what business we're in, how we compete, who our competitors are.

TABLE 4.5
The Strategic
Inventory

Defining the boundaries of the competitive environment
- What are the boundaries of our industry? What is our served market? What products and services do we provide?
- Who are the customers? Who are the noncustomers? What is the difference between them?
- Who are our competitors? Who are the noncompetitors? What makes one firm a competitor and the other not?
- What key competencies are required to compete in this industry? Where is the value added?

Defining the key assumptions
- Who is our customer? What kinds of things are important to that customer? How does he or she perceive us? What kind of relationships do we have?
- Who is the ultimate end user? What kinds of things are important to this end user? How does he or she perceive us? What kind of relationship do we have?
- Who are our competitors? What are their strengths and weaknesses? How do they perceive us? What can we learn from them?
- Who are the potential competitors? New entrants? What changes in the environment or their behavior would make them competitors?
- What is the industry's value chain? Where is value added? What is the cost structure? How does our firm compare? How about our competitors?
- What technologies are important in our industry? Product technologies? Production technologies? Delivery and service technologies? How does our firm compare? How about our competitors?
- What are the key factors of production? Who are the suppliers? Are we dependent on a limited number of sources? How critical are these relationships? How solid?
- What are the bases for competition in our industry? What are the key success factors? How do we measure up? How about our competitors?
- What trends and factors in the external environment are important to our industry? How are they likely to change? Over what time horizon?
- Are we able, in assessing our knowledge and assumptions, to separate fact from assumption?

Is our assumption set internally consistent?
- For each pair of assumptions, can we answer "yes" to the question, "If assumption A is true, does assumption B logically follow?"

Do we understand the relative importance of each of our assumptions in terms of
- Its potential impact on performance?
- Our level of confidence in its validity?
- The likelihood and expectation of near-term change?
- Its strategic impact?

Are our key assumptions broadly understood?
- Have we documented and communicated our key assumptions? To our key managers? To the boundary-spanners? To other key employees?

Do we have a process for reviewing and validating our key assumptions and premises?
- Is there a process in place? Are responsibilities assigned? Are periodic reviews scheduled?

FIGURE 4.5
The Cultural Web

Source: From Johnson et al. (2017), Pearson Education, Harlow, Essex.

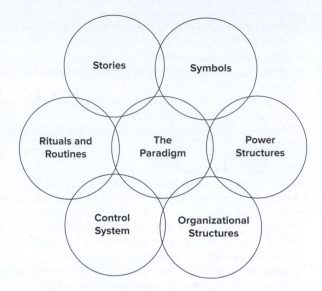

2. *Rituals and routines*. These concern how organizational members treat each other and, perhaps more importantly, the associated beliefs as to what is right and proper and valued in this regard.

3. *Stories*. As told by organizational members, stories are a form of oral history and communicate and reinforce core elements of the culture.

4. *Symbols*. Logos, office design, dress style, language use, and other symbols convey aspects of the culture.

5. *Control systems*. What is valued in the organization is communicated through what is measured and rewarded.

6. *Power structures*. These concern the most influential management groups in the organization.

7. *Organizational structure*. The formal and informal differentiation and integration of tasks.

As a change diagnostic, this approach highlights the value of "mapping" the organization's cultural web. First, exposing issues that are rarely discussed is a useful way of questioning traditional norms and habits. If what is taken for granted is never questioned, then change will be difficult. Second, cultural mapping can highlight potential barriers to change. Third, it may also be possible through this approach to identify aspects of the culture that are especially resistant to change. Fourth, a culture map can be the basis for considering the changes that will be necessary to pursue a new strategy. Finally, practical ideas for managing those changes can then be developed.

The unit of analysis for the cultural web is the organization as a whole. The change manager with a specific initiative in a particular division, therefore, may not find this approach helpful in identifying ways to increase the probability of success of that change project.

LO 4.3 Diagnosing Readiness for Change

The diagnostics that we have discussed so far have been designed to help decide whether or not an organization has to change and, if so, to determine what has to change. It is often appropriate to ask two other questions before pressing ahead with implementation. First, is the organization as a whole receptive to change? We will explore this question through the concepts of *receptive organizational context* and *absorptive capacity*. We will also discuss the technique of *force-field analysis* to assess how receptive an organization is to a particular change. Exercise 4.3 offers another readiness diagnostic. Second, are those who will be affected ready for these changes? In this section, therefore, we will explore both organizational receptiveness (or readiness) and individual readiness (or receptiveness) to change. The aim, of course, is not simply to establish levels of organizational and individual readiness. Understanding why readiness may be low is a platform for remedial action to strengthen receptiveness and readiness where appropriate.

The Receptive Organizational Context

Organizations vary in receptiveness to change, which depends on several conditions (Eccles, 1994):

1. What pressures are there for change?
2. Is there a shared vision of the goals, benefits, and direction?
3. Is there coordination and trust between those concerned?
4. Is there the will and power to act?
5. Do we have enough capable people with sufficient resources?
6. Do we have defined accountability and suitable rewards?
7. Have we identified the first steps that we need to take?
8. Is the organization able to learn and adapt?

Where the answers to these questions are "yes," organizational receptiveness is high and resistance to change is likely to be limited. However, without pressure, clear goals, trust, power to act, resources, and so on, receptiveness is likely to be low, and the changes will be more difficult to implement. It is important to note that an organization as a whole may be more or less receptive to change, regardless of the attitudes of individual members.

This simple assessment of receptiveness highlights two practical issues. The first is timing. Some conditions (growing pressure, for example) may improve simply by waiting. The second concerns action, to strengthen the conditions when receptiveness is low. Remedial actions could involve:

- Ensuring that the rationale for change is strong and understood.
- Articulating a clear vision of goals and benefits.
- Confidence-building measures to develop interpersonal and interdivisional trust.
- Ensuring that key positions are held by dynamic, high-performing individuals.
- Developing change management capabilities across the organization.

- Providing adequate resources (people, technology, training) to support the proposed changes.
- Aligning performance management and reward systems with change goals.
- Clearly establishing the initial action plan.
- Developing learning organization capabilities.

The key point is that organizational receptiveness to change can be managed, by taking steps to change the conditions that lower receptiveness. Most of those steps are cost-neutral.

Absorptive Capacity

Wesley Cohen and Daniel Levinthal (1990) developed the related concept of "absorptive capacity," which they defined as the ability of an organization to value, to assimilate, and to apply new knowledge. Absorptive capacity depends on an organization's existing stock of knowledge and skills and a "learning organization culture" with leadership and norms that support the acquisition, sharing, and application of new ideas. From their review of work on this abstract and complex concept, Zahra and George (2002, p. 185) redefine absorptive capacity as "a dynamic capability pertaining to knowledge creation and utilization that enhances a firm's ability to gain and sustain a competitive advantage." They argue that absorptive capacity has four dimensions:

1. *Acquisition*. The ability to find and to prioritize new knowledge and ideas quickly and efficiently
2. *Assimilation*. The ability to understand new knowledge and to link it to existing knowledge
3. *Transformation*. The ability to combine, convert, and recodify new knowledge
4. *Exploitation*. The ability to use new ideas productively.

Acquisition depends on the organization's external links and networks, which are often available only to a small number of professional staff and senior management. Assimilation, transformation, and exploitation rely more on internal capabilities, relationships, and systems. These four dimensions can also be managed. Actions to increase an organization's absorptive capacity include: widening the exposure of staff to external networks; the use of job rotation and cross-functional teams to encourage the sharing of knowledge and ideas across organizational boundaries; wider employee participation in management decision making; and relaxing rules, procedures, and routines that stifle exploration and experimentation (Jansen et al., 2005). Once again, many of these actions are cost-neutral.

Force-Field Analysis

Force-field analysis is a popular diagnostic, developed in the mid-twentieth century by Kurt Lewin (1943; 1951). As a change diagnostic, this tool has two main purposes. First, it can be used to assess whether or not an organization is ready for a particular change initiative. Second, if readiness or receptiveness is low, force-field analysis can help to identify and prioritize the preparation or "groundwork" that may be required before implementation can begin. The analysis involves identifying the forces that are, respectively, driving and restraining movement toward a given set of outcomes, called the "target situation." The "field" is usually drawn like this:

Target situation: develop customer-orientation

Driving Forces ⟶	⟵ Restraining Forces
static sales	difficult to recruit capable sales staff
increasingly aggressive competition	high turnover among part-time staff
rising number of customer complaints	trained and capable staff are "poached"
brand being criticized on social media	our competitors face similar problems
new chief executive supports this move	cost of customer relationships training

This example is artificial but used to illustrate the approach. It is unusual, for example, to have the same number of forces on the driving side as on the restraining side. Having constructed the field, the forces that have been identified can each be weighted or scored, say from 1 (weak) to 10 (strong), to produce a rough calculus to the balance of forces. This scoring procedure can give the analysis a false image of quantified rigor. More important than the forces and their scores is the discussion that produces the analysis. Who conducts this analysis is thus also important, often a project team or steering group. The underpinning discussion can expose wide differences in perception, both of the forces in play and of their strength. The debate helps to either resolve those differences or at least allow those involved to know how their opinions vary and how those differences have arisen.

If the driving forces are overwhelming, then the change can go ahead without significant problems. If the restraining forces are overwhelming, then the change may have to be abandoned, or delayed until conditions have improved. However, if the driving and restraining forces are more or less in balance, then the analysis can be used to plan appropriate action. The extent to which the force field is balanced is a matter of judgement. Used in a group setting, this method helps to structure what can often be an untidy discussion covering a wide range of factors and differing perceptions.

Managing a balanced force field to promote movement toward the target situation involves the following considerations:

1. Increasing the driving forces can often result in an increase in the resisting forces. This means that the current equilibrium does not change but instead is maintained with increased tension.
2. Reducing the resisting forces is preferable, as this allows movement toward the desired outcomes or target situation without increasing tension.
3. Group norms are an important force in resisting and shaping organizational change.

Individual Readiness for Change

Individual readiness for change is a predisposition, perhaps even impatience, to welcome and embrace change. Where individual readiness is high, change may be straightforward. But when readiness is low, as with organizational receptiveness, some "groundwork" may be required to increase levels of change readiness among those who are going to be affected.

Rafferty et al. (2013) view change readiness as an individual attitude that has both cognitive and emotional (or "affective") dimensions. "Collective readiness" for change, of a group or organization, is based on the shared beliefs that develop through social interaction and shared experiences. Underpinning an individual's change readiness, therefore, are five beliefs:

1. *Discrepancy.* The belief that change is needed.
2. *Appropriate.* The belief that the proposed change is an appropriate response.
3. *Efficacy.* The individual's perceived capability to implement the change.
4. *Principal support.* The belief that the organization (management, peers) will provide resources and information.
5. *Valence.* The individual's evaluation of the personal costs and benefits; no benefits, no overall positive evaluation of readiness.

Individual change readiness is demonstrated through support for, openness toward, and commitment to change. These attitudes and behaviors can be influenced by three sets of factors.

The first set of factors concerns external pressures, including industry and technology changes, new regulations, and professional group memberships. The second set of factors concerns what Rafferty et al. (2013) call "internal context enablers," including change participation and communication processes, and leadership. The third set of factors concerns personal characteristics and includes needs, values, and traits such as self-confidence, risk tolerance, dispositional resistance to change, and self-efficacy.

From a change management perspective, therefore, individuals' readiness for change can be assessed and can also be influenced. With regard to increasing readiness, research evidence points in particular to the power of the internal enablers. Individual readiness for change can be influenced by processes that are designed to enhance participation in decisions, by high-quality change communications, and by perceptions of the organization's history of change (previous experience, support for change, congruence of values). Again, there are practical steps that change managers can take to increase the probability that a change initiative will be welcome and successful—and most of those steps involve little or no expenditure.

Stakeholder Mapping

Another approach to assessing individual responses to change is stakeholder mapping, which focuses on power and interests. A stakeholder is anyone who is likely to be affected by an organizational change and who can influence the outcomes, directly or indirectly. Those stakeholders may be members of the organization, or external groups and agencies, or other organizations. Stakeholder mapping is used to decide how to manage those different individuals and groups. This approach involves categorizing stakeholders on two dimensions. The first concerns power and influence. Can a particular individual or group give strong support or pose a serious threat to the initiative? Or perhaps they have little influence, and their views will not count for much. The second concerns what those individuals and groups expect to win or lose from the change; some may have high stakes, and others a low level of interest. Stakeholders can be plotted on the matrix shown in Figure 4.6 (a development of the approach suggested by Grundy, 1997).

FIGURE 4.6

Stakeholder Mapping Matrix

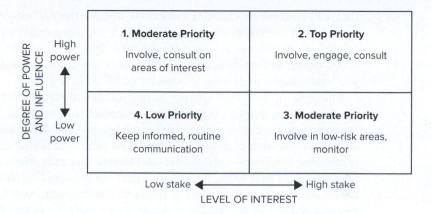

Change managers should pay close attention to influential stakeholders with a high level of interest in the outcomes of the change (those in quadrant 2). This group has the power to "make or break" the change. However, degrees of power and stakes in change can themselves change. And such changes can be brought about by the way in which those stakeholders and the change process itself are managed. Those in quadrant 1, who are influential but with low interest, may find that their stakes in the outcomes are higher if components of the change are redesigned in ways that affect them. In this way, stakeholders in quadrants 1 and 4 can migrate to quadrants 2 and 3, respectively, creating either more support for the proposed changes or greater resistance.

Action to manage stakeholders for a given change initiative can then be based on this matrix:

- Can new stakeholders be added to change the balance?
- Can oppositional stakeholders be encouraged to leave?
- Can the influence of pro-change stakeholders be increased?
- Can the influence of antagonistic stakeholders be decreased?
- Can the change be modified in a way that meets concerns without undermining the change?
- If stakeholder resistance is strong, should the proposal be revisited?

Stakeholder mapping informs change managers about the likely responses of key stakeholders, and steps can then be taken to manage those stakeholders, to weaken opposition and strengthen support.

With regard to organizational receptiveness to change and individual readiness to change, the change manager does not have to accept the diagnosis. There are practical—and often inexpensive—actions that can be taken to increase receptiveness and readiness. The diagnostic approaches described in this section help to identify what those actions could involve.

LO 4.4 Agile Organization

The agile organization model offers another valuable diagnostic framework that is central to understanding and implementing change. An agile organization is deliberately designed to change naturally. In other words, it has structures, systems, and procedures that adapt, flex, and respond to changing conditions without the explicit need for formal change management interventions. Change is thus a key feature, a part of the organization's culture, the way things are done around here. Spotify, mentioned earlier in this chapter, is one example of an agile organization. But is the agile organization model suitable for your organization or at least for sections of it?

The agile organization appears to be "the new dominant organizational paradigm" (de Smet, 2018, p. 80). The traditional paradigm is challenged by a rapidly changing environment, the constant introduction of disruptive new technologies, the digitization and democratization of information, and competition for skilled staff. To respond quickly to changing conditions—opportunities and threats—hierarchy, bureaucracy, detailed instructions, and silos have to go. Instead, organizations are adopting flexible resourcing, nonintrusive leadership, and networks of empowered teams with front-to-back responsibility for meaningful parts of the workflow. Along with Spotify, Gore and ING have adopted this approach with apparent success (Aghina et al., 2017).

This trend is not surprising, as the external environment for most organizations has become VUCA: Volatile, Unpredictable, Complex, and Ambiguous. Agility can be defined as "the ability to quickly reconfigure strategy, structure, processes, people, and technology toward value-creating and value-protecting opportunities" (Ahlbäck et al., 2017, p. 1). Agile ways of working include flat or nonexistent management hierarchies, self-managing teams, cross-functional teams, skunk works and scrums (autonomous project groups), knowledge communities, innovation hubs, integrator roles, and hackathons (rapid and intense periods of collaboration). These practices are designed to encourage timely and creative responses to problems and opportunities among those who are directly involved, without first having to refer issues to more senior management and wait for instructions.

Tomorrow It Will Be Relevant for You

Agility has always been important for companies. Take the high-tech sector, where I've done most of my work. In that sector, you're often only as good as your last product. That means you have to be agile. Now, you could think, 'I'm not in the high-tech sector, so that's less relevant for me.' But with today's levels of uncertainty, ambiguity, volatility in the markets, and globalization, this is starting to be true for any company. It's critical to be agile and quickly respond to change and actually benefit from change. And if you think that you're still in a corner where this doesn't hold true, wait for the disruption to come. Tomorrow it will be relevant for you. (Aghina et al., 2015, p. 2)

The concept of the flexible, adaptive, agile organization that responds quickly to environmental trends is not new. Burns and Stalker (1961), in a study of the Scottish electronics industry, distinguished between mechanistic (hierarchical, rigid) and organic (decentralized, flexible) management systems. Mechanistic systems, they argued, are appropriate for organizations whose environments are stable and predictable. Organic systems are more effective in complex, turbulent environments. As mentioned earlier, Kanter (1983) distinguished between segmentalist (mechanistic) and integrative (organic) organizational cultures, arguing that the latter are more open to innovation and change. Worley and Lawler (2006; 2009) distinguish between rigid "built to last" and adaptable "built to change" organizations. The concept of self-managing teams (or autonomous groups) dates from the seminal work of the Tavistock Institute in London in the mid-twentieth century (Emery, 1959).

ING is a Dutch multinational banking and financial services company based in Amsterdam. Since 2015, it has been implementing an agile organization model. The aims were to reduce time to market for new products, increase employee engagement, develop staff skills, minimize bureaucracy, increase productivity, and ultimately improve the customer experience. New digital distribution channels had changed the behavior of customers whose expectations were being influenced by companies in other sectors. ING wanted to offer seamless service for customers using a combination of digital and other channels, such as visiting a branch for advice and then making investments online.

ING "gave up traditional hierarchy, formal meetings, overengineering, detailed planning, and excessive 'input steering' in exchange for empowered teams, informal networks, and 'output steering'" (Mahadevan et al., 2017, p. 10). Starting with their headquarters staff, ING created 350 "squads" or self-managing teams, which each belong to one of 13 groups. Focusing on customer needs, each multidisciplinary team has "end to end" responsibility for their section of the workflow. Teams include marketing, product and commercial specialists, user-experience designers, data analysts, and IT engineers. The old departmental silos have gone. Teams of IT and commercial staff work together in the same building, testing products that might be offered to customers, without a management presence that could slow down collaboration. To the company's surprise, older employees adapted more rapidly to agile working than their younger colleagues. ING also introduced peer-to-peer hiring; teams recruit their own members, which increased team diversity in terms of gender, character, and skills. Chief operating officer Bart Schlatmann, said, "In the beginning, I think the [banking sector] regulators were at times worried that agile meant freedom and chaos; that's absolutely not the case. Everything we do is managed on a daily basis and transparent on walls around our offices" (Mahadevan et al., 2017, p. 8).

The Agile Army

The British Army, like any traditional organization, had a structured hierarchy with clearly defined silos. Decisions were made at the top and flowed down the structure. During World War II, everyone knew their place in what Field Marshall Bernard Montgomery called "a tidy battlefield." He also spoke of "the orchestra of war," with one conductor and the different instruments doing what they were told to do. But this rigid structure is not suited to the changing nature and pace of modern warfare. For example, during the Falklands War in 1982, soldiers waited to be told exactly what to do, when casualties could have been avoided if they acted on their own initiative. "At the end of that war, people asked themselves, Why did intelligent people sit there, waiting to be told what to do? Why didn't they just get on and do it?" (Theunissen and Maciejewski, 2019, p. 2)

To become more flexible, the army adopted "agile" organization principles, with networks of teams using rapid decision making and learning cycles (Brosseau et al., 2019). In the new "Mission Command" system, teams have decision rights to act on information available to them. Unnecessary bureaucracy was eliminated (with difficulty), and a degree of standardization was retained, so that everyone has a common frame of reference and knows what to expect from others. The aim is to combine speed and flexibility with efficiency and stability. This means "giving people the tools to make rapid decisions to disrupt the enemy. The idea was that you

(Continued)

could defeat a larger enemy by getting inside their decision cycle, moving so quickly that their cohesion is disrupted and they begin to fall apart" (Theunissen and Maciejewski, 2019, p. 2). This is how this works in practice:

> In the old world, leaders wrote down what they wanted people to do in quite a precise way. People were given tasks that fit within an overall operation or mission. A mission today is not a set of tasks, because, in a dynamic situation, people should revert to the purpose rather than the task. Situations change; the enemy's done something. That's my purpose—that's what I'm going to go after—rather than in the old system, where people would literally do their task and wait to be told what to do next. If you imagine that philosophy being replicated across an organization of 80,000 people at every level, it dramatically changes the performance. Everyone at every level is thinking, What if it changes? How do I respond? It's very disempowering to have targets without any real context of how that target fits into the bigger picture. (Theunissen and Maciejewski, 2019, p. 3)

Military commanders and their soldiers have changed the way in which they operate in the field. The same agile principles apply to commercial organizations facing complex and turbulent environments.

One novel aspect of the current agile concept is that, for many organizations, it has become a strategic priority, not just "nice to have." A second novel dimension concerns the blending of agility and stability: "To be agile, an organization needs to be both dynamic and stable. Dynamic practices enable companies to respond nimbly and quickly to new challenges and opportunities, while stable practices cultivate reliability and efficiency by establishing a backbone of elements that don't need to change frequently" (Ahlbäck et al., 2017, p. 4). Agility combines stable and dynamic practices. Stable practices include, for example, a shared vision and purpose, standardized ways of working, shared leadership, and a performance orientation. Dynamic practices include rapid iteration and experimentation, continuous learning, flexible resource allocation, and role mobility.

According to Ahlbäck et al. (2017, p. 12), the main challenges for an organization managing an agile transformation include:

- inconsistency between agile ways of working and day-to-day job requirements
- lack of collaboration between levels and departments
- resistance to change

How can management create an "agile friendly culture"? First, identify those parts of the organization that need to become agile, assess which stable and dynamic practices need to be strengthened, decide on resourcing and timescale for the change to maintain momentum, and also

1. Establish thinking (mindsets) and behaviors consistent with agile working.
2. Role model these new behaviors.
3. Support employees to develop required new skills.
4. Provide formal reinforcement, including rewards and incentives for demonstrating new behaviors.

From their research, Ahlbäck et al. (2017, p. 3) claim that, on average, respondents working in agile units are much more likely to report better financial performance relative to their peers and much better nonfinancial measures.

To Be Truly Agile

In our experience, truly agile organizations, paradoxically, learn to be both stable (resilient, reliable, and efficient) and dynamic (fast, nimble, and adaptive). To master this paradox, companies must design structures, governance arrangements, and processes with a relatively unchanging set of core elements—a fixed backbone. At the same time, they must also create looser, more dynamic elements that can be adapted quickly to new challenges and opportunities. (Aghina et al., 2016, p. 59)

Teams and Personality Traits

The core components of agile organizations are small self-managing, multidisciplinary, performance cells or teams. These teams have autonomy over their work, for which they are accountable. Unlike teams in traditional organizations, they can be quickly created and dissolved and are devoted to specific value-creating activities and performance outcomes. There are three types of agile teams or cells. First, flexible cross-functional cells work on specific projects, products, or activities, combining the necessary skills and knowledge within the team. Second, stable self-managing teams work on common tasks, such as frontline activities, setting their own goals and priorities. Third, "flow-to-work" groups handle different tasks based on need and priority, such as human resource management teams (Brosseau et al., 2019). The best approach is therefore tailored to the context and the task.

A False Sense of Control

Well, when you are a leader and for 20 years you have been in a managerial hierarchy, what do you do when you really get fearful and uncertain? You go back to what's worked in the past. You exert control, add things, add rules, add processes, add structure. What you should do is actually a real act of leadership: you have to take things away. You have to reduce the structure, the processes. But that's really difficult. It's much easier and more comfortable to add things because that gives you a, maybe false, sense of control. (Aghina et al., 2015, p. 2)

Self-managing teams create problems for supervisors and middle managers, whose traditional responsibilities are eroded but whose skills and experience are still valuable to the organization. The agile teams themselves absorb tasks such as project planning, task allocation, progress monitoring, and performance appraisal. However, the management task in an agile organization is to create the environment in which teams can work effectively. There may be some problems—remaining bureaucratic barriers, for example—that teams cannot overcome on their own initiative. Management oversight is therefore still required, but with "a light but consistent touch" (Bossert et al., 2018, p. 68). Middle managers thus help teams to define goals, focus on problem-solving rather than decision making, spend more time on coaching and learning, and act as stewards rather than as superiors. These redefined hands-off roles, with different job titles (coach, developer, mentor), may be difficult for managers with experience in traditional organizational structures (De Smet et al., 2019).

Are particular personality traits needed for agile working? Based on interviews with team members, Aghina et al. (2019) found that people who work well in agile settings have three attributes. They cope well with ambiguity, focus on outcomes rather than on process, and are "team players." The personality trait of "agreeableness" is also important:

> The prominence of agreeableness was the most surprising result. Agreeableness is the secret sauce of great agile teams. Most cultures teach and reinforce a culture of competition, but we are increasingly seeing other ways to build a high-performing, agile organization. Being agreeable is not about blindly agreeing without any thinking; in fact, research has found that increased diversity at work is associated with healthy conflict that allows room for group members to test ideas and listen to various alternative perspectives, which improves task performance. Agreeableness means saying "yes, and ..." instead of "yes, but." Rather than avoiding conflict, agreeableness is about empathetic listening to the team and their ideas and being attuned to feedback from customers. (p. 4)

Team research has consistently demonstrated that the best performing teams do not necessarily include the most skilled and experienced members, but those with an appropriate combination of personality and behaviors (Isaac and Carson, 2016). The same appears to be true for agile teams.

EXERCISE 4.1

Scenario Planning

LO 4.3

Here is one structured methodology for scenario planning, for your own organization, or for one with which you are familiar:

1. Brainstorm the range of environmental factors that have the potential to impact on the performance of your organization. In the spirit of brainstorming, accept all suggestions at this point and suspend judgement as to the significance of any suggested factor.

2. Ask individuals to identify which factors from this list they believe to be the "key drivers" of the organization's performance over a specified time period—say, five years.

3. Aggregating these individual responses, identify the five most commonly cited key drivers; these could be, for example, exchange rates, new technologies, entry by new competitors, mergers, competition for key staff, and costs and/or shortages of raw materials.

4. Using these key drivers as the core elements, construct three future scenarios for the organization: the most likely, an optimistic scenario, and a pessimistic one. The "most likely" scenario is constructed on the basis of the best guess as to what will happen to each of the five key drivers over the specified time frame. Note that "best guess" does not imply a casual approach; best guess can be based on sophisticated market intelligence and forecasting. The "optimistic" and "pessimistic" scenarios focus attention on how the organization might respond to each of those outcomes. The construction of the scenarios requires skill, and it is not uncommon for organizations to employ external consultants who are experienced in scenario development. Scenarios need to be compelling and plausible narratives, even if they are unlikely to happen. This is necessary if they are to form the basis of discussion concerning the organization's response to those three possible futures.

5. Finally, outline the different organizational change agendas that will be required to deal with each of those three possible futures.

EXERCISE 4.2

Readiness for Change Analysis

LO 4.3

The purpose of this diagnostic is to assess whether a *specific* organizational change initiative, project, or program has been well planned. Before you begin this assessment process, therefore, you must agree on a description of the proposed change or changes.

> The change proposal being considered is:

You can carry out this assessment on your own or with colleagues in the organization—your steering group or project team, for example. Study the following items and circle the appropriate number on the scale. The number that you circle should reflect your view of the quality of the work carried out on that item, with respect to this change, so far. Keep the agreed definition of the proposed change in mind throughout this analysis.

This is a generic assessment tool, and the wording may not apply directly to your organization. If you feel that an item is not relevant to your circumstances, either ignore it, or think of a way in which that item should be reworded to make it more appropriate.

If you are working on this assessment with other members of your program, project, or change management team, complete this analysis individually before sharing and discussing your scores. You may find that different team members see things differently. Exploration of those differences can be extremely valuable in developing a shared understanding of the proposals and in determining where the action priorities lie.

Source: This analysis is based on Woodcock and Francis (1992).

1. The change proposal has been financially justified as giving an adequate return on investment.

no financial justification	1	2	3	4	5	6	7	full financial justification

2. The assumptions on which the financial justification is based have been fully defined.

assumptions not defined	1	2	3	4	5	6	7	assumptions clearly defined

3. The costs of the proposed change have been realistically predicted—that is, all possible costs have been identified.

costs not identified	1	2	3	4	5	6	7	all costs identified

4. The costs of disruption to the present systems have been specifically identified.

disruption costs not identified	1	2	3	4	5	6	7	disruption costs identified

5. The leadership of the proposed change has been identified.

change leaders not identified	1	2	3	4	5	6	7	change leaders identified

6. The leaders of the proposed change are willing volunteers.

change leaders are not willing volunteers	1	2	3	4	5	6	7	change leaders are willing volunteers

(Continued)

7. A comprehensive implementation plan for the proposed change has been prepared.

no comprehensive plan	1	2	3	4	5	6	7	comprehensive plan prepared

8. All of those who could comment on the plan have had adequate time to study it.

no adequate comment	1	2	3	4	5	6	7	full comments available

9. Care has been taken to ensure that the risks inherent in the proposed change have been identified and assessed.

risks not identified or assessed	1	2	3	4	5	6	7	risks identified and assessed

10. Outside comment from impartial specialists has been invited on the wisdom of the proposed change.

no external comment invited	1	2	3	4	5	6	7	comprehensive external comment invited

11. Consideration has been given to the new skills that will be required for the effective implementation of the proposed change.

no consideration of skills requirement	1	2	3	4	5	6	7	full consideration of skills requirement

12. All those who could inhibit or stop the proposed change have been identified.

potential blockers not identified	1	2	3	4	5	6	7	potential blockers identified

13. A strategy has been devised for winning over all those who could inhibit or stop the proposed change.

no winning-over strategy identified	1	2	3	4	5	6	7	comprehensive winning-over strategy identified

14. The proposed change can be linked directly with the strategic plans of the organization.

no clear links with strategic plans	1	2	3	4	5	6	7	clear links with strategic plans

15. Those responsible for the proposed change have studied the nature and outcomes of similar initiatives in other organizations.

no other organizations visited or reviewed	1	2	3	4	5	6	7	several other organizations visited and reviewed

16. Although based on similar initiatives elsewhere, the need to tailor the proposed changes to the local context is recognized.

no allowances made for customization	1	2	3	4	5	6	7	realistic allowances made for customization

17. Clear success criteria and success measures have been identified.

no success criteria or measures identified	1	2	3	4	5	6	7	comprehensive success criteria and measures identified

18. Procedures have been established to help the organization to learn from the experience of implementing these changes.

no learning procedures in place	1	2	3	4	5	6	7	comprehensive learning procedures in place

19. Top management is deeply committed to the success of the proposed changes.

no top management commitment	1	2	3	4	5	6	7	full top management commitment

20. The overall leadership of the proposed change is able and willing to exercise decisive leadership.

uncertain overall leadership	1	2	3	4	5	6	7	superior overall leadership

Scoring

Simply add the numbers that you have circled to produce a score between 20 and 140. If several members of your group or team have completed this analysis, then add all their individual scores and calculate the average. What does the resultant score suggest?

20–40	Considerable anxiety should be experienced about the proposed changes.
41–80	Much work needs to be done to develop an effective change program.
81–100	The proposal is well developed, but change management can be improved.
101–140	This is a well-planned change proposal.

Action

Where are the main problems and blockages, and what can we do to address those? Identify those items that you scored five points or less, or use the average item scores for the group or team as a whole. Select the five lowest-scoring items. Prioritize these, and then brainstorm appropriate actions to address each of them in turn to improve readiness.

Problem Item	Appropriate Actions
1.	
2.	
3.	
4.	
5.	

Additional Reading

Blenko, M.W., Mankins, M.C., and Rogers, P. 2010. The decision-driven organization. *Harvard Business Review* 88(6):54–62. Argues that links between organization structure and performance are weak and that decision-making processes and decision quality are more important. Offers a diagnostic based on links between structure, roles, culture, and decisions.

Holbeche, L. 2018. *The agile organization: How to build an innovative, sustainable and resilient business.* 2nd ed. London: Kogan Page. Describes how to create agility at individual, team, and organizational levels, drawing on a wide range of case examples, including ING. Also includes practical checklists and guidelines.

Wilkinson, A., and Kupers, R. 2013. Living in the futures: How scenario planning changed corporate strategy. *Harvard Business Review* 94(5):118–27. Describes how Shell developed scenario planning in the 1960s, and assesses the company's use of the method. Finds that "a sustained scenario practice can make leaders comfortable with the ambiguity of an open future. It can counter hubris, expose assumptions that would otherwise remain implicit, contribute to shared and systemic sensemaking, and foster quick adaptation in times of crisis" (p. 127).

Roundup

Reflections for the Practicing Change Manager

- Do you feel that you now have knowledge of a number of diagnostic tools and models?

- Do you believe that you could apply those tools and models when necessary?

- If you were to select two or three favorite tools or models, which would they be and why?

- Is there a key area of organizational activity where you'd like a diagnostic tool that is not provided in this chapter? Where might you go to find such a tool?

- To what extent does your image(s) of change influence which diagnostic tools you are most comfortable using or see as most relevant?

This chapter has introduced a range of diagnostic tools that can contribute to the management of change by providing a perspective on a range of organizational situations. Models of "how organizations work" complement the implicit models that managers and others have in their heads. No one model is "correct" or "best," but each offers the opportunity to view the organization from a particular perspective. Choice of approach is therefore likely to be influenced by the image or images of change of those managers who are responsible for making the decisions. The models, frameworks, and tools from this chapter are summarized in table 4.1, which suggests when each may be useful.

Here is a short summary of the key points that we would like you to take from this chapter, in relation to each of the learning outcomes:

LO 4.1 * *Understand the use of diagnostic models in planning organizational change.*
We explained several organizational models: six-box model, 7-S framework, star model, and four-frame model. Not difficult to apply in practice, these models serve many purposes. They simplify complexity, highlight priorities, identify interdependencies, provide a common language, and offer a guide to the change implementation process.

LO 4.2 * *Use strategic analysis tools to assess the need for organizational change.*
We explained several strategic analysis tools: gap analysis, the PESTLE framework, scenario planning, the elements of strategy framework, the strategic inventory, and the cultural web. Gap analysis is a simple, but powerful, tool for assessing the need for change. The other tools in this section generate more detailed assessments on need for and nature of change, based on more in-depth questioning of current strategy and future goals.

LO 4.3 * *Diagnose organizational receptiveness to and individual readiness for change, and use those assessments as the basis for action to increase receptiveness and readiness.*

We explored the features of the receptive organizational context and the concept of "absorptive capacity." We identified the steps that can be taken to strengthen receptivity and increase absorptive capacity. Force-field analysis can often be a useful technique in this respect. Organizational receptiveness may be necessary but is not sufficient, and we also explored the factors that influence individual readiness for change and how those can be influenced to strengthen readiness. Stakeholder mapping can often be a useful framework in this context.

LO 4.4 * *Diagnose the degree of "agility" that an organization requires to operate effectively in an often uncertain and unpredictable business context.*

How responsive and adaptable—or agile—does a particular organization need to be? Do different sections or departments of an organization need to be more or less agile? We contrasted "traditional" principles of organization design with contemporary agile principles, which involve flat structures, self-managing teams, and the combination of stable and dynamic organization properties. In an agile organization, continuous change is "business as usual" and does not have to involve a planned transition from one state to another. In short, the agile model of the organization challenges conventional change management methods. Given the design principles involved, any organization could potentially develop agility. But agility entails uncertainty, which may not be suitable for all organizations or for all parts of one organization.

References

Aghina, W., Ahlbäck, K., De Smet, A., Fahrbach, C., Handscomb, C., Lackey, G., . . ., Woxholth, J. 2017. *The five trademarks of agile organizations*. London: McKinsey & Company.

Aghina, W., De Smet, A., and Weerda, K. 2016. Agility: It rhymes with stability. *McKinsey Quarterly* (1):59–69.

Aghina, W., De Smet, A., Murarka, M., and Collins, L. 2015. *The keys to organizational agility*. New York: McKinsey & Company.

Aghina, W., Handscomb, C., Ludolph, J., West, D., and Yip, A. 2019. *How to select and develop individuals for successful agile teams: A practical guide*. London and New York: McKinsey & Company.

Ahlbäck, K., Fahrbach, C., Murarka, M., and Salo, O. 2017. *How to create an agile organization*. New York and London: McKinsey & Company.

Bolman, L., and Deal, T. 2017. *Re-framing organizations: Artistry, choice, and leadership*. 6th ed. San Francisco, CA: Jossey Bass.

Bossert, O., Kretzberg, A., and Laartz, J. 2018. Unleashing the power of small, independent teams. *McKinsey Quarterly* 3:67–75.

Brosseau, D., Ebrahim, S., Handscomb, C., and Thaker, S. (2019). *The journey to an agile organization*. New York and London: McKinsey & Company.

Burke, W. W. 2013. *Organizational change: Theory and practice*. 4th ed. Thousand Oaks, CA: Sage Publications.

Burns, T., and Stalker, G. M. 1961. *The management of innovation*. London: Tavistock Publications.

Cohen, W. M., and Levinthal, D. A. (1990). Absorptive capacity: A new perspective on learning and innovation. *Administrative Science Quarterly* 30:560–85.

de Smet, A. (2018). The agile manager. *McKinsey Quarterly* 3:76–81.

de Smet, A., Smith, C., and Tofano, D. (2019). *How companies can help midlevel managers navigate agile transformations*. London: McKinsey & Company.

Eccles, T. (1994). *Succeeding with change: Implementing action-driven strategies*. London: McGraw Hill.

Emery, F. E. (1959). *Characteristics of socio-technical systems: Document 527*. London: Tavistock Institute of Human Relations.

Galbraith, J., Downey, D., and Kates, A. 2002. *Designing dynamic organizations*. New York: AMACOM.

Grundy, T. 1997. Accelerating strategic change: The internal stakeholder dimension. *Strategic Change* 6(1):49–56.

Hambrick, D. C., and Fredrickson, J. W. 2001. Are you sure you have a strategy? *Academy of Management Executive* 15(4):48–59.

Higgins, J. M. 2005. The eight "s's" of successful strategy execution. *Journal of Change Management* 5(1):3–13.

Houghton, E., and Spence, P. 2016. *People measurement and reporting: From theory to practice*. London: Chartered Institute for Personnel and Development.

Isaac, M., and Carson, K. 2016. *A guide to Belbin team roles: How to increase personal and team performance*. Marysville, OH: Bridge Publishing.

Jansen, J. J. P., Ven Den Bosch, F. A. J., and Volberda, H. W. 2005. Managing potential and realized absorptive capacity: How do organizational antecedents matter? *Academy of Management Journal* 48(6):999–1015.

Johnson, G., Whittington, R., Scholes, K., Angwin, D., and Regnér, P. 2017. *Exploring strategy: Text and cases*. 11th ed. Harlow, Essex: Pearson Education.

Kamer, J. 2018. How to build your own "Spotify Model." *The Ready*, February 9. https://medium.com/the-ready/how-to-build-your-own-spotify-model-dce98025d32f.

Kanter, R. M. 1983. *The change masters: Corporate entrepreneurs at work*. London: George Allen & Unwin.

Lewin, K. 1943. Defining the field at a given time. *Psychological Review* 50(3):292–310.

Lewin, K. (ed.) 1951. *Field theory in social science: Selected theoretical papers by Kurt Lewin*. London: Tavistock Publications (UK edition published 1952, edited by Dorwin Cartwright ed.).

Linders, B. 2016. Don't copy the Spotify model. *InfoQ*, October 6. https://www.infoq.com/news/2016/10/no-spotify-model.

Mahadevan, D., Jacobs, P., and Schlatmann, B. 2017. ING's agile transformation. *McKinsey Quarterly* 1(January):42–51.

Morrison, M., and Weeks, A. 2017. *Pestle analysis factsheet*. London: Chartered Institute for Personnel and Development.

Picken, J. C., and Dess, G. G. 1998. Right strategy—wrong problem. *Organizational Dynamics* 27(1):35–48.

Rafferty, A. E., Jimmieson, N. L., and Armenakis, A. A. 2013. Change readiness: A multilevel review. *Journal of Management* 39(1):110–35.

Theunissen, R., and Maciejewski, J. 2019. How the British army's operations went agile. *McKinsey Quarterly* (October):1–8.

Verity, J. 2003. Scenario planning as a strategy technique. *European Business Journal* 15(4):185–95.

Waterman, R. H., Peters, T. J., and Phillips, J. R. 1980. Structure is not organization. *Business Horizons* (June):14–26.

Weisbord, M. R. 1976. Organizational diagnosis: Six places to look for trouble with or without a theory. *Group & Organization Studies* 1(4):430–47.

Woodcock, M., and Francis, D. 1992. *Change*. Aldershot: Gower Publications.

Worley, C. G., and Lawler, E. E. 2006. Designing organizations that are built to change. *Sloan Management Review* 48(1):19–23.

Worley, C. G., and Lawler, E. E. 2009. Building a change capability at Capital One Financial. *Organizational Dynamics* 38(4):245–51.

Zahra, S. A., and George, G. 2002. Absorptive capacity: A review, reconceptualization and extension. *Academy of Management Review* 27(2):185–203.

PART 2

Implementation: The Substance and Process of Change

CHAPTER 5   What Changes?

CHAPTER 6   Purpose and Vision

CHAPTER 7   Change Communication Strategies

CHAPTER 8   Resistance to Change

CHAPTER 9   Organization Development and Sense-Making Approaches

CHAPTER 10   Change Management Perspectives

The central theme of the six chapters in Part 2 is *implementation*. What is the substance of the changes that are to be introduced? What is the organization's purpose or mission, given the desire of many employees, especially Millennials and Gen Z, for work that makes a meaningful contribution to the wider society? What is the vision for the organization's future, given the external environment, technology developments, regulatory changes, and other trends? Is that vision interesting, exciting, compelling, motivating? Through what strategies should the mission, vision, and substance of change proposals be communicated to an organization's stakeholders? What is the nature of resistance and, if necessary, how should that be managed—to capture the potential benefits of competing ideas as well as to address the concerns of resisters? There are several approaches to change implementation, each drawing on different theoretical perspectives, with different implications for practice. We first explore organization development and sense-making approaches. We then consider change management checklist approaches, stage models, and process and contingency theory perspectives. What are the benefits and drawbacks of these approaches? How can the change manager choose between them?

5

What Changes?

Learning Objectives

On completion of this chapter you should be able to:

LO 5.1 Explain several ways of categorizing different types of change.

LO 5.2 Identify practical implications of different types of change for the change manager.

LO 5.3 Understand the difference between sustaining and disruptive innovation, and explain the practical implications of this distinction for change management.

LO 5.4 Assess the significance of organizational culture with regard to organizational performance and reputation and the role of leaders as culture architects.

LO 5.5 Assess the organizational impact of digital transformations, including the adoption of social media tools, and the implications for change management.

"I can't understand why people are frightened of new ideas. I'm frightened of the old ones."

John Cage, composer

LO 5.1 What Changes?

What changes? Well, anything and everything, from an individual's job description, to a whole organizational system, which could involve other organizations as well. Here are some examples:

artificially intelligent systems	pay and reward systems
aspirations	performance appraisal and management systems
attitudes to risk and innovation	
automated equipment	performance targets
budgeting procedures	power bases
business model	product design
collaboration and conflict	role of customers/clients
culture of the organization	role of middle management
downsizing	service delivery models
external relationships such as partnerships and joint ventures	skill mix
	staff engagement
information systems	structure of the organization
leadership and management style	success criteria
location and layout of facilities	support services in-house or outsourced
manufacturing processes	teamworking
materials used in products and service delivery	technology
	workforce composition
merger or acquisition	working practices

The short version of this list might say that changes can include strategy, structure, technology, systems and procedures, human resource management practices, internal and external relationships, leadership style, and culture. These issues are not independent. In practice, they are closely coupled and should be mutually reinforcing. They can, however, be contradictory, which is also potentially damaging. Common contradictions include:

- expecting high performance teamwork while basing rewards on individual performance
- encouraging middle management autonomy while withholding vital performance information
- demanding cross-functional information exchange in a strong "organizational silos" structure
- combining a staff engagement policy with an autocratic top-down leadership style

It is also apparent that changes in one domain may have "knock-on" or "ripple" effects, creating or requiring changes in other areas. New technologies, for example, are likely to change skill mix requirements, working practices, rewards, and performance appraisal and management systems, and may also require supportive changes in leadership and management behavior. These examples of knock-on effects are obvious, but they emphasize that "What doesn't change?" is also a relevant issue. In practice, the ripples from even simple changes in an organization can be difficult to predict, and thus difficult to manage. One example concerns the redesign of working practices in one area, which leads to performance improvements, which lead to pay increases for those involved, which trigger jealousy and anger in the areas that were not involved in the initiative. Extending the changes to those other areas should reduce the tension, but the anger and perceived sense of betrayal (Why were we not chosen?) can be stored in the corporate memory for some time.

In sum, "What changes?" is a deceptively simple question, with potentially complex answers. There are several ways in which the content or substance of change can be categorized. For example, some changes are *planned*, while others are *emergent*. *Planned changes*, as the term suggests, are those that are implemented in anticipation of, or in response to, known trends and developments. Changes in motor vehicle engine design and manufacturing methods (technology, materials, and working practices) are likely to be prompted by legislation regulating carbon emissions. *Emergent changes* are those that just happen, or have to happen, in response to unforeseen events, such as the sudden opening

Yellow Card for Thai Union

The seafood conglomerate Thai Union is the world's largest producer of canned tuna and is based in Thailand. It is a global business, with revenues of $4.5 billion and 50,000 employees. Half of the shareholders and 90 percent of sales are from outside Thailand. Most consumers have probably never heard of the company, but they will know its brand names: Chicken of the Sea in the United States, John West in the United Kingdom, Mareblu in Italy, or Petit Navire in France.

In 2015, the Associated Press (AP) issued a report accusing the company of exploiting slave labor in its shrimp peeling sheds. Migrant workers from Myanmar, including children, were working long hours for low pay in dirty and cramped conditions and were in debt to labor brokers. For Thai Union, this was a public relations disaster. Thirapong Chansiri, the company's chief executive, was shocked. Thai Union came under immediate pressure from American and British customers—Costco, Sainsbury, Tesco, Walmart—and was criticized by human rights watchdogs and the environmental group Greenpeace. The U.S. State Department downgraded Thailand's ranking on Trafficking in Persons to the lowest score. The European Union gave Thailand a "yellow card" for fishing practices, and threatened to ban its exports.

What Changed?

Several aspects of the organization had to change. Most importantly, Chansiri had to restore the company's reputation. He cancelled contracts with shrimp processors, bringing that business in-house. He developed a "conduct and sustainability" code of practice, with targets, that applied to Thai Union and its suppliers. Thai Union was the first Thai seafood company to adopt a "zero recruitment fee" policy, preventing labor brokers from exploiting migrant workers. A commitment to sustainability changed labor and fishing practices on the company's boats. Thai Union introduced "traceability" of all its tuna and improved working conditions on its fishing fleet. In 2017, the company signed an agreement with Greenpeace to remove "exploitative and unsustainable practices" from its supply chain, changing its adversarial relationship with the environmental group.

The Outcomes

Activists have continued to criticize the company. But Greenpeace and the International Labour Organization have supported the changes that have been introduced. Thai Union is listed on the Dow Jones Sustainability Index of Emerging Markets and the FTSE4Good Emerging Index. The company plans to increase sales to $8 billion by 2020. Reflecting the changes that had taken place, the chief executive said, "Sustainability and innovation became part of our business strategy. Because of the effort we have made so far, I want to turn it into a positive element for the company that differentiates us from the others in the industry."

Based on Reed (2018).

of new market opportunities, or accidents and failures, or major geopolitical developments. It is difficult to plan ahead for those events in other than very general terms.

As we discussed in chapter 2, it is possible to argue that emergent change is now more common, given the complex, fluid, and unpredictable nature of the environment in which most if not all our organizations are operating. In contrast, much of the practical advice on change implementation assumes a carefully considered and planned approach.

We also need to distinguish between *incremental change*, which is gradual and small scale, and *transformational change*, which is radical and groundbreaking and can often be rapid. There is a widespread perception today that organizational change up to the mid-twentieth century was typically incremental and infrequent, and that from the late twentieth century to the present, change has become more common and traumatic. However, as noted in chapter 1, some commentators argue that radical, transformational change is not new, but was also a feature of the first half of the twentieth century—if not before. But, there is a more important question here: Is too much attention now lavished on large-scale transformational change, while the role of small-scale changes is overlooked?

Some commentators use the terms *first-order change* and *second-order change* to describe the difference between incremental and transformational (Coghlan and Rashford, 2006).

First-order change involves a specific initiative that solves a problem and/or makes improvements, in ways that do not present a challenge to current methods and thinking. First-order change is adaptive and implies a degree of continuity and order. This is captured in
the expression, "Change to stay the same." The incorporation of a growing range of safety
features in motor vehicles—from seat belts to electronic proximity sensors—is a series of
first-order changes that improve the product without making any major changes to it.

Second-order change leads to organizational transformation by introducing new products, services, and ways of doing business, based on creative lateral thinking, which alters current
core assumptions. Second-order change is disruptive and discontinuous and is captured in
the expression, "Move to a new position." The development of electric-powered self-driving
motorcars, made by companies that are not considered to be in the automotive sector, is
an example of second-order change.

David Coghlan and Nicholas Rashford (2006) also identify *third-order change*, based on the habitual questioning of assumptions and points of view, contributing to what can be a chaotic process of continual adaptation, self-renewal, and self-organization. Walmart and other retail supermarkets sell motorcars, thus threatening established dealer networks. What will follow electric and driverless cars and "phone app taxi services"? Given current global trends in house prices, will property developers and real estate agents offer discounted or free motorcars with house and apartment purchases as an inducement to customers? Will dealers in congested cities (Beijing, London, Mumbai, New York) provide free motorcycles with the cars that they sell so that customers can make their own "park and ride" arrange-ments to get to work? Will we continue to own cars anyway or hire them when we need them, ordering them by smartphone? These developments, and others more difficult to pre-dict, are examples of third-order change that, in some sectors, could become the norm.

The categories of change that we have discussed so far have involved simple dichotomies ("either this or that type") with third-order change offering another option. These are helpful categories, but they may be too simplified to deal with the complex patterns of contemporary organizational change. Depth is another metaphor that can be used to categorize different

FIGURE 5.1
Assessing Depth of Change

Off the scale ↑	Disruptive innovation Frame-breaking, mold-breaking Redraw dramatically organization and sector boundaries
Deeper	Paradigm shift, strategic change, *third-order change* New ways of thinking and solving problems, whole system change New ways of doing business
Deep change	Change the mission, vision, values, the organization's philosophy, to symbolize a radical shift in thinking and behavior, *second-order change*
	Change the organization's definition of success Create new goals, objectives, targets
Sustaining innovation	Improve business planning to symbolize a shift in thinking Tighten up on documentation, reporting, controls
	Reallocate resources Grow some departments, cut others, create new units
Shallow change	Incremental, fine-tuning: cut costs, find efficiencies, *first-order change* Constantly "nibble away" making minor improvements
Not on the scale ↓	"Sweat the small stuff"—quickly solve the minor annoying problems that nobody has bothered to fix; "grease the wheels"

types of change, as shown in Figure 5.1. At the bottom of this figure sits the "small stuff" that may not even be regarded as "change." Midscale includes "sustaining innovation" that involves improving on current practices. At the top of the scale is "disruptive innovation," which involves radically new business models and working methods (Christensen and Overdorf, 2000). It is not difficult to locate incremental and first-order change (shallow, sustaining), second-order or transformational change (deep, strategic), or third-order change (off the scale, disruptive) on this scale. The depth metaphor simply provides a richer picture of the patterns of change that we are likely to see in most organizations.

LO 5.2   What are the practical change management implications of these categories of change? The first, and most obvious implication, concerns matching solutions with problems. Despite the current fashion for deep transformational change, simple problems that are well understood can usually be resolved with simple, shallow, incremental changes. Addressing fundamental strategic opportunities and threats with fine-tuning, however, will typically lead to disappointment.

A second implication concerns the nature of the change management task. The management of shallow change typically requires less management capability and fewer resources than implementing frame-breaking initiatives. The former are likely to involve few departures from the familiar, may be relatively low in both cost and perceived risk, and pose little threat to the status quo with which people are comfortable. In contrast, deep, disruptive, or "off the scale" change is often abrupt, painful, risky, and expensive and can stimulate stronger and more widespread resistance, potentially creating a major management challenge.

A third practical issue concerns management reputation. Change management experience and capability have become "core selection factors" for candidates seeking promoted positions in many organizations (Beeson, 2009). Candidates who can answer those interview questions with accounts of the deep changes in which they have played a role are more likely to be preferred to those whose previous roles have involved them in only shallow, incremental initiatives. We have only anecdotal evidence to suggest that deeper changes can often be driven as much by personal career motives as by corporate need. Figure 5.1 can therefore be read, not just as a change typology, but also as a personal positioning tool for ambitious change managers. Assess the profile of changes in which you are currently engaged. If this involves shallow initiatives, explore how you can become involved with, or personally generate, deep changes that you can then discuss at the next job or promotion interview.

As discussed earlier, a lot of attention has been paid to deep, disruptive, transformational change. However, in most organizations, at any given time, changes are likely to be taking place across the range covered in Figure 5.1. Small changes can contribute to and support deeper initiatives. Some changes may start small but develop with experience into larger-scale initiatives. Deep changes demand time and resources, diverting attention from those necessary smaller-scale projects.

This pattern of shallow to deep change raises a fourth challenge, to coordinate those initiatives, to avoid duplication, overlap, and unnecessary cost. Research once suggested that most organizations experienced periods of stability that were interrupted on occasion by more profound changes. This was known as the theory of "punctuated equilibrium" (Romanelli and Tushman, 1994). That theory was based, however, on evidence from computer companies in the 1960s. That may not be the case today, as the pattern of change has become more programmatic. In response, many organizations have set up corporate program management offices (PMOs) to support and coordinate their initiatives (Ward and Daniel, 2013).

Initiative Overload and How to Avoid It

Organizations face pressure to change from many directions. The result can be initiative overload—too many projects. This can be expensive and lead to employee burnout. Hollister and Watkins (2018) identify seven causes of initiative overload:

1. *Impact blindness*. Top management may not be aware of all the initiatives in progress or the impact these are having on managers and employees.

2. *Multiplier effects*. Departments starting their own initiatives may not understand the impact on neighboring functions, some of whose resources may be required.

3. *Political logrolling*. Executives strike deals with each other—"I'll support your projects if you support mine"—leading to a collection of promises and projects that won't die.

4. *Unfunded mandates.* Executives ask management to meet key goals without providing the necessary resources, so these projects develop slowly over long periods.

5. *Band-Aid initiatives.* Initiatives are set up to provide partial fixes for major problems, resulting in lots of projects, none of which deal with the root causes.

6. *Cost myopia.* Staff is cut, but there is no change in the workload, so those who remain have more to do.

7. *Initiative inertia.* Some organizations have no mechanisms for stopping initiatives once they have started, even though the original purpose no longer applies.

To prevent initiative overload, they suggest the following solutions:

- Count the number of current initiatives, to confirm whether there is a problem.

- Identify the business need, resourcing, and impact of each of these initiatives.

- Have senior leaders prioritize these.

- Create a "sunset clause" for each initiative, with an end date for funding, so that projects do not continue to consume resources unless they are achieving their objectives.

- Have initiatives reapply for resources annually, by demonstrating their value to the business.

- Let the organization know that stopping an initiative does not mean that it was a failure—just that there is a limit to how many good ideas the organization can pursue.

Hollister and Watkins (2018, p. 71) conclude, "Of course, the best way to avoid initiative overload is to not allow it in the first place."

There is no standard PMO model, and this varies between organizations in terms of structure, location, and roles. The Philadelphia-based Project Management Institute (2012) identifies four factors contributing to the effectiveness of PMOs. First, they need a senior executive champion. Second, their role must be clearly understood. Third, the change professionals who staff the PMO must have the respect of functional departments. Finally, PMOs need to collaborate with functional departments in the development of initiatives, and not act as "change police."

For example, at State Auto Insurance Companies in Ohio, change projects would appear at random, and the company had no mechanism to ensure that projects stayed within budget and met their objectives. A PMO was made responsible for methodology, governance, change management, delivery, and portfolio management. Units that want to launch change projects have to construct a business case showing their alignment with corporate strategy. At the National Cancer Institute in Bethesda, Maryland, the PMO head found that teams working on early-phase drug development projects started every project plan from scratch. But there was a lot of overlap, with 80 percent of the work activities being either identical or similar from one project to another. The PMO designed a system to avoid this duplication. Previously, the teams held 16 four-hour meetings to develop their project plan. This was cut to only four meetings (Project Management Institute, 2012).

We have identified different types of change, reaching beyond a simple categorization (first-order, second-order). We have described other ways to conceptualize change (using a depth metaphor) and to assess the profile of change in an organization at any one time. These categories and concepts have implications for change management practice: matching solutions to problems, assessing the complexity of the change management task, linking involvement in change to personal reputations and careers, and coordinating a wide portfolio of change through a program management office.

In the rest of this chapter, we will develop these themes, first exploring different kinds of innovation and the distinction between sustaining and disruptive innovation. We then turn attention to changes that are likely to confront many organizations: culture change and technology-driven change. These are often seen as second-order changes, but this depends on the perspective from which they are interpreted. The kinds of changes that can take place with regard to organizational culture and to how new technologies are used can be profound and transformational. Throughout, the challenges for change managers posed by innovation, culture change, and technology developments will be considered. The most obvious challenges, perhaps, involve maintaining the pace of change, while ensuring effective implementation and sustained gains.

LO 5.3   Innovation

One of the key drivers of change is *innovation*. This term is not confined to new products. Other important innovations concern ways to organize, better working practices, and new ways to provide services. The word thus tends to be used in a broad sense, to mean the adoption of any product, system, process, program, service, or business model *new to this organization*. An idea may have developed elsewhere, but it can be seen as an innovation *here*.

How Simple Rules Encourage Innovation

To illustrate how simple rules can foster innovation, consider the case of Zumba Fitness. That company's fitness routine was developed when Alberto Pérez, a Columbian aerobics instructor, forgot to take his exercise tape to class and used what he had at hand—a tape of salsa music. Today, Zumba is a global business that offers classes at 200,000 locations in 180 countries to over 15 million customers drawn by the ethos, "Ditch the workout. Join the party."

Zumba's executives actively seek out suggestions for new products and services from its army of over 100,000 licensed instructors. Other companies routinely approach Zumba with possible partnership and licensing agreements. In fact, it is deluged by ideas for new classes (Zumba Gold for Baby Boomers),

music (the first *Zumba Fitness Dance Party* CD went platinum in France), clothing, fitness concerts, and video games, such as Zumba Fitness for Nintendo Wii. Zumba's founders rely on two simple rules that help them quickly identify the most promising innovations from the flood of proposals they receive. First, any new product or service must help the instructors—who not only lead the classes but carry Zumba's brand, and drive sales of products—to attract clients and keep them engaged. Second, the proposal must deliver FEJ (pronounced "fedge"), which stands for 'freeing, electrifying joy' and distinguishes Zumba from the 'no pain, no gain' philosophy of many fitness classes." (Sull, 2015, pp. 2–3)

It is helpful to identify different kinds of innovation. We can distinguish between product innovations (new gadgets) and operational innovations. Michael Hammer (2004) describes operational innovation as finding new ways to lead, organize, work, motivate, and manage. He describes a vehicle insurance company that introduced "immediate response claims handling," operating 24 hours a day. This involved scheduling visits to claimants by claims adjusters who worked from mobile vans and who turned up within nine hours. Previously, with office-based adjusters, it took a week to inspect a damaged vehicle. Handling 10,000 claims a day, adjusters were empowered to estimate damage and write a check on the spot. These operational innovations led to major cost savings, with fewer staff members involved in claims handling, lower vehicle storage costs, better fraud detection, and reduction in payout costs. Customer satisfaction and loyalty also improved.

Clayton Christensen and Michael Overdorf (2000) distinguish between sustaining and disruptive innovations. Sustaining innovations improve existing products and processes: a more efficient motorcar, a mobile phone that can shoot video as well as still photos. Disruptive innovations introduce wholly new processes and services: electric cars, social networking websites. Innovations that are disruptive do not necessarily mean chaos and upheaval; what is disrupted is often traditional ways of thinking and acting and old business models. Truly disruptive innovations may be harder to manage because they are riskier and because there are no established routines for handling them.

Christensen et al. (2015, p. 46) have complained that disruptive innovation has been misunderstood. As we have done here, the term is often applied to any major or radical change. However, the original concept meant something more specific:

> "Disruption" describes a process whereby a smaller company with fewer resources is able to successfully challenge established incumbent businesses. Specifically, as incumbents focus on improving their products and services for their most demanding (and usually most profitable) customers, they exceed the needs of some segments and ignore the needs of others. Entrants that prove disruptive begin by successfully targeting those overlooked segments, gaining a foothold by delivering more-suitable functionality—frequently at a lower price. Incumbents, chasing higher profitability in more-demanding segments, tend not to respond vigorously. Entrants then move upmarket, delivering the performance that incumbents' mainstream customers require, while preserving the advantages that drove their early success. When mainstream customers start adopting the entrants' offerings in volume, disruption has occurred.

In other words, disruption is a *process*—not just a new product or service. Christensen et al. (2015) argue that we need to understand the nature of innovation to manage it effectively. Small competitors, for example, can often be ignored—unless they are on a "disruptive trajectory," and then the incumbent has to act to counter the threat. This is different from head-on competition for an incumbent's traditional customers.

Disruptive Innovation in the Nineteenth Century *The Stethoscope*

That it [the stethoscope] will ever come into general use, not withstanding its value, I am extremely doubtful; because its beneficial application requires much time, and it gives a good deal of trouble both to the patient and practitioner, and because its whole hue and character is foreign, and opposed to all our habits and associations. It must be confessed that there is something ludicrous in the picture of a grave physician formally listening through a long tube applied to a patient's thorax, as if the disease within were a living being that could communicate its condition to the sense without.

Source: John Forbes, in the preface to his translation of *De L'Auscultation Médiate; ou Traité du Diagnostic des Maladies des Poumons et du Coeur* [A Treatise on Diseases of the Chest and on Mediate Auscultation], by R. T. H. Laennec, T&G Underwood, London, 1821.

Challenges for the Change Manager—Operational Innovations

Operational innovations can be more difficult to implement than product innovations. Potential users can see and touch a new product—a smartphone, for example—and they can try it out for themselves. An operational innovation, however, has to be implemented before anyone can really see how it is going to work—a streamlined process that will reduce time to market. This means that the benefits can take time to appear, particularly when the initial specification has to be adjusted with experience. Convincing others of the value of an operational innovation, therefore, is not always straightforward. Hammer (2004) argues that business culture undervalues operations, which are seen as boring and low status. Operations are not as glamorous, or as easily understood, as deal-making or new technology and are therefore not regarded as a source of competitive advantage. A further problem is that the "ownership" of an operational innovation may be vague, because it crosses functional boundaries.

Everett Rogers (2003) famously noted that adoption of innovations follows a pattern. First, small numbers adopt, followed by "takeoff," achieving a critical mass of adopters. Finally, the pace slackens as saturation is reached, typically short of 100 percent (you never convince everyone). Rogers argues that the five groups in Table 5.1 influence this pattern.

TABLE 5.1
From Innovators to Laggards

Innovators	Usually the first in their social grouping to adopt new approaches and behaviors; a small category of individuals who enjoy the excitement and risks of experimentation
Early adopters	Opinion leaders who evaluate ideas carefully, are more skeptical, and take more convincing, but also take risks, help to adapt new ideas to local settings, and have effective networking skills
Early majority	Those who take longer to reach a decision to change but are still ahead of the average
Late majority	Even more skeptical and risk averse; wait for most of their colleagues to adopt new ideas first
Laggards	Viewed negatively by others; the last to adopt new ideas, even for reasons they believe to be rational

Change is thus often dependent on innovators and early adopters in particular. Hammer (2004) offers four suggestions for accelerating the incidence of operational innovation. First, look for role models in other sectors. Second, challenge constraining assumptions ("This will never work because . . ."). Third, turn the "special case" into the norm. And finally, fourth, rethink the core dimensions of the work—who does it, where, when, how thoroughly, with what results; how can these dimensions be redesigned to make the process more effective?

Challenges for the Change Manager—Disruptive Innovations

Disruptive innovations can be more difficult to implement than sustaining innovations, as they are often viewed as risky. Christensen and Overdorf (2000) note that drastic change involving disruptive innovation can jeopardize an organization's business model and core capabilities. A further challenge is that disruptive products and services are often not as good as those in current use. The service provided by the low-cost business model of Southwest Airlines may not be as good as that of conventional carriers, but it is simpler, more accessible, and cheaper. The quality of images produced by the first digital cameras was much poorer than that from film cameras. In addition, most organizations have no routine processes for dealing with disruptive organizations. As just noted, disruptive innovations are thus often introduced by smaller new entrants or start-ups in a sector rather than by the older, larger, and dominant incumbents (Hwang and Christensen, 2008), but see "Case Study: David Solomon and Goldman Sachs" in the next section.

In contrast with disruptive innovations, it is easier to convince others of the value of sustaining innovations, which make existing processes, products, and services work better. Rogers (2003) argued that the probability of an innovation being accepted is increased when it has these properties:

1. advantageous when compared with existing practice
2. compatible with existing practices
3. easy to understand
4. observable in demonstration sites
5. testable
6. adaptable to fit local needs

One cannot easily demonstrate these properties with operational innovations—which can be difficult to understand, cannot be observed and tested, and cannot be compared with current practice until after they have been implemented. For the organization seeking to develop the capabilities for handling disruptive innovation, Christensen and Overdorf (2000, p. 7) make the following suggestions: Consider acquiring an organization that already has these capabilities; create an independent organization to deal with the problem; or create new structures, such as dedicated, cross-functional teams.

Change Manager as Disruptive Innovator

What advice is there for change managers seeking to develop and implement disruptive innovations to their organizations? Dyer et al. (2011) argue that anyone can be innovative by using the right approach. Innovators use the five habits shown in table 5.2.

These habits are not confined to a small number of special people; they can be developed. The change manager can thus become more innovative by following this advice and by

TABLE 5.2
The Five Habits of Disruptive Innovators

Associating	Are good at seeing connections between things that do not appear to be related, drawing ideas together from unrelated fields
Questioning	Are always challenging what others take for granted, asking, "Why is this done this way—why don't we do it differently?"
Observing	Watch the behavior of customers, suppliers, competitors—looking for new ways of doing things
Experimenting	Tinker with products and business models, sometimes accidentally, to see what happens, what insights emerge
Networking	Attend conferences and other social events to pick up ideas from people with different ideas, who may face similar problems, in other fields

collaborating with "delivery-driven" colleagues. Dyer and colleagues argue that organizations also need to encourage these habits, stimulating employees to connect ideas, to challenge accepted practices, to watch what others are doing, to take risks and try things out, and to get out of the company to meet others. See Intuit and the Nonsense Findings, which describes the practices that employees in that organization use for the company to be a "self-disrupter."

Intuit and the Nonsense Findings

Intuit is an American company that makes business and personal financial software. Market capitalization in May 2020 was $75 billion. In 2017, Intuit was listed in *Fortune*'s "Future 50" list of companies identified as best placed to significantly grow their revenue in coming years. Intuit was an oddity on this list, being 34 years old and operating in a "brutally competitive" industry. Colvin (2017, p. 78) refers to Intuit as "the Tom Brady of its industry—performing at the top of its game at an age when its onetime peers have long since stopped playing." (Tom Brady, over 40 years old, is a successful American football quarterback.)

Intuit has been able to continue to perform at a high level because of its approach to change. This involves being a "self-disrupter," which means not waiting for the need to respond to the actions of competitors, or to some form of crisis, before deciding to change itself.

Intuit does not just rely on customer surveys. The company uses a "follow-me-home" approach, in which staff visit the homes or offices of customers to watch them use Intuit products. The aim is to observe how customers actually use the products, instead of relying on what customers might say about their usage.

To understand their customers better, Intuit staff members are trained to "focus on the finding that makes no sense" and to "embrace anomalies." Rather than ignore information that doesn't fit with the company's beliefs about how its products are used, Intuit staff members are encouraged to "savor the surprise" and to work out the implications for the company. This approach is the opposite to what happens in most organizations where "nonsensical" information is typically ignored on the grounds that customers must have misunderstood. Colvin (2017) cites the example of Intuit staff finding that some users of Mint, an online money management system, were not using it in the way that was expected of the target market of young professionals. An investigation found that users were self-employed, gig economy workers, with organizations such as Uber and Lyft. Intuit quickly responded by producing a version of its market-leading QuickBooks accounting software for the gig economy market.

Other Intuit practices include:

- New ideas are initially developed by a "discovery team" of three or more people who report directly to a division general manager rather than up the chain of command.

- Where practices found outside Intuit seem to be relevant to an initiative that the company is considering, Intuit managers investigate and share their findings with other managers.

- Decisions are made quickly; if a decision cannot be made at a particular level of the organization within 24 hours, it must be escalated to a higher level within another 24 hours.

- Mistakes are not punished. Senior managers model this policy. They identify and discuss failures with which they have been associated, so that others will be more open about where something needs improvement.

- Groups of senior managers investigate the corporate implications of major trends. Recent trends investigated in this way have included how consumers under age 10 use technology, conversational user interfaces, artificial intelligence, and blockchain.

Case Sources

Colvin, G. (2017). How Intuit reinvents itself. *Fortune* 176(6):76–82.

https://www.macrotrends.net/stocks/charts/INTU/intuit/market-cap.

In Defense of Sustaining Innovation

As argued in chapter 1, it would be a mistake to think that transformational, disruptive innovation is the solution to most current organizational problems, for at least two reasons. First, considerable business benefit can be achieved through small-scale initiatives and sustaining innovations. Many healthcare organizations have imported "lean" techniques from manufacturing and made significant performance improvements that benefit patients, staff, and the organization as a whole (Graban, 2009). Second, many organizations have highly profitable businesses based on traditional products, such as Harris Tweed, Swiss watches, and Samuel Adams Boston Lager. Some traditional technologies, having once been overtaken by innovative replacements, have reemerged, such as vinyl LPs and green "environment-friendly" city trams. New technology does not simply displace past technologies. The appeal of some old technologies is enduring (sailing boats, paper books), and some items are bought for their aesthetic value, regardless of price.

These considerations further complicate our answer to this chapter's question: What changes? There are different kinds and degrees of innovation. The challenge for the change manager is to determine which (or which combination) is appropriate to a particular organization, at a given time.

LO 5.4 Organizational Culture

Are people enthusiastic about working for this organization? Do they feel valued? Are there development and career opportunities? Are customers and clients valued and given good-quality service? Are leaders and managers respected and trusted? Is information shared openly? Is teamwork and collaboration between divisions the norm? Do staff agree with the purpose of the organization? These are just some of the indicators of an organization's culture. When the answers to those questions turn to "no," then organizational effectiveness suffers.

Yang Yuanqing, Chief Executive of Lenovo

Lenovo [Chinese multinational computer manufacturer] *is often cited for sustaining a healthy corporate culture. What's the secret to that?*

"We focus on three elements. The first is an ownership culture: we try to empower people to think for themselves, to make decisions for themselves. Everyone is an engine. The second is a commitment culture: if you commit to something, you must deliver. The third is a pioneer culture: we encourage our people to be more innovative."

How do you actually promote innovative behavior?

"There are a lot of ways to do it. For example, I hold monthly brainstorming sessions with our R&D team. At each session we focus on one topic—it might be a product, a service, or a technology. Another approach is through the budget. For our R&D people, we allow 20% of the budget to be flexible, so they can decide which areas they want to focus on and what they want to develop." Interview by *Harvard Business Review* (Yuanqing, 2014, pp. 107–108).

One definition of organizational culture, therefore, is "the way we do things around here." A more technical definition regards organizational culture as the shared values, beliefs, and norms that influence the way employees think, feel, and act toward others, both inside and outside the organization. It is also argued that organizations each have their own distinct "personality," style, ideology, or climate, which gives them their unique identity. For example, walk into a McDonald's restaurant and note the atmosphere, décor, lighting, staff attitude toward customers, style and variety of food and drinks, speed of service, cost, and any other details that catch your attention. Next, walk into one of McCormick & Schmick's restaurants and pay attention to those same factors; you will see a different culture. Ann Cunliffe (2008) argues that organizational culture is important because it:

- shapes the public image of an organization
- influences organizational effectiveness
- provides direction for the company
- helps to attract, retain, and motivate staff

This issue can be the cause of many problems. Falling sales, customer complaints, staff absenteeism and turnover, and poor public reputation, for example, can often be attributed to organizational culture. It is therefore not surprising that culture change programs have become popular. Some theorists argue that organizations cannot have distinct cultures in the way that human societies do. But we can accept that criticism and still find practical value in the concept, if organizational culture is simply taken to cover the values, beliefs, and norms that shape employee—and management—behavior. If those behaviors are inappropriate or dysfunctional in some way, then "culture" offers a useful lens through which we can understand why and what action we can take to change those behaviors.

We can also make a distinction between strong and weak organizational cultures (Gordon and DiTomaso, 1992). A strong culture is one in which the organization's values are widely shared and intensely held and thus guide behavior. A weak culture, in contrast, displays little agreement about core values or about expected behaviors. Strong cultures thus suggest emotional attachment and commitment to an organization, unity in approach, and "walking the talk." Much of the commentary on this topic thus assumes that companies with strong cultures perform better. The quotes that opened this section, from Lenovo's chief executive, support this view.

We also know that organizational culture can cause serious problems. What happened with the oil exploration company BP provides an iconic example of what can happen when culture goes wrong.

Organizational Culture and the *Deepwater Horizon* Disaster

The movie *Deepwater Horizon* (2016, director Peter Berg), which stars Mark Wahlberg and Kurt Russell, is based on actual events. On April 20, 2010, when a blowout preventer failed a mile under water, the explosion and fire on the 33,000-ton *Deepwater Horizon* drilling rig in the Gulf of Mexico killed 11 of the 126 crew members on board and seriously injured 17 others. Oil poured from the Macondo wellhead on the seabed, drifting toward the Louisiana coast 50 miles away, threatening wildlife and the local fishing and tourism industries. Around 5 million barrels of crude oil spilled into the Gulf before the flow was stopped on July 15. This was the biggest environmental disaster in the United States since the *Exxon Valdez* spilled 750,000 barrels of crude oil in Prince William Sound in 1989. The investigation blamed leadership and management for creating the conditions in which this accident was allowed to happen. Here is what the accident investigation said about BP's culture (National Commission, 2011, emphasis added):

> The immediate causes of the Macondo well blowout can be traced to a series of identifiable mistakes made by BP, Halliburton, and Transocean that reveal such systematic failures in risk management that *they place in doubt the safety culture of the entire industry.* (p. vii)
>
> Investments in safety, containment, and response equipment and practices failed to keep pace with the rapid move into deepwater drilling. Absent major crises, and given the remarkable financial returns available from deepwater reserves, *the business culture succumbed to a false sense of security. The Deepwater Horizon disaster exhibits the costs of a culture of complacency.* (p. ix)
>
> In the wake of the BP Deepwater Horizon disaster—a crisis that was unanticipated, on a scale for which companies had not prepared to respond—*changes in safety and environmental practices, safety training, drilling technology, containment and clean-up technology, preparedness, corporate culture, and management behavior will be required* if deepwater energy operations are to be pursued in the Gulf—or elsewhere. (p. 215)

If an organizational culture is dysfunctional, the potential outcomes, from these examples, include:

- loss of life and serious injury
- widespread economic and environmental damage
- damage to the reputations and careers of senior management
- loss of public trust and confidence in the organization, if not the whole sector
- massive fines for misconduct

Failure to manage organizational culture can cost lives, reputations, careers—and money, affecting the wider community and the economy, as well as causing internal organizational damage. Another possible outcome is that the organization is faced with a transformational change agenda. The *Deepwater* investigation said that BP's culture of complacency had to change, to avoid further incidents and to regain public trust. (Crisis management at BP is explored in chapter 7.)

Changing an organizational culture is in many respects similar to managing any other form of change. However, culture is usually defined in terms of shared values, beliefs, and norms. Those are attributes of individuals and groups that are difficult to change directly. Most approaches to culture change thus advocate action to change behavior, through new working practices, systems, and human resource policies. This approach assumes that, once the benefits of those new behaviors become clear, the values, beliefs, and norms that reinforce those behaviors will adjust naturally.

For example, Emily Lawson and Colin Price (2003) argue that the success of change relies on persuading individuals to change their "mindsets"—to think differently about their jobs and how they work. This first involves changing behavior. They identify three levels of change. First, some outcomes (increased revenue) can be achieved without changing working practices (selling noncore assets). Second, staff can be asked to change working practices in line with current thinking (finding ways to reduce waste). The third level involves fundamental changes in organizational culture, in collective thinking and behavior—from reactive to proactive, hierarchical to collegial, inward-looking to externally focused. They identify four conditions for changing mindsets at the third level:

> The surrounding structures (reward and recognition systems) must be in tune with the new behaviour. Employees must have the skills to do what it requires. Finally, they must see people they respect modelling it actively. Each of these conditions is realized independently; together they add up to a way of changing the behaviour of people in organizations by changing attitudes about what can and should happen at work. (Lawson and Price, 2003, p. 32)

In other words, "mindsets" may not be altered directly but can be changed by a careful rethinking of structures, skills, and role models.

Risky Culture

Inside Job (2010, director Charles Ferguson, narrated by Matt Damon) examines the global financial crisis of 2008. Over the previous decade, deregulation allowed the finance sector to take risks that older rules would have discouraged. As you watch this film, identify the various stakeholders (including academics), their competing interests, their relationships, and their efforts to conceal sensitive information. How did those competing interests, relationships, and "information games" contribute to the crisis? The film concludes that, despite this crisis, the underlying culture has remained much the same. How has the sector been able to avoid fundamental changes to financial regulation? What does this account reveal about the nature of organizational culture?

Many organizations today, therefore, are concerned that their culture is appropriate, in the context of corporate strategy, performance, external scrutiny and regulation, and reputation. Culture change programs often target staff engagement, teamwork and collaboration, and information sharing and creativity, as well as costs, revenues, and customer service. For the change manager, it is important to remember that the role of the board, and of senior leadership in general, is key in this context.

Recent developments at Goldman Sachs illustrate several aspects of organizational culture change. As you read this case account, consider the following question: How can "the soft stuff" concerning an organization's culture influence the bottom line concerning revenue and profitability?

Case Study: David Solomon and Goldman Sachs

The Context

Goldman Sachs is a multinational investment bank based in New York, with branches in 30 countries. The business is divided into four main sectors: investment banking (for which it is most famous), institutional client services, investing and lending, and investment management. The company has 38,000 employees, with around 400 partners, generating annual revenue of around $40 billion. Clients include governments, companies, financial institutions, and individuals. Founded in 1869, Goldman Sachs celebrated its 150th birthday in 2019. It is the oldest of the Wall Street banks still trading under its original name, and it is the fourth largest bank in America.

Known for its high salaries and bonuses, Goldman Sachs was extremely profitable in the decade before the global financial crisis in 2008. Seen as "too big to fail" following that crisis, the company received a $10 billion bailout from the U.S. Treasury. The bailout (which was repaid the next year) led to angry criticism from the media, trade unions, and politicians. An article in *Rolling Stone* magazine compared Goldman Sachs to a blood-sucking vampire squid.

The Problem

The financial crisis led other banks to rethink their business models. Goldman Sachs had been so successful for so long, however, it did not feel the need to change. The company was profitable in 2008 and 2009, but revenues fell from 2010 onward, due to tighter financial regulation and the development of electronic trading. Trading in bonds and commodities generated over 70 percent of Goldman Sachs' revenues in 2009. That business is now automated and generated only 37 percent of revenues in 2018. The company's overall revenue fell 6 percent between 2010 and 2018 and has continued to fall further. In 2018, the company was implicated in the 1Malaysia Development Berhad (1MDB) scandal, which involved the theft of billions of dollars from a Malaysian infrastructure investment fund. Two former Goldman Sachs executives were indicted, and a $5 billion settlement was likely.

The Solution

David Solomon was appointed chief executive in October 2018 and chairman in January 2019. His task was to grow the company's revenues and to change the company's secretive, hierarchical culture. Solomon was an unconventional chief executive, working in his spare time as a DJ ("D-Sol"), donating the earnings to charity. Unlike other senior executives, he travels around New York on the subway and makes his own coffee in the office. Colleagues who want to see him can come straight to his door, rather than having to navigate receptionists and sit in a waiting room. Not concerned about breaking rules or challenging conventions, he has an aggressive, combative, strong-willed leadership style. He also has a reputation for navigating the organization's politics and for developing junior colleagues. Complimenting him, an executive colleague said, "I don't have any sense that he's a status quo kind of guy" (Wieczner, 2019, p. 162). Another senior colleague said, "There are very few leaders in the financial services business who are very detail-oriented and at the same time strategic. David is one of those who does both" (Wieczner, 2019, p. 165).

Solomon wanted to simplify the organization hierarchy and reduce the bureaucracy. On his first day as chief executive, he sent out an email describing "One Goldman Sachs," challenging the traditional silos around which the business was organized. Staff members were to be rewarded for bringing in business from anywhere in the company, regardless of their position. Shortly after the email was sent, the chair of the investment banking division got 50 phone calls from employees across the organization, including back-office staff, with ideas to sell to clients. In 2019, he dropped the company's dress code—35 pages of strict rules about suits, ties, and shoes. Goldman Sachs used to ban staff from taking photographs in the office. Solomon now posts such pictures to his Instagram account.

Solomon introduced three- to five-year strategic planning. This was innovative, because Goldman Sachs used to work with annual budgets, in the belief

(Continued)

that markets were too unpredictable. Solomon started expanding services to previously overlooked markets, such as providing banking services for less wealthy customers and small businesses. The high-net-worth and consumer arms of the business were merged, to serve both sets of customers with a common web platform. Retail banking was given a $1.3 billion investment in new technology. Automated trading was expanded, and backroom operations were consolidated to reduce staff costs. In 2019, the company launched a new credit card—the Apple Card, designed to be used with an iPhone—in partnership with Apple.

Solomon addressed the company's gender gap by first asking his investment bankers to ensure that 50 percent of new analysts were women, later extending this policy to all new recruits. If a manager succeeded in increasing their proportion of female staff from 40 percent to 49 percent, they would not receive a bonus, as they had failed to make the target. The banking division's analysts recruited in 2019 were the first to achieve gender parity, and Goldman Sachs is expected to recruit more women than men in 2020. A colleague said, "He is really breaking glass" (Wieczner, 2019, p. 164).

Remuneration was Goldman Sachs' biggest expense, amounting to 35 percent of revenue. Previously, annual bonuses and promotion to partner were based solely on the revenue that the individual generated for the company. Solomon wanted to strengthen cooperation, so bonuses became linked to three-year goals and diverse hiring, as well as to the overall performance of the company. Senior bankers now fly economy rather than business class. Only partners can take company cars to outside meetings. Everyone else takes a taxi.

The Outcome

Around 10 percent of the company's partners have left since Solomon took over, and more are expected to leave, unhappy with the changes that he has made. However, their departure has created openings for a younger generation of executives, and Solomon's approach was popular with the Millennials and Generation Z employees who now comprise 75 percent of the company's workforce. Goldman Sachs now manages $50 billion in online deposits for 4 million customers. The company's quarterly returns and share price, however, are still watched closely by investors.

Case Sources

Burroughs, C., and Khan, Y. 2018. The bizarre story of 1MDB, the Goldman Sachs-backed Malaysian fund that turned into one of the biggest scandals in financial history, December 20. *Business Insider*, https://www.businessinsider.com.au/1mdb-timeline-the-goldman-sachs-backed-malaysian-wealth-fund-2018-12.

Campbell, D. 2019. Read the full memo David Solomon sent to Goldman Sachs employees explaining why he's moving his management team out of stuffy offices and into open seating. *Business Insider*, December 25. https://www.businessinsider.com/goldman-sachs-open-executive-office-full-memo-2019-12.

Clark, A. 2019. Goldman Sachs pays off bailout bill. *The Guardian*, July 23. https://www.theguardian.com/business/2009/jul/23/goldman-sachs-repays-government.

McFarlane, G. 2019. How Goldman Sachs makes money. *Investopedia*, September 24. https://www.investopedia.com/articles/markets/041315/how-goldman-sachs-makes-its-money.asp.

Scipioni, J. 2019. Goldman Sachs' CEO takes the subway, gets his own coffee and has a side hustle as a DJ. *CNBC*, Decmber 5. https://www.cnbc.com/2019/12/05/why-goldman-sachs-ceo-david-solomon-takes-subway-gets-his-own-coffee.html.

Wieczner, J. 2019. Ripping up the rules at Goldman Sachs. *Fortune* 180(6):158–68.

Find on *YouTube*, "Interns meet our chairman and CEO, David Solomon, during an 'Explore GS' session" (2019, 15 minutes). David Solomon talks about his "foundational experiences," his career, and his approach to running Goldman Sachs, including the technology-based shift to commercial banking. Disrupters, traditionally, are outsiders and newcomers who threaten incumbents. Solomon describes Goldman Sachs, however, as a "disruptive insider."

LO 5.5   Digital Transformation and the Social Matrix

As we discussed in chapter 3, new technologies are key drivers of organizational change. However, Lindsay et al. (2018) argue that, due to current technology developments, the fundamental nature of organizational change is itself changing. Compared to traditional organizational change, which might involve process redesign or a new organizational structure, digital transformations require different change management capabilities, and implementing digital solutions means focusing on different priorities. Lindsay et al. (2018, p. 8) define digital transformation broadly, as "any changes—either internal or externally facing—that involve the use of digital tools or technologies, such as automating formerly manual work, improving methods to track work with digital tools, or expanding the functionality of digital customer interfaces."

The main challenge for change management concerns the scope and scale of digital transformations, which typically affect several business units or functions; the knock-on or ripple effects can be pervasive. Traditional transformations are often (but not always) focused on specific parts or aspects of the business. Implementing digital solutions requires piloting and prototyping skills, for testing major changes in smaller, controlled environments. These skills are now in short supply. Lindsay et al. (2018, p. 2) identify seven "core capabilities" for implementing digital transformations:

1. focusing the organization on a prioritized set of changes
2. having sufficient resources and capabilities to implement the changes
3. ensuring ownership of and commitment to the changes at all levels of the organization
4. planning from the start for long-term sustainability (see discussion in chapter 11)

Jeff Immelt, Chief Executive of GE (2001–2017) *You Are in the Information Business, Like It or Not*

You think about a jet engine today or a locomotive or an MRI scanner. A new jet engine might have a hundred sensors on it. These sensors have the capability to take continuous data about the heat of an engine, fuel consumption, the wear of the blades, the environment it's taking off in—a series of things. And one flight between New York City and Chicago produces a terabyte of data. So industrial companies are in the information business whether they want to be or not.

Our locomotive customers, they have a phrase called "velocity." Every CEO of a railroad could tell you their velocity. The velocity tends to be, let's say, between 20 and 25 miles per hour. This tends to be the average miles per hour that a locomotive travels in a day—22. Doesn't seem very good. And the difference between 23 and 22 for, let's say, Norfolk Southern, is worth $250 million in annual profit. That's huge for a company like that. That's one mile [per hour]. So that's all about scheduling better. It's all about less downtime. It's all about not having broken wheels, being able to get through Chicago faster. That's all analytics.

Immelt and Kirkland (2015).

5. establishing clear accountability for implementation

6. maintaining continuous improvement during and after implementation, and taking rapid corrective action when necessary

7. using standard change processes and effective program management

These capabilities apply to any organizational change. However, from their survey of over 1,500 managers across a range of sectors, Lindsay et al. (2018) found that among those organizations whose digital transformations had been successful, 85 percent had used all seven capabilities. Four-fifths of respondents whose transformations had not been successful had only used some of them. Of those who were successful, particular emphasis was placed on establishing commitment, sustainability, and continuous improvement. The key to commitment concerned communicating clear goals. The key to sustainability concerned embedding the key performance indicators (KPIs), echoing the saying, "What gets measured gets done." Lindsay et al. (2018) argue that the focus on KPIs is important in a changing environment; rapid corrective action is required when targets turn out not to be appropriate. The ongoing success of digital transformations was supported when employees across the organization were allowed to refine and improve the new systems.

Furr and Shipilov (2019) note that digital transformation is not a new challenge: Computers and software have been around for decades. However, the nature of current innovations, the opportunities that are being created, and the rapid pace of development are creating new challenges. They also argue that digital transformation does not have to be disruptive or involve a reinvention of the core business: "Change is involved, and sometimes radical replacements for manufacturing processes, distribution channels, or business models are necessary; but more often than not, transformation means incremental steps to better deliver the core value proposition" (p. 96). In other words, for most organizations, the needs of customers will not change much, and the challenge is to find the best way to meet those needs using new digital tools. They offer this example from the shipping container company Maersk:

> The costs of shipping are affected by global trade barriers and inefficiency in international supply chains. The industry also suffers from a lack of transparency. These are familiar challenges. What digital did for Maersk was provide a new way of overcoming them. The company partnered with IBM and government authorities to deploy blockchain technology for fast and secure access to end-to-end supply chain information from a single source. The technology, coupled with an ability to receive real-time sensor data, allows trustworthy cross-organization workflows, lower administrative expenses, and better risk assessments in global shipments. This shift allows Maersk to serve its core customers better. But Maersk has not been transformed into Google. It remains a company whose value proposition is providing a fast, reliable, cost-efficient shipping service—one with the potential to be more streamlined and transparent, thanks to a smart leveraging of digital technology. (Furr and Shipilov, 2019, p. 97)

In other terms, digital transformation is not mainly about the technology, but about finding better ways to meet customer needs. This often requires major changes to organizational structures, especially to break down corporate silos and increase flexibility.

Jeff Immelt, Chief Executive of GE *It's Not All about Technology*

This is something I got wrong. I thought it was all about technology. I thought if we hired a couple thousand technology people, if we upgraded our software, things like that, that was it. I was wrong. Product managers have to be different; salespeople have to be different; on-site support has to be different. We've had to change a lot about the company. It's infecting everything we do. It's infecting our own IT. It's infecting our own manufacturing plants. It's infected everything we're doing, I think in a positive way.

We started our digital initiative maybe five or six years ago. What we found was our culture was too complicated to get the work done the way we needed to get it done, both in terms of how we were trying to digitize and how we were trying to survive in terms of a more highly regulated world. So what

we've tried to do inside the company is drive what we call a "culture of simplification": fewer layers, fewer processes, fewer decision points. And we're democratizing information inside the company. The notion is that, in the digital age, sitting down once a year to do anything is weird, it's just bizarre. So whether it's doing business reviews or strategic planning, it's in a much more continuous way. We still give a lot of feedback. We still do a lot of analysis of how you're performing. But we make it much more contemporary and much more 360-degree. So somebody can get interactions with their boss on a monthly basis or a quarterly basis. And the data you get is being collected by your peers, the people who work for you, in a much more accurate and fluid way.

Immelt and Kirkland (2015).

The Social Matrix

Social media tools are one of the defining—we could say *redefining*—features of our lives, with the potential to change working practices and the way that organizations function. We now live in a *social matrix*—an environment in which any online activity can be social, influencing actions, solving problems, innovating, and creating new types of organizations that are not constrained by traditional boundaries. Social media are "low friction" tools: They are everywhere, they are flexible, and you don't need any training. They have changed the way in which we interact with each other, how we share information, the kinds of information that we share (ideas, pictures, music, videos), and how we form opinions. They potentially shift power and decision-making responsibility to frontline staff members who can now access the same information as everybody else. The mobile Internet and cloud storage mean that we can interact and share where and when we want, without relying on corporate computing. For many people, social media is now the main source of news about what is going on in the world.

These technologies have spread rapidly. The social networking service Facebook was launched in 2004. In 2019, Facebook had around 2.5 billion users, WhatsApp had 1.5 billion, Twitter 330 million, and Snapchat 203 million. WeChat, the Chinese mobile text and messaging service, had a billion users—three times the population of the United States and 15 times the population of the United Kingdom.

The list of potential organizational applications of social media tools is long (Gifford, 2014):

building shared purpose and workplace community
creating interconnections and networks

developing collaboration, cooperation and information sharing

drawing on insight and experience from across the organization

encouraging distributed leadership

encouraging openness, egalitarianism, and a lack of rigidity

facilitating employee voice

getting the right information to the right people

improving employee relations

increasing top team visibility

shaping organization culture

strengthening advocacy of the organization

strengthening the employer reputation and brand

supporting corporate communications

transforming learning and development

widening the recruitment pool

A study by the McKinsey Global Institute concluded that social media could increase the productivity of knowledge workers by 20 to 25 percent, simply by reducing the time spent looking for information. McKinsey also predicts that social media could save companies $1.3 trillion, through improvements in intra-office collaboration (Chui et al., 2013). With regard to recruitment, social networking sites can reveal (to potential employers) information about candidates' abilities and characteristics and display (to potential employees) an organization's culture, goals, and priorities, such as attitudes to environmental issues and corporate social responsibility.

Leonardi and Neeley (2017) cite a study of 4,200 American organizations that found that over 70 percent used social media tools. The reported benefits included promoting collaboration and knowledge sharing, speeding up decisions, developing innovative ideas for products and services, increasing employee engagement, establishing relationships between employees in different locations, and avoiding the duplication of work. However, they argue that organizations can fall into four traps:

1. Assuming that Millennials want to use social media at work; they see social media as tools for self-expression and communication with friends and family.

2. Prohibiting informal discussion of nonwork topics on internal organization sites; personal interactions make it easier to access other people and work-related information.

3. Not recognizing the difference between *direct learning* (knowing *how* to do something, like solve a problem), and *metaknowledge* (learning *who* has the expertise that you need); informal communication is important in developing metaknowledge.

4. Treating visible information as the most valuable; staff with technical skills may be more highly valued than those with cultural and political skills—but the latter are just as useful.

When we think of social media, we think of the online platforms that are available to everyone. However, the potential of these technologies may in future rely on *enterprise-specific* networks. Facebook launched its corporate social network platform *Workplace*

Antisocial Media—Operational Innovations

One large UK bank had a company intranet that gave staff the opportunity to give feedback to senior management. During a major reorganization, which involved cutting costs and the closure of many branches with job losses, the bank's human resources director decided to assess staff morale. He posted an intranet article that praised employees' commitment and flexibility. Staff members were asked to leave comments, and hundreds responded. Most of the feedback was negative:

If you want promotion do every extracurricular task that you can. Don't worry about the quality of the work as it is irrelevant.

Either execs are lying, or somewhere down the line people are misrepresenting what is being communicated from above.

Why should we trust you after what you did on pensions?

Most complaints concerned the decision to close the generous final salary pension scheme. This happened at the same time as the chief executive was awarded a large pension contribution as part of his multimillion pound annual package and was seen as showing double standards. Staff also criticized the excessive bureaucracy and lack of top management support. The corporate intranet makes it easy for management to capture staff feedback. That feedback, however, may be unfavorable, particularly when management actions are seen as inconsistent or unfair.

in 2016. Other popular enterprise networking platforms include *Yammer, Chatter, Jive,* and *Slack*. With these tools, employees can be involved in two-way discussions using a secure "gated" corporate networking platform for incubating ideas and feeding these to senior management. This can also be used to facilitate communication and collaboration. Social networking can be a more engaging medium than traditional organization communication tools to send corporate messages, quickly capture employee reactions, check that messages have been understood, and for information-sharing in general. A corporate social network can strengthen the sense of shared purpose, by celebrating achievements, reinforcing mission and values, and fostering identification with the organization.

One application of social media concerns encouraging *employee voice*, "where everyone in an organization feels they have a say, are listened to and have their views taken into account" (Simms, 2018, p. 41). Unlike the annual staff satisfaction survey, social media can capture real-time information, continuously. Dromey (2016) reports research that explored the extent to which employers in the United Kingdom use social media to promote and access employee voice. The study found that half of employers were using social media tools, but mainly for marketing and customer engagement purposes. Only one in six had internal enterprise social networks, and these were used mainly to provide organizational updates rather than to collect employee views. But where enterprise networks were in use at work, few employees said that this was effective in sharing knowledge and ideas or to encourage employee voice. Interestingly, employees in organizations with enterprise networks said that they felt less able to influence decisions than in organizations not using social networks. Dromey concludes that the benefits of these technologies are not being fully exploited.

Holland et al. (2016) explore the implications of social media for employee voice in Australia. They argue, "The understanding and management of social media at work are not well developed" (p. 2629). Their research examined the relationship between social media use and job satisfaction and found that social media was not commonly used to voice concerns about work. They suggest that this is an untapped resource for workplace communication, which could give management "real time" feedback on workplace issues. They conclude that:

> The challenge for management is whether to embrace this form of communication which is now ubiquitous outside the workplace and harness the ability to increase knowledge and understanding of workplace issues and improve the employment relationship in real time. The alternative is to ignore the opportunity such a medium provides and potentially allow social media to develop its own culture with the potential to be a focus for negative issues in the workplace and about the organization. (p. 2630)

Many failures and scandals might have been avoided had managers listened to and acted upon what employees were saying. The UK employee engagement movement, Engage for Success (2018), claims that employee voice is "the cheapest smoke alarm you can ever install in an organization." Engage for Success also found that over 60 percent of employees say that they have more to give to their organizations, but no one is asking them (see chapter 9). Research has demonstrated that people who feel that their opinions matter are more likely to be satisfied and productive (Bosak et al., 2017). Employees have to feel that it is safe to voice their opinions, even with gated enterprise social networks, so employee feedback has to be managed carefully. Simms (2018, p. 42) describes two cases where management ignored psychological safety:

> When Google engineer James Damore posted a memo about the firm's diversity initiatives last year to highlight what he saw as a left-wing bias that was silencing alternative views, he was fired. Similarly, at a town hall meeting at a technology company in Ireland, the chief executive claimed he wanted people to ask him questions, but when a male employee stood up and asked a question, he was asked: "Are you still here?" The next day, he wasn't.

Simms (2018) cites a positive example. The food company Danone UK encourages employee voice through three channels: Workplace by Facebook, its own intranet, and live events. Facebook—which is popular with younger staff—is especially effective, with over 90 percent of employees being active on Workplace every week, to share documents, minute meetings, and exchange other information.

The organizational applications of social media are not without problems, and management may want to assess carefully the balance of risks and opportunities. It is possible that senior (older) managers neither use nor understand the technology and its potential. The links between social media and corporate goals may not be obvious. The benefits of social media are difficult to quantify. Jobs may not be designed to make good use of social media. Management may feel that using social media at work encourages "cyberloafing" or "cyberslacking." Cybersecurity is a growing concern; one-fifth of cyberattacks involve insiders (employees, contractors, third-party suppliers) who have easy and legitimate access to an organization's systems and more opportunities to disrupt operations and steal intellectual property. Employees can be targeted by "bad actors" through social media.

Antisocial Media—Disruptive Innovations

Social media has many useful organizational applications, for communicating, sharing information, and collaborating. An investigation by the *Financial Times* newspaper, however, found that social media is contributing to sexual harassment in the workplace (Noonan and Ram, 2018). Employees share personal details through social media, and some organizations have their own internal enterprise networks, such as Workplace by Facebook, that allow potential stalkers to track the location of their colleagues in real time, through their online calendars. A financial service sector employee said:

> It's great to connect people across the world to form cross-border teams and share expertise. But if some guy at the company is persistently trying to ask you out on a date, or pressuring you into sex, it means he has loads of tools to stalk you online, get tons of information about you and find your whereabouts,

which is really scary. And because all these systems are company mandatory, you can't block the guy, switch messenger off, or hide your profile from him. At least if you're harassed on Twitter or Facebook, you can block people or close your account.

One employee was hounded on Facebook after she made a complaint about sexual harassment—a complaint that was widely publicized through the social network. Organizations may need to set up and enforce "acceptable use" policies that prohibit misuse of social media. Privacy controls and blocking functions can be introduced to allow individuals to protect themselves, although these steps could reduce the networking and collaboration benefits of social media. A participant in this study pointed to one benefit of sexual harassment through social networks: "It gives a great trail of the abuse should a person choose to report it" (extracts from Noonan and Ram, 2018).

Another problem is that social media exposes organizations to greater transparency and scrutiny, which are beyond management control. The jobs listing website Glassdoor.com was launched in 2008 and since 2018 has been owned by a Japanese company. As well as listing vacancies, it provides an anonymous platform where individuals can share salary information and rate their organizations on a scale from 1 to 5. Job applicants can find out the percentage of employees who approve of a company's leadership. The site has 33 million reviews of more than 700,000 companies in 200 countries. Glassdoor has altered the power dynamics between employees and employers in the same way that Ratemyprofessor.com altered the relationship between students and university lecturers. Beneath each company logo are accounts of interdepartmental feuds, managerial chaos, insecure bosses, toxic company cultures, building smells, employee confessions and pleas, as well as accounts of "boys' club" dynamics (uncomfortable hugs and demands for sexual favors).

The evidence suggests that up to 80 percent of job seekers in the United States read Glassdoor company reviews, and it is common for job interviewees to ask interviewers, "I read this on Glassdoor, how do you respond?" Changes in company practices can drop a company from a five-star to a one-star rating overnight. Glassdoor insists that reviews and scores on its website are "a mirror that reflects back on companies" (Widdicombe, 2018).

EXERCISE 5.1

The Mattel Toy Story

LO 5.1

This is an account of the changes that Ynon Kreiz, chief executive at Mattel since 2018, plans to implement to grow the company, which has been in decline for some time. As you read this case account, consider the following questions:

- Which of the changes at Mattel are emergent, and which are planned?
- Where do the changes that Kreiz is making sit on the continuum from shallow to deep change?
- What is your assessment of Ynon Kreiz's changes, given the challenges facing the company?
- What image—or images—of change management does Ynon Kreiz illustrate?

The Context

Founded in 1945, Mattel is an American multinational toy manufacturer based in California. With $1.4 billion annual revenue and 27,000 employees, it is one of the world's largest toymakers. Mattel's "power brands" are Barbie, Hot Wheels, American Girl, Fisher-Price, and Thomas & Friends. These were introduced between 1930 and 1986, and Mattel had not created another hit product for some time. Barbie dates from 1959. Smaller brands were incorporated in what Mattel called "toy box," an "everything else" category that included Polly Pocket dolls, Uno (a card game), and toys linked to the video game *Minecraft*. Mattel's traditional competitive advantage was based on making incremental product improvements and on manufacturing cost advantage.

Mattel's most important brand is Barbie, who still generates 20 percent of the company's sales despite being 60 years old. Half of Barbie sales are "nonoriginal body" or non-Caucasian, and Barbie dolls in the image of K-pop band BTS have been successful. The company also now sells gender-neutral dolls with the brand name Creatable World.

The Problem

Revenues at Mattel have been falling, from over $6 billion in 2007 to $4.5 billion in 2018. Mattel's stock price fell from $50 in 2014 to $10 at the end of 2018. Revenue growth was expected to be flat in 2019. Barbie and Hot Wheels continue to sell well, but American Girl dolls, once famous, are in decline. The company's falling sales are accompanied by rising debt. Earlier in the decade, American Girl was selling well, linked to Disney's *Frozen* franchise. But this success took sales away from Barbie. Sales of Monster High merchandise generated hundreds of millions of dollars, but suddenly collapsed when the brand became unfashionable. Sales of Hot Wheels have also stalled.

Manufacturing and supply chain management at Mattel had not changed. Along with other toymakers (apart from Lego), Hasbro closed factories and started outsourcing, but Mattel made its own products. Hasbro—Mattel's main competitor—has similar sales and employs 6,000 people; Mattel has 40,000 employees at peak factory output. Hasbro's gross margins are 51 percent; Mattel's are 39 percent.

The Changes

Ynon Kreiz, the company's fourth chief executive since 2012, joined Mattel in 2018. Colleagues describe him as "sure and steady, disciplined, and unflappable" (Lashinsky, 2019,

p. 101). His vision is to transform Mattel from toy maker to high-margin media company, basing movies on its familiar brands. Toy manufacturers earn only a small percentage of movie revenues, most of which go to studios and distributors. But movies can revive old brands and increase sales of merchandise.

One of Kreiz's first actions as chief executive was to reduce the workforce by 22 percent. To reduce costs further, he also planned to sell 12 of Mattel's 13 factories. He also reduced a three-inch-thick strategy document to one page, identifying three priorities: cut costs, fix broken brands, and capture the value of the company's intellectual property. Following practice in the rest of the sector, Kreiz abandoned the "toy box" concept and grouped Mattel's brands into two categories: toy-industry leaders (dolls, vehicles, infant/preschool) and challengers (games, construction, action figures).

The idea of making movies based on Mattel brands was not new. But movies that were to be based on Hot Wheels and on the Rock 'Em Sock 'Em Robot were never made. In 2016, Sony started to develop a live-action Barbie comedy, but the star, Amy Schumer, dropped out. Mattel was not the only toy company to adopt this strategy. Hasbro, for example, has based movies on Transformers and G.I. Joe and planned to buy the Canadian media production company Entertainment One.

Kreiz hired an experienced movie producer, Robbie Brenner, who identified Barbie, Hot Wheels, and American Girl as initial projects, along with Magic 8 Ball—an old "toy box" product that gives advice and had been almost forgotten. In 2019, Mattel announced eight film projects with four studios, including Warner Bros and MGM. Paramount will make a live-action movie starring Tom Hanks based on the astronaut Major Matt Mason, who was created by Mattel in 1966. In 2019, Mattel announced that Margot Robbie would star in its Barbie movie, with a script written by the prestige team of Greta Gerwig (*Little Women*, 2019) and Noah Baumbach (*Marriage Story*, 2019).

In October 2019, Mattel posted its first positive cash flow in three years. Revenues appeared to be increasing again. Performance would have been better, but Fisher-Price had to recall five million "Rock and Play Sleepers" at a cost of $34 million, when the product was alleged to have caused 30 infant deaths. Rising sales, cost cutting, and improved financial forecasts lifted the company's share price. Will Kreiz be successful in rewriting Mattel's toy story?

Case Sources

Gul, E. 2019. Can Barbie adopt frontier technologies? Mattel's innovation challenge. *The Startup*, July 18. https://medium.com/swlh/can-barbie-adopt-frontier-technologies-mattels-innovation-challenge-e4b97bc1b15e.

Lashinsky, A. 2019. Rewriting a toy story. *Fortune* 180(6):98–103.

Mattel. *Wikipedia*, https://en.wikipedia.org/wiki/Mattel.

Find on *YouTube*, "Mattel execs on toy film franchises: 'We create experiences,'" (2019, 26 minutes). Ynon Kreiz explains his turnaround strategy for Mattel. Robbie Brenner describes her approach to developing movies based on Mattel brands, and Barbie in particular.

EXERCISE 5.2

Organizational Culture Assessment

LO 5.4

1. What words would you use to describe the positive and negative dimensions of your organization's culture or that of an organization with which you are familiar?

2. How can you explain the negative aspects of that organizational culture? Why have those dimensions developed in that way? What factors are causing, supporting, or reinforcing those dimensions?

3. What are the consequences of the negative dimensions of this organizational culture? In what ways are they harmful to the organization, its employees, suppliers, and customers?

4. What actions can you take to change the dysfunctional aspects of the culture? The 7-S framework (chapter 4) is a good place to start. What changes need to be made to the "hard" factors: strategy, structure, systems? What changes need to be made to the "soft" factors: style, staff, skills, shared values? How does senior leadership behavior have to change?

5. What would those actions cost?

EXERCISE 5.3

How Will Digital Transformation Affect Your Organization?

LO 5.5

Briefing—Operational Innovations

- You have decided to leave your organization tomorrow, to set up your own business in competition with your large, out-of-date, slow-moving, bureaucratic former employer.

- You have identified your organization's main weaknesses and vulnerabilities. Critically, you have worked out how a combination of digital transformation and social media tools could be used to undermine your organization's traditional business model. Or, customers may have "after-market" needs that your organization is not fulfilling.

- Describe your new business model. What digital tools and social media tools will you use to attract customers or clients from your previous employer to your business—and perhaps from other organizations in the sector? How quickly can you set up this business? What will it cost you to set up this business?

Briefing—Disruptive Innovations

- OK, you are not leaving the organization after all. That briefing was designed to make you think about potential threats to your organization from agile and innovative "out of sector" competitors. Let us assume that the new business model that you have just described is real and that somebody else has already thought about it—and may already be setting it up. How can your organization respond to that threat? Better still, how can your organization counter that threat before it emerges?

- Draw up an internal action plan for transforming the organization's current business model or for creating a separate unit or division to develop your new business model alongside the existing one.

Additional Reading

Furr, N., and Shipilov, A. 2019. Digital doesn't have to be disruptive. *Harvard Business Review* 97(4):94–103. Argues that digital transformation is about the customer, not about the technology, and does not need to involve a reinvention of an organization's core business. But digital transformations require organizational flexibility, respect for incremental change, and awareness that new skills and technology must be acquired and protected.

Hollister, R., and Watkins, M. D. 2018. Too many projects. *Harvard Business Review* 96(5):64–71. Offers advice, also discussed in this chapter, on how to avoid having too many change initiatives running at the same time, which can increase costs and the chance of staff burnout.

Schein, E. H. 2016. *Organizational culture and leadership.* 5th ed. San Francisco, CA: Jossey-Bass. Classic and recently revised text exploring the nature and significance of organizational culture and the crucial role of leaders as "architects" of culture.

Warrick, D. D., Milliman, J., and Ferguson, J. 2016. Building high performance cultures. *Organizational Dynamics* 45(1):64–70. Case study of the culture-building efforts of the chief executive of Zappos, the online retailer.

Roundup

Reflections for the Practicing Change Manager

- In what kinds of change initiatives are you currently involved—shallow, deep, mixed? If your current involvement concerns mostly shallow initiatives, how will that affect your ability to answer questions about your change management experience at the next job or promotion interview? Do you need to "reposition" your profile to include deeper changes?

- If you are involved in shallower changes, can you show how these are linked to and support the major, strategic changes that the organization is implementing?

- Does your personal comfort zone favor involvement in major, transformational, deep changes? Why? Or are you more comfortable implementing lower-risk, shallow changes—which can of course still be highly effective? In your judgment, what are the personal and organizational implications of your preferences?

- In your judgment, does your organization need disruptive innovation, in which areas, and why? Or would those changes be too "disruptive" and less effective than continuing to implement sustaining innovations?

- Does your organization have the capabilities for successful digital transformation? What form is that transformation taking? If there are capabilities lacking, how will you acquire or develop those? What are the benefits and risks of digital transformation?

- Does your organization use social media tools, for internal and external information sharing and communication? Have you opened up new sources of information, feedback, and fresh communication channels between management and staff? Has this led to information overload? Have social media tools been used to share information that has damaged the reputation of the organization or its staff? How will you manage reputational threats in future?

In answer to the question, "What changes?", this chapter has introduced terms for describing different types of change, based on the metaphor of depth; some changes are shallow, others are deep. We then focused on three areas of organizational change: innovation, culture, and digital transformation. These are not the only dimensions of organizational change, of course, but they are issues that most, if not all, organizations will face for some time. Why have these particular themes acquired such a high priority? A failure to innovate can lead to organizational decline. Dysfunctional organizational cultures can have disastrous consequences. Digitization and social media tools have the potential to create new and disruptive business models, making many established business models obsolete. The "controlling" images of change management—director, navigator, caretaker—may be less useful in this context. Dealing with a rapidly developing, uncertain, and unpredictable climate, the "shaping" images of change management may be more appropriate—coach, interpreter, navigator.

Here is a short summary of the key points that we would like you to take from this chapter, in relation to each of the learning outcomes:

LO 5.1   * *Explain several ways of categorizing different types of change.*

Organizational changes are typically varied and multifaceted. Change one aspect of an organization, and the interdependencies lead to "knock-on" or "ripple" effects that lead to further change elsewhere. We introduced a number of different ways of describing and classifying change, and these are summarized in table 5.3. The concepts of transformational change and disruptive innovation have become fashionable. Given the rapid pace of technology development, and of change driven by other socioeconomic, cultural, and legislative pressures, transformation and disruption appear to be attractive options. However, we have to recognize that less profound, shallow, simple changes can often be valuable in context. Small changes can also underpin and trigger major initiatives. The potential organizational value of shallow change should therefore not be underestimated.

TABLE 5.3
Different Types of Change

Type of Change	Description
Planned	Implemented in anticipation of, or in response to, known developments
Emergent	Just happens, or has to happen, in response to unforeseen events
Incremental	Gradual, small scale
Transformational	Radical, ground-breaking, disruptive
First-order	Solves a problem using methods based on current assumptions
Second-order	Transforms the organization with creative thinking and new business models
Third-order	Habitual overturning of assumptions, continual adaptation, and self-renewal
Shallow	Another label for incremental, small-scale change, fine-tuning
Deep	Another label for transformational, disruptive change, mold-breaking

LO 5.2   * *Identify practical implications of different types of change for the change manager.*

One practical implication of our change classification system concerns, as just mentioned, the potential of small changes to deliver benefit in their own right and to contribute to deeper initiatives. A second implication for the change manager is that shallow changes are likely to be more straightforward to implement; less costly, less risky, less disruption, less resistance. Organizational transformations present a different order of change management challenge. A third implication, however, is that a change manager's involvement in deep change is more likely to contribute to experience, reputation, and career than managing small initiatives. This leads to the suspicion that some deep changes could be designed to address personal interests rather than corporate needs.

At any given time, especially in larger organizations, there are likely to be many change initiatives under way, across the spectrum of Figure 5.1, from shallow, to midrange, to deep. The problem of coordinating such a pattern of change has led to the establishment of program management offices (PMOs) in many organizations. PMOs can thus support change and help to avoid the duplication of effort and cost. Where they are seen as "change police," their contributions may be curtailed.

LO 5.3   * *Understand the difference between sustaining and disruptive innovation, and explain the practical implications of this distinction for change management.*

Sustaining innovations improve current practice, while disruptive innovations introduce wholly new ways of doing things. From a change management perspective, it is usually easier to persuade others of the value of sustaining innovations; disruptive innovations are more difficult to explain, and because they make current practice obsolete, they may be seen as more risky. Most organizations do not have established procedures or routines for handling disruptive innovations—which are thus often implemented by small start-up companies rather than large established organizations.

The change manager can become a "disruptive innovator" by adopting five habits: associating, questioning, observing, experimenting, and networking. These are habits that anyone can develop, with practice.

LO 5.4   * *Assess the significance of organizational culture with regard to organizational performance and reputation and the role of leaders as culture architects.*

Some commentators regard organizational culture as an abstract concept with limited organizational use. Defining culture as "the way we do things," however, it seems that some organizations have dysfunctional cultures, which can lead to highly undesirable consequences. We saw how the dysfunctional culture at BP contributed to loss of life and serious injury, widespread economic and environmental damage, damage to the reputations and careers of senior management, loss of public trust and confidence in the organization, and massive fines for misconduct. Culture change, where necessary, becomes a priority in the face of such evidence, and culture change programs have consequently become popular. However, we also saw how culture change at Goldman Sachs was potentially contributing to corporate revenue growth and profitability, with David Solomon—the current chief executive—as the company's culture architect.

LO 5.5   * *Assess the organizational impact of digital transformations, including the adoption of social media tools, and the implications for change management.*

Developments in technology and consumer needs and expectations mean that most organizations are now in "the information business." The process of implementing digital transformations means that the nature of change itself is changing, as the scope and scale of organizational change expand. New change management capabilities are required: gaining commitment, ensuring sustainability, and encouraging continuous improvement. But digital transformations do not have to be disruptive or involve the reinvention of business models. Digital transformations are often less about the technology and more about the customer, and change should focus on meeting customer needs more effectively with evolving digital technologies.

Social media tools have many organizational applications, with reported benefits including promoting collaboration and knowledge sharing, speeding up decisions, developing innovative ideas, increasing employee engagement, establishing relationships between employees in different locations, and avoiding the duplication of work. Strengthening employee voice is another potential benefit, but management may not always like the feedback that is generated in this way. Social media are largely beyond management's direct control, but they open up organizations to greater scrutiny as information about an organization's actions can be widely and rapidly shared. Greater control may be achieved with the development of enterprise-specific networks. However, there are corporate risks in using social media tools, with regard to online stalking and harassment and cybercrime.

References

Beeson, J. 2009. Why you didn't get that promotion: Decoding the unwritten rules of corporate advancement. *Harvard Business Review* 87(6):101–105.

Bosak, J., Dawson, J., Flood, P., and Peccei, R. 2017. Employee involvement climate and climate strength: A study of employee attitudes and organizational effectiveness in UK hospitals. *Journal of Organizational Effectiveness: People and Performance* 4(1):18–38.

Christensen, C. M., and Overdorf, M. 2000. Meeting the challenge of disruptive change. *Harvard Business Review* 78(2):66–76.

Christensen, C. M., Raynor, M., and McDonald, R. 2015. Disruptive innovation. *Harvard Business Review* 93(12):44–53.

Chui, M., Manyika, J., Bughin, J., Brown, B., Roberts, R., Danielson, J., and Gupta, S. 2013. *Ten IT-enabled business trends for the decade ahead.* New York: McKinsey & Company/McKinsey Global Institute.

Coghlan, D., and Rashford, N. S. 2006. *Organizational change and strategy: An interlevel dynamics approach.* Abingdon, Oxon: Routledge.

Colvin, G. 2017. How Intuit reinvents itself. *Fortune* 176(6):76–82.

Cunliffe, A. L. 2008. *Organization theory.* London: Sage Publications.

Dromey, J. 2016. *Going digital? Harnessing social media for employee voice.* London: ACAS.

Dyer, J., Gregersen, H., and Christensen, C. M. 2011. *The innovator's DNA: Mastering the five skills of disruptive innovators.* Boston, MA: Harvard Business School Press.

Engage for Success. 2018. http://engageforsuccess.org/employee-voice.

Furr, N., and Shipilov, A. 2019. Digital doesn't have to be disruptive. *Harvard Business Review* 97(4):94–103.

Gifford, J. 2014. *Putting social media to work.* London: Chartered Institute for Personnel and Development.

Gordon, G. G., and DiTomaso, N. 1992. Predicting corporate performance from organizational culture. *Journal of Management Studies* 29(6):783–98.

Graban, M. 2009. *Lean hospitals: Improving quality, patient safety, and employee satisfaction.* Boca Raton: CRC Press.

Hammer, M. 2004. Deep change: How operational innovation can transform your company. *Harvard Business Review* 82(4):84–93.

Holland, P., Cooper, B. K., and Hecker, R. 2016. Use of social media at work: A new form of employee voice? *International Journal of Human Resource Management* 27(21):2621–34.

Hollister, R., and Watkins, M. D. 2018. Too many projects. *Harvard Business Review* 96(5):64–71.

Hwang, J., and Christensen, C. M. 2008. Disruptive innovation in health care delivery: A framework for business-model innovation. *Health Affairs* 27(5):1329–35.

Immelt, J. R., and Kirkland, R. 2015. *The CEO Interview: GE's Jeff Immelt on digitizing in the industrial space.* New York: McKinsey & Company.

Lawson, E., and Price, C. 2003. The psychology of change management. *The McKinsey Quarterly* (Special edition: *The value in organization*):31–41.

Leonardi, P., and Neeley, T. 2017. What managers need to know about social tools. *Harvard Business Review* 96(5):118–26.

Lindsay, B., Smit, E., and Waugh, N. 2018. *How the implementation of organizational change is evolving.* New York and London: McKinsey & Company.

National Commission on the BP Deepwater Horizon Oil Spill and Offshore Drilling. 2011. *Deep Water: The Gulf Oil disaster and the future of offshore drilling.* Washington, DC: National Commission.

Noonan, L., and Ram, A. 2018. Social media use fuels rise in sexual harassment. *Financial Times* (January 3):14.

Project Management Institute 2012. *The project management office: In sync with strategy.* Philadelphia PA: PMI Inc.

Reed, J. 2018. Cleaning up an abusive supply chain. *Financial Times* (April 22):24.

Rogers, E. 2003. *The diffusion of innovation.* 5th ed. New York: Free Press.

Romanelli, E., and Tushman, M. L. 1994. Organizational transformation as punctuated equilibrium: An empirical test. *Academy of Management Journal* 37(5):1141–66.

Simms, J. 2018. Is anybody actually listening? *People Management* (February):40–43.

Sull, D. 2015. The simple rules of disciplined innovation. *McKinsey Quarterly*, May 1, (3):86–97.

Ward, J., and Daniel, E. 2013. The role of project management offices (PMOs) in IS project success and management satisfaction. *Journal of Enterprise Information Management* 26(3):316–36.

Widdicombe, L. 2018. Rate your boss! *The New Yorker* (January 22):22–28.

Yuanqing, Y. 2014. I came back because the company needed me. *Harvard Business Review* 92(7/8):104–108.

Source of the chapter opening quote: *The Quotations Page,* http://www.quotationspage.com.

Chapter opening silhouette credit: CharlotteRaboff/Shutterstock

Chapter 6

Purpose and Vision

Learning Objectives

By the end of this chapter you should be able to:

LO 6.1 Explain the arguments for and against the concepts of purpose (or mission) and vision and how approaches to these issues depend on the image of managing organizational change.

LO 6.2 Explain the value of a clear organizational purpose or mission statement.

LO 6.3 Identify the characteristics of effective visions.

LO 6.4 Apply different methods and processes for developing visions.

LO 6.5 Explain why some visions fail.

LO 6.6 Explain the contribution of purpose and vision to organizational change.

"This is a new year. A new beginning. And things will change."

Taylor Swift, singer

175

LO 6.1 Missions and Visions: Fundamental or Fads?

A Crisis of Purpose

It's hard to imagine how your employees can perform if they don't understand your company's purpose. How can they come to work every day ready to further the business if they don't know what your organization is trying to accomplish and how their jobs support those goals? Yet in a recent survey of more than 540 employees worldwide conducted by PwC's strategy consulting business, Strategy&, only 28 percent of respondents reported feeling fully connected to their company's purpose. Just 39 percent said they could clearly see the value they create, a mere 22 percent agreed that their jobs allow them to fully leverage their strengths, and only 34 percent thought they strongly contribute to their company's success. More than half weren't even "somewhat" motivated, passionate, or excited about their jobs. (Blount and Leinwald, 2019, p. 134)

There is confusion between the terms *mission*, *purpose*, and *vision*. Missions and visions are difficult to disentangle. For most commentators, mission statements concern the overriding *purpose* of the organization (Quinn and Thakor, 2018). Broadly, they answer the question, *"What business are we in?"* Vision, in contrast, concerns the *future state* of the organization, an aspiration that can mobilize the energy and passion of the organization's members. Visions answer the question, *"What do we want to achieve?"* As mission statements concern the organization's purpose, they are action-oriented. Visions, in contrast, describe an ultimate goal (Kolowich, 2019):

Mission: Warby Parker — To offer designer eyewear at a revolutionary price, while leading the way for socially conscious businesses

Vision: Alzheimer's Association — A world without Alzheimer's disease

These are the definitions of mission (purpose) and vision (future aspiration) that we will use in this chapter. We will use the terms *mission* and *purpose* to mean the same thing. Both missions and visions can drive organizational change. The change management perspectives explored in chapter 10 emphasize the importance of clear missions and meaningful visions; we need to know what business we are in, and if we don't know where we are headed, it doesn't matter which direction we take. But there is debate over whether the concepts of mission and vision are fundamental to effective change, or whether these are just fads—items with which to decorate the reception area at the company head office and the inside front page of annual reports. If you do a Google search for "mission and vision statements," most hits will take you to management consultancy sites offering advice on how to write these statements; telling them apart can be challenging—and confusing.

As we will see, missions and visions can be linked to strategy and competitive advantage, enhancing organizational performance and sustaining growth. Clear missions should enable boards to determine how well organizational leaders are performing and which new business opportunities to pursue. Visions should help staff identify with the organization and inspire the motivation to achieve personal and corporate objectives. The process of determining missions and visions can enhance the self-esteem of those who are involved, because they can see the outcomes of their efforts.

A confused mission and a lack of vision, on the other hand, can be linked to organizational decline and failure. The absence of clear and compelling mission and vision may explain why some companies fail to exploit their core competencies despite having access to adequate resources. Business strategies lacking in purpose and vision may fail to identify when organizational change and a fresh direction are required. Lack of an adequate process for translating shared vision into collective action may be associated with the failure to produce transformational organizational change.

The concept of vision is particularly powerful. However, it remains controversial and invites cynicism when every organization has the same bland vision that includes "excellence," "corporate responsibility," "empowered employees," and "delighted customers." Although there is a lot of advice on how to develop missions and visions, there is little or no consensus on effective approaches. Some commentators have argued that the preoccupation with these statements has meant that the terms have been overused and trivialized and are in danger of losing any value they may have had.

Debates around definition and substance do not themselves invalidate these concepts. The challenge for the change manager is to avoid abstract statements that give little detail. On the other hand, statements that focus in-depth on short-term goals are also of limited value. We need to work between these two extremes. These arguments point to a deeper understanding: The links between mission, vision, and change depend on the image of change management in use. Table 6.1 summarizes the different understandings of each

TABLE 6.1
Change Management Image, Mission, and Vision: Links and Focus

Image	Missions/Visions-Change Link	Focusing Attention On
Director	Missions/visions are essential to successful change and must be articulated at an early stage by leaders.	There is a need for clear missions/visions to drive change linked to strategy and goals. Analytical and benchmarking processes should be used. Context affects the impact of missions/visions. There is a top-down responsibility to tell/sell the missions/visions.
Navigator	Missions/visions are important but can be compromised by competing views of different stakeholders.	Missions/visions are the product of debate. The change manager has to handle "mission/vision collision" when competing groups disagree.
Caretaker	External forces shape the change process, and missions/visions rarely have a major influence.	Visionary or charismatic leaders have limited impact when missions/visions are not related to the events driven by those external forces.
Coach	Missions/visions emerge through the leader's facilitation skills, shaping agendas and desired futures.	Missions/visions emerge through consultation and co-creation. Missions/visions will fail without participation.
Interpreter	Missions/visions articulate the core values and ideology that underpin the organization's identity.	Missions/visions are developed intuitively through imagery and imagination, using framing, scripting, and staging techniques. Missions/visions emerge through change.
Nurturer	Missions/visions are always temporary, emerging from the clash of shifting and unpredictable forces for change.	Visionary change leaders cannot predict accurately the outcome of systemic forces. Missions/visions are organizational properties, not an individual product, and can survive chaos.

image. You can use this table to identify how different images focus attention on some issues and approaches, and not others.

In this chapter, we will first explore the concept of organizational mission or purpose, what this means, how this drives organizational change, the benefits of being a "purpose-driven" organization, and the language in which mission or purpose statements are best expressed. We will then turn to the concept of vision, which may have even more impact as a driver of change. This depends on the content of the vision and the process through which the vision is developed. We then identify why visions can fail to produce their desired effects. Finally, we focus on three controversial issues concerning the role of vision in organizational change. First, does vision initiate and drive change, or does it emerge as change unfolds? Second, does vision help or hinder change? Third, is vision best understood as an attribute of heroic leaders or of heroic organizations? The perceptive reader will note that these debates also apply to missions, but we have avoided duplicating this discussion.

LO 6.2   Mission: Why Are We Here?

Why Do We Come to Work?

As much as you may try to motivate employees with slogans or extrinsic rewards, you won't achieve excellence if your people don't know why they are coming to work every day at your firm. The clearer you can be about what value your company creates and for whom, the greater your ability to inspire your workers. And the more you align the right talent, operating model, and financial resources to support your purpose, the better able employees will be to deliver on it. Purpose is the key to motivation—and motivated employees are the key to realizing your purpose. (Blount and Leinwand, 2019, p. 139)

Many employees—not just Millennials and Gen Z—want to work for organizations whose missions and business philosophies resonate with them intellectually and emotionally (see chapter 3). Senior management needs to communicate why the company exists (what value it creates and for whom) in a way that is easy for employees to understand. But mission or purpose statements often talk about "being the company of choice" or "maximizing shareholder value." These vague statements do not say what the organization does or who its customers are. The confusion between mission, purpose, and vision can lead companies to produce several different statements, causing further confusion. However, a powerful statement of purpose meets two objectives: clearly articulating strategic goals and increasing workforce motivation. Blount and Leinwand (2019, p. 134) argue that, to achieve those objectives, purpose statements have to answer questions such as, *"What is your reason for existing?" "What value are you giving your customers?"* and *"Why is your firm uniquely capable of providing it?"*

IKEA is often cited as a company with a clear message about its purpose. It promises "to create a better everyday life for the many people"—as distinct from the affluent few—by "offering a wide range of well-designed, functional home furnishing products at prices so low that as many people as possible will be able to afford them." Henry Schein, who provides products and services for medical and dental practitioners, also has a well-defined purpose: "To provide innovative, integrated health care products and services, and to be trusted advisors and consultants to our customers, enabling them to deliver the best quality patient care and enhance their practice management efficiency and profitability" (Blount and Leinwand, 2019, p. 136). Blount and Leinwald suggest that board members should be asking the management team these questions:

- If we were to put our purpose statement alongside a competitor's, could our employees identify which one was ours?
- If we asked our employees, how many could say what our purpose is?
- Do our employees have the resources required to deliver on our promises to customers?

How Chobani Makes a Difference

Chobani, America's leading Greek yogurt brand, has developed a "purposeful organization culture." The company's purpose is "better food for more people." Workers in Chobani's New York factory are paid double the minimum wage, and they own 10 percent of the company through its equity-sharing scheme. Chobani's founder, Hamdi Ulukaya, believes that people take pride and ownership in the brand and are more highly motivated when they have a stake in the company. The brand also funds start-ups in health and wellness through the Chobani Foundation and the Chobani Incubator. Chobani also hires and supports refugees, in coalition with 80 companies with the same aim. Ulukaya says, "The minute they got the job, that's the minute they stopped being refugees." Most employees today want more than a wage. Millennials in particular want to work for organizations like Chobani that make a meaningful contribution to society (based on Mainwairing, 2018).

Find on *YouTube*, "Chobani CEO Hamdi Ulukaya on how businesses can step up for refugees" (2019, 7 minutes).

Research into rapidly growing companies in America, Europe, and India by Malnight et al. (2019, p. 72) suggests that purpose is a driver of organizational growth (along with creating new markets, serving broader stakeholder needs, and "changing the rules of the game"). Purpose is not just a decorative statement; it can generate sustained profitable growth. They note (p. 77) that "a compelling purpose clarifies what a company stands for, provides an impetus for action, and is aspirational."

For Malnight et al. (2019), purpose plays two strategic roles—both potential drivers of change. The first role is *redefining the playing field*. Instead of competing for a share of a defined market, high-growth companies, guided by their purpose, look for other, broader market opportunities. Malnight et al. (2019, p. 74) cite the contrast between Nestlé Purina Petcare, the leading company in North America, and Mars Petcare, the global leader in this sector. The purpose of Purina is "better with pets." Petcare's purpose is "a better world for pets." Purina has continued to focus on petfoods. But Mars Petcare has diversified into pet health, by investing in veterinary services, and is now the largest and fastest-growing business division in Mars Incorporated. This change worked because the transformation was consistent with the company's core purpose.

The second role is *reshaping the value proposition*. When competition erodes margins, most organizations look for innovative new products, services, and business models. This can generate short-term gains, but these are limited by existing market structures—the "ecosystem"—in which an organization operates. A purpose-driven approach helps the organization grow into new ecosystems. Malnight et al. (2019) suggest that there are three ways in which this growth can happen, by responding to trends, building on trust, and "focusing on pain points":

1. *Responding to trends.* Securitas AB, a Swedish security company, offered a traditional security guard service. The changing nature of risk, rising labor costs, and cheaper technology, however, encouraged the company to start using electronic security systems, offering enhanced protection using remote surveillance, with digital reporting. Going beyond reactive security, in 2018 the company started to develop predictive security systems, which continued to build on their core purpose, with stronger client relations and higher margins.

2. *Building on trust.* To grow sales of vehicle financing in largely uninsured rural markets, Mahindra Finance had to build trust with new customers. This involved determining the creditworthiness of poor, illiterate customers, who had no bank accounts or collateral. This also meant setting up branches in new locations and recruiting employees who could speak local dialects and work on their own initiative. The company also had to redesign loans, customer approvals, and repayment terms, and organize cash repayments. Having built trust with those customers, Mahindra started to sell equipment, life, and health insurance to farmers, in a market where insurance penetration is below 4 percent. This expansion was driven by the company's purpose, which is to improve customers' lives, captured by the word "Rise." The chief executive, Anand Mahindra hopes that the company's purpose "will inspire employees to accept no limits, think alternatively, and drive positive change" (Malnight, 2019, p. 75).

3. *Focusing on pain points.* In search of other ways to "create a better world for pets," Mars Petcare has developed ways of diagnosing and preventing pet health problems. They bought a company that made smart collars for activity monitoring and location tracking ("Fitbit for dogs"). Combining data analytics, machine learning, and veterinary expertise, this approach identifies changes in behavior that could identify health problems, leading to early treatment.

Malnight et al. (2019, p. 77) suggest that there are two approaches to defining corporate purpose:

- A *retrospective* approach has an internal focus and is based on the organization's current reason for being, based on its past history. "Where have we come from? How did we get here?"
- A *prospective* approach takes an external perspective and redefines the organization's purpose by looking forward. "Which trends affect our business? What new opportunities lie ahead?"

They identify three benefits to the organization of clarifying and communicating purpose. First, a clear purpose can unify the organization and help staff to understand the direction that the organization is taking. Second, purpose is motivating. As already noted, employees in general, and Millennials in particular, expect their work to contribute to a higher cause—a purpose—which can also increase the trust that customers, suppliers, and other stakeholders place in the organization. Third, clarity of purpose can have a significant impact on organizational change and performance.

Find on *YouTube*, "Put purpose at the core of strategy—interview with IMD Professor Thomas Malnight" (2019, 3 minutes).

Research by the management consulting firm Deloitte (O'Brien et al., 2019, pp. 7–8) suggests that purpose-driven companies have:

- stronger gains in market share
- higher productivity and growth rates
- a more satisfied workforce
- higher customer satisfaction
- 30 percent higher levels of innovation than their competitors
- 40 percent higher levels of employee retention than their competitors

Purpose and Performance at Unilever

In 2019, our consumer survey showed that price and quality remain the biggest factors driving customer decisions. However, many of the same respondents (55 percent) believe businesses today have a greater responsibility to act on issues related to their purpose. Those failing to do so risk being displaced by purpose-driven disruptors. For example, Unilever's 28 "sustainable living" brands (i.e., brands focused on reducing Unilever's environmental footprint and increasing social impact) such as Dove, Vaseline, and Lipton delivered 75 percent of the company's growth and grew 69 percent faster on average than the rest of its businesses in 2018 (compared to 46 percent in 2017). Soap, petroleum jelly, and tea are everyday household essentials, but by promoting sustainable living, these products became differentiated as they embody the company's purpose. (O'Brien et al., 2019, p. 8)

The Language of Mission Statements

The language that an organization uses to communicate its purpose or mission can affect employee commitment and performance. But as we have discussed, many organizations use mission statements that use abstract, conceptual terms. Murphy and Clark (2016) note that organizations tend to use the same corporate-speak: "striving for excellence" or "delivering cutting-edge services in a global marketplace." They cite a bank whose mission statement reads:

> The mission of People's Community Bank is to be the preferred independent community bank which meets and exceeds the expectations of our customers and communities, by providing excellent customer service, products and value, while maximizing shareholder return, along with maintaining the well-being and satisfaction of our employees.

TABLE 6.2
The Language of Mission Statements

Statements Using Imagery	Statements Using Abstractions
To put joy in kids' hearts and a smile on parents' faces	To be the world leader in . . .
To detect a previously undetectable tumor inside a human lung by asking a patient to breathe into a device like ours	To be the recognized performance leader in . . .
	To be the most trusted provider of . . .
To make people laugh	To be a leading company delivering improved shareholder value
To ensure the security and freedom of our nation from undersea to outer space, and in cyberspace	Create a better everyday life for many people
We believe in long candlelit baths, filling the world with perfume	To create long-term value for customers, shareholders, employees
A computer on every desk and in every home	To create a better future every day

For a mission statement to encourage a *shared* sense of purpose, it has to use vivid concrete imagery that people can visualize and interpret in the same way. They cite the mission statement of a manufacturer of wearable robotic prosthetic devices:

> One day, our robotic exoskeletons will be a viable and accessible option for the millions of wheelchair users who want the option to stand up and walk.

Table 6.2 shows examples of real company mission statements, using concrete imagery and abstractions. Which will be more effective in creating a shared sense of the organization's purpose?

The evidence suggests that many companies ignore this advice. In their annual review of corporate governance, the UK Financial Reporting Council (2020, p. 9) concluded that:

> Too many companies substituted what appeared to be a slogan or marketing line for their purpose or restricted it to achieving shareholder returns and profit. Reporting in these ways suggests that many companies have not fully considered purpose and its importance in relation to culture and strategy, nor have they sufficiently considered the views of stakeholders in their purpose statements. The best reporting described purpose by considering it alongside culture and strategy in a way that demonstrated the company had thought about purpose effectively.

Mission Statements: *The Best and the Worst*

Gabrielle Bosché (2019) offers the following examples of "best" and "worst" mission statements from leading American organizations. Do you agree with her assessment, or not? Why?

The Best

Amazon   To be Earth's most customer-centric company, where customers can find and discover anything they might want to buy online, and endeavors to offer its customers the lowest possible prices

Asos   To become the number 1 fashion destination for 20-somethings globally

Intuit   To improve our customers' financial lives so profoundly, they couldn't imagine going back to the old way

Whole Foods	Our deepest purpose as an organization is helping support the health, well-being, and healing of both people—customers, Team Members, and business organizations in general—and the planet	**Sony**	To be a company that inspires and fulfills your curiosity
Walmart	We save people money so they can live better	**Cisco**	Shape the future of the Internet by creating unprecedented value and opportunity for our customers, employees, investors, and ecosystem partners
American Red Cross	To prevent and alleviate human suffering in the face of emergencies by mobilizing the power of volunteers and the generosity of donors	**Home Depot**	The Home Depot is in the home improvement business and our goal is to provide the highest level of service, the broadest selection of products and the most competitive prices
Southwest	To provide authentic hospitality by making a difference in the lives of the people we touch every day		
The Worst		**MOMA***	To collect, preserve, study, exhibit, and stimulate appreciation for and advance knowledge of works of art that collectively represent the broadest spectrum of human achievement at the highest level of quality, all in the service of the public and in accordance with the highest professional standards
Disney	To be one of the world's leading producers and providers of entertainment and information, using its portfolio of brands to differentiate its content, services and consumer products		

*Museum of Modern Art, New York.

LO 6.3 Vision: Where Are We Going?

The Magic of Vision

Creating a unifying vision for an organization is a fundamental skill for leaders. A simple, bold, inspirational vision can feel almost magical: it brings people throughout the company together around a common goal and provides a focal point for developing strategies to achieve a better future. (Ashkenas and Manville, 2019, p. 2)

The evidence suggests that effective vision statements have positive consequences, but what makes visions "visionary' is not clear. Some commentators focus on the content of vision statements. Others explore the context in which visions are used. The roles of leaders in articulating visions, and the process by which visions are developed, have also attracted attention. Here, we will consider the content of visions, including their style and other attributes.

Vision Attributes

Table 6.3 shows several definitions of organizational vision. As we discussed earlier, most of these definitions refer to a future or to an ideal to which organizational change should

TABLE 6.3
Vision Definitions

Definitions	Sources
A leader's statement of a desired, long-term future state for an organization	Kirkpatrick (2017, p. 87)
Image of an "ideal future." It is aspirational and idealistic, a guiding star with dreamlike qualities	Haines et al. (2005, p. 139)
A picture of the future of our organization	Auster et al. (2005, p. 50)
A detailed description of a desired future that provides clarity as to how the organization will need to operate differently in order to meet the changing conditions of its markets, customers, and overall business environment	Belgard and Rayner (2004, p. 116)

be directed. The vision itself is presented as a picture or image that serves as a guide to that future. Visions can thus be inspiring, motivational, emotional, or analytical, depending on whose definition we are using.

Definitions do not necessarily help to determine the actual content of visions. Kimberly Boal and Robert Hooijberg (2001) argue that visions have two components:

- *Cognitive* (intellectual). Based on information and expresses outcomes and how these will be achieved
- *Affective* (emotional). Appeals to values and beliefs, and thus underpins the motivation and commitment that are key to implementation

Table 6.4 summarizes the views of commentators on the components of an effective vision. Most commentary points to similar attributes, suggesting that visions should be aspirational, clear, desirable, distinctive, easy to communicate, feasible, flexible, future-focused, inspiring, meaningful, memorable, and motivating, and it should recognize the problems facing the organization.

To be motivating, a vision may need another, counterintuitive component. Change managers are often advised to make clear how bad things are and emphasize the urgency of change. This is "burning platform" theory, in which a break with the past promises a bright new future. This sounds logical and positive. But people also value coherence, consistency, and continuity. Visions that offer to break with the past may be threatening and discourage support. Venus et al. (2019) argue that people are likely to resist changes that they see as threatening to their sense of organizational continuity. Visions that offer major changes, however exciting and innovative, can be demotivating. So how can change managers motivate with vision? The answer is that a vision that promotes continuity as well as change will reduce uncertainty and reduce resistance. Venus et al. (2019, p. 684) explore the implications for change management practice in the following terms:

> Unlike engaging in strategies such as creating a dissatisfaction with the status quo, and consequently, a need for change, and portraying change as highly attractive, managers ought to emphasize also that which is not going to change. If unwillingness to contribute to change is rooted in concerns about a potential discontinuity of the central aspects of the organizational identity, then managers ought to assure employees that this will not be

TABLE 6.4
The Characteristics of Effective Visions

Characteristics	Advocates
Provides a clear sense of continuity of organizational identity	Venus et al. (2019)
Uses image-based rhetoric to paint a concrete picture of the future	Carton and Lucas (2018)
Future focused. What will our business look like in 5 to 10 years time? *Directional*. Describes where the organization is going *Clear and easily understood*. Guides decisions and independent action *Relevant*. Reflects the past as well as current challenges *Purpose-driven*. Connecting to a meaningful sense of purpose *Values-based*. Shared beliefs that influence behavior and attitudes *Challenging*. Stretch goals that set a high standard *Unique*. Reflects what makes the organization different *Vivid*. Provides a striking mental image of the future *Inspiring*. Captures the heart, and engages people to commit to a cause	Ambler (2013)
Imaginable. Conveys a picture of the future *Desirable*. Appeals to stakeholder interests *Feasible*. Embodies realistic, attainable goals *Focused*. Guides decision making *Flexible*. Enables initiative and response to changing environments *Communicable*. Can be explained in five minutes	Kotter (2012)

a concern. Arguably, this critical shift in focus requires that development programs teach managers how to frame change such that it will be perceived as a continuation, reaffirmation, or preservation of who "we" are as a collective.

The Value of Effective Visions

Over 50 studies demonstrating the positive impact of an effective vision statement have been conducted across a variety of samples, including students and managers who served as laboratory study participants, military combat and noncombat leaders; top-, middle-, and lower-level managers; work teams; entrepreneurs; educational leaders; national leaders; and political leaders. These studies find positive, significant effects of vision statements on organizational as well as team performance. At the individual level, follower attitudes, such as commitment to the organization, trust in the leader, and satisfaction, are also positively affected by the presence of a vision statement. (Kirkpatrick, 2017, p. 88)

Carton and Lucas (2018) note that when we think about the future, we tend to think in abstract terms. Senior managers may be advised to think in this way when creating their organization's vision, which often turns out to be something like "aiming for excellence," "change the world," or "serve the community." Visions like these are vague; there are too many different interpretations. However, this means that they are not truly "visionary." This happens because, when we think about how we are going to use language, we activate *the meaning-based system*, which handles abstract concepts such as "better customer service." The meaning-based system relies on abstract rhetoric.

The use of abstract rhetoric leads to what Carton and Lucas call "blurry vision bias." This is based in part on how we think about the future. As it has not happened yet, we cannot see or feel it, so we tend to rely on an abstract understanding of what it will mean: providing excellent customer service. Carton and Lucas argue that this tendency is particularly marked in those who are most likely to be responsible for crafting the organization's vision—senior managers—because those in positions of power tend to think in broad, abstract terms about the organization's strategy.

In contrast, *the experience-based system* processes sensory information about the world and allows us to imagine real-life experiences such as "seeing customers smile as they eat in our restaurants." This system uses image-based rhetoric—language that depicts objects (cars), actions (driving), and events (landing on the moon). Image-based rhetoric also engages the emotions, is more memorable, and is therefore more motivating, and is likely to encourage action:

> Meeting a person who benefits from one's help is more motivating than reading about it; seeing one person die up close affects moral judgment more than does dropping a bomb on thousands from a distance; and observing a measuring cup containing the amount of sugar in one soda deters soft drink consumption more than reading about caloric content. A story of a single hungry child elicited more charitable giving compared to statistics about thousands of starving villagers, and people were more likely to quit smoking when they read about how their habit caused people to "reel back in disgust from the smoker's putrid odor" than when they read about its adverse health effects. (Carton and Lucas, 2018, p. 2108)

Blurry vision bias happens because managers rely more heavily on the meaning-based system in their choice of language. This can be overcome by relying instead on the experience-based system and image-based rhetoric. The latter describes how the world will look, sound, and feel when the organization's vision is achieved. However, this involves more than a simple change in the choice of language in which to express the vision. Carton and Lucas argue that, if you don't have a concrete image in mind, you are still likely to end up with abstract blurry vision bias.

To overcome blurry vision bias, Carton and Lucas (2018, p. 2107) suggest the deliberate use of the technique of *temporal projection*, which means:

> mentally projecting oneself to a moment in the distant future, akin to mental time travel—that targets the experience-based system rather than the meaning-based system. Rather than contemplate the distant future abstractly, this tactic impels leaders to imagine the future in vivid detail, as if they are directly observing a future scenario through firsthand observation. By vividly depicting an event or outcome that an organization can one day realize, image-based rhetoric reflects the notion that a vision is a "portrait" of an ideal future and underscores the very essence of the word "vision"—the ability to see. (Carton and Lucas, 2018, p. 2107)

In a series of experiments, Carton and Lucas found that senior managers who imagined what it would be like to see their organizations achieve their vision one day in the future developed visions with greater imagery, without weakening other aspects such as achievability, specificity, and values.

Twenty-First-Century Vision Statements

Consider the following sample of vision statements. With reference to the criteria shown in table 6.4, which of these statements are in your judgment effective, and which are not? Based on their vision statements, for which of these companies would you want to work? Whose visions would turn you away? Why? How do you explain your preferences and dislikes with regard to these visions?

Airbnb	Belong anywhere.
Apple	We believe that we are on the face of the earth to make great products and that's not changing.
CNN	We bring the world's breathtaking diversity into cinematic focus, telling stories that are revealing and inspiring.
Coca-Cola	Inspiring each other to be the best we can be by providing a great place to work.
Disney	To be one of the world's leading producers and providers of entertainment and information.
eBay	Our vision for commerce is one that is enabled by people, powered by technology, and open to everyone.
Google	To provide access to the world's information in one click.
Netflix	Becoming the best global entertainment distribution service. Licensing entertainment content around the world, creating markets that are accessible to film makers and helping content creators around the world to find a global audience.
Nike	To bring inspiration and innovation to every athlete in the world.
Spotify	We envision a cultural platform where professional creators can break free of their medium's constraints and where everyone can enjoy an immersive artistic experience that enables us to empathize with each other and to feel part of a greater whole.
Starbucks	To establish Starbucks as the premier purveyor of the finest coffee in the world while maintaining our uncompromising principles while we grow.
Walmart	Be the destination for customers to save money, no matter how they want to shop.

From Mission Statement Academy. 2019. https://mission-statement.com.

Vision and Market Strategy

Some commentators argue that, to create competitive advantage, an organization's vision and strategy must be unconventional, perhaps even counterintuitive, and must also be distinct from those of other companies. Visions have both external and internal dimensions. The external dimension concerns how markets work, what drives customers, competitors, industry dynamics, and macroeconomic trends. As we saw in chapter 5, the toy manufacturing company Mattel traditionally regarded its core business as selling toys that were made in its own factories. Falling sales and the behavior of competitors, however, encouraged Mattel to outsource production and develop into a media business. Mattel has had to develop new internal capabilities to realize this new vision. Customers can expect to see movies based on Mattel brands such as Barbie, Hot Wheels, American Girl, Magic 8-Ball, and Major Matt Mason appear on cinema screens in the 2020s (Lashinsky, 2019).

Having a well-specified external vision helps to identify how the company will grow and compete. Only then can an internal vision be developed, pointing to the capabilities that need to be acquired to compete, and also to what the organization seeks to become. External and internal dimensions of the vision thus have to be aligned.

The Big Picture

Inspire people by presenting a compelling vision for the future. During times of uncertainty, people experiencing change want a clear view of the path ahead. It's important to share what you know—including what's changing, when, and how. But for most change initiatives, it is also helpful to start with a narrative or story that clearly articulates the "big picture"—why change is important and how it will positively affect the organization long-term. This should serve as the foundation for how you communicate about the change moving forward. (Galbraith, 2018, p. 3)

LO 6.4   How Visions Are Developed

How are visions developed? We will consider three answers to this question, exploring approaches to "crafting" a vision, the kinds of questions that can help to develop a vision, and connecting the vision to the organization's "inner voice."

Crafting the Vision

Lawrence Holpp and Michael Kelly (1988, p. 48) argue that crafting a vision is "a little like dancing with a 500-pound gorilla. It takes a little while to get the steps down, but once the dance is over, you know you've really accomplished something." There are different approaches (or dances) to crafting or creating a vision, and some of these are outlined in table 6.5 (based on a concept similar to the "leadership styles continuum," discussed in chapter 10, table 10.7).

TABLE 6.5
Approaches to Vision-Crafting

Approach	What It Means	Used When
Tell	Chief executive creates the vision and gives it to staff.	Involvement is not seen as important.
Sell	Chief executive has a vision that he or she wants staff to accept.	Chief executive is attracted to the vision and wants others to adopt it.
Test	Chief executive seeks feedback on ideas about a vision.	Chief executive wants to see which aspects of the vision find support.
Consult	Chief executive seeks the creative input of staff, within set parameters.	Chief executive needs help to develop the vision.
Co-create	Chief executive and staff create a shared vision.	Chief executive wants to identify shared visions throughout the organization.

TABLE 6.6
Guidelines for Structuring the Vision Process: Core Steps in Creating a New Vision

	Deetz et al. (2000)	Davidson (2004)	Belgard and Rayner (2004)
1	Use a qualified facilitator.	Develop trial vision statements.	Leadership team defines the timeline.
2	Assess where you have been and where you are.	Discuss these with staff and customers.	Scan for environmental threats and opportunities.
3	Think about a new direction.	Revise the vision.	Develop interview questions.
4	Co-construct a statement about the organization's future direction.	Rediscuss the vision.	Use questions to interview leadership team to obtain their ideal vision of the future.
5	Identify roadblocks.	Repeat the process until an agreed vision is produced.	Draft a vision of the future.
6	Take action quickly to capitalize on enthusiasm; develop a strategic plan to integrate vision throughout organizational practices.		Get feedback from across the organization.
7	Develop a system for monitoring and adjusting the vision such as performance review workshops.		Develop a second draft.
8			Share vision with leadership team to gain commitment. Develop a catch-phrase that captures its essence, and a communication plan
9			Assess implications and develop action plans.

Three sets of structured guidelines or "routines" for producing a vision are summarized in table 6.6. Although similar in style, they provide different levels of detail with regard to the nature of the process and the steps that should be involved. There is no "one best way" to do this.

Ashkenas and Manville (2019) suggest that anyone in an organization can contribute to vision-crafting. This is not necessarily a top-management responsibility. Others can be involved in three ways. First, by helping to shape the vision work of senior leaders. The top team members are often removed from customer experiences and operational realities, and there is value in using the insights of those who are more closely connected. Second, by translating the corporate vision for your own team members. Third, by developing a new frontline team vision that can be "cascaded up" through the organization. Ashkenas and Manville (2019, p. 3) also note, "Each of these [modes of involvement in vision-crafting] can propel your professional development, leading to bigger responsibilities over time." An inclusive approach to vision-crafting can help to ensure "ownership" of the end result. Ates et al. (2019) argue that the potentially positive impact of visionary leadership can be lost when middle managers are not aligned with the top management vision and that this lack of alignment can cause strategic change efforts to break down or fail.

Asking the Right Questions

Discussion of different degrees of involvement in the development of an organization's vision do not directly address the question of how to develop the substance of the vision itself. Holpp and Kelly (1988) identify three different approaches and sets of questions through which vision may be developed. They label these approaches *intuitive*, *analytical*, and *benchmarking*.

The *intuitive* approach relies on the use of imagination and imagery to encourage staff to participate in vision development. Managers are asked to imagine doing their jobs in such a way that they really achieve what they want from themselves and from the other people with whom they work:

> First, they are asked to list up to ten things that they want to achieve personally and professionally, and then to prioritize these, focusing on the top two or three.

> Second, they focus on their current situation as a way to identify the tension between their current lived experiences and their desired image.

> Third, they are provided with support to help identify and implement structured action plans to work toward achieving their vision.

The *analytical* approach sees visions as defined in relation to organizational or departmental missions and roles. Vision is thus related to purpose and focuses on the following questions:

• Who is served by the organization?
• What does the organization do?
• Where does the organization place most of its efforts?
• Why does the organization focus on particular work and goals?
• How does the organization operationalize these efforts?

The aim of these questions is to guide the organization as a whole, and individual departments, from the current situation to a desired future state.

The *benchmarking* approach bases the vision on the actions and standards of the organization's toughest competitors. This involves asking:

• What do our competitors do well?
• How can we surpass this?
• What quantitative and qualitative measures would indicate that we had achieved this?
• What will it be like, and how will it feel, when those standards have been achieved?

The benchmarking approach is more externally focused, compared with the intuitive and analytical approaches, which have an internal focus. Here are some of the problems with these approaches:

- The intuitive approach, which follows an organization development perspective, may produce personal visions that are not connected to the core business of the organization and to current or anticipated industry trends.

- The analytical approach serves more to align the vision to the mission of the organization but pays less attention to the values and guiding logics of the organization. By aligning too tightly with mission, the analytical approach may neglect the inspirational element of visions.

- The benchmarking approach assumes that the organization's future will be linked to current competitors. However, it may be more valuable to identify who will be the new competitors in the future, especially where an organization and a sector are facing transformational change.

"Bread and Salt": Connecting to the Organization's "Inner Voice"

Robert Quinn (1996, p. 197) makes an interesting contribution to the process of identifying change visions. He points out that, in many organizations, people want to know what the vision is and look to the chief executive to provide it. Paradoxically, however, where vision statements are available, such as on corporate business cards, these are likely to be rejected as being in name only; they are not what people are "willing to die for." He argues that developing a vision to guide organizational actions has to go beyond superficial statements and "confront the lack of integrity that exists in the system," an exercise for which few managers are well equipped.

To illustrate this view, he tells the story of a speech given by Mahatma Gandhi at a political convention in India. When he rose to speak, many in the audience also rose, left their seats, and paid little attention to him. However, as he spoke about what Indians really cared about—not politics, but bread and salt—the audience sat down again and listened. His message was unusual: "This small, unassuming man had journeyed through their heartland and captured the essence of India. He was vocalizing it in a way they could feel and understand. Such articulation is often at the heart of radical, deep change" (Quinn, 1996, p. 199). For Quinn, it is this ability to find the organization's "bread and salt" that makes a vision appealing, passionate, and beyond the superficial. This search for the "inner voice' of the organization is necessary, to develop visions that resonate and narrow the gap between "talk and walk." Such "bread-and-salt" visions are achieved in a circular manner involving a bottom-up and top-down dialogue to reach the "inner voice" of the organization.

Adopting a similar position, Rogers (2007, p. 229) maintains that "vision is as much about insight as far sight." Visions need to connect with people's desires, feelings, and ambitions, as well as with the organization's intentions. Resonating with the *interpreter* image of change management, this implies that visions are important in encouraging the members of an organization to develop and explore "new ways of seeing," to gain fresh insights, make new connections, and to be better prepared to work with the challenges that a new vision is likely to bring.

LO 6.5   Why Visions Fail

Visions can fail for a number of reasons. For example, this can happen when a vision is:

- *Too specific.* Fails to appreciate the inability to control change, and the degree of uncertainty often associated with outcomes
- *Too complex.* Difficult to understand
- *Too vague.* Fails to act as a landmark toward which change actions are directed
- *Inadequate.* Only partially addresses the presenting problem
- *Irrelevant.* Clear picture, not firmly attached to the business
- *Blurred.* No clear picture of the future
- *Unrealistic.* Perceived as not achievable
- *A rearview mirror.* Pictures the past, extrapolated into the future

Todd Jick (2001, p. 36) adds that a vision is likely to fail when leaders spend 90 percent of their time articulating it (but not necessarily in clearly understood terms) and only 10 percent of their time implementing it. Table 6.7 suggests other reasons why visions fail. The box "A Lack of Shared Vision" tells a short story about the absence of a shared vision. We will now consider two further reasons for vision failure: inability to adapt over time, and the presence of competing visions.

Be Specific   *Alan Lafley at P&G*

The chief executive of Procter & Gamble (P&G), Alan Lafley, is reflecting on his five years of leading change inside the company. One of his key comments is that he found it important to provide more than just a briefly stated vision, because people responded better to specifics:

> So if I'd stopped at "We're going to refocus on the company's core businesses," that wouldn't have been good enough. The core businesses are one, two, three, four. Fabric care, baby care, feminine care, and hair care. And then you get questions: "Well, I'm in home care. Is that a core business?" "No." "What does it have to do to become a core business?" "It has to be a global leader in its

industry. It has to have the best structural economics in its industry. It has to be able to grow consistently at a certain rate. It has to be able to deliver a certain cash flow return on investment." So then business leaders understand what it takes to become a core business.

Why did this extra detail help? For Lafley, there were two factors. One was the size and diversity of the P&G workforce—100,000 people from over 100 cultures. The second was that, for managers with so much going on in their businesses, the provision of more detail on the implications of the vision helped them to focus on what was needed to implement it (Gupta and Wendler, 2005, p. 3).

Failure to Adapt

Some visions stand the test of time and remain applicable and adaptable to new situations and environments. Others, however, need to be overhauled to remain relevant. This

TABLE 6.7
Why Visions Fail

Source: Based on
Lipton (1996,
pp. 89–91).

Visions Fail When . . .	Because . . .
The walk is different from the talk.	When managers do not match their words with actions, staff members treat the vision as an empty slogan.
They are treated as the "holy grail."	The expectations will be unrealistic, and visions are not magic solutions.
They are not connected to the present.	Visions need to recognize current obstacles if they are to be believable and seen as achievable.
They are too abstract, or too concrete.	Visions must be idealistic, realistic, and tangible.
Development does not involve a creative process.	It is often the process as well as the final vision that helps to secure the organization's future.
Participation is limited.	Consensus must be built around the vision, which has to be diffused throughout the organization.
People are complacent.	Visions that are projected too far into the future are not seen as urgent.

A Lack of Shared Vision

John Symons (2006) tells the following humorous story:

> The man in the hot air balloon was lost. Descending sufficiently he shouted to a walker on the ground asking where he was. "You are 30 feet up in the air," was her immediate response before she walked away.
>
> Asked subsequently by a companion to explain this unhelpful behavior she said: "He was a typical manager. He didn't know where he was, or how to get to where he wanted to go without the help of those underneath him." Somewhat mischievously she added, "Why should I do more than necessary to help someone who got to where he was by hot air and did not tell me where he was planning to go?"

As John Symons comments:

> She obviously did not know or share the balloonist's vision. The lesson for managers is clear. As well as enthusing those underneath them, the leader needs to communicate where he or she is in relation to achieving the vision.

situation is illustrated by the investigation by Lloyd Harris and Emmanuel Ogbonna (1999) into two medium-sized UK retail companies and the impact of the founders' visions on strategic change. In both cases, the company founder established the vision well over 100 years ago and there was evidence of an escalation of commitment to the vision by subsequent management. In one company, the vision was paternalistic (commitment toward staff) and focused on prudent growth. This led to a strong focus on sales and profitability in each new store location. These characteristics were still present in the current management of the company. The vision itself was seen as flexible and responsive to the prevailing environmental conditions facing the company. The researchers label the founder's vision in this case as providing a "strategic dividend" for subsequent management.

By contrast, in the other company, the founder's vision was to have a store in every town in a particular region. A second aspect of this vision concerned family control of the company. The researchers argue that this original vision continued to drive senior management. However, in contrast to the first company, this vision served as a "strategic hangover." The closed nature of the vision led successive management teams to make decisions that were out of step with changes in the environmental conditions facing the sector, such as the movement of large retail stores into the region and a shift in focus of such stores from price to quality and service. As a result, the company almost faced financial ruin on two separate occasions. In relation to subsequent strategic change actions taken by management in these two companies, the authors argue that "whether the original vision of the founder results in a legacy or a hangover is clearly dependent on the original flexibility of the strategy and the later environmental appropriateness" (Harris and Ogbonna, 1999, p. 340).

Presence of Competing Visions

Visions may also fail due to what Kanter et al. (1992) call "vision collisions," where multiple visions conflict with each other. This happens, for example, when the vision is crafted by strategists who are convinced of the need for change, but where this sense of urgency is not shared by those who will implement or be affected by the change (who may still be trying to embed previous changes). Vision collisions can also occur where there is a gap between the visions of management and stakeholders. In the mid-1980s, the vision of Nike, the sportswear company, was to make athletic footwear. However, the company found that a different market segment was buying their shoes; not athletes, but people who were wearing Nike trainers instead of casual shoes. Nike responded by introducing its own brand of casual shoes. This strategy failed because Nike had not understood that customers were buying expensive "overengineered sneakers" because they appealed to their image. In other words, the company's vision was out of step with its customers' vision of Nike. Multiple and conflicting visions can also arise with company mergers. Colin Mitchell (2002), for example, cites the failure in 2000 of the merger between Deutsche Bank and Dresdner Bank. In this merger, there was a "failure of management to persuade Deutsche's investment bankers of the vision for how the newly merged company would compete. Many key employees left, and the threat of mass walk-out forced Deutsche to abandon the deal after considerable damage to the share price of both companies" (p. 104).

LO 6.6 Linking Vision to Change: Three Debates

In this section, we explore three debates concerning the links between vision and organizational change. First, we ask if vision is a driver of change, or if vision emerges through the change process. Second, we ask whether vision helps or hinders change. Third, we assess whether vision is better attributed to heroic, charismatic leaders, or is better understood as an organizational attribute.

Debate One—Vision: Driving Change or Emerging during Change?

Vision Drives Change

The change management approaches and frameworks described in chapter 10 give vision a prominent role in underpinning and implementing organizational change.

- For Kanter et al. (1992), establishing a vision is the first step toward change. Without a vision, changes may seem arbitrary and unnecessary. Vision provides clarity about the goals of change, avoiding the perception that this is just another cost-cutting exercise. The vision can motivate staff to embrace change, engaging in what may seem to be daunting or risky actions.

- For Pendlebury et al. (1998), vision determines the scope, depth, and time frame of change, and the areas that will be affected. Having a vision at the start of change is needed for both transformational change (outlining the broader strategic intent to which all actions are directed) and incremental or adaptive change (where the vision can be more specific in terms of specifying change objectives and procedures).

The need for vision at the start of change is also embedded in the strategy literature, where the term *strategic intent* is often used to represent vision. This is usually associated with the work of Gary Hamel and C. K. Prahalad (1989, p. 4), who argue that "strategic intent envisions a desired leadership position and establishes the criterion the organization will use to chart its progress." They point to Komatsu's "Encircle Caterpillar" and Canon's "Beat Xerox" as visionary statements that capture strategic intent. The strategic intent behind such statements was long term and encompassed a number of different change programs and actions over the short and medium terms that were designed to work toward the longer-term vision. The strategic intent expressed the desired end result without specifying or prescribing the necessary steps for achieving it.

Vision Emerges during Change

Although important, it may not be possible to articulate a clear vision at an early stage during transformational or discontinuous change. Robert Shaw (1995) argues that organizational structures and management processes may require fundamental change. It may not be possible to develop a vision until after the process has begun to unfold because the relevant information may not be available in the current configuration (customer expectations, competition). In other words, discontinuous change has to be under way to make that information available to inform the development of vision. Those who are leading the change are surrounded by the presenting problems and are able to make real-time adjustments in the context of the results of their ongoing efforts. Quinn (1996, p. 83) describes this as "building the bridge as you walk it."

Is "the vision thing" overrated in terms of driving change? It is possible to argue that effective business planning leads to successful change, and not vision, or visionary leaders. Is "vision rhetoric" used just to make management decisions appear to be more acceptable?

Debate Two—Vision: Help Change or Hinder Change?

Vision Helps Change

Lipton (1996) identifies five tangible benefits that skillful visions can bring to an organization:

* *Enhance performance.* The studies by Collins and Porras (1991; 1996; 2005) found that companies labelled as visionary were likely, over time, to deliver a greater dividend to shareholders compared to others.
* *Facilitate change.* Visions provide road maps, which assist the transition process.
* *Enable sound strategic planning.* Plans that have embedded within them imagery of the future are more likely to inspire people to action.
* *Recruit talent.* This applies particularly to the Generation Xers who want to maximize their incomes while feeling that they are engaging in challenges greater than simply making a profit.
* *Focus on decision making.* Vision helps to identify competencies that characterize an organization.

Emmanuel Metais (2000) supports this position arguing that "strategic vision" helps to produce stretch in an organization by creating a sense of incompetence resulting from the gap between the future and the current reality. This perceived incompetence encourages creativity and the search for new ways of acquiring and using resources. At the same time, vision can also help to leverage these resources by stimulating innovative ways of using them. Stretch and leverage combined, Metais argues, can be used to identify new strategies for achieving the vision, including actions such as:

Flanking. Exploiting a weakness in a dominant competitor

Encircling competitors. Gaining greater control of the market

Destabilizing the market. Changing the competitive rules

Paul Schoemaker (1992) also links strategic vision with helping to decide the products that an organization should make and the markets in which it should operate. Performance appraisals and incentive systems can then be managed so that they align with the vision.

Vision Hinders Change

Vision can impede the process of organizational change when visionary or charismatic leaders use emotional appeal as the basis for engagement and neglect the operational details needed to make change work. A related problem is that vision focuses on the future, diverting attention from current problems (see the box "Lou Gerstner on Vision"). One example is the failure of the UK Internet company Boo.com, which raised $135 million to deliver its vision which was to have a global presence in online clothes shopping (Lissack and Roos, 2001). It launched operations in 17 different countries but had problems with slow software, which frustrated potential buyers:

> Boo's vision called for a broadband world of cool kids with large budgets. Boo's reality consisted of 56k modems, fussy buyers, and tight budgets. Boo was consistent with its vision but out of sync with its present landscape. (Lissack and Roos, 2001, p. 61)

Vision can thus be a drawback when the wrong vision drives the change, when leaders exaggerate perceptions of crisis, and when the vision fails to deliver on its promise and followers become disillusioned and lose confidence in both the leader and the organization. Further problems will arise when there is a significant gap between the vision and the organizational capabilities that would be required to realize it.

Lou Gerstner on Vision

Louis V. Gerstner Jr., chief executive of IBM, argued in a press conference in the mid-1990s that "the last thing IBM needs right now is a vision." He later wrote that this was "the most quotable statement I ever made." This statement has often been cited as evidence that he downplayed or even dismissed the role of vision in organizational change. For example, Raynor (1998, p. 368) argues, "For a good many critics Gerstner's comment was greeted with a heartfelt "it's about time"—that is, it is about time that a senior executive had the courage to speak up and put all that rhetoric about visions and missions in its place."

Gerstner argues, however, that those who have portrayed this view of him have misinterpreted (or even misquoted) him, often failing to pay attention to the "right now" part of the statement. He maintains that IBM had a number of vision statements. It was now time to implement these, rather than engage in further visioning exercises because by that time "fixing IBM was all about execution."

Based on Gerstner (2003).

Vision development approaches that do not involve the people who will be affected are thought to have negative consequences for producing successful organizational change. For example, Harvey Robbins and Michael Finley (1997, p. 175) point out:

> Where organizations go wrong is in assuming that the vision is some precious grail-like object that only the organizational priests are privy to—that it appears in a dream to the executive team, who then hold it up high for the rank and file to ooh and ahh over. The problem with the priestly approach to vision-and-mission is that the resulting vision is often a lot of garbage. The outcome, instead of being a useful reminder to keep to the change track, is a paragraph held to be so sacred that no one dares change it.

Vision can further hinder change where, once developed, senior management becomes so committed to it that they are unwilling to reevaluate and test its ongoing utility and relevance. To do this could challenge the assumptions that the top team is truly in control, that they have better foresight than anyone else, and that they do indeed have a clear and compelling vision of the organization's future. Senior management may feel uncomfortable questioning those issues.

Visions can hinder organizations when they have been developed using sense-making processes that are linked to current or past practices. Lissack and Roos (2001) argue that this approach is flawed, because predicting the future on this basis reifies the desired outcome without enabling future changes to be built into it. Vision is based on the world in the future being stable and predictable. Outcomes are locked in and goals are set. The problem is that the vision may prevent the organization pursuing new, unanticipated opportunities that may emerge.

For Lissack and Roos (2001), the concept of vision is limited by other assumptions. One assumption is that organizational boundaries are well defined: staff, customers, suppliers. In a world of fuzzy organizational networks, this assumption is questionable. A second assumption is that the identity of the organization is fixed, with the vision built around that identity. We think of Lego, for example, as a toy company. However, corporate identity—what the organization does—is constantly changing; as we saw in chapter 5, Lego is also now an online games company. Lissack and Roos (2001, p. 61) prefer the term "coherence" to vision. Coherence involves, "acting in a manner consistent with who you are given your present spot in the business landscape." An interesting argument, but it is unlikely that the term *coherence*, emphasizing debates around boundaries and organizational identity, will replace the concept of vision, which is deeply embedded in change management thinking.

How does vision impact individual rather than organizational identity, and can this propel or impede change? This issue has generated debate. Landau et al. (2006) note that staff may identify strongly with an organization's original vision and with the underlying beliefs and assumptions. However, when an attempt is made to inject a new vision, this is likely to be resisted if it disrupts individual images and self-definitions. The new vision will therefore hinder change. This problem can be addressed if it is possible to ensure that new objectives and goals remain consistent with the values and beliefs that under-pinned the original vision.

Jeffrey Ford and William Pasmore (2006) question this position for two reasons. First, it is not clear that vision does directly affect individual identity-forming processes. This is an empirical question that needs to be examined and is likely to vary across organizations. Second, even if we accept that there is a direct relationship between individual identity and vision, the problem lies with staff members who are deeply committed to an existing identity, which they are reluctant to change, despite the need for a new vision (and perhaps, therefore, a new identity)—even if the new vision is necessary to secure the organization's survival. They note, "People should be entitled to their identities, but at the same time, organizations do need people who are committed to a viable, sustainable vision to survive" (p. 176). This argument reminds us that changes in vision may challenge individual identities, thereby producing resistance to change. When developing a new vision, therefore, it is important to assess, first, whether this will enable or disable identity-forming processes, and second, whether this will encourage or discourage those affected to become involved in the change.

Debate Three—Vision: An Attribute of Heroic Leaders or Heroic Organizations?

Vision Is an Attribute of Heroic Leaders

Some commentators argue that successful organizational change depends on effective leadership. For Nadler and Shaw (1995, p. 219), "heroic leaders" energize and support their followers and provide them with a vision that "provides a vehicle for people to develop commitment, a common goal around which people can rally, and a way for people to feel successful." As we have already noted, the vision has to be clear, compelling, challenging, and credible, but it must also be reflected in the expressions and actions of the leader who is articulating it. Nadler (1998, p. 276) points to visionary leaders such as Jamie Houghton at the U.S. technology company Corning who painted "an engrossing picture of a culture in which Corning would be one of the most competent, profitable, and respected corporations in the entire world." He also identifies Scott McNealy of Sun Microsystems (now part of Oracle) as envisioning "an information world where people would be free to choose from a range of vendors rather than held captive by a single, all-powerful mega-corporation." Ironically, some of those who are cited as visionary leaders do not see themselves as visionary or heroic and have challenged the significance of vision:

Robert Eaton, when he was CEO of Chrysler, downplayed vision in favor of measurable short-term results.

Bill Gates, one of the founders of Microsoft, once declared that "Being visionary is trivial." (Lipton, 1996, p. 86)

Nevertheless, those leaders are often praised for articulating clear, appealing, challenging images of the future of their organizations—the hallmarks of effective visions.

Gardner and Avolio (1998) argue that effective charismatic, visionary leaders create "identity images" that are valued and desired by others, incorporating trustworthiness, credibility, morality, innovativeness, esteem, and power. Drawing on a dramaturgical perspective, they argue that charismatic leaders enact (or perform) their visions through four processes:

1. *Framing*. The art of managing meaning, influencing others to accept the leader's interpretation of the vision, by stressing its importance, and aligning it with their values
2. *Scripting*. The process of coordinating and integrating more specific sets of ideas and actions including:
   - casting of the appropriate key roles
   - dialogue, using various rhetorical devices, such as metaphors and stories, to increase the appeal of the message
   - providing direction, using verbal and nonverbal behavior and emotional displays
3. *Staging*. The selection of symbols, artifacts, props, and settings to reinforce the vision
4. *Performing*. Enacting the vision by personally demonstrating the behaviors required to achieve the vision

It is important to note that, although having a vision is considered by many commentators to be a prerequisite for successful change leadership, others disagree. Vision may be a necessary component of inspirational leadership, but it may not be sufficient. Robert Goffee and Gareth Jones (2000) argue that, to complement energy and vision, other qualities are necessary including:

- revealing personal weaknesses to followers to gain their trust
- sensing how things are in the organization and the wider environment, picking up and interpreting subtle cues and signals
- showing "tough empathy," passionate, caring, but realistic, focusing on what others need rather than what they want
- daring to be different, signalling and maintaining their uniqueness, while maintaining social distance

It has also been argued that visionary leaders are needed at an everyday level throughout the organization, and not just at the top. Such individuals provide what Rogers (2007) calls "supervision," using interactions, conversations, and role modelling to demonstrate:

Perspective. Concerning the challenges facing the organization

Purpose. Both personal and organizational

Processes. Respond more effectively to customers

Possibilities. Challenge current constraints

Potential. Concerning personal contributions

Passion. Channel energies in meaningful ways

In this perspective, therefore, to maintain engagement and motivation, providing vision must be a day-to-day activity involving many leaders across the organization, and not an occasional process led by a single senior figure or a small top team.

Vision Is an Attribute of Heroic Organizations

Collins and Porras (2005) argue that visionary leaders are not necessary to create visionary companies, claiming that the role of charisma in setting vision has been exaggerated. A charismatic leader may even be an impediment to the creation of a visionary organization; sustained organizational effectiveness depends on embedded visions, values, and ideologies, rather than on pronouncements from one senior figure. The leader's role is to act as a catalyst, facilitating the development of, and commitment to, the vision. This is a process that can be achieved through a variety of leadership and management styles. It is more important to create an organization with a vision than to have a charismatic chief executive with a personal vision.

In this perspective, vision incorporates core ideology, which is unchanging, and defines what the organization stands for and why it exists. An envisioned future is what the organization aspires to and changes toward over time. Ideology comprises core values and core purpose. Core values are durable guiding principles: "the HP Way," Walt Disney Company's "imagination and wholesomeness," Procter & Gamble's "product excellence," and Nordstrom's "customer service." Collins and Porras (2005) note that most companies have only three to five shared core values. Core purpose on the other hand defines the reason for the organization's existence.

Core purpose should be durable (designed to last a century, perhaps) and differs from goals and business strategies, which change constantly over time. The purpose may not change, but it should inspire change, development, and progress. The envisioned future, in contrast, consists of "BHAGs"—Big, Hairy, Audacious Goals, or daunting challenges with specified timelines that can involve:

- *Common enemy logic*. Philip Morris in the 1950s wanted to "knock off RJR as the number one tobacco company in the world"; Nike in the 1960s aimed to "crush Adidas."
- *Role model logic*. Stanford University in the 1940s wanted to become "the Harvard of the West."
- *Internal transformation logic*. The goal for GE in the 1980s was to "become number one or number two in every market we serve, and revolutionize this company to have the strengths of a big company combined with the leanness and agility of a small company"; Rockwell in 1995 wanted to "transform this company from a defense contractor into the best diversified high-technology company in the world."

A further component of envisioned future, vivid descriptions, consists of vibrant, passionate, and engaging descriptions of what it will be like in the future when goals are achieved. Envisioning the future is a creative process, engaging staff across the organization.

The Complete Vision at Merck

Collins and Porras (2005) argue that complete visions have three components: a core ideology (values and purpose), an envisioned future (big, hairy, audacious goals), and vivid descriptions. They offer the following example from the pharmaceutical company Merck in the 1930s:

Core Ideology	Envisioned Future
Core values. Social responsibility, excellence, and science-based innovation	*BHAG.* To transform from a chemical manufacturer to a world drug company with research capacity rivaling major universities.
Purpose	**Vivid Description**
To preserve and improve human life	With the tools we have supplied, science will be advanced, knowledge increased, and human life win ever greater freedom from suffering and disease.

The work of Collins and Porras offers a sensitive treatment of the relationship between vision and change. Vision (which they also call "industry foresight") is broken down into component parts, some of which remain stable and some of which change over time. Many change models that refer to the need for vision to guide organizational change lack this degree of sophistication. Vision is often presented as something that guides change, handed down to the organization by the chief executive and the top-management team. However, for Collins and Porras, vision (as core ideology) serves as an enduring background component, not so much guiding change as reflecting how change will be achieved (by following core values, for example). It is the envisioned future of vision that offers concrete change direction, concerning what should be changed, and how.

EXERCISE 6.1

Interviewing Change Recipients

LO 6.1

Your task is to interview three employees; they can be in the same or a different organization. Ask them to think back to an organizational change that they experienced and to answer the following questions:

1. Were they presented with an organizational vision for this change? If so:
   What was the vision?
   What effect did this have on them?
   Were they involved in developing the vision?
   To what extent did the vision motivate them to engage in the change?
   How central was the vision to implementing the change?

2. If your interviewees were not given an organizational vision for this change, ask them:
   Would a vision have helped them to understand and become involved in the change?
   How important is vision to achieving organizational change?

When you have completed your interviews, consider the responses that you have documented. What general conclusions emerge regarding the relationship between vision and organizational change? What have you learned from this exercise?

EXERCISE 6.2

Analyze Your Own Organization's Mission and Vision

LO 6.2   LO 6.3

Consider your own current organization, or another with which you are familiar, which could be the institution where you are studying. Go to the website of the Mission Statement Academy: https://mission-statement.com. Note how they assess the mission and vision statements of leading organizations. Using their style as a template, and recalling the discussion of effective missions and visions in this chapter, assess your own chosen organization's approach to these issues.

- Does your organization's mission statement set out a meaningful and challenging purpose that will excite, attract, retain, and motivate staff?
- Does your organization's vision statement have the characteristics identified in table 6.4?
- Do your organization's mission and vision help to drive change, or not? Why?
- Are your organization's mission and vision just a "public relations" exercise, or are they used in practice? How can you tell?
- What changes (if any) would you make to your organization's mission and vision?

EXERCISE 6.3

The Role of Vision at Mentor Graphics

LO 6.5

As you read this case, consider the following questions:

1. How would you describe the way vision was used at Mentor Graphics?
2. Did it strengthen or weaken the company? How? Why?
3. Of the reasons discussed in this chapter concerning why visions fail, which are applicable to Mentor Graphics?
4. What is your assessment of the vision content and the process through which it was introduced in the Mentor Graphics context? What lessons emerge from your assessment?
5. Based on what happened at Mentor Graphics, what are the implications for the three debates discussed in this chapter: whether vision drives change or emerges during change; whether vision helps or hinders change; and whether vision is an attribute of heroic leaders or heroic organizations?
6. Of the six change images outlined in table 6.1, which images of vision can be applied to this case study? What lessons emerge from this?

Founded in 1981, Mentor Graphics (now Mentor, a Siemens Business) is a U.S. electronic design automation business. It was acquired for $4.5 billion by the German multinational Siemens in 2017 and had revenues of $3 billion in 2018. According to company president Gerard Langeler, the role of vision was important from the beginning. The company started with an unarticulated vision to "Build Something That People Will Buy." On this basis, they spent several months interviewing potential customers and designing a computer-aided engineering workstation product. At the same time, a competitor, Daisy Systems, was engaged in the same task and, in the early years, outcompeted Mentor Graphics. Eventually, "Beat Daisy" became the new vision, driven by the need to survive as a business.

By 1985 Mentor's revenues were higher than Daisy's; their vision had been realized. The company continued to grow despite the recession, but suffered from typical growth problems, including decline in product quality, and problems of internal company coordination. Stock value also suffered, and a number of staff approached Langeler seeking a new vision for the company.

The new vision was developed based on "Six Boxes," which represented the six different businesses in which the company sought market leadership. The "Six Boxes" became a company mantra, but in the late 1980s, one of the businesses—computer-aided publishing—was not paying dividends. However, the fact that it constituted one of the "Six Boxes" meant that they could not shut it down and be left with a "Five Boxes" vision. In this case, the existence of the vision disrupted the ability to make sound financial judgements. It also stopped them from moving more quickly to using Sun platforms, something they thought was too conventional for them.

A new vision was developed—the "10X Imperative"—that mirrored the push other companies were making toward quality through six-sigma and other similar quality programs. However, customers did not really understand the new vision. It was too abstract and elusive.

In 1989, yet another vision emerged: "Changing the Way the World Designs Together." In retrospect, Langeler depicts this vision as "the final extension of vision creep that began with Six Boxes." It was very grand and had little to do with the actual businesses in which Mentor Graphics operated, including the development of its new 8.0 generation of software.

The realization, by the early 1990s, that the company's vision detracted from what the company was actually trying to achieve led to the dumping of the vision and its replacement with one that echoed the early beginning of the company: "Our current short-, medium-, and long-term vision is to build things people will buy." This was seen as a more pragmatic vision for a company that had lost its way, caught up in a cycle of visions that were increasingly irrelevant to the core business and that inhibited their ability to make sound business decisions.

Additional Reading

Hollensbe, E., Wookey, C., Hickey, L., and George, G. 2014. Organizations with purpose. *Academy of Management Journal* 57(5):1227–34. Discusses vision and purpose in terms of the "greater good" and the organization's contribution to society. The authors argue that an organization's sense of purpose must recognize the interdependence of business and society.

Ibarra, H. 2015. *Act like a leader, think like a leader*. Boston: Harvard Business Review Press. Offers advice on thinking strategically and avoiding the distractions of short-term priorities. Citing George W. Bush and his dismissive comment about "the vision thing," Herminia Ibarra argues that "the ability to envision possibilities for the future and to share that vision with others distinguishes leaders from nonleaders" (p. 40).

Malnight, T. W., Buche, I., and Dhanaraj, C. 2019. Put purpose at the core of your strategy. *Harvard Business Review* 97(5):70–79. Explains how a clear statement of the organization's mission or purpose contributes to performance and competitive advantage.

Venus, M., Stam, D., and van Knippenberg, D. 2019. Visions of change as visions of continuity. *Academy of Management Journal* 62(3):667–90. As discussed in this chapter, offers the counterintuitive argument that good vision statements should emphasize continuity as well as change. Change means uncertainty, which can be demotivating. Continuity and stability are reassuring and can help to overcome potential resistance to change.

Roundup

Reflections for the Practicing Change Manager

- How do you distinguish mission (or purpose) from vision? Is this an important distinction? In your organization, how aligned are your purpose and vision? Are there competing missions and visions in your organization? How are these resolved?

- What criteria do you use to decide whether mission and vision statements are likely to be useful in your organization? What other criteria might you wish to take into account?

- Do your organization's mission and vision statements meet those criteria? If not, how would you recommend changing them?

- Looking at the language of your mission statement, is it abstract and vague, or does it use interesting imagery? How could you improve your organization's mission statement?

- Does your vision promise a break with the past and a brighter future? Could employees feel threatened by this? Would it be helpful to emphasize continuity—what isn't changing?

- What process have you used, or seen in use, to craft an effective vision? Do you have a personal preference toward an intuitive or an analytical approach to vision development? Why?

- Is there an "inner voice" in your organization? What are the "bread-and-butter" issues? Are there "undiscussable" issues in your organization?

- What is your judgment: when do visions fail, and when does their effectiveness fade? Can visions be revitalized? How?

- What is your position: do mission and vision drive change? Do mission and vision help change? In particular, does vision need visionary leaders?

Here is a short summary of the key points that we would like you to take from this chapter, in relation to each of the learning outcomes:

LO 6.1   *   *Explain the arguments for and against the concepts of purpose (or mission) and vision and how approaches to these issues depend on the image of managing organizational change.* Mission is a statement of purpose: Why are we here? Vision is a future aspiration: What do we want to achieve? Some commentators argue that statements of mission and vision are indispensable, giving purpose, direction, motivation, inspiration, and change. There is evidence that a clear sense of organizational purpose can contribute to organizational performance and sustained competitive advantage. Other commentators argue that these concepts are too abstract and vague and that they have become meaningless, attracting cynicism when most organizations have similarly bland statements about excellence, social responsibility, empowered employees, and delighted customers.

The concepts of mission and vision vary with the image of change management that is in use. For example, the director image assumes that responsibility for framing mission and vision statements lies with senior leaders. The caretaker assumes that the organization's mission and vision are shaped primarily by external forces. The coach facilitates the consultation and co-creation process through which mission and vision are developed by staff from across the organization. The nurturer sees missions and visions emerging from the clash of unpredictable forces and as temporary constructs.

LO 6.2   *   *Explain the value of a clear organizational purpose or mission statement.*
An organization's purpose is its reason for being in business. Having a clear purpose has become important as more employees—Millennials in particular—are looking for meaningful work with a purpose that contributes to society. Purpose can have strategic benefits, helping the organization to identify and exploit new market opportunities that are consistent with that purpose. Evidence suggests that purpose-driven organizations gain higher market share, have higher productivity and growth, have better job satisfaction and employee retention, and are more innovative. For greater impact and memorability, mission statements should use concrete imagery and not abstractions.

LO 6.3   *   *Identify the characteristics of effective visions.*
Evidence and experience suggest that, to be effective, visions should be clear, appealing, vivid, ambitious, and attainable, providing a sense of direction and guiding decision making, but also flexible enough to accommodate initiative and change. Effective visions also describe a desirable—perhaps ideal—future for the organization. Further emotional properties of the effective vision, although difficult to define, are that it "feels good" and that it emphasizes continuity, as a "complete break with the past" can be seen as threatening and demotivating. Research demonstrates that visions expressed in image-based terms are more motivating and memorable than those that use vague abstractions. "Blurry vision bias" can be overcome using the technique of temporal projection, which involves imagining how the organization will look, feel, and act in the future.

LO 6.4   *   *Apply different methods and processes for developing visions.*
There are many approaches to developing vision, ranging on the familiar continuum from "tell" (the chief executive determines the vision) to "co-create" (everyone participates in the development). There is no "one best way," and choice is influenced by the change management image in use. Leader-dominated methods can be rapid, and may be inspirational, but are not consistent with the concepts of employee empowerment and engagement. Most commentators suggest that co-creation methods, where the role of senior leaders is to "orchestrate" the vision-crafting process, are more likely to produce better visions and more successful change. Staff who are not directly responsible for creating an organization's vision can nevertheless become involved in the process, by helping to shape senior leaders' ideas, by translating the corporate vision for the members of a given team or department, and by developing a frontline team vision that can be transmitted up the organization.

Other approaches to crafting vision have been described as intuitive, analytical, and benchmarking. Intuitive approaches rely on imagination and creative imagery: What are our personal and organizational priorities, and what do we need to do to work toward our desired future? An analytical approach links vision to purpose and goals, using questions such as: Who do we serve? What do we do? Where do we place most of our efforts? How do we operationalize those efforts? A benchmarking approach is more externally focused and develops vision in relation to key competitors: What do our competitors do well? How can we do better than them? How should we measure our achievement? What will it be like when those standards have been met?

LO 6.5   * *Explain why some visions fail.*

Visions can fail for many reasons: too specific, too vague, too complex, fails to address known problems, detached from the business, unrealistic, and does not offer a clear view of the future. Lack of adaptation to changing circumstances can make a vision obsolete, contributing to decisions that are not consistent with new environmental conditions and constraints. Visions also fail because of "vision collisions"—the presence of too many competing visions for an organization.

LO 6.6   * *Explain the contribution of purpose and vision to organizational change.*

We explored three key debates. First, does vision drive change, or does vision emerge from the organizational change process? Second, does vision contribute to or hinder the organizational change process? Third, are visions attributes of heroic leaders or heroic organizations? With compelling arguments on both sides of these debates, the answers are not clear.

The traditional view sees the vision of the heroic, charismatic leader driving and contributing positively to the organizational change process. There is evidence and argument to challenge that perspective. The importance of charisma and vision may have been exaggerated. Charismatic senior figures perhaps contribute less to sustained organizational effectiveness than embedded visions, core values, and enduring ideologies. Visions are emergent because it is difficult to articulate a clear image of the future at the start of a disruptive transformational change process. Visions can impede change by making strong emotional appeals to the future instead of focusing on current operational problems and where organizational capabilities are inadequate to achieving the vision.

The change manager must be aware of these debates and tensions and take these considerations into account before embarking on a vision development process at a particular time in a specific context. The weight of commentary, from academic research and management consultants, appears to endorse the value of articulating clear and compelling visions. However, this perspective should not be taken for granted, and a more cautious, skeptical, critical approach is perhaps advisable. The role and need for vision should be assessed in relation to each specific organizational change situation. What has been effective for one organization, given its history, current challenges, and future aspirations, may not be wholly appropriate for another organization with a different background, a different set of problems, and a different desired future.

References   Ambler, G. 2013. 10 characteristics of an effective vision, online blog. http://www. georgeambler.com/10-characteristics-of-an-effective-vision (accessed October 14, 2014).

Ashkenas, R., and Manville, B. 2019. You don't have to be CEO to be a visionary leader. *Harvard Business Review*, digital article (April):1–6.

Ates, N. Y., Tarakci, M., Porck, J. P., van Knippenberg, D., and Groenen, P. 2019. Why visionary leadership fails. *Harvard Business Review*, digital article (February):2–5.

Auster, E. R., Wylie, K. K., and Valente, M. S. 2005. *Strategic organizational change: Building change capabilities in your organization*. New York: Palgrave Macmillan.

Belgard, W. P., and Rayner, S. R. 2004. *Shaping the future: A dynamic process for creating and achieving your company's strategic vision*. New York: Amacom.

Blount, S., and Leinwand, P. 2019. Why are we here? *Harvard Business Review* 97(6):132–39.

Boal, K. B., and Hooijberg, R. 2001. Strategic leadership research: Moving on. *Leadership Quarterly* 11(4):515–49.

Bosché, G. 2019. The 7 best and 5 worst mission statements of America's top brands. *LinkedIn*, January 2. https://www.linkedin.com/pulse/7-best-5-worst-mission-statements-americas-top-brands-bosché.

Carton, A. M., and Lucas, B. J. 2018. How can leaders overcome the blurry vision bias? Identifying an antidote to the paradox of vision communication. *Academy of Management Journal* 61(6):2106–29.

Collins, J. C., and Porras, J. I. 1991. Organizational vision and visionary organizations. *California Management Review* 34(1):30–52.

Collins, J. C., and Porras, J. I. 1996. Building your company's vision. *Harvard Business Review* 74(5):65–77.

Collins, J. C., and Porras, J. I. 2005. *Built to last: Successful habits of visionary companies*. 2nd ed. New York: HarperCollins.

Davidson, H. 2004. *The committed enterprise: How to make vision, values and branding work*. 2nd ed. London: Routledge.

Deetz, S. A., Tracy, S. J., and Simpson, J. L. 2000. *Leading organizations through transitions: Communication and cultural change*. Thousand Oaks, CA: Sage Publications.

Financial Reporting Council 2020. *Annual Review of the UK Corporate Governance Code*. London.

Ford, J. D., and Pasmore, W. A. 2006. Vision: Friend or foe during change? *Journal of Applied Behavioral Science* 42(2):172–76.

Galbraith, M. 2018. Don't just tell employees organizational changes are coming—explain why. *Harvard Business Review*, digital article (October):1–5.

Gardner, W. L., and Avolio, B. J. 1998. The charismatic relationship: A dramaturgical perspective. *Academy of Management Review* 23(1):32–58.

Gerstner, L. V. 2003. Who says elephants can't dance? Inside IBMs historic turnover. New York: Harper Business.

Goffee, R., and Jones, G. 2000. Why should anyone be led by you? *Harvard Business Review* 78(5):63–70.

Gupta, R., and Wendler, J. 2005. Leading change: An interview with the CEO of P&G. *McKinsey Quarterly* (July):1–6.

Haines, S. G., Aller-Stead, G., and McKinlay, J. 2005. *Enterprise-wide change: Superior results through systems thinking*. San Francisco: Pfeiffer.

Hamel, G., and Prahalad, C. K. 1989. Strategic intent. *Harvard Business Review* 67(3):2–14.

Harris, L. C., and Ogbonna, E. 1999. The strategic legacy of company founders. *Long Range Planning* 32(3):333–43.

Holpp, L., and Kelly, M. 1988. Realizing the possibilities. *Training and Development Journal* 42(9):48–55.

Jick, T. D. 2001. Vision is 10%, implementation the rest. *Business Strategy Review* 12(4):36–38.

Kanter, R. M., Stein, B. A., and Jick, T. D. 1992. *The challenge of organizational change: How companies experience it and leaders guide it*. New York: Free Press.

Kirkpatrick, S. A. 2017. Toward a grounded theory: A qualitative study of vision statement development. *Journal of Management Policy and Practice* 18(1):87–101.

Kolowich, L. 2019. 17 truly inspiring company vision and mission statement examples. *HubSpot*, https://blog.hubspot.com/marketing/inspiring-company-mission-statements (accessed December 19, 2019).

Kotter, J. P. 2012. *Leading change*. 2nd ed. Boston, MA: Harvard University Press.

Landau, D., Drori, I., and Porras, J. 2006. Vision: Friend and foe during change: A rejoinder to reviewers' comments. *Journal of Applied Behavioral Science* 42(2):177–81.

Langeler, G. H. 1992. The vision trap. *Harvard Business Review* 70(2):5–12.

Lashinsky, A. 2019. Rewriting a toy story. *Fortune* 180(6):98–103.

Lipton, M. 1996. Demystifying the development of an organizational vision. *Sloan Management Review* 37(4):83–92.

Lissack, M., and Roos, J. 2001. Be coherent, not visionary. *Long Range Planning* 54(1):53–70.

Mainwairing, S. 2018. Purpose at work: How Chobani builds a purposeful culture around social impact. *Forbes* (August 27):1–5. https://www.forbes.com/sites/simonmainwaring/2018/08/27/how-chobani-builds-a-purposeful-culture-around-social-impact.

Malnight, T. W., Buche, I., and Dhanaraj, C. 2019. Put purpose at the core of your strategy. *Harvard Business Review* 97(5):70–79.

Metais, E. 2000. SEB group: Building a subversive strategy. *Business Strategy Review* 11(4):39–47.

Mitchell, C. 2002. Selling the brand inside. *Harvard Business Review* 80(1):99–105.

Murphy, C., and Clark, J. R. 2016. Picture this: How the language of leaders drives performance. *Organizational Dynamics* 45(2):139–46.

Nadler, D. A. 1998. *Champions of change: How CEOs and their companies are mastering the skills of radical change.* San Francisco: Jossey-Bass.

Nadler, D. A., and Shaw, R. B. 1995. Beyond the heroic leader. In *Discontinuous change: Leading organizational transformation,* ed. D. A. Nadler, R. B. Shaw, and A. E. Walton (217–31). San Francisco: Jossey-Bass.

O'Brien, D., Main, A., Kounkel, S., and Stephan, A. R. 2019. Purpose is everything. In *2020 Global Marketing Trends,* ed. D. O'Brien, A. Main, S. Kounkel, and A. R. Stephan (7–13). London: Deloitte Development LLC.

Pendlebury, J., Grouard, B., and Meston, F. 1998. *The ten keys to successful change management.* London: John Wiley & Sons Ltd.

Quinn, R. E. 1996. *Deep change: Discovering the leader within.* San Francisco: Jossey-Bass.

Quinn, R. E., and Thakor, A. V. 2018. Creating a purpose-driven organization. *Harvard Business Review* 96(4):78–85.

Raynor, M. E. 1998. That vision thing: Do we need it? *Long Range Planning* 31(3):368–76.

Robbins, H., and Finley, M. 1997. *Why change doesn't work: Why initiatives go wrong and how to try again—and succeed.* London: Orion.

Rogers, C. 2007. *Informal coalitions: Mastering the hidden dynamics of organizational change.* New York: Palgrave Macmillan.

Schoemaker, P. J. H. 1992. How to link strategic vision to core capabilities. *Sloan Management Review* 34(1):67–81.

Shaw, R. B. 1995. The essence of discontinuous change: Leadership, identity and architecture. In *Discontinuous change: Leading organizational transformation,* ed. D. A. Nadler, R. B. Shaw, A. E. Walton, and Associates (66–81). San Francisco: Jossey-Bass.

Symons, J. 2006. The vision thing. *E.learning Age* (April):18–19.

Venus, M., Stam, D., and van Knippenberg, D. 2019. Visions of change as visions of continuity. *Academy of Management Journal* 62(3):667–90.

Source of opening quote from Taylor Swift, https://www.goodreads.com/quotes/tag/change

Chapter opening silhouette credit: FunKey Factory/Shutterstock

Chapter 7

Change Communication Strategies

Learning Objectives

By the end of this chapter you should be able to:

LO 7.1 Identify key elements in the change communication process.

LO 7.2 Understand how gender, power, and emotion affect change communication processes.

LO 7.3 Understand the power of language in influencing responses to change.

LO 7.4 Explain and assess appropriate strategies for communicating change.

LO 7.5 Understand how successful communication processes vary with the type and stage of organizational change.

LO 7.6 Assess the utility of a range of different change communication channels, including applications of social media.

"They always say time changes things, but you actually have to change them yourself."

Andy Warhol, artist

LO 7.1 The Change Communication Process

Change-related communication can be defined as "Regular two-way communication specifically about the change initiative, its implementation, related successes, challenges and their resolution" (Whelan-Berry and Somerville, 2010, p. 181). The ways in which changes are presented and discussed are critical to success. The approaches to change management explored in chapters 9 and 10 all give communication a key role in the process. Communication is one of the most frequently identified change drivers, explaining the need for change and how it will be achieved. Poor communication is a leading explanation for change failure. The evidence suggests that change communication should be two-way—telling and listening—or problems may not be identified and addressed. Communication is important throughout the change process—not just at the beginning—and should be resourced accordingly by addressing resistance, encouraging adoption and support, and sustaining momentum.

Lars Christensen and Joep Cornelissen (2011) offer a counterintuitive view of the significance of change communication. They first note that communication has attracted increasing attention due to a number of factors: the nature and consequences of stakeholder communications; the emergence of ideas such as corporate social responsibility, sustainability, and corporate citizenship; and the growing numbers of corporate communication professionals, procedures, and systems. Communication, therefore, is "an important force of organizing" and "the building block of organizations" (p. 398) because the act of communicating constructs or defines the change in the understanding of those who are going to be involved. Change communication is part of the process of collective sense-making.

Change communication, they note, aims to influence the opinions of many different audiences, inside and outside the organization. This suggests that clarity and consistency are important. However, Christensen and Cornelissen (2011, pp. 402–403) argue that organizations have to work with many voices, with different views and ideas (technical term: "polyphony"). In other words, it may often be desirable for change communications to be ambiguous and inconsistent, for the following reason:

> [V]ague and equivocal language allows organizations to talk about themselves in ways that integrate a variety of members and stakeholders without alienating anyone. Too much clarity and consistency in the formulation of "shared values" may actually prevent managers from establishing accord with some corporate audiences. Although writings in corporate communication and branding call for organizations to eliminate ambiguity, ambiguity is essential in promoting "unified diversity," the ability for differences to coexist within the unity of the organization. Ambiguity and polyphony may even be a conscious management strategy designed to foster identification and reduce tension by allowing different audiences to apply different interpretations to what is seen as one corporate message.

The process of communicating change—what is going to happen and why—can therefore be more complex than first appears. In this chapter, we explore the communication process and then discuss different communication strategies, before considering the evolving role of social media in organizational change management. First, we will consider how images of change management influence communication strategies and the implications for change managers.

One of the challenges for communicators concerns expectations with respect to what can be achieved. A "director" image has dominated our understanding, linking corporate communication with control and manageability. However, communication in the current turbulent organizational environment is perhaps better understood in terms of chaos and complexity—a "nurturer" image. Acceptance of the nurturer image may reduce the frustration of not being able to control events in the way that a director image assumes. Change managers may be able to shape, but not always control, the communication of change. More generally, each of the six images of change outlined in chapter 2 is associated with a different strategy for communicating change; see table 7.1.

We will first outline a classic model of the communication process, indicating how language, power, gender, and emotions are central to an understanding of how this works. We will then consider how this model applies to change communication and explore the dilemmas facing the manager designing a change communication strategy. Is it possible

TABLE 7.1

Change Images and Communication Purpose

Image	Purpose of Communication
Director	Ensure that people understand what is going to happen and what is required of them. Answer the why, what, who, how, and when questions. Present the "value proposition" of the change. Modify leadership style and information to "fit" the type of change and organizational levels affected. Avoid "spray and pray" methods, which lead to message overload. Do not distort the message.
Navigator	Outline the nature of the change, paying attention to the range of interests affected, power relationships, and actions that could disrupt the change. Problems identified can thus be addressed, and the change "replotted" if necessary, to generate the best outcomes in the situation. To win staff over, "tell and sell" communication methods are appropriate.
Caretaker	Let people know the "why" of the changes, their inevitability, and how best to cope and survive. This involves the use of reactive communication methods, recognizing employee concerns and responding accordingly ("identify and reply").
Coach	Ensure that people share similar values and understand what actions are appropriate to those values. Model consistency in actions and words. The director "gets the word out"; the coach "gets buy-in" to change by drawing on values and positive emotions. Team-based communications are effective (not top-down led by the chief executive). Key messages are emphasized to check understanding and encourage two-way dialogue ("underscore and explore").
Interpreter	Give employees a sense of "what is going on" through storytelling and metaphors. Recognize the multiple sense-making that occurs in different groups with regard to change. Present a persuasive account of the change to ensure that as many people as possible will have a common understanding. Recognize that not everyone will accept the change story. Aim to provide the dominant account using "rich" personal and interactive communications (discussed in the section "Media Richness" later in this chapter).
Nurturer	Reinforce the view that change processes cannot always be predicted and that creative and innovative outcomes can be achieved, even though few in the organization could have anticipated these.

to communicate too much? How can communication strategy be tailored to the type of change and to the phases of the change process? Should the aim be to "get the word out" or to "get buy-in" or both? Where should responsibility for communicating change lie? The different images in table 7.1 are likely to offer different answers to these questions. Finally, as explained earlier, we will assess the use of different media for communicating change, including the evolving use of different forms of social media technologies.

Communication Is Not a "Soft" Function

The American consulting company Towers Watson (2013) argues that communication is key to organizational performance. From a global survey of 650 organizations, it found that those with effective communication practices were three times more likely to show superior financial performance, compared with those that did not use those practices. The best practices were:

1. Helping employees to understand the business
2. Educating employees about organization culture and values
3. Providing information on financial objectives and organizational performance
4. Integrating new employees
5. Communicating how employee actions affect customers
6. Providing information about the value of individuals' total compensation package
7. Asking for rapid feedback from employees about their opinions of the company

Borrowing from consumer marketing, Towers Watson also argues that effective organizations categorize employees into groups based on the value of their skills and on personal characteristics. This approach to employee "segmentation" means that communication strategy can be tailored to focus on behaviors that are critical to performance. The most effective companies pay close attention to employees when they are planning change, evaluating culture, and assessing employee readiness and the

impact that change will have. Middle and frontline managers need to be good at: articulating what employees need to do differently to be successful, communicating what change means to individual employees, and creating a sense of ownership about change initiatives.

Three factors in particular put a premium on "communication effectiveness":

- *Workforce.* Increasingly diverse workforce, with rising expectations of the employment deal
- *The stakes.* The competitive advantage to be gained from "discretionary effort"—the willingness of employees to "go the extra mile" to improve company performance
- *Shorter timelines.* The need to communicate rapidly, driven by developments in technology and globalization, tighter resources, and increased concerns for security

Towers Watson concludes:

Today, top-performing organizations are building community—fostering the sense that employees at all levels are in it together. These organizations create the opportunity for social interaction using the latest new media technologies, display the appetite and courage to hear from employees, and establish ongoing forums conducive to collaboration rather than top-down communication. Those that do this well typically see better financial performance. (Towers Watson, 2013, p. 9)

Modelling the Communication Process

Interpersonal communication typically involves much more than the simple transmission of information. Pay close attention to the next person who asks you for information about something. You will often be able to tell how they are feeling, about why they want to know, if they are in a hurry, perhaps, or if they are anxious or nervous. In other words, their question has a purpose or a meaning. Although it is not always stated directly, we can often infer that meaning from the context and from their behavior. The same considerations apply to your response. Your reply suggests, at least, a willingness to be helpful, may imply friendship, and may also indicate that you share the same concern as the person asking the question ("I'm worried about that, too"). However, your reply can also indicate frustration and annoyance ("Why are you asking me?"). Communication thus involves the transmission of both information and meaning.

Figure 7.1 shows the components of the process of interpersonal communication. This is based on the seminal work of Shannon and Weaver (1949), who worked on signal processing in electronic systems, rather than with organizational communication. However, their model has general applicability.

FIGURE 7.1
Exchanging Meaning: A Model of the Communication Process

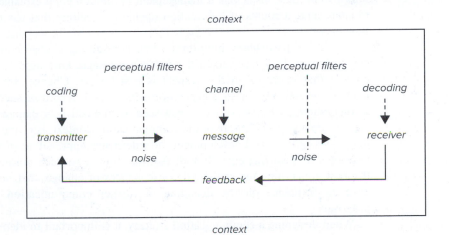

At the heart of this model, we have a *transmitter* sending a *message* through an appropriate *channel* to a *receiver*. We will consider the range of change communication channels later. It is helpful to think of the way in which the transmitter phrases and expresses the message as a *coding* process. The success of communication depends on the accuracy of the receiver's *decoding*; did they understand the language used and also the tone and implications of the message? *Feedback* is therefore critical to check understanding. Communication often fails where transmitters and receivers have different frames of reference and do not share experience and understanding, even if they share a common language. We make judgments—which may or may not be accurate—about the honesty, integrity, trustworthiness, and credibility of others, and decode their messages and act on them accordingly. When communicating details of a major change initiative, therefore, it cannot be assumed that all the recipients of the message will have the same understanding as each other, and of the transmitter.

Perceptual filters also play a role here, particularly affecting our decoding. This can involve, for example, a readiness or predisposition to hear, or not to hear, particular kinds of information. Preoccupations that are diverting our attention can also filter information. Past experience affects the way in which we see things today and can influence what we transmit and how, and what we receive. In an organizational setting, people may have time to reflect, or they may be under time pressure, or "communication overload," which again means that some content may be filtered out.

The physical, social, and cultural *context* in which change communication takes place is also significant. In organizations where staff members are widely dispersed across a number of locations, the ability to share and compare views is more difficult than when everyone is in the one place. The logistics of communicating with a large number of dispersed staff can be complex and costly. The casual remark by a colleague across a café table ("we could all be redundant by the end of the year") could be dismissed with a laugh. The same remark made by a manager in a formal planning meeting could be a source of alarm. If an organization's culture emphasizes openness and transparency, staff may become suspicious if communication is less informative than expected. However, staff may also become suspicious if management (without a good explanation) suddenly starts to share large amounts of information openly in a culture that has in the past been less transparent.

Context is particularly important when considering change communication, as this can influence how receivers will decode a message. One aspect of an organization's context that is critical in this respect is past history. Change communication is more likely to be welcome in an organization with a track record of successful changes than in one where past changes have been seen as ineffective or damaging. Current circumstances are also a key feature of the communication context. Is change a positive response to business growth and development, or a defensive approach to problems that will lead to budget and staffing cuts? If staff feel that they have been misled by management in the past concerning the goals and consequences of change, that perception is likely to have an influence on the decoding of further communication concerning change proposals.

When designing a communication strategy, it is important to identify issues that could affect the coding and decoding and to design the message content and channels accordingly. Baczor (2019) suggests than an effective internal communication strategy should be cohesive and strategic and should support a culture of trust and openness. In particular, successful communication:

- emphasizes shared purpose
- is aligned with the organization's strategy
- is supported fully by top management
- is based on genuine dialogue
- uses a range of digital channels and tools
- is assessed regularly for effectiveness

Although most organizations recognize the importance of communication, 40 percent of employees say that they get little or no information about their organization's strategy (Baczor, 2019). This may be because, faced with a complex and unpredictable external environment, managers struggle to communicate clearly about the organization's direction. Managers may not have the skills, confidence, or time to communicate effectively. Traditional clumsy "static" intranets are not designed for employees who are accustomed to on-demand, personalized content in their private lives.

Anything that interferes with a communication signal is called *noise* by electronics experts, and this applies to interpersonal and organizational communication, too. This does not just refer to the sound of equipment or other people talking. Noise includes coding and decoding problems and errors, perceptual filters, and any other distractions that damage the integrity of the communication channel, including issues arising from the context. Relationships can introduce noise, affecting the style and content of conversation (formal or informal) and what we are prepared to share. Status differences can introduce noise; we do not reveal to the boss what we discuss with colleagues. Motives, emotions, and health can also constitute noise; coding and decoding are affected by anxiety, pressure, stress, and also by levels of enthusiasm and excitement. This last point is particularly significant, as change communication itself can, of course, generate anxiety and stress or stimulate excitement.

LO 7.2 Gender, Power, and Emotion

The basic communication model that we have discussed can help to explain why communication sometimes breaks down. However, we also need to understand the impact of gender, power, and emotion on communication in general and on change communication in particular.

Gender

Gender differences also affect the communication process. Here are two examples:

Confidence and boasting. Women tend to emphasize their doubts and uncertainty, but men tend to express greater confidence and play down their doubts.

Asking questions. Women are more likely to ask questions than men; the downside is that male managers may interpret women as knowing less than their male peers.

An assessment by a male manager of how well a woman is coping with change, compared with male colleagues, may thus conclude: "She seems very uncertain since she is always asking questions." However, this assessment may have more to do with gender differences related to a willingness to question (about the change) than to real differences in attitude toward the change itself.

Deborah Tannen (1995, p. 141) also observes that even the apparently simple choice of which pronoun to use can influence who gets the credit:

In my research in the workplace, I heard men say "I" in situations where I heard women say "We." For example, one publishing company executive said, "I'm hiring a new manager. I'm going to put him in charge of my marketing division," as if he owned the corporation. In stark contrast, I recorded women saying "we" when referring to work that they alone had done. One woman explained that it would sound too self-promoting to claim credit in an obvious way by saying, "I did this." Yet she expected—sometimes vainly—that others would know it was her work and would give her the credit she did not claim for herself.

Reinforcing Tannen's findings, Heath et al. (2014) studied successful and ambitious women who said that they were not being taken seriously in critical high-level meetings. They were ignored and found it hard to break into the conversation, so their ideas were overlooked. Some men are aware of this problem. After a meeting, one male manager said to a female colleague, "Stop acting like a facilitator. Start saying what you stand for." Their research found that, although men and women agreed on the problems, they disagreed on the causes. For example, men said that they were concerned that women would respond negatively to criticism. Women, on the other hand, complained that they did not get feedback, even when they asked for it. Men said that women should be more concise when making a point. Women said that they did not want to repackage old ideas or to state the obvious. Men observed that women were more emotional than men, but women said, "It's not emotion—it's passion."

Heath et al. (2014, pp. 120–21) suggest three steps to help women become more comfortable and effective in what are still male-dominated settings.

- *Groundwork*. Ideas are tested, and decisions are taken in informal meetings that happen before the main meeting. That is why men often arrive for meetings early and leave late, to sound people out and build alliances. Women also need to "master the pre-meeting."
- *Preparation*. Women prefer formal presentations, which men avoid. However, key points, relevant comments, and interesting questions can be written down in advance, and "off-the-cuff" remarks can be rehearsed. Women should "*prepare* to speak spontaneously."
- *Emotion control*. Passion can be persuasive, but when women felt passionate about an idea, men saw "too much emotion." Women must appear to be in command, speak with an even tone, accept that confrontation is not personal, and avoid signaling frustration.

The differences between women and men are not always as clear as this brief discussion suggests. Research findings are often expressed in terms of averages, tendencies, and predispositions. Many women do not fit the Tannen profile. And Heath et al. (2014, p. 119) suggest that "men with more reserved personalities" will find their advice useful, as will members of racial and ethnic minorities.

Other gender differences relate to how feedback is given and received, how compliments are exchanged, and whether the communication is direct or indirect. Kate Ludeman and Eddie Erlandson (2004) argue that many senior managers are "alpha" males: fast thinkers who have opinions on every topic, analytical, data-driven, impatient, and think that they are smarter than most other people. As a result, their communication style can intimidate those around them. Alpha males are not good listeners, they miss subtleties, and they put others under extreme pressure to perform. The alpha male communication style can be softened with coaching (see Exercise 7.1), but this is not an easy transformation. When a male manager changes to a communication style that is not direct, competitive, confrontational, and authoritative, they can be seen as "going soft," becoming "touchy-feely," and "losing their grip" (Linstead et al., 2005, p. 543). The change manager may therefore need to find a balance between maintaining credibility with colleagues, while adopting a communication style that is appropriate to the change context and to those who are involved.

Power

The use of language can also reflect underlying power and gender relationships—factors that can also interfere with the change communication process (as with communications in general). For example, the manner in which change managers seek staff comments on proposals can reinforce power differentials. Telling staff to provide input may result in responses different from those obtained when the request conveys respect for their opinions. Power differences are normally a barrier to communication. Those who are more powerful may not wish to disclose information that could make them appear to be less powerful or that could weaken their power base. Those who are less powerful may not wish to disclose information that could potentially be used against them.

The term *power tells* describes the various signs and clues that indicate how powerful someone is—or how powerful they want to be. The power tells of dominant individuals include:

- sitting and standing with legs far apart (men)
- appropriating the territory around them by placing their hands on their hips
- using open postures
- using invasive hand gestures
- smiling less, because a smile is an appeasement gesture
- establishing visual dominance by looking away from the other person while speaking, implying that they do not need to be attentive
- speaking first, and dominating the conversation thereafter
- using a lower vocal register, and speaking more slowly
- more likely to interrupt others, more likely to resist interruption by others

The power tells of submissive individuals include:

- modifying speech style to sound more like the person they are talking to
- more frequent hesitations, using lots of "ums" and "ers"
- adopting closed postures
- clasping hands, touching face and hair (self-comfort gestures)
- "leakage tells," which reveal stress and anxiety: blushing, coughing, dry mouth, heavy breathing, heavy swallowing, increased heart rate, lip biting, rapid blinking, and sweating

We can thus "read" the power signals of others. More importantly, however, change managers may need to control their own "tells," to appear less dominant and less powerful, particularly when communicating change in a manner that will encourage staff feedback, engagement, and support.

Emotion

Communication models have been criticized for ignoring the role of emotions in organizational change, focusing instead on the rational and cognitive dimensions of communication. Nevertheless, change managers need to be aware of, to understand, and where appropriate to respond to emotional responses to change. Emotions can interfere with the communication process, but emotions can also be a positive resource, contributing to staff willingness, commitment, and support for change.

Shaul Fox and Yair Amichai-Hamburger (2001) stress the importance of consistency between understanding of change and emotional perceptions. Emotional appeals communicate vision and urgency and can aid the formation of powerful change coalitions. Table 7.2 summarizes the steps that can help to establish the "positive emotions" that generate "excitement and anticipation" around a change program.

TABLE 7.2
How to Get Emotional Commitment to Change

Address These Issues	Use These Tactics
The Core Message	
Emotional arguments	Positive words signal future success; negative terms indicate what will happen if change fails.
Metaphors	The use of familiar metaphors can help staff to picture the future and make it appear less strange or unusual.
Packaging the Message	
Emotional mode	Capture attention with music, color, slogans, pictures—but avoid excessive use of any one mode.
Humor	Humor can reduce the gap, and tension, between manager and staff.
Display emotion	Use feelings, tone of voice, body language, and facial expressions to generate warmth and confidence.
Change leader characteristics	Messages are perceived as more credible and attractive when they are consistent with leader behavior.
Change Manager Behavior	
Fairness and justice	Decisions should be seen to be fair and follow legitimate, recognized procedures, with opportunities to raise issues.
Setting	
Group dynamics	Use groups and teams to strengthen commitment to change.
Ceremonies	Stimulate emotions and reinforce the benefits of change with celebrations that also signal departure from the past.
Atmosphere	Speak in warm, informal terms, to produce positive feelings toward the change (not formal and cold).

Based on Fox and Amichai-Hamburger (2001).

Michele Williams (2007) suggests that the anticipation that change will be personally threatening or harmful can generate negative emotions and a loss of trust in management, thus making cooperation and engagement difficult to achieve. Change managers can avoid this situation by:

- *Perspective taking.* Thinking about how others are likely to think and feel about a change.
- *Threat-reducing behavior.* Engaging in intentional, interpersonal interactions with staff members to minimize their perceptions that changes are likely to lead to harm for them.

- *Reflection*. Participating in self-evaluation, to reduce the emergence of negative emotions and to identify corrective actions where necessary.

Understanding the emotional side of change is important. However, whether change managers can produce positive emotional responses to change is open to question for four reasons. First, there is an underlying assumption that emotions are produced and contained within the organization. The impact of external factors (how friends and family talk about a change, how change is presented in the media) can be overlooked. Second, an underlying assumption is that all people respond in the same way to the same emotional appeals. This view overlooks differences in work motivation and how these influence perceptions of change. With increasing workforce diversity, we also have to be aware of cultural differences in modes of emotional expression and response. Third, not all change managers have the skills or the credibility to manage the emotional responses of staff to change, and to achieve positive emotional responses. Finally, it may be easier to achieve positive emotional responses to some (exciting, developmental, progressive) changes and not others (routine, tedious, defensive).

Table 7.3 summarizes the main barriers to successful organizational change communication.

The communication process appears to be simple, but it is prone to errors arising on both sides of the exchange. We cannot confidently assume that receivers will always decode our messages in a way that gives them the meaning that we intended to transmit. Communication is central to organizational change, but this claim has practical implications. It seems that organizations function better where:

- communications are open
- relationships are based on mutual understanding and trust

TABLE 7.3
Barriers to Effective Organizational Change Communication

Language	Choice of words and tone of message can lead to misunderstandings and misinterpretations.
Gender differences	Men and women use different communication styles, which can lead to misunderstanding; men tend to talk more; women ask more questions.
Power differences	Research shows that employees distort upward communication and that superiors often have a limited understanding of subordinates' roles, experiences, and problems.
Context	Organizational culture and history, as well as physical setting, can color the way in which change communications are transmitted and interpreted.
Cultural diversity	Different cultures have different expectations concerning formal and informal communication; lack of awareness of those norms creates misunderstanding.
Emotion	Emotional arousal interferes with message transmission and receipt, and emotional responses to change communication can be negative (anxiety, anger) or positive (exciting, stimulating).

- interactions are based on cooperation rather than competition
- people work together in teams
- decisions are reached in a participative way

These features are not universal and are not present in all countries, cultures—or organizations.

LO 7.3 Language Matters: The Power of Conversation

As we discussed at the beginning of this chapter, communication does not just involve a transfer of information or ideas. The language that we use to describe reality also helps to create—or to constitute—that reality for others; communication thus involves the creation and exchange of *meaning*. For example, Tannen (1995) points out that language reflects and reinforces underlying social relationships. She offers the following illustrative statements, which each require the same response, but signal different information about the relationship between those involved:

"Sit down!" This signals higher status of the person uttering the statement, perhaps indicating anger, and informal conversation is not appropriate.

"I would be pleased if you would sit down." This signals respect, or possibly sarcasm, depending on the tone of voice and the situation.

"You must be so tired. Why don't you sit down?" This signals either a concern and closeness for the person or condescension.

Language is particularly important in organizational change contexts due to the sensitivity of the issues ("Will I lose my job?") and the possibility for confusion ("That is not what management said last week"). The choice of language that the change manager uses can therefore affect whether proposals will be seen as exciting or routine, as clear or muddled, as progressive or mundane, as threatening or developmental. These

There's Nothing Like a Good Story

As chief executive at Hewlett-Packard (HP), Mark Hurd (then chief executive at Oracle Corporation from 2010) wanted the company to develop a more sales-oriented culture. To reinforce this message, he told the story about how, in his first week as a newcomer at NCR Corporation, he made a successful sale to a San Antonio tractor maker for some printing equipment. However, he failed to fill in the order form correctly and the person in the NCR billing department refused to process the order because of a minor mistake that he had made in the paperwork. When Hurd informed his manager about the situation, his manager phoned the guy in billing:

"Hey, did my man just come down here with an order?" asked the manager as Hurd listened. "The next time he does, I want you to get your ass out from behind your desk, and I want you to shake his hand. And I want you to thank him for keeping your ass employed. If there's anything wrong with the order, I want you to fix it so that he can get about the job of continuing to keep you employed." (Lachinsky, 2006, p. 93) meanings can be shared in documentation and through formal meetings. However, for the change manager, the understanding of change is typically shared in a range of formal and informal meetings and conversations. Even brief, unplanned, casual conversations can be powerful channels for exchanges of ideas and understanding between the change manager and those who are involved in the proposals. Silence during a conversation also sends signals.

Managing change also involves different conversations at different stages of the change process. Conversations across those stages, however, must have "linguistic coherence," and managers should try to align their use of language with the type of change that is being implemented. It is also important to create a shared language of change among the stakeholders who are involved.

Talking in Stages

Communication is not simply a tool for producing intentional change; rather, it is through communication that change happens. In other words, "the management of change can be understood to be the management of conversations" (Ford and Ford, 1995, p. 566). Drawing on "speech act theory," Ford and Ford argue that change takes place through four types of conversation.

Initiative conversations draw attention to the need for change, whether reactive or proactive, and can take the form of:

Assertion: "We have to bring the finances under control."
Request: "Can you restructure your division to achieve greater operating efficiencies?"
Declaration: "We are going to increase market share."

Conversations for understanding help others to appreciate the change issues and the problems that need to be addressed, through three main elements:

Specifying the "conditions of satisfaction" that will make the change successful: "We need to make sure that there are no more than two customer complaints per thousand units produced."
Enabling the involvement of those affected by the change
Confirming interpretations and enabling shared meaning and understanding

Conversations for performance focus on producing the change and involve the action stage when:

Promises are made.
Obligations are entered into.
Accountabilities are established.
Deadlines are set.

Conversations for closure signal the completion of the change and facilitate the movement of people into new projects and initiatives. These conversations involve:

Acknowledgments
Celebrations
Rewards

Breakdowns in change and conversations occur when:

- Initiative conversations are held with people who are not in a position to proceed with the change.
- There is a lack of shared understanding about the intended changes and the expectations for the "conditions of satisfaction."
- There is shared understanding, but performance conversations do not take place, so people do not know who is accountable for specific actions.
- Requests for action and performance are not rigorous and fail to specify intentions regarding results and deadlines.
- Closure conversations do not take place, and people feel that they are still involved with the change, while being asked to move on to new initiatives.

Ford and Ford (1995) emphasize that change managers need skills in handling change conversations, while recognizing that not all change conversations take place in a linear manner; some stages may be skipped during the process. The practicing change manager thus needs to consider the following:

- Where managers are engaged in multiple change processes, there will be issues relating to how smoothly they are able to transition themselves among the different conversations.
- The stages of the conversations may be open to multiple interpretations among participants. Where managers assume that some conversations are complete and that it is appropriate to move on to another stage in the change conversations, others may have differing views.
- It is not clear whether it is possible to train all managers or if the managers will be able to exhibit all these conversation skills successfully. For example, some managers may have more affinity with initiative conversations rather than performance conversations, and so on.
- Change managers need to confront the notion of power. The willingness of participants to be involved meaningfully in each of the four change conversations may be affected by significant power imbalances. Some understandings may thus need to be enforced rather than shared.

IBM's Script for Offshoring Jobs

Internal IBM documents reported in *The Wall Street Journal* in January 2004 suggested that IBM was planning to move high-cost programming jobs offshore to countries such as Brazil, India, and China where labor costs were lower (Bulkeley, 2004). Rather than pay $56 per hour in the United States, the documents indicated that a comparable programming job would cost only $12.50 per hour in China. The documents also revealed that IBM was aware that this "offshoring" process was a sensitive issue and provided managers with a draft "script" for presenting information to affected staff.

One memo instructed managers to ensure that any written communication to employees should first be "sanitized" by communications and human resource staff ("Do not be transparent regarding the purpose/intent") and also directed that managers should not use terms such as "onshore" and "offshore." Part of the "suggested script" for informing staff members that their jobs were being moved offshore was to say, "This is not a resource action" (an IBM euphemism for being laid off), and that the company would try to find them jobs elsewhere. This script also proposed that the news should be conveyed to staff by saying, "This action is a statement about the rate and pace of change in this demanding industry. It is in no way a comment on the excellent work you have done over the years." And, "For people whose jobs are affected by this consolidation, I understand this is difficult news."

Aligning Language with the Change

Change may fail when the imagery and metaphors used by managers are not aligned with the type of change being implemented. This lack of alignment confuses those who are involved in the change. Robert Marshak (1993) describes a situation where a large corporation had to reposition fundamentally its business due to a decline in the government contracts that had been a mainstay of the company. Unfortunately, when communicating the need for this change to middle management, the chief executive's explanation was based on the need to build on the company's past success, as a way of developing into the future. Instead of shifting the company in radically new directions, middle managers continued to develop past practices. The imagery of "developing" was not aligned with the "transformational" change that was necessary.

To avoid such problems, Marshak advises managers to align their language closely with the planned change. He identifies four different images of change and the language appropriate to each:

- *Machine imagery.* Based on a "fix and maintain" view, portraying the organization as "broken" and the change as a "fix." The change manager is the repairperson; terms such as *repair*, *adjust*, and *correct* are aligned to this type of change.
- *Developmental imagery.* Based on a "build and develop" view, in which the organization has to improve performance by building on past and current practices. The change manager is trainer or coach; terms such as *nurturing*, *growing*, and *getting better* are aligned to this type of change.
- *Transitional imagery.* Based on a "move and relocate" view, in which change is designed to alter how the organization operates, for example, by introducing online sales and services. The change manager is a guide or planner; terms such as *moving forward* and *leaving the past behind* are aligned to this type of change.
- *Transformational imagery.* Based on a "liberate and re-create" view, where change involves reinvention or radical change to the nature of the business or market in which the organization trades. The change manager is visionary, helping to discover new possibilities; terms such as *reinvention*, *re-creation*, and *adopting a new paradigm* are aligned to this change.

These insights concerning the need to align language and change highlight how change managers can easily communicate mixed signals. Change managers are thus advised to reflect on how their metaphors for communicating about their organizations and changes may be influenced by dominant metaphors. New insights, actions, and unanticipated directions can be generated by adopting new language and new metaphors (see the box "The NASCAR Model"). We must also be aware that managers may not always be able to introduce metaphors that will resonate with staff. New metaphors often compete with dominant logics, embedded ways of operating, ingrained ways of perceiving, and formal policies and

The NASCAR Model

Apparelizm (pseudonym) is a *Fortune* 500 retailer, with over 1,000 stores nationwide, which began a major organizational change effort resulting from a review of its strategy. As part of the effort to build support, the change team drew from a National Association for Stock Car Auto Racing (NASCAR) analogy, this being a sport well understood and liked by many of the staff. The change team argued that store staff members were like a NASCAR race crew. Past store practice was likened to a race crew member driving the car, pumping the gas, and changing the tires during the race. A "pit crew" would do the ordering and receiving of goods and put them on the shelves after they arrived. The "drivers" would be responsible for helping customers as they moved around the store. The "racetrack manager" would monitor the traffic flow in the store, removing the "multicar pile-ups" that happened when sales associates ("drivers") congregated together (rather than servicing customers). The metaphor was further extended to a parallel between the need for NASCAR racing teams "to be fast, responsive and knowledgeable" if they were to be successful. A similar point was made with regard to the need for excellent communication between the "drivers," "pit crew," and so on.

The metaphor worked well. Staff members understood and accepted the analogy and saw how the changes would help them to work more like an effective racing team (based on Roberto and Levesque, 2005).

procedures. Change managers need to focus on redesigning old policies, systems, and processes that are going to conflict with the new language of the change. For example, if change concerns "leaving the past behind," then transformational metaphors may be weakened if, say, compensation and performance appraisal systems are still based on past practice.

Creating a Common Change Language

Managers are not alone in using—or misusing—terms and phrases in ways that cause amusement and confusion. It is important to check the assumption that different individuals and groups involved in change have a shared view of the terms—the language—being used (see the box "Misused Terminology?").

Misused Terminology?

Term	Meaning?
Emergent strategy	Justifies a lack of strategic thinking; if a strategy does emerge, we do not have to do anything.
Learning organization	We were right to neglect training; all we have to do is tell employees that we like them to learn for themselves.
Empowerment	A magic word that, if we repeat it often enough, will make a downsized and delayered structure work without any further effort from us.
Culture	This is what we say we will change when we cannot think of anything else to do.

Based on Hussey (1998)

The change manager's choice of terms has a significant impact on the way in which an issue, such as organizational change, is understood by others. Problems will thus arise when those who are responsible for managing a change cannot among themselves adopt a "common language." Checking the shared meanings of concepts in use is thus important to avoid confusion and conflict. For example, Loizos Heracleous and Michael Barret (2001) attribute the failed implementation of an electronic risk management system in the London insurance market to the lack of shared language and meaning among the parties that were involved. Over a period of five years, they studied the language of the main stakeholders, including market leaders, brokers, and underwriters, and also observed how the language of those stakeholders changed over time.

Heracleous and Barrett distinguish between "surface-level" communication and the underpinning "deep discursive structures." Deep structures include interpretive schemes, central themes, root metaphors, and rhetorical strategies. A focus on the different discursive structures explains the resistance of brokers and underwriters to the new system, and the failure of the project:

> [W]e saw stakeholder groups talking past each other, rather than to each other, because of their almost diametrically opposed discourses, at both the deeper structure levels and communicative action levels, and their lack of common ground on which to base a dialogue. (Heracleous and Barrett, 2001, p. 774)

Culture, Language, and Change in General Motors Poland

General Motors (GM) began to develop its Opel Polska car plant on a greenfield site in Poland in 1996. One of the key tasks for management was to develop working practices consistent with a car plant that could be competitive in the twenty-first century. Although part of the challenge was due to the lack of exposure to competition during decades as part of the Soviet bloc, there seemed to be a more fundamental issue rooted in hundreds of years of Polish culture. A high value was placed on *fantazja* (imaginativeness), which was directly opposed to the idea of being systematic or well organized—the latter being equated with boring and unnecessary. *Fantazja* was also associated with independence and freedom from subjugation—the opposite to following standard operating procedures.

The practices designed for the new plant clearly required a high level of discipline and coordination. Managers were concerned that while *fantazja* could contribute to the continuous improvement processes that were to be part of the plant's operating model, the cultural tolerance for disorder could be damaging.

There was no shortage of Polish workers: 46,000 applied for 1,800 positions in the new plant, which meant that the company was in a very powerful position (but threats of job loss for noncompliance were not to be used). The European managers met with their new employees (along with translators). Although cultural values and linguistics appeared to lie at the heart of employee resistance to GM's working practices, the solution was also found in the same roots. As in English, the term *development* in Polish can mean "to start something" and also "to progress." In turn, "to progress" is the opposite of stagnation. For the Poles, stagnation is something that lacks *fantazja*. Through discussion, "disciplined organization" was positively reframed using concepts and values that were already part of Polish culture. By 2000, the plant had the best quality and performance figures of all GM plants, worldwide.

Based on Dobosz-Bourne and Jankowicz (2006)

Change managers need to understand the deep discursive structures that underpin the surface communication of stakeholders, to support major organizational changes. Surface agreement may be artificial and tenuous where there is a lack of understanding of those deeper structures, which can explain inertia or resistance. Although they acknowledge that understanding the interpretive schemes of different stakeholders will not guarantee success, Heracleous and Barrett (2001, p. 774) conclude, "Uncovering and appreciating other stakeholders' deep structures, however, can be of help in avoiding dead ends and self-defeating compromises in change implementation." For further discussion of the relationship between surface-level changes and deep structures, see Heracleous and Bartunek (2020).

LO 7.4 Change Communication Strategies

The Importance of High-Quality Communication

Researchers have focused on the importance of effective communication with employees during change. Empirical research has demonstrated that high-quality change communication increases acceptance, openness, and commitment to change. Furthermore, the failure to provide sufficient information or providing poor-quality information can result in a number of problems, including cynicism about change and widespread rumors, which often exaggerate the negative aspects of change. (Rafferty et al., 2013, p. 122)

In this section, we will focus on the communication strategy questions facing the change manager: Can you communicate too much? How do you get "buy-in"? When should you use communication strategies other than "spray and pray"? Who will take responsibility for communicating the change? We will also explore two contingency approaches to communication strategy, one based on the type of change and the other related to different phases of the change process.

Can You Communicate Too Much?

A common claim is, "We need more communication around here." Many commentators argue that it is not possible to over-communicate, but this view is not shared by all change managers and researchers. Geigle and Bailey (2001) describe a reengineering project that affected 400 employees in a federal agency. The change team was committed to open, organization-wide communication regarding the project, to a degree that was unprecedented in the organization's history. The outcome of this strategy was change recipient anxiety and cynicism about the change, for two reasons.

First, staff suffered information overload. One staff member said, "It's almost like they know with all this information, we won't read it." Information overload can be problematic in organizations where employees are already in receipt of a high volume of other information. Second, the agency's communication strategy did not involve real participation. The change team had no strategy for incorporating feedback into the change program: "I feel like they may be informing me of everything that's going on, but I have absolutely zero say in what goes on." Geigle and Bailey (2001) conclude that that there may be symbolic importance in pursuing an open communication strategy but that this is not sufficient for success. They argue that a change team is at its best when acting not as reporters, but as sense-makers, facilitating understanding for change recipients and helping them to identify (filter and distill) what is important. This distinction is instructive. From her research, Lewis (1999) argues that change managers act more often as reporters, disseminating information, than as sense-makers, seeking and processing feedback during planned change processes. For a more detailed exploration of the perspective that sense-making brings to organizational change, see chapter 9.

Getting the Word Out, or Getting Buy-In?

The federal agency example illustrates the difference between "getting the word out" (providing information about a change) as opposed to "getting staff buy-in" (support and involvement). Both are important (Guaspari, 1996). We cannot always assume that management alone has all the good ideas concerning what is required to make a change successful. We do know, however, that those who are going to be affected by change need to be informed about what is happening and that when frontline staff are allowed to take the initiative to drive change, the success rate is higher (Keller et al., 2010).

Communication designed to generate "buy-in" involves capturing from staff members information that will be useful in delivering the change, identifying what is important to them, and discovering what they see as the costs and benefits. It is therefore important to identify a clear "value proposition" that addresses the interests and motives of individual staff. Examples include (Guaspari, 1996, p. 35):

> As a result of the new skills you'll learn in order to perform your job in the newly reengineered organization, you will have significantly increased your value internally and your marketability externally.
>
> The work will be backbreaking. The pace will be relentless. You stand to make a ton of money.
>
> We are making these changes to enable us to rewrite the rules in our industry, to improve by orders of magnitude the value we can create for our customers.

Getting "buy-in" depends on what people are being asked to purchase. Do they see this as having personal value? Have the changes been adequately justified? The evidence indicates that explaining and justifying the need for change relates positively to perceived fairness with regard to both the change process and the outcomes. From his study of 183 employees in companies that had relocated to Chicago, Daly (1995) found that management's justification was particularly important when the move was viewed unfavorably by staff. However, that justification was not as important when the move was welcomed. Daly (1995, p. 426) concludes that some managers may thus be tempted to avoid explaining change decisions to employees if they think that the change outcomes will be welcome anyway. However, that may not apply to staff judgments about the change process.

> [E]mployees are likely to expect an explanation for a change decision regardless of whether the outcomes are positive or negative. If those employees are not given an explanation, they are likely to feel that the procedures used to make and implement the decision were unfair, leading in many cases to resentment against the decision process and the decision makers.

Daly's (1995) findings are consistent with other research that has found that managers are more likely to be trusted by staff when they:

- provide accurate information and feedback
- adequately explain the basis for their decisions
- use open communication, enabling an exchange of ideas

Beyond "Spray and Pray"

Clampitt and colleagues (2000) locate communication strategies on a continuum. At one end of this continuum is "spray and pray," transmitting lots of information, to little effect. At the other extreme, "withhold and uphold" offers little information and is also ineffective. All five strategies on this continuum are summarized in table 7.4. The authors argue that "underscore and explore," which involves dialogue, is more likely to succeed, by allowing staff concerns to be combined with management initiatives. They note that some organizations mix these strategies. For example, in one organization, "spray and pray" (also known as the "communication clutter" approach) was used to "bombard" staff with information on organizational performance. However, when faced with

TABLE 7.4
The Communication Strategies Continuum

Strategy	Actions
spray and pray	Shower employees with a range of information; more is better. Managers pray that staff will see what needs to be done. *Benefit*: staff members are exposed to company information. *Downside*: staff members are overloaded with information, may not be able to identify what is more important, and may be able to understand what is happening, but not why.
tell and sell	Limit the information provided to core issues. Management tells staff members about the changes and "sells" them on why these are necessary. *Benefit*: can be done rapidly. *Downside*: staff members are passive recipients, and no dialogue opens potential for staff scepticism and cynicism.
underscore and explore	Focus on fundamentals, but engage employees in dialogue to identify obstacles and misunderstandings that need to be addressed. *Benefit*: staff engagement solves problems, strengthens support for change, and can generate useful ideas. *Downside*: takes time.
identify and reply	Defensive approach to identifying and responding to rumors and innuendo, and to reduce staff confusion about changes. *Benefit*: can resolve problems at an early stage. *Downside*: reactive approach that assumes (sometimes incorrectly) that staff understands the organizational problems that the changes need to address.
withhold and uphold	Withhold information until it is absolutely necessary to communicate. Management publicly defend the change strategy. Information is not disclosed openly. *Benefit*: management retains a high degree of control. *Downside*: staff bitterness and resentment.

Source: Based on Clampitt et al. (2000).

downsizing and operational changes, a "withhold and uphold" strategy was used, to avoid exposing staff to promises about the future that management was not able to meet. This dual approach led to discontent and mistrust, as staff members saw management providing them with significant amounts of information, but avoiding the issues about which they cared the most.

This argument supports the use of "underscore and explore" change communication strategies, the benefits of which arise from dialogue and engagement. This approach, however, takes time to organize. This may not be appropriate—and could cause damaging delays—if rapid organizational change is necessary. The best strategy may thus depend on the situation.

LO 7.5 Contingency Approaches to Change Communication

Two main contingencies—or dependencies—that affect communication strategy concern the type of change and the stage of change.

Communication Strategy and Type of Change

Doug Stace and Dexter Dunphy (2001) argue that a communication strategy must reflect the type of organizational change that is being proposed:

- *Developmental or incremental transitions* aim for widespread involvement, emphasizing face-to-face communication and the use of change teams to identify initiatives and broaden commitment.
- *Task-focused transitions* seek to align employee behavior with management initiatives, so these are primarily top-down in nature, using formal communication channels such as email broadcasts and memos.
- *Charismatic transformations* need to stimulate emotional commitment to new ways of working and thus require more personalized top-down forms of communication, ideally combined with at least symbolic two-way communication.
- *Turnarounds* tend to follow from organizational crises and draw on formal, top-down modes of communication that attempt to force compliance with the new direction.

Stace and Dunphy describe how these approaches vary in terms of communicating goals, who is to be involved, the issues to be addressed, the communication channels and directions (top-down, lateral, one-way, or two-way), and the balance of power that will need to be managed among relevant parties.

Each of these strategies makes different demands on the capabilities of the change manager. Developmental transitions need sophisticated social and interpersonal skills. Task-focused transformations rely on carefully crafted formal messages. Charismatic transformations need to be underpinned by visionary and inspiring messages. In the interests of speed and effectiveness, post-crisis turnarounds may require a directive, autocratic style, with which many experienced change managers may be uncomfortable, especially if they are accustomed to more participative, engaging modes of change communication and implementation.

Open the Files

Think back to a recent change in your organization, and consider the following questions:

1. Did your organization have a strategy for initially announcing the change?

2. What strategy was used to communicate information during the change process? Was one or more of the strategies from Table 7.4 used? Was this strategy adopted consistently and for all members across the organization?

3. On a scale from 1 (ineffective) to 5 (very effective), how would you rate the communication strategy overall?

4. With hindsight, what changes would you have made to improve the effectiveness of the change communication strategy?

5. To what extent will those recommendations apply to future changes in this organization? To what extent will that depend on the further changes that are proposed?

Bill Quirke (2008, p. 236) also argues that communication strategy should take into account the degree of change that is going to be implemented. The more significant the change, the more employees need to be involved. He uses the "communication escalator" (see Figure 7.2), a guide to designing communications strategy. Degrees of involvement range from awareness to support and to commitment.

FIGURE 7.2
The Com-munication Escalator

Source: Quirke (2008).

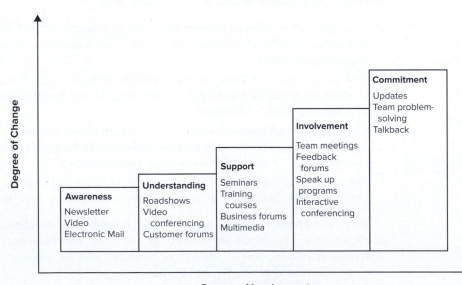

The escalator indicates the communications methods appropriate to each degree of involvement (suggestions—these are not comprehensive). For commitment, the organization should consider using all those types of communication methods, and any others that are available. At the awareness level, the focus is simply on providing information. However, for involvement and commitment, communication also needs to concentrate on improving the quality of interactions and relationships.

Communication Strategy and Stage of Change

Adopting a differing contingency focus, Kathleen and Kevin Reardon (1999) suggest that the most appropriate communication strategy depends on the stage of the change process. First, they identify four leadership styles, which each use different communication processes and strategies:

- *Commanding style.* Leaders are performance- and results-oriented, and their communication style is directive.
- *Logical style.* Leaders explore the available strategic options through analysis and reasoning, and their communication style involves explaining their intentions and their plans.
- *Inspirational style.* Leaders develop a vision of the future around which they seek to encourage cohesion, and their communication style involves creating trust and mobilizing people around the change program.
- *Supportive style.* Leaders are concerned with creating an open and consensual environment, and their communication style is based on involvement.

Reardon and Reardon (1999) argue that different modes of communicating should be used at different stages of the change process. Using a five-stage process, their argument is summarized in table 7.5.

TABLE 7.5
Stages of Change and Leadership Style

Stage	Leadership Style
Planning	Focus on identifying what needs to change requires a combination of logical and inspirational leadership styles.
Enabling	As people are selected and trained in relation to the change process, a combination of logical, inspirational, and supportive styles is required.
Launching	As change unfolds, combine logical and commanding styles.
Catalyzing	Use inspirational and supportive leadership styles to motivate and engage.
Maintaining	To encourage staff to continue with a change effort, perhaps in the face of obstacles, inspirational and supportive leadership styles are helpful.

This framework recognizes that no one individual is likely to have all the change management skills required at different stages of a change process. More than one style—or more than one image of change management—may be necessary. As discussed in chapter 8, however, change management can often be more of a team effort than a solo performance. Team members may thus have different strengths—or styles—that they can use to compensate for each other.

This framework has some drawbacks. First, change rarely unfolds in the logical manner shown in table 7.5 (see also chapter 10). Second, there may be several changes unfolding at once, but each at a different pace in an organization, raising questions about the management styles of those involved in more than one initiative. Third, it can be difficult to identify when one stage has ended and another has begun as these can overlap significantly. Fourth, the model offers clear advice but without supporting evidence. Finally, to apply this framework, change managers are required to have a good self-understanding of their leadership and communication preferences and styles. As with many such frameworks, this is useful as long as it is treated as a guide and not as a rigid set of rules.

Communication in a Crisis   *What Can We Learn from BP's Mistakes?*

Communication in a crisis is critical, affecting the organization's reputation and performance. Aikaterini Valvi and Konstantinos Fragkos (2013) assess BP's communication after the explosion on the *Deepwater Horizon* oil drilling rig in the Gulf of Mexico in April 2010. The incident killed 11 of the 126 crew members and injured 17 others. Oil poured from the wellhead on the seabed and drifted toward the Louisiana coast, threatening wildlife and the local fishing and tourism industries. Spilling 5 million barrels of crude oil into the Gulf, the *Deepwater Horizon* incident was the biggest environmental disaster in the United States since the *Exxon Valdez* spilled 750,000 barrels in Prince William Sound in 1989. With financial penalties and reputational damage, BP struggled to restore profitability.

Crises are expected to trigger significant organizational change, to prevent a recurrence. Many stakeholders are involved—employees, shareholders, local businesses, the public, regulatory agencies, government. Tony Hayward, BP's chief executive, took personal responsibility for providing information following the *Deepwater* incident. He was slow to respond to the crisis and made five other mistakes in his communication with the media, government, and public:

1. *The fake images.* Fake photographs were given to the press, claiming that these related to blank spots on the video; original images were quickly supplied, but this damaged BP's credibility.

2. *"I want my life back."* Under pressure from various sources, Hayward in a television interview in May said, "I want my life back." As the *Deepwater* incident had caused 11 deaths, this damaged his credibility and reputation.

3. *The incident with the yacht.* With oil still spilling into the Gulf, Hayward took time off to watch his yacht "Bob" compete in the UK Isle of Wight island race.

4. *We were not prepared.* Speaking to the *Financial Times* in Texas, Hayward said, "We did not have

the tools you would want in your toolkit"—not a reassuring statement.

5. *Self-interest.* During a hearing with the U.S. Cabinet, Hayward appeared to show an overriding concern with his own position, which he believed was not under threat, saying that he was ignoring press and television accounts of the disaster, so as not to "cloud his judgement."

U.S. President Barack Obama criticized BP for spending $50 million on radio, television, and on-line advertising during the crisis, suggesting that it would have been better to spend that money on dealing with the oil spill. The company made this worse by issuing a statement claiming that "not a cent" had been diverted from their response to the oil spill to pay for advertising. BP's communication with its own employees was ineffective. When staff involved in the oil cleanup operation were hospitalized with dizziness, headaches, and respiratory problems, Hayward blamed food poisoning, showing lack of concern for their well-being. Strategies for communicating with shareholders were more effective, reminding them of BP's past record, blaming other companies for the disaster, and promising to meet long-term dividend obligations. Nevertheless, Hayward was replaced in October 2010.

What advice can other organizations take from this experience? Develop a crisis communication plan. Appoint experienced staff to work from a designated public relations office. Communications with the media must be direct and sincere. Use press conferences, a crisis webpage, and social network accounts. Monitor media reports closely, and respond immediately to clarify issues when appropriate. Do not run advertising campaigns to promote your image during a crisis. Concentrate on restoring trust. Finally, make it clear from the start that "things will change."

(Other aspects of this incident are discussed in chapter 5.)

LO 7.6   Communication Channels and the Impact of Social Media

At the heart of our model of communication (see Figure 7.1) sits a key issue that we have not directly discussed: the channel, or the medium through which the message will be transmitted. This is not a mere technical issue. As Marshall McLuhan (1964) argued, "the medium is the message," suggesting that the properties of a chosen medium can influence the meaning of a message and its interpretation. The change manager selecting an inappropriate medium with which to transmit important information to key groups affected by a change proposal may not be taken seriously, may be seen as insensitive, and may strengthen disaffection. In the final section of this chapter, therefore, we will consider the characteristics of different media and how these can affect change communication. We then explore the impact on change communication of developments in social media.

Media Richness

One of the main characteristics on which communication media vary is "information richness," a concept originally developed by Lengel and Daft (1988). Richness concerns the amount and the kind of information that can be transmitted. The three characteristics of a communication medium that affect richness are (1) the ability to handle many items of information at the same time, (2) the availability of rapid feedback, and (3) the ability to establish a personal focus. Based on these characteristics, they classify media on the "hierarchy of richness" shown in Figure 7.3.

Face-to-face is the richest communication medium because it meets all three criteria: multiple information cues, immediate feedback, and personal focus. Moving down the hierarchy, online video chat and meeting technologies, such as FaceTime, Skype, and Zoom, provide some of the information cues that are available from nonverbal behavior. This includes body language such as eye contact, posture, gesture, and head movements. But many of the subtleties and nuances of in-person communication are not so evident when using these media, and some cues may not even be seen given the limited visual framing of the parties to the conversation and the sometimes poor sound quality. Telephone calls, conventional email, and interactive blogs allow some personalization and

Getting the (Change) News   *What Works Best for You?*

You are an employee of a large organization about to go through a major restructuring. Consider these questions:

1. What do you think you need to know about the restructuring?

2. From whom would you like to get this information? Why?

3. Would you prefer to receive this information in person or in a group setting?

4. What for you would be the best channel (e.g., management briefing, email, video, intranet) for receiving this information? Why?

5. As a change manager, how will you use your answers to these questions to help design a communication strategy?

FIGURE 7.3
Media Richness
Hierarchy

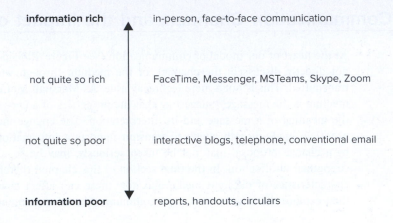

information rich	in-person, face-to-face communication
not quite so rich	FaceTime, Messenger, MSTeams, Skype, Zoom
not quite so poor	interactive blogs, telephone, conventional email
information poor	reports, handouts, circulars

feedback but are limited in the amount of information that can be transmitted. At the other extreme, impersonal written communications, such as reports and circulars, are limited on all three criteria and are therefore information poor or "lean."

This is not an argument in favor of rich communications. On the contrary, the degree of richness that is appropriate depends on the nature and content of what is being communicated, and in particular on where the issue lies on a continuum from routine to nonroutine. Routine issues are commonplace, simple, rational, straightforward, and contain no surprises. Nonroutine issues, in contrast, concern novel, complex, unexpected events, and are often characterized by time pressure, ambiguity, and surprise. The potential for misunderstanding is thus greater with nonroutine issues, and a richer exchange of information is therefore necessary to establish a common frame of reference. Lengel and Daft (1988, pp. 229–231) suggest six rules for "matching" media richness to the message:

Rule 1.   Send nonroutine, difficult communications through a rich medium—preferably face to face.

Rule 2.   Send routine, simple communications through a lean medium.

Rule 3.   Use rich media to extend your personal presence throughout the organization.

Rule 4.   Use rich media for implementing company strategy.

Rule 5.   Don't let the media in use "censor" information about critical issues; formal written reports simplify multidimensional issues and mask the nonroutine.

Rule 6.   Evaluate new communication technology as one channel in the media spectrum.

For the change manager, these rules indicate that incremental changes that simply build on current practice may be comparatively routine, and they should be communicated as such, using lean media. This is more suited, for example, to the transmission of factual or technical information. On the other hand, information-rich media should be used when changes are novel, more complex, and widespread in their implications. Information richness may be more difficult to achieve in a large organization, and the change manager may need to consider a wider range of options, including the use of the social technologies discussed shortly. In most instances of nonroutine change, it is likely that a portfolio of communication strategies will be desirable, tailored to the circumstances.

Adopting a different contingency approach, Bill Quirke (2008) suggests that different change communication media are better suited to some audiences than to others. With regard to change communication, he suggests that there are four types of target audience, whose needs differ:

- *Waking up.* They will be affected by the change, but have not noticed, yet.
- *Engaging.* They know that they will be affected and are interested and concerned.
- *Educating.* They will be affected marginally, and only need to be told about what is happening.
- *Reassuring.* They will also be marginally affected but are concerned nevertheless.

Media-rich face-to-face communication needs to be directed toward those who will be most impacted by change—those who need waking up, and those who need to be engaged. Leaner forms of communication can be used with those who only need education or reassurance.

A New Range of Tools—The Impact of Social Media

As discussed in chapter 5, social media gives management new tools for external and internal communication, reaching out to customers and suppliers and encouraging employee voice. Social media is "information rich," close to the top of the hierarchy in Figure 7.3, and is in widespread use. Until recently, most organizations have focused on the external uses of social media, which in some sectors have been disruptive (see the box "The Beauty Industry"). However, social media can also potentially disrupt change management processes, by engaging employees in new ways. Organizations can use public social media platforms or develop enterprise-specific networking platforms or both. Internally developed corporate platforms may, however, be easier for management to control and may minimize the risks inherent in using public online tools.

Rick (2015) argues that social media can contribute to change management in several ways:

- help to make better and faster decisions about change management actions
- open up conversations across organizational levels, functions, and locations
- engage employees by asking for creative ideas to support transformation programs
- support changes in management and employee behavior—which become more visible
- through early recognition, help to manage criticism and resistance to change

The Beauty Industry

The global beauty industry is worth around $250 billion. Hudson et al. (2018) argue that digital marketing and social media have disrupted this industry more severely than most other consumer-goods sectors. This is because "born digital" brands (Anastasia Beverly Hills, NYX) are capturing the attention of beauty-conscious customers with social media tools. These brands now account for 10 percent of the color cosmetics market, and born digital brands are growing faster than established "legacy players." These new brands have been able to build a following using online videos (vlogs) and influencer marketing through social media—channels that younger customers are more likely to use than older consumers. This social media approach also makes customers feel like they are part of a community, reinforcing brand loyalty.

Rick argues that personal communication, management support, and coaching are still critical with regard to maintaining trust, morale, and performance during change programs. However, social media is now a key part of the process. Clayton (2015) also argues that social media should be a key component of the change communication plan. Her research found that over half of employees who had experienced a change at work said that they would have welcomed more online engagement as well as face-to-face communication. She suggests four ways in which social media can be used as a change management tool:

1. *Social media can reduce the distance between top management and employees.* We discussed the importance of clearly communicating an inspiring vision of the future in chapter 6. But Clayton's research found that only 17 percent of employees rate highly the communications they receive about change from senior leaders.

2. *Social media tools flatten the organization*, giving employees opportunities to communicate directly with top management, who in turn can improve its understanding of what is happening in the organization. Clayton (2015, p. 3) gives this example:

   > Consider Zappos CEO Tony Hseih, who announced layoffs for 8 per cent of the company's workforce on Zappos' external blog immediately after sending an internal email. Employees appreciated the transparency and later engaged with Tony, each other, and Zappos' stakeholders over Twitter. The open conversation provided Zappos with insight into how best to handle sensitive situations, fostered thoughtful, public interaction between management and employees, and even helped some laid off workers find future employment with other companies.

3. *Employees can help to shape the organization's future, through social media tools.* Feeling powerless in the face of change is a major employee criticism, and few feel that senior management takes their ideas and opinions seriously. Clayton (2015, p. 3) gives this example:

   > When long-time Cisco CEO John Chambers stepped down to serve as chairman in July and was replaced by Chuck Robbins, the company started two simultaneous Jive threads— one inviting employees to thank John and another asking: "What advice or suggestions do you have for Chuck Robbins as he transitions to CEO?" Within four days the two posts drew over 1,000 comments and over 20,000 views. Similar employee crowdsourcing efforts have been used to redefine company values (at IBM) and generate ideas for cutting operational costs (at BASF).

4. People need time to work through uncertainty. *Social media tools create opportunities to discuss, collaborate, and share experiences.* These kinds of interactions are important during major changes. Clayton (2015, p. 4) gives this example:

   > When Pfizer undertook a major restructuring in 2007, they turned to ten employees to tell their stories. Each representing a different role in the new organizational structure, these employees were given video cameras and asked to share their real-life experience, warts and all, through a series of video diaries over a three-month period. Pfizer employees looked forward to following the journeys of their colleagues who were experiencing the same uncertainties they were facing. The ten employees became internal celebrities of sorts and pulse surveys tracked an upswing in employees' understanding of the change and confidence in the future. Those clips were delivered to employees on CDs. (Yes, CDs!) What could the same type of intervention mean for companies in the era of YouTube?

These applications rely on enterprise networks, especially where discussion topics are likely to include commercially sensitive information. When enterprise networks fail,

Clayton argues, the main reason is lack of top management engagement; the organization needs a group of socially minded executives who lead the way, even if this does not include the chief executive. From a study of seven organizations with internal networks, Gifford (2014) offers this helpful advice:

- Enterprise networks need a clear rationale or purpose if they are to be used and become embedded. They need to support day-to-day activities.
- The process of identifying uses is better developed bottom-up, coming from staff themselves. But effective uses need to be identified and replicated if they are to spread and be sustained.
- It helps if there is a key individual, or a team of "community champions," guiding and encouraging the use of social media until this reaches critical mass.
- Enterprise social networks are time-efficient ways for senior leaders to engage with large numbers of staff and to increase their visibility. However, the effects will be negative if senior management challenges or criticizes comments with which it disagrees.
- Social networks should be self-managed and not censored; policies should be "light touch" (with an expectation that posts will be "respectful"); negative comments should be dealt with frankly and openly; employees should be informed if comments have caused offence.

Social media thus offers the change manager a novel range of powerful, flexible, "information-rich" communication channels. Organizations that have experimented with these technologies have achieved significant benefits. Most of the tools are public and require little skill to use. To develop beneficial applications, it also seems that creativity, innovation, and experimentation will be necessary to tailor these new methods to local conditions and organizational goals.

When they were developing their theory of media richness, Lengel and Daft (1988) may not have foreseen the development of social media and mobile technologies in the twenty-first century. However, their conclusions with regard to computing technology in general speak to the change manager today. They observed that "electronic media" were just one potential channel in the media spectrum. All the other channels have their uses and advantages. They also concluded that "there is no electronic substitute for face-to-face discussions when issues are nonroutine" (Lengel and Daft, 1988, p. 231). Social media can therefore be misused. They should not, for example, be used to provide an excuse to avoid difficult interpersonal conversations—about forthcoming organizational changes perhaps or other controversial or sensitive issues.

EXERCISE 7.1 *Listen to Who's Talking*	The ways in which we communicate reinforce power and gender differences. This can affect our interpretations of what we think is happening in a particular situation.
	1. Observe a work meeting, preferably with up to 10 people.
	2. Listen to the language being used. What different types of languages in use can you observe: such as commanding, respectful, demonstrating concern, displaying condescension?
LO 7.2	3. Do individuals tend to use one type of language in their interactions?
LO 7.3	4. To what extent does the talk convey information about power and gender differences? For example, who takes credit, who exudes confidence?
	(Continued)

5. What conclusions can you draw from your analysis about the way language constructs and reinforces differences within the organization?

6. As a change manager, how will your awareness of these differences influence your future interactions with staff?

EXERCISE 7.2

How Defensive Are You?

LO 7.2

Many alphas think that looking interested when someone speaks to them demonstrates a high degree of openness when, in fact, that's just the bare minimum one must do not to be labeled defensive. Alphas can use this tool to chart their progress toward a more constructive state of mind and to see how their behavior appears to others.

Are you open or defensive? What are your normal behaviors? Where are your preferences? What do you need to change? How would this improve your relationships and personal effectiveness?

Highly Open

+10 ▬ Plan the change, engage others, set milestones, and implement.

+9 ▬ Communicate genuine enthusiasm about making a change.

+8 ▬ Think out loud, making new associations about the problem.

+7 ▬ Take full responsibility for the problem and its ramifications.

+6 ▬ Request information and examples about the problem.

+5 ▬ Openly wonder about your role in creating the problem.

+4 ▬ Express genuine curiosity about the issue and how to resolve it.

+3 ▬ Express appreciation for the messenger, regardless of delivery.

+2 ▬ Summarize key points without interjecting your own thoughts.

+1 ▬ Look interested, breathe, demonstrate an open posture.

Breakthrough: choosing curiosity over being right

−1 ▬ Show polite interest while inwardly preparing your rebuttal.

−2 ▬ Provide a detailed explanation of your point of view.

−3 ▬ Justify actions with compelling logic and an interpretation of events.

−4 ▬ Interrupt to give your perspective.

−5 ▬ Interpret comments as attacks and feel misunderstood.

−6 ▬ Convince them that you're right and they're wrong.

−7 ▬ Make snippy replies and show your irritation nonverbally.

−8 ▬ Blame or complain about someone who's not present.

−9 ▬ Intimidate or attack the messenger.

−10 ▬ Appear to comply, with no intention of doing what you say you'll do.

Highly Defensive

Source: Ludeman, K., and E. Erlandson. "Highly Open/Highly Defensive." *Harvard Business Review* 83, no. 5 (2004). Copyright ©2004 Harvard Business School Publishing. Harvard Business Publishing is an affiliate of Harvard Business School.

EXERCISE 7.3

Social Media at the Museum

LO 7.5

In the past, institutional mission and strategic vision were reviewed every four years; now, they are reviewed every time someone posts to Facebook, comments on a blog, or opens a new Twitter account. (Allen-Greil et al., 2011)

Social media could itself trigger dramatic organizational changes, as well as creating new channels of change communication. For example, social media is changing the ways in which museums interact with the public, and also how museum staff members communicate and work with each other. Allen-Greil and colleagues (2011) argue that, used effectively, social media can further the mission of the organization and foster more agile and collaborative organizational cultures. There are many wider cultural, political, and social pressures encouraging openness and collaboration. Social media offers a new set of tools with which organizations can respond to those pressures.

Allen-Greil and colleagues studied three museums: The Smithsonian's National Museum of American History (NMAH); Monticello, a historic house and research institution; and the J. Paul Getty Trust (the Getty). These museums have adopted different approaches to the use of social media.

At NMAH, social media contributes to *public programming*, focusing on education and visitor services, complementing the existing email newsletter, website, and other online communications. At Monticello, the focus lies with *relationships building*, and in particular on increasing the organization's "social media outreach." This means using social media to increase the number of "online visitors." In contrast, the Getty is using social media to "*get off the hill*." The Getty has a reputation for being inaccessible as it is located on a hill above the 405 freeway, and visitors have to take a quarter-mile tram ride to get up there. Social media thus allows the Getty to "take the collections and programs into the community" and to promote its educational and research work.

Sometimes the Best Thing Managers Can Do Is Get Out of the Way

Staff members who have collaborated on social media projects in these museums have created new channels of communication and new ways of thinking and working with each other. The leadership of these initiatives was mainly "bottom-up" and did not rely on senior management experts. Allen-Greil and colleagues note, "Effective collaboration means staff members need to cross lines traditionally drawn between different working groups, and probably across lines drawn between hierarchical levels within the institution." Social media may thus lead to flatter hierarchies and "horizontal working." The study also found that an increased level of online engagement with the public led to an increase in face-to-face conversations among staff. Why? Social media project staff had to meet with colleagues across the organization: human resources, legal department, registrars, publishers, and educators. The authors argue, "Social media are pushing us together in a very personal way. New conversations between staff members who have never had any reason to talk before are establishing new relationships and new lines of engagement."

A Perpetually Beta State of Mind

Senior managers need to encourage staff to experiment with social media, to develop more efficient and effective processes. However, at the Getty, the use of different social media platforms, by different groups of staff, meant that initiatives were often uncoordinated and some even competed with each other: "In a large, hierarchical institution, this kind of testing, rapid prototyping, and risk-taking is pushing the boundaries of the usual, highly-controlled content development processes." Although exciting for staff, spontaneous experimentation may not be sustainable. However, Allen-Greil and colleagues ask

(Continued)

us to consider, "What would it *really* be like if we could work in a *perpetually beta* state of mind? If we could try, fail, and try again? We are closer than you think because it's already happening at every museum that uses social media."

Now that you have read this case, consider the following questions:

1. In what ways could social media applications contribute to the mission of your organization?

2. How could social media change or strengthen the culture of your organization, with regard to widening collaboration and becoming more agile and responsive?

3. To what extent will your current organization silos and hierarchies inhibit the communication and collaboration opportunities opened up by social media? Or, will social media help you to break down those silos and hierarchies and encourage more "horizontal working"?

4. How should your organization balance the need for management control with the desire to open up conversations more widely across the organization to encourage experimentation with social media?

5. In your assessment, would your organization benefit or suffer from working in a "perpetually beta" state of mind, constantly experimenting, learning—and improving—from the mistakes?

Additional Reading

Keller, S., Meaney, M., and Pung, C. 2010. *What successful transformations share.* Chicago and London: McKinsey & Company. Identifies the tactics that lead to successful change. Emphasizes the power of widespread employee engagement, collaboration, co-creation, sense of ownership, and in particular the importance of ongoing communication and involvement.

Lewis, L. 2019. *Organizational change: Creating change through strategic communication.* John Wiley & Sons: London. Explores the theory and practice of change implementation from a communication perspective, highlighting the roles of informal and formal communication. Also shows how individuals and groups, as well as senior management, can influence the substance and process of change.

Rafferty, A. E., Jimmieson, N. L., and Armenakis, A. A. 2013. Change readiness: a multi-level review. *Journal of Management* 39(1):110–35. Stresses the role of communication to influence cognitive and emotional responses to increase change readiness. Argues that, to influence emotions, the use of pictures (see the following recommendation), color, music, and atmosphere are helpful. Concludes that high-quality change communication can increase readiness and that poor communication can damage the change process.

Sibbet, D. 2013. *Visual leaders: New tools for visioning, management, and organizational change.* Hoboken, NJ: John Wiley & Sons. Introduces an innovative range of visual tools for improving corporate communications and visual IQ. Demonstrates how visualization can engage, inspire, and contribute to thinking. Argues that these tools are particularly useful in driving organizational change. Describes with case studies (the GM Saturn project; the quality improvement program at HealthEast) a "storymapping" approach for anticipating, managing, and communicating the stages of the change process.

Roundup

Reflections for the Practicing Change Manager

- In what ways does your personal use of language reinforce power and gender differences in your organization? What effect do you think this has in terms of how your change messages are received? What modifications to your approach would help you to communicate change more effectively?

- Do you see yourself as a reporter of change information? Or are you a sense-maker, helping staff to understand change actions and seeking input from them?

- To what extent do you focus on getting the word out, rather than seeking staff buy-in? Do you tend to use the same communication methods, or do you adopt different approaches depending upon the type of change? Do you "spray and pray" information or "underscore and explore"?

- Are you more comfortable using "rich" communication media (face to face), or "leaner" media (email)? Do you use different forms of communication depending on the type or stage of change? With which communication media have you had the most success, and why?

- Does your organization have a strategy for using social media? If so, how would you assess the effectiveness of this approach? What recommendations would you make to strengthen the benefits of using social media tools? If not, how would you advise your organization in developing a social media strategy, balancing the benefits and risks?

Here is a short summary of the key points that we would like you to take from this chapter, in relation to each of the learning outcomes:

LO 7.1 * *Identify key elements in the change communication process.*
We emphasized the argument that communication is not a "soft" topic, but one which has a direct impact on organizational effectiveness and financial performance. We introduced a well-known model of the change communication process—a process for exchanging meaning as well as transmitting information. A transmitter codes a message, which is transmitted through a chosen channel to a receiver, who then decodes that message and, depending on the channel, provides feedback. A number of factors can interfere with this apparently simple process: perceptual filters, noise, and the wider organizational context in which communication takes place. The organization's past history of change is important, as this can influence responses to current change proposals.

LO 7.2 * *Understand how gender, power, and emotion can affect change communication processes.*
The use of language, gender and power differences, and emotional responses can all have an effect on the success of the communication process. Men and women tend to communicate in different ways. Women tend to emphasize doubts and uncertainties, and men tend to display confidence and minimize concerns. Women tend to ask more questions, which men can mistakenly interpret as a comparative lack of knowledge. Power differences are also a barrier to effective communication as the powerful may not wish to disclose information that could weaken their power, and the less powerful

may not disclose information that could be damaging to them. Change managers must be alert to the significance of emotional responses to change proposals. We identified a number of strategies for strengthening emotional commitment to change.

LO 7.3　*　Understand the power of language in influencing responses to change.*
We explored the proposition that the management of change involves the management of conversations. For the change manager, even informal conversations are powerful tools for exchanging meaning and influencing perceptions of change proposals, as well as ways of assessing responses. Choice of language in such conversations is therefore critical. That language may need to reflect the stage of the change process; we discussed different conversations for initiating, understanding, performing, and finally closing change initiatives. There is clearly a need for coherence and for shared understanding to avoid confusion. It is also appropriate, we argued, to align choice of language and imagery with the type of change that is proposed, once again in the interests of avoiding "mixed signals."

LO 7.4　*　Explain and assess appropriate strategies for communicating change.*
We addressed a number of key practical questions:

Is it possible to communicate too much? Probably not, as long as information overload is avoided and the communication process is two-way, capturing and exploring concerns and ideas as well as transmitting information.

Is it more important to get the word out, or to get buy-in? Both are important; but without buy-in, the chances of change failure are increased.

Which strategies are more effective than others? A communication strategy of "underscore and explore," which involves a genuine dialogue with those involved, is the most effective approach. Two strategies in particular, "spray and pray" and "withhold and uphold," are likely to be less effective because the communication is one-way, and the staff who are going to be affected have no opportunity to comment or discuss.

Who should be responsible for communicating the change? The obvious answer, the chief executive, may not always be the correct answer. This indeed may not be the right question, which is concerned with how to manage the conversation between those who lead the change and those who will have to implement it. The role of opinion leaders in the organization may be key, whether these are senior staff or first-line supervisors, or dedicated transition teams.

LO 7.5　*　Understand how successful communication processes vary with the type and stage of organizational change.*
Communication should be tailored to the *type* of change. Widespread face-to-face communication is effective with developmental changes. However, task-focused transitions and post-crisis turnarounds may need to be driven with formal top-down communication. Charismatic transformations also require top-down communication, but with a more personalized approach, allowing dialogue. The "communication escalator" also suggests that the degree of employee involvement, and the range of communication media used, should reflect the degree of change: significant change calls for a wider range of communication and a high degree of staff involvement.

Communication and leadership style should also be tailored to the *stage* of the change process. At the planning stage, a combination of analytical and inspirational styles. At the enabling stage, a combination of analytical and supportive styles. At the launch stage, a combination of analytical and commanding styles. At the catalyzing stage, inspirational and supportive styles. At the maintenance stage, inspirational and supportive styles. One change manager may not have all the skills and the behavioral flexibility required, reinforcing the importance of building a capable change team.

LO 7.6 * *Assess the utility of a range of different change communication channels, including applications of social media.*

Communication media varies in terms of "information richness," which involves handling many items of information simultaneously, rapid feedback, and personal focus. Face-to-face communications are information-rich; reports and flyers are lean. Information-rich media is more appropriate when dealing with complex, nonroutine issues. Lean media is more appropriate for simple routine matters. Social media tools are information-rich, allowing two-way communication across organizational levels, function, and locations, and encouraging information sharing, networking, and collaboration. Social media thus has the potential to transform change communication, and organizations that have experimented with these tools have achieved significant benefits. The use of enterprise-specific networking platforms, over which management has greater control compared to public platforms, may further help to realize the potential of these technologies, while managing the risks.

References   Allen-Greil, D., Edwards, S., Ludden, J., and Johnson, E. 2011. "Social media and organizational change," paper presented at *Museums and the Web 2011 Conference*, Philadelphia, April http://museumsandtheweb.com/mw2011/papers/social_media_and_organizational_change (accessed February 5, 2015).

Baczor, L. 2019. *Employee communication factsheet*. London: Chartered Institute for Personnel and Development.

Bulkeley, W. M. 2004. IBM documents give rare look at sensitive plans on offshoring, *The Wall Street Journal*, January 19, http://www.wsj.com/articles/SB107438649533319800 (accessed March 9, 2015).

Christensen, L. T., and Cornelissen, J. 2011. Bridging corporate and organizational communication: Review, development, and a look to the future. *Management Communication Quarterly* 25(3):383–414.

Clampitt, P. G., DeKoch, R. J., and Cushman, T. 2000. A strategy for communicating about uncertainty. *Academy of Management Executive* 14(4):41–57.

Clayton, S. 2015. Change management meets social media. *Harvard Business Review*, d*igital online article*, November 10.

Daly, J. P. 1995. Explaining changes to employees: The influence of justifications and change outcomes on employees' fairness judgments. *Journal of Applied Behavioral Science* 31(4):415–28.

Dobosz-Bourne, D., and Jankowicz, A. D. 2006. Reframing resistance to change: Experience from General Motors Poland. *International Journal of Human Resource Management* 17(12):2021-34.

Ford, J. D., and Ford, L. W. 1995. The role of conversations in producing intentional change in organizations. *Academy of Management Review 20*(3):541-70.

Fox, S., and Amichai-Hamburger, Y. 2001. The power of emotional appeals in promoting organizational change programs. *Academy of Management Executive* 15(4):84-95.

Galbraith, M. 2018. Don't just tell employees organizational changes are coming—explain why. *Harvard Business Review, digital article*, October 5.

Geigle, S. L., and Bailey, M. R. 2001. When communication fails: An analysis of the influence of communication practices during change," paper presented at Western Academy of Management Conference, Sun Valley, Idaho, April 5-7.

Gifford, J. 2014. *Putting social media to work: Lessons from employers*. London: Chartered Institute for Personnel and Development.

Guaspari, J. 1996. If you want your people to buy-in to change, you have to sell them—yes, sell them. *Across the Board* 33(5):32-36.

Heath, K., Flynn, J., and Holt, M. D. 2014. Women, find your voice. *Harvard Business Review* 92(6):118-21.

Heracleous, L., and Barrett, M. 2001. Organizational change as discourse: Communicative actions and deep structures in the context of information technology implementation. *Academy of Management Journal* 44(4):755-78.

Heracleous, L., and Bartunek, J. 2020. Organization change, failure, deep structures and temporality: Appreciating wonderland. *Human Relations* (in press).

Hudson, S., Moulton, J., and Kim, A. 2018. Lessons from the beauty upstarts. *McKinsey Quarterly* (4):36-37.

Hussey, D. E. 1998. Words, sentences and self delusion. *Strategic Change* 7(8):435-36.

Keller, S., Meaney, M., and Pung, C. 2010. *What successful transformations share.* Chicago and London: McKinsey & Company.

Lachinsky, A. 2006. The Hurd way. *Fortune* 153(7):92-102.

Lengel, R. H., and Daft, R. L. 1988. The selection of communication media as an executive skill. *Academy of Management Executive* 2(3):225-32.

Lewis, L. K. 1999. Disseminating information and soliciting input during planned organizational change: Implementers' targets, sources, and channels for communicating. *Management Communication Quarterly* 13(1):43-75.

Linstead, S., Brewis, J., and Linstead, A. 2005. Gender in change: Gendering change. *Journal of Organizational Change Management* 18(6):542-60.

Ludeman, K., and Erlandson, E. 2004. Coaching the alpha male. *Harvard Business Review* 82(5):58–67.

Mcluhan, M. 1964. *Understanding media: The extensions of man.* New York: McGraw Hill.

Marshak, R. J. 1993. Managing the metaphors of change. *Organizational Dynamics* 22(1):44–56.

Quirke, B. 2008. *Making the connections: Using internal communication to turn strategy into action.* 2nd ed. Aldershot: Gower Publishing.

Rafferty, A. E., Jimmieson, N. L., and Armenakis, A. A. 2013. Change readiness: A multilevel review. *Journal of Management* 39(1):110–35.

Reardon, K. K., and Reardon, K. J. 1999. "All that we can be: Leading the US Army's gender integration effort," *Management Communication Quarterly* 12(4):600–17.

Rick, T. 2015. Top 10 ways social media can facilitate change management. *Meliorate*, https://www.torbenrick.eu/t/r/lnb.

Roberto, M. A., and Levesque, L. C. 2005. The art of making change initiatives stick. *MIT Sloan Management Review* 46(4):53–60.

Shannon, C. E., and Weaver, W. 1949. *The mathematical theory of communication.* Urbana, IL: University of Illinois Press.

Stace, D. A., and Dunphy, D. 2001. *Beyond the boundaries: Leading and re-creating the successful enterprise.* 2nd ed. Sydney: McGraw Hill.

Tannen, D. 1995. The power of talk: Who gets heard and why. *Harvard Business Review* 73(5):138–48.

Towers Watson. 2013. *How the fundamentals have evolved and the best adapt: Change and Communication Report 2013–2014.* New York: Towers Watson.

Valvi, A. C., and Fragkos, K. C. 2013. Crisis communication strategies: A case of British Petroleum. *Industrial and Commercial Training* 45(7):383–91.

Whelan-Berry, K. S., and Somerville, K. A. 2010. Linking change drivers and the organizational change process: A review and synthesis. *Journal of Change Management* 10(2):175–93.

Williams, M. 2007. Building genuine trust through interpersonal emotion management: A threat regulation model of trust and collaboration across boundaries. *Academy of Management Review* 32(2):595–621.

Source of the chapter opening quote: The Philosophy of Andy Warhol, Goodreads, https://www.*goodreads*.com/quotes/tag/change.

Chapter opening silhouette credit: CharlotteRaboff/Shutterstock

Chapter 8

Resistance to Change

Learning Objectives

On completion of this chapter you should be able to:

LO 8.1   Explain the benefits of resistance to change, as well as the disadvantages.

LO 8.2   Understand the causes of resistance to change.

LO 8.3   Identify the symptoms of resistance to change.

LO 8.4   Recognize and diagnose middle-management resistance to change, which could be a blockage or could be highly beneficial.

LO 8.5   Understand and apply different approaches to managing resistance.

"We can't be afraid of change. You may feel very secure in the pond that you are in, but if you never venture out of it, you will never know that there is such a thing as an ocean, a sea. Holding onto something that is good for you now, may be the very reason why you don't have something better."

C. JoyBell C., author and poet

WIIFM, WAMI, and the Dimensions of Resistance

More Adaptive Than You Think

Workers seem to be more adaptive and optimistic about the future than their leaders recognize. The conventional wisdom, of course, is that workers fear that technology will make their jobs obsolete. But our survey revealed that to be a misconception. A majority of the workers felt that advances such as automation and artificial intelligence would have a positive impact on their future. When asked why they had a positive outlook, workers most commonly cited two reasons: the prospect of better wages and the prospect of more interesting and meaningful jobs. Both automation and technology, they felt, heralded opportunity on those fronts—by contributing to the emergence of more-flexible and self-directed forms of work, by creating alternative ways to earn income, and by making it possible to avoid tasks that were "dirty, dangerous, or dull." (Fuller et al., 2019, p. 122)

WIIFM stands for "What's In It For Me?" (or sometimes "What's In It For Them?"). WAMI stands for "What's Against My Interests?" If "it" is an organizational change, and if there is nothing in it for me but frustration and grief, then I will resist. If it is not in my interests, then I will resist. Convince me of the benefits, and persuade me that it is in my interests, then you have my support. Managing resistance to change can be seen as no more complex than that. Is it really so simple?

Resistance might explain the high failure rate of organizational change. Many commentators see resistance to change as a problem to be solved, a barrier to overcome, an enemy to defeat. Resistance stimulates strong emotions, and strong language, and has traditionally been seen in negative terms. For example, Foote (2001) described resistance as "one of the nastiest, most debilitating workplace cancers," claiming that "there isn't a more potent, paradoxical or equal-opportunity killer of progress and good intentions." Maurer (2010, p. 23) observed, "The mere mention of the word unleashes a torrent of negative thoughts—fear, opposition, conflict, hassles, pain, annoyance, anger, suspicion." This kind of language encourages an adversarial approach to resistance, which can make the problem worse. However, those negative views are now widely seen as outdated. Research and experience show that resistance is not always damaging, and it can be constructive.

Change can fail for many other reasons, even when widely supported. Attributing problems to resistance can obscure the ways in which management practices contribute to change implementation problems. We thus have to explore the various dimensions of what is commonly termed *resistance*, and ask whether this term, with its negative connotations, is still a helpful one.

Following this introduction, this chapter has five sections. First, we explore the argument that resistance to change, when seen and managed as a resource rather than as a problem, can often be helpful and beneficial. Second, we will explore the causes of resistance. Causes can include resistance to the substance or *content* of change, and resistance to the way in which changes are implemented, or the change *process*. Third, we then consider the signs or symptoms of resistance, some of which are public and easily recognizable, and some of which are covert and harder to detect. Fourth, we examine the stereotype of middle managers as "change blockers." The evidence suggests that this

TABLE 8.1
Individual Readiness and Stakeholder Analysis—A Reminder

Five Components of Individual Readiness	Five Components of Stakeholder Management
Belief that change is necessary.	Identify all stakeholders.
Belief that change is an appropriate response.	Establish what they expect to gain or lose.
Perceived individual capability to implement.	Check their "track record" on response to change.
Belief that resources will be provided.	Use planned benefits to strengthen support.
Personal evaluation of costs and benefits.	Address concerns by reducing losses.

popular view is often wrong. Middle managers can subvert changes proposed by senior executives when they believe that those proposals are ill-advised, but they then implement more effective initiatives of their own.

Finally, we consider strategies for managing resistance to change, which will be necessary in some settings despite the argument that resistance is beneficial. The concepts of individual readiness for change and stakeholder management were covered in chapter 4, so we will not repeat that discussion here. Table 8.1 provides a brief reminder of those issues.

LO 8.1 Benefits

Resistance Is Necessary

We come now to a most important point. Resistance to change is not only normal but in some ways even desirable. An organization totally devoid of resistance to change would fly apart at the seams. It must be ambivalent about radical technical innovation. It must both seek it out and resist it. Because of commitments to existing technology and to forms of social organization associated with it, management must act against the eager acceptance of new technical ideas, even good ones. Otherwise, the organization would be perpetually and fruitlessly shifting gears. (Schön, 1963, p. 82)

Is resistance to change a "natural" human response? If that were true, then we would never become bored with our jobs or look for promotion and more challenging work. If that were true, then manufacturers, from Apple to Ford, would have problems bringing new products to market. Does resistance to change strengthen with age? If that were true, then we would not see retirees set up new businesses, build "portfolio" or "encore" careers, and develop other new skills and interests. Research by Kunze et al. (2013) shows that resistance to change *decreases* with age. From a survey of employees in 11 countries, exploring the future of work, Fuller et al. (2019) found that employees are more welcoming to change, retraining, and new opportunities than management believes they are. Resistance is a topic shrouded in myths. Another of these myths is that resistance is a problem.

Resistance is not inevitable. As noted earlier, change is unlikely to be challenged if those who are going to be affected believe that they will benefit in some way—if "WIIFT" is clear and positive. Outcomes that can encourage support for change thus include (Kirkpatrick, 2001):

- *Security.* Increased demand for particular skills; stronger organizational competitive position and improved job security
- *Money.* Higher remuneration
- *Authority.* Promotion, power, more discretion in decision-making
- *Status.* Prestige assignments with matching job titles, a bigger office
- *Responsibility.* Increased job scope, visibility
- *Better conditions.* Improved physical environment, new equipment
- *Self-satisfaction.* Greater sense of challenge and achievement
- *Personal contacts.* More chances to meet and work with influential people
- *Less time and effort.* Operational efficiencies

Resistance, when it does occur, is not necessarily damaging. Donald Schön (1963) argued that resistance was not just desirable, but necessary, to prevent the implementation of weak ideas and ineffective proposals. Unity and consensus are often viewed as desirable, while conflict and disagreement are bad. However, in some settings, a divergence of opinions can be constructive if this exposes the dimensions of an argument or the full range of consequences—positive and negative—of a change proposal. We thus need to recognize the value of resistance. For example, Maurer (2010, p. 23) says, "Sometimes we need to hear the resistance in order to know that our plans are doomed to failure."

Jeffrey and Laurie Ford (2009) argue that resistance to change provides valuable feedback on what is being proposed. Resistance is a resource, even if it sounds like complaints and arguments. They suggest that there is no point in blaming resisters. Treated as a threat, they become defensive and uncommunicative, and the resource is no longer available. On the contrary, it is important to understand resistance, which can often be well founded. Resistance is not always irrational or self-serving. Ford and Ford (2009, p. 100) argue, "Even difficult people can provide valuable input when you treat their communication with respect and are willing to reconsider some aspects of the change you're initiating." What to you as the change manager is an annoying complaint, may be a genuine expression of concern from the person who raised it. Resisters believe that they are being helpful and constructive, while you believe that they are being negative and disruptive.

Pragmatic Resistance

McCabe et al. (2019) studied a badly managed change in which "pragmatic resistance" benefitted the organization. Pragmatic resistance can be defined as the "multiple, informal, unorganized, non-confrontational, unauthorized, pervasive, ongoing, sporadic subversions of official guidelines" (p. 19). This means refusing to do what the changes require, in order to be able to carry out the "real work."

The researchers studied a 100-employee UK manufacturing company. Its American parent organization launched a management initiative: Striving for Standardization (STS). But this was implemented quickly, with unclear aims, inadequate preparation, poor infrastructure, and a lack of coordination. The initiative also came with a lot of jargon, bureaucracy, and documentation, and it was implemented in an autocratic manner without any consultation. Staff saw the STS initiative as "irrational, disorganized and chaotic," and described it as "madness, ridiculous, stupid and a mess." The changes that staff was asked to make were seen as counterproductive, a distraction, and interfered with normal tasks and activities. They felt that UK managers were implementing STS because they had been told to do so, rather than to achieve any particular objective.

As a result, staff members prioritized their real work at the expense of STS requirements. Pragmatic resistance in this case, therefore, was not "anti-work" but "a pragmatic means of getting on with the daily demands of the job" (p. 16); "processes and procedures were ignored, figures fabricated, and image took precedence over substance" (p. 19).

Pragmatic resistance in this case was productive and constructive, opposing unnecessary bureaucracy, allowing staff to get on with the job. The researchers suggest that pragmatic resistance may be more widespread than is often thought. Indeed, pragmatic resistance—or *productive resistance*—may be responsible for rectifying management mistakes more often than for wrecking management plans.

Furthermore, different people interpret change, and therefore respond to change, in different ways, at different times, depending on their current role and past experience (Ford et al., 2002). We may resist your current proposals because your previous initiative did not work. We may find some parts of your proposals exciting and welcome, while being horrified by some of your other change ideas.

Ford and Ford (2009) identify five ways in which resistance can be used productively:

1. *Encourage dialogue.* Keep the conversation alive—even with complaints—to increase awareness of the change ideas and allow those affected to think through the implications.

2. *Clarify the purpose.* Ensure those affected understand why their roles have to change.

3. *Consider new possibilities.* Assess and, if appropriate, accept the ideas of those who are resisting; the most outspoken are often closest to the operations affected, and they care about getting it right.

4. *Listen to the voices.* Encourage participation and engagement; people want to be heard, and noting concerns can generate novel and valuable options.

5. *Deal with the past.* Current responses to change can be based on previous failures, in which today's managers were not involved; it may be necessary to resolve any "leftover" issues before going ahead with new plans.

For some change managers, adopting a "welcoming" approach to resistance to change may sound unrealistic and personally challenging. However, Todd Jick and Maury Peiperl (2010) suggest that change managers should "rethink" the concept of resistance, recognizing this as a natural part of the process of adapting to change, and thus as a potential source of energy and feedback. Maurer (2010) argues that resistance can be used to build support for change. Treating resisters with respect strengthens relationships and improves the chances of success. He also advises the change manager to relax, to resist the temptation to "push back" when attacked, to learn from the resistance, to look for common ground. Maurer (2010) also accepts that there are situations where focusing attention on dissent can be counterproductive. This can occur, for example, where challenges to the change proposals are not well informed or where change is necessary for organizational survival.

Find on *YouTube*, "Learn with Rick Maurer: An elaboration on resistance to change" (2018, 2:10 minutes).

For the benefits to be gained, resistance must be active. But resistance can sometimes be passive and involve silence and withholding cooperation and information. Encouraging complaints and challenges may sound perverse, but by encouraging the dialogue, active resistance can be stimulated, and the feedback and ideas can then be used constructively.

This section has focused on the positive dimensions of resistance. We also have to recognize the damage that resistance can cause, to an organization, its members, and sometimes even to those who are resisting; job security, for example, may be jeopardized by a failure to introduce new systems, procedures, practices, and technology. It is important, therefore, to adopt a balanced perspective on this topic, recognizing the negative as well as the positive implications.

LO 8.2 Causes

Resistance can have seriously damaging organizational and individual consequences, leading to reduced performance and competitiveness, failure to acquire new capabilities, and job loss. Why then do people resist change? There are probably as many answers to that question as there are members of organizations faced with change. Broadly, the reasons fall into three categories concerning the *content* or substance of the change, the *process* through which change is implemented, and the *uncertainty* that change can generate (Hughes, 2010). We will explore in this section the common causes of resistance. Be aware that this is not an exhaustive list. It is important, however, for the change manager to diagnose the cause—or causes—of resistance before taking action.

Innate Dislike of Change

This is the starting point for many explanations of resistance: some of us just do not like change. It is common to hear the complaint that the main barrier that managers face in introducing change is that people dislike change and will resist it. We have already argued, however, that this view is oversimplified and doesn't explain why people sometimes welcome and even seek change. It is not wise to assume that a dislike of change is necessarily an innate human characteristic that we all share. As individuals, we vary in our approach or "disposition" to change. Some of us prefer routine, become tense and anxious when confronted with change, do not like to change our plans, and are more rigid in our thinking. Those who have high dispositional resistance toward change are therefore less likely to accept change in general and are more likely to resist when change is imposed. But some of us dislike routine, are animated by new ideas and plans, and are comfortable with changing our minds when presented with fresh information.

Although our individual disposition toward change may be a relatively stable personality trait, context is also important. Oreg (2003; 2006), for example, argues that trust in management and having the right amount of information can positively influence dispositions toward change. Information overload, however, can reinforce negative perceptions and strengthen resistance. Another significant feature of the context concerns the substance or content of the changes. You may find some ideas attractive, even if you have high dispositional resistance to change in general. We therefore cannot automatically predict your reaction to the next change based on your response to current proposals.

For most of us, therefore, our responses are more likely to depend on the organizational context and the characteristics of the proposed changes than on our personality. If correct,

Find on *YouTube*, "An affect-based model of recipients' responses" by Shaul Oreg, Jean Bartunek, Gayoung Lee, and Boram Do (2018, 3:21 minutes).

this conclusion has profound practical implications for the change manager. We cannot manage your personality. We can, however, change our proposals, and we can manage or adjust aspects of the organizational context. The change manager has to accept, however, that some individuals, in some contexts, may have extremely high dispositional resistance to change, which cannot easily be altered.

Low Tolerance of Uncertainty

Do you enjoy being taken by surprise? You look forward to the "mystery tour," destination unknown. Or do you need to know precisely what will happen next? You want to know all the journey details in advance. There are individual differences in our tolerance of uncertainty and ambiguity. If you are not confident that you have the skills and capabilities that the proposed changes will demand, then the uncertainty will be magnified. Uncertainty can of course be reduced, and support strengthened, by making clear the strategic intent of the change and the actions that are expected of those involved. The key point here is that lack of support for change may not be due to overt resistance, or apathy, but to uncertainty and ambiguity, based on lack of information—a lack that can be remedied.

This Is Not in My Interests

We noted earlier that resistance can be based on the perception that change will work against the interests of those who will be affected. The term *interests* can cover a range of factors: authority, status, rewards (including remuneration), opportunities to apply expertise, membership of friendship networks, autonomy, and security. People find it easier to support changes when their interests are not threatened and may resist when they perceive that their interests will be damaged.

The key term here is *perception*. Seen from a different standpoint (long-term job security, for example), proposed changes may support the interests of those involved, whose focus on short-term implications (loss of currently valued skills, for example) may take priority. It is the perceptions of those who are involved that determine their responses to change, and not the perceptions of others. Perceptions are difficult to manage and to change, but the quality and volume of available information, and the roles of opinion leaders and networks, can be significant in this regard.

Entrepreneurs Also Resist Change

As discussed in chapter 3, market feedback in the early stages of a start-up organization sometimes requires a "pivot"—a change of strategy, but not of vision, based on new knowledge of the business, its products and services, and its customers. Ries (2019) identifies three reasons why entrepreneurs may resist such pivotal changes:

1. Over-reliance on "vanity measures," which paint a positive picture, rather than on metrics that offer deeper insights into the sustainability of the business.

2. Focusing on early results, which are often ambiguous, and which do not give clear evidence that the business is failing, thus discouraging the major change that a pivot involves.

3. An unwillingness to acknowledge failure, by admitting that the business concept will have to be abandoned before it has had time to prove itself; a pivot itself may be seen as an admission of failure.

Find on *YouTube*, "Erik Ries explains The Pivot" (2012, 3:35 minutes).

Attachment to Organizational Culture and Identity

The "image" of the organization as a cultural system is a popular one. A cultural system includes beliefs, values, artefacts, and beliefs concerning "the way we do things around here." Resistance to change can thus be influenced by the degree of attachment to the existing culture. Reger et al. (1994, pp. 33–34) argue that members of an organization interpret change proposals through their existing mental models:

> A particularly powerful mental model is the set of beliefs members hold about the organization's identity. Identity beliefs are critical to consider when implementing fundamental change because organizational identity is what individuals believe is central, distinctive, and enduring about their organization. These beliefs are especially resistant to change because they are embedded within members' most basic assumptions about the organization's character.

Reger et al. (1994) also argue that two mental barriers can undermine the acceptance of change initiatives that are seen as inconsistent with the current organizational identity. First, passive resistance (apathy, anxiety) can occur when the meaning and purpose of the change have not been made clear. Second, active resistance can be triggered when change is seen to be in direct conflict with key aspects of the organization's identity. The attachment to an organization's culture and identity can be even greater where that attachment involves an individuals' sense of self and self-esteem. That is, there is a certain "psychological ownership" of elements of the current state that are seen as threatened by a proposed change (Cocieru et al., 2019).

Change managers cannot assume that other members of the organization share their mental models concerning the need for change. Strong resistance may therefore be triggered by change proposals that are perceived as threatening basic assumptions. One strategy for the change manager, therefore, is to avoid changes that carry such threats. A second approach concerns presenting proposals in a way that minimizes challenges to the current order. Third, it may be necessary to develop an overwhelmingly compelling case for fundamental culture change, if threats to current assumptions cannot be minimized or avoided.

Perceived Breach of Psychological Contract

Our understanding of the nature of the reciprocal relationship that we have with an employer has been called the "psychological contract" (Coyle-Shapiro and Shore, 2007; Woodrow and Guest, 2020). A breach of this contract occurs when employees believe that the employer is no longer honoring its side of the deal. The psychological contract is defined partly by a formal agreement (job description, terms and conditions, performance appraisal) and also in part by informal social and psychological dimensions. The informal aspects are not put into writing. These concern expectations concerning organizational values, trust, loyalty, and recognition—features that can have just as significant an effect on employee perceptions as formal written terms. Perceived breaches of the psychological contract can thus lower performance and reduce adaptability to change (McDermott et al., 2013).

Research has explored relationships between psychological contract and responses to change. From their study in a textiles company in Scotland, Pate et al. (2000) found a link between perceived breaches of psychological contracts and resistance to strategic and organizational change. They conclude, "When organizations fail to respect employee interests, the low-trust relationships and levels of cynicism that invariably result severely constrain the potential for effective strategic change" (p. 481). Sjoerd van den Heuvel and René Schalk (2009, p. 283), in a study of Dutch organizations, conclude, "The more the organization had fulfilled its promises in the employee's perception, the less the employee resisted organizational change. By maintaining good psychological contracts with employees, organizations can build trust, which could prevent resistance to change."

Lack of Conviction That Change Is Necessary

The work of the change manager is more straightforward if there is widespread belief across the organization that change is needed. However, what seems obvious to some ("We have to change") is not necessarily viewed in the same way by others ("What's the problem?"). There are many reasons for complacency: a past track record of success, the absence of a visible crisis, inconsistent top-management comments. We react negatively to change when we feel that there is no need for it.

Lack of Clarity as to What Is Expected

Sometimes proposed changes, and particularly strategic changes, are not accompanied by clear information about the implications for those who will be affected. How will my role change? What new knowledge, skills, and behaviors will be required? Where questions such as those are not answered, there is a heightened probability of resistance and lack of support from those who feel that they have not been adequately informed. In other words, "A brilliant business strategy is of little use unless people understand it well enough to apply it" (Gadiesh and Gilbert, 2001, p. 74). For the change manager, the key point is that resistance may not be due to opposition to the changes that have been proposed. The absence of support may instead be due to a lack of clear understanding of what will be involved for those who are going to be affected.

Belief That the Proposed Changes Are Inappropriate

Those affected by a proposed change are likely to form a view that it is either an appropriate response to current issues ("We need to do this") or a bad idea ("Whose crazy plan is this?"; "It's a fad"). This view is likely to influence readiness for change. As change advocate and manager, it is easy to see those who support the change as astute and to criticize those who do not as blinkered. The latter are then categorized as "resistant to change." However, this is not necessarily an accurate label, because resistance to *this* change does not necessarily mean resistance to *all* change. We should also consider that, in some cases, the resisters may be right; the changes may have been poorly thought through and inadequately planned. This is another situation where resistance is valuable.

Organizational Change and Insider Threats

Searle and Rice (2018) have been exploring the effect of organizational change on counterproductive work behavior (CWB). CWB can be minor: time wasting, holding back information. But CWB can also be extremely damaging: destroying systems, removing confidential documents, passing information to malicious others, "playing dumb." Can this behavior be predicted and avoided?

(Continued)

Searle and Rice studied a "security critical" UK organization that was undergoing continual and significant physical and cultural changes. Some staff were engaged through these changes, but others became disengaged and behaved in deviant ways. As well as conducting a workforce survey, the researchers interviewed senior and middle managers, staff, and stakeholders who had been involved with insider threats. They found that the changes had four characteristics, which had reduced trust in management, triggered cynicism and feelings of injustice, and encouraged CWB:

1. The changes created an unpredictable working environment, which was distracting.

2. There was inadequate communication—incomplete, inaccurate, or untimely.

3. Leadership at all levels was seen to be inconsistent.

4. The change processes were seen as poor or unfair, and this was felt most severely by those who lost power and influence.

The researchers identified four types of CWB perpetrators:

• *Omitters*. Break rules unintentionally without realizing the implications of their actions.

• *Slippers*. Occasionally commit CWB—removing documents, being rude to others.

• *Retaliators*. Angry individuals who cause deliberate harm through small acts, as either *passive withdrawers*, reducing effort, cooperation, and attention, or *active revengers*, deliberately sabotaging organization systems.

• *Serial transgressors*. Disengaged individuals who routinely commit a range of CWB, undermining management and increasing security risks.

Searle and Rice conclude that organizations can develop resilience and reduce the chance of CWB during change by:

• making sure that HR processes are fair and consistent

• encouraging the reporting of CWB as part of the organization's culture and values

• communicating change initiatives regularly, consistently, and transparently

• assessing the vulnerability of individuals and teams affected by change

• having leaders act as role models, demonstrating acceptable behaviors, such as concern for others

Change can also be seen as inappropriate due to fundamental differences in "vision," which is achieved through the organization's strategy. Change, as a key component in the enactment of strategy, can thus expose widely divergent views of how to achieve that vision.

Perception That the Timing Is Wrong

The change may be welcome, but the timing may be seen as wrong; "yes, but not now." This may be due to change fatigue (see next section "Too Much Change"). Or it may be that, if the change were to be implemented now, it would have a negative impact on, say, customers or suppliers or employees or joint venture partners. Change the timing, and those undesirable outcomes would be avoided.

Too Much Change

Too much change can of course induce "initiative fatigue," "initiative overload," and burnout, especially when new initiatives are launched before the last changes have been fully embedded. Those suffering from initiative fatigue are likely to feel overworked and under pressure and are unlikely to welcome further change, regardless of how desirable it may seem.

Does Your Organization Have an Acceleration Culture?

If you answer "yes" to five or more of these questions, you may be caught in the acceleration trap:

- Are activities started too quickly?

- Is it hard to get the most important things done because too many other activities diffuse focus?

- Is ending activities considered a sign of weakness?

- Are projects carried out pro forma because people fear ending them publicly?

- Is there a tendency to continually drive the organization to the limits of its capacity?

- Is it impossible for employees to see the light at the end of the tunnel?

- Does the company value attendance at work and meetings more than goal achievement?

- Does it value visibly hard effort over tangible results?

- Are employees made to feel guilty if they leave work early?

- Do employees talk a lot about how big their workload is?

- Is "busyness" valued?

- Are managers expected to act as role models by being involved in multiple projects?

- Is "no" a taboo word, even for people who have already taken on too many projects?

- Is there an expectation in the organization that people must respond to emails within minutes?

- Do countless people routinely get copied on emails because employees are trying to protect themselves?

- In their free time, do employees keep their cell phones or messaging devices on because they feel they always need to be reachable?

(From Bruch and Menges, 2010, p.85)

Heike Bruch and Joche Menges (2010) argue that intense market pressures have increased the number and pace of change initiatives, which becomes "the new normal." This can lead an organization, they claim, into "the acceleration trap"; the pressure is unrelenting, staff are demotivated, focus is scattered, and customers become confused. They identify three damaging patterns.

Overloading.	Staff are asked to do too much and have neither the time nor the resources to do it.
Multiloading.	Staff are asked to cover too many different kinds of activities, reducing the focus on what they do best.
Perpetual loading.	The organization is operating close to capacity, denying staff any chance to escape or to "recharge": "When is the economizing going to come to an end?"

Organizations caught in this acceleration trap are thus likely to encounter more resistance to further change than organizations that have avoided or escaped from this trap. Escape strategies include halting the less important work, clarifying strategy, and having a system for prioritizing projects. At one company, the chief executive cut the number of top-priority goals that managers set from ten, down to a maximum of three "must-win battles," to focus attention and energy.

Find on *YouTube*, "Acceleration trap: Myths vs reality of speed" (by Heike Bruch) (2016, 19:34 minutes).

Yong-Yeon Ji et al. (2014) support this argument. From their study of 4,900 U.S. organizations in 18 industries, they conclude that unstable employment reduces organizational performance. However, they also found that very low instability could damage competitiveness; stable organizations are rigid and inflexible. They advise a "slow and steady" response to external conditions, rather than acting too quickly and aggressively.

The Cumulative Effects of Other Life Changes

Readiness for change at work is affected by what else is going on in an individual's life. Measures of stress, for example, typically include elements from a range of aspects of one's life, and not just those associated with employment. As a result, people may resist organizational change in the belief that this will add to the burden of pressures that they are already experiencing.

Perceived Ethical Conflict

Sandy Piderit (2000) argues that resistance is multidimensional and can often be motivated by a desire to act ethically. Resistance to change may thus be based on positive intentions, designed to protect the interests of the organization and its employees. The belief that some individuals or groups will be disadvantaged or unreasonably pressured by proposed changes could lead to resistance. Piderit (2000) also notes, however, that resistance in these situations is likely to be covert if perceived threats to job security and promotion discourage open expressions of concern.

The Legacy of Past Changes

Past experience is one predictor of responses to current change proposals. As our experiences shape expectations of the future, resistance may be grounded in previous bad experiences of change, while support may be strengthened by past successes. From a sense-making perspective (see chapter 9), we learn "how change works in this organization" and use that understanding as a lens through which further change initiatives are assessed. The change manager can thus be the fortunate beneficiary, or the unfortunate victim, of sense-making experiences in which they played no part and of which they may be unaware. The impact on responses to current change proposals may be more intense where the same organization, managers, and staff are involved. Sense-making based on personal past experience is more credible, and more powerful, than the reassurances of today's change managers.

Where past experience of change has been bad, cynicism and resistance may be default responses to fresh initiatives. Stensaker et al. (2002, p. 304) note that BOHICA ("Bend Over, Here It Comes Again") is a response based on learning from experience. Cynicism can be particularly difficult to deal with because it is usually accompanied by strong emotions such as anger, resentment, and disillusionment.

Managing Change, Managing Memories

1. Begin change initiatives with a systematic inquiry into organizational members' memories of past changes.
2. Do not tell people to leave their past behind. That is not going to happen. The power and credibility of past experiences cannot be erased to order. Attempts to suppress those experiences may mean that they "go underground," but they will remain influential.

3. If past experiences are impediments to change, their influence will only be challenged if those involved are directly and fully engaged with current proposals, in ways that enable them to learn that the change experience this time can be different—and positive.

Based on Geigle (1998).

Disagreement with How the Change Is Managed

The idea that resistance to change—that is, to the *substance* of change—is a natural human response, diverts attention away from the nature of the change management *process*. "Overcoming natural resistance to change," in some situations, may actually involve "overcoming natural resistance to poor management," or "highlighting change management mistakes."

In other words, labelling behavior as "resistance to change" may be an example of the fundamental attribution error—blaming individuals while overlooking the context (Ross, 1977). If those who are managing change can attribute unsatisfactory outcomes to the behavior (resistance) of others, the spotlight may not then fall on inadequate change management practices. This "blame game" can also work in the opposite direction, with organization members attributing change failures to management faults, rather than to their own behavior.

It is easy to understand how a change manager can be attracted to the proposition that the lack of success of a change program was due to resistance. This shifts attention away from management capabilities and practices and onto the change recipients. The popular notion that people have a natural resistance to change also makes this a plausible explanation. As we argued earlier, resistance may be a natural response to change that has not been adequately considered and planned. If such resistance prompts a review, then it will have been valuable. Mark Hughes (2010) argues that the term *resistance* has negative connotations and is thus misleading and inappropriate. He suggests that it should now be "retired" in favor of "employee responses" to change, recognizing the broad spectrum of potential reactions—positive, neutral, negative—to organizational change initiatives.

LO 8.3 Symptoms

Despite assertions to the contrary, people aren't against change—they are against royal edicts.
(Hamel and Zanini, 2014, p. 2)

How can resistance to change be detected? The answer to this question is not as straightforward as it might seem, because the symptoms—the signs and clues—can be difficult to detect and to interpret. For example, resistance can be overt and visible, but it can also be covert and hidden. Open criticism and heated debate are easier to detect than

TABLE 8.2
Active and Passive Resistance

Symptoms of Active Resistance	Symptoms of Passive Resistance
Being critical, finding fault, ridiculing, arguing	Agreeing in person but not following through
Appealing to fear, starting rumors	Failing to implement change
Using facts selectively, distorting facts	Procrastinating, dragging one's feet
Blaming, accusing, intimidating, threatening	Feigning ignorance
Manipulating, sabotaging	Withholding information, suggestions, support
Blocking, undermining	Standing by and allowing change to fail

based on Hultman (1995)

whispered private conversations. Given the potential benefits of challenges to change proposals, overt resistance may be of more value to the organization, to the change manager, and ultimately to the change process. Resistance is also three-dimensional, with emotional, cognitive, and behavioral components (Oreg, 2003). In short, the change manager has to be sensitive to how people *feel* about change, how they *think* about it, and what they intend to *do* about it (see the box "Merger in Adland").

Kenneth Hultman (1995) draws a useful distinction between active and passive resistance. Table 8.2 identifies typical active and passive resistance behaviors. This illustrates the distinction, but these lists are not comprehensive, and the various symptoms are not necessarily mutually exclusive (ridiculing, and being critical, for example). Nevertheless, the change manager must be alert to the various ways in which resistance to change can be demonstrated. Hultman also reminds us that identifying the symptoms does not explain why people are resisting change and that it is important to be clear about symptoms and causes (as in this chapter) and not to confuse one with the other.

Merger in Adland: Symptoms of Resistance?

When the Australian advertising agencies Mojo and MDA merged, they decided to locate all staff in the same building. However, as an interim step, all the creative staff (copywriters, art directors, production) moved into the Mojo offices and management ("the suits") went to the MDA offices.

One of the Mojo people required to move was the finance director, Mike Thorley. Mike was one of the original Mojo employees and had come to think of himself more as a partner in the business than as an employee. However, he was quickly disabused of this notion when, with all the other Mojo employees, he was given no warning of the merger. He reacted with shock and anger. To add insult to injury, he

had to move to the MDA offices—which felt like banishment—where he would report to MDA's finance director, who was now in charge of finance for the merged organization.

The Mojo culture was much less formal than that of MDA. Mojo staff would often have a few drinks together after work, sitting around an old white bench in the office. In an attempt to make Thorley and his Mojo colleagues feel at home, a modern black laminate bar was installed in the MDA offices. One morning, Mike Thorley arrived at work with a chainsaw and cut the bar in two.

Based on Coombs (1990)

LO 8.4   Managers as Resisters

Most discussions of resistance present managers as advocates of change and cast employees in the role of resisters. However, resistance is not monopolized by "the managed." Managers can also resist change, for all the reasons identified earlier, and therefore, they are not always passionate advocates of change. In fact, the most senior managers in an organization are often those who, because of their position, are most able to prevent a change occurring if they believe it is unnecessary. CEOs and other senior managers may be sincerely and deeply committed to the organization's existing strategy, believing it to be "the right thing to do." However, sincere and deeply committed does not always mean correct in terms of their "reading" of how competitive conditions are evolving (see the box "Even Very Smart, Very Senior People Sometimes Get It Wrong").

Even Very Smart, Very Senior People Sometimes Get It Wrong

Joe Kennedy, chief executive of Pandora, was quoted in 2012 as saying, "We haven't seen evidence of Spotify or any other player affecting the growth that we're seeking—services such as Spotify are fundamentally complementary to Pandora."

Tom Anderson, founder of MySpace, said in 2008, "I wouldn't single out Facebook as a concern because we've got different local competitors around the world."

Steve Ballmer, chief executive of Microsoft, said, in 2005, "Google's not a real company. It's a house of cards."

Source: Corporate Venture Capital. 2019. Foot in mouth: 59 quotes from big corporate execs who laughed off disruption when it hit. *CB Insights*, November 12, https://cbinsights.com/research/big-company-ceos-execs-disruption-quotes.

Managers can be considered collectively, as a group, but sometimes differences within management can be significant. Changes proposed by one department or division may be opposed by another. Changes directed by top management may not be welcomed by middle managers. In other words, managers, at least as much as any other category of employee, are likely to have within their ranks a range of opinions concerning proposed changes. Even where there is no question as to the dedication of managers to the long-term interests of the organization, it is normal to find different views as to which initiatives or changes are most appropriate.

The stance of middle managers in particular can have a critical effect on the outcome of change initiatives because middle managers are often responsible for implementation. It is not unusual for this role to involve tensions for middle managers who are likely to be both recipients of change initiatives from senior management, as well as implementers.

Middle managers have long been stereotyped as change blockers. However, research has consistently painted a different picture. The positive contributions of middle management to innovation and change are now widely recognized, partly due to the influential work of Wooldridge and Floyd (1990; Wooldridge et al., 2008). They argue that middle management involvement in shaping strategy leads to better decisions, higher degrees of consensus, improved implementation, and better organizational performance. They also emphasize the coordinating, mediating, interpreting, and negotiating roles of middle managers, arguing that it is the pattern of influence of middle managers that affects performance. The mediating role, combining access to top management with knowledge of frontline operational capabilities, gives middle management a valuable perspective, where appropriate acting as a counter to the strategic view of the top executive team. (See the box "Change: Does It Matter Who Initiates and Who Executes?")

Change: Does It Matter Who Initiates and Who Executes?

Heyden et al. (2017) surveyed 1,795 respondents in 468 organizations undergoing change. They found that top-down change was not met with above-average employee support, regardless of who implemented the change—top or middle managers. However, support for change was higher when it was initiated by middle managers and executed by either top or middle managers. The strongest support for change occurred when middle managers initiated and top managers executed—although this situation was rare. Why should this be the case? Middle managers are closer to frontline employees and have a better understanding of operations, so they have an advantage in initiating change. Top managers, in contrast, may have a better understanding of context and have power to allocate resources, so they may be more effective in executing change. The traditional assumption is that top managers initiate and middle managers execute—but this may not be the best way to do it.

With regard to blocking change, Inger Boyett and Graeme Currie (2004) report how middle managers in an Irish telecommunications firm subverted the intent of senior management, by designing an alternative strategy that was more profitable. Julia Balogun (2008) argues that, even when middle managers are "change recipients," the way in which directives are interpreted and implemented may differ from—and significantly improve upon—senior management intentions. From their study of change in the Irish health service, Edel Conway and Kathy Monks (2011) describe how ambivalent middle managers who resisted top-down directives played a vital role by championing and implementing their own initiatives. Those initiatives assisted in dismantling outdated structures and processes and provided solutions to the problems that those directives had identified in the first place. Aoife McDermott et al. (2013) show how middle managers and other change recipients often tailor, add to, and adapt top-down change directives so that they will work in particular local contexts.

Social Gaming

Cramer et al. (2019) explain how "social games in the cabinet room" block transformational change in public-sector organizations, such that government initiatives fail to deliver the promised outcomes. This also happens in private-sector corporate boards. Contrary to the assumptions of many senior leaders, strategy processes are not an intellectual enterprise based on the dispassionate analysis of data, trends, and opportunities; "social dynamics playing out in the background are often a major driver of what gets decided" (p. 2). These social games include:

- *Sandbagging.* To maintain my track record and my reputation, I will only approve a plan that I know I can deliver.

- *The short versus the long game.* I need to get results now and move on with my career—someone else will be running this three years from now—or

I will be working here for the next decade, long after you have gone.

- *My way or your problem.* I know this business inside out, so you will just have to take my advice.

- *I am my numbers.* Make sure that targets are achievable—I am going to work just hard enough to hit them.

To counter these games, management should ensure that "noble failures" are not punished, that a number of strategies are under discussion with different teams working on each, that initiatives are limited to those that can realistically be delivered, and that budgeting adapts to changing priorities.

The negative middle-management stereotype thus has to be adjusted in two respects. First, middle managers are likely to attempt to block or undermine senior management directives if they believe that those proposals will not work well. This is a reasonable "self-defense" position because, were those senior management plans to be put in place and then fail, middle management would probably be blamed for mishandling the implementation. Second, where middle managers have better ideas and plans of their own, they are likely to attempt to implement those instead of senior management proposals. Employee resistance is more likely to arise at the point of implementation, by which stage it may be too late. Management resistance, however, is more likely to occur at the conceptualization and planning stage, when options still remain open. We are thus faced with yet more examples of pragmatic or positive resistance, where middle management "change blocking" is not as disruptive as the label implies, but can lead to improved organizational outcomes.

LO 8.5 Managing Resistance

How widespread is the problem of resistance to change? In 2010, the consulting company McKinsey surveyed 1,890 executives who had recent experience of organizational redesign. One-third of those who replied said, "employees actively resisted change or became demoralized," and a quarter said, "leaders resisted, undermined, or changed the plans for reorganization" (Ghislanzoni et al., 2010, p. 6). The problem most frequently cited as harmful in those organizations where redesign had been successful concerned senior managers undermining the change. One explanation is that "redesign that fundamentally changes the way the organization works frequently upsets those who rose to the top in the old system" (Ghislanzoni et al., 2010, p. 7).

Does it matter if some people resist a particular change? Not necessarily. Senge (1990) argues that dispositions toward change vary on a continuum from commitment, through varying degrees of compliance, to noncompliance, and apathy (see table 8.3). From a change management perspective, it is useful to understand the dispositions of those who are going to be affected. It is also important to be aware that dispositions can change, as understanding of the implications develops.

It may be reassuring to have everyone fully committed to an organizational change. Senge argues, however, that this is not necessary. Rather than attempt to persuade everyone to "commit," it can be more useful to analyze the level of support required from each of those individuals and groups who are involved and to direct change management's

TABLE 8.3
The Commitment–Compliance Continuum

Disposition	Response to Change
Commitment	Want change to happen and will work to make it happen Willing to create whatever structures, systems, and frameworks are necessary for it to work
Enrollment	Want the change to happen and will devote time and energy to making it happen within given frameworks Act within the spirit of the framework
Genuine compliance	See the virtue in what is proposed and will do what is asked of them and think proactively about what is needed Act within the letter of the framework
Formal compliance	Can describe the benefits of what is proposed and are not hostile to the changes—they do what they are asked and no more Stick to the letter of the framework
Grudging compliance	Do not accept that there are benefits to what is proposed and do not go along with it, but do enough of what is asked of them not to jeopardize their position Interpret the letter of the framework
Noncompliance	Do not accept that there are benefits and have nothing to lose by opposing the proposition, so will not do what is asked of them Work outside the framework
Apathy	Neither support nor oppose the proposal, just serving time Do not care about the framework

Based on Senge, 1990, pp. 204–205

attention and energies to winning that support. With a critical mass of support in place, the noncompliance or apathy of others may have little or no impact.

Despite what we have said regarding the benefits, and the misleading nature of the label, resistance to change can be self-interested, deliberately disruptive, badly informed—and a problem for the change manager. How can such resistance be managed effectively? Given what we know about the many possible causes of resistance, there is no "one best way" to handle this situation, and it is not possible to "match" causes of resistance with specific solutions. We will therefore explore three approaches to this task, suggesting that these should be seen as complementary rather than as competing and that their use relies on the informed judgement of the change manager in a particular context:

1. *Let nature take its course.* Allowing those who will be affected by change to recognize and to adjust to the implications in their own time.
2. *Attraction strategies.* Utilizing approaches that can overcome or avoid resistance before it develops by finding novel aspects of the changes that recipients find attractive and are drawn to.
3. *Contingency approach.* Choosing and using methods that are appropriate to the context and to those who are involved.

Let Nature Take Its Course

Individual reactions to change typically involve working through a series of natural psychological stages. This progression is known as the coping cycle, and models of this process are often based on the work of Elizabeth Kübler-Ross (1969), who studied human responses to traumatic events such as the death of a close relative. The application of her work to change management is based on the assumption that, for at least some people, major organizational and career changes can also be very traumatic. Under those conditions, resistance to change is predictable. Cynthia Scott and Dennis Jaffe (2006), for example, describe a change coping cycle with four stages:

- *Denial.* Refusal to recognize the situation; "this can't be happening," "it will all blow over." The person is not receptive to new information and refuses to believe he or she needs to behave differently or is prepared to make only minor adjustments.
- *Resistance.* Recognition that the situation is real; the past is mourned; active and passive forms of resistance may appear. This can be seen as a positive stage, as the individual lets go of the past, and becomes confident in his or her ability to deal with the future.
- *Exploration.* Reenergizing and a willingness to explore the possibilities of the new situation.
- *Commitment.* Focusing attention on new courses of action.

This is an "ideal" picture of the coping cycle. There are individual differences in the experience of this cycle. Different people work through these stages at a different pace, some moving more quickly, as others become "stuck." The context can also affect progress, through sharing experiences with others and encountering fresh information. If individual responses conform broadly to this pattern, then one approach to managing resistance is to step back, to monitor what is happening, and to let nature take its necessary course. However, if key individuals become "stuck," say at the resistance stage, then doing nothing may be unwise, and some form of intervention may be helpful. Table 8.4 offers a guide to dealing with different expressions of resistance.

Attraction Strategies

From their work with healthcare professionals in U.S. hospitals, Paul Plsek and Charles Kilo (1999, p. 40) conclude that "Change is not so much about resistance, as it is about creating attraction." What is often described as "resistance," they note, is actually "attraction" to aspects of the current system. The change manager's task is to find new attractors or to effectively use those that already exist. To identify appropriate attractors, change managers must have a good understanding of the issues and concerns that are important to those whose behavior they want to change—and those issues may differ from those of the change manager. Close relationships are therefore important: "Attractors are easier to create when working together in cooperative, positive relationships of trust" (Plsek and Kilo, 1999, p. 42). The focus should lie with system changes and improvements, rather than with changing the behavior of individuals in an existing system (see the box "Find the Attractor"). Questions that can be helpful in identifying the attractors in a particular situation include:

- How will this change benefit individual staff, the team, customers/clients?
- How will current problems and frustrations be addressed?

TABLE 8.4
Individual Resistance and Management Responses

The Person Says . . .	Comment	Your Response . . .
I don't want to. ("the block")	An authentic response, unambiguous, and easy to handle.	Why? What's your concern?
Tell me exactly what you want me to do. ("the rollover")	Ambiguous—may be a genuine request for information or passive resistance: "If you don't tell me, I'm not responsible for the outcomes."	Tell me what you need to know.
I'll get on it first thing next week. ("the stall")	May reflect lack of awareness of urgency or indicate a desire to avoid complying.	Is there anything serious that would prevent you from starting tomorrow?
Wow, what a great deal! ("the reverse")	May be genuine, but resisters will say this to keep you happy with no intention of supporting.	I am pleased that you feel this way. What exactly can I count on you to deliver, and when?
I think it would be better if this were implemented first in X division. ("the sidestep")	Could be correct, but resisters use this to shift the pressure to change onto somebody else.	I understand your concern, but we have other plans for X. What I specifically want you to do is this.
X isn't going to like this. ("the projected threat")	Implies the threat that someone important will not be happy (could be true).	X has been part of this process and is fully supportive *or* I'll be speaking to X about this, but at the moment I'm more interested in your views.
You owe me one. ("the press")	Involves asking to be exempt as reciprocity for a past favor.	I haven't forgotten that, but I need your support right now.
See what you're making me do. ("the guilt trip")	An attempt to deflect attention by focusing on the change manager's actions.	I am sorry that you have a problem, and we can discuss how to help, but it is important for this change to go ahead.
But we've always done it the other way. ("the tradition")	Traditions should only be maintained if they still work; but old ways often feel safer, less threatening.	The other way has served us well for a long time, but things have changed. What could we do to incorporate the best of our traditional approach?

Based on Karp (1996).

- How does this relate to the interests and priorities of staff?
- How will those involved gain recognition for their efforts?
- How will performance be improved?
- How could efficiency gains be used to make further improvements?

Find the Attractor

Physician leader Roger Resar, MD, tells of an office assistant who resisted a change that would offer same-day appointments to patients and reduce the booking of future appointments. The assistant was attracted to the existing scheduling system, chaotic though it was, because she understood it so well.

> Rather than labelling her a "resister," Resar spoke to her about the most appealing and unappealing aspects of her job. One prominent dislike was having to call 30 or more patients to reschedule appointments when the doctor needed to be away. When Resar pointed out that the open access system would virtually eliminate the need for this activity, the assistant became actively attracted to the new idea—the same idea that she was seen as resisting just moments before. The proposed change was now associated with the comfort attractor and the resistance vanished. (Plesk and Kilo, 1999, p. 41)

Martin Lippert, chief executive of the Danish telecommunications company TDC, describes how middle management resistance to the introduction of "lean management" was addressed:

> It was a big change for them. Before, middle managers spent only about 10 or 15 percent of their time on real leadership—performance management, coaching, finding out what's going on in their organization. Instead, almost all of their time was consumed by projects, mostly to fix problems. That's a very inefficient way of working. We needed to reverse those numbers so that managers could spend 80 percent of their time being managers and leaders. Some of the managers were truly unable or unwilling to make the change. But eventually most of them saw that what we were providing was a set of techniques that they could adapt as they needed. In working together with the front line and senior leadership to design the transformation in their teams, the managers gradually came to recognize how the whole system of lean management could help them accomplish more. It took time, of course, but once they did, we saw more involvement from them than ever before. (McKinsey & Company, 2014, p. 157)

As noted previously, resistance to change can be due to employees having a strong attachment to the organization's identity. In this situation, attraction can be provided if the change vision being communicated by organizational leaders is one that assures employees that the proposed changes are consistent with core elements of that identity. From this perspective, in "selling" the vision for change, leaders should "frame change such that it will be perceived as a continuation, reaffirmation, or preservation of who 'we' are as a collective" (Venus et al., 2019, p. 684).

W. Chan Kim and Renée Mauborgne (2003, p. 62) also claim, "Once the beliefs and energies of a critical mass of people are engaged, conversion to a new idea will spread like an epidemic, bringing about fundamental change very quickly." In other words, that critical mass forms a "tipping point," beyond which change can be straightforward and rapid. They further note:

> The theory suggests that such a movement can be unleashed only by agents who make unforgettable and unarguable calls for change, who concentrate their resources on what really matters, who mobilize the commitment of the organization's key players, and who succeed in silencing the most vocal naysayers.

Kim and Mauborgne (2003) illustrate their theory using the experience of Bill Bratton, a well-known American police chief known for his achievements in "turning around" failing or problem forces, such as in Boston and New York. One of the main hurdles to overcome, they argue, is motivational. This concerns establishing the desire to implement change, as well as making clear the need. One of the most powerful strategies that Bratton used to motivate change involved targeting the small number of key influencers in the organization. In the New York Police Department, that meant the city's 76 precinct commanders, who were each responsible for up to 400 staff members. The key influencers are people with power, based on extensive networks inside and outside the organization, and on their influencing skills. Once the key influencers become attracted to the change program, they complete the task of persuading and motivating others, freeing the change manager to focus on other issues.

Attraction strategies suggest, therefore, that resistance can be avoided if the change manager is able to design and present proposals in ways that are appealing to and compelling those who will be involved. We will meet this argument again, in a different form, in chapter 10 (implementing change). One way in which to ensure that change is attractive is to involve those who will be directly affected in deciding what and how to change in the first place.

Contingency Approaches

There is no "one best way" to manage resistance. As suggested in the last section, action to deal with resistance should be based on a diagnosis of the cause or causes; people may resist change for more than one reason. Those resisting a particular change may do so for different reasons; different stakeholders thus have to be managed differently. Allies and supporters need to be "kept on side." Opponents need to be converted or neutralized. These observations point to the need for a contingency approach, with actions tailored to the circumstances and the context.

One of the most widely cited contingency approaches to managing resistance was developed by John Kotter and Leo Schlesinger (2008). Their approach has two dimensions, concerning pace and management strategies. They advise the change manager to decide the optimal pace or speed of the change; how quickly or how slowly should this happen? They suggest moving quickly if there is a crisis affecting performance or survival. They suggest moving slowly where:

- information and commitment from others will be needed to design and implement
- the change manager has less organizational power than those who will resist
- resistance will be intense and extensive

They then identify the six strategies for managing resistance summarized in table 8.5: education, participation, facilitation, negotiation, manipulation, and coercion. Those strategies each have advantages and drawbacks. Education is time consuming—a disadvantage. Coercion can be quick—a key advantage in some contexts. Personal values and social norms suggest that the first three of those strategies will be more common. But in practice, there are times when negotiation, manipulation, and coercion should be considered. The conditions in which each strategy is appropriate are also identified in the last column of table 8.5, and these strategies can be used in combination, if appropriate.

Christensen et al. (2006) also advocate a contingency approach to managing resistance. They argue that the organizational context of change varies on two main dimensions. The

TABLE 8.5

Strategies for Dealing with Resistance to Change

Strategies	Advantages	Disadvantages	Use When Resistance Is Caused By
Education and communication	Increases commitment, reconciles opposing views	Takes time	Misunderstanding and lack of information
Participation and involvement	Reduces fear, uses individual skills	Takes time	Fear of the unknown
Facilitation and support	Increases awareness and understanding	Takes time and can be expensive	Anxiety over personal impact
Negotiation and agreement	Helps to reduce strong resistance	Can be expensive and encourage others to strike deals	Powerful stakeholders whose interests are threatened
Manipulation and co-optation	Quick and inexpensive	Future problems from those who feel they were manipulated	Powerful stakeholders who are difficult to manage
Explicit and implicit coercion	Quick and overpowers resistance	Change agent must have power; risky if people are angered	Deep disagreements and little chance of consensus

Source: Kotter and Schlesinger (2008)

first concerns the extent to which people agree on the outcomes or goals of change. The second concerns agreement on the means, on how to get there. Low agreement and high agreement contexts need to be managed in different ways. Where there is low agreement concerning both goals and means, they argue–along with Kotter and Schlesinger–that coercion, threats, fiat, and negotiation become necessary.

Building Commitment to Change: Make the Process Attractive

Attraction strategies to overcome resistance can focus on the change process as well as the substance of the changes. Rosabeth Moss Kanter (1985, p. 55) suggests how to do this:

- Allow room for participation in the planning of the change.
- Leave choices within the overall decision to change.
- Provide a clear picture of the change, a "vision" with details about the new state.
- Share information about change plans to the fullest extent possible.

- Divide a big change into manageable and familiar steps; let people take a small step first.
- Minimize surprises; give people advance warning about new requirements.
- Allow for digestion of change requests—a chance to become accustomed to the idea of change before making a commitment.
- Repeatedly demonstrate your own commitment to the change.
- Make standards and requirements clear—tell exactly what is expected of people in the change.

(Continued)

- Offer positive reinforcement for competence; let people know they can do it.
- Look for pioneers, innovators, and early successes to serve as models and reward them.
- Help people find or feel compensated for the extra time and energy change required.

- Avoid creating obvious "losers" from the change. (But if there are some, be honest with them—early on.)
- Allow expressions of nostalgia and grief for the past—then create excitement about the future.

When dealing with resistance, the change manager thus has a range of tools and approaches. Give those affected time to come to terms with what is required and the implications. Find ways to avoid resistance by identifying the features that will make change attractive to those who will be involved. Select an appropriate strategy or strategies depending on the cause or causes of the resistance. These three broad sets of approaches are not mutually exclusive, and it may be appropriate to deploy a number of approaches, at the same time, with the same or different individuals and groups.

EXERCISE 8.1

Diagnosing and Acting

LO 8.2

Consider a change in which you were involved and that was seriously affected by resistance.

1. When did you first become aware of resistance?
2. What form did the resistance take?
3. What were your first thoughts (anger, betrayal, confusion, relief)?
4. What made you decide that you had to do something?
5. What actions did you take?
6. What was the impact in (a) the short term and (b) the long term?
7. If you could "rewind the tape," what would you do differently?

EXERCISE 8.2

Jack's Dilemma

LO 8.5

Jack White is the newly appointed general manager of the pet food division of Strickland Corporation. He has completed a strategic review that has convinced him that the division needs to undergo rapid and substantial change in a number of areas, given the recent strategic moves of key competitors.

Although Jack is new, he is familiar enough with the company to know that there will be significant resistance to the changes from a number of quarters. He also suspects that some of this resistance will come from people with the capacity to act in ways that could seriously impede successful change.

Jack reflects on the situation. He believes that it is important to introduce the proposed changes soon, but he also recognizes that if he acts too quickly, he will have virtually no time to have a dialogue with staff about the proposed changes, much less involve them in any significant way.

One option is to act speedily and to make it clear that "consequences" will follow for anyone not cooperating. He certainly has the power to act on such a threat. The risk, Jack knows, is that even if no one shows outright resistance, there is a big difference between not cooperating and acting in a manner that reflects commitment. He knows that he needs the cooperation of key groups of staff and that sometimes "minimum-level compliance" can be as unhelpful as resistance when it comes to implementing change. "But maybe I'm exaggerating this problem," he thinks to himself. "Maybe I should just go ahead with the change. If people don't like it, they can leave. If they stay, they'll come around."

But Jack is not sure. He considers another option. Maybe he should spend more time on building up support at least among key groups of managers and staff, if not more broadly across the organization. "Maybe," he reflects, "the need to change is not quite as immediate as I think. I just know that I'd feel a whole lot better if this consultation could happen quickly."

Your Task

Jack respects your opinion on business matters and has asked you for your views on his situation. What would be your recommendation? What factors should Jack take into account in deciding what course of action to take?

EXERCISE 8.3

Moneyball

LO 8.2

LO 8.3

LO 8.5

The *New York Times* bestseller *Moneyball* (Lewis, 2003) is a book about baseball. It describes how Billy Beane, the general manager of the Oakland Athletics, revolutionized Major League Baseball (MLB) by introducing a new approach (sabermetrics) to assessing the value of a player to a team (see Wolfe et al., 2006). The established approach to assessing player talent favored future potential, but sabermetrics focused on past performance. Also, the established approach focused on the statistics of batting average (BA) and earned run average (ERA). The new approach was based on the argument that different statistics such as on-base percentage and slugging percentage (OSP) were better predictors of a player's performance. Beane introduced sabermetrics, but the underlying concept was not his. The writer Bill James had argued (and been ignored) for three decades that research attested to its superiority as a basis for determining a player's true value to a team.

Beane's application of the new approach was successful, and the Oakland Athletics moved close to the top of the league despite being outspent by most of their competitors. As a result, the team had approaches from many interested businesses and sporting bodies including teams from the NFL and MLB, *Fortune* 500 companies, and Wall Street firms.

However, other MLB teams continued to show a lack of interest in the new approach, and some were openly hostile to it. Why? The MLB was bound in tradition and characterized by deep respect for convention and precedent. Sabermetrics challenged treasured orthodoxies for two reasons. First, it questioned the value of established predictors of performance. Second, sabermetrics based decisions on statistics and thus reduced the importance of professional judgment. In other words, sabermetrics sidelined the field managers who had previously enjoyed significant control over talent selection and in-game tactics. Sabermetrics thus threatened the job security of many who had been appointed on the strength of their knowledge of individual characteristics and aspects of the game that were no longer considered to be important.

We can explore how the introduction of sabermetrics affected team management and players in the movie *Moneyball* (2011, director Bennett Miller). Brad Pitt plays Oakland's manager, Billy Beane, who is losing his star players to wealthier clubs. The Athletics' owner Stephen Schott (Bobby Kotick) will not provide more money. How can he build a competitive team with a limited budget? Beane hires an economics graduate, Peter Brand (Jonah Hill). Brand introduces him to James' statistics-based approach to picking talent,

(Continued)

looking at the complementary skills of the players in the team as well as focusing on individual capabilities. Using this method, Beane puts together a team of previously unknown players. However, Bean's senior manager Art Howe (Philip Seymour Hoffman) will not allow Beane to use these recruits and refuses to discuss the matter. The team's talent scouts do not like the new method either. As you watch this movie, consider the following questions:

1. Who is resisting this change and why?
2. What behaviors are used to demonstrate that resistance?
3. What role do emotions play, on both sides of this argument?
4. What tactics and behaviors do Billy Beane and Peter Brand use to overcome resistance to their new approach?
5. What lessons can you take from this experience concerning the nature of resistance and methods for overcoming resistance to change?

Additional Reading

Battilana, J., and Casciaro, T. 2013. The network secrets of great change agents. *Harvard Business Review* 91(7/8):62–68. Explores the importance of the change agent's networks in dealing with resisters and fence-sitters, as well as with those who support the change.

Fuller, J. B., Wallenstein, J. K., Raman, M., and de Chalendar, A. 2019. Your workforce is more adaptable than you think. *Harvard Business Review* 97(3):118–26. Discusses the results of a survey that suggests that management concerns over resistance to new technology in particular are exaggerated and that employees recognize and welcome new opportunities.

Harvey, T. R., and Broyles, E. A. 2010. *Resistance to change: A guide to harnessing its positive power*. Lanham, MD: R&L Education. Develops the view that resistance is natural, positive, and necessary, rather than destructive, offering practical guidance with illustrations.

Maurer, R. 2010. *Beyond the walls of resistance*, 2nd ed. Austin, TX: Bard Books. An easy-to-read "no nonsense" practical guide to resistance, its benefits, its causes, and its management.

Roundup

Reflections for the Practicing Manager

- What symptoms of resistance to change have you observed? Have you observed both active and passive forms? Have you as a recipient resisted change? Have you experienced resistance while responsible for initiating and managing a change?

- In your experience, what are the most common causes of resistance to change?

- As a change manager, what are the three most difficult forms of resistance that you have to deal with? What approaches do you use?

- When senior managers resist change at the strategic level, they are in a position to cause more damage than employees resisting change at an operational level. Have you worked in an organization where you believe that there was management resistance to change? As a manager, what action would you take to prevent this?

- Which particular approaches to the management of resistance attract you? Why do you make this choice? Do you think those approaches are more

effective, or do your choices relate to your views about how people should be managed?

- From your experience as a change manager, what are the three main pieces of advice that you would give to someone new in this role concerning diagnosing and managing resistance?

Resistance is a multi-faceted topic. The negative label suggests damage, but we have seen how resistance can be constructive, and we have argued that the term itself is thus potentially misleading. Resistance can have a number of different causes, takes several different forms, and reveals itself in a range of symptoms. However, there are several approaches or strategies available for managing resistance effectively, where that becomes necessary and depending on a diagnosis of the situation. In sum, resistance is not the change manager's worst nightmare, as some commentary has suggested.

Here is a short summary of the key points that we would like you to take from this chapter, in relation to each of the learning outcomes:

LO 8.1   * *Explain the benefits of resistance to change, as well as the disadvantages.*

Resistance can threaten organizational performance, competitiveness, and survival, and lead to job loss in some cases. Resistance can also mean a failure to learn new skills and abilities, with long-term implications for individual employability. However, those who resist are those who are going to be affected directly by change and therefore have a good understanding of how it might work. Their feedback can be particularly valuable in identifying whether or not change has been adequately considered and planned. "Pragmatic" or productive resistance can therefore be seen not as damaging, but as helpful and constructive. This may not always happen; there can be many reasons behind displays of resistance. However, the change manager who views resistance positively, and who listens with genuine interest to the concerns and challenges raised, is more likely to implement effective change, while improving relationships with those involved.

LO 8.2   * *Understand the causes of resistance to change.*

There are many potential causes for resistance, and we have only explored a number of the most common in this chapter. Diagnosing cause in a given situation is a key task for the change manager. In making that diagnosis, the change manager must be aware of two issues. First, resistance may be underpinned by several causes, not just one (although there may be one main concern). The management response thus has to take this into consideration. Second, the cause or causes of resistance can change over time, as an initiative develops, as other parallel initiatives are introduced, and as new information is uncovered. The task of diagnosing resistance is thus an ongoing one.

LO 8.3   * *Identify the symptoms of resistance to change.*

Once again, there are many potential symptoms of resistance, which can be active or passive. The passive resistance may be more difficult to detect. Paradoxically, active resisters—those who shout and complain the loudest—may be more valuable. At least the change manager knows what they are thinking and can address that, and they may have genuine concerns that could inform and improve change design, planning, and implementation.

LO 8.4   * *Recognize and diagnose middle-management resistance to change, which could be a blockage or could be highly beneficial.*

We know that managers at all levels can sometimes resist change and that such behavior is not restricted to frontline or operational staff. However, the stereotype of the middle manager as a change blocker is not consistent with the evidence. Middle managers often subvert or block top-leadership directives but only to put in place something more effective.

LO 8.5   * *Understand and apply different approaches to managing resistance.*

We explored a range of resistance management strategies: allow people naturally to adjust, develop "attractors" to avoid or minimize resistance in the first place, and develop a contingency approach depending on the cause or causes of the resistance. As in most management contexts, there is no "one best way," and action has to be based on a diagnosis of the problem.

We have seen how resistance to change can be viewed from a number of different perspectives. How in turn is this phenomenon interpreted by different images of the change manager? The different images perspectives are summarized in table 8.6. Which of these perspectives most closely fits your own view of organizational change, resistance, and change management?

TABLE 8.6
Images of Change Management and Perspectives on Resistance

Image	Perspective on Resistance
Director	Resistance is a sign that not everybody is on board in terms of making the change. Resistance can and must be overcome to move change forward. Change managers need specific skills to ensure that they can deal with resistance.
Navigator	Resistance is expected. It is not necessarily a sign of people being outside their comfort zone, but that there are different interests in the organization and some of these may be undermined by the change. We cannot always overcome resistance, but this should be achieved where possible.
Caretaker	Resistance is possible but likely to be short-lived and ultimately futile. This is because changes will occur in spite of attempts to halt them. At best, resistance might temporarily delay change rather than halt its inevitable impact.
Coach	Resistance needs to be recognized and expected as change takes people out of their comfort zones. Change managers need to work with resistance to show how these actions are not consistent with good teamwork.
Interpreter	Resistance is likely where people do not fully understand what is happening, where the change is taking the organization, and the impact it will have on those involved. Making sense of the change, helping to clarify what it means, and linking individual identity with the process and the expected outcomes of the change will help to address the underlying problems that led to the resistance.
Nurturer	Resistance is irrelevant to whether or not change happens. Changes will occur but not always in predictable ways. Therefore, resisting change will be a matter of guesswork by the resister as change often emerges from a clash of chaotic forces and it is usually not possible to identify, predict, or control the direction of change.

References   Balogun, J. 2008. *When organisations change: A middle management perspective on getting it right*. London: Advanced Institute of Management Research.

Boyett, I., and Currie, G. 2004. Middle managers moulding international strategy: An Irish start-up in Jamaican telecoms. *Long Range Planning* 37(1):51–66.

Bruch, H., and Menges, J. I. 2010. The acceleration trap. *Harvard Business Review* 88(4):80–86.

Christensen, C. M., Marx, M., and Stevenson, H. H. 2006. The tools of cooperation and change. *Harvard Business Review* 84(10):73–80.

Cocieru, O. C., Lyle, M. C. B., Hindman, L. C., and McDonald, M. A. 2019. The "dark side" of psychological ownership during times of change. *Journal of Change Management* 19(4):266–82.

Conway, E., and Monks, K. 2011. Change from below: The role of middle managers in mediating paradoxical change. *Human Resource Management Journal* 21(2):190–202.

Coombs, A. 1990. *Adland: A true story of corporate drama*. Melbourne: Heinemann.

Coyle-Shapiro, J. A-M., and Shore, L. 2007. The employee-organization relationship: Where do we go from here? *Human Resource Management Review* 17(2):166–79.

Cramer, D., Hirscher, J., Scherf, G., and Smit, S. 2019. *From promise to delivery: Overcoming the strategy problem in the public sector*. Amsterdam and Berlin: McKinsey & Company.

Foote, D. 2001. The futility of resistance (to change). *Computerworld*, January 15, https://www.computerworld.com/article/2589854/the-futility–of-resistance—to-change-.html (accessed January 3, 2020).

Ford, J. D., and Ford, L. W. 2009. Decoding resistance to change. *Harvard Business Review* 87(4):99–103.

Ford, J. D., Ford, L. W., and McNamara, R. T. 2002. Resistance and the background conversations of change. *Journal of Organizational Change Management* 15(2):105–21.

Fuller, J. B., Wallenstein, J. K., Raman, M., and de Chalendar, A. 2019. Your workforce is more adaptable than you think. *Harvard Business Review* 97(3):118–26.

Gadiesh, O., and Gilbert, J. L. 2001. Transforming corner-office strategy into frontline action. *Harvard Business Review* 79(5):72–79.

Geigle, S. 1998. Organizational memory and scripts: Resistance to change or lessons from the past. Paper presented to the *Annual Conference of the Academy of Human Resource Development*, Chicago, March.

Ghislanzoni, G., Heidari-Robinson, S., and Jermiin, M. 2010. *Taking organizational redesign from plan to practice*. London: McKinsey & Company.

Hamel, G., and Zanini, M. 2014. *Build a change platform, not a change program*. London: McKinsey & Company.

Heyden, M. L. M., Fourné, S. P. L., Koene, B. A. S., Werkman, R., and Ansari, S. 2017. Rethinking "top-down" and "bottom-up" roles of top and middle managers in organizational change: Implications for employee support. *Journal of Management Studies* 54(7):961–85.

Hughes, M. 2010. *Managing change: A critical perspective*. London: Chartered Institute for Personnel and Development.

Hultman, K. E. 1995. Scaling the wall of resistance. *Training and Development* 49(10):15–18.

Ji, Y.-Y., Gutherie, J. P., and Messersmith, J. G. 2014. The tortoise and the hare: The impact of employee instability on firm performance. *Human Resource Management Journal* 24(4):355–73.

Jick, T. J., and Peiperl, M. 2010. *Managing change: Cases and concepts. 3rd ed.* New York: McGraw Hill.

Kanter, R. M. 1985. Managing the human side of change. *Management Review* 74(April):52–56.

Karp, H. B. 1996. *The change leader*. San Francisco: Pfeiffer.

Kim, W. C., and Mauborgne, R. 2003. Tipping point leadership. *Harvard Business Review* 81(4):60–69.

Kirkpatrick, D. L. 2001. *Managing change effectively*. Boston: Butterworth-Heinemann.

Kotter, J. P., and Schlesinger, L. A. 2008 (first published 1979). Choosing strategies for change. *Harvard Business Review* 86(7/8):130–39.

Kübler-Ross, E. 1969. *On death and dying*. Toronto: Macmillan.

Kunze, F., Boehm, S., and Bruch, H. 2013. Age, resistance to change, and job performance. *Journal of Managerial Psychology* 28(7/8):741–60.

Lewis, M. 2003. *Moneyball: The art of winning an unfair game*. New York: W.W. Norton & Co.

McCabe, D., Ciuk, S., and Gilbert, M. 2019. There is a crack in everything: An ethnographic study of pragmatic resistance in a manufacturing organization. *Human Relations, published online first*, pp. 1–28.

McDermott, A. M., Fitzgerald, L., and Buchanan, D. A. 2013. Beyond acceptance and resistance: Entrepreneurial change agency responses in policy implementation. *British Journal of Management* 24(S1):93–225.

McDermott, A. M., Conway, E., Rousseau, D., and Flood, P. C. 2013. Promoting effective psychological contracts through leadership: The missing link between HR strategy and performance. *Human Resource Management* 52(2):289–310.

McKinsey & Company. 2014. *The lean management enterprise: A system for daily progress, meaningful purpose, and lasting value*. New York: McKinsey Practice Publications.

Maurer, R. 2010. *Beyond the walls of resistance*. 2nd ed. Austin, TX: Bard Books.

Oreg, S. 2003. Resistance to change: Developing an individual differences measure. *Journal of Applied Psychology* 88(4):680–93.

Oreg, S. 2006. Personality, context, and resistance to organizational change. *European Journal of Work and Organizational Psychology* 15(1):73–101.

Pate, J., Martin, G., and Staines, H. 2000. Exploring the relationship between psychological contracts and organizational change: A process model and case study evidence. *Strategic Change* 9(8):481–93.

Piderit, S. K. 2000. Rethinking resistance and recognizing ambivalence: A multidimensional view of attitudes towards an organizational change. *Academy of Management Review* 25(4):783–94.

Plsek, P., and Kilo, C. M. 1999. From resistance to attraction: A different approach to change. *Physician Executive* 25(6):40–2.

Reger, R. K., Mullane, J. V., Loren T., Gustafson, L. T., and DeMarie, S. M. 1994. Creating earthquakes to change organizational mindsets. *Academy of Management Executive* 8(4):31–43.

Ries, E. 2019. *The lean startup.* New York: Penguin Random House.

Ross, L. 1977. The intuitive psychologist and his shortcomings: Distortions in the attribution process. In *Advances in experimental social psychology,* ed. L. Berkowitz (173–220). New York: Academic Press.

Schön, D. A. 1963. Champions for radical new inventions. *Harvard Business Review* *41*(2);77–86.

Scott, C. D., and Jaffe, D. T. 2006. *Change management: Leading people through organizational transitions.* 3rd ed. Cincinnati, OH: Thomson Learning.

Searle, R., and Rice, C. 2018. *Assessing and mitigating the impact of organisational change on counterproductive work behaviour: An operational (dis)trust based framework.* Coventry: Centre for Research and Evidence on Security Threats/Economic and Social Research Council.

Senge, P. 1990. *The fifth discipline: The art and practice of the learning organization.* New York: Doubleday Currency.

Stensaker, I., Meyer, C. B., Falkenberg, J., and Haueng, A. C. 2002. Excessive change: Coping mechanisms and consequences. *Organizational Dynamics* 31(3):296–312.

van den Heuvel, S., and Schalk, R. 2009. The relationship between fulfilment of the psychological contract and resistance to change during organizational transformations. *Social Science Information* 48(2):283–313.

Venus, M., Stam, D., and van Knippenberg, D. 2019. Visions of change as visions of continuity. *Academy of Management Journal* 62(3):667–90.

Wolfe, R., Wright, P. M., and Smart, D. L. 2006. Radical HRM innovation and competitive advantage: The Moneyball story. *Human Resource Management* 45(1):111–26.

Woodrow, C., and Guest, D. E. 2020. Pathways through organizational socialization: A longitudinal qualitative study based on the psychological contract. *Journal of Occupational and Organizational Psychology* 93(1):110–33.

Wooldridge, B. J., and Floyd, S. W. 1990. The strategy process, middle management involvement, and organizational performance. *Strategic Management Journal* 11(3):231–41.

Wooldridge, B., Schmid, T., and Floyd, S. W. 2008. The middle management perspective on strategy process: Contributions, synthesis, and future research. *Journal of Management* 34(6):1190–221.

Source of the chapter opening quote: "Change Quotes," *Good Reads,* https://www.goodreads.com/quotes/tag/change.

Chapter opening silhouette credit: FunKey Factory/Shutterstock

Chapter 9

Organization Development and Sense-Making Approaches

Learning Objectives

By the end of this chapter you should be able to:

LO 9.1 Appreciate more clearly the organizational change approaches underpinning the coach and interpreter images of managing change.

LO 9.2 Understand the Organization Development (OD) approach to change.

LO 9.3 Be aware of extensions of the OD approach such as Appreciative Inquiry, Positive Organizational Scholarship, and Dialogic OD.

LO 9.4 Understand the sense-making approach to change.

"When the world changes around you and when it changes against you—what used to be a tail wind is now a head wind—you have to lean into that and figure out what to do because complaining isn't a strategy."

Jeff Bezos, CEO

LO 9.1 Alternative Approaches to Managing Change

Of the six images of managing change, the *caretaker* and *nurturer* images have their foundations in the field of organization theory; the other four images—*director, coach, navigator,* and *interpreter*—have stronger foundations in the organizational change field. This chapter and chapter 10 delve further into the foundations of the four images that are rooted in the organizational change field and explore their implications for how to manage organizational change. They are also the four images that, in various ways, assume that the change manager has an important influence on the way change occurs in organizations. In contrast, the first two images, *caretaker* and *nurturer,* have in common an assumption that change managers *receive rather than initiate* change. Therefore, this chapter and chapter 10 explore the four images that assume that change managers have an active role in the initiation, support, and outcomes of organizational change. This chapter considers the foundational approaches associated with the *coach* and *interpreter* images; chapter 10 considers the foundational approaches associated with the *director* and *navigator* images.

Underpinned by the *coach* image, the Organization Development (OD) approach is one where its adherents present their developmental prescriptions for achieving change as being based, at least traditionally, upon a core set of values, ones that emphasize that change should benefit not just organizations but the people who staff them.

OD has played a central role in the organizational change field for over half a century. In their 2012 review of OD, Burnes and Cooke (p. 1396) argue that it "has been, and arguably, still is, the major approach to organizational change across the Western world, and increasingly globally." However, as this chapter and chapter 10 illustrate, different images of change management are associated with different ideas about what sort of approaches (and techniques) should be used to try to bring about change within organizations. It is not surprising, therefore, that OD's long history has been accompanied, from time to time, by expressions of concern as to its continuing relevance, leading some writers to raise the question of whether OD is "in crisis"; both the *Journal of Applied Behavioral Science* [40(4), 2004] and *OD Practitioner* [46(4), 2014] have had special issues focused on the question of OD's ongoing relevance. A long-standing criticism of OD has been the claim that it has been sidelined from the concerns of the business community because of its preoccupation with humanistic values rather than with other issues such as business strategy (Hornstein, 2001; Beer, 2014).

Approaches to managing change other than OD have emerged, For example, underpinned by the *interpreter* image, the sense-making approach maintains that change emerges over time and consists of a series of interpretive activities that help to create in people new meanings about their organizations and about the ways in which they can operate differently in the future.

We commence this chapter considering the approaches underpinned by the *coach* image and then move on to the *interpreter* image. Further approaches to managing change are addressed in chapter 10.

LO 9.2 Organization Development (OD)

In this section, we consider the underlying tenets of the OD approach to managing change along with the role of the OD practitioner. We then review a number of challenges that have been directed at OD including the continuing relevance of the values underlying the

OD approach, the universal applicability of these values, and the relevance of OD to large-scale change.

Traditional OD Approach: Fundamental Values

OD as a change intervention approach has developed over time and incorporated a number of different perspectives (see table 9.1), each of which is discussed in this chapter.

In drawing together the common threads of traditional OD, Beckhard (1969) depicts the classic OD approach as one that has the following characteristics:

- *It is planned* and involves a systematic diagnosis of the whole organizational system, a plan for its improvement, and provision of adequate resources.
- *The top of the organization* is committed to the change process.
- *It aims at improving the effectiveness* of the organization to help it achieve its mission.
- *It is long term,* typically taking two or three years to achieve effective change.
- *It is action oriented.*
- *Changing attitudes and behavior* is a focus of the change effort.
- *Experiential-based learning* is important as it helps to identify current behaviors and modifications that are needed.
- *Groups and teams* form the key focus for change.

Though it is commonly presented as being aimed at incremental, developmental, first-order change, other writers claim that what unifies the OD field, at least traditionally, is an emphasis on a core set of values. These values build upon humanistic psychology and emphasize the importance of developing people in work organizations and helping them to achieve satisfaction (Nicholl, 1998a). Three value sets are involved:

- *Humanistic values* relate to openness, honesty, and integrity.
- *Democratic values* relate to social justice, freedom of choice, and involvement.
- *Developmental values* relate to authenticity, growth, and self-realization (Nicholl, 1998c).

TABLE 9.1
The Evolution of Organization Development

Period	Approach	Perspective
1940s+	Traditional OD	Improve organizational performance through a focus on individual and group behavior, and apply humanistic and democratic values.
1990s/2000s+	Large-scale change	Enable whole organization engagement rather than focusing on individual and group level.
2000s/2010s+	Appreciative inquiry	Begin by focusing on the best of the current organization rather than on its problems.
2000s/2010s+	Positive organizational scholarship	Emphasize interventions that improve "the human condition."
2010s+	Dialogic OD	Identify and acknowledge different organizational members' views as to the existing reality, and encourage "conversations" on the change issues.

Human development, fairness, openness, choice, and the balance between autonomy and constraint are fundamental to these values (Burke, 1997). It is said that these values were radical and "a gutsy set of beliefs" in relation to the time in which they were developed; that is, in the 1940s and 1950s when organizational hierarchy was dominant, emphasizing authority, rationality, and efficiency rather than humanism and individuality (Burke, 1997). In this sense, the traditional practice of OD has as its focus people and is not necessarily meant to solely focus on the interests of management or the profitability of the firm (Nicholl, 1998a).

The OD Practitioner

Central to the traditional OD approach is the role of the "OD practitioner" who may be either internal or external to the organization. A typical OD practitioner helps to "structure activities to help the organization members solve their own problems and learn to do that better" (French and Bell, 1995, p. 4). Where this is based upon action research, it involves a variety of steps such as (Cummings and Worley, 2019):

1. *Problem identification.* Someone in the organization becomes aware of what he or she thinks is a problem that needs to be addressed.
2. *Consultation with an OD practitioner.* The client and the practitioner come together with the latter endeavoring to create a collaborative dialogue.
3. *Data gathering and problem diagnosis.* Interviews, observations, surveys, and analysis of performance data occur to assist in problem diagnosis. Each of these techniques is recognized as an intervention in itself in the sense that it involves an interaction with people.
4. *Feedback.* The consultant provides the client with relevant data, at the same time protecting the identity of people from whom information was obtained.
5. *Joint problem diagnosis.* As part of the action research process, people are involved in consideration of information and discuss what it means in terms of required changes.
6. *Joint action planning.* The specific actions that need to be taken are identified.
7. *Change actions.* The introduction of and transition to new techniques and behaviors occur.
8. *Further data gathering.* Outcomes of change are determined and further actions identified.

In coaching people through such change processes, Cummings and Worley (2019) argue that OD practitioners need a variety of skills, including:

1. *Intrapersonal skills.* Having a well-developed set of values and personal integrity including the ability to retain their own health in high-stress organizational situations.
2. *Interpersonal skills.* Skills that are needed to work with groups, gain their trust, and "provide them with counseling and coaching."
3. *General consultation skill.* Including knowledge about intervention techniques to assist them in diagnosing problems and designing change interventions.
4. *Organization Development theory.* Ensuring that they have a current understanding of the specialist field of which they are a part.

A key idea underpinning many OD interventions is psychologist Kurt Lewin's three-step model of change: *unfreezing* how the organization operates, *changing* the organization in specific ways, and then *refreezing* the changes into the operations of the organization. [While some critics, in particular Cummings et al. (2016), have argued that the three-step model is more a creation of Lewin's followers than of Lewin himself, more recent research by Burnes (2020) has shown the three-step concept to be well-embedded in Lewin's work.] How the three-step model of change relates to the actions of the OD practitioner is set out in table 9.2.

TABLE 9.2
Classic OD Change Intervention Processes

Three-Step Change Process	OD Action Research Change Process
Unfreezing: Establishing the need for change	• Identification of problems
	• Consultation with OD practitioner
	• Gathering of data and initial diagnosis
Movement: To new behavior through cognitive restructuring	• Client group feedback
	• Joint problem diagnosis
	• Joint planning of change actions
	• Engagement in change actions
Refreezing: Integrating new behaviors into social and organizational relationships	• Post-action data gathering and evaluation

Sources: Adapted from French and Bell (1995) and Cummings and Worley (2019).

Criticisms of OD

As the application of OD as an approach to managing change became more widespread, so did attention to its limitations. Even advocates of the OD approach began to acknowledge that there are problems in the field. For example, French and Bell (1995) identified six of these:

1. *OD definitions and concepts.* OD may consist of single or multiple interventions over different periods of time, so establishing the relationship between "OD" and its ability to enhance "organizational effectiveness" is difficult, especially given that the latter term itself also lacks precise definitions.
2. *Internal validity problems.* This relates to whether the change that occurred was caused by the *change intervention or a range of other factors.*
3. *External validity problems.* This is the generalizability question and relates to whether OD and its techniques are appropriate to all organizational settings.
4. *Lack of theory.* There is no comprehensive theory of change to assist researchers in knowing what to look for in what they study.

OD and the Challenge of Managing Covert Processes

Bob Marshak is a very experienced and highly regarded OD consultant. For Marshak, one of the great OD challenges is dealing with what he describes as "covert processes," those "powerful processes that impact organizations but remain unseen, unspoken, or unacknowledged [and which] include hidden agendas, blind spots, organizational politics, the elephant in the room, secret hopes and wishes, tacit assumptions, and unconscious dynamics" (Marshak, 2006, p. xi).

To reduce the likelihood that covert processes thwart an attempt to bring about organizational change, Marshak (2006) identifies five "keys" to dealing with covert processes in the context of an OD intervention:

1. *Create a (psychologically) safe environment.* Do whatever you can to create a climate of trust and respect where people feel safe to reveal their thoughts and beliefs.

2. *Seek movement not exposure.* Focus on moving the situation forward, not being judgmental about the matter revealed (i.e., progress not punishment).

3. *Assume that people are trying their best.* Put the focus on inquiry rather than judgment.

4. *Look in the mirror.* Be self-aware so that your behavior as the consultant is driven by the situation of the people you are working with and not your own covert norms and beliefs.

5. *Act consistently with expectations.* Stay within the scope of your brief as explained to participants at the outset unless you explicitly renegotiate expectations with them.

5. *Problems with measuring attitude changes.* Using pre-change and then post-change surveys to measure attitudinal changes are problematic as people may view the scale differently when they answer it a second time.

6. *Problems with normal science approaches to research.* The ability to use these techniques (hypothesis testing, assessing cause–effect relationships, etc.) is questioned in relation to OD being a process based on action research.

French and Bell (1995, p. 334) adopted an optimistic view of this situation, arguing that "these do not appear to be insurmountable problems at this time, although they continue to plague research efforts." However, other writers were critical of such optimism, pointing out that the approach is largely descriptive and prescriptive, often failing to adequately consider the inherent limitations and underlying assumptions of its own techniques (Oswick and Grant, 1996). OD has been presented with a range of other criticisms relating to the extent to which it deals adequately with issues such as leadership, strategic change, power, and reward systems (Cummings and Worley, 2019). Three further criticisms relate to the current relevance of OD's traditional values, the universality of those values, and the ability of OD to engage in large-scale change. Each of these issues is addressed next.

Current Relevance of OD's Traditional Values

Despite its longevity, or perhaps because of it, the issue of the ongoing relevance of the values underlying OD continues to be a matter of debate (see, e.g., Jamieson and Marshak, 2018). Going back 20+ years, prominent OD thought leader Warner Burke (1997, p. 7) argued that, for many experienced OD practitioners, "the profession has lost its way—that its values are no longer sufficiently honored, much less practiced, and that the unrelenting emphasis on the bottom line has taken over." This sentiment was a reaction to the growing role of some OD practitioners as advisers on corporate restructurings, mergers and takeovers, and so on, despite the lack of evidence of the values core to OD being central to such changes.

As a result, a view formed that "OD has lost some of its power, its presence, and perhaps its perspective" (Burke, 1997, p. 7). An editor of *OD Practitioner* at the time, Dave Nicholl, agreed with Burke's general assessment, pointing to how many of the values of OD are confrontational to many of the values held in our organizations, leading to "stark contrasts" between being relevant and value-neutral or being value-laden and marginal (Nicholl, 1998c). Nicholl argued that OD practitioners need to remind themselves of the dilemma they face, of assisting both individual development and organizational performance—which he characterizes as "contradictory elements." By delving back into OD's heritage, Nicholl (1999) suggested that they regain their humility and present to clients not certainty but educated conjecture. Finally, he proposed the need for a paradigm shift in how the corporation is viewed and rebuilt, allowing space to recognize that corporations are not necessarily just institutions for profit but social institutions.

Other OD writers have challenged managers to make their organizations more inclusive (multiple levels of involvement in decision making), to create mutual accountability (linking performance remuneration to adherence to core values, stakeholders, and corporate sustainability), to reinforce interdependence (between individuals, organizations, and the wider society), to expand notions of time and space (such as considering the impact of decisions for future generations), to ensure the wise use of natural resources (such as consideration of renewable and nonrenewable resources), and to redefine the purpose of the organization in terms of multiple stakeholders (including customers, stockholders, community, planet, descendants, organizational leaders, employees, and directors) (Gelinas and James, 1999).

OD Values *An Anachronism or Something Worth Preserving?*

The valuing of inclusion, open communication, collaboration, and empowerment has caused OD to struggle in recent decades in the face of a perception that these are values from a "gentler" time and inconsistent with fiercely competitive markets where only rapid change, driven by top-down edict, can give hope of survival. However, Burnes and Cooke (2012) query this characterization of OD. Instead they ask, "Are we in a time when the issue of values has never been more important?" They suggest that many countries are struggling with the impact of organizations exhibiting unethical, and financially or environmentally unsustainable, practices. If this is so, Burnes and Cooke (2012, p. 1417) argue, OD "with its humanist, democratic and ethical values, wide range of participative tools and techniques, and experience in promoting behavior changes, is ideally placed . . . to play a leading role in the movement to a more ethical and sustainable future."

Similarly, widely experienced professor and consultant, Harvard Business School's Mike Beer (2014, p. 61), argues:

With the corporate scandals of the past decade, clear evidence that we are doing damage to our planet, and the great recession of 2008 . . . higher ambition CEOs are reframing the purpose of their firm from increasing shareholder value to contributing to all stakeholders . . . . This trend is opening up new opportunities for the field of OD to help these higher ambition leaders to create a better world. Higher ambition companies integrate head, heart, and hands.

Are OD Values Universal?

One challenge leveled at OD is whether the approach and the values underpinning it are relevant outside of the United States, where it was predominantly developed. As with the issue of the continuing relevance of OD values over time (as previously discussed), debate over the global appropriateness of OD values continues (see, e.g., Sorenson and Yaeger, 2014).

Some advocates portray OD change values as being universal, with cultural differences serving as "a veneer which covers common fundamental human existence" (Blake et al., 2000, p. 60). For example, Blake et al. (2000) claim that the classic *Managerial (or Leadership) Grid* framework developed by Robert Blake and Jane Mouton in the 1960s has been applied successfully in many different countries. For Blake et al. (2000, p. 54) this framework was "probably the first systematic, comprehensive approach to organizational change" and had played a central role in the development of OD. They argue that the grid sustains and extends core OD values in seeking greater candor, openness, and trust in organizations. The grid maps seven leadership styles that vary in terms of their emphasis on people versus results: controlling, accommodating, status quo, indifferent, paternalist, opportunist, and sound—the latter style being preferred insofar as it portrays a leadership style that is concerned for both results and people (Blake et al., 2000).

The grid has been used as the basis for change leadership seminars, helping to establish both individual awareness and skills. In response to the question of the grid's applicability outside of the United States, they claim that it has been used extensively in a variety of countries (including within Asia), in part because of "its ability to effectively employ a universal model of effective management and organization development within diverse cultures" (Blake et al., 2000, p. 59). Similarly, for Sorenson and Yaeger (2014, p. 58) the evidence from years of application of OD in diverse countries is that national cultural values are more akin to "a veneer that covers more fundamental and universal needs, needs which are reflected in the fundamental values of OD."

However, other OD advocates are more circumspect about how far the OD approach is relevant across cultural boundaries. For example, Marshak (1993) contends that there are fundamentally different assumptions underlying Eastern (Confucian/Taoist) and Western (Lewinian/OD) views of organizational change. These differences are outlined in table 9.3. Marshak's (1993) view is that OD practitioners need to view with care any assumptions they may hold that OD practices have universal applicability, while Mirvis (2006) recommends that OD become more open to a pluralism of ideas by drawing from both Eastern and Western styles of thought. Similarly, Fagenson-Eland, Ensher, and Burke (2004, p. 461), based on the findings of a seven-nation study, conclude that "OD practitioners should carefully consider dimensions of national culture when recommending specific OD interventions."

Engaging in Large-Scale Change

One of the biggest challenges to the traditional OD field was the criticism that it was ill suited to handle large-scale organizational change. Traditional OD techniques focused on

TABLE 9.3 Is OD Change Culture-Bound?	Lewinian/OD Assumptions	Confucian/Taoist Assumptions
	• Linear (movement from past to present to future)	• Cyclical (constant ebb and flow)
	• Progressive (new state more desirable)	• Processional (harmonious movement from one state to another)
	• Goal oriented (specific end state in mind)	• Journey oriented (cyclical change, therefore no end state)
	• Based on creating disequilibrium (by altering current field of forces)	• Based on maintaining equilibrium (achieve natural harmony)
	• Planned and managed by people separate from change itself (application of techniques to achieve desired ends)	• Observed and followed by involved people (who constantly seek harmony with their universe)
	• Unusual (assumption of static or semi-static state outside of a change process)	• Usual (assumption of constant change as, in the yin-yang philosophy, each new order contains its own negation)

Source: Adapted from Marshak (1993).

working with individuals and group dynamics through processes such as survey feedback and team building. Such methods came under attack as being insufficient to deal with the large-scale changes needed by organizations to cope with the hypercompetitive business world that confronts them (Manning and Binzagr, 1996, p. 269). OD was seen as "too slow, too incremental and too participative" to be the way to manage change at a time when organizations often faced the need to make major change and to do so with speed (Burnes and Cooke, 2012, p. 1397).

As a result of such criticisms, many OD practitioners began to move their focus from micro-organizational issues to macro, large-system issues, including aligning change to the strategic needs of the organization (Worley et al., 1996). This has led to the development of a range of techniques designed to get the whole organizational system, or at least representatives of different stakeholders of the whole system, into a room at one and the same time.

Whole system techniques take a variety of forms and names, including search conference (see table 9.4), future search, real-time strategic change, world café, town hall meetings, simu-real, whole-system design, open-space technology, ICA strategic planning process, participative design, fast-cycle full participation, large-scale interactive process, and appreciative future search (Axelrod, 1992; Bunker and Alban, 1992, 1997; Dannemiller and Jacobs, 1992; Emery and Purser, 1996; Fuller, Griffin and Ludema, 2000; Holman, Devane and Cody, 2007; Klein, 1992; Levine and Mohr, 1998). Such techniques are typically designed to work with up to thousands of people at one time.

The various techniques do entail differences. Some techniques assume that organizational participants can shape and enact both their organization and its surrounding environment; others are based on the assumption that the environment is given (although its defining characteristics may need to be actively agreed upon) and that organizations and their participants join together democratically to identify appropriate adaptation

TABLE 9.4
An Example of a
Search
Conference
Format

Phase 1	Identifying relevant world trends = shared understanding of global environment
Phase 2	Identifying how trends affect a specific issue, organization, institution = how global trends impact on operations of the system
Phase 3	Evolution of issue, organization, institution = creation of its history including its chronology (timeline)
Phase 4	Future design of issue, organization, institution = use of small-group creativity and innovation to design a consensus scenario for the way forward

Source: Adapted from Baburoglu and Garr (1992).

World Café

World Café is a large-scale OD intervention technique developed by Juanita Brown and David Isaacs (2005). It has been described by Jorgenson and Steier (2013, p. 393) as "one of a new generation of methods that attempt to achieve collective change by bringing all members or stakeholders of a system together in one place, using a highly structured process of movement to create flexible and coevolving networks of conversations."

Typically, the event is held away from the normal workplace and uses small face-to-face groupings seated at a collection of small café-like tables as the basis for rounds of conversations. Convened by one or more facilitators, the World Café involves a series of issues and questions being addressed by participants. Table membership changes between various rounds (of questions) although one person usually remains as the "table host." Each table usually "reports back" (verbally) to the group as a whole between rounds, and the meeting culminates in the whole group discussing what has occurred.

Jorgenson and Steier (2013, p. 393) note:

The event is densely symbolic. Tables are often covered with red and white checked tablecloths reminiscent of an Italian restaurant as well as bud vases with flowers. Sheets of butcher block paper laid on each table along with colored markers or crayons are intended to evoke an atmosphere of play and allow participants, if they desire, to capture emerging ideas with sketches or notes.

Adapted from Jorgenson and Steier (2013).

processes. Other differences relate to the extent to which the technique includes a majority of organizational members and stakeholders. Some techniques are highly structured and use a consultant who manages the process, whereas others utilize a more flexible self-design approach (Manning and Binzagr, 1996).

Although designed, as the name suggests, for application in large-scale system-wide situations such as that represented in the World Trade Center example given in the box "Large-Scale Interventions," these methods have also been applied in smaller-scale situations such as that described in the box "World Café on a Small Scale."

Large-Scale Interventions *"Listening to the City": Town Hall Meeting on Rebuilding the World Trade Center after 9/11*

In New York City on July 20, 2002, over 4,300 New York citizens came together for what has been billed as the largest town hall meeting ever held. The meeting was organized by *AmericaSpeaks,* at that time a nonprofit organization headed by Carolyn Lukensmeyer, who used twenty-first-century town hall meetings to design and facilitate large-scale dialogues on public issues. She would group up to 5,000 people into one room. She profiled participants so that the group as a whole represented the various interests and stakeholders associated with the issues for discussion and debate and arranged participants into small groups of around a dozen people, each having a facilitator. Each group had a networked computer that recorded the ideas of the participants and a wireless network within the room to transfer these data to a central computer. This enabled a "theme team" to read the data from each group, identify key themes in real time, distill them, and present them back to the whole room via large overhead video screens. Each participant in the room had a wireless keypad that he or she could then use to vote in relation to the distilled themes. This provided instant feedback to the entire group, which, at the conclusion of the day, received a summary of the major issues and outcomes. Involving key decision makers in the meeting was an important way of trying to ensure that the outcomes of the day had a meaningful input into public policy.

In the case of the World Trade Center, the town hall meeting was held after five months of organizing, sponsored in part by the Lower Manhattan Development Corporation (LMDC) and the Port Authorities of New York and New Jersey. During this period, a representative sample of New Yorkers was identified and invited to the July 20 meeting, which was titled "Listening to the City." The room contained 500 tables, each with a facilitator. Theme team members provided feedback throughout the day, and issue experts were on hand to answer specific questions from participants. Representatives from various federal, state, and city agencies also were present. A key outcome of the meeting was an expression of dissatisfaction with the six memorial site options being considered and a demand for one having more open space; the meeting also made recommendations regarding expansion of the transit service and more affordable housing. The outcome was that the LMDC began a new planning process for the World Trade Center, and the Port Authority agreed to reduce the amount of commercial development planned for the site to enable more space for hotel and retail. As reported by the *New York Daily News* (July 21, 2002), "the process was an exercise in democracy."

Based on Lukensmeyer and Brigham (2002).

World Café on a Small Scale *The Museum of Science and Industry*

The Museum of Science and Industry (MOSI) is in Tampa, Florida, and has used a World Café format for various purposes including meetings that involved staff and members of the local community in the discussion of planning and design matters. Having had World Café experience, a decision was made to try this format for a meeting of its

30-member executive board that was scheduled to explore possible futures—and identify "actionable ideas"—for MOSI. World Café was seen as an approach that would signal to members that this was intended to be a very different sort of meeting from the highly structured ones that were the executive board norm in its usual setting (a traditional

(Continued)

boardroom with members seated around one large elliptical table).

Participants sat at small round tables (seating four). The presenters explained the purpose of the event and the World Café process, and the first round began with the presenters asking the participants to discuss their own experiences of really good conversations and what it was about those conversations that made them "really good." In future rounds, presenters asked respondents to discuss questions such as "What could MOSI be like in five years?" and "We're now five years in the future and MOSI has attained these goals. What did we do to get here" (Jorgenson and Steier, 2013, p. 396).

Postscript: Reactions to this use of World Café differed between participants. Although several board members agreed with one colleague's enthusiastic response that "this was the first time in a long time that we really talked to each other" and that "maybe this is what a board meeting *could* be like," another responded rather ambiguously, "Yes, this has been great but now let's get down to business" (Jorgenson and Steier, 2013, p. 396). For some people, an experience like World Café opens up a new set of possibilities as to how they could work with each other in the future; for others it is dismissed as a (possibly interesting) diversion before they return to "business as usual."

Jorgenson and Steier (2013)

Proponents of large-scale intervention approaches are glowing, sometimes almost evangelical, in expounding their benefits. Weisbord (1992b, pp. 9–10) claims that Future Search conference outcomes "can be quite startling" and produce restructured bureaucratic hierarchies in which "people previously in opposition often act together across historic barriers in less than 48 hours." Results emerge "with greater speed and increased commitment and greatly reduced resistance by the rest of the organization" (Axelrod, 1992, p. 507) enhancing "innovation, adaptation, and learning" (Axelrod, 2001, p. 22).

However, alongside testaments to the success of these techniques are disagreements regarding both the origin of large-scale, whole-system change techniques and their likely effectiveness in highly volatile environments. Some writers disagree with the version of "OD history" that depicts the field as having moved over time from a micro to a macro focus. They maintain that large-scale techniques have always been part of the OD approach and that "ODers have a strong tendency to neglect their past" (Golembiewski, 1999, p. 5). Others such as Herman (2000) maintain that because of the need for more rapid responses, systemwide culture change programs are less relevant today than more specific, situational interventions such as virtual team building and management of merger processes.

Aligned with this critique is the issue of the feasibility of systemwide changes in an era when "[t]he old model of the organization as the center of its universe, with its customers, share-owners, suppliers, etc. rotating around it, is no longer applicable in 'new-era' organizations" (Herman, 2000, p. 110). As one OD practitioner argues, "I'm not sure that 'system wide' change is really possible, since the real system often include[s] a number of strategic partners who may never buy into changes that fit one company but not another" (cited in Herman, 2000, p. 109).

However, others disagree. For OD consultant Susan Hoberecht and her colleagues (2011), the increasing centrality of inter-organizational alliances and networks in the business world provides an opportunity for change methods with a systemwide focus because in such an environment a greater than ever premium is placed on the effective operating of interdependencies. In such an environment, Hoberecht et al. (2011) argue, large-scale interventions have particular relevance.

For an empirically based assessment of various aspects of the effectiveness of large-scale interventions, see Worley et al. (2011).

LO 9.3 Appreciative Inquiry (AI)

Techniques of "inclusion" appropriate to large-scale or large-group intervention techniques led to them being labeled as part of a new "engagement paradigm" (Axelrod, 2001, p. 25), a "new type of social innovation" (Bunker and Alban, 1992, p. 473), a "paradigm shift" (Dannemiller and Jacobs, 1992, p. 497), and "an evolution in human thought, vision and values uniquely suited to our awesome 21st Century technical, economic, and social dilemmas" (Weisbord, 1992b, p. 6). They represented a shift from the emphasis on problem-solving and conflict management, common to earlier OD programs, to a focus on joint envisioning of the future. For example, Fuller, Griffin, and Ludema (2000, p. 31) maintain that with a problem-solving approach comes the assumption that "organizing-is-a-problem-to-be-solved," one that entails steps such as problem identification, analysis of causes and solutions, and the development of action plans.

Contrary to this logic, Fuller et al. (2000) point to the assumptions underlying the Appreciative Inquiry (AI) approach to change, which seeks to identify what is currently working best and to build on this knowledge to help develop and design what might be achieved in the future. They outline the technique as involving four steps:

- *Discovering* or appreciating the best of what is currently practiced.
- *Building* on this knowledge to help envision (or dream) about what the future could be.
- *Designing* or co-constructing (through collective dialogue) what should be.
- *Sustaining* the organization's destiny or future.

The technique is also depicted diagrammatically in Figure 9.1. An illustrative sample of questions for this four-step process is provided in table 9.5.

In these techniques the act of participation or inclusion of a wide variety of voices itself constitutes a change in the organization. The "what" to change and the "how" to change cannot be easily separated.

In their outline of the benefits of Appreciative Inquiry, Fuller et al. (2000, p. 31) claim that it "releases an outpouring of new constructive conversations," "unleashes a self-sustaining learning capacity within the organization," "creates the conditions necessary for self-organizing to flourish," and "provides a reservoir of strength for positive change." These are not minor claims. Certainly, the techniques have been reportedly used successfully in a variety of organizational settings (Weisbord, 1999b). However, whether these approaches are successful in achieving their outcomes is difficult to establish, being based most often on the assertions of their proponents rather than on rigorous research evidence.

FIGURE 9.1
Appreciative
Inquiry 4-D
Cycle

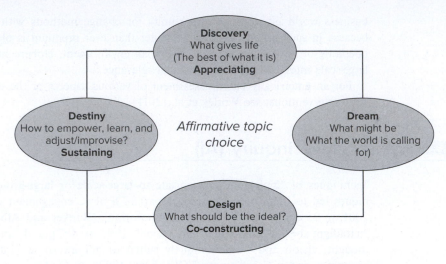

TABLE 9.5

An Illustrative Sample of Appreciative Inquiry Questions
The following questions were part of an AI-based OD engagement that consultant Meghana Rao (2014, p. 81) carried out in a U.S. social services agency.

Stage	Questions
Discovering	"Describe a time when you were most proud to be a member of your organization. What was the situation? Who was involved? What made it a proud moment?"
Dream	"Imagine yourself and your organization have been fast-forwarded by five years. What do you see around you? What does the structure look like? How have clients been created, retained, and expanded?"
Design	"What will your ideal organizational structure look like?—people, systems? . . . What structures need to be in place for the organization to sustain and employees to flourish?"
Destiny	"What are the action items that we need to cover to create the organization of the future? What additional resources will be needed?"

Appreciative Inquiry at Roadway Express

Roadway Express, a North American industrial and commercial transportation company, adopted an Appreciative Inquiry approach to change its culture and management. Working with Case Western Reserve University, the company embarked on a major leadership-training program to develop skills and capabilities for sustained economic performance. In what was called the Breakthrough Leadership Program, 150 Roadway Express leaders went through personal discovery exercises involving developing personal vision statements, identifying personal strengths and weaknesses, developing personal learning plans, and experimenting with these back in the work setting. Executive coaches served to facilitate these processes.

In the next phase, David Cooperrider, who co-founded Appreciative Inquiry, worked with them in convening summits (large group meetings), each held over two days and consisting of a cross section of stakeholders (customers, staff, suppliers, and others). The aim of these summits was to identify what the "ideal" was for the organization in relation to a variety of business issues. Each summit went through the four AI stages (discovery, dreaming, designing,

and delivering) to facilitate cooperation and collaboration throughout the organization. From 2000 to 2004, 8,000 Roadway people experienced this process with over 70 summits being held in this time. At the end of each summit, in what was referred to as the "open microphone" segment, participants "publicly pledged their commitment to each other to see the changes embodied in the action plans through to completion" (Van Oosten, 2006, p. 712).

Van Oosten (2006)

LO 9.3 Positive Organizational Scholarship (POS)

Dubbed as a "new movement in organizational science," Positive Organizational Scholarship (POS) is an umbrella term that emerged in the early 2000s to encompass approaches such as Appreciative Inquiry and others, including positive psychology and community psychology (Cameron and Caza, 2004, p. 731). POS developed out of a view that for most of the history of OD, attention had mainly been paid to identifying instances of "negatively motivated change" (or problems) in organizations and designing change programs to eliminate them (Cameron and McNaughtan, 2014). Following this line of argument, thinking about the positive aspects of organizational life—and building change programs to spread these aspects elsewhere in organizations—has been relatively neglected.

To take a POS perspective involves what one of its founders, Kim Cameron, describes as "four connotations" (Cameron and McNaughtan, 2014, p. 447):

1. "Adopting a positive lens," which means that whether one is dealing with celebrations/successes or adversity/problems, the focus is on "life giving elements."
2. "Focusing on positively deviant performance," which means investigating outcomes that are well in excess of any normally expected performance, that is, outcomes that are spectacular, surprising, or extraordinary.
3. "Assuming an affirmative bias" involves holding the view that positivity generates in individuals, groups, and organizations the capacity for greater achievements.
4. "Examining virtuousness" involves assuming that all "human systems" are inclined toward "the highest aspirations of mankind."

In line with the coaching metaphor, POS can be depicted as coaching organizations to identify their "best plays," to understand the behaviors and dynamics underlying them, and then to work out how to spread them to other parts of their "game" (the organization).

POS has had its critics. Fineman (2006, pp. 270–73) raises four issues that question whether POS can really live up to its "positive" aims. First, he questions whether we can really agree on which behaviors are "positive." What passes for being positive will vary in different environments. For example, in reviewing a number of research studies, he points out how "'courageous,' 'principled' corporate whistle-blowers are also readily regarded as traitors, reneging on the unspoken corporate code ('virtue') to never wash one's dirty linen in public."

Second, he (2006, pp. 274–75) questions whether the positive can be separated from the negative or whether they are really "two sides of the same coin, inextricably welded and mutually reinforcing." For example: "Happiness may trigger anxiety ('will my happiness last?'). Love can be mixed with bitterness and jealousy. Anger can feel energizing and exciting." By focusing on positive experiences, he maintains, approaches such as Appreciative Inquiry fail "to value the opportunities for positive change that are possible from negative experiences, such as embarrassing events, periods of anger, anxiety, fear, or shame."

Third, he (2006, p. 276) points to how what are regarded as positive behaviors and emotions differ, not just in different organizational environments but also across different cultural environments. Drawing on the work of writers on culture, he points out how "[e]ffusive hope, an energizing emotion in the West, is not a sentiment or term prevalent in cultures and sub-cultures influenced by Confucianism and Buddhism."

Fourth, he (2006, p. 281) suggests that there is "an unarticulated dark side to positiveness." This occurs where there is a lack of recognition that there are different interests in organizations and that not all people respond well to so-called positive programs like empowerment and emotional intelligence or practices that impose a "culture of fun" in the workplace. These programs "have a mixed or uncertain record, and some can produce the very opposite of the self-actualization and liberation they seek" (Fineman, 2006, p. 281).

In response to these criticisms, defenders of POS argue that their perspective complements and expands rather than replaces the perspective of those who "only wrestle with the question of what's wrong in organizations" (Roberts, 2006, p. 294). Indeed, those whose focus is on the latter question "may inadvertently ignore the areas of human flourishing that enliven and contribute value to organizations, even in the face of significant human and structural challenges" (Roberts, 2006, p. 295). POS is presented as "concerned with understanding the integration of positive and negative conditions, not merely with an absence of the negative" (Cameron and Caza, 2004, p. 732). Rather than assume that there are no universally positive virtues, the task of POS is to "discover the extent to which virtues and goodness are culturally influenced (Roberts, 2006, p. 298). Roberts (2006) suggests that criticism of POS may be due to a combination of the critics not wanting to step outside of their comfort zone—an approach to managing change that is focused on identifying problems—and lack of consideration for the relative infancy of POS as an area of practice.

Where does this leave the manager of change? On the one side, proponents of POS wish to change organizations with "an implicit desire to enhance the quality of life for individuals who work within and are affected by organizations" (Roberts, 2006, p. 294). On the other side are critical scholars who do not lay out an alternative call to action for agents of change so much as caution them if they assume that they will be successful in their "positive" ventures. Instead, the critics of POS urge POS advocates to recognize how underlying power relationships and interests in organizations (and beyond) will limit their actions; they also are urged to recognize that what passes as being positive will vary in different contexts and may not be shared by all. However, such critical reflections do not seem to have dented, in any significant way, the increasing momentum that the POS movement has gained, at least in North America. Whether it achieves the same momentum outside of the United States remains to be seen.

Cameron and McNaughtan (2014, p. 456) revisit the findings of a decade of application of POS ideas to organizational change covering such variables as virtuous practices (e.g., compassion), humanistic values, the meaningfulness of work, high-quality interpersonal communication, hope, energy, and self-efficacy. They summarize the results as "provid[ing] support for the benefits of positive change practices in real-world work settings." Quinn and Cameron (2019) provide a summary, description, and discussion of POS' distinctive approach to organizational change.

LO 9.3 Dialogic Organization Development

As OD developed through its various manifestations, such as Large Group Interventions and Appreciative Inquiry, it was moving more and more away from the classic, diagnosis-driven, approach to OD (as described in the initial sections of this chapter). Gervase Bushe and Bob Marshak (2009) characterized this change by contrasting the traditional "Diagnostic OD" with what they described as "Dialogic OD."

Bushe and Marshak (2009) contrast the characteristics of Diagnostic and Dialogic OD. Whereas traditional, or Diagnostic, OD emphasizes that any problem requiring change could be addressed by first applying an objective diagnosis of the circumstances of the situation, Dialogic OD treats reality as subjective so that the priority in intervening in an organization was to identify and acknowledge different stakeholders' interpretations of what for them was "reality." In parallel with this, the role of the OD consultant moved from being the provider of data for fact-driven decision making to being the facilitator of processes that encouraged "conversations" around change issues (Marshak, 2013; Bushe and Marshak, 2015) (see the box "From the Originators of Dialogic OD, Gervase Bushe and Bob Marshak").

From the Originators of Dialogic OD *Gervase Bushe and Bob Marshak*

By 2005 each of us had separately concluded that various OD change methods were being practiced that didn't follow the basic orthodoxies found in OD textbooks. Although we didn't really know each other at that time, we decided to collaborate on defining the premises and practices we believed underlay approaches as disparate as Open Space Technology, Appreciative Inquiry, and the Art of Hosting, to name a few. In a 2009 article we originated the name and concept of "Dialogic OD," based on the principle that change comes from changing everyday conversations and contrasted it with the foundational form of OD we named "Diagnostic OD."

Later we articulated key ideas derived from the interpretive and complexity sciences that lead to a Dialogic OD Mindset and the "secret sauce" of ingredients that in combination produce transformational change. Those ingredients, occurring in no specific order, include: disruption of ongoing patterns of social agreement such that the emergence of new patterns of organizing become possible; introduction of a "generative image," for example *sustainable development,* that stimulates new thinking and possibilities not previously considered; and development of new narratives that become part of the day-to-day conversations that guide how organizational actors think about and respond to situations.

We believe Dialogic OD is especially effective in a VUCA [volatility, uncertainty, complexity, ambiguity] world of continual change. Given those conditions,

(Continued)

instead of trying to control the uncontrollable, Dialogic OD asks leaders to enrich stakeholder networks, promote open-ended inquiry and support groups that self-generate small experiments that challenge conventional wisdom and may lead to new outcomes not previously considered. Leaders stay involved by amplifying and embedding new ideas and practices that work. In brief, leaders become sponsors and framers of dialogic processes that stimulate innovation and invention, rather than trying to maintain illusory control as directors or managers of planned change.

Private correspondence from Bob Marshak to the authors, March 11, 2015.

Central to the Dialogic OD approach is the view that "real change" only occurs when mindsets are altered and that this is more likely to occur through "generative conversations" than persuasion by "facts." Altered mindsets are represented by changes at the level of language and associated changes at the level of actions taken by organization members. This changed approach is also associated with moves from (1) seeing change as a relatively manageable, plannable, linear process to one that could be unpredictable with far from predictable moves from diagnosis to outcomes and (2) "the shift from fixing a problem to cultivating a system capable of addressing its own challenges" (Holman, 2013, p. 20) (see table 9.6).

As OD continues to evolve, it remains a major "school of thought" as to how organizational change should be managed. Although debates exist as to what form of OD is optimal, Tenkasi (2018, p. 67) argues the virtues of OD as follows:

> The idea of top down centralised change leadership is becoming more and more obsolete as we devolve from monolithic organizational structures to nimble and agile decentralised structures. The need of the hour is involving communities of stakeholders, empowerment across a broad swath of the organization, and facilitating poly-vocal conversations to determine the scope and the process of change.

TABLE 9.6
How Dialogic OD and Diagnostic OD Are Different: Base Assumptions

	Dialogic OD	Diagnostic OD
How the OD practitioner influences the organization	Working with people in a way that creates new awareness, knowledge, and possibilities	Carrying out diagnosis of the organizational situation before intervening
What makes change happen?	Engaging with stakeholders in ways that disrupt and shift existing patterns of norms, beliefs and behaviors leading to the emergence of new possibilities and associated commitments	Applying known expertise to identify, plan, and manage the change in a systematic unfreeze-change-refreeze sequence
The consultant's orientation	As an involved facilitator who becomes part of the situation being changed	As a neutral facilitator who retains a separateness and distance from those being affected

Source: Adapted from Marshak, R. J. 2015. My journey into Dialogic organization development. *OD Practitioner* 47(2):47–52 (from table 1, p. 48).

However, not all OD practitioners are sure that a move from [Diagnostic] OD to Dialogic OD is sufficient to position OD optimally for being able to have an influence on how change in organizations is managed. For example, both Worley (2014) and Bartunek and Woodman (2015) argue that the diagnostic–dialogic dichotomy is unhelpful and that "we should be talking about whether a comprehensive and systematic diagnostic OD can be integrated with a really good dialogic OD to create a powerful change process" (Worley, 2014, p. 70). For Worley (2014, p. 70), the dialogic–diagnostic focus places too much attention on "OD as process"; he argues that for OD "to capture its full potential" practitioners must complement their process skills with skills and knowledge "related to the principles and frameworks of strategy and organization design."

Dialogic OD in Practice *Using Organizational Theatre*

As part of a change that involved the implementation of a new customer relationship management (CRM) system, the employees of a financial services organization were asked to request customers to make an appointment at which their financial situation would be reviewed free of charge. Employees were to make this request during the course of regular over-the-counter transactions. However, the targeted number of appointments was not being reached, and it appeared that the barrier was employees not feeling confident about making the required approach.

In response the financial institution arranged for a theatre company to craft and present a play that illustrated the conversations and interactions involved in the interface between customer and employee. A half-day theatre workshop was then conducted in which participating employees were invited to ask questions of the actors and to suggest changes to the script to make the play more "realistic." A second workshop followed at which employees volunteered scenarios that would make the play even more typical of the customer interface situations in which they were involved. The employees then joined the theatre actors in acting out the roles in the evolved script. Following the workshops, a collective discussion took place on proactive customer conversations.

Measures made following employee participation in the theatre process showed a significant improvement in both self-efficacy beliefs and task performance compared to a control group of employees who did not participate in the theatre.

Badham et al. (2015)

What OD Must Do to Be Influential

Michael Beer, Professor Emeritus at HBS and co-founder of consulting firm TruePoint Partners—reflecting on 50 years in OD (Beer, 2014)—argues that OD is at a crossroads in terms of its ability to be influential. According to Beer, even if an OD engagement directly involves just one of the following processes, the OD practitioner must consider how what they are doing will enhance all three of the following:

1. *Performance alignment.* High performance that flows from the organization's design, processes, and capabilities being aligned with its strategy

2. *Psychological alignment.* The commitment of people that follows from alignment between the organization's culture and humanistic values

3. *Capacity for learning and change.* The organization supporting, on an ongoing basis, honest conversations on any matters that inhibit the first two items in the list.

OD in Different Settings

1. **Law enforcement**
   Pyle, B. S., and Cangemi, J. 2019. Organizational change in law enforcement: Community-oriented policing as transformational leadership. *Organization Development Journal* (Winter):81–88.

2. **Hospital**
   Kamolsiri, P., Tayko, P. R. M., and Mullin, V. 2018. The impact of OD interventions on high-performing teams in hospitals. *Organization Development Journal* (Summer):51–74.

3. **Small to medium enterprises**
   Stewart, S., and Gapp, R. 2017. The role of organizational development in understanding leadership to achieve sustainability practices in small to medium enterprises. *Organization Development Journal* (Summer):33–57.

4. **Media organization**
   Birmingham, C. 2012. How OD principles of change still matter in an impossible situation. *OD Practitioner* 44(4):61–64.

5. **The U.S. Army**
   Koknke, A., and Gonda, T. 2013. Creating a collaborative virtual command centre among four separate organizations in the United States Army. *Organization Development Journal* (Winter):75–92.

6. **Nonprofit organizations**
   Gratton, P. C. 2018. Organization Development and strategic planning for non-profit organizations. *Organization Development Journal* (Summer):27–38.

7. **Mergers and acquisitions**
   Marks, M. L., and Mirvis, P. H. 2012. Applying OD to make mergers and acquisitions work. *OD Practitioner* 44(3):5–12.

8. **China**
   Tang, Y. 2018. Theory S: A Chinese transformative OD framework. *Organization Development Journal* (Winter):77–98.

LO 9.4 Sense-Making

As discussed in chapter 2, the *interpreter* image emphasizes the role of the change manager as a "manager of meaning"; that is, it emphasizes that a core skill of a change manager is the capacity to frame meaning for those involved. Times of change can be confusing to those affected, and a key element of what change managers do through their various actions and communications is convey a sense of "what's going on." Organizational change is a process that is "problematic" in terms of its outcomes "because it undermines and challenges [people's] existing schemata, which serve as the interpretive frames of reference through which to make sense of the world" (Lockett et al., 2014).

Change often means that the leaders of an organization are seeking to take it in a significantly new direction and/or to have the organization function in a significantly different manner. To do so, the sense-making process is likely to involve a sequence that Mantere and colleagues (2012) describe as beginning with "sense-breaking" (as the leaders challenge the appropriateness of the status quo), followed by "sense-giving" (their attempts to reshape people's understandings of the direction they should be heading).

Managers lacking self-awareness will often convey a message that is other than they would intend. People in organizations interpret managers' actions symbolically, and, particularly where formal communications leave ambiguity, such interpretations will fill the "meaning gap." Good change managers are likely to have a high level of self-awareness and recognize that their capacity to provide a narrative along the lines of "what's going on and why?"—that is, acting as an interpreter—can meet a need. What is at stake, according to Iveroth and Hallencreutz (2015, p. 3), is that sense-making is central to creating "the necessary awareness, understanding and willpower needed to make people change."

Drawing on the *interpreter* image of managing organizational change, Karl Weick's (2000; Weick et al., 2005) sense-making model provides an alternative approach to the OD school. Weick's (2000) point of departure is to argue against three common change assumptions.

The first is the *assumption of inertia.* Under this assumption, planned, intended change is necessary to disrupt the forces that contribute to a lack of change in an organization so that there is a lag between environmental change and organizational adaptation. He suggests that the central role given to inertia is misplaced and results from a focus on structure rather than a focus on the structuring flows and processes through which organizational work occurs. Adopting the latter perspective leads one to see organizations as being in an ongoing state of accomplishment and re-accomplishment with organizational routines constantly undergoing adjustments to better fit changing circumstances.

The second *assumption is that a standardized change program is needed.* However, Weick (2000) says that this assumption is of limited value because it fails to activate what he regards as the four drivers of organizational change. As outlined in chapter 2, these drivers are:

- *Animation.* Whereby people remain in motion and may experiment, e.g., with job descriptions
- *Direction.* Including being able to implement, in novel ways, directed strategies
- *Paying attention and updating.* Such as updating knowledge of the environment and reviewing and rewriting organizational requirements
- *Respectful, candid interaction.* Occurs when people are encouraged to speak out and engage in dialogue, particularly when things are not working well

These drivers emerge from a sense-making perspective that assumes "that change engages efforts to make sense of events that don't fit together" (Weick, 2000, p. 232). For Weick, most programmed or intentional changes fail to activate one or more of these sense-making forces that assist individuals in managing ambiguity.

The third *assumption is that of unfreezing,* most often associated with Kurt Lewin's unfreezing–changing–refreezing change formula. Unfreezing is based on the view that organizations suffer from inertia and need to be "unfrozen." However, "if change is continuous and emergent, then the system is already unfrozen. Further efforts at unfreezing could disrupt what is essentially a complex adaptive system that is already working" (Weick, 2000, p. 235). If there is deemed to be ineffectiveness in the system, then his position is that the best change sequence is as follows:

- *Freeze.* To show what is occurring in the way things are currently adapting
- *Rebalance.* To remove blockages in the adaptive processes
- *Unfreeze.* To enable further emergent and improvisational changes to occur

In this view of organizational change, change agents are those who are best able to identify how adaptive emergent changes are currently occurring, much of which often are dismissed as noise in the system.

As noted in chapter 2, from a sense-making perspective, it is up to managers of change "to author interpretations and labels that capture the patterns in those adaptive choices [and] within the framework of sense-making, management sees what the front line says and tells the world what it means" (Weick, 2000, p. 238). Sense-making is "a social process of meaning construction and reconstruction through which managers understand, interpret, and create sense for themselves and others of their changing organizational context and surroundings" (Rouleau and Balogun, 2010, p. 955).

In a landmark study in using and extending the sense-making framework to the management of organizational change, Jean Helms Mills (2003) looked at the organizational changes at Nova Scotia Power, a large electrical utility company based on the eastern shore of Canada. From 1982 to 2002, Nova Scotia Power went through a variety of major organizational changes, including the introduction of:

- a cultural change program
- privatization
- downsizing
- business process reengineering
- strategic business units
- balanced scorecard accounting

Jean Helms Mills (2003) found that there were a variety of interpretations within the organization about these change programs. Drawing on the work of Weick (2000), she argues that these differing sense-making activities across the organization are indicative of the importance of understanding change as the accomplishment of ongoing processes for making sense of organizational events. She uses Weick's (2000) eight features of a sense-making framework to show how they impacted on understandings of organizational changes in the company. She draws out from each feature their implications for change managers (see table 9.7).

Similarly, in a study of downsizing in Telenor, Norway's main telecom organization, Bean and Hamilton (2006) point to the way its corporate leaders used sense-making to frame changes to the company in terms of making it an innovative, flexible, learning organization. After the downsizing, while some staff accepted the corporate "alignment" frame, others adopted an "alienated" frame, feeling marginalized and fearing for their job security. The researchers suggest that framing of change is fragile, with employees' interpretations of senior management pronouncements varying from *frame validating* (accepting) to *frame breaking* (challenging). That is, when the change manager acts as an interpreter, there is no guarantee that the manager's interpretations will not be contested.

As noted in chapter 8 on the topic of resistance to change, people in organizations can hold very strong views about an organization including what it "stands for" and how it should operate, and that these views ("mental models") can make people resistant to change that they see as inconsistent with these views. Another way of expressing this same point is that people in organizations can be disinclined to accept the change manager's

TABLE 9.7

Eight Features of a Sense-Making Framework

Sense-Making Framework Feature	Definition	Implications for Change Managers
Sense-making and identity construction	The different ways in which people make sense of the same organizational change events and how it is related to their understanding of the way their identities are constructed within organizations (Helms Mills, 2003, p. 126).	The "top-down initiatives requiring dramatic changes of self (i.e., from humanist to efficiency focused) are highly problematic and need either to be avoided or handled with great skill" (Helms Mills, 2003, p. 145).
Social sense-making	The need that people have to make sense of their situations not just as individuals but as social individuals is connected to a variety of influences on them such as supervisors, management, and trade unions.	An understanding of social sense-making highlights the need for managers to identify the social factors that influence sense-making in their organizational contexts.
Extracted cues of sense-making	The need for managers of change to be aware of the way people draw on a variety of "cues" or ideas and actions, perhaps taken from the external environment, to make sense of various decisions.	Change managers need to identify appropriate cues and match them to intended change programs. The way in which these cues are interpreted, however, may inadvertently create problems for staff in accepting the legitimacy of the change program and its intended purposes.
Ongoing sense-making	Sense-making changes over time as new cues are experienced and events addressed.	Change managers need to understand "that on-going sense-making stabilizes a situation and how change acts as a shock, generating emotional response and new acts of sense-making" (Helms Mills, 2003, p. 164).
Retrospection	Reference to Karl Weick's argument that people make sense of their actions retrospectively.	Change managers need to understand that different groups will apply their own retrospective sense-making to understand emerging organizational events.
Plausibility	The way that change management programs need to be sold so that the "story" about the change is plausible rather than necessarily accurate.	Change managers need to understand the way the context and power relations impact on their ability to provide plausible stories that gain widespread acceptance of the need for change.
Enactment	Whereas the above aspects of sense-making act as influences on sense-making, "enactment is about imposing that sense on action" (Helms Mills, 2003, pp. 173–74).	Enactment alerts change managers to the need to connect sense-making to actions.
Projective sense-making	The ability of a powerful actor to project sense-making onto a situation, shaping the interpretations of others.	The implication of this is that using legitimate power to impose sense-making on parts of the organization may be an important aspect of understanding the implementation of change.

Source: Based on Helms Mills (2003).

construction of events (i.e., his or her interpretation). As noted in chapter 7 on change communication strategies, the communicated message is not necessarily the message as understood by the receiver. In regard to the construction of events as provided by the change manager, it is not just that there may be some misunderstanding of the "story" the manager is seeking to communicate—the story may be well and truly understood—but it may not be accepted as "the facts of the situation."

The sense-making approach alerts change managers to the different facets that influence interpretations of events. At the same time, it is clear that these influences are often deeply embedded and less tangible than a clear set of steps that can be followed. From this perspective, managers of change need to be what Bolman and Deal (2017) describe as more artistic than rational, interpreting experience and expressing it in forms that can be felt, understood, and appreciated by others.

Change managers who are comfortable with these concepts are likely to find the sense-making framework of assistance to them in exploring the "tangled underbrush" of organizational change (Bolman and Deal, 2017). At the same time, they need to be mindful of organizational limitations on their sense-making abilities. This point is made by Balogun and Johnson (2004, p. 545) in their study of sense-making by middle managers when they "question the extent to which leaders can manage the development of change recipients' schemata, particularly in the larger, geographically dispersed, modularized organizations we are increasingly seeing."

Contested Interpretations in Metropolitan Police Department

Metropolitan (a pseudonym) police department began a change process that involved an organizational restructuring in which an increased share of resources was allocated to pro-active policing (intelligence gathering) and to a mode of organizing that prioritized having the capacity to rapidly deploy police when and where they were needed. The change managers' narrative emphasized the importance of the need to make these specific changes so that the police could be more "flexible" and by so doing deal more effectively with organized crime, which was demonstrating a capacity to speedily form and/or disband criminal teams to meet current needs.

However, the framing of the need for change as a matter of needed "flexibility" was not viewed that way by many of the police because they experienced the change as involving the regular turnover in squad membership. The significance of this experience was that consistency and longevity of squad membership were seen by many police as vital elements in producing both deep knowledge about specific areas of crime (e.g., armed robbery) and deep relations of trust (between squad members), which they saw as central to effective policing.

Dunford et al. (2013)

In chapter 8, we made the point that the simple dichotomy "managers lead change, workers resist change" was simplistic and did not serve us well if we wished to have a deeper and more useful understanding of resistance to organizational change. A similar and equally simplistic dichotomy is sometimes applied to the role of managers in regard to sense-making and sense-giving. In times of change, an organization's managers are commonly assumed to be the sense-givers who contribute—often to a major extent—to the sense-making by employees. However, the category of "manager" can apply to a large and diverse body of people, many of whom are not part of their organization's most senior leadership team and not fully aware of all details of "what's going on." Consequently, in some change situations, a subset of an organization's managers are likely to see themselves as more on the receiving end of change ("change recipients") than part of the team that is the architect of the change (see the box "Brand Corporation: Where You 'Sit' Influences Your Sense-Making, Even for Managers").

Brand Corporation *Where You "Sit" Influences Your Sense-Making, Even for Managers*

Brand Corporation, the European division of a fast-moving consumer goods (FMCG) multinational, announced that it was reorganizing in response to declining financial performance. Sales and marketing strategy, which had up to that point been determined at country level, was centralized at the Europe level, with other functions (finance, IT, HR) to follow.

As the centralization process continued, members of the UK management team began to define their situation as one in which they had, in effect, become middle managers responsible for strategy implementation, a lesser status than the senior managers they had been when they had strategy creation authority. They saw their new role as one in which they were rarely consulted and were on the receiving end of decisions that were predominantly

presented to them as fait accompli. These interpretations of the situation were accompanied and reinforced by a view that European managers were largely invisible.

This negative interpretation of the change expanded to include the belief that local and national knowledge and practices were being devalued and that the "people-based values" they saw themselves as practicing pre-change were not held by those at the center. For the UK management team this meant that, in turn, the change was defined as producing an organization in which people were not considered to be important, leading to a disengaged organization.

Balogun et al. (2015)

In reviewing the sense-making framework, it is clear that it provides less a set of prescriptions for managers of change and more a set of understandings about how to proceed. It acknowledges the messiness of change and accepts that competing voices mean that not all intended outcomes are likely to be achieved. However, critical to engaging these competing voices is the ability to shape and influence how they make sense of organizational events.

Although (as noted earlier in this chapter) OD has been subject to critique as it has evolved, this is much less the case for sense-making. For an exception, see Sandberg and Tsoukas (2015).

Can Sense-Making Success Become a Problem?

"The Office" is a Nordic firm that began a change process as a result of an announced forthcoming merger. As part of the change process, the top management of The Office put a lot of effort into convincing staff that the current organization was substantially underperforming due to being overly bureaucratic and as a result failing to be the innovative organization that it was intended to be. The strategy of The Office was presented by top management to staff as outdated and inappropriate.

The discrediting of the current arrangements at The Office—as described above—provided the basis for "sense-breaking." "Sense-giving" occurred through top management framing the merger as a way in which the staff of The Office would become part of a new and much higher performing entity, capable of operating with a quality, flexibility and level of customer service that The Office could not deliver in its present form. This sense-giving succeeded, and the staff of The Office bought into the message.

Unfortunately, complications then arose in the inter-organizational negotiations, and the merger was abruptly cancelled less than a week before the planned merger date. The Office's top management presented the failed merger as a good outcome and announced the reintroduction of a strategy almost identical to the one they had been following for 10 years. The reaction from The Office staff was "a sullen lack of enthusiasm" (Mantere et al., 2012, p. 186), even a sense of betrayal.

The top management had done such a good job of sense-breaking and sense-giving that the pre-merger version of The Office had been reframed by staff as no longer appropriate or acceptable, and this interpretation was not changed just because the merger had not proceeded.

Based on Mantere et al. (2012).

Managing Change from a Sense-Making Perspective   *Some Basic Advice*

1. Change managers should try to provide a clear narrative that articulates the what, why, and how of a proposed change.

2. Humans are creatures who abhor a "meaning vacuum"; in the absence of clear communication, they will draw conclusions, i.e., attribute meaning to fill the void. This is something that an organization should try to avoid at a time of change as all sorts of misconstructions might take hold and make change more difficult to achieve.

3. There is no guarantee that change managers' attempts at sense-giving will be successful as organizational members live in a world of multiple narratives and, regardless of authority structures, the interpretation being presented by a change manager need not have greater credibility than other narratives. For example, some organizations are characterized by a very strong sense of identity, which can give the "what we stand for, how we do things, what we value," an almost moral quality that can make organizational members very disinclined to "switch narratives."

4. Managers (including those in a change management role) in an organization are "interpreters" whether they like it or not. They cannot choose to opt out of having this role. Their only choice is how consciously or explicitly they play this role. Managers' actions have symbolic meaning and will be interpreted (by other organizational members) in this way. In this regard see Exercise 9.4.

EXERCISE 9.1

Reports from the Front Line

LO 9.2

This exercise requires you to interview two Organization Development practitioners about how they go about doing their work. Compare and contrast them in terms of the following issues:

- their background
- values they espouse
- steps they say they use in approaching a consulting assignment
- tensions they identify in working as an OD practitioner
- their perceptions of the way the OD field has changed and likely changes into the future

What general conclusions do you draw about the practice of OD?

EXERCISE 9.2

Designing a Large-Scale Change Intervention

LO 9.2

Choose a current issue in your local neighborhood. This exercise gets you to figure out how you would design a large-scale change intervention program in relation to this issue. Give consideration to the following issues:

- How many people would it make sense to involve?
- Where and when would you hold it?
- How would you ensure that you have a representative cross sample of relevant people in the room at the same time? What data sources would you need to achieve this?
- Who are the key decision makers in relation to this issue? What arguments will you use to get them to attend the meeting?
- How will you structure the agenda of the meeting? What would be the best way of doing this so that people who attend on that day have appropriate buy-in to it?
- How would you run the actual meeting?
- What technology would you need to make it work well?
- What would people take away from the meeting?
- What follow-up actions would you plan to ensure that actions and decisions flowed from it?
- What possible funding sources might you draw on to finance the meeting?
- As a result of considering such questions, what new issues emerge for you, as a large-scale change intervention agent, to consider? What specific skills would you need to make such an event work well? Which of these skills would you need to develop more?

EXERCISE 9.3

Making Sense of Sense-Making

LO 9.4

Identify a current change in an organization with which you are familiar. Alternatively, identify a current public issue about which "something must be done." In relation to the change issue, think about what sense-making changes might need to be enacted and how you would go about doing this. Assess this in terms of the eight elements of the sense-making framework suggested by Helms Mills (2003) and as set out in table 9.6:

- Identity construction
- Social sense-making
- Extracted cues
- Ongoing sense-making

- Retrospection
- Plausibility
- Enactment
- Projection

What ones did you feel you might have the most and least control over? Why? What implications does this have for adopting a sense-making approach to organizational change?

EXERCISE 9.4

Interpreting the Interpreter: Change at Target

LO 9.4

Target in 2019 was one of the 10 largest retailers in the United States (Walmart was no. 1), but it has had to deal with some difficult times. In the decade to 2014, Target's earnings dropped from $3.2 billion to $1.5 billion with net income as a percentage of sales similarly dropping from 4.6 percent to 2 percent during this period. These were key elements of the context into which Brian Cornell arrived in August 2014 as Target's new CEO. Some of the actions he then took included:

1. He made an impromptu and incognito visit to a Target store in Dallas to talk to customers. Not recognized by store employees or customers, he sought candid opinions from shoppers. This action by the CEO was a surprise to Target executives because it was a significant departure from past practice. Prior to Cornell's arrival, store visits had occurred—supposedly as intelligence-gathering exercises—but they had been "meticulously planned affairs, only less formal than, say, a presidential visit" with the store managers notified in advance and "the 'regular shoppers' handpicked and vetted" (Wahba, 2015, p. 86).

2. When he first arrived at Target's headquarters (in Minneapolis), Cornell was allocated the newly refurbished CEO's suite, but he insisted on moving to a smaller office close to Target's global data nerve center. The 10 staff members in this center monitored live feeds from social media—including Pinterest, Facebook, and Twitter—and from TV stations to locate stories and information on product launches, customer comments, etc. The nerve center staff watched social media on large screens and used software to aggregate data for later analysis.

3. With the intention of putting pressure on Amazon and Walmart, Cornell changed Target's policy to one offering free shipping for online orders during the holidays, a "decision that was made in a matter of days rather than the months it would have taken in the past" (Wahba, 2015, p. 88).

4. It was not unusual for Cornell to ask colleagues about their "work–life" balance and especially their workout habits. He encouraged colleagues to take time for fitness activities and wasn't "the type who exalts the machismo of outlandish hours" (Wahba, 2015, p. 88).

5. Cornell relaxed the company's dress code and ate in the company café where he mixed with staff.

6. He moved the company's recruitment policy to change the situation from one where Target was "long populated by lifers" to one making more effort to "recruit outsiders with fresh ideas" (Wahba, 2015, p. 94).

Consider the proposition that managers' actions have symbolic meaning and will be interpreted (by other organizational members) in this way:

1. What do you see as the symbolism associated with Target CEO Brian Cornell's actions?

2. If you had been a Target employee, what might you have concluded about the nature of the change happening in Target?

Case Source
Wahba (2015).

EXERCISE 9.5

Change at DuPont

LO 9.2, 9.3, 9.4

As we walked through the manufacturing areas of DuPont, the plant manager, Tom Harris, greeted each worker by name. The plant was on a site that stretched over 10 acres beside the South River on the edge of town, and it was the major employer in the community.

The plant seemed to be a permanent fixture, or at least more permanent than most things. There had been changes, big ones, but the plant was still the plant. The Orlon manufacturing operation had been shut down, the equipment dismantled and sent to China. As far as I could find out early in my work there, these changes, despite their magnitude, were seen as doing the regular business of the enterprise. No one framed the changes as needing unusual attention, so there was no change management design. The projects—getting rid of one operation and installing another—were planned and executed just like any project. Change management was not a rubric used to either accomplish or explain what was going on. More changes were coming, whether there was any formal practice of change management or not. The plant would soon enough look very different from what I saw on that first tour with Tom.

I first met Tom when he came to the University of Virginia seeking to make contact with the academic community in order to bring some of the latest thinking in business to his operation. His interest lay in introducing his managers to new ideas and in applying those ideas to improving the plant. He was not, he said, looking for solutions to specific problems, but rather in improving overall organization effectiveness. This was important because he was under increasing pressure to do more with less.

In February, this general bulletin was sent to all employees, and I began the fieldwork from which a portrayal of the work culture would be built.

Gib Akin, a professor from the University of Virginia, will be spending time at the plant. He has been asked to give us some new perspectives on our work and our organization that we might use to help us develop people and continually improve. Most importantly, he is here to help us appreciate and develop what goes right, assist us in building on our strengths, to make the plant work better for everybody. His presence is not due to any particular problem but is a result of our desire to continuously improve.

Over the next six months, I conducted interviews with workers and managers, spending time in the workplace, and learning about everyday life there. This yielded a thick description of the shared stock of knowledge that organizational members used to interpret events and generate behavior. What we made explicit with this process was the local, widely used, every day, common-sense model of work performance, unique to this scene. In a sense, this was the local organization theory that people used for getting along at work.

Of course, this theory was more important than any imported academic theory of organization, because it had to work well or the users would not be successful in their work. This was the practical theory in use every day and by everyone. Such culturally embedded theory also tends to create what it is intended to explain, thus making it even more powerful and generative. For example, in this plant, the local model of teamwork was organized around a southern stock-car racing metaphor, which was not only used to explain teamwork but was also the pattern for accomplishing it. And since everyone knew the metaphor, and used it, it became so.

Tom and the other managers were surprised to learn of the NASCAR (the premier stock-car racing organization) metaphor, but it explained why they had not recognized existing teamwork in the workplace (they had a different metaphor for teamwork) and

(Continued)

gave them a language in which to introduce change for improvement. Similarly, illumination of the local meaning of effective supervision, high performance, and what constituted a good day at work gave those with leadership roles constructs to work with for making improvements and the language for introducing change.

Managers, and particularly first-line supervisors, were asked to use this new understanding gained from the findings of the study. Their new understanding could be used to interpret the local meaning of effective work to capitalize on strengths to expand and develop existing good practices in order to swamp problems, that is, to render problems less troublesome even if unsolved.

The findings of the study also could be used as the basis for experiments. Members of the so-called Leadership Core Team were instructed to introduce change as an experiment—something to be tried and watched closely, and after a designated time, if it is not working as hoped, it can be stopped. Framing changes as experiments requires thinking through what is expected and how and when to measure the results. And by interpreting the possible results before they happen, all outcomes can be positive. Even if things don't go as hoped, what does happen can yield learning. All experiments are successes at one level or another.

Tom embraced the framing of change as experiment, and it was probably his most pervasive concept regarding change. "A notion I use all the time is that everything is an experiment. If you describe every change as an experiment, the ability of people to digest it goes up an order of magnitude. And that goes for officers as well as people on the shop floor. As a matter of fact, nothing is forever anyway."

Case Source

Personal correspondence from Gib Akin.

Questions

1. To what extent are the following approaches to change embedded in the DuPont story (justify your answer, providing specific examples):

   a. OD

   b. Appreciative Inquiry

   c. Sense-making

2. In your opinion, how compatible are these three approaches? Why? What evidence is there in the DuPont story for your answer? As a change manager, to what extent could you utilize insights from each approach?

3. Imagine you are an OD practitioner brought into DuPont at the time of the Orlon manufacturing operation closure. Describe the steps you would take to help manage this change based upon action research.

4. As a class, decide on a fictional large-scale change that could affect DuPont. Divide the class into three groups (and role-play the situation in two acts). In Act 1, one group will take a problem-solving approach and introduce the change with the second group (DuPont staff affected by the change). In Act 2, a third group (the Appreciative Inquiry group) will introduce the change with the second group (DuPont staff affected by the change). After the exercise, compare and contrast the steps taken in each approach. From the point of view of group two (DuPont staff), which approach seemed to work better? Why? From the point of view of groups one and two, how easy or difficult was it adopting this approach? What broad conclusions can be drawn?

Additional Reading

Bunker, B. B., and Alban, B. T. 2006. *The handbook of large group methods: Creating systemic change in organizations and communities.* San Francisco, CA: Jossey-Bass. Provides details on methods used in large group interventions and multiple cases studies illustrating the successful use of large group methods in a range of industries and countries.

Bushe, G. R., and Marshak, R. J. (eds.). 2015. *Dialogic Organization Development: The theory and practice of transformational change.* Oakland: CA, Berrett-Koehler. A comprehensive introduction to the evolving field of Dialogic OD from the originators of this approach to managing organizational change.

Cooperrider, D. L., Whitney, D., and Stavros, J. M. 2008. *The Appreciative Inquiry handbook: For leaders of change.* 2nd ed. San Francisco, CA: Berrett-Koehler. A detailed guide to the application of AI, including rationale and examples, from originators of the concept.

Cummings, T. G., and Worley, C. G. 2019. *Organization Development and change.* 11th ed. Stamford, CT: Cengage Learning. A comprehensive and classic textbook on Diagnostic OD.

Kraft, A., Sparr, J. L., and Peus, C. 2018. Giving and making sense about change: The back and forth between leaders and employees. *Journal of Business Psychology* 33:71–87. Provides a framework that identifies employee sense-making needs at different points in the organizational change process and the associated leader sense-giving activities.

Quinn, R. E., and Cameron, K. S. 2019. Positive Organizational Scholarship and agents of change. *Research in Organizational Change and Development* 27:31–7. Focuses on the role of the change agent from a Positive Organizational Scholarship perspective.

Roundup

Reflections for the Practicing Change Manager

- Do you model the change behavior you desire?
- Whose interests do you serve when you engage in change?
- Is your approach value-laden or value-neutral? If value-laden, can you articulate what these values are? Are you comfortable with them?
- What do you mean when you talk about a change being successful? What criteria do you use? Do they relate to organizational performance? How can you determine this?
- Are there other people, inside or outside your organization, who have differing perspectives on such questions? What would you say are the criteria they use to evaluate change? Is your organization open to having conversations around this issue?
- If you manage across different countries, to what extent have you observed the necessity for different ways of engaging in organizational change in those countries? Why is this the case?
- Can you identify different sense-making activities going on during organizational change? What ability do you have to influence these? Do you exercise power in your attempts to influence the interpretations others have of change situations? With what success? What are the implications of this?

Here is a short summary of the key points that we would like you to take from this chapter, in relation to each of the learning outcomes:

* *Appreciate more clearly the organizational change approaches underpinning the coach and interpreter images of managing change.*

While two of the change images—*caretaker* and *nurturer*—present change managers as receiving rather than initiating change, the other four images—*director, coach, navigator,* and *interpreter*—present the change manager as having an active, as opposed to reactive, role in how change occurs in organizations. The image of the change manager as *coach* is particularly strong in the approach to change that has developed with what is known as Organization Development (OD) and its derivatives, including Appreciative Inquiry (AI), change as viewed from within the perspective of Positive Organizational Scholarship (POS), and Dialogic OD. The coach link is that each of these approaches involves encouraging a willingness to change and the developing of change capabilities in people, rather than seeking to bring about change by top-down edict. The image of the change manager as *interpreter* links closely to a sense-making view of the role of the change manager

* *Understand the Organization Development (OD) approach to change.*

Underpinned by the *coach* image, the Organization Development (OD) approach is one where its adherents present their developmental prescriptions for achieving change as being based, at least traditionally, upon a core set of values: values that emphasize that change should benefit not just organizations but the people who staff them.

* *Be aware of extensions of the OD approach such as Appreciative Inquiry, Positive Organizational Scholarship, and Dialogic OD.*

In chapter 2, we suggested that the coach image is a metaphor for thinking about the Organization Development approach. OD practitioners coach organizations and the people in them toward intentional outcomes. These outcomes are shaped by a set of values that emphasize humanistic, democratic, and developmental aspirations. In recent times, these values have been placed under the microscope in terms of their universal applicability, in particular regarding their applicability in an environment that appears to demand radical, not developmental change—an era where the bottom line rather than democratic values appears to have a higher priority for engaging in change. Of course, there does not necessarily have to be a dichotomous choice between a focus on people and a focus on the bottom line; one may lead to the other. Nevertheless, adherents to the OD approach have had to reassess how their approach to managing change can be adapted to the changing times.

Chapter 10 will pick up this theme in more detail; suffice it to say that we expect that the OD approach is likely to remain a strong contender for managing change in the future. However, it is also likely that it will lose its distinctive, traditional character as it is molded in different ways. Some changes move OD more in the direction of delivering tangible, measurable outputs, while others such as POS explicitly assert the importance of organizational interventions that improve the "human condition" in ways that are not reducible to "traditionally pursued organizational outcomes" such as profitability (Cameron and McNaughtan, 2014). This evolution of OD has led some commentators to suggest that there needs to be greater recognition that OD is now not one approach but a plurality of approaches. If so, then greater clarity will be needed in how OD is talked about, including whether classic or newer versions of OD—such as Dialogic OD—are being referred to when the term is being used.

LO 9.4   *   *Understand the sense-making approach to change.*

In chapter 2, we depicted the sense-making approach to organizational change as drawing upon an image of the change manager as *interpreter*. In this chapter, we have been able to delve deeper into the different elements of this image. As Helms Mills' (2003) study of Nova Scotia Power showed, there are a number of different levels on which the change manager as *interpreter* operates, each of which requires attention. At the same time, this approach does not imply that mastering each of these levels will always enable intended outcomes to be achieved. Wider forces, both inside and outside the organization, will ensure that there will always be competing forces vying for a privileged place in providing for organizational members an interpretation of "what's going on here" as well as "what needs to go on here." The interpreter image therefore points out to change agents the need to have a realistic view of what can be achieved in undergoing organizational change. Although managers of change may find the sense-making approach to be more difficult given that it is less tangible in terms of "what needs to be done," it is also likely to give other managers comfort in reaffirming their experience of the messiness of change and identification of new ways of approaching it.

References

Axelrod, D. 1992. Getting everyone involved: How one organization involved its employees, supervisors, and managers in redesigning the organization. *Journal of Applied Behavioral Science* 28(4):499–509.

Axelrod, R. H. 2001. Terms of engagement: Changing the way we change organizations. *Journal for Quality & Participation* (Spring):22–27.

Baburoglu, O. N., and Garr, M. A. 1992. Search conference methodologies for practitioners: An introduction. In *Discovering common ground,* ed. M. R. Weisbord (72–81). San Francisco: Berrett-Koehler.

Badham, R.J., Carter, W. R., Matula, L. J., Parker, S. K., and Nesbit, P. L. 2015. Beyond hope and fear: The effects of organizational theatre on empowerment and control. *Journal of Applied Behavioral Science* 51:1–28.

Balogun, J., and Johnson, G. 2004. Organizational restructuring and middle manager sense-making. *Academy of Management Journal* 47(4):523–49.

Balogun, J., Bartunek, K. M., and Do, B. 2015. Senior managers' sensemaking and responses to strategic change. *Organization Science* 26(4):960–79.

Bartunek, J. M., and Woodman, R. W. 2015. Beyond Lewin: Toward temporal approximation of organization development and change. *Annual Review of Organizational Psychology and Organizational Behavior* 2:157–82.

Bean, C. J., and Hamilton, F. E. 2006. Leader framing and follower sense-making: Response to downsizing in the brave new workplace. *Human Relations* 59(3):321–49.

Beckhard, R. 1969. *Organization Development: Strategies and models.* Reading, MA: Addison-Wesley.

Beer, M. 2014. Organization Development at a crossroads. *OD Practitioner* 46(4):60–61.

Blake, R., Carlson, B., McKee, R., Sorenson, P., and Yaeger, T. F. 2000. Contemporary issues of grid international: Sustaining and extending the core values of O.D. *Organization Development Journal* 18(2):54–61.

Bolman, L. G., and Deal, T. E. 2017. *Reframing organizations: Artistry, choice, and leadership.* 6th ed. San Francisco, CA: Jossey-Bass.

Brown, J., and Issacs, D. 2005. *The World Café.* San Francisco, CA: Berrett-Koehler.

Bunker, B. B., and Alban, B. T. 1992. Editors' introduction: The large group intervention— a new social innovation? *Journal of Applied Behavioral Science* 28(4):473–579.

Bunker, B. B., and Alban, B. T. 1997. *Large group interventions: Engaging the whole system for rapid change.* San Francisco: Jossey-Bass.

Bunker, B. B., and Alban, B. T. 2006. *The handbook of large group methods: Creating systemic change in organizations and communities.* San Francisco: Jossey-Bass.

Burke, W. W. 1997. The new agenda for Organization Development. *Organizational Dynamics* 26(1):7–20.

Burnes, B. 2020. The origins of Lewin's three-step model of change. *Journal of Applied Behavioral Science* 51(1):32–59.

Burnes, B., and Cooke, B. 2012. Review article: The past, present and future of Organization Development: Taking the long view. *Human Relations* 65(11):1395–429.

Bushe, G. R., and Marshak, R. J. 2009. Revisioning Organization Development: Diagnostic and dialogic premises and patterns of practice. *Journal of Applied Behavioral Science* 45(3):348–68.

Bushe, G. R., and Marshak, R. J. (eds.). 2015. *Dialogic Organization Development: The theory and practice of transformational change.* Oakland, CA: Berrett-Koehler.

Cameron, K. 2006. Good or not bad: Standards and ethics in managing change. *Academy of Management Learning and Education* 5(3):317–23.

Cameron, K. S., and Caza, A. 2004. Contributions to the discipline of positive organizational scholarship. *American Behavioral Scientist* 47(6):731–39.

Cameron, K., and McNaughtan, J. 2014. Positive organizational change. *Journal of Applied Behavioral Science* 50(4):445–62.

Cooperrider, D. L., and Whitney, D. 2005. *Appreciative Inquiry: A positive revolution in change.* San Francisco: Berrett-Koehler.

Cooperrider, D. L., Whitney, D., and Stavros, J. M. 2008. *The Appreciative Inquiry handbook: For leaders of change.* 2nd ed. San Francisco, CA: Berrett-Koehler.

Cummings, S., Bridgman, T., and Brown, K. G. 2016. Unfreezing change as three steps: Rethinking Kurt Lewin's legacy for change management. *Human Relations* 69(1):33–60.

Cummings, T. G., and Worley, C. G. 2019. *Organization Development and change.* 11ᵗʰ ed Stamford, CT: Centage Learning.

Dannemiller, K. D., and Jacobs, R. W. 1992. Changing the way organizations change: A revolution of common sense. *Journal of Applied Behavioral Science* 28(4):480-98.

Dunford, R., Cuganesan, S., Grant, D., Palmer, I., Beaumont, R., and Steele, C. 2013. "Flexibility" as the rationale for organizational change: A discourse perspective. *Journal of Organizational Change Management* 26(1):83-97.

Emery, M., and Purser, R. E. 1996. *The search conference.* San Francisco, CA: Jossey-Bass.

Fagenson-Eland, E., Ensher, E. A., and Burke, W. W. 2004. Organization Development and change interventions: A seven-nation comparison. *Journal of Applied Behavioral Science* 40(4):432-64.

Fineman, S. 2006. On being positive: Concerns and counterpoints. *Academy of Management Review* 31(2):270-91.

French, W. L., and Bell, C. H. 1995. *Organization Development: Behavioral science interventions for organization improvement.* Englewood Cliffs, NJ: Prentice Hall.

Fuller, C., Griffin, T., and Ludema, J. D. 2000. Appreciative future search: Involving the whole system in positive organization change. *Organization Development Journal* 18(2):29-41.

Gelinas, M. V., and James, R. G. 1999. Organizational purpose: Foundation for the future. *OD Practitioner* 31(2):10-22.

Golembiewski, R. 1999. Process observer: Large-system interventions, II: Two sources of evidence that ODers have been there, been doing that. *Organization Development Journal* 17(3):5-8.

Helms Mills, J. 2003. *Making sense of organizational change.* London: Routledge.

Herman, S. 2000. Counterpoints: Notes on OD for the 21st century, Part 1. *Organization Development Journal* 18(2):108-10.

Hoberecht, S., Joseph, B., Spencer, J., and Southern, N. 2011. *OD Practitioner* 43(4):23-27.

Holman, P. 2013. A call to engage. *OD Practitioner* 45(1):18-24.

Holman, P., Devane, T., and Cody, S. (eds.). 2007. *The change handbook: Group methods for shaping the future.* 2nd ed. San Francisco, CA: Berrett-Koehler.

Hornstein, H. 2001. Organizational development and change management: Don't throw the baby out with the bath water. *Journal of Applied Behavioral Science* 37(2):223-26.

Iveroth, E., and Hallencreutz, J. 2015. *Effective leadership through sensemaking.* New York: Routledge.

Jamieson, D. W., and Marshak, R. J. 2018. Reasserting what OD needs to be. *Organization Development Journal,* Fall:91-103.

Jorgenson, J. and Steier, F. 2013. Frames, framing, and designing conversational processes: Lessons from the World Café. *Journal of Applied Behavioral Science* 49(3):388-405.

Klein, D. C. 1992. Simu-Real: A simulation approach to organizational change. *Journal of Applied Behavioral Science* 28(4):566-78.

Kraft, A., Sparr, J. L., and Peus, C. 2018. Giving and making sense about change: The back and forth between leaders and employees. *Journal of Business Psychology* 33:71-87.

Levine, L., and Mohr, B. J. 1998. Whole system design (WSD): The shifting focus of attention and the threshold challenge. *Journal of Applied Behavioral Science* 34(3):305-26.

Lewin, K. 1947. Frontiers in group dynamics. *Human Relations* 1:5-41.

Lockett, A., Currie, G., Finn, R., Martin, G., and Waring, J. 2014. The influence of social position on sense-making about organizational change. *Academy of Management Journal* 57(4):1102-29.

Lukensmeyer, C. J., and Brigham, S. 2002. Taking democracy to scale: Creating a town hall meeting for the twenty-first century. *National Civic Review* 91(4):351-66.

Maitlis, S., and Christianson, M. 2014. Sense-making in organizations: Taking stock and moving forward. *Academy of Management Annals* 8(1):57-125.

Manning, M. R., and Binzagr, G. F. 1996. Methods, values, and assumptions underlying large group interventions intended to change whole systems. *International Journal of Organizational Analysis* 4(3):268-84.

Mantere, S., Schildt, H. A., and Sillince, J. A. 2012. Reversal of strategic change. *Academy of Management Journal* 55(1):172 -96.

Marshak, R. J. 1993. Lewin meets Confucius: A re-view of the OD model of change. *Journal of Applied Behavioral Science* 29(4):393-415.

Marshak, R. J. 2006. *Covert processes at work*. San Francisco, CA: Berrett-Koehler.

Marshak, R. J. 2013. The controversy over diagnosis in contemporary organization development. *OD Practitioner* 45(1):54-59.

Marshak, R. J. 2015. My journey into Dialogic Organization Development. *OD Practitioner* 47(2):47-52.

Mirvis, P. 2006. Revolutions in OD: The new and the new, new things. In *Organization Development: A Jossey-Bass reader, ed.* J. V. Gallos *(39-88)*. San Francisco, CA: Jossey-Bass,

Nicholl, D. 1998a. From the editor: Is OD meant to be relevant? Part I. *OD Practitioner* 30(2):3-6.

Nicholl, D. 1998b. From the editor: Is OD meant to be relevant? Part II. *OD Practitioner* 30(3):3-6.

Nicholl, D. 1998c. From the editor: Is OD meant to be relevant? Part III. *OD Practitioner* 30(4):3-6.

Nicholl, D. 1999. From the editor: A new profession for the next millennium. *OD Practitioner* 31(4).

Oswick, C., and Grant, D. 1996. Organization Development and metaphor—mapping the territory. In *Organization Development: Metaphorical exploration*, ed. C. Oswick & D. Grant (1–3). London: Pitman.

Quinn, R. E., and Cameron, K. S. 2019. Positive Organizational Scholarship and agents of change. *Research in Organizational Change and Development* 27:31–37.

Rao, M. 2014. Cultivating openness to change in multicultural organizations: Assessing the value of appreciative discourse. *Organization Development Journal* (Fall):75–88.

Roberts, L. M. 2006. Shifting the lens on organizational life: The added value of positive scholarship. *Academy of Management Review* 31(2):292–305.

Rouleau, L., and Balogun, J. 2010. Middle managers: Strategic sense-making, and discursive competence. *Journal of Management Studies* 48(5):953–83.

Sandberg, J., and Tsoukas, H. 2015. Making sense of the sense-making perspective: Its constituents, limitations, and opportunities for further development. *Journal of Organizational Behavior* 36:S6–S32.

Sorenson, P. F., and Yaeger, T. F. 2014. The global world of OD. *OD Practitioner* 46(4):56–59.

Tenkasi, R. V. 2018. Revisiting the past to re-imagine the future of organizational development and change. *Organization Development Journal* (Winter):61–75.

Van Oosten, E. B. 2006. Intentional change theory at the organizational level: A case study. *Journal of Management Development* 25(7):707–17.

Wahba, P. 2015. Back on target. *Fortune* (March):86–94.

Weick, K. E. 2000. Emergent change as a universal in organizations. In *Breaking the code of change, ed.* M. Beer and N. Nohria (223–41). Boston: Harvard Business School Press.

Weick, K. E., Sutcliffe, K. M., and Obstfeld, D. 2005. Organizing and the process of sense-making. *Organizational Science* 16(4):409–22.

Weisbord, M. R. 1992a. Preface. In *Discovering common ground, ed.* M. R. Weisbord (pp. xi–xvi). San Francisco: Berrett-Koehler.

Weisbord, M. R. 1992b. Applied common sense. In *Discovering common ground, ed.* M. R. Weisbord (3–17). San Francisco, CA: Berrett-Koehler.

Worley, C. G. 2014. OD values and pitches in the dirt. *OD Practitioner* 46(4):68–71.

Worley, C. G., Hitchin, D. E., and Ross, W. L. 1996. *Integrated strategic change: How OD can create a competitive advantage.* Reading, MA: Addison-Wesley.

Worley, C. G., Mohrman, S. A., and Nevitt, J. A. 2011. Large group interventions: An empirical field study of their composition, process, and outcomes. *Journal of Applied Behavioral Science* 47(4):404–31.

Source of the chapter opening quote: Tan, J. 2020. 69 Of the Best Jeff Bezos Quotes, Sorted by Category, Referral Candy, https://www.referralcandy.com/blog/jeff-bezos-quotes.

Chapter opening silhouette credit: CharlotteRaboff/Shutterstock

Chapter 10

Change Management Perspectives

Learning Objectives

By the end of this chapter you should be able to:

LO 10.1 Understand and identify the factors that can cause change to fail.

LO 10.2 Assess the strengths and limitations of checklists for managing change effectively.

LO 10.3 Evaluate the advantages of stage models of change management.

LO 10.4 Assess the theoretical and practical value of the process perspective on change.

LO 10.5 Understand and apply contingency approaches to change management.

"The question isn't who's going to let me; it's who is going to stop me."

Ayn Rand, writer and philosopher

Options for Managing Change

Change Is Disruptive—Live with It

A true transformation is disruptive. It doesn't just work with the existing governance, the existing processes, the existing budgeting cycle, the existing ways of doing things. It is going to disrupt. And it's going to create challenge and tension and friction in the organization. Because it is so disruptive, it's also a top priority of the organization. This is not something that can be third or fourth down in the CEO's list of things he or she must do. We view those characteristics as being necessary co-travellers to delivering a true transformation of the company. (Bucy et al., 2017a, pp. 2–3).

The perspectives discussed in this chapter include change management checklists, stage models, and process and contingency theories. They offer advice on managing change, but make no mention of the personal styles and preferences of individual change managers. Let us first fill this gap.

The Director and Navigator Images of Change Management

Two of our six images of change management are particularly relevant to the approaches explored in this chapter. The *director* image underpins the change management approaches associated with the work of large consulting companies, and also of academics who work as change consultants in this field. Those who adopt such approaches take a strategic view, adopting a pragmatic, managerialist approach to achieving lasting organizational change. The checklists and stage models that we explore fall into this category. They suggest that change can be managed and controlled in a predictable manner as long as the correct steps are taken, in more or less the correct sequence. However, given the number of different sets of recipes and frameworks that are available, it is not always clear which to adopt, or the criteria on which the choice should be made.

Contingency frameworks can also be seen as consistent with the *director* image. Rather than claiming to have discovered "the one best approach," however, these frameworks argue that "it depends" on a number of context factors, such as the scale and urgency of the proposed changes. For example, one of these contingency frameworks, the change kaleidoscope (Balogun et al., 2016) does not offer prescriptive advice on how to implement change in particular contexts. That framework instead highlights for the change manager the contextual issues to consider when reaching an informed judgment with regard to change implementation design options. This approach is also consistent to some extent with the *navigator* image of change management. Change can be controlled in part, but external factors (contextual enablers and constraints, competing interests) can generate emergent and unintended outcomes over which the change manager has little or no influence.

The idea of establishing "fit" between change implementation and organizational context is not consistent with a processual view of change. Process theories see change unfolding over time in a messy and iterative way and thus rely on the image of change manager as *navigator*. Here, the change outcomes are shaped by a combination of factors including the past, present, and future *context* in which the organization functions; the *substance* of the change; the implementation *process*; *political behavior*, inside and outside the organization; and the interactions between these factors (Dawson and Andriopoulos, 2017). The role of the change manager is not to direct, but to identify options, accumulate resources, monitor progress, and to *navigate* a path through the complexity.

It is therefore important for change managers to be aware of, and perhaps on many occasions to put to one side, their preferred image of change management. It is also important that managers are comfortable with their actions, with regard to both personal capability and how actions are perceived to fit with the context. However, implementation design decisions should ideally be more heavily influenced by the context factors that we explore in this chapter than by personal considerations.

LO 10.1 Why Change Fails

Anyone who has never made a mistake has never tried anything new. (Albert Einstein)

Trying is the first step towards failure. (Homer Simpson)

In this chapter, we explore approaches to implementing organizational change effectively, drawing on a range of change management, processual, and contingency perspectives. First, however, we will explore why change fails. If we understand the common mistakes, perhaps we can avoid them.

Ask a group of managers to reflect on their experience and to identify what to do to make organizational change fail. Their response usually comes in two stages. First, they laugh. Second, they generate without difficulty a list of practical actions to guarantee that an initiative will not be successful. Table 10.1 illustrates the typical results of such a discussion. This suggests two conclusions. First, ensuring that change fails—should one wish to do that—is not difficult. There are many tools at one's disposal, involving a combination of actions and inactions. Second, if we have such a good understanding of what can go wrong, then getting it right should be easy. Just turn the negatives around: clear vision,

TABLE 10.1
How to Make Change Fail: A Management View

Choose the most expensive way to do it	Commitment without leadership support
Demotivate the group	Do not recognize the power of the team
Distort the vision	Divert attention and resources
Don't buy into the process	Don't follow the process
Highlight past failures	Highlight the negatives
Lack of honesty	No communication
Political games	Set up silos
Team up with others	Too many policies and procedures

commitment and leadership support, honest communication, simplicity, break down the silos, highlight successes and positives—and so on. Sadly, while this approach is helpful, "getting it right" is not this easy.

From his research into over 100 companies (most but not all American), John Kotter (2007; 2012a) argues that transformational changes often fail because of the mistakes that are identified in table 10.2. Understanding what not to do, Kotter turns these mistakes into a positive model of successful transformation. That involves careful planning, working through these issues more or less in sequence, and not missing or rushing any of them—which takes time. However, given the rapid pace of contemporary change, many organizations perhaps try to take too many shortcuts, to put change in place quickly, and get it wrong as a result.

Although it may be an oversimplification to claim that successful change just means avoiding these mistakes, they should be avoided nevertheless. It is also important to recognize that there are many of these mistakes, and that in any particular setting, several of those factors may be combining to ensure that the change program fails. Success or failure can rarely be explained with reference to only a single factor. What are the costs involved in avoiding these mistakes? Almost all the remedies are cost-neutral, involving changes in leadership and management style and in organizational policies and procedures. In short, while ensuring that change will fail involves little or no cost, most of the actions required to "get it right" are also free.

TABLE 10.2
Why Transformation Efforts Fail*

Mistakes	Nature and Remedy
No urgency	If employees don't see the need, then they will not be motivated to change; management must create a sense of urgency.
No coalition	One or two people acting on their own can't drive big change; management must create a coalition with the expertise and the power to make it happen.
No vision	Without a picture of the future that is easy to explain and understand, a change program becomes confusing; change needs a clear vision.
Poor communication	Giving people an important message once is not enough; the vision must be communicated repeatedly by management, in words and actions.
Obstacles not removed	Structures, design of jobs, reward and appraisal systems, and key individuals can get in the way; the obstacles must be confronted and removed.
No wins	Change takes time, and momentum can be lost without interim achievements to celebrate; management should create and reward short-term wins.
Premature victory	The job is not done when improvements appear; it is a mistake to "declare victory" too soon, before the changes are embedded.
No anchoring	Change that is not seen to be beneficial will decay, and the next generation of managers may not continue the work; the change must be seen to have worked, and successors must champion the changes of their predecessors.

*based on Kotter (2007 and 2012a)

LO 10.2 # Change by Checklist

> *There is a certain relief in change even though it be from bad to worse; as I have found travelling in a stage-coach, it is often a comfort to shift one's position and be bruised in new places.*

> (Washington Irving)

The landscape of practical advice for the change manager is dominated by simple checklists. These have also been described as "*n*-step recipes," where *n* is the number of items on the list. This approach is open to the criticism that it oversimplifies a complex process. However simplified, it is probably accurate to claim that, in most cases, if the change manager does not follow most of the advice in these checklists, then the change program could run into trouble.

Checklist approaches to change management assume that the process is logical and linear and can therefore be controlled by planning and then following the correct set of steps. This "rational linear" model of change has been widely criticized, but it remains popular with professional bodies and management consultancies. This is probably because these checklists or recipes codify what is usually a messy and iterative process and thus offer the busy change manager straightforward advice on what to do to improve the chances of success. In this section, we will consider three typical checklists and consider how the change agent should choose between them.

The Boston Consulting Group's DICE Model

Management consulting companies typically develop their own recipes, often with a memorable acronym. The DICE model developed by the Boston Consulting Group, for example, identifies four factors that determine whether a change program will "fly or die": Duration, Integrity, Commitment, and Effort. These four factors are outlined in table 10.3 (Sirkin et al., 2005).

TABLE 10.3
DICE—Will Your Change Program Fly or Die?

DICE Factor	Meaning
Duration	The duration of time until the program is completed if it has a short life span; if not short, the amount of time between reviews or milestones
Integrity	The project team's performance integrity; its ability to complete the initiative on time, which depends on members' skills relative to the project's requirements
Commitment	The commitment displayed by top management and employees who are affected
Effort	The effort required that is over and above the usual demands on employees

Based on Sirkin et al., 2005

Change managers are advised to calculate scores for each of the DICE factors. For example, Duration scores highly if the overall project timescale is short with frequent reviews but gets a low score if reviews are more than eight months apart. Integrity scores well if a skilled and motivated project team has a capable and respected leader and scores badly if those features are absent. Are those who will be affected by the change enthusiastic and supportive (high Commitment score), or are they concerned and obstructive (low score)? Does the project require a small amount of additional work (high Effort score) or a lot of extra effort on top of an already heavy load (low score)? The combined scores reveal whether a project is in the *win zone*, the *worry zone*, or the *woe zone*. Knowing where the weaknesses are, management can develop an action plan to move the change into the *win zone*.

Reducing the task to four dimensions provides reassurance that, in spite of the uncertainties and untidiness, change can be controlled and managed effectively in a more or less logical and predictable manner. Also, having to handle such a small number of issues appears to lessen the scale of the challenge that the change manager has to face. Success appears to be pretty much guaranteed.

Prosci's ADKAR Model

The ADKAR change model was developed by the consulting company Prosci (Hiatt, 2004; 2006; Hiatt and Creasey, 2012). The acronym is based on five elements: Awareness, Desire, Knowledge, Ability, and Reinforcement. Many commentators have observed that organizations change by changing one person at a time (e.g., McFarland and Goldsworthy, 2013). Following that premise, the focus of the ADKAR model lies with the *individuals* who will be involved in and affected by change. In other words, the change manager is advised to concentrate on individual Awareness, individual Desire, individual Knowledge, individual Ability, and the extent to which Reinforcement is meaningful and relevant to the individual. The ADKAR elements are described in table 10.4.

TABLE 10.4
ADKAR–Five Elements Influencing Change Success

ADKAR Elements	Factors Influencing Change Success
Awareness of the need for change	Individual views of the current state and problems Credibility of those sending the awareness messages Circulation of rumors or misinformation Contestability of the reasons for change
Desire to support and participate in change	The nature and impacts of the change Perception of the context or environment for change Each individual's personal situation Intrinsic motivators
Knowledge of how to change	The individual's knowledge base Personal capability to absorb new knowledge Education and training resources available Access to the required information
Ability to apply new skills and behaviors	Psychological blocks and physical capabilities Intellectual capability Time available to develop the required skills Availability of resources to support skills development
Reinforcement to sustain the change	Meaningful and specific to the person affected Link with demonstrable progress No negative consequences Accountability system to continually reinforce the change

Source: Hiatt, J. 2006.

As with DICE, the change manager can use ADKAR as a diagnostic and planning tool, to identify areas of potential resistance, to develop communication and staff development strategies, and to strengthen change implementation by addressing gaps and problems. Paying close attention to individual perceptions, strengths, and weaknesses is a strength of the ADKAR approach, particularly with regard to generating enthusiasm, overcoming resistance, and developing new skills. In addition, this is one of the few models that explicitly address the issue of sustaining change (which we will explore in chapter 11). However, ADKAR pays less attention to the nature and implications of the wider organizational context and the process of change—factors that are emphasized in other models.

Stouten's Evidence-Based Approach

Noting that the failure rate of planned organizational change is high, Stouten et al. (2018) suggest that managers should not use the available research evidence when making decisions about proposed changes to organizational practices. They argue that an evidence-based approach is more appropriate. Their review of that evidence, focusing on practical guidelines and underlying theory, identifies 10 steps that the change manager is advised to follow:

1. Diagnosis (1): Gather the facts concerning the nature of the problem.
2. Diagnosis (2): Assess the organization's readiness for change.
3. Identify solutions: Implement evidence-based change interventions.
4. Develop effective change leadership throughout the organization.
5. Develop and communicate a compelling change vision.
6. Work with social networks, and use their influence.
7. Use enabling practices—goal setting, learning, employee participation, and transitional structures—to support implementation that should also be fair and just.
8. Encourage small-scale initiatives and experimentation, to allow local adjustments to broad change plans.
9. Assess change progress and outcomes over time.
10. Institutionalize the change to sustain its effectiveness.

This general advice has to be adapted to specific local circumstances, but the researchers argue that an approach that follows the evidence carefully is more likely to succeed than one that does not. It is interesting to note that this approach is broadly consistent with other guidelines, such as, for example, those from Kotter (2012a): Establish the need and readiness for change, communicate a compelling vision, assess progress, institutionalize or embed the change.

Checking the Checklists

There are many "how to" checklists in circulation. How should the change manager choose between them? Their contents are similar, but they each highlight different issues. DICE (Sirkin et al., 2005) asks the change manager to calculate scores for the change timing, team, commitment, and demands on staff. ADKAR (Hiatt, 2006) focuses on individual perceptions, motivations, and capabilities. Stouten et al. (2018) want the change manager to follow the research evidence across 10 steps.

One response concerns "fit"; some approaches are more appropriate than others to a given context. This depends on the size of the organization, the nature, scale and urgency of change, the problems to be solved, numbers affected, the organization's history of change, and so on. If change timing and demands on staff are key concerns, and the organizational culture has a preference for quantified methods, the DICE model may be appropriate. The ADKAR approach may apply in situations where individual concerns are seen as central to the success of change. The evidence-based approach of Stouten et al. (2018) may contribute to the credibility of the change manager in organizational cultures where changes themselves have to be seen to be supported by evidence, such as engineering, research and development, and healthcare settings.

Resourcing Organizational Change

It may seem obvious to argue that changes need to be adequately resourced, with funds, people, and other appropriate support, if they are to have any chance of success. Research suggests the opposite.

Weidner et al. (2017) were interested in the support provided for organizational changes, as inadequate resourcing is often used to explain (or excuse) failure. Confidence in and commitment to change, and experimentation with different options, can be encouraged by having access to the right financial and human resources. Experience shows, however, that the success of major changes is not guaranteed even where significant resources are made available.

The researchers studied links between available resources and the success of change in three healthcare settings in the UK National Health Service (NHS). These involved hospital services, community care, and mental health services. The NHS had been under pressure to cut costs, while maintaining quality, at a time when demand for healthcare was rising. Changes to the hospital and community care practices were felt to be strategic priorities, so they were well resourced, and their change agents had a lot of freedom. In contrast, mental health services were not seen as a priority, and budget and administrative support resources for these services were cut. The researchers gathered information over four years,

using a combination of observation, interviews, and a wide range of organizational documents.

Which services experienced the most profound changes, and why? Weidner et al. (2017) found:

- Despite being very well resourced, hospital and community care services were largely unchanged over the period of this study.

- Mental health services changed and improved to such a degree that they became a local and national showpiece for strategic change initiatives.

- Those working in mental health benefitted from the lack of interest in what they were doing, as this allowed them to implement changes quickly, without becoming involved in lengthy debates and negotiations.

The initiatives that were prioritized and well resourced attracted the attention of a wide range of powerful stakeholders. As a result, these changes came under more intense scrutiny and challenge. Change agents had to devote more time to managing the needs and demands of all the interested parties and spent less time implementing the actual changes.

Contrary to most change management advice, this evidence suggests that, if you want a department, service, or unit to make dramatic changes, consider giving it inadequate resources to do so.

Another answer to "how to choose?" may simply be–does it matter? As long as advice in this form is used as a structured starting point, then the details and issues that are relevant to a specific change in a particular organization should emerge in the discussion and the planning. A final response is–why choose? Why not work through more than one of these approaches and assess their value in use? Two or more approaches applied to the same change program may suggest similar–or widely different–implications for practice. The similarities can be reassuring. The differences may trigger further insights and investigation and contribute to better implementation planning.

These models are "high-level" guides, not detailed "best practice" road maps. They are useful as long as they are used in that way. Unlike a recipe in your kitchen cookbook, these guidelines list the ingredients without explaining how to make the dish. You have to work that out for yourself. This can be frustrating for change managers seeking concrete advice on "what works and what doesn't." Checklists just identify factors that need to be addressed; the challenge is to construct a change implementation process that fits the organizational context. That is the hard part. Change from this perspective is to some extent a technical exercise, understanding the issues to consider, but also requires a blend of local knowledge, informed judgment, and creative flair.

LO 10.3 Stage Models

> *Kanter's Law: Welcome to the miserable middles of change. Everything looks like a failure in the middle. Everyone loves inspiring beginnings and happy endings; it is just the middles that involve hard work.* (Kanter, 2009)

Change can be seen, not just as a checklist of to-dos, but as a series of stages unfolding over time, from initiation, through implementation, to conclusion. This stage approach does not necessarily disqualify the checklists and recipes. However, stage models suggest the actions that the change manager is advised to take will vary over the implementation cycle. The steps necessary to initiate change thus will be different from those required during the implementation stage, and different actions again will be necessary to conclude and sustain the change. Stage models can thus complement the checklist approach by introducing this temporal dimension.

Lewin's Three-Stage Model

One of the best-known models of change was developed by Kurt Lewin (1951), who argued for the need to *unfreeze* the current state of affairs, to *move* to a desired new state, and then to *refreeze* and stabilize those changes (Burnes, 2020; Cummings et al., 2016):

unfreeze   Change attitudes by making people feel uncomfortable about the way things are because they could be improved, and so establish the motive to change.

move   Implement the change to move to the desired new state.

refreeze   Embed or institutionalize the new behaviors, to prevent people from
                    drifting back to previous ways of doing things.

Each of these stages makes different demands on the change manager. First, convincing those who will be involved of the need to change. Second, putting the change in place. Third, redesigning roles, systems, and procedures to discourage a return to past practice. One important observation of this model is that, if people are happy with the way things are, they will be reluctant to change. The change manager's first task in this approach, therefore, is to make people unhappy. But this is a "positive dissatisfaction," which encourages people to believe that "we can do better."

Find on *YouTube*, "Unfreezing change as three steps: Rethinking Kurt Lewin's legacy for change management" (2019, 7:36 minutes).

Lewin's second stage—move—can invoke Kanter's law (see the box "Kanter's Law), which says that change often looks like a failure in the middle. Schneider and Goldwasser (1998), who plotted "the classic change curve," captured this law (see Figure 10.1). In the middle of the curve sits the "valley of despair." Those who are affected start to realize that this could mean loss and pain for them. Schneider and Goldwasser (1998, p. 42) argue that this is probably inevitable, but that it is useful to be aware of this and to weaken the impact if possible:

> A leader of change must anticipate employees' reactions, another key factor in the process. As shown [Figure 10.1], these reactions occur along a "change curve." The blue line represents what is, unfortunately, typical. Unrealistically high expectations at the outset of a programme lead to a relatively deep "valley of despair" when change doesn't come as quickly or easily as anticipated. Over time, employees do see a "light at the end of the tunnel" and the change eventually produces some positive results. The red line illustrates what is possible with effective change management: a less traumatic visit to the valley and greater results as the programme reaches completion. Can you avoid the "valley of despair" altogether? Probably not. All change programmes involve some loss. The best approach is to acknowledge that employees will mourn the loss of business as usual, much as people experience stages of grieving when trauma invades their personal lives.

Kotter's Eight-Stage Model

Probably the most widely cited, and widely applied, stage model of change is the one developed by John Kotter (2007; 2012a), mentioned earlier in this chapter. Kotter's model is summarized in table 10.5. It is sometimes presented as another checklist, but this is a misrepresentation. Note how his eight-stage approach to transformational change opens with "create a sense of urgency" (unfreeze), passes through "empower people to act" (move), and ends with "institutionalize new approaches" (refreeze). Lewin's echo can be heard in this model, too.

Kotter advises the change manager to work through those eight stages more or less in sequence. To rush or to miss out on any of the stages increases the chance of failure. However, Kotter also recognizes that this is an "ideal" perspective, as change is often untidy and iterative. As with the checklists, this model codifies the stages of change in a clear and easily understood manner. However, the change manager still has to combine

FIGURE 10.1
The Classic Change Curve

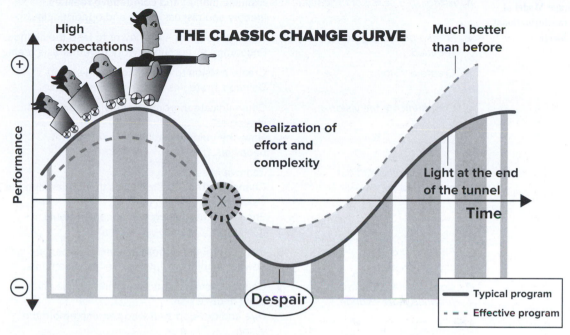

Source: Schneider, D. M., and Goldwasser, C. 1998.

local knowledge with creative thinking to translate this advice into practical actions that are appropriate to the organizational context and to the nature of the changes that are being proposed. There are many ways, for example, in which to "create a sense of urgency" or to "communicate the vision" or to "institutionalize new approaches." As with checklists, these stage models are also "high level" guides, rather than detailed "best practice" frameworks.

Appelbaum et al. (2012) reviewed the evidence relating to the effectiveness of Kotter's model and found support for most of the individual steps. However, despite Kotter's argument about integrating the eight stages, no studies had evaluated the framework as a whole. On the other hand, there was no evidence to challenge the practical value of the approach, which remains popular. The authors argue that "Kotter's change management model appears to derive its popularity more from its direct and usable format than from any scientific consensus on the results" (Appelbaum et al., 2012, p. 764). They conclude, therefore, that Kotter's model is useful in change implementation planning but should be complemented by other tools to adapt the change process to local conditions.

Kotter (2012b, p. 52) subsequently revised his framework, arguing that the components identified in table 10.5 should be seen as "change accelerators" to speed up change. The new argument has three aspects. First, Kotter argues that the accelerators must operate concurrently, rather than in sequence. Second, change must not rely on a small powerful

TABLE 10.5
Kotter's Eight-Stage Model of Transformational Change

Stage	What Is Involved
1. *Establish a sense of urgency.*	Examine market and competitive realities. Identify and discuss crises and opportunities.
2. *Form a powerful guiding coalition.*	Assemble a group with power to lead the change. Encourage this group to work together as a team.
3. *Create a vision.*	Create a vision to direct the change effort. Develop strategies to achieve that vision.
4. *Communicate the vision.*	Communicate thoroughly the vision and strategies. Have the guiding coalition model the new behaviors.
5. *Empower others to act on the vision.*	Remove obstacles to change. Change systems or structures that undermine the vision. Encourage risk taking and unconventional thinking.
6. *Plan for and create short-term wins.*	Plan for visible performance improvements. Reward employees involved in improvements.
7. *Consolidate gains and produce more change.*	Change systems, structures, and policies that don't fit the vision. Hire and develop staff who can implement the vision. Maintain momentum with new themes, projects, and change agents.
8. *Institutionalize new approaches.*	Link the new behaviors clearly with corporate success. Ensure leadership development and succession.

Source: Kotter (2007 and 2012a)

core group but on many change agents from across the organization. Third, flexible and agile networks must complement traditional hierarchy. Kotter is not alone in advocating the use of multiple levers to pursue goals, adopting a "distributed" approach to change leadership, and strengthening organizational flexibility.

The McKinsey 5A Model

The stage approach to transformational change advocated by the management consultancy firm McKinsey focuses on "hard and soft" elements—the performance and health of the organization (Keller and Schaninger, 2019a; 2019b). Performance concerns what the organization does to improve its operational and financial results. Health concerns how well people work with each other. If large-scale change is to be successful, the change manager must emphasize performance and health equally.

Keller and Schaninger (2019a; 2019b) advocate a "5A" approach that divides change implementation into five manageable stages. At each stage, there is a key question. When that question has been answered, the change can proceed to the next stage. The five stages are:

Aspire   Where do we want to go?

Assess   How ready are we to go there?

Architect   What must we do to get there?

Act   How do we manage the journey?

Advance   How do we continue to improve?

This model offers guidelines for managing both the hard performance and soft health issues. The five guidelines for managing performance are:

1. *Strategic objectives (aspire).* Create a compelling long-term change vision, set midterm aspirations along the path, and guard against biases in the process.
2. *Skill-set requirements (assess).* Forecast demand for skills, and understand their supply dynamics; then decide how to close gaps.
3. *Bankable plan (architect).* Define the portfolio of initiatives that will realize your strategic objectives, and meet your skill requirements; then sequence your actions and reallocate resources accordingly.
4. *Ownership model (act).* Establish strong governance, decide how to scale your change initiatives, monitor their progress, and dynamically adjust them throughout implementation.
5. *Learning infrastructure (advance).* Institutionalize processes and expertise so that the organization shares knowledge, constantly improves, and continually learns how to do new things (Keller and Schaninger, 2019a, p. 8).

The five guidelines for managing health are:

1. *Health goals (aspire).* Objectively check your organization's health, choose where to be exceptional, and target areas that need immediate improvement.
2. *Mindset shifts (assess).* Pinpoint helping and hindering behaviors for priority health areas, explore the underlying mindset drivers, and prioritize a critical few "from-to" mindset shifts.
3. *Influence levers (architect).* Use four levers to reshape the work environment: role modelling, understanding and conviction, reinforcement mechanisms, and confidence-building efforts. Then ensure that performance initiatives are engineered to promote the necessary mindset and behavioral shifts.
4. *Generation of energy (act).* Mobilize influence leaders, make the change personal for employees, and maintain high-impact, two-way communication.
5. *Leadership placement (advance).* Prioritize ongoing roles by their potential to create value, match the most important ones to the best talent, and make the talent-match process business as usual (Keller and Schaninger, 2019a, p. 8).

Even if this highly detailed prescription is followed carefully, transformation can still disappoint. According to McKinsey research, adopting a "pipeline" analogy, problems often arise through "leakage," which may explain the 70 percent failure rate of planned change:

It's all about avoiding leakage. So at the aspiration stage, folks don't go for their full potential. They go for seven out of ten of it. And then in the planning and execution, they let some things slide. They don't see some things all the way through. And they do seven out of ten of it. Then, finally, they don't build in the changes that are necessary for the initiative to be sustained. They get it seven out of ten right. Well, if you multiply that together, those sevens out of tens, you quickly get to about a 30 percent success rate. That's what we've seen, again and again. You have to, at each step of the process, go for the 100 percent and be able to realize the full potential of the business in order for the transformation to be successful. (Bucy et al, 2017a, p. 3)

Bucy et al. (2017b) offer three pieces of advice for keeping the pipeline intact and transformational change on target. First, *be relentless*, assuming that most initiatives will deliver less than they promise at the start. And ensure that time is allocated to smaller initiatives. To reinforce this point, they use an interesting "boulders, pebbles, and sand" analogy. "Boulders" are initiatives that are each expected to contribute at least 5 percent of the program's total value. "Pebbles" are expected to contribute between 0.5 and 5 percent. All initiatives expected to contribute less than 0.5 percent of the total value are "sand." McKinsey research suggests that 50 percent of the total value of many transformation programs typically comes from sand. Focusing effort on the boulders—the large, high-profile initiatives—is therefore risky. In addition, it is usually quicker and easier to implement the "sand," which may involve fewer layers of approval and less cumbersome coordination.

Second, *focus resources*, and do not expect your best change managers to run more than three initiatives at the same time. And control the number of metrics and milestones, many of which are never used and become unnecessary burdens. Third, *plan and adapt*; expect some projects to be delayed, and manage this with weekly actions for initiative owners.

Appraising the Stage Models

Stage models complement the checklist approach by highlighting the way in which change unfolds over time. This leads to the McKinsey observation that changes fail to deliver their promises due to "leakage in the pipeline" as change unfolds. As we have noted, change is likely to make different demands on the change manager—and on those who are affected by change—at each of the different stages. Although change is rarely tidy, knowing the probable sequence of events, and how that may be disrupted, allows the change manager to anticipate and prepare for potential difficulties.

Stage models are open to three criticisms. First, despite the emphasis on events unfolding over time, these models rarely refer to what has gone before the current intervention. What has happened in the past, however, with regard to previous change attempts, will influence responses to current proposals. Consider, for example, the change management actions that may be required to "create a sense of urgency" in an organization that has seen many previous unsuccessful changes that senior management drove with "a sense of urgency" and where top team credibility is now low. Contrast this with the organization where the opportunity or threat is clear to all staff members, who, on the basis of recent experience of change, place a high degree of trust in the top team. It may thus often be helpful to extend the timeline backward and to identify (and if necessary, to compensate for) previous events and outcomes that may influence today's action plans.

Second, it may also be helpful to extend the timeline forward, beyond "consolidate" and "institutionalize." Even changes that are successful will eventually decay without appropriate maintenance. Paradoxically, successful changes can also inhibit the implementation of further innovation, which may be seen as novel, risky, and a threat to currently effective operations. The issues that arise in managing the sustainability of change are explored in chapter 11.

Finally, as with change checklists, stage models offer further "high level" guidance, leaving the change manager to determine how in practice to apply that advice in a given context. There is no clear, unambiguous statement of "this is what to do." The contingency approaches to change management explored in the next section, however, seek to advise the change manager how to adjust implementation strategies effectively to different contexts and conditions.

LO 10.4 The Process Perspective

Change is a process, and not an event. This is a straightforward observation and is reflected in the stage models of change management discussed in the previous section. Process perspectives, however, highlight other significant aspects of organizational change and draw the attention of the change manager to issues not covered by either checklists or stage models. Although potentially making change appear to be more complex, process thinking encourages the change manager to adopt a more comprehensive approach to designing, planning, implementing, and reviewing change activities.

One of the architects of the processual perspective, Andrew Pettigrew (1985; 1987), cautioned against looking for single causes and simple explanations for change. Instead, he pointed to the many related factors—individual, group, organizational, social, political— that can affect the nature and outcomes of change. Pettigrew observed that change was a complex and "untidy cocktail" that included rational decisions, mixed with competing individual perceptions, often stimulated by visionary leadership, and spiced with "power plays" to recruit support and to build coalitions behind particular ideas.

In this view, the unit of analysis is not "the change": a new organization structure, or new technology, or new working practices. The unit of analysis is "the process of change in context": how a new structure will be implemented and developed in this particular organizational setting. This subtle shift in perspective has two related implications. First, this means paying attention to the flow of events and not thinking of change as either static or neatly time-bounded with defined beginning and end points. Second, this also means paying attention to the wider context in which change is taking place and not thinking in terms of a particular location in time and geography (this new machine in this factory bay). In short, process perspectives argue that, to understand organizational change, one has to understand how the substance, context, and process interact over time to produce the outcomes.

Patrick Dawson and Constantine Andriopoulos (2017) have further developed this processual perspective. They make it clear that to understand change we need to consider the following issues:

1. The *context*—past, present, and future—in which the organization functions, including external and internal factors, and the organization's history as past events shape current responses

2. The *substance* of the change and its scale and scope, which could be new technology, process redesign, a new payment system, or changes to structure and culture

3. The *transition process*, including tasks, activities, decisions, timing, and sequencing

4. *Political* activity, within and outside the organization, shaping decisions, securing support

5. The *interactions* between these factors, which shape both the change process and the outcomes

This perspective incorporates the role of power and politics in shaping organizational change. This is a feature that the perspectives we have examined so far either do not mention or deal with only briefly. As organizations are political systems, and as change is inevitably a politicized process, the process perspective argues that the change manager must be willing to intervene in the politics of the organization. In this respect, the key task is to legitimize change proposals in the face of competing ideas. The management of change can thus be described as "the management of meaning," which involves symbolic attempts to establish the credibility of particular definitions of problems and solutions and to gain consent and compliance from other organization members. Part of this task, therefore, is to do with "the way you tell it," or more accurately with "the way you *sell* it" to others.

Dawson and Andriopoulos (2017) identify eight lessons from a process perspective concerning change management practice:

1. There are no universal prescriptions or simple recipes for how best to manage change.

2. Change is a political process, and change leaders need to be politically sensitive and astute.

3. Time, planning, and flexibility are essential in changing attitudes and behaviors and in gaining commitment for change.

4. They advocate "critical reflection," challenging taken-for-granted assumptions; for example, with regard to resistance, which may be desirable if it subverts a weak initiative.

5. It is important to learn from both positive and negative experiences.

6. Education, training, and development should be aligned with new operating procedures.

7. Communication is fundamentally important in steering processes in desired directions.

8. "Contradictions provide health food for critical reflection." Change requires constant adaptation to contextual circumstances.

Most of this advice echoes the guidance from checklists and stage models. However, where the checklists say "do this," process accounts advise, "be aware of this," noting that there are no "best practice" recipes for change. The process perspective differs in the emphasis placed on the role of power and politics in shaping change outcomes. One implication of this emphasis is that the change manager must be politically skilled and be willing and able to use those skills. The capabilities of the change manager are explored in chapter 12.

From Hot Breakfasts to Strategic Change *How Did That Happen?*

Process theory argues that the outcomes of change are produced by the interactions of several factors over time in a given context. What does this look like in practice? Donde Plowman and colleagues (2007) give a fascinating account of what they call "radical change accidentally." They studied the turnaround of *Mission Church*, a failing organization in a large southwestern U.S. city.

The organizational context was unstable. The church was faced with a potentially terminal problem. Seen as a traditional "silk stockings" church, the organization was asset rich but cash poor. Attendance and membership were declining. There were ongoing conflicts involving a KKK plaque, the playing of jazz in the church, and whether gays and lesbians should be accepted as members. The purpose and identity of the church created further tensions, particularly with regard to including the homeless and others who were excluded. With several previous changes in leadership, there had been two pastors in three years, resulting in the controversial appointment of two co-pastors.

How did change begin? A group of youngsters, who did not like the traditional church school program, had the idea of providing hot breakfasts for homeless people on Sunday mornings. Some of those youngsters were not even church members; they were soon serving 500 people every Sunday. The hot breakfasts idea was never intended to produce radical change. However, Plowman and colleagues argue that small actions such as this were "amplified" by the unstable context.

What were the outcomes? Church membership recovered, involving a wider range of the local population including the homeless and minorities. Homeless individuals joined the church, sang in the choir, and served as ushers. The style of worship, formality of dress, and music changed as did the profile of the congregation; this was no longer a "silk stockings" church. The church got city funding to provide a day center for several thousand homeless and was soon serving over 20,000 meals a year. In addition to breakfasts and clinics, the church provided legal assistance, job training, laundry services, and shower facilities. The church motto changed to include "justice into action."

Why did this happen? The "contextual configuration" that encouraged ongoing change included:

- Dissatisfied youngsters came up with the hot breakfasts idea.

- A doctor working as a volunteer offered to treat medical problems instead and soon recruited others, leading to full-scale medical, dental, and eye clinics as part of the Sunday activity.

- The church removed the KKK plaque—a major symbolic act.

- Leaders acted as "sense-givers," providing meaning rather than directing changes, and chose the language labels: "purging," "recovering," "reaching out to the marginalized."

- Affluent members left as the church focused increasingly on the homeless, and new (less affluent) members were attracted by the message of inclusivity.

The features of the organizational context encouraged a series of small changes to emerge and amplified these into an unplanned, radical, and successful change process. There was no top-down transformation designed by senior leaders. This is a good example of a processual account of change unfolding over time, illustrating how factors at different levels of analysis interact to produce the outcomes. Plowman et al. (2007) offer the following advice for the change manager. First, be sensitive to context. Second, be prepared to be surprised; the emergence of small changes is not an orderly process. Third, view those small changes opportunistically, in terms of how they might be developed.

The process perspective on change thus appears to have three strengths:

1. It recognizes the complexity of change, drawing attention to the interaction between many factors at different levels, shaping the nature, direction, and consequences of change.

2. It recognizes change as a process with a past, a present, and a future, rather than as a static or time-bounded event or discrete series of events.

3. It highlights the political nature of organizations and change, emphasizing the importance of political skill to the change manager.

However, the process perspective has three limitations:

1. Change in this perspective is in danger of being presented as overcomplex and overwhelmingly confusing, and thus as unmanageable.

2. Those who are involved in the change process are sometimes portrayed as minor characters in the broad sweep of events, relegated to the role of sense-givers and interpreters controlled by social and contextual forces, rather than as proactive "movers and shakers."

3. It does not lend itself readily to the identification of specific guidelines, focusing on awareness rather than prescription. Advice is thus limited to those issues to which change management should be sensitive: complexity, process, context, political influences, opportunity.

LO 10.5 Contingency Approaches

Dawson and Andriopoulos (2017) are not alone in noting that there are no universal "one best way" prescriptions for managing change. This has led to the development of contingency approaches, which argue that the best way to manage change depends on the context. We will explore four contingency approaches: *Where to start?*, *the change leadership styles continuum*, *the Stace–Dunphy contingency matrix*, and *the Hope Hailey–Balogun change kaleidoscope*.

Where to Start?

The problem has been diagnosed, and appropriate organizational changes have been agreed. What to do next? Where to begin? Hope Hailey and Balogun (2002, p. 158) discuss this briefly in their contingency model (explained below) arguing, "Change can start from top-down, bottom-up, or some combination of the two, or as another alternative, be developed from pockets of good practice. Should change be implemented throughout the organization simultaneously, or can it be delivered gradually through pilot sites?" The change manager is thus faced with a range of options.

Adopting a novel approach to the question of where to start, Marco Gardini et al. (2011) argue that change should begin with those staff whose contributions will have the most significant impact on the aspects of performance that need to change. Identifying those "pivotal roles" is vital, but this is not always obvious. They reached this "pivotal roles" conclusion from experience with a large European retail bank. This bank, with 6,000 branches, faced increasing competition from more "customer-friendly" local banks. To deal with this threat, management developed a new organizational model, which reduced central supervision and control and gave branch managers more autonomy to tailor their marketing, promotions, and offerings to their local areas. The new model was communicated quickly to all staff, and the way in which the new roles would work was explained. Top management did this through road shows, memos, intranet articles, and by publishing the new organization charts. Everyone received the same information, and the changes were all to happen at the same time.

Reviewing progress a few months later, however, most staff members had not changed their working practices. In particular, the branch managers were still using the previous structure and procedures because they were afraid of making mistakes or annoying more senior staff. The regional supervisors were meant to act as coaches to the branch managers, but many did not have coaching skills, and many branch managers did not have the skills to run their own branches and make their own decisions. Realizing that they had tried to change too much at the same time, top management decided to focus on those who could deliver the change the fastest. The regional managers, perhaps, or the branch supervisors? Neither of those groups qualified; they had no impact on daily branch activities, could therefore not affect results, and had little credibility with frontline staff. The branch managers themselves had the greatest influence on the outcomes of the planned changes because:

- Their work had direct and significant impact on the revenue stream.
- They were connected with many other groups across the organization.
- They could decide how people got things done.

In other words, the branch managers combined managerial impact with local control, but they lacked the skills and attitudes to drive change quickly. The implementation plan was redesigned, focusing initially on the 6,000 branch managers. The training designed especially for them began with their role in the new organizational model and covered commercial skills, credit and asset management capabilities, quality and customer satisfaction principles, and other skills such as managing people, communications, and conflict resolution. Only when the branch managers were ready—six months later—did the bank start to work with other staff and supervisors, with different programs designed for different roles. This time the results were much better. Eighteen months later:

- The number of products sold per branch had risen by 15 percent.
- The time spent making credit decisions had fallen by 25 percent.
- Branch relationship managers were spending 30 percent more time with customers due to the streamlined process.
- Customer responses to marketing campaigns doubled, with a national survey showing a 20 percent improvement in customer satisfaction.
- Knowledge sharing and mutual support increased, and the bank became more receptive to ideas from frontline staff.

Gardini et al. (2011) conclude that change is more likely to be successful if implementation has two key components. First, start with the "pivotal people," whose work is closest to the activities that need to be improved. Second, design a comprehensive program with clear and meaningful goals, linking those in pivotal roles with the changes that the rest of the organization has to make. This question of "where to start?" is not addressed explicitly by the checklists, stage models, or process approaches. This, of course, is not the only contingency affecting the appropriate mode of change implementation.

The Change Leadership Styles Continuum

One of the oldest contingency approaches addresses the question of change management style, which can range over a continuum from autocratic to democratic, or, as Tannenbaum and Schmidt (1958) described this, from leader-oriented to follower-oriented leadership (see Figure 10.2). The cultures—or, at least, the management textbooks—of developed western economies have endorsed participative approaches to change management, for which evidence has long established the benefits (e.g., Coch and French, 1948). Those who are involved in the design and implementation of change are more likely to contribute to its success than those on whom change has been imposed. However, the change manager should be aware of the range of options available with regard to style and of the disadvantages and advantages of these (see table 10.6). For example, "telling" people without participation is quick and decisive, but it may cause resentment and does not capture staff ideas. On the other hand, "inviting participation" increases commitment and access to useful information, but it is time consuming and involves a loss of management control. In a crisis where a rapid response is required, "inviting participation" can be damaging. In an organization that values the knowledge and commitment of its staff, the resentment caused by "telling" staff about planned changes can also be damaging. Choice of change management style thus needs to reflect the context.

The Stace–Dunphy Contingency Matrix

Participative approaches to change management have also been challenged by the work of two Australian researchers, Doug Stace and Dexter Dunphy (Stace and Dunphy, 2001). Their approach begins by establishing a scale of change, from "fine tuning" to "corporate transformation" (see table 10.7 and Figure 1.1, "Assessing Depth of Change," in chapter 1). They then identify four styles of change (see table 10.8).

FIGURE 10.2
Tannenbaum–Schmidt Leadership Continuum

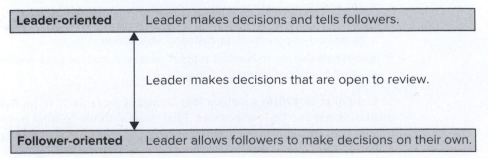

Leader-oriented   Leader makes decisions and tells followers.

Leader makes decisions that are open to review.

Follower-oriented   Leader allows followers to make decisions on their own.

TABLE 10.6
Change Management Styles—Disadvantages and Advantages

Style	Disadvantages	Advantages
Tell	May cause resentment. Does not use staff experience and ideas.	Quick, decisive, unambiguous. Management in full control.
Tell and sell	May be seen as cosmetic. Especially a disadvantage if consequences for staff are negative and serious.	Selling can be fairly quick. Management remains in control.
Consult	Time consuming. Resentment if staff views are then ignored.	More information, better decisions. Staff commitment higher if views have influenced decisions.
Invite participation	Time consuming. Logistics can be problematic. Conflicts with concept of management accountability. Management loses some control over outcomes.	Uses all available information. Should lead to better decisions. Higher commitment from staff members who share ownership of the decision-making process.

TABLE 10.7
Scale of Change

Fine-tuning	Refining methods, policies, and procedures, typically at the level of the division or department
Incremental adjustment	Distinct modifications to strategies, structures, and management processes, but not radical enough to be described as strategic
Modular transformation	Restructuring departments and divisions, potentially radical, but at the level of parts of the organization and not the whole
Corporate transformation	Strategic change throughout the organization, to structures, systems, procedures, mission, values, and power distribution

TABLE 10.8
Styles of Change

Collaborative	Widespread employee participation in key decisions
Consultative	Limited involvement in setting goals relevant to areas of responsibility
Directive	The use of authority in reaching decisions about change and the future
Coercive	Senior management imposes change on the organization

Plotting scale of change against style of change produces the matrix in Figure 10.3. This identifies four strategies: participative evolution, charismatic transformation, forced evolution, and dictatorial transformation. Figure 10.3 also advocates the use of different change management styles depending on the attributes of the context. Stace and Dunphy (2001) thus argue that participative strategies are time consuming as they expose conflicting views that are difficult to reconcile. Where organizational survival depends on rapid and strategic change, dictatorial transformation is appropriate. Stace and Dunphy (2001, p. 185) cite the example of a police chief appointed to stamp out corruption and modernize a police department who, in his own words, initially adopted a management style that was "firm, hard and autocratic, and it had to be that because that is what the organization understood."

Once again, we have a contingency perspective that argues that, while collaborative-consultative modes will work well under some conditions, there are circumstances where directive-coercive modes of change management are likely to be more appropriate and effective. In particular, where major changes are necessary for survival, time is short, and those affected cannot agree on the changes, then dictatorial transformation may be the necessary choice of style. Inviting participation under those conditions would take time and be unlikely to produce any agreement.

FIGURE 10.3
The Stace–Dunphy Contingency Approach to Change Implementation

Scale of change:	Incremental change strategies	Transformative change strategies
Style of change:	*Participative evolution*	*Charismatic transformation*
Collaborative— consultative modes	Use when the organization needs minor adjustment to meet environmental conditions, where time is available, and where key interest groups favor change	Use when the organization needs major adjustments to meet environmental conditions, where there is little time for participation, and where there is support for radical change
	Forced evolution	*Dictatorial transformation*
Directive—coercive modes	Use when minor adjustments are required, where time is available, but where key interest groups oppose change	Use when major adjustments are necessary, where there is no time for participation, where there is no internal support for strategic change, but where this is necessary for survival

Source: Stace and Dunphy (2001).

The Hope Hailey–Balogun Change Kaleidoscope

Veronica Hope Hailey and Julia Balogun (2002; Balogun et al., 2016) also advocate a context-sensitive approach to the design and implementation of change. Their framework identifies the characteristics of the organizational context that should be taken into consideration when making change implementation design choices. They describe this framework as "The Change Kaleidoscope," shown in Figure 10.4 (Hope Hailey and Balogun, 2002, p. 156).

FIGURE 10.4
The Change Kaleidoscope

Organizational change	
Context factors: enablers and constraints	**Implementation options**
Timing	What type of change is required?
Scope	Where should we start?
Need for continuity	What implementation style will we use?
Diversity of attitudes	What targets are we aiming for?
Capability of those involved	What intervention strategies will be appropriate?
Capacity of the organization	What change implementation roles are needed?
Readiness for change	
Power of the change manager	

The argument that change implementation should reflect the organizational context is not a novel one, but Hope Hailey and Balogun argue that other contingency models focus on too narrow a range of factors such as type of change, time frame, the power of the change manager, and the degree of organizational support for change. The eight context factors in the change kaleidoscope are:

Time	Depending on urgency, what is the necessary speed of the change?
Scope	How narrow or broad is the scope of the change agenda?
Preservation	Is there a need to maintain a degree of continuity on some dimensions, in some areas?
Diversity	Are the attitudes and values of those affected similar or are there diverse subcultures?
Capability	Do the individuals involved have the necessary skills and knowledge?
Capacity	Does the organization have the resources to implement more change?
Readiness	What degree of acceptance of or resistance to change is there?
Power	What is the power of the change manager relative to other stakeholders?

These eight context factors can be either constraints (e.g., shortage of time, low capability) or enablers (e.g., broad agreement on need for change, powerful change manager). The point is that the design of the change implementation process should be influenced by the nature of those context factors. Hope Hailey and Balogun (2002, p. 161) identify the six design options summarized in table 10.9.

TABLE 10.9
Change Kaleidoscope Implementation Options

Design Options	Meaning
Type	The scope and speed of the proposed change
Start point	Top-down, bottom-up, a combination, or pilot sites and pockets of good practice
Style	From coercive to collaborative, varied by staff group and phase of change
Target	Focus on changing outputs, behaviors, attitudes, and values
Interventions	Levers and mechanisms: technical, political, cultural, education, communication
Roles	Responsibility for implementing: leadership, change teams, external facilitation

As well as offering a diagnostic approach to understanding context and identifying the range of options, Hope Hailey and Balogun (2002, p. 154) also argue that the kaleidoscope "encourages an awareness of one's own preferences about change and how this limits the options considered." In other words, the change manager who adopts a *director* image may use the kaleidoscope in a manner quite different from the manager adopting the *navigator* image.

The aim of this framework, therefore, is to trigger a questioning approach to the context and an informed approach to choosing design options. There is no mechanistic way to "read" a particular configuration of design choices from the results of an analysis of the context. As with all the approaches in this chapter, the change manager's local knowledge and informed judgment are key to choosing the contextually appropriate change design from the wide range of options available, as Hope Hailey and Balogun (2002, p. 163) explain:

> Understanding the contextual constraints and enablers is key to understanding the type of change an organization is able to undertake as opposed to the type of change it needs to undertake, and therefore what sort of change path is required. Similarly, understanding the contextual constraints and enablers is central to making choices about startpoint and style. More participative change approaches require greater skills in facilitation, a greater readiness for change from those participating, more time, and therefore, often, more funds. Choices about the change target and interventions may obviously be affected by the scope of change, but also by, for example, capacity. Management development interventions can be expensive and may not be accessible to organizations with limited funds. In reality choosing the right options is about asking the right questions and exercising change judgement.

The argument that "the best approach" depends on context is an appealing one. Contingency approaches, however, are not beyond criticism. First, the idea of "fitting" change implementation to a particular type of change in a given context may be easier to explain in theory than to put into practice. As the change kaleidoscope implies, the change manager needs considerable depth and breadth of understanding of the change context to make informed judgments. Second, contingency approaches are more ambiguous and difficult to explain than the simpler "off the shelf" competition from checklists and stage models. Third, contingency approaches require a degree of behavioral flexibility, especially with regard to style, with which some senior managers may be uncomfortable if they lack the necessary capabilities. Fourth, if managers adopt different approaches at different times and in different conditions, will this weaken their credibility with staff? Finally, is everything contingent? Are there no "universals" when it comes to organizational change?

EXERCISE 10.1

Develop Your Own Change Model

LO 10.2–10.5

In this chapter, we have explored three change checklists, three stage models of implementation, the process approach to change, and four contingency frameworks. These approaches are similar in some respects and different in others. Can they be combined? Try the following experiment:

1. Bring the advice from these different models into a single list, omitting the overlaps.

2. Reflecting on your own experience and knowledge of organizational change, consider what issues and steps are missing from these guidelines; add these to your master list. Now create your own composite change management model; if possible, do this as a group activity.

3. Can you prioritize this advice? What items are more important, and which are less important? Taking a contingency approach, in which organization contexts do particular items become more or less significant?

4. Can you identify a preferred sequence of change implementation steps? And can you explain and justify this recommendation?

5. Looking at your composite change management model, identify three management skills associated with each of the elements. Use this as the basis of a personal assessment; what are your strongest and your weakest change management skills?

6. Looking at the elements in your composite change management model, and reflecting on your own experience of organizational change, which elements are usually handled well, and which are often handled badly? Why do you think this is the case?

EXERCISE 10.2

Getting Boeing Back in the Air

LO 10.2–10.5

As you read this case, consider the following questions:

1. Can organizational culture be blamed for plane crashes? Will those crashes prompt Boeing to change its culture, or could they be a barrier to culture change?

2. With hindsight, moving the top-management team to Chicago looks like a mistake. But how do you assess the reasoning behind that move? Was the explanation a good one?

3. To get Boeing "back in the air," what will be the priorities of David Calhoun, the new chief executive? What steps do you think he will need to take to implement "deep culture redesign"?

(Continued)

4. Check your online news sources and bring this case history up to date. Has David Calhoun been able to change the culture at Boeing? Have there been any more accidents? What is your assessment of David Calhoun's change leadership?

The American company Boeing makes airplanes, rockets, satellites, telecommunications equipment, and missiles. Defense production is based in St. Louis, Missouri, and the aerospace business is in Long Beach, California. Passenger jets are made in Seattle, Washington, on the northwest coast, where the company's 40,000 engineers are based. Boeing is one of America's biggest exporters. A million people work either for Boeing or for one of its suppliers, and it has been described as "too important to fail" (McNulty and Marcus, 2019, p. 2). Boeing's main competitor in the passenger jet market is Airbus; other competitors include Lockheed Martin, Northrop Grumman, Raytheon, General Dynamics, SpaceX, BAE Systems, Bombardier, Embraer, and Loral Space & Communications.

Boeing's new 737 Max aircraft was introduced in 2017. In October 2018, a Lion Air Boeing 737 Max crashed, killing 189 people. Five months later, in March 2019, an Ethiopian Airlines 737 Max crashed, killing 157 people. Investigators found that the plane's new Maneuvering Characteristics Augmentation System (MCAS) automatically forced the aircraft to stall and nosedive. This system had been omitted from flight manuals and crew training. The U.S. Federal Aviation Authority (FAA) grounded the 737 Max. Boeing's reputation was damaged. But chief executive Dennis Muilenburg decided to keep making the 737 Max, to demonstrate confidence in the plane, even though they could not be sold. Boeing fired Muilenburg at the end of 2019, and David Calhoun took over as CEO.

To understand how this could have happened, we have to go back to 1997, when Boeing acquired McDonnell Douglas, a competitor with a "finance first ethos." Boeing took on many McDonnell Douglas executives including their chief executive, Harry Stonecipher, who was known for his aggressive cost cutting. In 2001, Boeing's chief executive and then president, Phil Condit and Harry Stonecipher, decided to put some distance between the company's 500 senior management and staff and the plane-makers and moved the headquarters to Chicago—2,000 miles from Seattle. They explained that senior management was being drawn into day-to-day operational decisions when they were so close to the manufacturing base. In a large, modern, multinational company, they felt that senior executives should not have such contact with engineers. Stonecipher said, "When people say I changed the culture of Boeing, that was the intent, so that it's run like a business rather than a great engineering firm. It is a great engineering firm, but people invest in a company because they want to make money" (Useem, 2019). Stonecipher became chief executive of Boeing in 2003 (but was forced to resign in 2005 following an improper relationship with a female executive).

The previous close proximity of managers and engineers meant, however, that senior executives had a good understanding of engineering issues. They "spoke the language of engineering and safety as a mother tongue," and they could see for themselves what was happening. As Useem (2019) points out, "The present 737 Max disaster can be traced back two decades—to the moment Boeing's leadership decided to divorce itself from the firm's own culture." With Stonecipher as president, the new slogans became "a passion for affordability" and "less family, more team." One aerospace analyst said that "You had this weird combination of a distant building with a few hundred people in it and a non-engineer with no technical skills whatsoever at the helm." In other words, "a company once driven by engineers became driven by finance" (Useem, 2019).

Signalling the shift to a "shareholder-first culture," between 2014 and 2019, Boeing spent $43.4 billion on stock buybacks, and only $15.7 billion on research and development for commercial airplanes (Catchpole, 2020, p. 56). This culture placed short-term rewards to shareholders ahead of engineering decisions and longer-term strategy. Boeing's board even approved a further $20 billion buyback in December 2018, two months after the first 737 Max crash (but that decision was later reversed).

The immediate causes of the 737 Max crashes were technical—faulty software. But other factors had played a role. In the interests of cost and time to market, Boeing had decided to modify the 737 rather than design a new aircraft from scratch. To avoid regulatory delays, Boeing maintained that no additional pilot training was required for the 737 Max. Boeing engineers were surprised when some software development tasks (not specific to MCAS) were outsourced to college graduates employed by an Indian subcontractor in Seattle earning $9 an hour. Ed Pierson, a former Boeing manager, claimed that, before the fatal crashes, the 737 Max had experienced more than a dozen other safety incidents. Pierson said, "Something happened in the translation from, 'let's build a high-quality safe product' to 'let's get it done on time'" (Diss, 2020). There was pressure on 737 engineers and test pilots and also a lot of pressure on production employees. Pierson saw tired workers doing jobs for which they were not trained, and making mistakes. He asked management to shut down the 737 factory, but they refused. The software failures were thus symptoms of a wider management problem.

In March 2020, the House Transportation Committee, of the U.S. Congress, released its preliminary findings following a year of investigation into the 737 Max crashes. Concluding that these tragic accidents were due to multiple factors, the Committee's report focused on five issues:

- The implementation of aggressive cost cutting and excessive pressure on employees to maintain the production pressure, due to competition from Airbus.
- Boeing's faulty assumptions about critical technologies, and the MCAS system in particular, which relied on a single sensor and was not classed as a safety-critical system.
- Boeing's culture of concealment, withholding critical information from the FAA, customers, and pilots.
- Conflicts of interest among Boeing employees who were authorized to carry out aviation safety certification work on behalf of the FAA.
- Boeing's influence on the FAA's oversight; FAA management rejected safety concerns raised by their own experts.

The House Transportation Committee (2020, p. 13) concluded, "These preliminary investigative findings make clear that Boeing must create and maintain an effective and vigorous safety culture and the FAA must develop a more aggressive certification and oversight structure to ensure safe aircraft designs and to regain the confidence of the flying public." The focus on finance had changed the relationships between Boeing management and engineers: "It was the ability to comfortably interact with an engineer who in turn feels comfortable telling you their reservations, versus calling a manager 2,000 miles away who you know has a reputation for wanting to take your pension away. It's a very different dynamic. As a recipe for disempowering engineers in particular, you couldn't come up with a better format" (Useem, 2019). Boeing's "moral compass" was broken, and the focus on "making the numbers" put quality and safety at risk. McNulty and Marcus (2019, p. 4) claim that "Boeing should engage in a deep culture redesign process." Edmondson (2019) argues, "What's required is more than operational fixes. It is nothing less than a full organizational culture change."

(Continued)

Find on *YouTube*, "New Boeing CEO David Calhoun takes the reins by developing fresh strategy" (2020, 3:21 minutes).

Case Sources

Catchpole, D. 2020. Boeing's long descent. *Fortune* 181(2):56–58.

Diss, K. 2020. Troubled 737 Max Boeing airplane had at least 13 other safety incidents, ex-employee says. *ABC News*, February 14, https://www.abc.net.au/news/2020-02-15/ex-boeing-manager-says-one-in-25-737-max-had-safety-incident/11957634.

Edmondson, A. C. 2019. Boeing and the importance of encouraging employees to speak up. *Harvard Business Review*, May 4, https://hbr.org/2019/05/boeing-and-the-importance-of-encouraging-employees-to-speak-up.

McNulty, E. J., and Marcus, L. J. 2019. Flying safe: Boeing's values and culture need to change. *EHS Today*, October 7, https://www.ehstoday.com/safety-technology/article/21920393/flying-safe-boeings-values-and-culture-need-to-change.

Stacey, K. 2019. Senators castigate Boeing over anti-stall system. *Financial Times* (October 30):12 (U.S. edition).

The Economist. 2019. Boeing's misplaced strategy on the 737 MAX. *The Economist*, December 18, https://www.economist.com/leaders/2019/12/18/boeings-misplaced-strategy-on-the-737-max.

The House Committee on Transportation and Infrastructure. 2020. *The Boeing 737 MAX aircraft: Costs, consequences, and lessons from its design, development, and certification*. Washington.

Useem, J. 2019. The long-forgotten flight that sent Boeing off course. *Ideas*, November 20, https://www.theatlantic.com/ideas/archive/2019/11/how-boeing-lost-its-bearings.

EXERCISE 10.3

Did Heinz Choke on the 3G Recipe?

LO 10.5

As you read this case, consider the following questions:

1. What is your assessment of the strengths and limitations of the 3G approach to change?

2. If you were advising the board of Kraft Heinz on how to "invigorate" the company today, what changes would you recommend, and why? Use the dimensions of the change kaleidoscope to frame your advice concerning timing, scope, need for continuity, diversity of attitudes, capability of those involved, capacity of the organization, readiness for change, and power of the change manager.

3. What mistakes would you advise the board to avoid when implementing the changes that you are recommending (refer to tables 10.1 and 10.2)?

In 2013, Heinz, the iconic food company with an annual revenue of $11.6 billion, was bought for $29 billion by Warren Buffett's Berkshire Hathaway and the Brazilian private equity firm 3G Capital. The new owners wasted no time making changes. Eleven of the twelve most senior executives were replaced, 600 staff were laid off, the corporate planes were sold, individual offices were dispensed with, executives when travelling were to stay at a Holiday Inn hotel and not at the Ritz-Carlton, and much longer working hours were expected. Micro-management limited each staff member to 200 copies a month; printer usage was tracked. Executives were allowed only 100 business cards a year.

Heinz employees referred to "an insular management style in which only a small inner circle knows what is really going on." One said, "It's a bit like God—you feel there's a grand plan, but you aren't sure what it is" (Reingold and Roberts, 2013, p. 189). On the other hand, 3G had a young team of mostly Brazilian executives, who moved as directed from company to company across countries and industries, loyal to 3G, not Heinz, and driven to work hard to receive bonuses or stock options.

The driving force behind these changes was "The 3G Way"—which 3G had used to manage change in previous acquisitions such as Burger King. Efficiency was key, everything was measured, and costs were slashed. In this perspective, "leanest and meanest" wins, and human capital was not seen as a key component of corporate success. The assumption was that employees were motivated by the economic returns that came from owning company shares rather than by any sense of purpose or mission.

Those likely to be affected by a 3G deal often saw a "how to" guide written by consultant Bob Fifer as a "must read," because it had been popular with the partners at 3G (as it had been with Jack Welch, the iconic chief executive at GE). The guide was titled, "Double Your Profits: 78 Ways to Cut Costs, Increase Sales, and Dramatically Improve Your Bottom Line in 6 Months or Less." Chapter titles included "Cut Costs First, Ask Questions Later" and "Don't Be Afraid to Use a Shotgun."

However, in the minds of many food industry experts, while some of 3G's previous acquisitions would have been prime candidates for a cost-cutting regimen, Heinz was not an obvious target for that "hack and slash" approach. The company had been through several years of efficiency improvements ("slimming and trimming"), and it was already a relatively lean and efficient operation.

Summing up the situation, business journalists Jennifer Reingold and Daniel Roberts (2013, p. 186) speculated that "the experiment now under way will determine whether Heinz will become a newly invigorated embodiment of efficiency—or whether 3G will take the cult of cost cutting so far that it chokes off Heinz's ability to innovate and make the products that have made it a market leader for almost a century and a half."

In 2015, Heinz and the food industry giant Kraft announced a merger that would create an entity with an annual revenue of $28 billion, the third largest food company in the United States and the fifth largest in the world. Annual cost savings of $1.5 billion were expected.

The merger was followed by more cost cutting. However, less attention was paid to changing customer preferences, such as for healthy organic food instead of processed cheese and lunch meat. Margins were also cut by supermarket purchasing strategies (La Monica, 2019). In an attempt to grow further, Kraft Heinz made an offer of $143 billion for Unilever in 2017—but the offer was rejected. Further cost cutting at Kraft Heinz failed, leading to falling sales, falling operating income, and a falling share price. Unilever, in contrast, was comparatively successful. Cox (2019) said, "How the tables have turned. The Cheez Whiz giant has melted down since offering to buy Unilever: its US$40 billion market value is now just a quarter of its erstwhile prey. Unilever, meanwhile, has blossomed into a US$155 billion behemoth." By 2018, Kraft Heinz was making losses, the share price had fallen by 60 percent in over two years, and the Securities and Exchange Commission was investigating its accounting practices.

Find on *YouTube*, "Warren Buffett on what he plans to do with his Kraft Heinz shares and 3G Capital" (2019, 8:31 minutes).

(Continued)

Case Sources

Carey, D., Dumaine, B., and Useem, M. 2019. CEOs are suddenly having a change of heart about what their companies should stand for—and the diverging fates of 2 major corporations show why. *Business Insider*, September 6, https://www.businessinsider.com.au/kraft-heinz-unilever-ceo-investments-economy.

Cox, R. 2019. Unilever can't help but mull a Kraft pounce. *Reuters*, March 8, https://www.reuters.com/article/us-kraft-heinz-unilever-breakingview.

Kell, J. 2017. Big food is going to get even bigger. *Fortune,* March 15, 175(4):11–12.

La Monica, P. R. 2019. What went wrong at Kraft Heinz? *CNN Business*, February 22, https://edition.cnn.com/2019/02/22/investing/kraft-heinz-stock-strategy/index.html.

Reingold, J., and Roberts, D. 2013. Squeezing Heinz. *Fortune* (October 28):184–92, https://www.forbes.com/sites/greatspeculation/2015/03/30/analysis-of-the-kraft-heinz-merger.

Additional Reading

Balogun, J., Hope Hailey, V., and Gustafsson, S. 2016. *Exploring strategic change.* 4th ed. Harlow, Essex: Pearson. Wide-ranging theoretical and practical text on change management, advocating a contingent approach that tailors change implementation to the context, based on the "change kaleidoscope" tool.

Dawson, P., and Andriopoulos, C. 2017. *Managing change, creativity and innovation.* 3rd ed. London: Sage Publications. A comprehensive and clearly explained account of a processual perspective on change and innovation, theoretical and practical.

Kotter, J. P. 2012. Accelerate! *Harvard Business Review* 90(11):44–52. Explains how to drive strategic, transformational change without disrupting daily operations. This is a development of Kotter's original eight-stage model of transformational change.

Roundup

Reflections for the Practicing Change Manager

- Do you work with a "one size fits all" approach to change management? To what extent do you adapt your approach to the scale and timing of the change, staff readiness, your own relative power, and other context features identified in this chapter?

- How capable are you in adopting more than one change image? Are you more comfortable with a top-down or a bottom-up approach—or somewhere in between? Do you need to develop any particular skills to achieve greater flexibility (assuming you believe that flexibility will give you an advantage)?

- Is there a dominant change approach in your organization? If so, how appropriate is it? What would you need to do to modify or replace that dominant approach?

- How do you handle the many different change initiatives that are unfolding in our organization or business unit at a given time—when these are all at different stages? Is this a problem? If not, why not? If it is, what is your preferred solution? If possible, share and discuss your responses to this question and the others in this "reflection" with colleagues.

Here is a short summary of the key points that we would like you to take from this chapter, in relation to each of the learning outcomes:

LO 10.1   * *Understand and identify the factors that can cause change to fail.*
Making change fail is relatively easy; there are many things that one can do, and not do, to achieve that result. John Kotter identifies eight main failure factors: lack of urgency, no supportive coalition, no vision, poor communication, obstacles to change not removed, no "wins" or achievements to celebrate, declaring victory too soon, and not anchoring or embedding the changes. Lack of communication is a particularly significant cause of change failure.

LO 10.2   * *Assess the strengths and limitations of checklists for managing change effectively.*
We introduced three checklists or "recipes" for managing change:

- Boston Consulting Group's DICE model
- Prosci's ADKAR model
- Stouten's evidence-based model

One strength of these approaches is that they provide clarity and simplicity in an area that can be complex and untidy. Another strength is that different checklists tend to offer much the same advice, which is reassuring. One limitation is that these checklists tend to lack any theoretical underpinning, relying often on an argument that sounds like, "This worked for us, so it should work for you." From a practitioner perspective, another limitation is that these are generic "high-level guides" and not detailed "best practice" road maps. The change manager is left with the challenging task of translating this guidance into a change implementation plan that will fit the organizational circumstances. These checklists do not substitute for local knowledge, informed judgment, and creativity.

We discussed the question concerning when to use each of these checklists. As they tend to offer broadly similar advice, it may not matter. However, they encourage different emphases—DICE on taking action based on scoring the issues, ADKAR on individual perceptions, and Stouten on following the research evidence base. A more appropriate question, perhaps, is how to use these checklists. They should be seen as high-level guides and not detailed road maps, and they will be helpful as long as they are not used in a tightly prescriptive manner, but to trigger discussion, diagnosis, and planning. It may be useful in some settings to apply more than one model to the same change program. These comments concerning when and how to use change management guidelines apply to all the models and frameworks in this chapter.

LO 10.3   * *Evaluate the advantages of stage models of change management.*
We introduced three stage models of change management:

- Lewin's three-stage model
- Kotter's eight-stage model
- McKinsey 5A model

Stage models complement a checklist approach by emphasizing how change unfolds and develops over time, making changing demands on the change manager and on those who are affected, at each stage. Although change rarely develops in a neat and tidy manner, approaching the process in this way encourages the change manager to anticipate and prepare for possible future problems. It also encourages a focus on the "pipeline" of change benefits and on how "leakage" during the process can lead to disappointing outcomes. It may also be helpful to consider a more extended time line, considering how past events could influence current proposals, and how changes will be sustained, and eventually decay, into the future.

LO 10.4   * *Assess the theoretical and practical value of the process perspective on change.*

The process perspective argues that the outcomes of change are shaped by the combination and interaction of a number of factors over time in a given context. Those factors include the context and substance of the change, the implementation process, and also the internal and external organization politics. One strength of the process perspective is that it emphasizes the role of organizational politics, which is often overlooked or regarded as marginal by other approaches. The practical advice flowing from this perspective is similar to that provided by checklists and stage models: plan, train, communicate, learn from mistakes, adapt to circumstances. However, where some change management advice recommends "do this," the process perspective says, "be aware of this," leaving the change manager with the task of reaching informed judgments with regard to appropriate action.

The process perspective highlights the complexity and politicized nature of change and sees change as a process with a past, present, and future, rather than as a static or time-bounded event. However, there are dangers in this perspective, in presenting change as overcomplex and unmanageable, in placing the focus on context at the expense of individual and team contributions, and in the focus on awareness rather than clear direction.

LO 10.5   * *Understand and apply contingency approaches to change management.*

We presented four contingency approaches:

- Where to start?
- Change leadership styles continuum
- Stace–Dunphy contingency matrix
- Change kaleidoscope

Contingency approaches argue that change implementation should take into account the attributes of the organizational context concerned. However, these approaches differ with regard to the contingencies—the key factors—that the change manager needs to consider. For example, "where to start?" argues that change should begin with the "pivotal roles," where changes will have the biggest impact on the behavior and performance that is of concern. Those "pivotal roles" will vary from one change initiative to another. The styles continuum suggests choosing a change leadership style based on considerations of available time, use of available expertise, and staff commitment. A dictatorial approach to management in general, and to change management in particular, probably runs counter to most management beliefs. However, the Stace–Dunphy contingency framework suggests that where change is vital, time is short, and consensus is unlikely, a dictatorial approach is more likely to be effective in achieving management outcomes. The most complex of these models, the change kaleidoscope, identifies eight sets of context factors and six sets of change implementation design options. The design options, this approach argues, need to reflect the context diagnosis.

It may seem obvious to argue that "the best approach" depends on the context. However, this idea of "fitting" change to the setting is easier to explain in theory than to put into practice. Detailed diagnosis of the context takes time and requires considerable local knowledge and insight. A contingency approach also demands flexibility in style from change leaders and managers who may in some instances be required to move out of their "comfort zones," and inconsistent behavior may weaken management credibility. Our two final questions are: Is everything contingent in this area? Are there no universals in organizational change?

References

Appelbaum, S. H., Habashy, S., Malo, J.-L., and Shafiq, H. 2012. Back to the future: Revisiting Kotter's 1996 change model. *Journal of Management Development* 31(8):764–82.

Balogun, J. 2006. Managing change: Steering a course between intended strategies and unanticipated outcomes. *Long Range Planning* 39(1):29–49.

Balogun, J., Hope Hailey, V., and Gustafsson, S. 2016. *Exploring strategic change*. 4th ed. Harlow, Essex: Pearson.

Bucy, M., Hall, S., Yakola, D., and Dickson, T. 2017a. Disruption, friction, and change: The hallmarks of a true transformation, Podcast. New York and London: McKinsey & Company.

Bucy, M., Fagan, T., Maraite, B., and Piaia, C. 2017b. *Keeping transformations on target*. New York and London: McKinsey & Company.

Burnes, B. 2020. The origins of Lewin's three-step model of change. *The Journal of Applied Behavioral Science* 56(1):32–59.

Coch, L., and French, J. R. P. 1948. Overcoming resistance to change. *Human Relations* 1:512–32.

Cummings, S., Bridgman, T., and Brown, K. G. 2016. Unfreezing change as three steps: Rethinking Kurt Lewin's legacy for change management. *Human Relations* 69(1):33–60.

Dawson, P., and Andriopoulos, C. 2017. *Managing change, creativity and innovation*. 3rd ed. London: Sage Publications.

Gardini, M., Giuliani, G., and Marricchi, M. 2011. *Finding the right place to start change*. Rome and Milan: McKinsey & Company.

Hiatt, J. M. 2004. *Employee's survival guide to change*. Loveland, CO: Prosci Research.

Hiatt, J. 2006. *ADKAR: A model for change in business, government, and our community*. Loveland, CO: Prosci.

Hiatt, J. M., and Creasey, T. J. 2012. *Change management: The people side of change*. Loveland, CO: Prosci Learning Center.

Hope Hailey, V., and Balogun, J. 2002. Devising context sensitive approaches to change: The example of Glaxo Wellcome. *Long Range Planning* 35(2):153–78.

Kanter, R. M. 2009. Change is hardest in the middle. *Harvard Business Review* Blog Network, August 12, http://blogs.hbr.org/2009/08/change-is-hardest-in-the-middl.

Keller, S., and Schaninger, B. 2019a. *A better way to lead large-scale change*. New York: McKinsey & Company.

Keller, S., and Schaninger, B. 2019b. *Beyond Performance 2.0: A proven approach to leading large-scale change*, Hoboken, NJ: Wiley.

Kotter, J. P. 2007. Leading change: Why transformation efforts fail. *Harvard Business Review* 85(1):96–103 (first published 1995).

Kotter, J. P. 2012a. *Leading change*. 2nd ed. Boston, MA: Harvard University Press.

Kotter, J. P. 2012b. Accelerate! *Harvard Business Review* 90(11):44–52.

Lewin, K. (ed.) 1951. *Field theory in social science: Selected theoretical papers by Kurt Lewin* London: Tavistock Publications (UK edition published 1952, ed. Dorwin Cartwright).

McFarland, W., and Goldsworthy, S. 2013. *Choosing change: How leaders and organizations drive results one person at a time*. New York: McGraw Hill Professional.

Pettigrew, A. M. 1985. *The awakening giant: Continuity and change in ICI*. Oxford: Basil Blackwell.

Pettigrew, A. M. 1987. Context and action in the transformation of the firm. *Journal of Management Studies* 24(6):649–70.

Plowman, D. A., Baker, L. T., Beck, T. E., Kulkarni, M., Solansky, S. T., and Travis, D. V. T. 2007. Radical change accidentally: The emergence and amplification of small change. *Academy of Management Journal* 50(3):515–43.

Schneider, D. M., and Goldwasser, C. 1998. Be a model leader of change. *Management Review* 87(3):41–45.

Sirkin, H. J., Keenan, P., and Jackson, A. 2005. The hard side of change management. *Harvard Business Review* 83(10):108–18.

Stace, D. A., and Dunphy, D. 2001. *Beyond the boundaries: Leading and re-creating the successful enterprise*. 2nd ed. Sydney: McGraw Hill.

Stouten, J., Rousseau, D. M., and De Cremer, D. 2018. Successful organizational change: Integrating the management practice and scholarly literatures. *Academy of Management Annals* 12(2):752–88.

Tannenbaum, R., and Schmidt, W. H. 1958. How to choose a leadership pattern. *Harvard Business Review* 36(2):95–101.

The House Committee on Transportation and Infrastructure. 2020. *The Boeing 737 MAX aircraft: Costs, consequences, and lessons from its design, development, and certification*. Washington.

Wiedner, R., Barrett, M., and Oborn, E. 2017. The emergence of change in unexpected places: Resourcing across organizational practices in strategic change. *Academy of Management Journal* 60(3):823–54.

Source of opening quote from Ayn Rand: https://blog.hubspot.com/sales/great-female-leader-quotes

Chapter opening silhouette credit: FunKey Factory/Shutterstock

Running Threads: Sustainability and the Effective Change Manager

CHAPTER 11   Sustaining Change versus Initiative Decay

CHAPTER 12   The Effective Change Manager: What Does It Take?

Part 3 focuses on two themes that are distinct from, but which run through, the first two parts of this book. The first of these "running threads" concerns the sustainability of organizational change. We know that even successful changes can "decay," with the benefits lost. What actions are necessary to ensure or at least improve the sustainability of change? In many of the implementation models that we explored in part 2, sustainability is treated as the final step in the change process. Chapter 11 argues that sustainability has to be considered from the start, built into the implementation process. In most cases, it will be too late to treat sustainability as an issue to be managed after implementation has been completed. The second running thread, the core theme that this text as a whole addresses, concerns what it takes to be an effective change manager. We consider who the change managers are in an organization and if they are necessarily senior leaders. The role of middle managers—traditionally seen as change blockers—turns out to be key in initiating and implementing change. Finally, we set out a six-step approach to developing personal change management capabilities.

Chapter 11

Sustaining Change versus Initiative Decay

Learning Objectives

By the end of this chapter you should be able to:

LO 11.1 Understand the causes of initiative decay—threats to the sustainability of change.

LO 11.2 Distinguish between change initiatives that are "blameworthy," and should not be sustained, and those that are "praiseworthy."

LO 11.3 Identify and apply actions that can contribute to the sustainability of change.

LO 11.4 Understand the pitfalls that can arise when seeking to sustain change.

"It's easy to make a buck. It's a lot tougher to make a difference."

Tom Brokaw, journalist

LO 11.1 Initiative Decay and Improvement Evaporation

Your reorganization was implemented successfully. Significant benefits were achieved. Revisiting the initiative some months later, however, you find that the new working practices and increased performance levels appear not to have been maintained. Things have gone back to where they were before you started. How did this happen? Unfortunately, this is a common story. Even successful initiatives can decay, leading to "the improvement evaporation effect" as the gains are lost.

For many organizations, it is a strategic imperative to embed, to have "stickability," and to maintain changes and their contribution to performance. This chapter focuses on the problems of sustaining change and on the practical steps that can be taken to increase the probability that changes once implemented will endure, that they will become institutionalized and regarded as normal practice. This is not a new problem, having been famously identified by Lewin (1951) as the need to "refreeze" behavior once change has taken place. The attention of practicing managers and academic researchers has focused on the first two stages of his model, "unfreezing" and "moving." The problem of refreezing, or sustaining change, is less well understood. There may be a widespread assumption that if changes have been successful, they will automatically be sustained. That assumption, however, appears to be incorrect. Sustaining change may in some cases be more difficult than implementing change in the first place.

Find on *YouTube,* "OCM: Sustaining Change" (2017, 3:33 minutes).

Sustainability implies that new working methods and performance levels are maintained for an appropriate period or that new practices and processes are routinized until they become obsolete. What are the causes of initiative decay? What steps can be taken to increase the probability that changes will be sustained and become embedded in the organization as routine practice? As we have explored in other chapters, what is considered to be achievable with regard to sustaining change depends on how managing change is understood. The views of sustainability from each image of change management are summarized in table 11.1.

TABLE 11.1
Images of Managing and Sustaining Change

Image	View of Sustainability
Director	It is the responsibility of the change manager to design the change process and direct others to comply, to ensure that planned objectives are achieved.
Navigator	The change manager designs the change process to fit the context, recognizing that modifications will be required and that the outcome may not be as intended.
Caretaker	Change outcomes will be determined primarily by contextual factors, and not by management intervention.
Coach	The change manager's main role is to help others to develop the capabilities necessary to achieve the intended outcomes of the change.
Interpreter	The change manager develops an understanding of the meaning and significance of the changes and what will count as successful outcomes.
Nurturer	Change outcomes are in constant flux and are largely beyond management control.

Momentum Busters

Robert Reisner (2002) examines the U.S. Postal Service, which during the 1990s, "transformed itself from the butt of sitcom jokes into a profitable and efficient enterprise" (p. 45). By 2001, however, morale and performance were low and losses were predicted. Why was the transformation not sustained? Reisner (vice president for strategic planning) blames three "momentum busters": the indifference of senior managers, who regarded some aspects of strategy as a "distraction"; resistance from trade unions, whose role and voice had been marginalized; and the inability to steer funding through a budget process that favored traditional initiatives over innovations. Innovation was also stifled by governance constraints. What one competitor, UPS, achieved, the U.S. Postal Service could not have initiated without a prior hearing process before the Postal Rate Commission, and major structural changes would have required Congressional sanction. The situation was exacerbated by a weak economy, problems with e-commerce, and terrorist assaults on the U.S. Postal Service.

Reisner's (2002, p. 52) conclusion is optimistic: "Despite the limits to any transformation effort, accomplishing meaningful change in even the largest, most complex, and traditionbound of organizations is achievable." However, the leadership, organizational, and contextual causes of initiative decay need to be addressed to sustain these changes (Buchanan et al., 2005).

We have to recognize that management may have no direct control over many of the factors that can jeopardize the sustainability of change. That does not mean, however, that it is not possible to anticipate and to counter those factors in some manner.

For changes to "stick," they must "seep into the bloodstream," become "the new norm," "baked into the organization," or, as Kotter (2007, p. 103) observes, accepted as "the way we do things around here." That is, it must become an integral part of the organizational culture, or what has also been described as the "mind-set" of the organization's members (Lawson and Price, 2003). This means that new structures, processes, and working practices are no longer seen as "change," with all the emotional, political, and operational connotations that accompany that term. Unless this happens, change may prove to be just a passing diversion, a temporary disruption. However, as we explored in chapter 5, culture change is not a straightforward process. As Lou Gerstner (2002, pp. 182 and 187) once said, referring to his leadership of the successful transformation of IBM:

> I came to see, in my time at IBM, that culture isn't just one aspect of the game—it is the game. Vision, strategy, marketing, financial management—any management system, in fact—can set you on the right path and can carry you for a while. But no enterprise—whether in business, government, education, health care, or any area of human endeavor—will succeed over the long haul if those elements aren't part of the DNA.
>
> What you can do is create the conditions for transformation. You can provide incentives. You can define the marketplace realities and goals. But then you have to trust. In fact, in the end, management doesn't change culture. Management invites the workforce itself to change the culture.

What are the main threats to the sustainability of change? Buchanan et al. (2007) identify the top ten factors that can lead to initiative decay:

1. *The initiators and drivers move on.* Managers who have been successful at implementing change may be more interested in moving on to the next change challenge than in staying around for a period of relative stability. In addition, experienced and

successful change agents may be sought by other divisions or organizations, which have other novel change agendas to progress. It can be difficult to turn down promotion opportunities such as these.

2. *Accountability for development has become diffuse.* The responsibility for driving change is normally (but not always) clear, with formal change or project management roles, often accompanied by steering groups, task forces, and implementation teams. Once the changes are in place and operational, those individuals and groups return to their normal roles. There are change managers, but organizations tend not to appoint "sustainability managers." Just who is accountable for ensuring that the changes are now embedded, that they become the new norm, is often unclear.

3. *Knowledge and experience with new practices are lost through staff turnover.* Staff training and development programs usually support change initiatives that involve new skills and knowledge. Everyone who is going to be affected will be invited to attend these programs, creating a "critical mass" of participants for training sessions. However, as individuals subsequently leave and are replaced, it may be difficult to repeat those development sessions for small numbers of participants. The knowledge that is lost when staff members leave is therefore not replaced.

4. *Old habits are imported with recruits from less dynamic organizations.* Linked to factor 3, new recruits bring with them habits and working practices from previous employers. Once again, they are unlikely to be offered retraining, but instead expected to learn new practices "on the job" by observation. The likelihood of initiative decay thus increases with the numbers of new recruits.

5. *The issues and pressures that triggered the initiative are no longer visible.* As we discussed in chapter 3, organizations usually change in response to a combination of internal problems, external environmental challenges, and new opportunities. Those triggers, however, may not be durable; the problems are solved, the challenges are addressed, the opportunities are developed. The rationale for change can thus fade with the triggers, and again lead to initiative decay.

6. *New managers want to drive their own agendas.* For personal satisfaction, visibility, and reputation, newly appointed managers often want to appear to be innovative and energetic and to "make a mark" on their new organization. This means enhancing their careers by designing and implementing their own change initiatives. Continuing with work that was started by others is less interesting and satisfying and could limit one's promotion prospects.

7. *Powerful stakeholders are using counter-implementation tactics to block progress.* Successful implementation does not always silence the power brokers. They may remain in their posts, and if they did not welcome the changes, they may wait for opportunities to undermine the changes. This becomes easier if factor 1 applies; the initiators are no longer there to protect their changes.

8. *The pump-priming funding runs out.* Many changes are allocated additional funding to support the implementation costs. This can include the temporary appointment of specialist staff or external consultants and the cost of training programs to provide new skills and knowledge. As those resources are consumed and the temporary appointments and the training come to an end, support for the changes is weakened and initiative decay becomes more likely.

9. *Other priorities come on stream, diverting attention and resources.* Most organizations today do not suffer a shortage of internal and external pressures for change. As other urgent problems and opportunities arise, the focus inevitably shifts away from past pressures and the changes that those prompted. If those past problems have indeed been addressed, then it may be appropriate for attention and resources to move to more urgent issues. However, this will generate problems if the shift in focus to new priorities simply re-creates the situation that past changes were implemented to address.

10. *Staff at all levels suffer initiative fatigue, and enthusiasm for change falters.* The experience, or the perception, of "too much change," successful or not, can threaten sustainability by generating a desire to "get back to normal." Initiative decay can result when management does not pay attention to the pace and timing of the changes that staff are expected to deal with and generate burnout and initiative fatigue by attempting to drive too many changes too rapidly.

Initiative decay can be caused by many factors, at different levels of analysis. Several of those factors may be operating in a given context at any one time. In the absence of proactive management steps to address those factors, initiative decay, and not sustained change, may be the norm.

LO 11.2 Praiseworthy and Blameworthy Failures

The failure of an intended change is not always a problem that needs to be solved. A change can fail because it was inappropriate for some reason. Marks and Shaw (1995) argue that "productive failure" is valuable, if an organization has the capacity to add the learning from such experiences to its store of knowledge, rather than to conduct a witch hunt to find whom to blame. A learning organization treats occasional failure as natural and as an opportunity to develop a better understanding and to improve future performance. Marks and Shaw (1995) also argue that an organization may gain more in the long term from a productive failure than from an "unproductive success"—a change that has gone well, but nobody quite knows why: "We must be doing something right."

Some changes, if they do not meet their intended goals, must therefore be allowed to decay. Most organizations, however, do treat such "failures" harshly. Those who were responsible may even be punished in some manner and perhaps find that their career opportunities have become more limited. In chapter 3, we discussed the work of Amy Edmondson (2011, p. 50), who describes a spectrum of reasons for failure (see table 11.2), from blameworthy at one extreme, to praiseworthy at the other. Not all these failure modes concern change, but those that do are more likely to be praiseworthy.

Most managers, Edmondson argues, do not distinguish blameworthy from praiseworthy failures, treating them all equally. This is not helpful, and is potentially wasteful:

> When I ask executives to consider this spectrum and then to estimate how many of the failures in their organization are truly blameworthy, their answers are usually in single digits—perhaps 2% to 5%. But when I ask how many are treated as blameworthy, they say (after a pause or a laugh) 70% to 90%. The unfortunate consequence is that many failures go unreported and their lessons are lost. (Edmondson, 2011, p. 50)

Productive Failure at McDonald's

In 2001, McDonald's opened two four-star Golden Arch hotels in Switzerland. They were distinctive, with a 24-hour McDonald's restaurant attached and rooms with a patented curved wall, arch-shaped headboards, and a cylindrical, see-through shower (that was partially in the bedroom). The idea had been proposed by the McDonald's Switzerland chairman, Urs Hammer, in response to a push from the parent company for diversification and new ideas.

The hotels were not a financial success. There were problems with the interior design (lack of privacy in the shower), and the phrase "golden arches" is not associated with McDonald's in German-speaking countries (it also didn't help that "arch," when pronounced by German speakers, sounded like a vulgar German word for posterior). Also, and more importantly, although the restaurant venture made use of many of the company's core competencies in areas such as franchising and real estate management, the McDonald's brand simply didn't work when applied to a four-star hotel.

However, international marketing professor Stefan Michel (2007) argues that the decision by McDonald's to pilot this initiative was not as bizarre as it seemed. For example: (1) diversifying into hotels gave McDonald's a chance to test the multi-billion-dollar restaurant industry; (2) it required what was a relatively small investment for McDonald's; (3) the damage to the McDonald's brand was limited through the use of the name Golden Arches and restricting the experiment to Switzerland; and (4) the losses on real estate and operations were insignificant in relation to the overall McDonald's business. Most significantly, the venture was a statement of support for entrepreneurial ideas within the company, and the outcome was treated as an important, and relatively inexpensive, learning experience.

Based on Michel (2007).

TABLE 11.2
A Spectrum of Reasons for Failure

Reason	Description	
Deviance	An individual chooses to violate a prescribed process or practice.	blameworthy
Inattention	An individual inadvertently deviates from specifications.	↑
Lack of ability	An individual doesn't have the skills, conditions, or training to execute a job.	
Process inadequacy	A competent individual adheres to a prescribed but faulty or incomplete process.	
Task challenge	An individual faces a task too difficult to be executed reliably every time.	
Process complexity	A process composed of many elements breaks down when it encounters novel interactions.	
Uncertainty	A lack of clarity about future events causes people to take seemingly reasonable actions that produce undesired results.	
Hypothesis testing	An experiment conducted to prove that an idea or a design will succeed fails.	↓
Exploratory testing	An experiment conducted to expand knowledge and investigate a possibility leads to an undesired result.	praiseworthy

From Edmondson (2011, p.50).

Changes that fail can therefore be valuable, discouraging further experiments of that kind and revealing what adjustments may be necessary to make the next attempt successful. To build such a learning culture, experimentation should be encouraged, and failures (including near misses) need to be detected and subjected to an analysis that looks beyond the obvious. It is also necessary to avoid making the "fundamental attribution error," which means blaming individuals and ignoring the context in which they were working (Ross, 1977).

Based on experience at a children's hospital in Minnesota, Edmondson (2011, pp. 52–53) describes five practices for building a "psychologically safe environment" in which to learn from failures:

1. *Frame the work accurately.* People need a shared understanding of the kinds of failures that can be expected to occur in a given work context (routine production, complex operations, or innovation) and why openness and collaboration are important for surfacing and learning from them. Accurate framing detoxifies failure.

2. *Embrace messengers.* Those who come forward with bad news, questions, concerns, or mistakes should be rewarded rather than shot. Celebrate the value of the news first, and then figure out how to fix the failure and learn from it.

3. *Acknowledge limits.* Being open about what you don't know, mistakes you've made, and what you can't get done alone will encourage others to do the same.

4. *Invite participation.* Ask for observations and ideas, and create opportunities for people to detect and analyze failures and promote intelligent experiments. Inviting participation helps defuse resistance and defensiveness.

5. *Set boundaries and hold people accountable.* Paradoxically, people feel psychologically safer when leaders are clear about what acts are blameworthy. And there must be consequences. But if someone is punished or fired, tell those directly and indirectly affected what happened and why it warranted blame.

Will adopting such a "soft" and "understanding" management approach to failures make staff more careless and encourage more mistakes? Edmondson (2011, p. 55) argues that a failure to encourage experimentation, combined with a failure to learn from the inevitable mistakes, poses greater risks to organizational change and effectiveness. Change initiatives that do not work cannot be sustained. However, if management wants to sustain the generation of further new ideas for change, then those who develop praiseworthy failures should be recognized and rewarded, and not blamed and punished.

Find on *YouTube,* "Building a psychologically safe workplace: Amy Edmondson TEDxHGSE" (2014, 11:26 minutes).

LO 11.3 Actions to Sustain Change

What actions will increase the probability that change will be sustained? No specific set of steps can guarantee success, but awareness of the threats to sustainability can lead to timely and effective responses. Action to secure sustainability is often identified as the final point in the "change recipes" that we discussed in chapter 10. For

Sustaining Successful Change Means Permanently Changing Mindsets

Emily Lawson and Colin Price (2003) argue that the success and sustainability of change rely on people thinking differently about their jobs, and not just on persuading them to change the way they work. This is particularly the case with fundamental changes to organizational culture, for example, from reactive to proactive, from hierarchical to collegial, from introspective to externally focused. There are four conditions for the necessary change in mindsets.

First, those who are affected by a change need to understand the purpose, and agree with it. There is no point in management telling people that things must be done differently: "Anyone leading a major change program must take time to think through its 'story'—what makes it worth undertaking—and to explain that story to all of the people involved in making change happen, so that their contributions make sense to them as individuals" (p. 33).

Second, reward and recognition systems need to be consistent with the new behaviors. Third, staff must have the necessary skills and be given time to absorb new information, link that to existing knowledge, and apply it effectively in practice.

And finally, "they must see people they respect modelling it actively" (p. 32). We all tend to model our behavior on "significant others" and especially those in influential positions. Managers at all levels thus become role models and must "walk the talk" if mindsets are to change (p. 35).

example, "institutionalize new approaches" is step 8 in Kotter's (2007) eight-step model of transformational change. However, sustainability depends not just on what happens after implementation, but also on the cumulative effects of decisions and actions during the change process. In other words, it is more effective to plan for sustainability from the beginning than to regard this as an issue that can be left until a later stage.

Here are eight sets of actions that should be considered when designing a change initiative, to build sustainability into the process from the beginning, or at least from an early stage.

Redesign Roles

Organizational change, particularly where new structures, processes, and technologies are involved, often leads to the redesign of existing roles and to the creation of new ones. However, these role changes may be a critical dimension of the process, and not just a product of change. Beer et al. (1990) argue that most change programs do not work because they focus on attempts to change attitudes and beliefs by introducing new perspectives. The assumption that underpins this approach, that changes in behavior will follow changes in attitudes, is in their view fundamentally flawed. The causal arrow, they suggest, runs in the opposite direction. Behavior is influenced by the context in which people find themselves—by their responsibilities, relationships, and roles. In short, first redesign roles, which require new behaviors, and attitude change will then follow. It is difficult to revert to past behavior with a new formal role

Busting the Momentum Busters

Reflecting on his experience of the "momentum busters" that derailed transformational change in the U.S. Postal Service, Robert Reisner (2002, pp. 51–52) identifies "four hard lessons" for organizations undertaking a major change initiative in a turbulent economic environment:

1. *Don't miss your moment.* We missed numerous market opportunities that competitors such as UPS seized. Furthermore, we let pass at least two chances to capitalize on high morale and momentum within the Postal Service, moments that provided the best opportunity to overcome organizational resistance to change.

2. *Connect change initiatives to your core business.* Most of the innovative programs we launched to boost revenue existed at the fringes of our business. And we never established a path for them to migrate to the heart of our operations.

3. *Don't mistake incremental improvements for strategic transformation.* [O]ur tremendous success in improving delivery times, which we enthusiastically celebrated, blinded us to the need for strategic change. For a time, we slipped into complacency, ignoring our competition and challenges and declaring ourselves the winner in a race with ourselves.

4. *Be realistic about your limits and the pace of change.* [I]n a change initiative, it is important to identify which obstacles are in your control and which aren't. Some of what we wanted to do may simply not have been possible, at least at the time. . . . While some of our constraints—our regulatory framework, if not our very size and complexity—are specific to us, every organization has limits of one kind or another. It may seem heretical to say so in the can-do environment of American business, but sometimes you need to accept those limits. A failure to acknowledge that you sometimes *can't* do certain things can breed discouragement and cynicism, ultimately undermining those change initiatives that are achievable.

definition, which is one of a network of similarly redesigned roles. Sustainability is not guaranteed by this approach but is significantly encouraged.

Redesign Reward Systems

Beer and Nohria (2000, p. 267) also observe that "there are virtually no fundamental changes in organizations that do not also involve some changes in the reward system." This is one consequence of redesigning roles and responsibilities. Fisher (1995, p. 122) cites the example of Integra Financial, a $14 billion (in assets) bank holding company that was formed through a merger. To reinforce the company's commitment to a teamwork initiative, management implemented a carefully designed evaluation and reward system "to discourage hot-dogging, grandstanding, filibustering, and other ego games" and to ensure that "the best team players get the goodies." Fisher (1995, p. 122) also notes, "One thing that you can count on: Whatever gets rewarded will get done." This also means that whatever is not rewarded (such as pre-change working practices) will not get done. Changing the reward system can thus contribute significantly to sustainability by removing the financial motivation to return to old behaviors.

Rewards should also include public recognition of behaviors that are consistent with the desired change. This both reinforces individual behavior and sends strong signals to others. The opposite also applies. Management's failure to respond to behavior that is in direct opposition to the change undermines the credibility of the program. Lack of action in this respect can increase rapidly the rate of initiative decay. The organization's pay system can thus support or derail a change initiative.

Link Selection to Change Objectives

Staff selection, and promotion processes, can be subtle but powerful ways in which to embed and sustain assumptions and values—to change and to maintain the organization's culture. As with the rewards system, appointments and promotions, particularly to key and influential roles, have symbolic significance in signalling whether top management really support a change, or not. A single inappropriate senior appointment during the change process can quickly derail all the implementation work that has already been undertaken.

To support organizational changes with selection, a number of organizations have adopted "values-based recruitment" systems, which seek to select staff whose motives, attitudes, and values support what the organization is trying to achieve. For example, Rapping (2009) describes a values-based recruitment, training, and mentoring program for selecting and developing public defenders to represent poor clients in criminal cases in Georgia. Poor defendants often have problems finding lawyers, who then refuse to visit them in jail. To change this traditional culture, recruitment and selection changed to emphasize values relating to enthusiastic and loyal representation, advocating the client's cause, studying and preparing the case, and communicating with the client.

Triggered by failures in quality of social care in the UK, Goode (2014) describes a values-based recruitment toolkit to help employers to find people with values appropriate to working in this sector. This toolkit includes sample job advertisements and an online personality profiling questionnaire and suggested values-based interview questions such as: "What excites you about working in adult social care?" "Can you give an example of where your understanding of what another person may be going through has helped you to develop your compassion for that person?" and "Tell me about a time when you have 'gone the extra mile' at work." The answers to these kinds of questions reveal candidates' behavior and their values with regard to care and compassion.

Walk the Talk

This is a well-known cliché. However, senior management can seriously jeopardize the sustainability of change if their words and actions are interpreted by employees as signalling, "We don't really mean it." In other words, if the top team does not support this change, why should we? Little is more damaging to the credibility of a change program than a lack of consistency between the statements and behaviors of the change advocates. Even if management did not mean to send negative signals, "unintentional hypocrisy" can be equally damaging (Fisher, 1995).

One indicator of consistency concerns changes in management practices that are clearly aligned with the goals of the change. For example, who is praised and promoted and why? Is management enthusiastically advocating teamwork while still rewarding individual performance? Where are resources—finance, staffing, expertise—being allocated?

Alan Lafley's Moment of Truth

Early in his time as chief executive at Procter & Gamble, Alan Lafley had to decide whether to approve a major marketing effort to launch several new products. This would require a significant commitment of funds, and P&G had just missed earnings targets two quarters in a row. But Lafley had been working hard communicating the message that innovation was P&G's lifeblood. Lafley describes his response: "So we locked arms and we went ahead. I had to make choices like these to convince P&G managers we were going to go for winning" (Gupta and Wendler, 2005, p. 4).

The commitment of resources to an initiative in such a way that to withdraw would be extremely costly conveys unambiguous management support (see the box "Alan Lafley's Moment of Truth"). All these management decisions and actions have symbolic as well as tangible effects. Schein (2010) argues that managers signal what is important by what they systematically pay attention to. "Communication" is not confined to conversations, meetings, presentations, and emails, but includes all management actions—and omissions—that send signals concerning goals and priorities (and we have also to recognize that those signals may or may not be interpreted in the manner that management intended).

Encourage Voluntary Acts of Initiative

Kotter (2012) emphasizes the value of having many change agents in an organization, and not just a small elite team, arguing that vision and strategy should be communicated in a way that creates buy-in and attracts a growing "volunteer army" (p. 52). From their study of change in six corporations, Beer et al. (1990) conclude that in encouraging change, the most effective senior managers specified the general direction in which they wanted the company to move, and left the details of specific changes to be decided "closer to the action," lower down in the organization. They found that change was more likely to become embedded if those at the operational level were supported when they developed for themselves the specific changes that they believed appropriate for their local circumstance.

Measure Progress

A focus on measurement is important for two reasons. First, metrics and milestones are fundamental to tracking the progress of change, highlighting the need for any corrective action. Second, what gets measured can significantly affect how people act, because measurement signals the importance of that aspect of performance. Less attention is paid to dimensions of performance that are not measured. From a survey of the change experiences of over 2,000 executives, Ghislanzoni et al. (2010, p. 8) found that two of the top five procedures used by organizations whose changes had been successful were "defining detailed metrics for reorganization's effect on short- and long-term performance and assessing progress against them" and "using detailed plan, split into workstreams with milestones for delivery and someone accountable for reaching each." Progress measurement is thus important both for implementation and for sustainability.

It is important to choose appropriate metrics (see the box "Change Metrics: The Continental Airlines Experience"). David Nadler (1998) argues that organizations should carry out a comprehensive progress check on major change initiatives within six months after they have begun, and then annually thereafter. These checks should use quantitative performance measures, attitude surveys, focus groups, and individual interviews. Kanter et al. (1992) suggest that two kinds of measures are particularly helpful. First, *results measures*: How will we know that we have achieved our objectives? Second, *process measures*: How will we know that we are doing what is necessary to achieve those objectives and how plans may need to be adjusted? The Price Waterhouse Change Integration Team (1995) argues that a balanced set of performance measures should include:

- *Leading measures*, which reveal the immediate results of a new initiative, such as changes in processing time, or time to market for new products
- *Lagging measures*, such as financial performance and corporate image, which can take time to become apparent
- *Internal measures*, focusing on intra-organizational processes and efficiencies
- *External measures*, such as the perspectives of stakeholders, customers, and suppliers, and how the organization compares with benchmark competitors
- *Cost-based measures*, which are directly financial
- *Noncost measures*, such as market share and brand image

Exercise 11.1 asks you to apply these measures to a current change in your own organization or to one with which you are familiar. Do all these measures apply? If not, why not?

Celebrate En Route

Months or years can pass before the outcomes of a change initiative are fully realized. Those involved expect to see evidence that their efforts are rewarded. A lack of clear evidence of success strengthens the views of those who initially resisted the change. Skepticism concerning the value of the change may thus be increased by delays in demonstrating the benefits. However, it is often the case that some tangible benefits can be identified at an early stage in the process. Kotter (2012, p. 52) thus argues that one of the "accelerators" of change is to celebrate significant short-term wins. Celebrating the early benefits, even if they are relatively small in scale, recognizes and rewards those who are involved, strengthens the credibility of the program, and helps to weaken the skepticism.

In addition, the links between changed systems and working practices and organizational performance should be made clear. Staff members who have to work out those links for themselves may not make accurate assumptions. And successes, if they are effectively publicized and widely understood, can act as catalysts for further changes (see the box "Celebrating Success at Sandvik"). A further implication of the focus on celebrating "en route" concerns the allocation of resources to priority areas; those areas that need the most urgent attention may provide the best opportunities to demonstrate clear and immediate benefits, which can then be celebrated as short-term wins. Failure to establish those priorities at an early stage in the change process may be a direct cause of change failure.

Change Metrics *The Continental Airlines Experience*

Continental was one of America's major airlines until 2010, when it merged with United. Before that, Continental had tough times. When Gordon Bethune became chief executive of Continental in 1994, it had been losing money for most of the previous decade, had a debt-to-equity ratio of 50-to-1, and had served some time in Chapter 11 of the federal bankruptcy code. During this period, Continental had emphasized competing on the basis of cheaper fares than its major competitors. However, although it achieved the lowest revenue per available seat mile (of the major airlines), it also had the lowest revenue per available seat mile and a loss overall. Bethune reflects on this situation:

> I firmly believe that what you measure is what you get. This is an example of a company that said that it couldn't compete with the big boys unless it was able to have cheaper fares. That set the culture and mind-set. So, we had a culture that said, "Cost is everything." That's the Holy Grail. We even had pilots turning down the air-conditioning and slowing down airplanes to save the cost of fuel. They made passengers hot, mad and late. That's a dysfunctional measure, a measure some accountant dreamed up who does not understand our business.

Bethune responded by investigating what factors most influenced passengers' level of satisfaction with airlines. This revealed that on-time performance was the most significant factor. Unfortunately, at the time of Bethune's arrival, Continental ranked tenth of the 10 largest U.S. carriers on this criterion. Nonetheless, Bethune changed the core metric used inside Continental to on-time performance:

We use that measure for two reasons. One because it is the single most vital sign of a functioning airline, and two, it's ranked by our Government and we can't screw the metrics.

To reinforce the centrality of this factor, a new system of rewards was established in which bonuses were paid to all staff each month that Continental was ranked in the top five of the 10 largest U.S. carriers for on-time performance. The cost of the bonus payments was more than covered by the reduction in the amount—that had risen to $6 million per month—that Continental had been paying to put passengers on other airlines, put them up in hotels, bus them across town, and so forth.

The next month, March 1995, we wound up in first place. We had never been in first place in 60 years. I mean, Continental, the worst company in America for the last 20 years, is first place in "on time" which is a metric everyone kind of understands.

By 1996 (and again in 1997), Continental had won the J.D. Power & Associates award for customer satisfaction as the best airline for flights of 500 miles or more and was in the top three in terms of fewest customer complaints and lost baggage. From 1995 to 1998, Continental's market capitalization rose from $230 million to $3 billion.

Case Source

Kurtzman, J. 1998. Paying attention to what really counts. *Art of Taking Charge* 3(1):1–12. Copyright © 1998 Joel Kurtzman. All rights reserved. Used with permission.

Fine-Tuning

Despite careful advance planning, most change initiatives do not unfold as anticipated. The need for corrective action is to be expected. Making timely modifications in the light of experience will normally be more effective than attempting not to deviate from the plan. Problems arise for two main reasons. First, by definition, the implementation of change always involves doing something new, something that has never been done before. A particular type of change program may, of course, have been implemented in another

Celebrating Success at Sandvik

Sandvik AB makes advanced alloys and ceramics, employs 42,000 people, and has sales in 160 countries. When a change program focusing on business processes was introduced, some of Sandvik's units achieved significant improvements. People from these units then visited other units, particularly where there was skepticism about the change. These visits spread knowledge of successes and helped other units see what improvements could be achieved through the change initiative. Later, when a key financial target was reached, this was acknowledged by having a photograph taken of the Sandvik management team standing on top of a pile of gravel. However, according to Sandvik President Peter Gossas, "When we looked at the photo we thought, 'Yes, success should be celebrated but hey, this is the wrong message.' So we added five bigger piles to symbolize mountains we have yet to climb" (Ahlberg and Nauclér, 2007, p. 4).

Case Sources

Ahlberg, J., and Nauclér, T. 2007. Leading change: An interview with Sandvik's Peter Gossas. *McKinsey Quarterly*, January:1–3.

https://www.home.sandvik (2019).

division, or another organization—but that change will always be new here, in this organization, in this division, at this time, for these reasons, with those resources, affecting our staff. In other words, change management always involves "building the plane as you fly," and it is not surprising if parts fall off. Second, organizational changes are multifaceted, affecting many different factors, which are themselves interlinked. It is therefore difficult to anticipate all the "knock on" effects or "ripples" that a change in one area will have elsewhere.

For the change manager, this means adjusting and refining aspects of the implementation process without this being seen as an admission of failure. This can be difficult in practice, because as "we have learned from experience" can also be described as, "you made mistakes in the planning." This can be addressed by communicating the fine-tuning in terms of consistency with the original goals. As we have noted elsewhere, part of the change management responsibility is to help others to make sense of what is happening, to shape and to retell the story, and to explain that the core principles that lie behind the change remain intact.

Fine-Tuning at Ford

In 1995, Ford Motor company introduced a series of changes to the way the company designed and manufactured its cars and trucks. This involved changing from an existing functional structure, consolidating activities into five vehicle centers, and using a reduced number of platforms for its vehicle range. After a year and a half, senior management decided to make modifications in light of the initial experience. However, some groups and individuals, both inside the company and in the financial community, viewed the changes with some skepticism. As a result, when the time came to announce the modifications (for example, consolidating further from five to three vehicle centers), the company paid a lot of attention to making sure that the further changes were presented as a refinement, that is, a logical adjustment completely in keeping with the spirit and intent of the original change (Nadler, 1988).

TABLE 11.3
Managing the Improvement Evaporation Effect

Sustainability Actions	Sustainability Cautions
Define what "sustainability" means in your context and over what timescale.	Do not defer sustainability planning, as some modes of development and change implementation will damage sustainability.
Identify the factors (contextual, temporal, organizational, political) that affect the sustainability of new methods in your context.	Do not expect changes to survive because they are now working; staff leave, resources are reallocated, novel ideas become familiar.
Determine what combination of factors you can control and adjust to increase the probability of sustaining change.	Do not ignore the risk factors; if you are unable to sustain successful changes, that will reduce the probability of other sites adapting the approach and jeopardize future changes.
Monitor the support conditions and implement an appropriate mix of preventive and developmental maintenance.	Do not allow efforts to sustain change to block the development of other good ideas.
Allow or encourage changes to decay when they no longer fit the context or when better methods become available.	Do not withdraw preventive and developmental maintenance as long as you wish the approach to be sustained.

Source: Based on Buchanan et al. (2007).

In this section, we have discussed eight sets of actions to consider when designing a change initiative, to build sustainability into the process from the beginning, or at least from an early stage. These include redesign roles, redesign reward systems, link selection to organizational objectives, walk the talk, encourage voluntary acts of initiative, measure progress, celebrate en route, and fine-tuning. Finally, based on a study by David Buchanan et al. (2007) of the UK National Health Service, one of the largest employing organizations in the world, table 11.3 summarizes key sustainability "actions and cautions." This research emphasizes that sustainability relies on local management judgement, and on two main forms of action: preventive maintenance and developmental maintenance. *Preventive maintenance* involves action to sustain the status quo, to keep new working practices operating as intended, and to meet predetermined targets and objectives. *Developmental maintenance* involves continuing to adapt the changes to local circumstances to sustain an improvement trajectory, to exceed expectations, and to meet higher targets. Preventive maintenance sustains the changes; developmental maintenance both sustains and builds on the benefits.

LO 11.4 Words of Warning

It can be difficult to manage sustainability after a change has been successfully implemented; by then, it may be too late. Building sustainability into a change initiative from the beginning provides no secure guarantees, but it is more likely to be an effective approach. However, there are a number of further factors about which the change manager needs to be aware.

Expect the Unanticipated

Most change initiatives will generate unanticipated consequences, unless the links between the changes and outcomes are controllable and predictable (which is rare). Unanticipated consequences may be positive and support the change process. For example, staff may demonstrate greater levels of enthusiasm and commitment to making the changes work than was initially anticipated; cost saving may be higher than planned; processing times may be cut more dramatically. On the other hand, support may be more limited than expected, causing disruption and delay; cost savings may not materialize; time savings may be minimal. Unanticipated outcomes are not necessarily a sign of management failure; in complex change processes, the unexpected is to be expected. No amount of careful preplanning is likely to overcome this.

The change management challenge is to respond in timely and appropriate ways to the unexpected, which, on some occasions, may be early warnings of more serious problems, requiring a combination of resilience and improvisation.

Unanticipated Consequences at FedEx

Federal Express (FedEx) introduced a new aircraft routing system with the intention of increasing the productivity of its pilots. More powerful computers and developments in scheduling algorithms made this seem feasible, the estimated savings in the hundreds of millions of dollars made it attractive, and the pilots had a record of supporting measures intended to improve competitive efficiencies.

However, things did not work out as planned. The new system produced flight plans that required pilots to cross the time zones of two hemispheres, undertake back-to-back trans-Pacific and trans-Atlantic flights, and spend hours travelling by land to change aircraft. Efforts by FedEx to improve the working of the new system failed to produce any improvement, but the company persisted with the new system. In response, the pilots' union, despite having a reputation for compliance with management requirements, threatened a work stoppage if the system was not abandoned. Then, having taken this stance, their demands extended to a substantial wage increase, fewer flying hours, and improved retirement benefits.

Faced with the prospect of a strike by the pilots—which would have been the first pilot strike in the company's history—FedEx management relented, and the new scheduling system was abandoned.

Based on Pascale et al. (2000).

Beware the Limitations of Measurement

The benefits derived from new ways of doing things (online customer satisfaction, brand image, and reputation) may not immediately be reflected in traditional measures (sales per square foot, stock turnover, market share). The credibility of a new idea may be threatened if it does not succeed on established criteria. However, in some circumstances, a change may be regarded as successful even where the intended aims have not been met—such as a major process redesign initiative that achieved few of the intended goals but that increased the organization's receptiveness to and capacity for further changes. Assessing the effectiveness of change is therefore complex and challenging.

"Premature measurement" can also create problems. As discussed earlier, celebrating short-term wins can be valuable, but measuring the overall success of a change initiative should be related to the timescale over which benefits are expected to be delivered. A focus on short-term gains and quick fixes can weaken the persistence that is often required to achieve gains that develop over a longer period. In addition, organizational change rarely flows in a linear fashion, and the outcomes tend to be shaped by the combination and interaction of multiple factors. At times, change may appear to be progressing rapidly, while at other times, it may appear to have stalled. In some instances, performance may deteriorate before it improves, as people learn how to adjust to and work with new structures systems, procedures, and practices. This initial dip followed by an uptick in performance is known as the "J-curve" (see Figure 11.1). This is also known as "Kanter's law" (chapter 10), which states that "Everything can look like a failure in the middle" (Kanter, 2009).

The shape of the J-curve, and the timescale over which it operates, will of course vary from one setting to another (performance may not dip in some cases and may never recover in others). Assessment of how well a change is progressing must consider not only which metrics to apply, but also the timing of those measurements. The J-curve can be helpful in managing the expectations of others, with regard to justifying a deterioration in performance, and also explaining the rate at which the benefits of the change are likely to become apparent.

FIGURE 11.1
The J-Curve

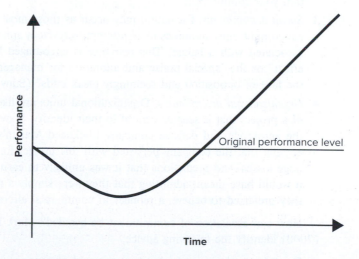

Beware Premature Declaration of Victory

Embedding and sustaining organizational culture change can take a considerable amount of time—years in some cases. For any transformational change, Kotter (2012, p. 52) advises the change manager to "never let up; keep learning from experience; and don't declare victory too soon." In other words, celebrate the wins, but do not declare overall victory. Until a change is firmly embedded, the possibility of a return to previous working practices will remain possible. There may be significant numbers of people who are hoping that the change will not succeed and that "things will return to normal." Those who feel this way may not make their views known. Anne Fisher uses the term "vicious compliance" to describe those who display support in public ("they will nod and smile and agree with everything that you say") but are resentful of the change and are waiting for the opportunity to return to the "old ways" of working to which they remain committed.

Beware the Escalation of Commitment

It is important to recognize that not all proposed changes are going to be beneficial (de Barros Teixeira et al., 2019). If a change is not producing the desired outcome, then this may be a "praiseworthy failure," which it would be wise to discontinue. However, it is also wise to guard against the understandable tendency of the advocates of this change to argue that failure to deliver is due to insufficient funding and that more time is needed to demonstrate the benefits. If those arguments are accepted, then further resources will be allocated to the initiative, creating an "escalation of commitment." Barry Staw and Jerry Ross (2004) identify four factors that can lead to escalation:

1. *Project determinants.* Commitment is likely to increase where the lack of progress is considered to be due to a temporary problem, where additional funding is considered likely to be effective, or where the relative payoff to come from additional investment is considered to be large.

2. *Psychological determinants.* "Sunk costs are not sunk psychologically." Escalation can result from self-justification biases. This happens when you have been personally responsible for a decision and want to avoid being associated with losses, so you maintain your commitment.

3. *Social determinants.* Escalation may occur as those most closely identified with a project commit more resources in an attempt to revive it and thereby save face by not being associated with a failure. This response is encouraged by the existence of "the hero effect" or the "special praise and adoration for managers who 'stick to their guns' in the face of opposition and seemingly bleak odds" (Staw and Ross, 2004, p. 209).

4. *Organizational determinants.* Organizational units are likely to resist the abandonment of a project that is seen as central to their identity. Staw and Ross cite the example of the aerospace and defense company Lockheed Martin's L1011 Tri-Star Jet program, arguing that the company persisted with this project for more than a decade, despite huge losses—and predictions that it was unlikely to earn a profit—because to abandon it would have meant admitting that they were simply a defense contractor and not, as they preferred to believe, a pioneer in commercial aircraft.

How can escalation of commitment be avoided? Mark Keil and Ramiro Montealegre (2000) identify the following advice:

- Don't ignore negative feedback or external pressure.
- Hire an external assessor to provide an independent view on progress.
- Don't be afraid to withhold further resources and funding; as well as limiting losses, it has symbolic value in that it is a fairly emphatic signal that there is concern with progress.
- Look for opportunities to redefine the problem and thereby generate ideas for courses of action other than the one being abandoned.
- Manage impressions. Frame the "de-escalation" in a way that saves face.
- Prepare your stakeholders because, if they shared the initial belief in the rationale for the change, their reaction to an announcement of the abandonment of the change may be to resist.
- Look for opportunities to deinstitutionalize the project, that is, to make clear that the project is not a central defining feature of the organization, so that "stepping back" does not imply any weakening of commitment to the central mission of the organization.

Dipankar Ghosh (1997) suggests three further steps that can help to reduce the escalation of commitment. First, *unambiguous feedback* on progress reduces escalation; where feedback is ambiguous, the tendency to filter information selectively can lead to escalation by those who are already committed to the change. Second, provide *regular progress reports*, including explanations for deviations from budget. If progress reports are not a requirement, then they will not necessarily be requested before further resources are committed. Third, provide *information on future benefits*. In the absence of these data, decisions will be too heavily influenced by historical costs.

Awareness of the phenomenon of escalation of commitment is the starting point for identifying solutions. However, this can be a challenging problem to manage as the line between an optimistic "can do" attitude and over-commitment can be difficult to establish.

Recognize Deep Structures

To understand what is involved in producing sustained organizational change, it is important to recognize two different and coexisting levels of analysis (Clausen and Kragh, 2019). First is the level of specific change projects that may be relatively surface-level phenomena, in the sense that they do not disrupt or significantly challenge key aspects of underlying cultural and power relationships. Second is the level of "deep structures" involving embedded senses of identity and normative beliefs that, as noted in chapter 8, can generate resistance. Surface-level changes still need to be well managed as they are not immune from negative reactions, but they are typically less complex forms of change to manage than those where deep structures are involved.

Sustainable Organizations

Jeffrey Pfeffer (2010) argues that, to build sustainable organizations, we need to treat human sustainability as seriously as we do environmental and ecological concerns. Organizational policies and management practices influence the human and social environment and affect employee well-being in various ways: provision of health insurance, effects of layoffs, working hours and work–life balance, job design and stress, income inequalities, organizational culture, and emotional climate:

> Companies that do not provide health insurance, lay people off, pay inadequate wages, and have work arrangements that stress and overwork their employees also impose externalities that others pay for even as they save on their own costs. (p. 42)

However, "green management," which is concerned with environmental awareness, energy efficiency, and carbon emissions, has not been matched by a parallel focus on employee welfare, "even though that might be an interesting and informative indicator of what companies are doing about the sustainability of their people" (p. 36). Actions affecting the physical environment are more visible:

> You can see the icebergs melting, polar bears stranded, forests cut down, and mountaintops reshaped by mining, and experience firsthand the dirty air and water that can come from company economic activities that impose externalities. Reduced life expectancy and poorer physical and mental health status are more hidden from view. Even the occasional and well-publicized act of employee or ex-employee violence has multiple causes and is often seen as aberrant behavior outside of the control and responsibility of the employer. (p. 41)

Pfeffer proposes a research agenda to explore the implications of "human sustainability" policies on both employee welfare and organizational effectiveness. What steps is your organization taking to address human and social sustainability? What further action would be desirable, and why?

EXERCISE 11.1

A Balanced Set of Measures

LO 11.3

It is helpful to consider appropriate measures of success for a change initiative. Thinking of a change initiative that is currently under way in your organization (or a change that is taking place in an organization with which you are familiar), identify the measures that you think should be applied, and list them in the following table. By ticking the appropriate column (✓), note which type of measures you have identified. It may be possible to classify any one measure in more than one category; brand image, for example, may be lagging, external, and noncost.

If the measures that you are proposing do not include all six types of measures, you need to explain why the "missing" types are not included. If you cannot give a good explanation, you may need to propose additional measures.

	Type of Measure					
Measure	Leading	Lagging	Internal	External	Cost	Noncost
1.						
2.						
3.						
4.						
5.						

EXERCISE 11.2

Treating Initiative Decay

LO 11.3

Earlier in this chapter, we identified the top ten causes of initiative decay. Which of these factors apply to the recent changes in your organization? What additional factors, not mentioned here, could cause initiative decay in your organization? Considering each cause in turn, what treatment would you prescribe to avoid or reduce the decay?

Cause	Prescribed Treatment
1. Initiators move on.	
2. Accountability becomes diffuse.	
3. Knowledge lost through staff turnover.	
4. Old habits imported with new recruits.	
5. Change triggers no longer visible.	
6. New managers with their own agendas.	
7. Power brokers blocking progress.	
8. Pump-priming funds have run out.	
9. Other priorities diverting attention.	
10. Initiative fatigue, lack of enthusiasm.	
11. Other.	
12. Other.	

EXERCISE 11.3

The Challenger and Columbia Shuttle Disasters

LO 11.4

We discussed the 2003 *Columbia* shuttle disaster in chapter 3. There, we explored reasons why organizations (in this case NASA) often fail to change following accidents such as this one, having previously lost the shuttle Challenger in 1986. We also explored the organizational culture at NASA in chapter 5, emphasizing that, while the blame for both shuttle losses was linked to technical problems, the more significant contributory factors lay with leadership, management, and organizational culture issues. This is a familiar pattern, seen in many major catastrophes. Here is a fuller account of both disasters, which contain lessons concerning organizational change in general and the sustainability of change in particular. Space exploration is unique in many respects, but from a change management perspective, the lessons from this experience are generic.

As you read this case account, consider the following questions:

1. What aspects of NASA practice revealed following the *Columbia* disaster suggest that the changes that were recommended following the *Challenger* disaster were not sustained?

2. This chapter has discussed actions that can be taken to sustain change. In your judgment, which of the following would have been most useful to NASA after the *Challenger* disaster?

   - Redesign roles.
   - Redesign reward systems.
   - Link selection to organizational objectives.
   - Walk the talk.
   - Encourage voluntary acts of initiative.
   - Measure progress.
   - Celebrate en route.
   - Fine-tuning.

3. This chapter has explained "words of warning" in terms of what to be alert to in regard to sustaining change. Which of the following do you see as most applicable to NASA?

   - Recognize productive, praiseworthy failures.
   - Expect the unanticipated.
   - Beware the limitations of measurement.
   - Beware premature declaration of victory.
   - Beware the escalation of commitment.

The *Challenger* Disaster

On January 28, 1986, the space shuttle *Challenger* rose into the sky, its seven crew members strapped into their padded seats while the 2,000-ton vehicle vibrated as it gained speed and altitude. The launch was going perfectly. Seventy seconds had passed since lift-off, and the shuttle was already 50,000 feet above the earth. From NASA Mission Control at Houston's Johnson Space Center, Spacecraft Communicator Richard Covey instructed, "*Challenger*, go at throttle up." "Roger, go at throttle up," replied *Challenger* Commander Dick Scobee.

In the next few seconds, however, *Challenger* experienced some increasingly violent maneuvers. The pilot, Mike Smith, expressed his sudden apprehension: "Uh-oh." In Mission

(Continued)

Control, the pulsing digits on the screen abruptly stopped. Mission Control spokesman Steve Nesbitt sat above the four console tiers. For a long moment he stared around the silent, softly lit room. The red ascent trajectory line was stationary on the display screen. Finally he spoke: "Flight controllers here looking very carefully at the situation. Obviously a major malfunction."

Headed by former Secretary of State William Rogers, the Presidential Commission that was set up to investigate the cause of the *Challenger* disaster had little trouble identifying the physical cause. One of the joints on a booster rocket failed to seal. The "culprit" was one of the synthetic rubber O-rings that were designed to keep the rockets' superhot gases from escaping from the joints between the booster's four main segments. When one of the O-rings failed, the resulting flames burned through the shuttle's external fuel tank. Liquid hydrogen and liquid oxygen then mixed and ignited, causing the explosion that destroyed *Challenger*.

However, the so-called Rogers Commission investigations also revealed a great deal about the internal workings of NASA. It was a geographically dispersed matrix organization. Headquarters were in Washington, DC, where its most senior managers, including its head, NASA administrator James Beggs, were mainly involved in lobbying activity, reflecting the dependence on federal funds (and its vulnerability to fluctuations in funding). Mission Control was located at the Johnson Space Center in Houston, Texas. All propulsion aspects—main engines, rocket boosters, fuel tanks—were the responsibility of the Marshall Space Center in Huntsville, Alabama. Assembly and launch took place at the Kennedy Space Center in Cape Canaveral, Florida.

These various centers existed in an uneasy alliance of cooperation and competition. The Marshall Center in particular was known for its independent stance based on its proud tradition going right back through the Apollo program to the early days of rocketry with Wernher von Braun. One manifestation of this pride, reinforced by its autocratic leader William Lucas, was that loyalty to Marshall came before all. Any problems that were identified were to be kept strictly "in-house," which at Marshall meant within Marshall. Those who failed to abide by this expectation—perhaps by speaking too freely to other parts of NASA—could expect to receive a very public admonishment. Marshall was also at the center of a "can-do" attitude within NASA, supporting the idea that great objectives are achievable if only the will is there. Born of the Apollo success, this took form in Marshall as pride in the achievement of objectives and strongly held views that if a flight was to be delayed for any reason, it would never be because of something caused by Marshall.

The Rogers Commission also concluded that NASA was working with an unrealistic flight schedule. The formal schedule demanded twelve flights in 1984, fourteen in 1985, seventeen in 1986 and again in 1987, and twenty-four in 1988. In practice, NASA had managed five launches in 1984 and eight in 1985. Congressional critics had begun to question the appropriateness of continuing the current (high) level of program funding when NASA was falling so far short in meeting its own goals. However, rather than revise its schedules, these were retained and senior NASA managers increased the pressure on staff and contractors to meet the schedules.

Most of the design and construction work in the shuttle program was contracted out. One of the contractors was Morton-Thiokol, a Brigham City, Utah-based company that had won the contract to produce the solid rocket boosters. At the time of the *Challenger* launch, Thiokol and NASA were in the middle of contract renewal negotiations.

The Rogers Commission revealed that there had been doubts about the reliability of the O-rings for some time. Since 1982, they had been labelled a "criticality 1" item, a label reserved for components whose failure would have a catastrophic result. However, despite evidence of O-ring erosion on many flights and requests from O-ring experts from both NASA and Thiokol that flights be suspended until the problem was resolved, no action had been taken. There was no reliable backup to the O-rings. This violated a long-standing NASA principle, but each time a flight was scheduled, this principle was formally waived.

A cold front hit Cape Canaveral the day before the scheduled launch. Temperatures as low as 18°F were forecast for that night. Engineers from Thiokol expressed their serious reservations about the wisdom of launching in such conditions because the unusually cold conditions at the launch site would affect the O-rings' ability to seal. As a result, a teleconference was called for that evening.

At the teleconference, Roger Boisjoly, Thiokol's O-ring expert, argued that temperature was a factor in the performance of the rings and Robert Lund, Thiokol's vice president for engineering, stated that unless the temperature reached at least 53°F, he did not want the launch to proceed. This position led to a strong reaction from NASA; from Lawrence Mulloy, Marshall's chief of the solid rocket booster program; and George Hardy, Marshall's deputy director of science and engineering. Hardy said that he was "appalled" at the reasoning behind Thiokol's recommendation to delay the launch, and Mulloy argued that Thiokol had not proven the link between temperature and erosion of the O-rings, adding, "My God, Thiokol, when do you want me to launch, next April?" A view expressed at the Commission was that the Thiokol engineers had been put in a position where, for a delay to be approved, they were being required to prove that the O-rings would fail, rather than to prove that they would be safe at the low temperatures, before a go-ahead was approved.

The teleconference took a break, to allow the Thiokol management team to consider their position. The Thiokol engineers were still unanimously opposed to a launch. Jerald Mason, Thiokol's senior vice president, asked Robert Lund to "take off his engineering hat and put on his management hat." Polling just the senior Thiokol managers present, and not any of the engineers, Mason managed to get agreement to launch. The teleconference was then reconvened, the Thiokol approval was conveyed, no NASA managers expressed any reservations, and the OK to launch was given.

Post-*Challenger* Changes at NASA

The Rogers Commission's recommendations included that NASA restructure its management to tighten control, set up a group dedicated to finding and tracking hazards with regard to shuttle safety, and review its critical items as well as submitting its redesign of the booster joint to a National Academy of Sciences group for verification. The official line within NASA was that the necessary changes had been successfully implemented. A NASA news release on January 22, 1988, stated:

> In response to various reviews of NASA safety and quality programs conducted in the aftermath of the Challenger accident and associated recommendations for improvements, NASA has acted to elevate agency emphasis on safety and implement organizational changes to strengthen SRM&QA [Safety, Reliability, Management & Quality Assurance] programs. There has been a 30 percent increase in NASA personnel assigned to SRM&QA functions since January 1986.

(Continued)

The *Columbia* Disaster

On February 1, 2003, the space shuttle *Columbia*'s braking rockets were fired as the shuttle headed toward a landing at Kennedy Space Center. As it passed over the United States, observers spotted glowing pieces of debris falling from the shuttle. At 8:59 am EST, commander Rick Husband replied to a call from Mission Control, but his acknowledgment ceased mid-transmission. About a minute later, *Columbia* broke up, killing its seven astronauts.

The Columbia Accident Investigation Board (CAIB or Board) was formed to identify what had happened. In its August 2003 final report, it identified the physical cause of the accident. A 1.67-pound slab of insulating foam fell off the external fuel tank 81.7 seconds after *Columbia* was launched (on January 16), hit the left wing, and caused a breach in the tiles designed to protect the aluminum wing from the heat of reentry. On reentry, the breach allowed superheated gas into the wing, which, as a result, melted in critical areas.

But the Board also addressed the nonphysical factors that contributed to the disaster. Because of no improvement in the level of NASA funding, NASA Administrator Daniel Goldin pushed a "Faster, Better, Cheaper" (FBC) initiative that impacted on the shuttle program.

The premium placed on maintaining an operational schedule, combined with ever-decreasing resources, gradually led shuttle managers and engineers to miss signals of potential danger. Foam strikes on the orbiter's thermal protection system (TPS), no matter what the size of the debris, were "normalized" and accepted as not being a "safety-of-flight risk."

The shuttle workforce was downsized, and various program responsibilities (including safety oversight) were outsourced. Success was measured through cost reduction and the meeting of schedules and the shuttle was still being mischaracterized as an operational rather than a developmental technology.

The Board particularly identified NASA's organizational culture as being as much to blame as the physical causes. According to the Board:

> Though NASA underwent many management reforms in the wake of the Challenger accident, the agency's powerful human space flight culture remained intact, as did many practices such as inadequate concern over deviations from expected performance, a silent safety program, and schedule pressure.

> Cultural traits and organization practices detrimental to safety and reliability were allowed to develop, including: reliance on past success as a substitute for sound engineering practices (such as testing to understand why systems were not performing in accordance with requirements/specifications); organizational barriers which prevented effective communication of critical safety information and stifled professional differences of opinion; lack of integrated management across program elements, and the evolution of an informal chain of command and decision-making processes that operated outside the organization's rules.

According to the Board: "NASA's blind spot is that it believes it has a strong safety culture [when in fact it] has become reactive, complacent, and dominated by unjustified optimism." The Board found that while NASA managers said that staff members were encouraged to identify safety issues and bring these to the attention of management, there was evidence to the contrary, including insufficient deference to engineers and other technical experts. Also, while NASA's safety policy specified oversight at headquarters combined with decentralized execution of safety programs at the program and project levels, the Board found that NASA had not been willing to give the project teams the independent status for this to actually work.

The external tank of the shuttle was designed with a layer of insulation tiles that were designed to stick to the tank, not to be shed. Similarly, the shuttle's heat shield was not designed to be damaged; the tiles were fragile, such that the shuttle was not allowed to fly in rain or stay outside in hail.

However, the experience of previous launches was that foam sometimes did fall off and tiles sometimes were damaged. But this was occurring without any noticeable negative effect on the functioning of the shuttle. Of 112 flights prior to the fatal *Columbia* flight, foam had been shed 70 times and tiles had come back damaged every time. Over time, NASA managers got used to the idea that such damage would occur and convinced themselves there was no safety-of-flight issue. The Board reported that "program management made erroneous assumptions about the robustness of a system based on prior success rather than on dependable engineering data and rigorous testing."

The report cites eight separate "missed opportunities" by NASA during the 16-day flight to respond to expressions of concern or offers that could have assisted. For example, engineer Rodney Rocha's email four days into the mission, asking Johnson Space Center if the crew had been directed to inspect *Columbia*'s left wing for damage, had been left unanswered. Also, NASA had failed to accept the U.S. Defense Department's offer to obtain spy satellite imagery of the damaged shuttle.

The Board faulted NASA managers for assuming that there would be nothing that could be done if the foam strike had indeed caused serious damage to the TPS. After the accident, NASA engineers, working at the request of the Board, concluded that it might have been possible either to repair the wing using materials on board *Columbia*, or to rescue the crew through a sped-up launch of the shuttle *Atlantis*. The Board also criticized NASA managers for not taking steps to ensure that minority and dissenting voices were heard, commenting:

> All voices must be heard, which can be difficult when facing a hierarchy. An employee's location in the hierarchy can encourage silence. Organizations interested in safety must take steps to guarantee that all relevant information is presented to decision makers. This did not happen in the meetings during the *Columbia* mission. Program managers created huge barriers against dissenting opinions by stating preconceived conclusions based on subjective knowledge and experience, rather than on solid data.

The NASA Intercenter Photo Working Group had recommended that the loss of foam be classified as an in-flight anomaly—a much more critical designation than it currently had—but this was not approved by the program requirements control board. The engineers were placed in the situation of having to prove that a safety-of-flight issue existed before the shuttle program management would take action to get images of the left wing. The Board found that this was just one example of a more general situation where those concerned with safety found themselves having to prove that a situation was unsafe, whereas it might be reasonably expected that the emphasis would be on proving instead that a high level of safety existed. The Board also concluded that there was an unofficial hierarchy among NASA programs and directorates that hindered the flow of communications:

(Continued)

Management decisions made during *Columbia*'s final flight reflect missed opportunities, blocked or ineffective communication channels, flawed analysis, and ineffective leadership. Perhaps most striking is the fact that management displayed no interest in understanding a problem and its implications. Because managers failed to avail themselves of the wide range of expertise and opinion necessary to achieve the best answer to the debris strike question—"was this a safety-of-flight concern?"—some space shuttle program managers failed to fulfil the implicit contract to do whatever is possible to ensure the safety of the crew. In fact, their management techniques unknowingly imposed barriers that kept at bay both engineering concerns and dissenting views, and ultimately helped create "blind spots" that prevented them from seeing the danger the foam strike posed.

The Board concluded that the post-*Challenger* changes "were undone over time by management actions" and that "the pre-*Challenger* layers of processes, boards and panels that had produced a false sense of confidence in the system and its level of safety returned in full force prior to *Columbia*."

Case Sources

Berger, B. 2003. Columbia report faults NASA culture, government oversight. *Space.com*, August 26. http://www.space.com/missionlaunches/caib_preview_030707-1.html.

Columbia Accident Investigation Board. 2003. *Columbia Accident Investigation Board Report, Volumes I to VI*. Washington, DC: National Aeronautics and Space Administration and the Government Printing Office.

Covault, C. 2003. Failure an option?: NASA's shallow safety program put Columbia and her crew on same path as Challenger. *Aviation Week & Space Technology* 159(9):27–35.

McConnell, M. 1987. *Challenger: A serious malfunction*. London: Simon & Schuster.

Magnusson, E. 1986. A serious deficiency. *Time* (March 10):34–36.

Morring, F. Jr. 2003. Culture shock. *Aviation Week & Space Technology* 159(9):31–34.

Additional Reading

Buchanan, D. A., Fitzgerald, L., and Ketley, D. (eds). 2007. *The sustainability and spread of organizational change: Modernizing healthcare*, London: Routledge. Reports a study of the problems of diffusing and sustaining new working practices in the UK National Health Service. Based on case studies of sustainability practice in different areas of healthcare, offers practical advice on the dissemination of new ideas and the steps necessary to sustain those once implemented. The organization and management issues—and implications for practice—apply to other organizations and sectors and are not confined to health.

Edmondson, A. 2018. *The fearless organization: Creating psychological safety in the workplace for learning, innovation, and growth*. Hoboken, NJ: John Wiley & Sons. Discusses the steps necessary to create a psychologically safe environment at work, in which people feel able to experiment and make mistakes without punishment.

Mahler, J. G., and Casamayou, M. H. 2009. *Organizational learning at NASA: The Challenger and Columbia accidents*. Washington, DC: Georgetown University Press. Offers a fresh analysis of the two NASA shuttle disasters, in terms of organizational learning. What did NASA learn from the *Challenger* disaster? How much of that learning was symbolic, and not substantive? What did NASA not learn? And what did NASA learn and then forget—thus contributing to the loss of the shuttle *Columbia*? External political and budgetary pressures were often to blame for the nonlearning and forgetting, and these are factors that also jeopardize the sustainability of the kinds of organizational changes that NASA was advised to make.

Pfeffer, J. 2010. Building sustainable organizations: The human factor. *Academy of Management Perspectives* 24(1):34–45. Argues that environmental sustainability has attracted most of the attention and that human and social sustainability are equally important. Suggests that, while "green management" can benefit an organization financially, and in terms of reputation, a similar focus on human sustainability should also generate returns. Proposes a research agenda, to explore links between human and social sustainability practices and organizational effectiveness.

Sull, D., Homkes, R., and Sull, C. 2015. Why strategy execution unravels—and what to do about it. *Harvard Business Review* 93(3):58–66. Strategy execution seems to be more problematic than developing strategy, because execution is misunderstood. The problem is not alignment, but coordination; research shows that people in other units (internal and external) are not reliable. Execution does not mean "sticking to the plan" where changing conditions demand flexibility. Communications from top management may be frequent but are often inconsistent; only half of middle managers can name any of their organization's top priorities. Does execution require a "performance culture"? Perhaps, but agility, teamwork, and ambition should also be rewarded. The idea that execution should be driven from the top is a myth; execution "lives and dies with managers in the middle—but they are hamstrung by the poor communication from above" (p. 66). Concludes that fostering coordination and building agility are key to strategy execution. The same guidelines apply to change implementation.

Roundup

Reflections for the Practicing Manager

- If you have been involved previously as a manager of change, how would you rate yourself in terms of your handling of the need to take actions that sustain change? What have you done well? What not so well?

- When you have been on the receiving end of the change initiatives of others, how well have they handled the need to take actions that sustain change? What have they done well? What not so well?

- Of the cases presented in this chapter, which one resonates best with you? What is it about this case that you can relate to? Are there any implications for how you would act in the future?

- How good are you at handling unanticipated outcomes? How could you improve in this area?

- If there was one main idea that you took away from this chapter that you believe can be of most use to you as a change manager, what would it be?

- If you were to add an idea, suggestion, or practice to the treatment of sustaining change that is provided in this chapter, what would be your contribution?

Here is a short summary of the key points that we would like you to take from this chapter, in relation to each of the learning outcomes:

LO 11.1   * *Understand the causes of initiative decay–threats to the sustainability of change.*
This chapter has emphasized that even changes that have been implemented successfully are liable to decay. Sustainability cannot be taken for granted. The "improvement evaporation effect," as the benefits from change are lost, is common. The change manager may have little direct control over the factors that lead to initiative decay, but measures can be put in place to counter those factors and to increase the probability that change will be sustained. Initiative decay can be caused by many factors, and we identified 10: initiators move on, accountability becomes diffuse, knowledge is lost with staff turnover, old habits are imported with new recruits, the change triggers are no longer visible, new managers have their own agendas, power brokers block progress, start-up funding runs out, other priorities emerge, staff suffer initiative fatigue–and enthusiasm for change drops. The change manager thus has to remain vigilant with regard to potential threats to sustainability such as these. Many of the change models and frameworks discussed in chapter 10 identify sustainability as a final step in the process. Managing sustainability as an afterthought, however, can be problematic. It is more appropriate to design sustainability into a change initiative from the start.

LO 11.2   * *Distinguish between change initiatives that are "blameworthy," and should not be sustained, and those that are "praiseworthy."*
We also emphasized that, when a change does not work out as planned, this is not necessarily a problem. Failures are not always bad. We discussed the distinction between blameworthy and praiseworthy failures. The former include deliberate or inadvertent deviations from prescribed practice. Experiments designed to improve performance, and reasonable actions that have undesirable but unpredictable outcomes, are praiseworthy–because they offer opportunities from which to learn. Many organizations, however, treat most failures as blameworthy. This is wasteful, because the lessons are lost, and those who are inappropriately punished are likely to be demotivated. The change management challenge is to establish a psychologically safe environment that welcomes experimentation, recognizes and rewards praiseworthy failures, and enables learning.

LO 11.3   * *Identify and apply actions that can contribute to the sustainability of change.*
Although some of the threats to sustainability are beyond direct management control, awareness of those threats and their impact can generate timely and appropriate responses. We discussed eight sets of possible actions to strengthen the sustainability of a given change: redesign roles, redesign reward systems, link staff selection to change objectives, "walk the talk," encourage voluntary acts of initiative, measure progress, celebrate "smaller wins" en route, and fine-tune the approach when the process (as almost always happens) does not unfold as anticipated. We also distinguished between sustaining the substance of change (new working practices, for example) and an improvement trajectory (further reductions in time to market, for example). Preventive maintenance involves action to sustain the former, to keep those practices operating as intended. Developmental maintenance, on the other hand, involves adapting to circumstances to gain increasing benefits.

LO 11.4 * *Understand the pitfalls that can arise when seeking to sustain change.*
We closed the chapter with a number of words of warning for the change manager. First, expect the unexpected and manage the (positive and negative) unintended consequences. Second, beware the limitations of measurement, and recognize the implications of the J-curve and Kanter's law, which states, "Everything looks like a failure in the middle." Third, beware the premature declaration of victory, which may divert energy and attention from the change process, but continue to celebrate the "small wins" as appropriate. Finally, beware the escalation of commitment to struggling change initiatives by accepting the requests of advocates for further resources when it is becoming clear that the initiative is not going to deliver the planned outcomes (but may be a praiseworthy failure).

References

Ahlberg, J., and Nauclér, T. 2007. Leading change: An interview with Sandvik's Peter Gossas. *McKinsey Quarterly* (January):1–3.

Beer, M., and Nohria, N. (eds.). 2000. *Breaking the code of change*. Boston, MA: Harvard Business School Press.

Beer, M., Eisenstat, R. A., and Spector, B. 1990. Why change programs don't produce change. *Harvard Business Review* 68(6):158–66.

Buchanan, D. A., Ketley, D., Gollop, R., Jones, J. L., Lamont, S. S., Neath, A., and Whitby, E. 2005. No going back: A review of the literature on sustaining organizational change. *International Journal of Management Reviews* 7(3):189–205.

Buchanan, D. A., Fitzgerald, L., and Ketley, D. (eds.). 2007. *The sustainability and spread of organizational change: Modernizing healthcare*. London: Routledge.

Clausen, B., and Kragh, H. 2019. Why don't they just keep doing it?: Understanding the challenges of the sustainability of change. *Journal of Change Management* 19(4):221–45.

de Barros Teixeira, J. A., Koller, T., and Lovallo, D. 2019. Knowing when to kill a project. *McKinsey Quarterly*, June 3.

Edmondson, A. 2011. Strategies for learning from failure. *Harvard Business Review* 89(4):48–55.

Fisher, A. B. 1995. Making change stick. *Fortune* 131(7):121–24.

Gerstner, L. V. 2002. *Who says elephants can't dance?: Inside IBM's historic turnaround*. New York: Harper Business.

Ghislanzoni, G., Heidari-Robinson, S., and Jermiin, M. 2010. *Taking organizational redesign from plan to practice*. London: McKinsey & Company.

Ghosh, D. 1997. De-escalation strategies: Some experimental evidence. *Behavioral Research in Accounting* 9:88–112.

Goode, J. 2014. *Value based recruitment toolkit: Evaluation of 12 month pilot final report.* London: The National Skills Academy for Social Care.

Gupta, R., and Wendler, J. 2005. Leading change: An interview with the CEO of P&G. *McKinsey Quarterly* (July):1-6.

Kanter, R. M. 2009. Change is hardest in the middle. *Harvard Business Review.* August 12.

https://hbr.org/2009/08/change-is-hardest-in-the-middl (accessed February 21, 2015).

Kanter, R. M., Stein, B. A., and Jick, T. D. 1992. *The challenge of organizational change,* New York: Free Press.

Keil, M., and Montealegre, R. 2000. Cutting your losses: Extricating your organization when a big project goes awry. *Sloan Management Review* 41(3):55-68.

Kotter, J. P. 2007. Leading change: Why transformation efforts fail. *Harvard Business Review* 85(1):96-103 (first published 1995).

Kotter, J. P. 2012. Accelerate! *Harvard Business Review* 90(11):44-52.

Kurtzman, J. 1998. Paying attention to what really counts. *Art of Taking Charge* 3(1):1-12.

Lawson, E., and Price, C. 2003. The psychology of change management. *McKinsey Quarterly,* (Special edition: *The value in organization*):31-41.

Lewin, K. (ed.) 1951. *Field theory in social science: Selected theoretical papers by Kurt Lewin* (UK edition published 1952, ed. Dorwin Cartwright). London: Tavistock Publications.

Marks, M. L., and Shaw, R. B. 1995. Sustaining change: Creating the resilient organization. In *Discontinuous change: Leading organizational transformation,* ed. D. A. Nadler, R. B. Shaw, and A. E. Walton (97-117). San Francisco: Jossey-Bass.

Michel, S. 2007. The upside of falling flat. *Harvard Business Review* 85(4):21-22.

Nadler, D. 1998. *Champions of change: How CEOs and their companies are mastering the skills of radical change.* San Francisco: Jossey-Bass.

Pascale, R., Millemann, M., and Gioja, L. 2000. *Surfing the edge of chaos: The laws of nature and the new laws of business.* New York: Crown Business.

Pfeffer, J. 2010. Building sustainable organizations: The human factor. *Academy of Management Perspectives* 24(1):34-45.

Price Waterhouse Change Integration Team 1995. *The paradox principles: How high-performance companies manage chaos, complexity, and contradiction to achieve superior results,* New York: McGraw Hill.

Rapping, J. 2009. You can't build on shaky ground: Laying the foundation for indigent defense reform through values-based recruitment, training, and mentoring. *Harvard Law & Policy* 3(Spring):161-84.

Reisner, R. A. F. 2002. When a turnaround stalls. *Harvard Business Review* 80(2):45-52.

Ross, L. 1977. The intuitive psychologist and his shortcomings: Distortions in the attribution process. In *Advances in experimental social psychology*, ed. L. Berkowitz (173–220). New York: Academic Press.

Schein, E. H. 2010. *Organizational culture and leadership* (4th ed.). San Francisco: Jossey-Bass.

Staw, B. M., and Ross, J. 2004. Understanding behavior in escalation situations. In *Psychological dimensions of organizational behavior*, ed. B. M. Staw (206–14). Upper Saddle River, NJ: Pearson Prentice Hall.

Sull, D., Homkes, R., and Sull, C. 2015. Why strategy execution unravels—and what to do about it. *Harvard Business Review* 93(3):58–66.

Source of opening quote from Tom Brokaw https://conantleadership.com/25-quotes-about-managing-change/

Source of the chapter opening quote: 25 Quotes about Managing Change, *Conant Leadership,* August 28, 2017, https://conantleadership.com/25-quotes-about-managing-change.

Chapter opening silhouette credit: CharlotteRaboff/Shutterstock

Chapter 12

The Effective Change Manager: What Does It Take?

Learning Objectives

By the end of this chapter you should be able to:

LO 12.1 Recognize the nature and significance of the contributions of change managers at all levels of an organization, regardless of their formal roles or responsibilities.

LO 12.2 Appreciate the challenges and rewards that accompany performing a change management role.

LO 12.3 Identify the competencies in terms of the skills, knowledge, and other attributes that are ideally required to be an effective change manager.

LO 12.4 Understand the significance of political skill to the role and effectiveness of change managers.

LO 12.5 Develop an action plan for improving your own change management capabilities.

"*Leadership is the ability to guide others without force into a direction or decision that leaves them still feeling empowered and accomplished.*"

Lisa Cash Hanson, blogger and digital marketer

387

LO 12.1 Change Managers: Who Are They?

This chapter explores the skills, knowledge, and other attributes that are required to design and implement change. First, we identify those who carry out these responsibilities, as this can involve significant numbers of people. Senior management, the chief executive or chief transformation officer, sometimes drives change, but this is rarely a solo performance. Some organizations create change support or delivery units (Wylie and Sturdy, 2018). Typically, many members of an organization, from across all levels, can be involved in initiating, encouraging, catalyzing, facilitating, and contributing to the implementation of change. That involvement does not have to mean a formal management job title. There may even be circumstances in which a formal title could be a barrier to getting support and instead stimulate suspicion and distrust. Having identified who an organization's change managers are likely to be, we then consider what kind of role this is, in terms of the challenges and rewards. We will then explore the competency requirements, one of which concerns political skill, "street smarts," "savvy," or political astuteness (Buchanan and Badham, 2020).

Champions, Deviants, and Souls of Fire

Several terms have been used to describe change managers and change agents, suggesting the nature of the role and the kinds of people and capabilities involved. These terms are summarized in table 12.1. Some offer clues about those who become change managers: catalysts, champions, deviants, evangelists, generators, shapers, sparks, and "souls of fire," which comes from the Swedish word *eldsjälar* meaning "driven by burning enthusiasm" (Stjernberg and Philips, 1993). Motivation and commitment matter as much as technical and professional capabilities.

These labels suggest that change relies on the complementary contributions, advice, and support of a number of different people. Some accounts suggest that change depends on transformational leaders—senior, powerful, visionary, charismatic individuals, who diagnose the organization's problems and implement solutions single-handed. However,

TABLE 12.1
Other Names for Change Managers

catalyst	product champion
change adopter	resource linker
change champion	shaper
change generator	solution giver
change implementer	souls of fire
evangelist	sounding board
executive champion	spark
patriarch	specialist
positive deviant	sponsor
process helper	technological entrepreneur

as we will see, transformational leadership has a "dark side," and there are advantages in allowing middle managers to take the lead in implementing both small- and large-scale initiatives.

Changing from the Top

With the perception that the pace of change was accelerating in the second half of the twentieth century, the role of heroic, powerful, visionary, charismatic leaders came to be seen as vital. These are senior management "superheroes" who orchestrate the large-scale organizational changes that global trends appear to dictate. James McGregor Burns (1978) described transformational leaders as charismatic individuals who inspire others to perform "beyond contract." Transactional leaders, in contrast, manage relationships with followers in terms of trade, swaps, or bargains; this style is more appropriate in less complex, stable business environments. It has been argued, therefore, that the three main roles of transformational leaders are recognizing the need for revitalization, creating a new vision, and institutionalizing change (Tichy and Devanna, 1986). For Bass and Avolio (1994), transformational leadership involves "the Four Is":

- *Intellectual stimulation.* Encourage others to see what they are doing from new perspectives.
- *Idealized influence.* Articulate the mission or vision of the organization.
- *Individualized consideration.* Develop others to higher levels of ability.
- *Inspirational motivation.* Motivate others to put organizational interests before self-interest.

As the pressures for major organizational change have intensified, the notion of transformational leadership remains popular today. A Google search for the term "transformational leadership" returns almost 36 million results. There are many leadership development programs based on the concept. In addition, charisma, which is at the heart of transformational leadership, can be learned (Cabane, 2013).

Find on *YouTube*, "Olivia Fox Cabane—Build your personal charisma" (2017, 44 minutes).

On the following pages, read our accounts of three twenty-first-century leaders, Tricia Griffith (Progressive insurance), Chip Bergh (Levi Strauss), and Dara Khosrowshahi (Uber). Are they transformational leaders? What other terms would you use to describe their styles? What aspects of their approaches to change leadership do you think you should copy in your own work? Do leaders have to be "transformational" to implement transformational change successfully?

If charismatic leaders inspire others, then more charisma is surely better. Vergauwe et al. (2018) challenge this claim. They defined charismatic leadership in terms of four personality tendencies: bold, mischievous, colorful, and imaginative. In behavioral terms, charismatic leaders are likely to challenge the status quo, take risks, and be self-confident, captivating, expressive, extraverted, energetic, optimistic, inspirational, and creative. Are charismatic leaders always effective? The researchers gathered information on 306 leaders in an international aerospace company. Subordinates, peers, and superiors assessed the effectiveness of these leaders. The leaders themselves completed a self-assessment to get a "charisma score." This study found that:

- More experienced leaders saw themselves as more effective and were perceived as more effective by subordinates and superiors.
- Leaders with higher charisma scores rated themselves as more effective.
- Subordinates, peers, and superiors rated leaders with low and high charisma scores as less effective than leaders with moderate levels of charisma.

This research contradicts the "more is better" principle. Charisma is a strength. But it can be a weakness when bold, mischievous, colorful, and imaginative behaviors are seen by others as attempts to overwhelm, intimidate, and manipulate. In other words, too much charisma confirms the "too much of a good thing" (TMGT) principle.

Since the concept was first introduced, transformational leadership has been widely seen as a positive, desirable approach—as a solution to the problem of driving major organizational changes quickly and successfully. Increased job satisfaction, employee well-being, and lower sickness absence can also result from transformational leadership. However, transformational leaders have been accused of generating too much change, leading to management and staff burnout. One commentator calls transformational leaders "a dangerous curse" (Khurana, 2002). Leaders who adopt this approach often put their followers under pressure to perform "above and beyond the call of duty." Are the outcomes for employee well-being always positive? Does transformational leadership have a "dark side"?

Tricia Griffith and Change at Progressive

Founded in 1937, Progressive, based in Mayfield, Ohio, is America's third largest auto insurance company, also covering motorcycles, boats, RVs, and commercial vehicles. Progressive used to sell home insurance through other companies, but in 2015 it acquired the home insurance company ASI to "bundle" auto and home insurance for customers more effectively.

Tricia Griffith was appointed chief executive in 2016, having worked for the company for 30 years. She is not a typical holder of this role. There are very few CEOs who started work as an entry-level employee in the same company (she began as a trainee claims adjuster), and she was one of only 24 female chief executives of *Fortune* 500 firms. Senior colleagues say that she is good at encouraging teamwork, and she has rapport with frontline staff (having worked on the front line herself), often joining groups of employees at random for lunch on a Friday.

Traditional insurance companies are not known for their dynamic organizational cultures. Griffith set out to change the culture at Progressive, which now is "not only inclusive and inspiring, it's—dare we say—exciting," with hackathons, innovation groups, and employee-run experimental labs (Jenkins, 2018, p. 126). In 2018, Progressive was nominated by *Fortune* magazine as one of the Best Places to Work in America.

Since Griffith took over, sales have grown steadily, to $30 billion in net premiums in 2018, up from $20 billion in 2015. Sales growth has been faster than that of either Apple or Microsoft. In 2018, the share price rose 50 percent and profits doubled. Griffith likes to "set audacious goals" around key projects and investments. The number of "bundle" auto and home insurance customers increased over two years from 400,000 to 1 million, following an unsuccessful decade trying to grow this business.

Griffith invested in artificial intelligence, introducing in 2017 an innovative mobile app that uses analytics that calculate drivers' premiums based on their driving style. This allowed Progressive to capture 1.5 million miles of driving data, which have been used to develop an algorithm to measure distracted driving, helping the company to better understand risks and losses in this sector. Also in 2017, the home insurance business launched a "HomeQuote Explorer" tool, so that customers could compare quotes from different companies.

Progressive faces two future challenges. One is climate change, which will affect home insurance.

The other is self-driving vehicles, which could reduce demand for auto insurance. But Griffith says, "The world is changing, so we have to change with it" (Jenkins, 2018, p. 127).

What image or images of the change manager does Tricia Griffith adopt? What capabilities and attributes make Tricia Griffith a successful change manager?

Find on *YouTube*, "Progressive moves in 2019: One-on-one with CEO Tricia Griffith" (2019, 3:21 minutes).

Nielsen and Daniels (2016) studied the leadership of groups of postal workers in Denmark, looking at sickness absence rates over three years. They found that transformational leaders had groups with higher sickness absence rates and that groups with higher levels of "presenteeism" (coming to work and working excess hours even when unwell) had even higher levels of sickness absence rates. Leaders with a transformational style may therefore increase sickness absence among healthy employees. Vulnerable employees may also be encouraged to work when they are not well, and this self-sacrifice could lead to more sickness absence in the long run.

Chip Bergh and Change at Levi's

Founded in 1853, and based in San Francisco, Levi Strauss & Co. is one of America's oldest companies, best known for its denim jeans. Chip Bergh took over as CEO in 2011. Sales in 2010 were $4.5 billion, down from $7 billion in 1997. Bergh said, "When I decided to accept the CEO role, I saw it as a noble cause. I wanted to leave a legacy and make the company great again."

Bergh first spent an hour with each of the top 60 executives, asking them four questions: "What are three things we should not change? What are three things we must change? What's one thing you're hoping I'll do? What's one thing you're afraid I may do?" He discovered that the company had no clear strategy; people were working on different things. He also found that most employees thought the company was performing really well. Bergh explained that the company was underperforming and that this was an opportunity to do better. The challenge was to be contemporary, while exploiting the company's heritage, in a business where product lines change every six months.

Early in his tenure, Bergh replaced 9 of the 11 members of the top management team. In his second month in the job, during a visit to Bangalore, Bergh arranged "in-home" meetings with customers to learn about lifestyle and interests. One young woman showing him the various pairs of jeans that she wore said, "You wear other jeans, but you live in Levi's." "Live in Levi's" became the company's advertising slogan. But the company also had to increase revenue and profits. Bergh's strategy had four "memorable and easy to understand" components:

- *Build the profitable core.* Eighty percent of profits came from men's denim jeans and Dockers (a brand of khaki garments); market share was high, but sales growth was slow.

- *Expand.* Market share in women's clothing was low, and sales were falling, especially in developing markets (Brazil, Russia, India, China); people usually buy three or four tops to every bottom, but at Levi's, the numbers were the opposite, and this was a growth opportunity.

(Continued)

- *Become a leading omnichannel retailer.* Levi's had 2,700 stores and online sales direct to customers (DTC). However, most sales were through department stores where margins were lower, and the brand was not always well presented. Levi's had to grow sales in its own stores and online, recognizing that the latter were becoming increasingly important.

- *Achieve operational excellence.* Bergh wanted to cut costs, become more data driven, and generate surplus to invest in technology and innovation. With a $2 billion debt, Levi's was spending more on interest payments than on advertising.

Levi's had an innovation lab in Turkey, but the designers were in San Francisco. In 2013, against the advice of his chief financial officer, Bergh moved the lab close to the company headquarters. The lab's first success was a line of women's "athleisure" wear, using a new type of soft, stretch denim. Annual sales of women's garments went from $800 million to $1 billion. One way of leveraging the company's history involved a partnership with Google to create a "wearable technology" version of Levi's classic trucker jacket. The wearer can control their iPhone from the sleeve. Sales of trucker jackets increased by 40 percent in 2018. One-third of Levi's sales are now DTC through their own stores and website, and this business has grown over 51 percent in five years. Bergh says, "Levi's lost a generation of consumers in the early 2000s, but today our customers are younger than ever—and we're gaining momentum as we bring them back" (Bergh, 2018, p. 39).

What image or images of the change manager does Chip Bergh adopt? What capabilities and attributes make Chip Bergh a successful change manager?

Find on *YouTube*, "Levi's CEO Chip Bergh on innovation, strategies to reach the next generation of consumers" (2019, 9:20 minutes).

The Chief Transformation Officer

Gorter et al. (2016) argue that we are seeing the emergence of a new kind of change management role—the chief transformation officer (CTO). The CTO is a "high-level orchestrator of a complex process. He or she acts as the face of the transformation, sets the tone, spurs enthusiasm, and challenges current wisdom." This means that:

> CTOs should be independent (certainly not associated with the decisions of the past), have experience of similar turbulent corporate environments in their earlier careers, and enjoy support from the board, the CEO, and top management. Their mandate—responsibility for ensuring that the full bottom-line target gets delivered—must be clearly defined at the outset. They should be fully integrated into the executive team (not side-lined to a separate transformation unit), and their compensation must be linked to performance, with a significant bonus for overdelivery. Ideally, they should behave like an extension of the CEO or even the board and as such be able to hold the top managers accountable.
>
> (Gorter et al., 2016, p. 1)

The CTO ideally requires a number of attributes. "Great CTOs accept nothing without facts and independent analysis. They are not only good problem solvers and business leaders; they have a high emotional quotient and strong interpersonal skills. The most successful transformations we have seen are the result of CTOs igniting passion and leveraging the efforts of a range of individual talents. They recognize and reward outperformance" (Gorter et al., 2016, p. 2).

Gorter et al. (2016, p. 3) note that CTOs have to deal with eight key issues if they are to be successful:

- They must have the backing and confidence of the chief executive and board.
- They have to deal with vested interests and challenge taken-for-granted norms.

- They need to establish a new pace for the business, to reset the "clock speed."
- They have to understand the perspectives and frustrations of frontline staff.
- They need to coach the top team with regard to how to lead the transformation.
- They need to be realistic about the benefits of the change, and about where compromises can and cannot be made.
- They should deliberately pick fights with senior leaders with a view to getting them to change.
- They need to understand the dominant culture of the organization and how this has to change.

The CTO role is probably one that will be found mainly in large organizations, implementing large-scale transformational changes. However, change managers in smaller organizations will almost always have to deal with the same issues, even with smaller-scale changes. One of the intriguing aspects of the CTO job description is that the change manager should "deliberately pick fights" with other senior managers. As we will suggest when discussing the political dimension of organizational change, conflict can be valuable in opening up discussion, confronting and dealing with resistance, and identifying innovative solutions (see the discussion of the benefits of resistance in chapter 8).

Dara Khosrowshahi and Change at Uber

In August 2017, following a period of bad publicity and upheaval, Dara Khosrowshahi replaced Travis Kalanick as chief executive of Uber, the taxi ride-hailing company. Kalanick had led a company known for its "Uber Way" involving a "take-no-prisoners, win-at-any-cost mentality." This had helped the company to grow rapidly to a $70 billion valuation. However, that same corporate culture had become associated with a series of public relations disasters that began to concern not just employees but also customers, regulators, and investors.

Uber's cultural norms included "always be hustlin," "toe-stepping" (i.e., "don't hesitate to challenge the boss"), and "champion's mind set" (i.e., "get Uber over the finish line"). These norms "took on a more sinister aspect in the workplace"; a former Uber employee said that "everyone used those values to excuse their bad behavior" (Wong, 2017). Former Uber engineer Susan Fowler wrote a blog that described a corporate culture that tolerated sexual harassment and sexism, with both being reinforced through disinclination to act on such behavior when it was brought to the attention of management. Following

Fowler's "bombshell blog," other Uber employees were emboldened to report their experiences and around 200 claims of sexual harassment were made against the company.

During the first half of 2017, many Uber employees left, not wanting to be associated with the scandals or because they felt that they had been mistreated by managers. Eric Schiffer, CEO of Reputation Management Consultants, said, "Travis had almost a Rambo-style approach to leadership, which made Uber giant. But it came with a lot of fallout."

Khosrowshahi started quietly, talking to people—drivers, customer support staff, and women engineers. In the words of Jessica Bryndza, Uber's global director of people experiences and employer brand, "He didn't come in guns blazing, he came in listening." Months later, he was still listening. He also "made nice" with lawmakers in response to their removal of Uber's license to operate in London, including stating in public, "On behalf of everyone at Uber globally, I apologize for the mistakes we've made." Meetings were held in

(Continued)

cities around the world where regulatory disputes were occurring—something that Kalanick had not done.

One journalist said that Khosrowshahi being a "measured and diplomatic leader, doesn't mean he's meek. He's dramatically reshaped Uber's famously 'toxic' corporate culture" (Kerr, 2018).

Find on *YouTube*, "Dara Khosrowshahi, CEO, Uber" (2018, 41:12 minutes).

Changing from the Middle

Change is often led from the middle. A transformational leader or chief officer may not always be the best solution for the organization implementing large-scale change. We discussed in chapter 8 the notion that middle managers are better placed to initiate change because they understand day-to-day operations better than the top team (Heyden et al., 2017). Research has consistently shown how middle managers play a key role in organizational change. In chapter 8, we challenged the stereotype of middle managers as change blockers. Joseph Bower (1970) was among the first to recognize the importance of middle managers as change drivers, exerting upward influence on strategy based on their knowledge of the frontline operational context, and by nurturing, testing, and championing initiatives. Kanter (1982, p. 95) argues that "a company's productivity depends on how innovative its middle managers are," adding that loosely defined roles and assignments encourage managers to develop and promote their own ideas.

Who Are Your Most Capable Strategic Change Leaders?

Research by the consulting firm Pricewaterhouse-Coopers (PwC) found that only 8 percent of senior managers have the strategic leadership capabilities required to drive organizational change (Lewis, 2015). From a survey of 6,000 managers in Europe, the highest proportion of strategic leaders were women over the age of 55—a group which has traditionally been overlooked in the search for change agent skills. PwC defines a strategic leader as someone who has "wide experience of settings, people, and also of failure, which engenders humility or perspective and resilience, so that they know what to do when things don't work" (Lewis, 2015, p. x).

Women over 55 were more likely to:

- see situations from multiple perspectives
- think and work outside the existing system
- identify what needs to change
- be able to persuade or inspire others to follow them
- use positive language
- be open to frank and honest feedback
- exercise power courageously

One consultant (female) at PwC said, "Historically women over the age of 55 would not have been an area of focus, but as the research suggests, this pool of talent might hold the key to transformation and in some cases, business survival" (Lewis, 2015).

Supporting those views, Susan Ashford and James Detert (2015, p. 73) argue that "Organizations don't prosper unless managers in the middle ranks identify and promote the need for change." When it comes to sharing those ideas, however, middle managers are often discouraged by the top leadership style ("if an idea was any good, we would

TABLE 12.2
Tactics for Leading Change from the Middle

Tactic	Base Your Approach on These Questions
Tailor your pitch	Where does my audience stand on this issue? What does my audience find most convincing or compelling?
Frame the issue	How can I connect my issue to organizational priorities? How can I best describe its benefits? How can I link it to other issues receiving attention? How can I highlight an opportunity for the organization?
Manage emotions	How can I use emotions to generate positive and not negative responses? How can I manage my audience's emotional responses?
Get the timing right	What is the best moment to be heard? Can I "catch the wave" by tapping into a trend in the outside world? What is the right time in the decision-making process to raise my issue?
Involve others	Which allies from my network can help me sell my issue? Who are my potential blockers; how can I persuade them to support me? Who are my fence-sitters; how can I convince them that my issue matters?
Adhere to norms	Should I use a formal approach, an informal casual one, or a combination?
Suggest solutions	Am I suggesting a viable solution? If not, am I proposing a way to discover one, instead of just highlighting the problem?

Source: Ashford and Detert (2015).

have already thought of it") and valuable opportunities are missed. Ashford and Detert asked middle managers to describe their experiences of selling three kinds of ideas: new products, processes, or markets; improvements to existing products and processes; and better ways to meet employees' needs. They identified seven influence tactics that middle managers use to attract senior executive attention and resources. These are summarized in table 12.2.

Ashford and Detert offer three further pieces of advice to middle managers. First, choose your audience; your immediate boss may not be the best place to start to promote your idea. Second, use several of these tactics rather than just one or two; they are more powerful in combination. Finally, choose your battles; some ideas can just be too difficult to sell.

The middle management role is not necessarily confined to implementing changes directed by others. McDermott et al. (2013) show how middle managers and other "change recipients" become change managers by tailoring, adding to, and adapting top-down directives so that they work better in particular local contexts. But middle managers may not always be free to play those organizational change roles. Donald Kuratko and Michael Goldsby (2004) identify the conditions that can discourage what they describe as *the entrepreneurial middle manager* from taking risks and innovating:

- systems and policies that encourage consistent, safe, conservative behavior
- complex approval cycles with elaborate documentation
- controls that encourage micromanagement
- top-down management and lack of delegated authority

Middle managers can be key to change. Their understanding of frontline operations is usually better than that of senior management. They are able to mediate between the frontline and top team. However, the organizational context has to allow them to make these contributions. Otherwise, they may be a misunderstood and underutilized resource. The stereotype of senior "transformational" leaders is only one model of change management. We have highlighted the importance of creativity, ingenuity, interpersonal relationships, communication skills, risk taking, and working below the corporate radar. The organization's most valuable change managers may not be visible and may not be those who have been formally appointed to change roles.

The Gang of Four: Middle versus Senior Management

Ole Hope (2010) examines how middle managers "redefined" senior management plans for change in the claims handling division of a Nordic insurance company. The claims handling process was time consuming and costly and was difficult for customers to use. Middle management, however, did not agree with senior management plans, and a back office management team, who called themselves "The Gang of Four," decided to implement their own proposals instead.

The "micro practices" that they used to influence the change outcomes included:

- disobeying management decisions about project representation
- handpicking loyal and skilled people to fill project roles
- taking control over the subproject staffing
- controlling information gathering by deciding what questions were to be asked
- producing a memo supporting their own position and aims
- holding back information, and distributing information selectively
- questioning the expertise of the external consultants
- taking advantage of the new division head and his lack of direct local experience
- rejecting unfavorable decisions and insisting on a "replay" to reach different outcomes

Middle management was thus able to implement their more effective proposals.

Change Support and Delivery Units

Given the scope and complexity of the change agenda, many organizations have established internal change departments or units. Wylie and Sturdy (2018) identify four main types of change units, each with distinctive characteristics, scope, impact, and challenges. These are transformers, enforcers, specialists, and independents.

Transformers are responsible for delivering large-scale change, and this kind of unit is relatively rare. They tend to work to a fixed timetable, using a consistent change methodology across a range of projects. Transformer units are likely to be "high profile" and may thus be expected to meet high expectations. They may face opposition from operational managers who wish to keep control over initiatives in their areas, leading to disputes over responsibility. As transformer units may have a limited timescale, they may be tempted to adopt directive, nonparticipative approaches to change.

Enforcers are embedded in the organizational structure, perhaps as a form of chief executive support or strategy unit. Their role is to help senior executives to translate strategy and vision into specific projects, with a policing role, exercising central control to ensure consistency. As they may be seen as the "eyes and ears of the CEO," operational managers who value their own links to top management may regard enforcers with suspicion.

Specialists are delivery units staffed by subject-matter experts, focusing on incremental change in specific functions and departments, and thus have more limited scope and impact. They are likely to be based in services such as human resources or IT, and they may have to overcome the negative stereotypes of those functions. Their narrow specialist focus may lead to limited problem-solving solutions where the change agenda does not align with their interests and expertise.

Independents are found where there is a need for a generalist change delivery unit. These units deliver specific, small projects within business units, and their impact tends to be localized. Unlike enforcers and specialists, they operate outside the management hierarchy, and they more closely resemble external consultancies. They may be expected to find their own work and be self-funding. The advantages of autonomy are thus offset by resource constraints. In setting up projects, a lot of time is likely to be consumed in relationship management.

Kaiser Permanente's Innovation Consultancy

Lew McCreary (2010) describes the innovation and improvement methods of Kaiser Permanente, a managed care consortium based in Oakland, California. The company set up an internal Innovation Consultancy unit, which employs change experts to observe people, ask them how they feel about their work, take notes and photographs, make drawings, and identify better ways of doing things. This involves, McCreary (p. 92) suggests, "a combination of anthropology, journalism, and empathy," exploring how staff and patients live, work, think, and feel before trying to solve a problem.

The approach involves "uncovering the untold story"—finding out "What is really going on here?" For example, to prevent nurses being interrupted during medication rounds and to reduce errors, a "deep dive" event was held, including nurses, doctors, pharmacists, and patients. This generated around 400 ideas and led to the design of a smock with the words "leave me alone" on it (known as "no-interruption wear") and a five-step process for ensuring the correct dispensing of medication. Another example is the exchange of patient information between nursing shifts. This used to take 45 minutes and delayed the next shift's contact with patients. Nurses would also compile and exchange information in idiosyncratic ways, potentially missing important details. The revised Nurse Knowledge Exchange is faster and more reliable, with new software and with information presented in standard formats.

Members of the Information Consultancy unit do not dictate the changes to be made but work with staff as "codesigners" on change projects. This approach allows Kaiser Permanente to achieve the aim of implementing innovation and change quickly and economically.

The model, or models, of delivery unit that an organization decides to introduce thus depends on the nature and timescale of the changes that are under consideration.

Identifying Your Souls of Fire

Studies of creative, innovative individuals have shown how to identify the "souls of fire" who are most likely to be passionate about development and change. But there is a problem. How many organizations want to employ people who are easily bored, act without permission, are not adaptable, and do not follow instructions? It is important to recognize that:

- Change managers can be difficult nonconformists, mavericks who take risks, and may not always present themselves well in an employee selection context.
- Change managers are often regarded as troublemakers who break rules, and they may be blamed when things go wrong.
- An organization needs a balance of personalities—too many radical innovators can be just as ineffective as having too many conformists who do what they are told.

Thomas Davenport et al. (2003) studied the *ideas practitioners* who bring new management ideas into an organization. Consistent with the findings of other research, they found this to be a diverse and scattered group but with common ways of working. Ideas practitioners seem to work in four stages:

Scouting	They read a lot, attend conferences, explore interdisciplinary perspectives, and look to other fields for ideas.
Packaging	They translate and tailor their ideas for a wider audience and express ideas in terms of key issues—innovation, efficiency, effectiveness—that will interest senior management.
Advocating	They sell, run marketing campaigns, find early adopters, and persuade other managers.
Implementing	They make things happen, rolling change out from the boardroom to the front line.

In terms of personality, ideas practitioners tend to be intelligent, optimistic, passionate about ideas, intellectually restless, mild mannered (not fanatical), and self-confident. They also tend to be boundary spanners with extensive personal networks.

Networks are a recurring theme in studies of change agents. From their study of change in Britain's National Health Service (one of the largest employing organizations in the world), Julie Battilana and Tiziana Casciaro (2013, p. 64) also found that the success of change managers depended on their informal networks. They identify different types of networks. In *cohesive networks*, the members know each other and their actions are easier to coordinate. The members of *divergent networks* are connected indirectly by their link to the change manager, and these networks can be a source of new ideas and information. Change managers were more successful where:

- they held central positions in the organization's informal network, regardless of their roles in the formal hierarchy.
- the nature of their network matched the type of change that they were pursuing.
- they had good relationships with "fence-sitters" who were ambivalent about the changes.

Case Study: *Boosting Factory Yields*

Aaron De Smet et al. (2012, p. 4) describe the following example of a change manager faced with a particularly difficult challenge. How would you assess his approach? Is this a style that you would be prepared to use in your own organization? Or would you consider this style to be too risky?

Conor, as we'll call one European plant manager, needed to boost yields using the company's new production system. In the past, the industrial giant would have assigned engineers steeped in lean production or Six Sigma to observe the shop floor, gather data, and present a series of improvements. Conor would then have told plant employees to implement the changes, while he gauged the results—a method consistent with his own instinctive command-and-control approach to leadership. But Conor and his superiors quickly realized that the old way wouldn't succeed: only employees who actually did the work could identify the full range of efficiency improvements necessary to meet the operational targets, and no attempt to get them to do so would be taken seriously unless Conor and his line leaders were more collaborative.

Workers were skeptical: a survey taken at about this time (in 2009) showed that plant workers saw Conor and his team as distant and untrustworthy. Moreover, the company couldn't use salary increases or overtime to boost morale, because of the ongoing global economic crisis.

Conor's leadership training gave him an opportunity to reflect on the situation and provided simple steps he could take to improve it. He began by getting out of his office, visiting the shop floor, and really listening to the workers talk about their day-to-day experiences, their workflows, how their machines functioned, and where things went wrong. They'd kept all this information from him before. He made a point of starting meetings by inviting those present to speak, in part to encourage the group to find collective solutions to its problems.

Conor explained: "As I shared what I thought and felt more openly, I started to notice things I had not been aware of, as other people became more open. We'd had the lean tools and good technology for a long time. Transparency and openness were the real breakthrough." As the new atmosphere took hold, workers began pointing out minor problems and additional areas for improvement specific to their corners of the plant; within just a few months its yields increased to 91 percent, from 87 percent. Today, yields run at 93 percent.

The organization chart is not a good guide to finding the champions, the ideas practitioners, the souls of fire, and the change managers. Lili Duan et al. (2014) argue that managers need to find these "hidden influencers." They claim, however, that managers asked to identify the influencers in their organizations are almost always wrong. Informal influencers are those to whom other staff turn to for advice, and they can have a major impact on attitudes to change. Retail cashiers, for example, can have considerable influence because they are well connected with many others. Spotting the change managers thus involves understanding the informal organizational networks and how these function.

LO 12.2 Change Managers: What Kind of Role Is This?

What kind of role is this? What challenges and rewards does it bring? From our discussion about who becomes a change manager, it is clear that this is not necessarily a formal appointment; the most effective change managers do not always occupy senior positions on the organization chart. In addition, much of the work may be done behind the scenes, below the radar.

The evidence shows that the experience of most change managers has two main dimensions. First, this can be a challenging, stressful, high-pressure, fast-paced, high-risk role. Senior management expects rapid results. There may be open and covert resistance from those who are affected. Any concerns, complaints, and anger may be directed at the change manager in person. Change managers thus have to be comfortable with and able to handle conflict. Those who need to be liked by others and who do not like to lose friends will be uncomfortable in a change management role. One study of an organization redesign program (Buchanan, 2003) found that change managers not only had to cope with personal stress, but also had to deal, at the same time, with the stress experienced by those involved in the change, who were described as "scarred" and as "hurt and bruised people."

Given the pressure, pace, stress, risks, and vulnerability of the role, change managers ideally need to be resilient. Resilience can be defined as "the successful adaptation to life tasks in the face of social disadvantage or highly adverse conditions" (Chartered Institute of Personnel and Development, 2011, p. 2). Conditions for change managers are not always" highly adverse" but are rarely problem-free. Other terms that describe resilience include adaptability, equanimity, perseverance, self-reliance, mental toughness, and bouncebackability. These are capabilities that we all benefit from on occasion. Change managers in particular, however, need to be able to "bounce back" when plans go wrong, and to persevere in spite of difficulties. Some of us are more resilient than others, but resilience is an attribute that can be developed. Exercise 12.2 provides a diagnostic, "How Resilient Are You?" This diagnostic invites you to assess your level of resilience and to consider actions to develop your resilience if necessary.

Confessions of a Change Manager

If the change manager's role is so demanding, why would anyone accept the responsibility? We met a Finnish woman who was working with a large utility company in South Australia. She described her change manager's role as risky, pressured, and stressful, just as we have discussed here. So we asked, "Why did you take this job?" This was her answer:

> I wanted a job to look forward to in the morning, and not want to leave in the evening.
> I saw it as a great opportunity to learn. I get charged up with more learning. I need that.
> I needed to get my hands dirty. It gave me a chance to show my capabilities. It is a very tiring and frustrating job. On the other hand, it gives you a great opportunity to excel.
>
> I am a risk taker. I need some excitement and power-play while at work. It gave me an opportunity to work with some highly motivated and committed individuals. Together we were able to make it happen. I believe that the only way to meet the challenges of the external business environment is to offer the customer what they really want.
>
> I have thick skin. I realized that I was going to make some enemies during the change process—as well as some very influential and powerful friends. I was able to accept the challenge due to the stage of my personal lifestyle (boyfriend overseas, dog at home). I sacrificed my spare time for the company—and for the financial and non-financial rewards.
>
> Even though I was an inexperienced change manager, I was confident that I had skills, knowledge and attributes to make it happen. Or that I could find an expert (internal or external) to assist me to make it happen. If I would fail, I could still work with [this organization]—or elsewhere, because I am tolerant of ambiguity.

This account reveals the second and more positive dimension of the change manager's experience. Especially with "deep" changes (see Figure 1.1), the change manager is exposed to a wider range of internal and external corporate and strategic issues than is the case in most general or operational management positions, which tend to be more narrowly constrained. The role of change manager can thus be challenging in an exciting, stimulating, energizing way. Here is an opportunity to demonstrate one's capabilities, pick up new knowledge, develop new skills, and add powerful and influential colleagues to one's network. Successful experience as a change manager has "resumé value."

Our Finnish change manager made several comments that reveal aspects of her personality: "I get charged up with learning"; "I need to get my hands dirty"; "I am a risk taker"; "I need excitement and power-play"; "I have thick skin"; "I realized that I was going to make enemies"; "I was confident that I would be able to make it happen"; "I am tolerant of ambiguity." These attributes appear to be appropriate for someone working in such a challenging role. Personality is only one factor contributing to personal effectiveness; capability and context are also important. However, the need for action, learning, excitement, and power play, along with tolerance of ambiguity, risk, and conflict, all appear to be useful personal attributes for a change manager to possess or to develop.

On the one hand, the role of the change manager is stressful and the position is a vulnerable one. On the other hand, the role can offer substantial opportunities for personal development and career progression. As we saw in chapter 1, when being interviewed for the next promotion, one is more likely to impress by telling stories about the success and impact of the (preferably deep) changes for which one has been responsible rather than tell stories about shallow initiatives—or no stories at all. Beeson (2009, p. 103) identifies the "core selection factors" for senior executive appointments. Most of these do not relate to business knowledge or technical ability but to "soft" skills. Here are four of those selection factors, all related to demonstrable change implementation capabilities:

- Setting direction and thinking strategically; spotting marketplace trends and developing a winning strategy that differentiates the company.
- Managing implementation without getting involved at too low a level of detail; defining a set of roles, processes, and measures to ensure that things get done reliably.
- Building the capacity for innovation and change; knowing when new ways of doing business are required; having the courage, tolerance for risk, and change-management skills to bring new ideas to fruition.
- Getting things done across internal boundaries (lateral management); demonstrating organizational savvy; influencing and persuading colleagues; dealing with conflict.

Change managers thus enjoy several intrinsic rewards: challenge, excitement, personal development, and job satisfaction. The extrinsic rewards in terms of career progression can also be substantial.

LO 12.3 Change Management Competencies

What competencies—skills, knowledge, and other attributes—do change managers ideally require? This question is significant for three reasons. First, change that is badly managed can cause serious damage to the organization and units involved, to those who are affected by the change, and to other stakeholders. Second, although full-time change managers and external consultants often carry out this work, many general and functional managers combine change responsibilities with their regular duties. Third, responsibility for change is increasingly distributed, and the demand for change management competencies is also now widespread.

When discussing this topic, it is difficult to escape from competency frameworks, which itemize the various skill and knowledge requirements. These lists can make tedious reading, especially when one framework says much the same as the next. These frameworks tend to agree, however, on two fundamental issues. First, the change manager's role is a multifaceted one. Second, change management roles make considerable demands on those who perform them.

Table 12.3 summarizes one of the most comprehensive competency frameworks, from the Change Management Institute (2017), a global not-for-profit organization headquartered in Australia. This model identifies 12 competencies relating to the full-time professional change manager who is heading up or working in a specialist corporate unit or has been hired as an external adviser or consultant.

TABLE 12.3
The CMI Change Manager Master Level—Competency Model

Skill Area	Demonstrates Understanding of/Capabilities in
Facilitating change	Principles of change; the environment Business focus; change readiness; culture awareness
Strategic thinking	Vision; assess readiness Strategic view; sustainable outcomes
Thinking and judgment	Analytical thinking; holistic perspective; decision making
Influencing others	Customer or stakeholder focus; professional presence Networking; interpersonal skills (selling ideas; use of power)
Coaching for change	Adult learning principles; change management Needs analysis; organizational capability to manage change Role model; champion new skills
Project management	Plan development; monitor and manage progress Cost management; risk and opportunity management; vendor management; review project outcomes
Communicating effectively	Relationships building; empathy; oral and written communication Measures effectiveness of communication
Self-management	Personal responsibility; prioritization and time management Resilience; flexibility; emotional intelligence
Facilitation—meetings	Design; participatory environment Structure (agenda, physical environment) Process (facilitation tools, inclusion, timing)
Professional development	Updates knowledge and develops skills Promotion of change management
Specialist expertise: Training and development	Needs identification; training plan Solution delivery; evaluation
Specialist expertise: Communication	Needs identification; plan; solution design and development Solution delivery; evaluation

Source: Change Management Institute (2017).

TABLE 12.4
Images of Change and Key Competencies

Image	Soundbite	Approach to Change	Key Competencies
Director	"This is what is going to happen."	Management choice, command and control.	Strategic thinking Facilitating change
Navigator	"I will tell you what I'd like to happen."	Plan with care, but expect the unexpected.	Facilitating change Project management
Caretaker	"Let us explore what might be possible."	Accept the force of external context and adapt as necessary.	Thinking and judgment Influencing others
Coach	"How can we develop the capability to deal with change?"	Shape systemic capabilities—values, skills, drills—to respond effectively to change.	Coaching for change Influencing others
Interpreter	"We need to think differently about this."	Managing meaning through interpretations that explain and convey understanding.	Learning and development Communication
Nurturer	"This is everybody's problem—how will we fix it?"	Develop resilience, and encourage involvement, continuous learning, and self-organizing.	Facilitation Learning and development Communication

This model identifies capabilities that we would expect to see: understanding the change process, interpersonal and communication skills, influence and persuasion, and self-management. The model also emphasizes a strategic perspective, expecting the "master" change manager to have environmental knowledge and stakeholder focus. Based on this model, table 12.4 identifies the two or three key competencies that are particularly relevant to each of our six images of change management. For the director, strategic thinking and facilitating change are critical. For the nurturer, facilitation, learning and development, and communication are more important. Self-management and professional development apply to all six images.

The Great Intimidators

Roderick Kramer (2006) challenges the view that change managers must be nice and not tough and should be humble and self-effacing rather than intimidating. Kramer argues that intimidation is an appropriate style when an organization has become rigid or unruly, stagnant or drifting, and faces inertia or resistance to change. Abrasive leadership, he argues, gets people moving. Intimidators are not bullies, but they can use bullying tactics when time is short and the stakes are high. Kramer (2006, p. 90) makes his positive view of intimidators clear when he argues, "They are not averse to causing a ruckus, nor are they above using a few public whippings and ceremonial hangings to get attention. They're rough, loud, and in your face."

Intimidators have what Kramer calls "political intelligence." Socially intelligent managers focus on leveraging the strengths of others, with empathy and soft power. Politically intelligent managers focus on weaknesses and insecurities, using coercion, fear, and anxiety. However, working intimidating leaders can be a positive experience. Their sense of purpose can be inspirational, their forcefulness is a role model, and intimidators challenge others to think clearly about their objectives. Kramer (2006, p. 92) quotes a journalist who said, "Don't have a reputation for being a nice guy—that won't do you any good." Intimidation tactics include:

- *Get up close and personal.* Intimidators work through direct confrontation, invading your personal space and using taunts and slurs to provoke and throw you off balance.
- *Get angry.* Called "porcupine power," this involves the "calculated loss of temper" (use it, don't lose it), using rage and anger to help the intimidator prevail.
- *Keep them guessing.* Intimidators preserve an air of mystery by maintaining deliberate distance. Transparency and trust are fashionable, but intimidators keep others guessing, which makes it easier to change direction without loss of credibility.
- *Know it all.* "Informational intimidators" who appear to have mastery of the facts can be very intimidating indeed. It doesn't matter whether "the facts" are correct, as long as they are presented with complete confidence at the right time.

This is a style that will not work well in all situations. Kramer is careful to suggest, however, that this approach may be appropriate—even necessary—to overcome either apathy or resistance to change. As a change manager, do you feel that intimidation is appropriate in some circumstances? Are you comfortable using the intimidation tactics that Kramer identifies?

A Great Intimidator at Work

The movie *The Devil Wears Prada* (2006, director David Frankel) is based on the novel of the same name by Lauren Weisberger. The movie tells the story of a naive, young aspiring journalist, Andrea Sachs (played by Anne Hathaway), who gets a job as an assistant to the famous editor-in-chief of the New York fashion magazine *Runway*. The magazine's powerful and ruthless editor, Miranda Priestly (Meryl Streep), is a legend in the industry. At the beginning of the movie, we see Andrea arriving for her job interview as "second assistant" with Miranda's "first assistant" Emily Charlton (Emily Blunt), but Miranda decides to conduct the interview herself. Watch the movie starting when Andrea comes out of the lift and heads for the *Runway* reception desk. Stop when Emily runs after Andrea and calls her back into the office.

1. How would you describe Miranda Priestley's management style?
2. What impact does Miranda's style have on the performance of those around her?
3. Good boss or bad boss: What is your assessment of this management style?
4. Given her style, why do so many people desperately want to work for Miranda?
5. Why do you think Miranda Priestly gave Andrea Sachs the job?

LO 12.4 Political Skill and the Change Manager

Organizations are political systems, and change is almost always a politicized process. Why? Individuals, groups, and divisions have to compete with each other for resources of different kinds, such as people, money, and space. Political tactics are tools that can be used in that competition. Change can often upset the established allocation of resources among stakeholders, thus triggering even more intense conflict. The change manager must be aware of the organizational politics but must also be prepared to engage with the politics—to "play the game." Political skill is particularly important in addressing resistance to change (see chapter 8). Maslyn et al. (2017) found that political behavior is not always viewed unfavorably but can be seen as positive when it benefits the organization and its members. Buchanan and Badham (2020) argue that the change manager who is not politically skilled will fail. It is rarely possible for the change manager to escape from this dimension of the role.

Age and Treachery Win

Bill Bratton is an American police chief known for his achievements in "turning around" failing or problem forces.

In 1980, at age 34 one of the youngest lieutenants in Boston's police department, he had proudly put up a plaque in his office that said: *Youth and skill will win out every time over age and treachery.* Within just a few months, having been shunted into a dead-end position due to a mixture of office

politics and his own brashness, Bratton took the sign down. He never again forgot the importance of understanding the plotting, intrigue, and politics involved in pushing through change.

(Kim and Mauborgne, 2003, p. 68)

The advice is: Know who the key players are, understand how they play the politics game, and know their attitudes and positions in relation to change proposals.

Organizational politics is a topic that is generally regarded as unsavory and damaging, associated with backstabbing and dirty tricks. "Machiavellian" is an insult, not a compliment. Mintzberg's (1983, p. 172) definition of politics is a popular one and has been widely cited:

> individual or group behavior that is informal, ostensibly parochial, typically divisive, and above all, in the technical sense, illegitimate—sanctioned neither by formal authority, accepted ideology, nor certified expertise.

This is one source of the enduring negative perception of politics—parochial, divisive, illegitimate. How could managers in general, and change managers in particular, be advised to develop capabilities such as these? However, research has revealed the positive, constructive uses of political tactics. This involves the use of political skill, sometimes called political astuteness (Manzie and Hartley, 2015). Ferris et al. (2000, p. 30) offer this definition of political skill:

> an interpersonal style construct that combines social astuteness with the ability to relate well, and otherwise demonstrate situationally appropriate behavior in a disarmingly charming and engaging manner that inspires confidence, trust, sincerity, and genuineness.

Ferris et al. call this "savvy and street smarts," and they argue that political skill has four key dimensions. *Social astuteness* concerns the ability to observe and to understand the behavior and motives of others. *Interpersonal influence* concerns the ability to engage and influence others in a compelling way. *Networking ability* involves building a variety of

TABLE 12.5
Dimensions of Political Skill

Dimension	Definition	Sample Inventory Items
Social astuteness	Attuned observers, good interpreters of behavior, self-aware, sensitive to others, clever	I understand people very well. I pay close attention to people's facial expressions.
Interpersonal influence	Subtle and convincing style, calibrate actions to the situation, to the "target," be flexible	I am able to make most people feel comfortable and at ease around me. I am good at getting people to like me.
Networking ability	Adept at using networks, develop friendships and build alliances easily, skilled in negotiation and conflict resolution	I spend a lot of time and effort at work networking with others. At work, I know a lot of important people and am well connected.
Apparent sincerity	Appear honest and open and to have integrity, authenticity, sincerity, genuineness, no ulterior motives	It is important that people believe I am sincere in what I say and do. I try to show a genuine interest in other people.

Source: Ferris et al. (2005a)

relationships across and outside the organization. *Apparent sincerity* means being seen as forthright, open, honest, and genuine. This model is summarized in table 12.5 (Ferris et al., 2005a; 2007; Brouer et al., 2006). They have also developed an assessment inventory to measure individual skills in those four areas. Studies using university staff and students as participants produced the following conclusions:

- Political skill correlates with measures of self-monitoring and emotional intelligence.
- Those who score high on political skill display less anxiety and are less likely to perceive stressful events as threatening.
- Political skill is not correlated with general intelligence.
- Political skill predicts job performance and subordinate evaluations of leadership ability.
- The dimension of political skill related most strongly to performance rating is social astuteness.

The Political Grandmaster

The politically skilled organizational grandmaster reads people and environments in ways that yield the detection of cues and thus opportunities that others simply cannot see. These masters operate on and enact with their environments in ways that create new opportunities. Finally, it is capitalization on these recognized opportunities that allows the politically skilled to achieve their objectives—much in the same way chess grandmasters leverage their skills—which translates into heightened job performance, enhanced reputation, and faster promotions.

(McAllister et al., 2015, p. 33)

To what extent do the statements in the "sample inventory items" column describe you? Are these not characteristics that all managers should perhaps have? Describing those with a high degree of political skill, Ferris et al. (2005b, p. 128) observe:

> Politically skilled individuals convey a sense of personal security and calm self-confidence that attracts others and gives them a feeling of comfort. This self-confidence never goes too far so as to be perceived as arrogance but is always properly measured to be a positive attribute. Therefore, although self-confident, those high in political skill are not self-absorbed (although they are self-aware) because their focus is outward toward others, not inward and self-centred. [. . .] We suggest that people high in political skill not only know precisely what to do in different social situations at work but how to do it in a manner that disguises any ulterior, self-serving motives and appears to be sincere.

Political skill is only one factor affecting the personal effectiveness of change managers, and of managers and leaders in general. Used effectively, political skill can be a powerful way to influence others and to motivate action to change, while strengthening the change manager's reputation. How does political skill work in practice? David Buchanan and Richard Badham (2020) identify 12 categories of political behavior, from relatively harmless image building to disreputable "dirty tricks" (see table 12.6).

TABLE 12.6
Categories of Political Behavior: A Typology

Image building	We all know people who didn't get the job because they didn't look the part—appearance is a credibility issue; highlight successes and achievements.
Information games	Withholding information to make others look foolish, bending the truth, white lies, massaging information, timed release.
Structure games	Creating new roles, teams, and departments, or abolishing old ones, to promote supporters, sideline adversaries and signal new priorities.
Scapegoating	Blaming another department, external factors, a predecessor, trading conditions, or a particular individual.
Alliances	Doing secret deals with influential others to form a critical mass, a cabal, to win support for and to progress your proposals.
Networking	Using lunches, coffees, dinners, and sporting events to get initiatives onto management agendas, improve visibility, gather information.
Intermediation	Asking someone with better connections and knowledge to advise you on how to approach another individual; having someone else approach that other individual on your behalf instead of making direct contact.
Compromise	All right, you win this time, I won't put up a fight and embarrass you in public—if you will back me next time.
Rule games	I'm sorry, but you have used the wrong form, at the wrong time, with the wrong arguments; we can't set inconsistent precedents.
Positioning	Switching and choosing roles where one is successful and visible; avoiding failing projects; position in the building, in the room.
Issue-selling	Packaging, presenting, crafting, enacting, and promoting plans and ideas in ways that make them more appealing to the target audience.
Dirty tricks	Keeping dirt files for blackmail, spying on others, discrediting and undermining, spreading false rumors, corridor whispers.

One category of political behavior in table 12.6 is networking. This is a key political skill, but it is often neglected by change managers: "This takes time, where is the pay-off?" Furnham (2015) argues that networking is key to career success, having a map of who's who and who holds power and influence, using "elevator" and "water cooler" moments to start up conversations. McAllister et al. (2015, p. 29) cite this example:

> F. Ross Johnson, the infamous former head of RJR Nabisco described as having a knack for corporate politics, recognized the importance of being embedded in networks comprised of influential individuals. Shortly after his move to New York as head of Standard Brands International (his first American corporate post), Johnson positioned himself among the major players in Manhattan by wrangling a coveted seat on the New Canaan Club Car, a hangout for executives on the commuter train. Further, Johnson immediately ingratiated himself with Standard Brands board members. This opportunity-rich network led to his promotion to president and a seat on the Standard Brands board 1 year after his arrival in New York.

As a practicing manager, you have been using these kinds of behaviors already. How you behave is of course dependent on your goals, the context, and those whom you are seeking to influence. Is image building harmless? This is also called "impression management" and involves behaving in a manner that presents the public image or "persona" that you want others to see. Dress and act differently, and others will see a different persona. Image building can be a good way to manipulate the perceptions, beliefs, and behavior of others. At the bottom of table 12.6, can you imagine circumstances in which "dirty tricks" could be seen as useful, ethical, appropriate, professional management actions?

Take a Moment and Think about a Leader

Take a moment and think about a leader in your organization whom you would consider to be political. How would you describe that leader? Some common descriptions that may immediately come to mind are self-serving, manipulative, phony, or untrustworthy. You may conjure up images of secret pacts made behind closed doors or on the golf course. Or, perhaps, you came up with descriptions such as influential, well connected, trustworthy, or concerned for others. Often, the idea of a leader being political is associated with negative perceptions and behaviors. In reality, though, political skill is a necessity and can be a positive skill for leaders to possess when used appropriately. Indeed, when we view political skill through this lens, it is difficult to envision any leader being effective without it.

(Braddy and Campbell, 2014, p. 1)

Issue-selling is a political tactic of particular interest to change managers. Many managers have a built-in bias against novelty. New ideas are risky and drain resources, assessment is often subjective, and there is not enough time for comprehensive evaluations. Most organizations find it difficult to resource all the ideas that are circulating at any one point in time. All these good ideas for improvement and change are competing with each other, and good ideas do not always sell themselves. How can you, as a change manager, increase the probability that your ideas are implemented? Jane Dutton et al. (2001) identify three sets of issue-selling tactics, which they call "behind-the-scenes moves to promote ideas for change." *Packaging moves* concern making ideas more appealing and urgent, for example by linking them to (wrapping them up with) profits or market share. *Involvement moves* concern using relationships to build support for ideas, knowing who to involve, clearing ideas with a senior sponsor, and using committees to legitimize ideas. *Process moves* concern groundwork before selling the issues: how much background information do I need, when should I move and when should I delay, and should I make formal or informal approaches?

Lu et al. (2019) argue that issue-selling methods alone are not enough. They explored the use of *idea enactment*, which is "the illustration of abstract ideas in more tangible forms using demos, PowerPoint presentations, or other physical objects such as prototypes, animating boards, drawings, mockups, and simulations" (p. 580). The aim is to present ideas in a concrete way, showing how they will work in practice. The researchers conducted a study with 200 employees in a video game and animation company in China and a lab experiment with 300 students in an American university. To attract favorable management assessments for new ideas, the combination of issue-selling and idea enactment was most effective. Lu et al. (2019, p. 599) conclude, "By putting their ideas into tangible forms and making persuasive arguments on their behalf, employees can make their ideas more intelligible and noticeable to their supervisors, thereby increasing the odds that their ideas will be recognized and ultimately implemented." The ideas themselves, of course, have to be novel and useful.

Political behavior is not always damaging, and it can benefit individuals and the organization. The nature of change puts a premium on political skill for those who manage the process. The change manager who is not comfortable playing politics will find the role challenging. Some managers argue that playing politics is a time waster and a diversion from the real work. For the change manager, dealing with the politics *is* the real work, and although this can take time, an investment early in the change process often means that events move more quickly at later stages, because barriers have been addressed and support has been won. Skilled organization politicians experience less anxiety and stress. Some change managers even enjoy the political dimension of the role.

Killer Gestures and Trigger Images

If you have an idea to "sell" to top management, you will be advised to write a business case. At some point, however, you will probably have to present the idea in person, and the business case alone may not be enough. For example, Cornelissen (2019) asked experienced investors to watch a video that showed an entrepreneur presenting an idea for a new product. There were four versions of this presentation. One used colorful language to make the presentation more dramatic and interesting, one included lots of hand gestures, one used both rich language and gestures, and one used neither. Those who saw the third video, with the gestures, were more interested in investing. Nonverbal communication is important. But why were the hand gestures significant?

When the "entrepreneur"—an actor we'd hired—used his hands to explain the idea, investors were more interested in it than when he described it in straightforward technical terms or with metaphors, analogies, and anecdotes. Gesturing had a more direct impact than either kind of language did. The data suggests that the hand motions gave them a better sense of what the product would look like and how it would work. The unfamiliar idea was made more concrete. We think this kind of information is especially important in uncertain, high-stakes contexts like pitch meetings, where investors are looking for a variety of cues that will help them evaluate ideas' potential. When we surveyed the investors who'd watched the pitches, we found that people who'd seen the gesturing version were more likely

(Continued)

to say they had a good understanding of the new device. (Cornelissen, 2019, p.36).

Cornelissen et al. (2019) suggest that you find some "killer gestures" that illustrate the nature and benefits of your idea. They also advise practicing the use of body language: "We've seen lots of tech entrepreneurs coming right out of university who just stand behind the lectern and give very dry, technical pitches, without any hand movements at all. These don't stand out as much as pitches by skilled presenters who gesture frequently" (p. 37). Change managers with new ideas should take note.

Visual imagery is often used to capture people's attention. Barberá-Tomás et al. (2019) studied a not-for-profit organization that was encouraging people to reject plastics instead of recycling them. The image that they used to trigger this behavior change was the "Midway albatross"—an iconic photo of a dead chick with its carcass opened to show plastic items lodged in its gut. The image was designed to trigger feelings of rage, sadness, and guilt, and the implicit messages were "plastics are harmful," "you are responsible," and "end the throwaway culture." Choice of image, they point out, is critical, to avoid alienating potential supporters. The not-for-profit used a multimodal approach, combining that image with briefings and talks and the use of social media. This is an extreme example of the use of a shocking photograph. However, the researchers argue that this "emotion-symbolic" approach can be used in organizational change situations to influence responses and behaviors.

How can the change manager develop political skill? This requires a combination of self-awareness, careful observation and modeling of the behavior of politically skilled colleagues, and practice. This also involves finding and nurturing your inner Machiavelli. Playing politics involves taking informed risks, and one has to be prepared to make mistakes—and to learn from those. Phillip Braddy and Michael Campbell (2014, p. 15) developed the self-assessment in table 12.7, based on the political skills model introduced earlier. More checks on the right indicate that you are already effectively using political skill. More checks on the left indicate room for improvement.

If necessary, how will you develop your profile? To develop *social awareness*, for example, focus on understanding the language and body language, feelings, motives and agendas of others, and on how your proposals can help them to meet their goals. To develop *interpersonal influence*, ask more questions, listen actively, use self-disclosure, play down power differences, learn about others' professional and personal interests, and sell your ideas instead of imposing them. *Networking ability* can be developed by monitoring whom you approach for advice, giving them something in return, building a more diverse network through new relationships outside your team or department, and taking time to maintain those relationships. To strengthen *apparent sincerity*, follow through on your commitments, ensure that others see you as authentic, do not appear to be withholding information, be prepared to reveal your emotions and vulnerabilities, and "Don't rush trust; it takes a long time to build and only a short time to lose" (Braddy and Campbell, 2014, p. 19).

Machiavelli's Memorandum

So if, in the coming months, you find that your enemies call you Machiavellian, do not be disheartened. It means you are doing something right.

(*The Economist*, 2013)

TABLE 12.7

Political Skills Assessment

Which statements describe you? For each pair of statements, place a check mark by the statement that best describes your behavior.

Do I Behave Like This?	Or Do I Behave Like This?
Social Awareness	
Focus primarily on my own agenda and myself	Try to understand other people's motives
Struggle with knowing how to present myself	Consistently make positive impressions on others
Have difficulty making small talk or carrying on conversations	Naturally know the right things to say to influence others in most situations
Interpersonal Influence	
Find it difficult to establish rapport with others	Put people at ease
Struggle to communicate with others	Interact easily and effectively with colleagues
Have difficulty getting to know others	Have a knack for getting others to like me
Networking	
Stay to myself and spend virtually all my time at work completing job-related tasks	Deliberately spend time networking with others at work
Primarily spend time with a close group of coworkers and friends with whom I feel comfortable	Invest in building relationships with diverse and influential people
Almost exclusively rely on formal processes for securing resources and getting things done	Often leverage my networks and relationships to secure valuable resources and get things done
Sincerity	
Only show interest in others when I need something from them	Take time to regularly show genuine interest in people at work
Come across as being manipulative because I say and do what is needed to get what I want	Act sincerely around others
Have a tendency to be very secretive and to keep people on a strict "need to know" basis	Communicate openly and transparently with others

Source: Braddy and Campbell (2014).

LO 12.5 Developing Change Management Expertise

We explored the development of political skill in the previous section. Finally, we will consider, using a six-step approach, the development of this and other change management capabilities.

1. Career Moves

First, is this the right role for you at this point in your career? You know what being a change manager involves, and you understand the capabilities that are required to be effective. But do you still want the job? This is not a job for everyone, because it can be

TABLE 12.8
Desirable and Undesirable Characteristics of the Change Manager

Desirable	Undesirable
Believes that this is the right thing to do	Sees this job as a stepping stone in career
Patient, persistent	Impatient, lacking persistence
Honest, trustworthy, reliable	Devious, unreliable, untrustworthy
Positive and enthusiastic	Unable to convey enthusiasm
Confident but not arrogant	Has high need for praise and recognition
Good observer and listener	Poor listener, insensitive to others' feelings
Flexible and resourceful	Inflexible, arrogant, cold, unapproachable
Not easily intimidated	Moral putty, changes view to fit context
Good sense of humor	Status-conscious
Willing to accept risks and challenges	Risk averse, protective of image and career
Recognizes and deals with office politics	Political and manipulative
Prefers an inclusive cooperative style	Prefers a secretive, adversarial style

demanding, tiring, and risky, as well as satisfying. David Hutton (1994) describes the desirable and undesirable characteristics of change managers (see table 12.8). The question is: Which of these profiles fits you? If you have more of the undesirable characteristics, then it may be advisable to consider other career choices or to change your behavior where appropriate. Become more persistent and enthusiastic, more flexible, and approachable. Become less impatient, less arrogant, less risk averse, and less adversarial.

2. Repositioning

Second, refer back to Figure 1.1 "Assessing Depth of Change" in chapter 1. Where does your past and present change management experience sit in that framework? Mostly shallow, mainly deep, or a mix? Although all experience can be useful, deep change is more challenging and risky, because there is a higher chance that things could go wrong. However, deep change offers much greater potential for personal development and also increases the visibility and reputation of the change managers responsible, as long as things go well. Interview panels and promotion boards are likely to be more impressed by involvement in successful deep change than in shallow change. Given this assessment and your recent and current roles, do you need to consider "repositioning" yourself with regard to current and forthcoming change initiatives in your organization? Do you need to become associated more closely with the deeper, high-impact changes, as long as you are confident that these are likely to succeed? Where possible, of course, avoid association with initiatives that are likely to fail.

3. The Politics

Third, are you comfortable with the political dimension of change management? As we have seen, some managers see this as unethical and time-wasting. However, this is an aspect of the change management role from which it is difficult to escape, and political skill is a prerequisite for success in most, if not all, general management and leadership positions. Given the contested nature of much organizational change, political skill is at a premium for the change manager. Political skill can be developed, as we explored in the previous section, but if you are not comfortable with these behaviors, these "games," then developing and using political skill will be difficult.

4. Strengths

Fourth, refer back to table 12.3 "The CMI Change Manager Master Level—Competency Model," and add intimidation and political skills to the list of competencies. Most of these competencies apply to most general management positions. As an experienced manager, you will probably find that you are already well equipped to handle the challenges of change, if you have not already done so. However, it may still be useful to confirm what skills, knowledge, and other attributes you already possess that are relevant to a change management role. The question here is: How do you plan to maintain and to build on those capabilities and strengths? Will this involve further training and development, careful "repositioning" with regard to future experience (step 2 above), or internal and external job moves to consolidate, diversify, and improve those existing skills?

5. Gaps

Fifth, looking again at table 12.3 and the other competencies identified in this chapter, where do you see personal gaps? Realistically, is it going to be possible for you to fill these gaps? Remember that this may not be necessary, as other colleagues are likely to have different and overlapping skill sets. Decide which areas of competence you feel that you must develop as a matter of priority, which areas are less important for you, and which you feel would be acceptable to avoid.

6. Action

Finally, prepare a personal action plan that covers these three issues:

1. *Building strengths*. How will I maintain and build on the strengths that I currently have as a change manager?
2. *Allowable weaknesses*. Which of my weaknesses will I not try to develop, as this would be unnecessary, time consuming, or particularly difficult for some reason?
3. *Filling gaps*. Which skills, knowledge, and attributes do I need to strengthen as a matter of urgency? What are my options for building those capabilities: taking on further change responsibilities, partnering with others in change management teams, secondments, networking, mentoring, specialist training and development, guided reading, other?

The actions required to develop change management capabilities are not necessarily costly. Most of the possibilities are free, because they are experience based, but they do involve a significant time commitment. In terms of personal and career development, however, that investment can generate returns in the form of personal skills development and career progression.

EXERCISE 12.1

Networking— How Good Are You?

LO 12.3

Networking is a core change manager capability. Use the following diagnostic to assess your own networking skills and to determine what action you may need to take to improve. Tick whether you agree, or disagree, with each of the following statements.

		Disagree	Agree
1	I enjoy finding out what other people do.	❏	❏
2	I feel embarrassed asking people for favors.	❏	❏
3	I send Christmas cards to ex-colleagues and business contacts.	❏	❏
4	I usually call or email former colleagues and contacts when I am struggling with a particularly difficult problem.	❏	❏
5	I do not like to waste time going to conferences.	❏	❏
6	I cannot remember the names and family details of all my team members.	❏	❏
7	I cut out articles from the press that I think might interest colleagues.	❏	❏
8	I prefer to write emails or letters to picking up the phone.	❏	❏
9	I am quick to return phone calls.	❏	❏
10	I pursue opportunities to work on committees, task forces, and projects.	❏	❏
11	I like to solve problems on my own.	❏	❏
12	I am happy to ask people for their business cards.	❏	❏
13	I go to social events with people outside my team.	❏	❏
14	I have lost touch with my ex-bosses.	❏	❏
15	I use the Internet to make contact with people in my field.	❏	❏
16	I do not mix work and social life.	❏	❏

Networking: How Did You Score?

Give yourself one point each if you *agreed* with these items, scoring up to 9:

1	3	4	7	9	10	12	13	15

Give yourself one point each if you *disagreed* with these items, scoring up to 7:

2	5	6	8	11	14	16

Add these two scores to produce your final total score out of 16:

❏

Score	Implications
0 to 5	You do not appear to do much networking, and you may need to be careful that you are not overlooked for promotion. What can you do to lift your profile, to make yourself more visible?
6 to 9	You network a little, but you could do more to develop relationships that would improve your career opportunities. Where are the gaps in your networking efforts, and how can you fill them?
10 to 13	You are a competent networker, but you could improve. What areas are you not covering? Do you need to do more external networking?
14 to 16	It looks like you are a natural networker. However, you may need to be careful not to overplay this aspect of your profile building, as there is a danger that this can annoy some people.

Source: Based on Yeung, R. 2003. *The ultimate career success workbook*. London: Kogan Page.

EXERCISE 12.2

How Resilient Are You?

LO 12.2

Rate your agreement with each of these 25 statements, and put your score in the right-hand column.

		Disagree					Agree		Score
1	When I make plans, I follow through with them.	1	2	3	4	5	6	7	
2	I usually manage one way or another.	1	2	3	4	5	6	7	
3	I am able to depend on myself more than anyone else.	1	2	3	4	5	6	7	
4	Keeping interested in things is important to me.	1	2	3	4	5	6	7	
5	I can be on my own if I have to.	1	2	3	4	5	6	7	
6	I feel proud that I have accomplished things in my life.	1	2	3	4	5	6	7	
7	I usually take things in my stride.	1	2	3	4	5	6	7	
8	I am friends with myself.	1	2	3	4	5	6	7	
9	I feel that I can handle many things at a time.	1	2	3	4	5	6	7	
10	I am determined.	1	2	3	4	5	6	7	
11	I seldom wonder what the point of it all is.	1	2	3	4	5	6	7	

(Continued)

		Disagree						Agree	Score
12	I take things one day at a time.	1	2	3	4	5	6	7	
13	I can get through difficult times because I've experienced difficulty before.	1	2	3	4	5	6	7	
14	I have self-discipline.	1	2	3	4	5	6	7	
15	I keep interested in things.	1	2	3	4	5	6	7	
16	I can usually find something to laugh about.	1	2	3	4	5	6	7	
17	My belief in myself gets me through hard times.	1	2	3	4	5	6	7	
18	In an emergency, I'm someone people generally can rely on.	1	2	3	4	5	6	7	
19	I can usually look at a situation in a number of ways.	1	2	3	4	5	6	7	
20	Sometimes I make myself do things whether I want to or not.	1	2	3	4	5	6	7	
21	My life has meaning.	1	2	3	4	5	6	7	
22	I do not dwell on things that I can't do anything about.	1	2	3	4	5	6	7	
23	When I'm in a difficult situation, I can usually find my way out of it.	1	2	3	4	5	6	7	
24	I have enough energy to do what I have to do.	1	2	3	4	5	6	7	
25	It's okay if there are people who don't like me.	1	2	3	4	5	6	7	

Your Total:

Resilience Scoring

Add the scores that you have given to each of the 25 items. Your resilience score total will lie between 25 and 175. Higher scores reflect higher resilience.

The scores of adults on this test normally lie between 90 and 175, with a mean of 140. A resilience score of 150 or above is considered to be high.

- If you have a low resilience score, say below 140, what steps do you think you could take to improve your resilience?
- How would you advise a colleague with a low resilience score?

Source: This diagnostic is based on Wagnild, G. M., and Young, H. M. 1993. Development and psychometric evaluation of the resilience scale. *Journal of Nursing Measurement* 1(2):165–78.

EXERCISE 12.3

How Political Is Your Organization?

LO 12.4

To what extent do the following statements describe your organization? Tick the appropriate box on the right.

		Disagree	Maybe	Agree
1	Who you know around here matters a lot more than what you know.	❑	❑	❑
2	The most competent people in the business don't always get promoted.	❑	❑	❑
3	Decisions are often taken outside formal meetings or behind closed doors.	❑	❑	❑
4	Resource allocations between departments are a source of argument and conflict.	❑	❑	❑
5	You have to be prepared to socialize to build effective networks and alliances.	❑	❑	❑
6	Information is jealously guarded and not shared openly between groups and departments.	❑	❑	❑
7	People suspect that there are "hidden agendas" behind management decisions.	❑	❑	❑
8	Some individuals always seem to be better informed than everyone else.	❑	❑	❑
9	Individuals are having their reputations damaged by "whispers in the corridors."	❑	❑	❑
10	Those who take the credit are not always those who made the biggest contribution.	❑	❑	❑
11	You have to know how to "play by the rules"— breaking and bending them—to get things done.	❑	❑	❑
12	When mistakes are made, people are quick to start putting the blame on others.	❑	❑	❑
13	Most people recognize that you're not going very far here unless you have the support of the key players.	❑	❑	❑
14	Being open and honest all the time can seriously damage your career.	❑	❑	❑
15	People will criticize others' ideas merely to help win support for their own proposals.	❑	❑	❑

Scoring

Give yourself:

- 1 point for each item where you ticked "disagree."
- 3 points for each item where you ticked "maybe."
- 5 points for each item where you ticked "agree."

Total

(Continued)

This will give you a score between 15 and 75.

The politics-free zone. If you score around 25 or lower, we are all coming to work with you. Your organization has a relatively low level of political behavior. Either that, or you are just not aware of the degree of politics going on behind your back. In such a *politics-free zone*, are you concerned that:

- There is not enough discussion and debate before key decisions are taken?
- There is not enough constructive conflict and debate to stimulate creativity?

The free-fire zone. If you score around 65 or above. There is a high level of political behavior in your organization. Either that, or you are reading too much into routine decisions and actions. In such a *free fire zone*, are you concerned that:

- Too much time and energy is going into the politics game, and not enough into strategic thinking and performance improvement?
- The discussions and debates are motivated more by personal goals and are less related to the organization's strategies and goals?

The average behavior zone. If you score between 30 and 60, your organization is typical, middle-of-the-road in terms of the degree of political behavior that you can expect to witness. In such an *average behavior zone*, are you concerned that:

- There is still too much political behavior to stimulate the quality of discussion and debate around key issues and decisions?

On the basis of your scoring, what advice applies to you and to other change managers with regard to dealing with the politics in your organization?

Source: Buchanan and Badham (2020).

Additional Reading

Battilana, J., and Casciaro, T. 2013. The network secrets of great change managers. *Harvard Business Review* 91(7/8):62–68. Describes the nature and functions of two different kinds of networks—cohesive and divergent. The power and influence of change managers depends not on formal title or seniority but on position in the organization's informal networks. Offers practical advice to change managers on developing and leveraging these networks effectively.

Buchanan, D. A., and Badham, R. 2020. *Power, politics, and organizational change: Winning the turf game.* 3rd ed. London: Sage Publications. Comprehensive discussion of the nature, tactics, and ethics of organizational politics. Describes the constructive use of political tactics to maintain personal reputation and further organizational objectives. Offers guidance on the use of political behavior and advice on the development of political skill or expertise.

Dutton, J. E., Ashford, S. J., O'Neill, R. M., and Lawrence, K. A. 2001. Moves that matter: Issue selling and organizational change. *Academy of Management Journal*

44(4):716–36. Describes the seminal research work that developed the "issue-selling" tactics described in this chapter–tactics for "successfully shaping change from below by directing the attention of top management" (p. 716).

Pfeffer, J. 2010. Power play. *Harvard Business Review* 88(7/8):84–92. Argues that power and influence are prerequisites for management success, and offers advice on leveraging power. Concludes:

> So, welcome to the real world. It may not be the world we want, but it's the world we have. You won't get far, and neither will your strategic plans, if you can't build and use power. Some of the people competing for advancement or standing in the way of your organization's agenda will bend the rules of fair play or ignore them entirely. Don't bother complaining about this or wishing things were different. Part of your job is to know how to prevail in the political battles you will face. (p. 92)

Roundup

Reflections for the Practicing Change Manager

- How would you describe your role as a change manager using the terms introduced in this chapter: champion, soul of fire, positive deviant, disruptive innovator, chief transformation officer? How is this reflected in your behavior? Would you become more or less effective as a change manager if you "dropped below the radar"?

- How effectively do you use your informal networks to drive change in your organization? How could you develop and make better use of those networks?

- Do you feel that you have the resilience required to operate effectively as a change manager? If necessary, what steps can you take to maintain and strengthen your resilience?

- As a practicing manager, you probably already have most of the required capabilities of the change manager. But how do you feel about using intimidation to motivate others to change? Are there circumstances when this would be appropriate in your organization?

- Are you politically skilled? Do you use political skills to advance your change agenda? What approaches and tactics do you use to "sell" ideas to colleagues and top management? Who are the other "politicians" in your organization? Are you able to manage their support and block their attempts to interfere with your change agenda?

Here is a short summary of the key points that we would like you to take from this chapter, in relation to each of the learning outcomes:

LO 12.1   * *Recognize the nature and significance of the contributions of change managers at all levels of an organization, regardless of their formal roles or responsibilities.*
Change managers can be found at all levels of an organization. Given the pace and scale of change in most organizations, the shared leadership of change has become a necessity. Contrary to the popular stereotype, middle managers are often among the most important change managers in an organization. The power and influence of many

change managers come not from a formal, senior title but from their position in the organization's informal networks. Those with more informal connections can be more influential, and the organization chart is not a good guide to identifying them. The terminology that commentators have used to describe this variety of change managers offers insights into the nature of the role and of those who take on these responsibilities: champions, evangelists, positive deviants, souls of fire, tempered radicals, stealth innovators, ideas practitioners, and disruptive innovators. Those innovators and souls of fire are highly motivated and assertive, but they are also nonconformists and do not follow instructions, so they can be difficult to manage.

LO 12.2   *   *Appreciate the challenges and rewards that accompany performing a change management role.*
The role of the change manager is often a demanding one: challenging, lonely, stressful, fast-paced, risky. Dealing simultaneously with senior management expectations and different modes of resistance from those who are going to be affected can make the role particularly pressured. However, the opportunities for personal development and career progression can be significant, and the role is especially satisfying and rewarding when the change process is successful. Given the pressures, a high degree of resilience is often required. Resilience can be developed, and Exercise 12.2 offers a personal diagnostic.

LO 12.3   *   *Identify the competencies in terms of the skills, knowledge, and other attributes that are ideally required to be an effective change manager.*
We considered the competency framework designed by the Change Management Institute. Their model identifies 12 competency headings: facilitation, strategic change, judgment, influencing, coaching, project management, interpersonal and corporate communications, self-management, facilitation, professional development, and learning and development. Although this appears to be a daunting specification, most of those capabilities are relevant to most general management positions. We also discussed "intimidation" as a change management style. Many managers feel uncomfortable with this approach, but it can be appropriate in certain circumstances, particularly when an organization has become rigid, apathetic, stagnant, and change-resistant. We also discussed a small number of intimidation tactics: confrontation; the "calculated loss of temper"; maintaining an air of mystery; and "informational intimidation," which involves the appearance of having mastered the facts.

LO 12.4   *   *Understand the significance of political skill to the role and effectiveness of change managers.*
Organizations are political systems, and change is a politicized process. Politics is often seen in negative terms, as damaging and unnecessary. However, effective leaders and change managers need political skill to exert influence over others. Change managers must be aware of the agendas and perceptions of other stakeholders and be able to engage them in consultation where their views are valuable, and also when necessary to counter attempts to subvert or resist change with political tactics. We identified several types of political tactics: image building, information games, structure games, scapegoating, alliances, networking, intermediation, compromise, rule games, positioning, issue-selling, and dirty tricks. One model of political skill identifies four key dimensions: social astuteness, interpersonal influence, networking ability, and apparent sincerity. We offered a self-assessment covering those four skill dimensions and suggested how to develop political skill.

LO 12.5 * *Develop an action plan for improving your own change management capabilities.*

We set out a six-step approach to personal development. First, do you still want this job, knowing how challenging and stressful it is, and what kinds of attributes contribute to success? Second, do you need to consider your personal positioning with regard to the depth of the change initiatives for which you are responsible or with which you are associated? Deeper changes can be more risky, but they offer greater opportunities for personal development. Third, make sure that you are comfortable with the political dimension of the role and follow the guidelines for developing political skill—if you feel this is relevant with regard to your current and future change management roles. Fourth, identify your strengths as a change manager and determine how to maintain those capabilities. Fifth, identify gaps in your capability profile and decide whether or not it is possible and desirable to address those—or to delegate those aspects of your change management role to other team members. Finally, develop a practical action plan to build on your strengths, recognize and manage allowable weaknesses, and address the gaps in your profile with further development.

References

Ashford, S. J., and Detert, J. 2015. Get the boss to buy in. *Harvard Business Review* 93(1/2):72–79.

Barberá-Tomás, D., Castelló, I., de Bakker, F. G. A., and Zietsma, C. 2019. Energizing through visuals: How social entrepreneurs use emotion-symbolic work for social change. *Academy of Management Journal* 62(6):1789–1817.

Bass, B. M., and Avolio, B. J. 1994. *Improving organizational effectiveness through transformational leadership*. Thousand Oaks, CA: Sage Publications.

Battilana, J., and Casciaro, T. 2013. The network secrets of great change agents. *Harvard Business Review* 91(7/8):62–68.

Beeson, J. 2009. Why you didn't get that promotion: Decoding the unwritten rules of corporate advancement. *Harvard Business Review* 87(6):101–105.

Bergh, C. 2018. The CEO of Levi Strauss on leading an iconic brand back to growth. *Fortune* 96(4):33–39.

Bower, J. L. 1970. *Managing the resource allocation process*. Boston, MA: Graduate School of Business Administration, Harvard University.

Braddy, P., and Campbell, M. 2014. *Using political skill to maximize and leverage work relationships*. Greensboro, NC: Center for Creative Leadership.

Brouer, R. L., Ferris, G. R., Hochwarter, W. A., Laird, M. D., and Gilmore, D. C. 2006. The strain-related reactions to perceptions of organizational politics as a workplace stressor: Political skill as a neutralizer. In *Handbook of organizational politics*, ed. E. Vigoa and A. Drory (187–206). Thousand Oaks, CA: Sage Publications.

Buchanan, D. A. 2003. Demands, instabilities, manipulations, careers: The lived experience of driving change. *Human Relations* 56(6):663–84.

Buchanan, D. A., and Badham, R. 2020. *Power, politics, and organizational change: Winning the turf game.* 3rd ed. London: Sage Publications.

Burns, J. M. 1978. *Leadership.* New York: Harper & Row.

Cabane, O. F. 2013. *The charisma myth: Master the art of personal magnetism.* London: Portfolio Penguin.

Change Management Institute. 2017. *CMI accreditation handbook.* Sydney: Change Management Institute.

Chartered Institute of Personnel and Development. 2011. *Developing resilience: An evidence-based guide for practitioners.* London: CIPD.

Cornelissen, J. 2019. When you pitch an idea, gestures matter more than words. *Harvard Business Review* 97(3):36-37.

Davenport, T. H., Prusak, L., and Wilson, H. J. 2003. Who's bringing you hot ideas and how are you responding? *Harvard Business Review* 81(2):58-64.

De Smet, A., Lavoie, J., and Hioe, E. S. 2012. Developing better change leaders. *McKinsey Quarterly* (April):1-6.

Duan, L., Sheeren, E., and Weiss, L. 2014. Tapping the power of hidden influencers. *McKinsey Quarterly* (March):1-4.

Dutton, J. E., Ashford, S. J., O'Neill, R. M., and Lawrence, K. A. 2001. Moves that matter: Issue selling and organizational change. *Academy of Management Journal* 44(4):716-36.

Ferris, G. R., Perrewé, P. L., Anthony, W. P., and Gilmore, D. C. 2000. Political skill at work. *Organizational Dynamics* 28(4):25-37.

Ferris, G. R., Davidson, S. L., and Perrewé, P. L. 2005a. *Political skill at work: Impact on work effectiveness.* Mountain View, CA: Davies-Black Publishing.

Ferris, G. R., Treadway, D. C., Kolodinsky, R. W., Hochwarter, W. A., Kacmar, C. J., Douglas, C., and Frink, D. D. 2005b. Development and validation of the Political Skill Inventory. *Journal of Management* 31(1):126-52.

Ferris, G. R., Treadway, D. C., Perrewé, P. L., Brouer, R. L., Douglas, C., and Lux, S. 2007. Political skill in organizations. *Journal of Management* 33(3):290-320.

Furnham, A. 2015. Seven steps to the stars: How to fly up the career ladder. *The Sunday Times Appointments Section* (January 18):2.

Gorter, O., Hudson, R., and Scott, J. 2016. *The role of the chief transformation officer.* New York and London: McKinsey & Company.

Heyden, M. L. M., Fourné, S. P. L., Koene, B. A. S., Werkman, R., and Ansari, S. 2017. Rethinking "top-down" and "bottom-up" roles of top and middle managers in organizational change: Implications for employee support. *Journal of Management Studies* 54(7):961-85.

Hope, O. 2010. The politics of middle management sensemaking and sensegiving. *Journal of Change Management* 10(2):195–215.

Hutton, D. W. 1994. *The change agent's handbook: A survival guide for quality improvement champions*. Milwaukee, WI: ASQC Quality Press.

Jenkins, A. 2018. Policy shift. *Fortune* 178(6):124–27.

Kanter, R. M. 1982. The middle manager as innovator. *Harvard Business Review* 60(4):95–105.

Kerr, D. 2018. Uber's U-turn: How the new CEO is cleaning house after scandals and lawsuits. *CNET*, April 27, https://www.cnet.com/news/ubers-u-turn-how-ceo-dara-khosrow-shahi-is-cleaning-up-after-scandals-and-lawsuits.

Khurana, R. 2002. The curse of the superstar CEO. *Harvard Business Review* 80(9):60–66.

Kim, W. C., and Mauborgne, R. 2003. Tipping point leadership. *Harvard Business Review* 81(4):60–69.

Kramer, R. M. 2006. The great intimidators. *Harvard Business Review* 84(2):88–96.

Kuratko, D. F., and Goldsby, M. G. 2004. Corporate entrepreneurs or rogue middle managers?: A framework for ethical corporate entrepreneurship. *Journal of Business Ethics* 55(1):13–30.

Lewis, G. 2015. Women over 55 best suited to lead transformational change, finds PwC. *People Management*, May 18, http://www.thewayahead.org.uk/women-over-55-best-suited-to-lead-transformational-change-finds-pwc (accessed January 13, 2020).

Lu, S., Bartol, K. M., Venkataramani, V., Zheng, X., and Liu, X. 2019. Pitching novel ideas to the boss: The interactive effects of employees' idea enactment and influence tactics on creativity assessment and implementation. *Academy of Management Journal* 62(2):579–606.

Manzie, S., and Hartley, J. 2013. *Dancing on ice: Leadership with political astuteness by senior public servants in the UK*. Milton Keynes: The Open University Business School.

McAllister, C. P., Ellen, B. P., Perrewe, P. L., Ferris, G. R., and Hirsch, D. J. 2015. Checkmate: Using political skill to recognize and capitalize on opportunities in the "game" of organizational life. *Business Horizons* 58(1):25–34.

McCreary, L. 2010. Kaiser Permanente's innovation on the front lines. *Harvard Business Review* 88(9):92–97.

McDermott, A. M., Fitzgerald, L., and Buchanan, D. A. 2013. Beyond acceptance and resistance: Entrepreneurial change agency responses in policy implementation. *British Journal of Management* 24(S1):93–225.

Maslyn, J. M., Farmer, S. M., and Bettenhausen, K. L. 2017. When organizational politics matters: The effects of the perceived frequency and distance of experienced politics. *Human Relations* 70(12):1486–513.

Mintzberg, H. 1983. *Power in and around organizations*. Englewood Cliffs, NJ: Prentice Hall.

Nielsen, K., and Daniels, K. 2016. The relationship between transformational leadership and follower sickness absence: The role of presenteeism. *Work & Stress* 30(2):193–208.

Stjernberg, T., and Philips, A. 1993. Organizational innovations in a long-term perspective: Legitimacy and souls-of-fire as critical factors of change and viability. *Human Relations* 46(10):1193–221.

The Economist. 2013. Machiavelli's memorandum. (September 28):53.

Tichy, N. M., and Devanna, M. A. 1986. *The transformational leader.* New York: John Wiley.

Vergauwe, J., Wille, B., Hofmans, J., Kaiser, R. B., and De Fruyt, F. 2018. The double-edged sword of leader charisma: Understanding the curvilinear relationship between charismatic personality and leader effectiveness. *Journal of Personality and Social Psychology* 114(1):110–30.

Wagnild, G. M., and Young, H. M. 1993. Development and psychometric evaluation of the resilience scale. *Journal of Nursing Measurement* 1(2):165–78.

Wong, J. C. 2017. Uber's "hustle-oriented" culture becomes a black mark on employees' resumes. *The Guardian*, March 7. https://www.theguardian.com/technology/2017/mar/07/uber-work-culture-travis-kalanick-susan-fowler-controversy.

Wylie, N., and Sturdy, A. 2018. Structuring collective change agency internally: Transformers, enforcers, specialists and independents. *Employee Relations 40*(2):313–28.

Yeung, R. 2003. *The ultimate career success workbook.* London: Kogan Page.

Source of opening quote from Lisa Cash Hanson, blogger and digital marketer https://fairygodboss.com/articles/inspiring-leadership-quotes

Source of the chapter opening quote: Inspiring Leadership Quotes, *Fairy Good Boss,* https://fairygodboss.com/articles/inspiring-leadership-quotes.

Chapter opening silhouette credit: FunKey Factory/Shutterstock

Name Index

A

Abbasi, K., 56, 58
Aghina, W., 126, 129, 130, 135
Ahlbäck, K., 126, 128, 135
Ahlberg, J., 368, 383
Alban, B. T., 289, 293, 311, 314
Allen-Greil, D., 241, 245
Aller-Stead, G., 208
Alsever, J., 72, 98
Ambler, G., 185, 206
Amichai-Hamburger, Y., 219, 246
Anderson, L. A., 47, 58
Anderson D., 47, 58
Andriopoulos, C., 4, 27, 38, 59, 321, 333, 334, 336, 348, 351
Angwin, D., 118, 120, 136
Ansari, S., 264, 278, 394, 422
Anthony, W. P., 405 422
Appelbaum, S. H., 329, 351
Armenakis, A. A., 61, 137, 242, 247
Ashford, S. J., 394, 395, 418, 421, 422
Ashkenas, R., 183, 189, 190, 206
Ates, N. Y., 190, 207
Auster, E. R., 184, 207
Avolio, B. J., 199, 207, 389, 421
Axelrod, D., 289, 292, 313
Axelrod, R. H., 292, 293, 313

B

Baburoglu, O. N., 290, 313
Baczor, L., 77, 102, 216, 245
Badham, R. J., 13, 26, 65, 98, 299, 313, 388, 405, 407, 418, 422
Bailey, M. R., 228, 229, 246
Baker, L. T., 335, 352
Bakker, F. G. A., 410, 421
Ball, J., 73, 98
Balogun, J., 37, 42, 58, 264, 277, 302, 304, 305, 313, 317, 320, 336, 341, 342, 348, 351
Barberá-Tomás, D., 410, 421
Barge, J. K., 42, 58

Barnard, S., 82, 100
Barrett, M., 227, 228, 246, 352
Barsoux, J. L., 25, 26
Bartol, K. M., 409, 423
Bartunek, J. M., 228, 246, 299, 313
Bartunek, K. M., 305, 313
Basford, T., 41, 58
Bass, A., 83, 98
Bass, B. M., 389, 421
Battilana, J., 56, 58, 274, 398, 418, 421
Bean, C. J., 302, 313
Beaudan, E., 37, 58
Beaumont, R., 304, 315
Beck, T. E., 335, 352
Beckhard, R., 283, 314
Beer, M., 282, 287, 299, 314, 362, 363, 365, 383
Beeson, J., 146, 172, 401, 421
Belgard, W. P., 184, 189, 207
Bell, C. H., 284, 285, 286, 315
Bennis, W. G., 33, 58
Bettenhausen, K. L., 405, 423
Bevere, L., 73, 98
Biacabe, B. T., 87, 102
Binzagr, G. F., 289, 290, 316
Bissell-Linsk, J., 85, 98
Blake, R., 288, 314
Blount, S., 176, 178, 179, 207
Boal, K. B., 184, 207
Boehm, S., 77, 101, 251, 278
Boje, D. M., 5, 28, 42, 62
Bolman, L. G., 31, 59, 111, 135, 304, 314
Bond, S., 71, 98
Bormann, U., 87, 102
Bosak, J., 164, 172
Bosché, G., 182, 207
Bossert, O., 129, 135
Bower, J. L., 394, 421
Boyett, I., 264, 277
Braddy, P., 408, 410, 411, 421
Brazeal, D. V., 39, 62
Brewis, J., 218, 246
Bridgman, T., 285, 314, 327, 351

Brigham, S., 291, 316
Brosseau, D., 37, 59, 127, 129, 135
Brouer, R. L., 406, 421, 422
Brown, B., 162, 172
Brown, J., 76, 94, 98, 290, 314
Brown, K. G., 285, 314, 327, 351
Bruch, H., 77, 101, 251, 259, 277, 278
Buchanan, D., 14, 26
Buchanan, D. A., 13, 27, 41, 59, 90,98, 256, 264, 278, 357, 383, 400, 421, 388, 405, 407, 418, 422, 395, 423
Buche, I., 179, 180, 203,208
Bucy, M., 12, 27, 34, 35,59, 320, 332, 351
Bughin, J., 69, 70, 86, 87, 101, 162, 172
Bulkeley, W. M., 224, 245
Bunker, B. B., 289, 293, 314
Burke, W. W., 107, 136, 284, 286, 287, 288, 314, 315
Burnes, B., 34, 40, 59, 282, 285, 287, 289, 314, 327, 351
Burns, J. M., 389, 422
Burns, T., 126, 136
Bushe, G. R., 297, 311, 314

C

Cabane, O. F., 389, 422
Calnan, M., 79, 98
Cameron, K. S., 61, 295, 296, 297, 311, 312, 314, 317
Campbell, M., 408, 410, 411, 421
Carlile, P. R., 25, 27
Carlson, B., 288, 314
Carson, K., 130, 136
Carter, W. R., 299, 313
Carton, A. M., 185, 186, 207
Casamayou, M. H., 88, 89,101, 380
Casciaro, T., 56, 58, 274, 398, 418, 421
Castelló, I., 410, 421
Caza, A., 295, 296, 314

Chand, M., 75, 99
Chatman, J., 56, 59
Checinski, M., 42, 59
Cheung-Judge, M.-Y., 33, 40, 59
Christensen, C. M., 17, 25, 27,
   145, 149, 150, 151, 172, 173,
   270, 277
Christensen, L. T., 212, 245
Chui, M., 162, 172
Ciuk, S., 35, 60, 252, 278
Clampitt, P. G., 230, 245
Clark, J. R., 181, 209
Clarke, R., 79, 99
Clausen, B., 373, 383
Clayton, S., 238, 245
Coch, L., 338, 351
Cocieru, O. C., 256, 277
Cody, S., 289, 315
Coghlan, D., 144, 172
Cohen, W. M., 122, 136
Collins, J. C., 196, 200, 201, 207
Collins, L., 126, 129, 135
Colvin, G., 152, 172
Conway, E., 256, 264, 277, 278
Cook, B., 40, 59
Cooke, B., 282, 287, 289, 314
Coombs, A., 262, 277
Coombs, C., 82, 100
Cooper, B. K., 164, 173
Cooperrider, D. L., 294, 295,
   311, 314
Cornelissen, J., 212, 245, 409,
   410, 422
Coyle-Shapiro, J. A-M.,
   256, 277
Cramer, D., 264, 277
Creasey, T. J., 324, 351
Cuganesan, S., 304, 315
Cummings, S., 285, 314, 327, 351
Cummings, T. G., 284, 285, 286,
   311, 315
Cunliffe, A. L., 31, 60, 154, 172
Currie, G., 264, 277, 300, 316
Cushman, T., 230, 245

D

Daft, R. L., 235, 236, 239, 246
Daly, J. P., 229, 230, 245

Daneshkhu, S., 75, 99
Daniel, E., 17, 28, 146, 174
Daniels, K., 391, 424
Danielson, J., 162, 172
Dannemiller, K. D., 289, 293, 315
Davenport, T. H., 82, 99, 398, 422
Davidson, H., 189, 207
Davidson, S. L., 406, 422
Dawson, J., 164, 172
Dawson, P., 4, 27, 38, 41, 59, 321,
   333, 334, 336, 348, 351
Deal, T. E., 31, 59, 111, 135,
   304, 314
de Barros Teixeira, J. A., 372, 383
de Chalendar, A., 74, 80, 86, 100,
   250, 251, 274, 277
De Cremer, D., 12, 28, 325, 326, 352
Deetz, S. A., 189, 207
De Fruyt, F., 389, 424
DeKoch, R. J., 230, 245
Dellot, B., 82, 85, 99
DeMarie, S. M., 256, 279
Denis, J. L., 27
Derousseau, R., 71, 99
De Smet, A., 130, 135, 136,
   399, 422
Dess, G. G., 117, 118, 137
Detert, J., 394, 395, 421
Detert, J. R., 30, 31, 33, 60
Devane, T., 289, 315
Devanna, M. A., 389, 424
Dhanaraj, C., 179, 180,203, 208
Dickson, T., 320, 332, 351
Dickson, W. J., 33, 61
Dillon, R., 42, 59
Di Maggio, P. J., 59
DiTomaso, N., 154, 173
Do, B., 305, 313
Dobosz-Bourne, D., 227, 246
Douglas, C., 406, 407, 422
Downey, D., 110, 111, 136
Dromey, J., 163, 172
Drori, I., 198, 208
Duan, L., 399, 422
Duke, S., 48, 59
Dunford, R., 32, 61, 304, 315
Dunphy, D., 37, 61, 231, 247, 338,
   340, 352
Dutton, J. E., 408, 418, 422
Dyer, J., 151, 173

E

Ebrahim, S., 37, 59, 127, 129, 135
Eccles, T., 121, 136
Edgecliffe-Johnson, A., 71, 99
Edmondson, A., 89, 99, 345, 346,
   359, 360, 361, 380, 383
Edwards, S., 241, 245
Eisenstat, R. A., 362, 365, 383
Ellen, B. P., 406, 408, 423
Emery, F. E., 127, 136
Emery, M., 289, 315
Ensher, E. A., 288, 315
Erlandson, E., 218, 247
Ewing, J., 65, 99

F

Fagan, T., 12, 27, 34, 35, 59, 332, 351
Fagenson-Eland, E., 288, 315
Fahrbach, C., 126, 128, 135
Falkenberg, J., 260, 279
Farmer, S. M., 405, 423
Fayol, H., 33, 59
Ferris, G. R., 405, 406, 407, 408, 421,
   422, 423
Fineman, S., 295, 296, 315
Finley, M., 197, 209
Finn, R., 300, 316
Fisher, A. B., 363, 364, 383
Fitzgerald, L., 256, 264, 278, 357,
   369, 380, 395, 423
Fletcher, S., 81, 99
Flood, P., 164, 172
Flood, P. C., 256, 264, 278
Floyd, S. W., 263, 280
Flynn, J., 217, 218, 246
Foote, D., 250, 277
Ford, J. D., 198, 207, 223, 224, 246,
   252, 253, 277
Ford, L. W., 223, 224, 246, 252,
   253, 277
Fourné, S. P. L., 264, 278, 394, 422
Fox, S., 219, 220, 246
Fragkos, K. C., 234, 247
Francis, D., 131, 137
Francis, T., 78, 99
Fredrickson, J. W., 116, 136
French, J. R. P., 338, 351

French, W. L., 284, 285, 286, 315
Frey, C. B., 81, 83, 86, 99
Friedman, W. H., 39, 62
Frink, D. D., 407, 422
Fuller, J. B., 74, 80, 86, 100, 250, 251, 274, 277
Furnham, A., 408, 422
Furr, N., 160, 168, 173

G

Gabriel, Y., 4, 25, 27
Gadiesh, O., 257, 277
Galbraith, J., 110, 111, 136
Galbraith, M., 188, 207, 246
Gardini, M., 336, 337, 351
Gardner, W. L., 199, 207
Garr, M. A., 290, 313
Geigle, S., 261, 277
Geigle, S. L., 228, 229, 246
Gelinas, M. V., 287, 315
George, G., 36, 59, 122, 137
Gerstner, L. V., 197, 207, 357, 383
Ghislanzoni, G., 265, 277, 365, 383
Ghosh, D., 373, 383
Gifford, J., 161, 173, 239, 246
Gilbert, J. L., 257, 277
Gilbert, M., 35, 60, 252, 278
Gilmore, D. C., 406, 421, 405, 422
Gioja, L., 370, 384
Giuliani, G., 336, 337, 351
Goffee, R., 199, 207
Goldsby, M. G., 395, 423
Goldsworthy, S., 324, 352
Goldwasser, C., 328, 329, 352
Golembiewski, R., 292, 315
Gollop, R., 357, 383
Goode, J., 364, 384
Gordon, G. G., 154, 173
Gorter, O., 392, 422
Grant, D., 286, 304, 315, 317
Gratton, L., 76, 100
Greenberg, E., 66, 67, 100
Gregersen, H., 151, 152, 173
Groenen, P., 190, 207
Groom, B., 78, 100
Grouard, B., 195, 209
Grundy, T., 124, 136
Guaspari, J., 229, 246

Guest, D. E., 256, 280
Gulick, L., 33, 59
Gupta, R., 192, 208, 365, 384
Gupta, S, 162, 172
Gustafson, L. T., 256, 279
Gustafsson, S., 37, 42, 58, 320, 341, 348, 351
Gutherie, J. P., 260, 278

H

Haas, M., 36, 59
Habashy, S., 329, 351
Hagen, N., 11, 27
Haines, S. G., 184, 208
Hall, S., 320, 332, 351
Hallencreutz, J., 301, 315
Hambrick, D. C., 116, 136
Hamel, G., 195, 208, 261, 277
Hamilton, F. E., 302, 313
Hammer, M., 148, 150, 173
Handscomb, C., 37, 59, 126, 129, 130, 135
Harris, L. C., 193, 194, 208
Harrison, M. I., 38, 39, 60
Hartley, J., 405, 423
Harwell, D., 96, 100
Hatch, M. J., 31, 60
Haueng, A. C., 260, 279
Heath, K., 217, 218, 246
Hecker, R., 164, 173
Heidari-Robinson, S., 265, 277, 365, 383
Helms Mills, J., 302, 303, 307, 313, 315
Heracleous, L., 227, 228, 246
Herman, S., 292, 315
Hewlett, S. A., 78, 100
Heyden, M. L. M., 264, 278, 394, 422
Hiatt, J., 324, 325, 351
Hiatt, J. M., 324, 351
Hieronimus, S., 42, 59
Higgins, J. M., 109, 136
Hindman, L. C., 256, 277
Hioe, E. S., 399, 422
Hirsch, D. J., 406, 408, 423
Hirscher, J., 264, 277
Hirt, M., 66, 67, 100

Hislop, D., 82, 100
Hoberecht, S., 292, 293, 315
Hochwarter, W. A., 406, 407, 421, 422
Hoefel, F., 78, 99
Hofmans, J., 389, 424
Holland, P., 164, 173
Hollinger, P., 81, 85, 100
Hollister, R., 67, 100, 146, 147, 169, 173
Holman, P., 289, 298, 315
Holpp, L., 188, 190, 208
Holt, M. D., 217, 218, 246
Homes, C., 86, 99
Homkes, R., 381, 385
Hooijberg, R., 184, 207
Hope, O., 36, 60, 396, 423
Hope Hailey, V., 37, 42, 58, 336, 341, 342, 348, 351
Hornstein, H., 282, 315
Houghton, E., 115, 136
Hudson, R., 392, 422
Hudson, S., 237, 246
Hudson Consulting, 78, 100
Hughes, M., 25, 27, 254, 261, 278
Hultman, K. E., 262, 278
Hussey, D. E., 226, 246
Hutton, D. W., 412, 423
Hwang, J., 151, 173

I

Ibarra, H., 40, 56, 60
Illanes, P., 79, 100
Immelt, J. R., 159, 161, 173
Isaac, M., 130, 136
Issacs, D., 290, 314
Iveroth, E., 301, 315

J

Jack, A., 74, 100
Jackson, A., 323, 352
Jacobs, P., 127, 137
Jacobs, R. W., 289, 293, 315
Jaffe, D. T., 267, 279
James, R. G., 287, 315
Jamieson, D. W., 286, 315

Jankowicz, A. D., 227, 246
Jansen, J. J. P., 122, 136
Jenkins, A., 65, 100, 390, 391, 423
Jermiin, M., 265, 277, 365, 383
Ji, Y.-Y., 260, 278
Jick, T. D., 192, 208, 366, 384
Jick, T. J., 253, 278
Jimmieson, N. L., 38, 61, 124, 137, 228, 242, 247
Johnson, E., 241, 245
Johnson, G., 118, 120, 136, 304, 313
Jones, G., 199, 207
Jones, J. L., 357, 383
Jorgenson, J., 290, 292, 315
Joseph, B., 293, 315

K

Kacmar, C. J., 407, 422
Kaiser, R. B., 389, 424
Kamer, J., 106, 136
Kanter, R. M., 65, 100, 126, 136, 194, 195, 208, 271, 278, 327, 351, 371, 384, 394, 423
Karp, H. B., 268, 278
Kates, A., 110, 111, 136
Katz, D., 32, 60
Keenan, P., 323, 352
Keil, M., 372, 384
Keller, S., 12, 27, 33, 60, 229, 242, 246, 330, 331, 351, 352
Kelly, M., 188, 190, 208
Kerr, D., 394, 423
Ketley, D., 357, 380, 383
Khurana, R., 390, 423
Kilo, C. M., 267, 269, 279
Kim, A., 237, 246
Kim, W. C., 269, 278, 405, 423
Kimes, M., 9, 27
King, L., 87, 101
Kirkland, R., 159, 161, 173
Kirkpatrick, D. L., 252, 278
Kirkpatrick, S. A., 184, 186, 208
Klein, D. C., 289, 316
Klier, J., 42, 59
Kniffin, K. M., 30, 31, 33, 60
Koene, B. A. S., 264, 278, 394, 422
Koller, T., 372, 383
Kolodinsky, R. W., 407, 422

Kolowich, L., 176, 208
Kotter, J. P., 30, 37, 60, 185, 208, 271, 278, 322, 325, 328, 329, 330, 348, 352, 357, 362, 365, 366, 371, 384
Kounkel, S., 181, 209
Kowitt, B., 6, 7, 27, 65, 95, 96, 100
Kragh, H., 373, 383
Kramer, R. M., 403, 404, 423
Kretzberg, A., 129, 135
Krishnan, M., 69, 70, 86, 87, 101
Kruse, K., 44, 60
Kübler-Ross, E., 267, 278
Kuiken, B., 43, 60
Kulkarni, M., 335, 352
Kunze, F., 76, 77, 100, 101, 251, 278
Kuratko, D. F., 395, 423
Kurtzman, J., 367, 384

L

Laartz, J., 129, 135
Lachinsky, A., 222, 246
Lackey, G., 126, 135
Laird, M. D., 406, 421
Lamont, S. S., 357, 383
Landau, D., 198, 208
Langeler, G. H., 202, 203, 208
Langley, A., 38, 27, 60
Lashinsky, A., 166, 167, 188, 208
Lavoie, J., 399, 422
Lawler, E. E., 68, 101, 126, 137
Lawrence, K. A., 408, 418, 422
Lawrence, M., 87, 101
Lawson, E., 42, 60, 156, 173, 357, 362, 384
Leinwand, P., 178, 179, 207
Lengel, R. H., 235, 236, 239, 246
Leonardi, P., 162, 173,
Leroy, H. L., 30, 31, 33, 60
Levesque, L. C., 226, 247
Levine, L., 289, 316
Levinthal, D. A., 122, 136
Lev-Ram, M., 65, 80, 93, 94, 101
Lewin, K., 122, 136, 285, 301, 316, 327, 352, 356, 384
Lewis, G., 394, 423
Lewis, L. K., 229, 246

Lewis, M., 273, 278
Lichtenstein, B. B., 43, 60
Linders, B., 106, 137
Lindsay, B., 159, 160, 173
Linstead, A., 218, 246
Linstead, S., 218, 246
Lipton, M., 193, 196, 199, 208
Lissack, M., 196, 197, 198, 208
Liu, X., 409, 423
Lockett, A., 300, 316
London, S., 69, 70, 101
Loren T., 256, 279
Lovallo, D., 372, 383
Lu, S., 409, 423
Lucas, B. J., 185, 186, 207
Ludden, J., 241, 245
Ludeman, K., 218, 240, 247
Ludolph, J., 130, 135
Lukensmeyer, C. J., 291, 316
Lund, S., 79, 100, 101
Lux, S., 406, 422
Lyle, M. C. B., 256, 277

M

Macaulay, S., 14, 26
Maccoby, N., 32, 60
Maciejewski, J., 127, 128, 137
Mahadevan, D., 127, 137
Mahler, J. G., 88, 89, 101
Main, A., 181, 209
Mainwairing, S., 179, 208
Malnight, T. W., 179, 180, 203, 208
Malo, J.-L., 329, 351
Manning, M. R., 289, 290, 316
Mantere, S., 300, 306, 316
Manville, B., 183, 189, 190, 206
Manyika, J., 69, 70, 86, 87, 101, 162, 172
Manzie, S., 405, 423
Maraite, B., 12, 27, 34, 35, 59, 320, 332, 351
Marin, D. B., 39, 62
Marks, M. L., 359, 384
Marricchi, M., 336, 337, 351
Marshak, R. J., 43, 61, 225, 247, 286, 288, 289, 297, 298, 311, 314, 315, 316
Martin, G., 256, 279, 300, 316

Marvell, R., 76, 101
Marx, M., 270, 277
Maslyn, J. M., 405, 423
Masters, B., 71, 101
Matula, L. J., 299, 313
Mauborgne, R., 269, 278, 405, 423
Maurer, R., 250, 252, 253, 274, 278
Mayo, E., 33, 61
McAllister, C. P., 406, 408, 423
McCabe, D., 35, 60, 252, 278
McCreary, L., 60, 397, 423
McDermott, A. M., 256, 264, 278,
    395, 423
McDonald, M. A., 256, 277
McDonald, R., 17, 27, 149, 172
McFarland, W., 324, 352
McKee, R., 24, 27, 288, 314
McKinlay, J., 184, 208
Mcluhan, M., 235, 247
McNaughtan, J., 295, 297,
    312, 314
Meaney, M., 229, 246
Menges, J. I., 76, 100, 259, 277
Messersmith, J. G., 260, 278
Meston, F., 195, 209
Metais, E., 196, 208
Meyer, C. B., 260, 279
Michel, S., 360, 384
Millemann, M., 370, 384
Milne, R., 84, 101
Mintzberg, H., 31, 33, 35, 61,
    405, 423
Mirvis, P., 288, 316
Mitchell, C., 194, 208
Mohr, B. J., 289, 316
Mohr, L. B., 4, 27
Mohrman, S. A., 68, 101, 289, 317
Monks, K., 264, 277
Montealegre, R., 372, 384
Moore, C., 13, 27, 90, 98
Morgan, G., 31, 61
Morrison, M., 114, 115, 137
Morse, N. C., 32, 60
Moulton, J., 237, 246
Mourshed, M., 79, 100
Muir, M., 69, 70, 86, 87, 101
Mullane, J. V., 256, 279
Muntz, A., 87, 102
Murarka, M., 126, 128, 129, 135
Murphy, C., 181, 209

N

Nadler, D. A., 198, 366, 384
Narasimhan, A., 25, 26
Nauclér, T., 368, 383
Neath, A., 357, 383
Neeley, T., 162, 173
Nesbit, P. L., 290, 299
Nevitt, J. A., 289, 293
Nicholl, D., 283, 284, 287, 316
Niehaus, G., 87, 102
Nielsen, K., 391, 424
Nohria, N., 363, 383
Noonan, L., 165, 173

O

O'Brien, D., 181, 209
Obstfeld, D., 301, 317
Oertel, S., 40, 61
Ogbonna, E, 193, 194, 208
Oliver, C., 42, 58
O'Neill, R. M., 408, 418, 422
Oreg, S., 254, 262, 279
Osborne, M. A., 81, 83, 86, 99
Oswick, C., 286, 317
Overdorf, M., 145, 149, 150,
    151, 172

P

Palmer, I., 32, 61, 304, 315
Parker, S. K., 290, 299
Pascale, R. T., 44, 56, 61,
    370, 384
Pasmore, W. A., 198, 207
Pate, J., 256, 279
Peccei, R., 164, 172
Peiperl, M., 253, 278
Pendlebury, J., 195, 209
Pentland, A. S., 36, 59
Perrewé, P. L., 405, 406,
    408, 422
Peters, T. J., 108, 109, 137
Pettigrew, A. M., 41, 58, 61,
    333, 352
Pfeffer, J., 373, 381, 384
Philips, A., 388, 424

Phillips, J. R., 108, 109, 137
Piaia, C., 12, 27, 34, 35, 59, 320,
    332, 351
Picken, J. C., 117, 118, 137
Piderit, S. K., 260, 279
Plowman, D. A., 335, 352
Plsek, P., 267, 279
Poole, M. S., 38, 62
Porck, J. P., 190, 207
Porras, J. I., 196, 198, 200, 201,
    207, 208
Powell, W. W., 40, 59
Prahalad, C. K., 195, 208
Price, C., 42, 60, 156, 173, 357,
    362, 384
Prusak, L., 398, 422
Pung, C., 229, 242, 246
Purser, R. E., 289, 315

Q

Quinn, R. E., 176, 191, 195, 209, 297,
    311, 317
Quirke, B., 232, 237, 247

R

Rafferty, A. E., 38, 61, 124, 137, 228,
    242, 247
Ram, A., 165, 173
Raman, M., 74, 80, 86, 100, 250, 251,
    274, 277
Rao, M., 294, 317
Rapping, J., 364, 384
Rashford, N. S., 144, 172
Rayner, S. R., 184, 189, 207
Raynor, M. E., 17, 27, 149, 172,
    197, 209
Reardon, K. J., 233, 247
Reardon, K. K., 233, 247
Reed, J., 143, 173
Reger, R. K., 256, 279
Regnér, P., 118, 120, 136
Reisner, R. A. F., 357, 363, 384
Reynolds, S., 89, 101
Rice, C., 257, 279
Rick, T., 237, 247
Ries, E., 88, 101, 255, 279

Robbins, H., 197, 209
Roberto, M. A., 226, 247
Roberts, C., 87, 101
Roberts, L. M., 296, 317
Roberts, R., 162, 172
Roethlisberger, F. J., 33, 61
Rogers, C., 191, 199, 209
Rogers, E., 150, 173
Romanelli, E., 146, 174
Ronanki, R., 82, 99
Roos, J., 196, 197, 198, 208
Ross, J., 372, 385
Ross, L., 261, 279, 361, 385
Rouleau, L., 302, 317
Rousseau, D. M., 12, 28, 256, 264, 278, 325, 326, 352
Rutherford, S., 79, 100

S

Salo, O., 126, 128, 135
Sandberg, J., 305, 317
Schalk, R., 257, 279
Schaninger, B., 12, 27, 33, 41, 58, 60, 330, 331, 351, 352
Schein, E. H., 30, 61, 365, 385
Scherf, G., 264, 277
Schildt, H. A., 300, 306, 316
Schlatmann, B., 127, 137
Schleier, C., 92, 94, 101
Schlesinger, L. A., 270, 271, 278
Schmid, T., 263, 280
Schmidt, W. H., 32, 61, 338, 352
Schneider, D. M., 328, 352
Schoemaker, P. J. H., 196, 209
Scholes, K., 118, 120, 136
Schön, D. A., 251, 252, 279
Schwartz, M., 73, 98
Scott, A., 76, 100
Scott, C. D., 267, 279
Scott, J., 392, 422
Scoular, A., 40, 56, 60
Searle, R., 257, 279
Semler, R., 43, 44, 61
Senge, P., 25, 266, 279
Seong, J., 69, 70, 86, 87, 101
Shafiq, H., 329, 351
Shannon, C. E., 215, 247
Sharan, R., 73, 98

Shaw, R. B., 195, 198, 209, 359, 384
Sheeren, E., 399, 422
Sherbin, L., 78, 100
Shipilov, A., 160, 168, 173
Shirom, A., 38, 39, 60
Shore, L., 256, 277
Sillince, J. A., 300, 306, 316
Simms, J., 163, 164, 174
Simpson, J. L., 189, 207
Sirkin, H. J., 323, 325, 352
Smallman, C., 4, 27, 38, 60
Smart, D. L., 273, 279
Smit, E., 159, 160, 173
Smit, S., 66, 67, 100, 264, 277
Smith, C., 130, 136
Solansky, S. T., 335, 352
Soler, G. J., 87, 102
Somerville, K. A., 212, 247
Sonenshein, S., 5, 28, 42, 62
Sorenson, P. F., 288, 314, 317
Sorkin, A. R., 74, 101
Southern, N., 293, 315
Spector, B., 362, 383
Spence, P., 115, 136
Spencer, J., 292, 293, 315
Stace, D. A., 37, 61, 231, 247, 338, 340, 352
Stacey, K., 65, 101
Staines, H., 256
Stalker, G. M., 126, 136
Stam, D., 184, 185, 203, 209, 269, 279
Staw, B. M., 372
Steele, C., 304, 315
Steier, F., 290, 292, 315
Stein, B. A., 194, 195, 208, 327, 351, 366, 371, 384
Stensaker, I., 260, 279
Stephan, A. R., 181, 209
Sternin, J., 44, 56, 61
Stevenson, H. H., 270, 277
Stjernberg, T., 388, 424
Stouten, J., 12, 28, 325, 326, 352
Sturdy, A., 17, 28, 388, 396, 424
Sull, C., 381, 385
Sull, D., 148, 174, 381, 385
Sumberg, K., 78, 100
Sun, K., 38, 62
Sutcliffe, K. M., 301, 317
Symons, J., 193, 209

T

Taneva, S., 82, 100
Tannen, D., 217, 222, 247
Tannenbaum, R., 32. 61, 338, 352
Tarakci, M., 190, 207
Tenkasi, R. V., 298, 317
Tetenbaum, T. J., 43, 61
Thaker, S., 37, 59, 127, 129, 135
Thakor, A. V., 176, 209
Theunissen, R., 127, 128, 137
Thommes, K., 40, 61
Tichy, N. M., 389, 424
Tofano, D., 130, 136
Toft, B., 89, 101
Towers Watson., 214, 247
Tracy, S. J., 189, 207
Travis, D. V. T., 335. 352
Treadway, D. C., 406, 407, 422
Tsoukas, H., 4, 5, 27, 38, 60, 305, 317
Tung, R. L., 75, 99
Tushman, M. L., 146, 174
Tyreman, M., 79, 100

U

Urwick, L., 33, 59

V

Vaara, E., 5, 28, 42, 62
Valente, M. S., 184, 207
Valvi, A. C., 234, 247
van den Heuvel, S., 257, 279
Van de Ven, A. H., 4, 27, 38, 60, 62
van Knippenberg, D., 184, 185, 190, 203, 207, 209, 269, 279
Van Oosten, E. B., 295, 317
Vaughan, D., 101
Ven Den Bosch, F. A. J., 122, 136
Venkataramani, V., 409, 423
Venus, M., 184, 185, 190, 203, 209, 269, 279
Vergauwe, J., 389, 424
Verity, J., 115, 137
Visser, N., 15, 16, 28
Volberda, H. W., 122, 136
von Brauchitsch, B., 87, 102

W

Wagnild, G. M., 416, 424
Wahba, P., 18, 28, 67, 102, 308, 317
Walgenbach, P, 40, 61
Wallace-Stephens, F., 82, 85, 99
Wallenstein, J. K., 74, 80, 86, 100, 250, 251, 274, 277
Ward, J., 17, 28, 146, 174
Waring, J., 300, 316
Wasik, J., 76, 102
Waterman, R. H., 108, 109, 137
Waters, J. A., 35, 61
Watkins, M. D., 67, 100, 146, 147, 169, 173
Waugh, N., 159, 160, 173
Weaver, W., 215, 247
Weeks, A., 114, 115, 137
Weerda, K., 129, 135
Weick, K. E., 41, 62, 301, 302, 303, 317
Weisbord, M. R., 107, 108, 137, 292, 293, 317
Weiss, L., 399, 422

Wendler, J., 192, 208, 365, 384
Werkman, R., 264, 278, 394, 422
West, D., 130, 135
Whelan-Berry, K. S., 212, 247
Whitby, E., 357, 383
White, M. C., 39, 62
Whitney, D., 294, 311, 314
Whittington, R., 118, 120, 136
Widdicombe, L., 165, 174
Wiedner, R., 352
Wille, B., 389, 424
Williams, M., 220, 247
Wilson, H. J., 398, 422
Wisskirchen, G., 87, 102
Woetzel, J., 69, 70, 86, 87, 101
Wolfe, R., 273, 279
Wong, J. C., 393, 424
Woodcock, M., 131, 137
Woodman, R. W., 58, 61, 299, 313
Woodrow, C., 256, 280
Wooldridge, B. J., 263, 280
Worley, C. G., 126, 137, 284, 285, 286, 289, 293, 299, 311, 315, 317
Woxholth, J., 126, 135

Wright, P. M., 273, 279
Wylie, K. K., 184, 207
Wylie, N., 17, 28, 388, 396, 424

Y

Yaeger, T. F., 288, 314, 317
Yaffe-Bellany, D., 95, 102
Yakola, D., 320, 332, 351
Yeung, R., 415, 424
Yip, A., 130, 135
Young, H. M., 416, 424
Yuanqing, Y., 153, 174

Z

Zahra, S. A., 122, 137
Zaleznik, A., 30, 62
Zanini, M., 261, 277
Zheltoukhova, K., 77, 102
Zheng, X., 409, 423
Zietsma, C., 410, 421
Zimmerli, P, 73, 98

Subject Index

A

Ability, ADKAR model, 323
Absorptive capacity
  acquisition, 122
  assimilation, 122
  defined, 122
  exploitation, 122
  transformation, 122
Acceleration trap, 14, 259
Accenture, AI used in, 83
Accountability, 358
Acquisition, 122
Act, McKinsey 5A model, 331
Action plan
  allowable weaknesses, 413
  building strengths, 413
  filling gaps, 413
Active resistance, 262
Adaptive thinking skill, 86
Adaptive workforce, 250
ADKAR (Awareness, Desire, Knowledge, Ability, and Reinforcement) model, 324–325
Advance, McKinsey 5A model, 331
Advocating, ideas practitioners and, 398
Affective component, vision, 184
Age discrimination, 76
Ageing population, 75–76
Agile organization, 125–130
Agility, 70
Agreeableness (personality trait), 130
Airbnb, 65, 187
Alliances, political behavior, 407
Alpha males, 218
Amazon, mission statement of, 182
American Red Cross, mission statement of, 183
Analytical approach, 190
Animation, 41, 301
Anti-globalization, 70
Antisocial media, 163, 165
Apathy, 266
Apparelizm, 226

Apparent sincerity, 406, 410, 411
Apple, 187
Appreciative inquiry (AI), 283, 293–295
  benefits of, 293
  building, 293
  designing, 293
  discovering, 293
  4-D cycle, 294
  questions, 294
  Roadway Express (example), 294–295
  sustaining, 293
Appropriate, 124
Architect, McKinsey 5A model, 331
Arenas, 116
Artificial intelligence (AI), 82–83. See also Automation
  business benefits, 82
  challenges in developments of, 83
  and cybersecurity, 83
  developments, 82
  robots with, 81
Asos, mission statement of, 182
Aspire, McKinsey 5A model, 331
Assess, McKinsey 5A model, 331
Assessment, political skills, 410–411
  apparent sincerity, 410, 411
  interpersonal influence, 410, 411
  networking ability, 410, 411
  social awareness, 410, 411
Assimilation, 122
Associating habit, of disruptive innovator, 151
Attention, 41, 301
Attitudes and behavior, changing, 283
Attitudinal changes, 286
Attraction strategies, 266, 267–270
Attractor, finding, 269
Authority, 252
Automation. See also Artificial intelligence (AI)
  complicating factors, 83–84
  effects of, 86

and unemployment, 83
and workless future, 85
Awareness, ADKAR model, 323

B

Baby Boomers, 78
Band-Aid initiatives, 147
Bankable plan, 331
Bankruptcy, 10, 11
Beauty industry, 237
Benchmarking approach, 190–191
Best Buy, transformation strategy, 67
Beth Israel Deaconess Medical Center (BIDMC), 53–56
Better conditions, 252
BHAGs (Big, Hairy, Audacious Goals), 200
Big Food, 95
BlackRock case study, 73–74
Blameworthy failures, 359–361
Bloomberg, AI used in, 83
Blue world, 115
Blurry vision bias, 186
Boeing, 65, 343–346
BOHICA ("Bend Over, Here It Comes Again"), 260
Boston Consulting Group, 323
BP, 154–156
Brand Corporation, 305
"Bread-and-salt" vision, 191
Buddhism, 296
"Burning platform" theory, 184
Business risk, climate change and, 73
Buy-ins, 229–230

C

Caesars, AI used in, 83
Canon, 195
Capability, 341
Capacity, 341
Career moves, 411–412

Caretaker image, 33, 38–40, 52
  communication and, 213
  diagnostic model, 104
  institutional theory, 40
  key competencies, 403
  life-cycle theory, 38–39
  missions/visions and, 177
  organization development and, 282
  population ecology theory, 39
  pressures for change and, 68
  sustaining change and, 356
Carnival Cruise Line, 72
Catalyzing stage, 233
Challenger disaster, 88–89, 374–377
Change agent, 30–31
Change communication
  barriers to, 221
  context and, 216
  power of conversation. *See* Power
    of conversation
  process of, 212
  significance of, 212
  target audience and, 237
Change communication strategies,
    228–231
  buy-ins, 229–230
  charismatic transformations, 231
  contingency approaches to,
    231–234
  continuum of, 230
  developmental/incremental
    transitions, 231
  getting the word out, 229–230
  identify and reply, 230
  leadership styles and, 233
  opening files, 232
  overcommunication, 228–229
  spray and pray, 230–231
  stage of change and, 233
  task-focused transitions, 231
  tell and sell, 230
  turnarounds, 231
  type of change, 231–232
  underscore and explore, 230
  value propositions, 229
  withhold and uphold, 230, 231
Change deviant, 388–389
Change kaleidoscope, 341–343
  context factors, 341–342
  implementation options, 342

Change leaders, 14–15, 30–31
Change management
  alternative approaches to, 282
  assessing depth, 16–18
  assumptions about, 46
  checklist approaches to.
    See Checklist approaches
  competencies. *See* Change
    management competencies
  contingency approaches, 37,
    336–343
  defensive, 90
  diagnostic models, 104–106
  digital transformation, 159–160
  director image of, 36–37, 52
  disagreement over, 261
  dominant images of, 46–47
  explicit models, 107
  frames for, 31–32
  general lessons for, 334
  "hard and soft" elements of, 33
  implications for, 184–185
  implicit models, 106
  power of conversation and.
    See Power of conversation
  processual theories, 37–38
  progressive, 90
  from sense-making perspective, 306
  six images of, 36–45. *See also*
    Images, change management
  social media and, 237–239
  stories about, 4–11
  styles, 339
  tension and paradox, 11–15
  unanticipated outcomes, 370
  vision. *See* Vision
  warnings at, 369–373
Change management capabilities,
    411–413
  action plan, 413
  career moves, 411–412
  gaps, 413
  politics and, 412–413
  repositioning, 412
  strengths and, 413
Change management competencies,
    401–403
  CMI change manager master level,
    401–402
  great intimidators, 403–404

Change Management Institute
  change manager master level,
    402–403
Change managers, 30–31
  assumptions about, 46
  boosting factory yields, 399
  as caretaker, 38–40, 52
  challenges for, 150–151
  as champions, 388–389
  CMI change manager master level,
    401–402
  as coach, 40, 52
  competencies, 401–404
  confessions of, 400–401
  context of change, 47
  defense of sustaining innovation, 153
  desirable characteristics of, 412
  as deviants, 388–389
  as director, 36–37, 52
  as disruptive innovator, 151–152
  dominant images of change, 46–47
  experience, 400
  heroic leaders, 198–200
  as ideas practitioners, 398
  and internal change departments/
    units, 396–397
  as interpreter, 40–42, 52
  managing emotions, 220–221
  middle managers, 394–396
  multiple images/perspectives,
    47–48
  names for, 388
  as navigator, 37–38, 52
  as nurturer, 42–45, 52
  phase of change, 47
  political skills and, 404–411
  resistance to change and, 253
  as resisters, 263–265
  role of, 399–401
  selection factors for, 401
  simultaneous involvement/multiple
    changes, 48
  as souls-of-fire, 388–389, 398–399
  top managers, 389–392
  undesirable characteristics of, 412
Change outcomes, 32–33
  images of, 32–35
  intended, 34–35
  Netflix, 94
  partially intended, 35

Starbucks, 6
unintended, 35, 36
Change process, and resistance to
change, 250
Change readiness. *See* Readiness
diagnostic
Change(s). *See also* Environmental
pressures; Organizational change
accelerators, 329
actions, 284
agile organization model, 125–130
blockers, 250
building commitment to, 271–272
cultural, 153–158
depth of, 144–145
diagnosing readiness for.
See Readiness diagnostic
disruptive, 320
emergent, 143, 144
first-order, 144
incremental, 144
and innovation. *See* Innovation
news, 235
organizational strategy and.
See Organizational strategy
planned, 143
practical implications of, 145–148
process perspectives on.
See Process perspectives
reason for failures, 321–322
resistance to. *See* Resistance
to change
scale of, 339
second-order, 144
stages of, 233
start-up's strategy, 88
styles of, 339
third-order, 144
transformational, 144
types of, 142–148
value proposition in, 229
vision and, 194–201
Channel, of communication.
See Communication channels
Chaos theory, 43, 44
Charismatic leaders, 199–200,
389–390
Charismatic transformations, 231
Chatter, 163
Checklist approaches, 323–327

ADKAR model, 324–325
checking, 325–327
DICE model, 323–324
evidence-based approach, 325
Chief Transformation Officer (CTO),
392–393
China, organization development
in, 300
Chobani, 179
Chrysler, 199
Cisco, mission statement of, 183
Classic change curve, 329
Climate change, 72–74
BlackRock case study, 73–74
and economic losses, 72
and insurance industry, 73
CMI change manager master level,
401–402
CNN, 187
Coach image, 33, 40, 52
communication and, 213
diagnostic model, 104
key competencies, 403
missions/visions and, 177
organization development and, 282
positive organizational scholarship,
295–297
pressures for change and, 68
sustaining change and, 356
Cobots (collaborative robots), 81
Coca-Cola, 187
Co-creating vision technique, 188
Coding process, 215
Coercive pressure, 40
Coercive style, 339
Cognitive component, vision, 184
Cognitive load management, 86
Cognitive work, 81
Coherence, 198
Cohesive networks, 398
Collaborative style, 339
Collectivity stage, 39
Columbia disaster, 88–89, 375,
378–380
Commanding leadership style, 233
Commitment, 266, 267
DICE model, 323
escalation of, 372–373
Commitment culture, 153
Common enemy logic, 200

Communication
change-related, 212
in crisis, 234
education and, 271
emotional commitment to, 220
high-quality, importance of, 228
importance of, 212, 216
not "soft" function, 214
power of conversation. *See* Power
of conversation
"surface-level," 227
Communication channels, 215
media richness, 235–237
and social media, 235–239
Communication escalator, 232
Communication process,
212–217
emotion and, 219–222
gender and, 217–218
modelling of, 214–217
power and, 218–219
Communication skills. *See* Change
communication strategies
Compromise, political behavior, 407
Confucian/Taoist assumptions, 289
Confucian/Taoist theory, 43, 44
Consensus, 118
Consultation, 284
Consultative style, 339
Consulting vision technique, 188
Consult style, change
management, 339
Content of vision, 178
Context, 38, 333
and change communication, 216
Continental Airlines, 367
Contingency approaches, 37, 320,
336–343
to change communication,
231–234
change leadership styles
continuum, 338
Hope Hailey-Balogun change
kaleidoscope, 341–343
to resistance management, 266,
270–272
scale of change, 339
Stace–Dunphy contingency matrix,
338–340
styles of change, 339

Control
  management as, 33
  sense of, 129
  systems, 118
Controlling activities, 33
Conventional wisdom, 30
Conversation for understanding, 223
Conversations for closure, 223
Conversations for performance, 223
Core business, 363
Core purpose, 200
Core selection factors, 146
Core values, 200, 201
Corporate code, 296
Corporate culture. *See* Organizational
  culture
Corporate purpose, approaches to
  define, 180
Corporate response, to divisive
  issues, 71
Corporate transformation, 339
Cost-based measures, 366
Cost myopia, 147
Counterproductive work behavior
  (CWB), effect of organizational
  change and, 257–258
Covert processes, organization
  development and, 286
COVID-19 pandemic, 67
  consequences, 90–91
Cross-border trade services, 70
Cross-cultural competency skill, 86
Cultural mapping, 120
Cultural web, 118, 120
Culture. *See* Organization culture
Cybersecurity, 164
  AI and, 83
Cynicism, 260

D

Danone UK, 164
Data gathering, 284
Decoding, 215
"Deep discursive structures," 227
Deep learning, 82
Deep structures, 373
Deepwater Horizon disaster, 154–156
Defensive change management, 90

Democratic values, 283
Demographic trends, 75–79
Denial, coping cycle stage, 267
Depth of change, 144–145
Design mindset skill, 86
Desire, ADKAR model, 323
Destabilizing the market, 196
Detroit
  bankruptcy, 10, 11
  change diagnostics, 23
  change leader, 14
  change story, 10–11
  "focusing on the boring"
    strategy, 11
  house parties, 10–11
  lessons from, 16
  population, 10
Deutsche Bank, 194
Developmental imagery, 225
Developmental/incremental
  transitions, 231
Developmental maintenance, 369
Developmental values, 283
Deviance, 360
"Deviant peers," 40
The Devil Wears Prada (movie), 404
Diagnostic organization development,
  297, 298
Dialogic organization development,
  283, 297–300
  diagnostic organization
    development *vs.*, 297, 298
  originators of, 297–298
  in practice, 299
DICE (Duration, Integrity,
  Commitment, and Effort)
  model, 323–324
Dick's Sporting Goods, Parkland
  incident and, 71
Differentiators, 116
Digital profile, globalization with,
  69–70
Digital transformation, 159–160, 168
Direction, 41, 301
Directive style, 339
Direct learning, 162
Director image, 33, 36–37, 52,
  320–321
  communication and, 213
  diagnostic model, 104

key competencies, 403
missions/visions and, 177
organization development and, 282
pressures for change and, 68
sustaining change and, 356
Dirty tricks, political behavior, 407
Discrepancy, 124
Discrimination, age, 76
Disney
  mission statement, 183
  vision statement, 187
Disruption, 66, 149
Disruptive, change as, 320
Disruptive innovation, 145, 149,
  150–151, 165
Disruptive innovator
  change manager as, 151–152
  habits of, 151–152
Distributed leadership, 14–15
Divergent networks, 398
Diversity, 341
Divisive issues, corporate response
  to, 71
Downsizing, 42
Dresdner Bank, 194
DuPont, 309–310
Duration, DICE model, 323

E

eBay, 187
Economic logic, 116
Economic losses, weather disasters
  and, 72
Education, and communication, 271
Efficacy, 124
Effort, DICE model, 323
Eight-stage model, 328–330
Elaboration stage, 39
Emergent changes, 143, 144
Emergent strategy, 226
Emotional commitment, 220
Emotion control, 218
Emotions, 219–222
Employee engagement, 34
Employee voice, 163
  implications of social media
    for, 164
Empowerment, 226

Enabling stage, 233
Enactment, 303
Encircling competitors, 196
Engagement paradigm, 293
Enrollment, 266
Entrepreneurial middle manager, 395
Entrepreneurial stage, 39
Entrepreneurs, and resistance to change, 255
Environmental pressures, 64, 66–88
  changing expectations of work, 74–75
  climate change, 72–74
  corporate response to divisive issues, 71
  demographic trends, 75–79
  globalization with digital profile, 69–70
  images of change and, 68
  technology, 79–88
Environmental threats, 72
Envisioned future, 200
Escalation of commitment, 372–373
  advice for, 372
  organizational determinants, 372
  project determinants, 372
  psychological determinants, 372
  regular progress reports, 373
  social determinants, 372
  steps to limit, 373
  unambiguous feedback, 373
Estée Lauder case study, 74–75
Ethical conflict, 260
Etsy, 18
Evidence-based approach, 325
Experience-based system, 186
Experiential-based learning, 283
Experimenting habit, of disruptive innovator, 151
Explicit/implicit coercion, 271
Explicit models, 107
Exploitation, 122
Exploration, 267
Exploratory testing, 360
External dimension, 187–188
External forces, 35
External measures, 366
External pressures, 124
Extracted cues of sense-making, 303
Extrapolation, 73

F

Facebook, 79, 161, 164
Face-to-face communication, 231, 235, 238
Facilitation and support, 271
Failures
  to adapt, 192–194
  change, causes for, 321–322
  learning from, 361
  management approach to, 361
  reasons for, 360
  vision, 192–194
Fast-cycle full participation, 289
Federal Express (FedEx), 370
Feedback, 215, 218, 284
  unambiguous, 373
Fine-tuning, 145, 339, 367–369
First-order change, 144
Flanking, 196
"Focusing on the boring" strategy, 11
Force-field analysis, 122–123
Ford Motor company, 368
Formal compliance, 266
Formalization stage, 39
Four-frame model, 111–112
  human resource frame, 111, 112
  political frame, 111, 112
  structural frame, 111, 112
  symbolic frame, 111, 112
Frames, 199
  breaking, 302
  for change management, 31–32
  validating, 302
Freezing, 301

G

Gap analysis, 113
Gaps, personal, 413
Gender differences, and communication process, 217–218
General consultation skill, 284
General Electric (GE), 200
General Motors (GM), 227
Generation of energy, 331
Generation X, 78
Generation Y, 78

Generation Z, 71, 77, 78–79
Genuine compliance, 266
Gestures, 409–410
Getting the word out, 229–230
Glassdoor.com, 165
Goldman Sachs, 157–158
Google, 187
Great intimidators, change managers as, 403–404
Greener cruising, 72
Green management, 373
Green world, 115
Groundwork, 218
Grudging compliance, 266

H

Harris Tweed, 153
Health goals, 331
Health management, guidelines for, 331
Heinz, 346–348
Helpful mechanisms, 107
Hero effect, 372
Heroic leaders, 198–200
Heroic organizations, 200
Hewlett-Packard (HP), 200, 222
High-quality communication, importance of, 228
Home Depot, mission statement of, 183
Hope Hailey-Balogun change kaleidoscope, 341–343
Hospital, organization development in, 300
Humanistic values, 283
Human resource frame, 111, 112
Hypothesis testing, 360

I

IBM
  offshoring jobs script, 224–225
  organization culture at, 357
  transformational change, 357
  vision, Gerstner's on, 197
Idea enactment, 409
Idealized influence, 389

Ideas practitioners, 398
Identify and reply strategy, 230
Identity construction, 303
IKEA, 178–179
Image building, political behavior, 407
Images, change management,
31–32, 282
assumptions about change, 46
caretaker image. *See* Caretaker image
coach image. *See* Coach image
communication and, 213
director image. *See* Director image
interpreter image.
See Interpreter image
key competencies, 403
management as control, 33
management as shaping, 33–34
multiple images and perspectives,
47–48
navigator image. *See* Navigator
image
nurturing image. *See* Nurturing
image
pressures for change and, 68
six-images framework, 32–35,
45–47
Impact blindness, 146
Implementing, ideas practitioners
and, 398
Implicit models, 106
Impression management, 408
Improvement evaporation effect,
356–359
managing, 369
Inattention, 360
Incremental adjustment, 339
Incremental change, 144, 363
Incremental transitions, 231
Individualized consideration, 389
Individual readiness, and stakeholder
analysis, 251
Individual resistance *vs.* management
responses, 268
Inequality, 79
Inertia, 301
Influence levers, 331
Information
on future benefits, 373
games, political behavior, 407
ING, agile organization model in, 127

Initiative conversations, 223
Initiative decay, 356–359
Initiative inertia, 147
Initiative overload, 146–147
Innovations, 148–153
disruptive, 145, 149, 150–151, 165
innovators to laggards, 150
operational, 148–149, 150, 163
rules encouraging, 148
sustaining, 145, 149, 151
Innovators to laggards, 150
Inside Job (movie), 156
Inspirational leadership style, 233
Inspirational motivation, 389
Institutional theory, 40
coercive pressure, 40
mimetic pressure, 40
normative pressure, 40
Insurance industry, climate change
and, 73
Integra Financial, 363
Integrative organizational cultures,
126–127
Integrity, DICE model, 323
Intellectual stimulation, 389
Intelligence augmentation (IA)
systems, 82
Intended change outcomes, 34–35
Interactions, 41, 301, 334
Intermediation, political
behavior, 407
Internal change departments/units,
396–397
Internal context enablers, 124
Internal dimension, 187–188
Internal forces, 35
Internal measures, 366
Internal organization change drivers,
64–66
importance in certain
circumstances, 64
Internal transformation logic, 200
Interpersonal influence, 405, 406,
410, 411
Interpersonal skills, 284
Interpreter image, 33, 40–42, 52
animation and, 41
attention and, 41
communication and, 213
diagnostic model, 104

direction and, 41
implementing change and,
300–306
interaction and, 41
key competencies, 403
missions/visions and, 177
organization development and, 282
pressures for change and, 68
sense-making approaches, 300–306
sustaining change and, 356
vision and, 191
Interventions, 342
Interviewing change recipients, 201
Intrapersonal skills, 284
Intraregional trade, 70
Intuit, 109, 152
mission statement of, 182
Intuitive approach, 190
Invite participation style, change
management, 339
Involvement moves, 408–409
Issue-selling, 407, 408–409
involvement moves, 408–409
packaging moves, 408
process moves, 409

J

J-curve, 371
Jive, 163
Johnson & Johnson, AI used
in, 83
Joint action planning, 284
Joint problem diagnosis, 284
*Journal of Applied Behavioral
Science,* 282

K

Kaiser Permanente, 397
Kanter's Law, 328, 371
Key performance indicators
(KPIs), 160
Killer gestures, 409–410
Knightscope security robot, 81
Knock-on effects, 142
Knowledge, ADKAR model, 323
Komatsu, 195

L

Labor
  cost of, 85
  growth in demand for, 86
Lack of ability, 360
Lack of clarity, 257
Lack of conviction, 257
Lack of shared vision, 193
Lack of vision, 176–177
Lagging measures, 366
Language
  aligning with change, 225–226
  common change, 226–228
  of mission statements, 181–182
  and power of conversation, 222–228
Large-scale change, and organization development, 283, 288–293
Large-scale interactive process, 289, 291
Launching stage, 233
Law enforcement, organization development in, 300
Leadership, 107. *See also* Change managers
  commanding style, 233
  communication processes and strategies, 233
  distributed, 14–15
  heroic leaders and, 198–200
  inspirational style, 233
  logical style, 233
  styles of, 233, 338
  supportive style, 233
  Tannenbaum–Schmidt leadership continuum, 338
  thinking about leader and, 408
Leadership placement, 331
Leading measures, 366
Learning, from failures, 361
Learning infrastructure, 331
Learning organization, 226
Legacy of past changes, 260
Lego, and computerization, 84
The Lego Movie, 84
Lego Universe (computer game), 84
Lehman Brothers, collapse, 39
Lenovo, 153
Less time and effort, 252

Let nature take its course, 266, 267
Levi Strauss & Co., 391–392
Lewinian/OD assumptions, 289
Life-cycle theory, 38–39
  collectivity stage, 39
  elaboration stage, 39
  entrepreneurial stage, 39
  formalization stage, 39
Life expectancy, 75, 77
Linguistic coherence, 223
Lockdown, 90
Lockheed, 372
Logical leadership style, 233
Lower Manhattan Development Corporation (LMDC), 291

M

Machiavelli's memorandum, 410
Machine imagery, 225
Machine learning, 82
Maersk, 160
Mahindra Finance, 180
Maintaining stage, 233
Management. *See also* Change management
  approach to failures, 361
  Chief Transformation Officer, 392–393
  as controlling, 33, 67
  "hard" dimension of, 33
  middle, 394–396
  reputation, 146
  as shaping, 33–34
  sustained change and, 364–365
  top, 389–392
"Management of meaning," 41
Managerial (or Leadership) Grid (Blake and Mouton), 288
Manipulation and co-optation, 271
Manual work, 81
Many perspectives, 12
Marjory Stoneman Douglas High School shooting, 71
Market strategy, vision and, 187–188
Mars Petcare, 179, 180
Mattel, 187–188
The Mattel Toy Story, 166–167

McCormick & Schmick's restaurant, 153
McDonald's, 48, 79, 95, 154
  productive failures at, 360
McKinsey 5A model, 330–332
McKinsey & Company, 34, 108, 265
Meaning, 222
Meaning-based system, 185–186
Mechanistic management systems, 126
Media literacy skill, 86
Media organization, organization development in, 300
Media richness, 235–237
  hierarchy, 236
Mental grid, 117
Mental models, 31–32
Mental organization images, 31–32
Merger in Adland, 262
Mergers and acquisitions, organization development in, 300
Message, 215
Metaknowledge, 162
Metropolitan Police Department, 304
Microculture image, 32
Microsoft, 199
Middle managers, 36, 394–396
  advice to, 395
  entrepreneurial, 395
  as key to change, 396
  roles of, 394
  senior management *vs.,* 396
  tactics for leading change, 395
Migration, 75
Millennials, 78, 181
Mimetic pressure, 40
Mindsets, conditions for changing, 42
Mindset shifts, 331
Minecraft (computer game), 84
Mission, 176–183
  analysis of, 202
  confused, 176–177
Mission statements
  best and worst, 181–182
  language of, 181–182
Modular transformation, 339
Mojang, 84
Momentum busters, 357
Money, 252

Moneyball (Lewis), 273–274
"More is better" principle, 390
Movement, 285
Moving, 328
Multiframe thinking, 111
Multiloading, 259
Multiple perspectives, 31–32
Multiplier effects, 146
Museum of Modern Art (MOMA),
    mission statement of, 183

N

Narrative knowing, 5
NASA, 375–380
NASCAR Model, 226
Navigator image, 33, 37–38, 52, .
    320–321
  communication and, 213
  diagnostic model, 104
  key competencies, 403
  missions/visions and, 177
  organization development
    and, 282
  pressures for change and, 68
  processual theories and, 37–38
  sustaining change and, 356
Negotiation, and agreement, 271
Nestlé Purina Petcare, 179
Netflix, 65, 92–94, 187
  change outcomes, 94
  content budget, 93
  slow growth problem, 92–93
Networking, 414–415
  ability, 405–406, 410, 411
  as habit of disruptive innovator, 151
  political behavior, 407, 408
Nike, 71, 187, 194
  automation in, 85
Noise, 217
Noncompliance, 266
Noncost measures, 366
Nonprofit organizations, organization
    development in, 300
Nonroutine work, 81
Nordstrom, 200
Normative pressure, 40
Nova Scotia Power, 302
"*N*-step" models, 36

O

Observing habit, of disruptive
    innovator, 151
Ocean plastic, 15
OD Practitioner, 282, 287
The Office, 306
Older workers/employees, 76–77
  approaches to attract/retain skills/
    knowledge of, 77
Omitters, CWB perpetrators, 258
Ongoing sense-making, 303
Open-space technology, 289
Operational innovations, 148–149,
    150, 163
Orange world, 115
Organic management systems, 126
Organizational capabilities, 14
Organizational change, 41
  Detroit story, 10–11
  effect on counterproductive work
    behavior, 257–258
  environmental pressures for.
    See Environmental pressures
  images of managing change.
    See Images, change management
  and insider threats, 257–258
  middle managers and, 394–396
  Netflix story, 92–94
  resourcing, 326
  Sears story, 7–10
  sensemaking theory of, 41
  Starbucks, 5–7
  technology and, 79–88
  vision and, 194–201
Organizational culture, 153–158, 226
  assessment of, 168
  at BP, 154–156

Deepwater Horizon disaster and,
    154–156
  defined, 154
  importance of, 154
  integrative, 126–127
  at Lenovo, 153
  mapping of, 120
  and resistance to change, 256
  risky, 156
  segmentalist, 126–127
  strong *vs.* weak, 154
Organizational determinants, 372
Organizational failures, 89
Organizational models, 104–107
  four-frame model, 111–112
  7-S framework, 108–109
  six-box, 107
  star model, 110–111
Organizational performance.
    See Performance measurement
Organizational politics, 65–66, 405
Organizational retention, 39
Organizational roles, redesign of,
    362–363
Organizational selection, 39
Organizational strategy, 112–120
  assumptions and, 118
  cultural web, 118, 120
  elements of, 116
  gap analysis, 113
  key evaluation criteria, 117
  PESTLE framework, 113–115
  scenario planning, 115
  strategic inventory, 117–118, 119
  testing quality of, 117
Organizational structure, 118
Organizational variation, 39
Organization development (OD),
    282–283
  appreciative inquiry, 283, 293–295
  characteristics of, 283
  classic change intervention
    processes, 285
  and covert processes, 286
  criticisms of, 285–286
  as culture-bound, 289
  definitions and concepts, 285
  diagnostic, 297
  dialogic, 283, 297–300
  in different settings, 299

evolution of, 283
fundamental values, 283–284
influential, 299
internal/external validity
    problems, 285
large-scale change, 283, 288–293
positive organizational scholarship,
    283, 295–297
relevance of traditional values,
    286–287
traditional, 283–284
values, 287–288
Organization development (OD)
    practitioner, 284–285
action research steps, 284
role of, 284
skills of, 284
Organization development theory, 284
Organization development (OD)
    theory, 40
Organizations after crises, 88–90
    Challenger disaster, 88–89
    Columbia disaster, 88–89
    organizational failures, 89
Overloading, 259
Ownership culture, 153
Ownership model, 331

                    P

Packaging, ideas practitioners
    and, 398
Packaging moves, 408
Paradigm, 118
Paradox, 11–15
Partially intended change
    outcomes, 35
Participation and involvement, 271
Participative design, 289
Passive resistance, 262
People practices, 110, 111
Perceptual filters, 215–216
Performance management, guidelines
    for, 331
Performance measurement, 365–366
    Continental Airlines example, 367
    cost-based measures, 366
    external measures, 366
    internal measures, 366

lagging measures, 366
leading measures, 366
limitations of, 370–371
noncost measures, 366
vision and, 196
Performing, 199
Perpetual loading, 259
Personal contacts, 252
Personality traits, teams and, 129–130
Personal skills, 14
Perspectives, 31–32
PESTLE framework, 104, 113–115
Physical risk, 73
Pioneer culture, 153
Planned changes, 143
Planning stage, 233
Plastics ban, in Vanuatu, 15–16
Plausibility, 303
Political behavior, 38
    categories of, 407
Political frame, 111, 112
Political logrolling, 146
Politically skilled organizational
    grandmaster, 406
Political skills, 413
    assessment of, 410–411
    change manager and, 404–411
    defined, 405
    dimensions, 405–406
    importance of, 405
Political tactics, 404–405
Politics, defined, 405
Politics of change, 334
Population ecology theory, 39
Positioning, political behavior, 407
Positive organizational scholarship
    (POS), 283, 295–297
Post-incident contexts, 90
Power, 341
    gender relationships and, 218–219
Power of conversation, 222–228
    aligning language with change,
        225–226
    breakdowns in, 224
    conversation for understanding, 223
    conversations for closure, 223
    conversations for performance, 223
    developmental imagery, 225
    GM Poland example, 227
    initiative conversations, 223

language and, 222–228
machine imagery, 225
misused terminology, 226
in stages, 223–224
transformational imagery, 225
transitional imagery, 225
Power structures, 118
Power tells, 219
Practical implications, 145–148
    management reputation, 146
    matching solutions with
        problems, 145
    punctuated equilibrium
        theory, 146
    shallow change management, 146
Pragmatic resistance, 252–253
Praiseworthy failures, 359–361
Preparation, to speak
    spontaneously, 218
Preservation, 341
Preventive maintenance, 369
PricewaterhouseCoopers (PwC)
    scenario planning used by, 115
    strategic change leaders, 394
Principal support, 124
Problem diagnosis, 284
Problem identification, 284
Process complexity, 360
Processed foods, 95–96
Processes and lateral capability,
    110, 111
Process inadequacy, 360
Process measures, 366
Process moves, 409
Process narratives, 4
Process perspectives, 333–336
    context, 333
    general lessons from, 334
    interaction between change
        factors, 334
    limitations of, 336
    politics of change, 334
    strategic change, 335
    strengths of, 335–336
    substance of change, 334
    transition process, 334
Process theories, 5
Processual theories, 37–38
Procter & Gamble (P&G), 192,
    200, 365

Productive failures, 359–361
 at McDonald's, 360
Program management offices
 (PMOs), 146–147
Progressive, 390–391
Progressive change management, 90
Project determinants, 372
Projective sense-making, 303
Project Management Institute, 146
Prospective approach, 180
Psychological contract, 256–257
Psychological determinants, 372
Pump-priming funding, 358
Punctuated equilibrium theory, 146
Purposeful organization culture, at
 Chobani, 179
Purposes, 107. *See also* Mission
 benefits to organization of
 clarifying/communicating,
 180–181
 strategic roles, 179–180

Q

Questioning habit, of disruptive
 innovator, 151

R

Racial bias, 5
Rapid change, 14
Readiness, 341
Readiness diagnostic, 121–125
 absorptive capacity, 122
 force-field analysis, 122–123
 individual readiness for change,
 123–124
 receptive organizational context,
 121–122
 stakeholder mapping, 124–125
Rebalance, 301
Receptive organizational context,
 121–122
Refreezing, 285, 328
Regular progress reports, 373
Reinforcement, ADKAR model, 323
Relationships, 107
Repositioning, 412

Resilience, 70, 400
Resistance, 267. *See also* Resistance
 to change
 active, 262
 managing. *See* Resistance
 management
 passive, 262
Resistance management, 265–272
 attraction strategies, 266, 267–270
 contingency approaches, 266,
 270–272
 finding attractor, 269
 individual resistance *vs.*
 management responses, 268
 let nature take its course, 266, 267
Resistance to change
 active *vs.* passive resistance, 262
 attachment to organizational
 culture and identity, 256
 benefits, 251–254
 change managers and, 253,
 263–265
 content of, 254
 cumulative effects, 260
 damaging patterns, 259
 dimensions of, 250–251
 disagreement with change
 management, 261
 dispositional, 254–255
 entrepreneurs and, 255
 ethical conflict and, 260
 excessive change, 258–260
 individual readiness and
 stakeholder analysis, 251
 innate dislike of change, 254–255
 interests and, 255
 lack of clarity, 257
 lack of conviction, 257
 legacy of past changes, 260
 managing resistance. *See*
 Resistance management
 need for, 251
 perceptions and, 255
 positive dimensions of, 254
 process, 254
 proposed changes, 257–258
 psychological contract breach,
 256–257
 substance/content, 250
 symptoms, 261–262

 uncertainty and, 254, 255
 WAMI of, 250
 ways to use, 253
 WIIFM of, 250
 wrong timing, 258
Responsibility, 252
Results measures, 366
Retaliators, CWB perpetrators, 258
Retention, organizational, 39
Retrospection, 303
Retrospective approach, 180
Reward system, 107, 110, 111,
 363–364
Ripple effects, 142
Risk, business, climate change
 and, 73
Rituals and routines, 118
Roadway Express, appreciative
 inquiry at, 294–295
Robotics, 81. *See also* Artificial
 intelligence (AI); Automation
 advantages/disadvantages of, 87
Role model logic, 200
Roles, 342
Routine work, 81
Rule games, political behavior, 407

S

Samuel Adams Boston Lager, 153
Sandvik AB, 368
Scale of change, 339
Scapegoating, political behavior, 407
Scenario planning, 104, 115, 130–133
Scope, 341
Scouting, ideas practitioners and, 398
Scripting, 199
Search conference format, 290
Sears Holdings Corporation
 business operating profit, 9
 change diagnostics, 21–22
 change leader, 14
 change story, 7–10
 falling profitability at, 7–9
 internal marketing, 7
 lessons from, 16
 managing merger, 7–8
 messy approach, 8
 online shopping, 7–9

Second-order change, 144
Securitas AB, 180
Security, 252
Segmentalist organizational cultures, 126–127
Selection, organizational, 39
Self-organization, 43, 144
Self-renewal, 144
Self-satisfaction, 252
Selling vision technique, 188
Semco, 43, 44
Senior management, middle managers *vs.*, 396
Sense-making approaches, 300–306
   assumption of inertia, 301
   change management from, 306
   contested interpretations, 304
   features of, 303
   freeze-rebalance-unfreeze, 301
   standardized change, 301
   success, as problem, 306
Sensemaking skill, 86
Sensemaking theory, of organizational change, 41
Serial transgressors, CWB perpetrators, 258
7-S framework, 108–109
   Intuit example, 109
   skills, 108
   staff/staffing, 108
   strategy, 108
   structure, 108
   style, 108
   superordinate goals, 108
   systems, 108
Shallow changes, 17
Shaping, management as, 33–34
Shell method, 115
Silence, 223
Six-box organizational models, 107
Skills, 108
   in demand, 86
   political. *See* Political skills
Skill-set requirements, 331
Slack, 163
Slippers, CWB perpetrators, 258
Small to medium enterprises, organization development in, 300
Snapchat, 161

Social astuteness, 405, 406
Social awareness, 410, 411
Social determinants, 372
Social distancing, 90
Social gaming, 264–265
Social intelligence skill, 86
Social matrix, 161–165
Social media, 162–165
   benefits of, 164
   communication channels and, 235–239
   impact of, 237–239
   implications for employee voice, 164
   at museum, 241–242
   tools, 161–162
Social sense-making, 303
Society expectations, from work organizations, 74–75
Sony, mission statement of, 183
Souls-of-fire, 388–389, 398–399
Southwest Airlines, 150–151
   mission statement of, 183
Speech act theory, 223
Spotify, 187
Spotify Model, 106
Spray and pray strategy, 230–231
Stace–Dunphy contingency matrix, 338–340
Staff and staffing, 364
Staff/staffing, 108
Stage models, 327–333
   appraising, 332–333
   eight-stage model, 328–330
   McKinsey 5A model, 330–332
   three-stage model, 327–328
Stage of change, and leadership style, 233
Staging, 116, 199
Stakeholder analysis
   resistance to change and, 251
Stakeholder mapping, 124–125
Stakeholders
   counter-implementation tactics by, 358
Starbucks
   change diagnostics, 20–21
   change leader, 14
   change outcome, 6
   change story, 5–7

   lessons from, 16
   mobile order and pay system, 6
   Philadelphia incident, 5, 6
   racial bias, 5
   sales growth, 6
   vision statement, 187
Star model, 110–111
Start point, 342
Start-ups, and change strategy, 88
State Auto Insurance Companies, 147
Status, 252
Stories, 118
Strategic change, 335
Strategic drift, 117, 118
Strategic intent, 195
Strategic inventory, 117–118, 119
Strategic objectives, 331
Strategy
   attraction, 266, 267–270
   organizational. *See* Organizational strategy
   organizational models, 108, 110, 111
   vision and, 196
Striving for Standardization (STS) initiative, 252–253
Structural frame, 107, 108, 110, 111, 112
Structure games, political behavior, 407
Styles, 108, 342
   of change, 339
Substance of change, 38, 334
Subway, 95–96
Sun Microsystems, 198–199
Superordinate goals, 108
Supportive leadership style, 233
"Surface-level" communication, 227
Sustainability actions, 369
Sustainability cautions, 369
Sustainable organizations, 373
Sustained change
   actions for, 361–369
   blameworthy failures, 359–361
   celebrating successes, 366
   fine-tuning, 367–369
   improvement evaporation effect, 356–359
   initiative decay, 356–359
   in management practices, 364–365

Sustained change (*continued*)
measure progress, 365–366
momentum busters, 357
praiseworthy failures, 359–361
reasons for failures, 360
reward system redesign, 363–364
role redesign, 362–363
staffing selection and change
objectives, 364
successful, 362
threats to, 357–359
vicious compliance and, 371
voluntary acts of initiative, 365
Sustaining innovation, 145, 149, 151
Swiss Re (reinsurance company), 73
Swiss watches, 153
SWOT (Strengths, Weaknesses,
Opportunities, and Threats)
analysis, 118
Symbolic frame, 111, 112
Symbols, 118
Systematic tools-based approach,
13–14
Systems, 108

T

Taoist theory, 43, 44
Target, 342
Task challenge, 360
Task-focused transitions, 231
Teams, and personality traits,
129–130
Technology, 79–88. *See also* Artificial
intelligence (AI); Automation
and Generation Z, 79
and organizational change, 79–88
robots, 81
and workforce transition, 79
Telenor, 302
Tell and sell strategy, 230
Tell and sell style, change
management, 339
Telling vision technique, 188
Tell style, change management, 339
Temporal projection, 186
Tension, 11–15
Testing vision technique, 188
Thai Union, 143

Third-order change, 144
Three-stage model, 327–328
Time, as context factor, 341
"Too much of a good thing" (TMGT)
principle, 390
Top-down hierarchical view of
management, 33
Top managers, 389–392
Transactional leaders, 389
Transdisciplinarity skill, 86
Transformation, 122
Transformational change, 13, 47, 144
IBM, 357
Kotter's eight-stage model of,
328–330
Transformational imagery, 225
Transformation efforts, failures in, 322
Transitional imagery, 225
Transition process, 334
Transition risk, 73
Transmitter, 215
Trends, responding to, 180
Trust building, 180
Turnarounds, 231
Twitter, 161
Type, change kaleidoscope
implementation options, 342

U

Uber, 393–394
UK National Health Service, 369
Unambiguous feedback, 373
Unanticipated outcomes, 370
Uncertainty, 360
low tolerance of, 255
resistance to change, 254
Underscore and explore strategy, 230
Unemployment, 79
automation potential and, 83
Unfreezing, 285, 301, 327
Unfunded mandates, 147
Unilever, purpose and performance
at, 181
Unintended change outcomes, 35, 36
Unretirement, 76
U.S. Army, organization development
in, 300
U.S. Postal Service, 357, 363

V

Valence, 124
Value propositions, 229
Values, organization development,
283, 287
as universal, 288
Values-based recruitment
systems, 364
Vanuatu, plastics ban in, 15–16
Variation, organizational, 39
Vehicles, 116
Veterans, 78
Vicious compliance, 371
Vinyl LPs, 153
Virtual collaboration, 86
Vision, 176–178, 183–191
adaptability of, 192–194
affective component, 184
analysis of, 202
analytical approach, 190
attributes, 183–187
benchmarking approach,
190–191
"bread-and-salt," 191
change and, 194–201
as change driver, 195
characteristics of, 185
cognitive component, 184
competing, 194
components of, 184
concept of, 177
content of, 178
crafting, 188–190
creation of, 183
defined, 183–184
development of, 188–191
emerging during change, 195
external dimension of, 187–188
failures of, 192–194
helping change, 196
heroic leaders and, 198–200
hindering change and, 196–198
inner voice and, 191
internal dimension of, 187–188
intuitive approach, 190
lack of, 176–177
market strategy and, 187–188
Merck example, 201
process, 189, 199

questions for, 190–191
role at Mentor Graphics, 202–203
value of effective, 185–186
Vision statements, 187
Visual imagery, 410
Vodafone, AI used in, 83
Volkswagen, 65
VUCA (Volatile, Unpredictable,
Complex, and Ambiguous), 126

W

Walmart, 144
mission statement, 183
vision statement, 187

Walt Disney, 200
WAMI, of resistance, 250
Weather disasters, and economic
losses, 72
Weberian "ideal type," 45
WeChat, 161
WhatsApp, 161
Whistle-blowers, 296
Whole Foods, mission statement
of, 183
Whole system techniques, 289
WIIFM, of resistance, 250
Win zone, 324
Withhold and uphold strategy,
230, 231
Woe zone, 324

Workforce diversity, 221
Workforce transition, technology
and, 79
World Café, 290, 291–292
Worry zone, 324

Y

Yammer, 163

Z

"Zero recruitment fee" policy, 143
Zumba Fitness, 148